A PUEBLO DIVIDED

D0937668

A Pueblo Divided

BUSINESS, PROPERTY,
AND COMMUNITY IN
PAPANTLA, MEXICO

Emilio Kourí

STANFORD UNIVERSITY PRESS

STANFORD, CALIFORNIA 2004

Stanford University Press
Stanford, California

Printed in the United States of America
On acid-free, archival-quality paper

Library of Congress Cataloging-in-Publication Data

Kourí, Emilio.
    A Pueblo divided : business, property, and community in
Papantla, Mexico / Emilio Kourí.
        p.   cm.
    Includes bibliographical references and index.
    ISBN 0-8047-3939-0 (cloth : alk. paper)
        1. Land tenure—Mexico—Papantla de Olarte—History—
19th century.   2. Vanilla industry—Mexico—Papantla de Olarte—
History—19th century.   3. Papantla de Olarte (Mexico)—Economic
conditions—19th century.   4. Papantla de Olarte (Mexico)—Social
conditions—19th century.   5. Papantla de Olarte (Mexico)—
History—19th century.   I. Title.
HD330.P36K68   2004
330.972'62—dc22   2004003968

Jacket illustration: *Señor de Papantla* (1934–35), by Manuel Alvarez
Bravo. © Familia Alvarez Bravo, courtesy of Colette Urbajtel

Original Printing 2004
Last figure below indicates year of this printing:
13   12   11   10   09   08   07   06   05   04
Typeset by Heather Boone in 10/12.5 Sabon

For my mother,
and also for my father

Contents

Illustrations

Acknowledgments

This book began thirteen years ago as a research project for my doctoral dissertation. It is not the book I had first intended to write, but I stumbled upon Papantla's seemingly improbable story and was compelled to follow it. Much changed along the way, not only in my understanding of the agrarian history of Porfirian Mexico but also in my life. I have been fortunate to count on the advice and encouragement of many teachers and friends, without which this study would never have been completed. John Womack's classes and writings made me want to be an historian. A generous adviser and insightful critic, much of what I know about Mexico I learned from him. John Coatsworth's probing questions and ample analytical scope helped me to grasp the larger significance of my work. Alfred Chandler taught me about business and its importance beyond economics. John Tutino's wise suggestions at key moments of decision made this a better book. Other scholars read part or all of the manuscript at various stages, offering valuable comments: Jeremy Adelman, Dain Borges, Jim Brennan, Jonathan Brown, Brodie Fischer, Heather Fowler-Salamini, Aurora Gómez, Friedrich Katz, Claudio Lomnitz, Jennie Purnell, Bill Taylor, John Watanabe, and the Press's readers. I am grateful to all of them.

In Xalapa, the recently opened Archivo General del Estado de Veracruz became my second home. A cheerful staff provided excellent service under less than ideal circumstances, and the archive's directors, first María Elena García Díaz and then Olivia Domínguez, allowed me to consult much uncatalogued material. Olivia generously assisted my research in many other ways as well, helping me gain access to documents held by several state agencies. The members of the Centro de Investigaciones Históricas (now Instituto de Investigaciones Histórico-Sociales) of the Universidad Veracruzana welcomed me warmly into their midst, sharing their knowledge of Veracruz, its history and peoples. Carmen Blázquez, Ricardo Corzo, Bernardo García Díaz, Feliciano García, and Adriana Naveda come specially to mind. Olimpia Gracia, research assistant and friend, devoted hundreds of hours to this project. Charming and tenacious, she achieved the impossible time and again, opening doors that might otherwise have remained closed to me. I can't thank her enough. Michael Ducey, Victoria Chenaut, Odile Hoffmann, and Helga Baitenmann talked to me about their work on Veracruz, sharing sources and ideas. Marisa Moolick invited me to stay in her beautiful house in Pacho, where I spent many happy weeks. In Papantla, Lic. Rufino Zárate kindly allowed me to examine the treasure trove of historical documents in his possession. Inside a small room on the second floor of his house, he kept piles of old papers bundled with rope, a nearly complete record of Papantla's land privatization. Moldy, buggy, crumbling into dust, they had not been read in nearly a century. Not even Don Rufino knew the story they told. I spent many long days poring over them in his living room, not far from the office where he notarized property transactions, still relying on the old *lote* maps drawn by Papantla's military surveyors, his Premio Simón Tiburcio (a high honor awarded by the municipality) hanging proudly on the wall. In Mexico City, Aurora Gómez and Antonio Escobar Ohmstede went out of their way to facilitate my research, and Alma Fuertes did some work for me at the Archivo General de la Nación. Aurora and her husband, César Hernández, offered me lodging and good conversation on numerous occasions. At Adolfo Castañon's request, Colette Urbajtel kindly allowed me to put Manuel Alvarez Bravo's *Señor de Papantla* on the jacket cover. Jean Meyer, José Ignacio González Manterola, Bernardo García Díaz, Malú Block, and Teresa del Conde also helped in this quest. A todos, mil gracias.

In Cambridge, friends and fellow graduate students Kathryn Burns, José Orozco, Michelle McKinley, Maren Niehoff, Tom Harsanyi, Elizabeth Boggs, Faviola Rivera, Renée González, and Betsy McIver made scholarship—and life—a less lonely endeavor. Widener Library was a dream come true. Up in New Hampshire, my colleagues at Dartmouth's History Department supported my work in every conceivable way. I could not have asked for more. Thanks to all, and in particular to Michael Ermarth, Marysa Navarro, Annelise Orleck, Christina Gómez, and Gail Vernazza. At the University of Chicago, Friedrich Katz, Claudio Lomnitz, Dain Borges, and Tamar Herzog provided the intellectual stimulus needed to finish the book. Out in the larger world of academia, Susan Gauss, Carlos Illades, Chris Boyer, and Andrew Wood kept me company. Norris Pope, Stanford's editor, took an early interest in this book project, and then waited patiently for me to deliver. The Press's Anna Eberhard Friedlander, Ruth Steinberg, and Kim Lewis Brown helped turn the manuscript into this book. Allow me to express my gratitude.

Financial assistance for this long undertaking came from many sources: Harvard University (Graduate Prize Fellowship, Dorothy Danforth-Compton Fellowship, History Department Research Grant, Tinker Foundation Field Research Grant, Frederick Sheldon Traveling Fellowship, Alfred D. Chandler, Jr. Traveling Fellowship, Whiting Fellowship in the Humanities); Dartmouth College (Walter Burke Research Award, Class of 1962 Faculty Fellowship); the U.S. Department of Education (Fulbright-Hays Doctoral

Dissertation Grant, Fulbright-Hays Faculty Research Grant); the American Historical Association (Albert Beveridge Research Grant); and the University of Chicago's Social Sciences Division and History Department. Their support is gratefully acknowledged.

Other debts are much harder to categorize. In more ways than they imagine, my mother and father, my brothers and sister, and my late grandmother Josefina nurtured in me a love of knowledge and a critical spirit. I hope I have not disappointed them. Thanks also to Félix Matos, Elizabeth Zachos, César Salgado, and Fernando Picó. Each will know why. Brodie Fischer has been with me all along, in Coatepec, Mexico City, Papantla, Cambridge, Hanover, Rio de Janeiro, Amherst, and Chicago. Muse, critic, resident lexicologist, *compañera*, she has done more for—and lived longer with—this book than anyone has the right to expect. I have been blessed with her, and with a lovely girl named Sofía.

La vainilla, fruto precioso, que es una fuente perenne de lucros, y que cosechada en su sazón sin los desórdenes que la codicia ha introducido, conservaría por sí solo el ser del partido.

—José María Bausa, "Bosquejo Geográfico y Estadístico del Partido de Papantla," 1845

A PUEBLO DIVIDED

Introduction

This is the story of how a Mexican *pueblo* changed. Woven together from the most diverse strands, it is at once deeply local and fundamentally international, vividly conflictual as well as coldly impersonal, seemingly predictable yet full of surprises. Remote and sparsely populated, almost forgotten by the conquering Spaniards, late-eighteenth-century Papantla was a place of indigenous family farmers. Totonac, not Spanish, was the sole language of the vast majority. Largely cut off from markets, much of what these people grew or picked or made was for their own consumption. The village lands were held collectively, and there was scant competition for them. Ecology, geography, and old customs shaped the social organization of economic life. But despite its local isolation, Papantla was connected to the wider world of commerce. That link was vanilla, the precious fruit of a native orchid coveted by wealthy Europeans who were enthralled by its delicate flavor. Light, expensive, and cultivable on a small scale by native farmers, the trade in vanilla would become Papantla's main business. As vanilla grew steadily more popular overseas, production and exports expanded hand in hand, in the process upsetting Papantla's long-established pattern of social relations. Money flowed in, land became more valuable, and those who stood to gain the most—both town merchants and Totonac entrepreneurs— eventually pushed to privatize the old village patrimony. It was not easily accomplished. By the late nineteenth century, land tenure had become the battleground of a rural society bound in violent struggle. How and why this happened is the subject of this book.

Long identified as one of the leading causes of the Mexican Revolution of 1910, the demise of communal landholding is one of the grand motifs of Mexico's nineteenth-century history. It is also, I think, among the least understood. Summarily explaining *pueblo* land disentailments as the product of liberal, pro-capitalist privatization laws and policies imposed from above by the State, historians have seldom bothered to examine these processes systematically from below, in their specific ecological, socioeconomic, cultural, and demographic contexts. As a result, a whole dimension of meaning (and explanation) has remained largely obscured. In particular, the role played by village residents in the subdivision of communal property—the internal impetus to privatization—has not received the analytical attention it deserves.[1] Judging from the case of Papantla, it is in fact what mattered most.

In the pages that follow, the end of communal land ownership in Papantla is depicted as part of a broader process of rural social change. To this end, I have carefully mapped out the area's physical features, the roots of its agricultural ecology, and the history of its human and economic geography; viewed from these intertwined perspectives, Papantla's distinctive historic pattern of social relations becomes intelligible. I have also reconstructed in detail the birth and growth of Mexico's international vanilla economy, especially its extraordinary development in the course of the nineteenth century. In and around Papantla, the business of vanilla—production, trade, and the networks of social ties built around these activities—became the main engine of economic and social transformation. As Papantla's vanilla economy evolved, so did the character of its social relations, including those concerning property. The conflicts, alliances, ambitions, and fears generated by these changes, I argue, paved the way for the privatization of communal land. Only in this context can the radical restructuring of land-use rights in Papantla—a protracted, persistently contested, crooked, and ultimately bloody process—be properly understood. The reader will have to judge whether this integrated approach to the study of rural social history is a convincing one.

The book begins with a comprehensive introduction to vanilla, the spice that put Papantla on the map and has been so intimately connected with its history. Chapter 1 chronicles the fortuitous emergence of native Mexican vanilla as a prized international commodity and sketches the evolution of the vanilla trade. It also explains how this forest orchid fruit is grown and turned into a delicate aromatic. Chapter 2 focuses on the Tecolutla River basin in northern Veracruz, of which Papantla is the historic capital. It describes the basin's terrain, climate, and vegetation, showing how a particular set of indigenous agricultural practices developed out of this context. The chapter goes on to examine the basin's colonial economy, society, and demography. I argue that the Spaniards were unable to found working haciendas or to establish strong urban centers in the Tecolutla basin, and that the Totonacs' subsistence-oriented agriculture and dispersed settlement patterns survived colonialism unchallenged and continued to prevail well into the nineteenth century. Prior to the ascendancy of vanilla, Papantla was an isolated backwater with a weak commercial economy and scant competition for land, a world of Totonac farmers and small-time Spanish or mestizo merchants and bureaucrats.

In light of these long-standing conditions, the impact of a rising vanilla business on Papantla's economic and social relations stands in sharp relief.

Chapter 3 investigates the early growth of the basin's lucrative vanilla exports, the ensuing process of local capital formation, and its effects on merchants as well as farmers. As production and business competition intensified, so did social conflicts, among Totonacs as well as between them and town merchants. By 1870, land had become a more valuable and coveted good and the stage was set for a struggle over the fate of communal property. Chapter 4 links the vanilla boom of the 1870s and 1880s to the conversion of the basin's communal lands into *condueñazgos*, private associations of share-holding landowners. It describes in detail the politics and the mechanics of these initial subdivisions, showing that Totonac bosses played a leading role in the creation of the *condueñazgos*, and that the process, though peaceful, was ominously flawed.

Following the establishment of the *condueñazgos*, Papantla's vanilla production soared and competition for control over land-based resources turned fierce. Chapter 5 analyzes the internal functioning of the land-holding associations, as well as the concurrent rise in social conflicts over business, land-use rights, tax increases, and the growing involvement of merchants in land matters. In these conflicts, the dividing lines were not primarily ethnic, but political and socioeconomic. By the mid-1880s several *condueñazgos* had become hotbeds of discord and an organized opposition began to emerge among groups of Totonac farmers. For more than a decade, these dissidents would strive—and even fight—to undo all the recent changes. At the start of the 1890s, amidst a downturn in vanilla prices and with social tensions sharply on the increase, some state and local officials, the basin's rapacious merchants, and groups of powerful Totonacs all pushed for the division of the ex-communal territories into individual private properties. Their means as well as their goals elicited a spirited resistance, some of it coming from the most unexpected sources. This is the subject of Chapter 6, which traces the tortuous dissolution of the troubled *condueñazgos* and the recurrent violence—including two large uprisings, both bloodily crushed—engendered by this ruthless process. By the turn of the century, the social strife unleashed by the profits of the vanilla trade had profoundly transformed the face of Papantla. The old communal lands of the Totonac *pueblo* had been fractionalized, but only after the land-holding community had itself been fractured.

The book ends, quite deliberately, in 1900, and not—as has been the norm in the historiography of the Porfiriato—with the Revolution of 1910. By the start of the twentieth century, a new social order had been firmly established in Papantla, the wrenched product of bitter struggles played out over three decades. From an historical perspective, the 1870s, 1880s, and 1890s stand out as Papantla's great season of change, its own long revolution. It was then—and not in the wake of 1910—that this *pueblo*'s socioeconomic relations were decisively reshaped. The years of the Mexican Revolution—while not uneventful—would not witness any comparable social transformations. By leaving the Revolution out of the book, I have sought to avoid conventional teleologies, emphasizing instead the neglected importance of internal village rifts and power shifts in the history of Porfirian Mexico.

With regard to Mexico's agrarian history, the broader analytical significance of Papantla's path of change remains to be settled. Although the push for—and the consequences of—village land disentailment have long been salient themes in standard narratives of the late nineteenth century and the Revolution, these have in fact received remarkably little scholarly scrutiny. There are many fine regional studies of land, labor, and agriculture in the Porfiriato, but few that look closely inside the villages. This is the first detailed account of *pueblo* land privatization anywhere in Mexico. It is therefore impossible, at least for now, to compare Papantla's experience to that of other land-holding communities, and hence to assess its typicality. It is highly improbable, however, that—local peculiarities aside—Papantla's transformation will turn out to be unique. An accelerated process of social differentiation driven by new business opportunities—that is, the rise to prominence of an indigenous agrarian middle class within the villages—may well be the key to understanding the dynamics of land disentailment and expropriation in many other *pueblos*. At odds with prevailing stereotypes of village history, the case of Papantla points to the need for a reexamination of the causes, process, and consequences of rural social change in pre-Revolutionary Mexico.

The full story of Papantla's late-nineteenth-century struggles has been buried for a long time, and in more ways than one. It was buried with the many Totonacs who were killed or exiled for opposing the usurpatory designs of the powerful, other Indians among them. It was buried again with the old municipal archive, which was used as landfill when the current town hall was built. And it has been buried by the dominant historical narratives about the *pueblos* of Porfirian Mexico, which left no room for complex and contradictory social transformations like the one depicted in these pages. I have unearthed as much of it as I was able to; I hope it will now find its place in history.

1 The Culture and Commerce of Mexico's Vanilla

Throughout the nineteenth century, and indeed for a good part of the eighteenth and twentieth centuries, the history of Papantla was inseparable from the history of its vanilla economy. To understand Papantla's past, one must understand vanilla. These pages trace the unexpected and somewhat fortuitous emergence of vanilla as a valuable spice of international commerce, showing how Papantla's vanilla economy acquired the characteristics that would define it in the nineteenth century. As will be seen, an historical examination of the economic botany, utilization, and commercial development of vanilla reveals the raison d'être not only of aspects of production as diverse and fundamental as ownership of the crop, division of labor, capital inputs, scale of cultivation, timing of the harvest, and credit and purchasing mechanisms, but also of the geography of production—within and outside Mexico—and the structure of export markets.

While ordinarily this information might be obtained by recourse to previous scholarship, the case of vanilla presents special difficulties. For one, precious little is known about the historical development of Mexico's vanilla industry. Remarkably, even though until at least the 1850s virtually all of the vanilla ever consumed in Europe and the United States came from Mexico, Alexander von Humboldt was the first to report any details about its cultivation, preparation, and commerce.[1] Its earlier history remains obscure. Witness the Abbé Raynal's rambling *Histoire philosophique et politique des établissemens et du commerce des europeéns dans les deux Indes*, which managed only to deplore the dearth of information about the vanilla economy of New Spain, flatly stating, "We are equally ignorant how many different species there are of it [vanilla]; which are the most valuable; what is the soil which suits them best; how they are cultivated; and in what manner they are propagated."[2] As Humboldt pointed out, Raynal was not able even to name the districts where vanilla was produced, indicating only that it "grows in the inaccessible mountains of New Spain."[3] One hundred years after Mexico achieved independence from Spain (1821), the literature on the

Mexican vanilla business had outgrown Humboldt's *Ensayo* only slightly. Even though the international vanilla economy changed profoundly between 1820 and 1920, only three slim grower's manuals—by Rossignon (1859), Fontecilla (1861), and López y Parra (1900)—date back to this period. Each described planting and curing techniques, but for the most part disregarded the social organization of the industry. Likewise, the natural and horticultural histories of vanilla have received scant attention. Although the notably complex economic botany of vanilla has undergone significant historical transformations, popular writings have tended to reduce it to a simple series of exotic vignettes; not surprisingly, various aspects of its development remain the subject of long-standing confusion.[4] In sum, there is little to rely on by way of previous studies.

Out of necessity, therefore, a fresh effort has to be made here to map out and integrate the intricate botanic and economic histories of vanilla. This chapter is devoted to that task. It examines the production and reproduction of vanilla, its uses and markets, and its transformation from fruit to spice. The ensuing panorama will make it possible to understand the historical development of Papantla's rural economy.

Out of the Wilderness: Production and Reproduction

The spice commonly known as "vanilla" is the cured and fermented fruit of a tropical orchid native to the Americas.[5] The "vanilla" used commercially is a flavoring extract made by combining glycerin, sugar, and alcohol with chopped or ground processed vanilla.[6] In Spanish and in English the word refers both to the plant and to the fruit. In French, however, *vanillier* is the name of the plant and *vanille* is reserved for the fruit. As will be seen, this is a useful distinction, setting apart the agricultural and the processing stages of vanilla production.

There is not just one kind of vanilla plant, but many. Numerous species of the genus *Vanilla* (*Orchidaceæ* family) are known to botanists, but according to a prominent student of the genus "only three . . . (*V. planifolia* Andrews, *V. pompona* Schiede and *V. tahitiensis* J. W. Moore) are of commercial importance as sources of vanilla."[7] In the process of curing, all three species develop vanillin, "the substance chiefly responsible for the peculiar fragrance and flavor of the vanilla bean."[8] However, the *planifolia* produces by far the best vanilla for flavoring, and this has long been recognized. As such, merchants always preferred and sought out *V. planifolia*, and the modern vanilla trade has concentrated almost exclusively on this species.[9] Yet before the late nineteenth century, when commercial standards were at last successfully enforced, it was quite common to sell other kinds, especially *V. pompona*, mixed in with and disguised as the legitimate sort,

V. planifolia.[10] Much of the early botanical research on vanilla in Europe was sparked by the desire to describe and classify the coveted "true vanilla of commerce," then synonymous with "the true Mexican vanilla of commerce," eventually labeled *Vanilla planifolia*.[11]

It was in Mexico that the conquering Spaniards first came in contact with vanilla and learned its various local uses, and vanilla from the Viceroyalty of New Spain was, for the most part, all that could be had anywhere in Europe until the mid-nineteenth century. This largely uncontested monopoly within the Americas is remarkable, considering that *V. planifolia* is indigenous not only to Mesoamerica but also to a good part of South America and perhaps the Caribbean.[12] *V. planifolia* is a climbing green vine whose aerial roots cling to neighboring trees for support; it is not, however, a parasitic plant, but rather an epiphyte. The supporting trees and shrubs shelter the vine from unfiltered sunlight and strong winds, which can impair growth or damage the delicate shoots, flowers, and fruits. The vine's leaves are thick and succulent, oblong-elliptic in shape, and it produces small yellowish flowers (orchids) in bunches, often numerous. It grows well in warm, humid climates where rain is abundant, provided that the distribution of precipitation is seasonal, so that flowering can take place during the relatively drier months.[13] The soil in which it grows requires high levels of superficial moisture, and it must also be light, porous, and well drained, since the vine's underground roots are shallow and rot easily. In the words of a Totonac vanilla grower from Tajín, near Papantla, Veracruz, "The soil must have a great deal of 'juice,' because the roots are on the surface."[14] Thus, low hillside forests rich in mulch are a common location, since the slopes aid the drainage and protect against the winds.

V. planifolia normally flowers only once a year; in Mexico this usually happens during April and May. The blooms live only for a day. Fruit develops only if fertilization of the fleeting flower succeeds. Due to their anatomy, however, this orchid, like most, is incapable of direct self-pollination. The structure of its pistil (female organs) prevents it. For fertilization to take place, the pollen must attach to the inner tissue of the stigma, which is connected to the ovary of the flower. In *V. planifolia*, however, the stigma develops a flap-like membrane over its mouth; this membrane (rostellum) covers the stigma's cavity and prevents the pollen held in the anther, directly above, from reaching the surface where it would germinate. In the words of the botanist whose discovery this was,

The flower of *Vanilla* has this peculiarity—that the retinaculum is highly developed, so that this organ forms a curtain suspended before and above the stigmatic surface, thus separating it completely from the anther, which in its turn encloses in two cavities, naturally shut, the pulverulent masses of pollen. From this structure it results, that all approximation of the sexes in this orchideous plant is naturally impossible.[15]

The fructification of vanilla therefore depends on the participation of an external agent in the pollination process. In the regions where *V. planifolia* is indigenous, bees and other insects seem to have performed this role exclusively well into the nineteenth century. If one considers that at least until the 1850s these regions were the only source of vanilla for commerce, the importance of these agents becomes evident. Yet precious little is known in detail about the natural pollination of *V. planifolia*. The French colonial botanist Arthur Delteil—an early expert on the systematic cultivation of vanilla—wrote that in Mexico small bees of the genus *Melipone* carried out fertilization while "collecting from the flower pollen and sugars used in the elaboration of their honey." Hummingbirds, he added, performed the same task. Although Delteil did describe these bees, it does not seem that he ever observed them, and his sources are not known. Nevertheless, his claim was supported by Charles Darwin's broad research on cross and self-fertilization, including his studies on the role of insects in the fertilization of orchids. Darwin noted that "much nectar [is] secreted from the bases of the flower-peduncles of Vanilla," and that insects were drawn to it.[16] Some decades later, a Mexican writer asserted that "the natural fertilization of the flowers of this orchid takes place and has taken place for many centuries, perhaps thanks to various species of bees and some other insects," adding that "it is also probable that hummingbirds, so common in our vanilla producing regions, are agents of fertilization for these flowers." However, these remarks have no empirical value since they are clearly borrowed from Delteil.[17]

Evidently, some kind of insect fertilization must have routinely occurred, but no direct observation of it in Mexico is recorded. Because this delicate operation was a crucial step in the natural and economic cycle of vanilla, botanists nonetheless sought to clarify it, resorting to educated speculations. In 1896 a prominent student of vanilla reasoned:

As regards *V. planifolia* it may be said that the flowers are fragrant, and that they secrete a large amount of honey at the bottom of the tube, which would naturally attract insects. The front lobe of the lip is reflexed and somewhat rough, and thus would afford a lighting place for the insect, which would then crawl into the tube to suck the honey. A small bee would easily get the front part of its body past the anther, because the appendages of the crest are all deflexed towards the base, but on retreating these would present an obstacle, and in order to pass them the bee would have to elevate its body, and thus would press against the incumbent anther and dislodge the pollinia. In what way these become attached to the insect in this case is perhaps not known, but it may be safely assumed that they do become so attached and are carried away. On retreating from the flower the bee would also lift up the flap-like rostellum which protects the stigma, and thus any pollen would inevitably be deposited on the latter and fertilize the flower.[18]

Regardless of what the exact procedure might have been, it is surely right that these agents not only enabled self-pollination to take place, but also, by taking pollen from one flower to the next, carried out cross-pollination. This fact illuminates an essential aspect of the natural and early economic history of the vanilla plant, namely, that it was able to reproduce itself in the wild. Cross-pollinated flowers bear seeds from which new plants can in turn grow; self-pollination, on the other hand, engenders sterile seeds.[19] The insects that so puzzled the minds of generations of botanists and would-be entrepreneurs were, in fact, the key element in understanding not only the production of the precious fruit but the entire life cycle of the species as well.

Until sometime in the eighteenth century, the vanilla plant was not culti-vated or cultured to any significant extent.[20] Its growth, health, or repro-duction were not generally the result of deliberate human intervention, which is to say that the plant did not habitually obtain any improvements from labor. The original vanilla economy seems to have operated exclu-sively on an extractive basis; that is, it did not include a horticultural cycle. Vanilla vines grew wild in forests and water meadows where ecological conditions were suitable for their development and propagation. Native gatherers simply searched for ripe fruits to pick, selling them for silver coins with which to supplement their subsistence economies.[21] Annually, some would trek to known spots to pick fruit from scattered vines, while others roamed nearby hills and streams hoping to find wayward clusters. The sum total of their haphazard findings constituted the season's harvest.

The early geography of vanilla collection is not precisely known; there are only brief colonial references to vanilla-picking in parts of Tabasco, Ve-racruz, Oaxaca, Campeche, Soconusco, and Guatemala.[22] "This fruit grows wild in the hills and is not owned or cared for by anyone," reads a 1744 document from Papantla, Veracruz, "for which reason those who trade it are mostly Indians who go out after it and they cut it."[23] In the 1770s the Veracruz-born Jesuit Francisco Javier Clavijero, exiled in Bologna, ob-served in his *Storia Antica del Messico* simply that "the vanilla, which the Mexicans call *tlilxochitl* and is so well known and much used in Europe, grows without culture in the *tierras calientes.*"[24] The scant specialized his-toriography is equally laconic. "In the beginning," states the first treatise on Mexican vanilla, "one harvested only what was produced spontaneously in the forests."[25]

Nonetheless, it is possible to discern a chronological pattern. Vanilla was used almost exclusively to flavor a drink made with cacao beans (chocolate). During the sixteenth century, the regular consumption of this beverage was customary only in southern and central New Spain, Chiapas, Soconusco, and Guatemala; although the cacao drink was already known in Spain, there it was still largely an unusual and exotic product. Thus, the demand for va-nilla was modest and overwhelmingly internal, and its exportation remained commercially insignificant. Under these conditions, the vigorous cacao trade originating in Soconusco and Guatemala—organized around elaborate networks and routes predominantly of pre-Hispanic origin—functioned also as the principal conduit for and the driving force behind the collection and commercialization of wild vanilla for the entire zone of chocolate consumption. Although in all likelihood some vanilla was concurrently extracted from zones unrelated to the production of cacao—for example, Totonacapan—it is fair to say that at this early stage the crop's commercial structure and geography were essentially ancillary to those of cacao.[26]

As long as the geographical distribution of the markets for the spice did not extend beyond Mesoamerica, the main cacao-producing regions remained as well the most dynamic sources of wild vanilla. However, in the course of the seventeenth century the exportation of vanilla to Spain—and through it to other European nations—became a lucrative economic activity. These new and expansive markets provided the impetus for the emergence and articulation of vanilla economies in regions better positioned to take advantage of an export trade obligatorily channeled through the port of Veracruz. Thus, by the eighteenth century, Misantla, Colipa, northeastern Oaxaca, southern Veracruz and—to a much lesser extent—Papantla begin to appear as the preeminent sources of wild vanilla, now destined mainly for export. Since vanilla was indigenous to these places as well, increasing the output initially required only the intensification of gathering forays. Mule packs linked these producing regions to Veracruz, and through them far-flung trading networks were established, gradually forging a strong vanilla business geographically and operationally independent from cacao.[27]

In some of these newly dynamic areas the botanical underpinning of the business would in time undergo a very significant transformation. Vanilla vines began to be planted and cultivated by Totonac Indians, many of whom eventually incorporated this new activity into their agricultural cycle. By the 1760s, there is mention for the first time of vanilla being planted in the hills surrounding the towns of Colipa and Papantla, northwest and uphill from the port of Veracruz. In a letter to the Viceroy, the Indian officers of San Francisco Colipa stated that most of the Indians in that locality kept vanilla plots in certain nearby hills, "which we have planted after much toil and travel,"[28] and which they therefore wanted to purchase. It is not clear when this practice started in those regions. In his pioneer essay on vanilla, Agapito Fontecilla noted that "despite having made some inquiries, I have not been able to find out, not even according to tradition, in what epoch cultivation started," but he added that "from some fragments that remain of the old archive of Papantla one can tell that by the year 1760 there were already cultivated vanilla fields (*vainillales*)."[29]

While the harvesting of wild vanilla in these parts of Veracruz would persist—albeit in a subsidiary role—well into the nineteenth century, the emergence and gradual spread of sustained planting marks an historic shift in the economic botany of this spice. The "care" and "assistance"[30] which the Indians of Colipa would need to bestow on their new vanilla fields denotes a radically different relationship between people and the plant, one that provided a more solid foundation for the vanilla business and modified the web of social relations that constituted it. There are no known accounts of any instances of this transition, nor any explicit explanations of its causes and proximate consequences. However, two commentaries are worth citing. Alexander von Humboldt speculated that planting came about in order to avoid lengthy and arduous gathering treks: "The Indians, who from the outset recognized how difficult the harvest was in spite of its abundance, due to the vast stretches of land they had to traverse every year, have propagated the species, bringing together a large number of plants into a more limited space."[31] Agapito Fontecilla, on the other hand, supposed that diminishing harvests of wild vanilla, combined with increased consumption, must have brought about planting: "In the beginning one harvested only what was produced spontaneously in the forests, and it is to be believed that as this gradually diminished and consumption progressively increased, the need to cultivate it arose, and the state of Veracruz excelled in this, being the first and perhaps the only one thus far to cultivate it in America."[32] Because any attempt to resolve these questions entails a detailed examination of the social organization of vanilla production and trade, it is best to postpone it momentarily. For now it will suffice to say that at least three issues deserve careful consideration: the constraints and uncertainties built into the economy of wild vanilla; changes in the use of and distribution of access to privately owned and communal woodlands; and the rise in the demand for vanilla overseas. Each will be analyzed in due course.

This practice of planting vanilla vines took hold selectively in the course of the eighteenth century. As noted, there is evidence that it became commonplace in areas in the northern part of the Intendancy of Veracruz, where there was already a tradition of trading in wild vanilla for export, that is, in Misantla and Colipa.[33] At the time of Humboldt's visit, these were the important zones of vanilla cultivation. If Fontecilla is right, the vine was also grown around Papantla, where the gathering of wild vanilla appears not to have been nearly as important an activity. On the other hand, planting was not widely or systematically adopted in the old *alcaldía mayor* of Teutila, in northeastern Oaxaca. Its rugged lands down the eastern slopes of the Sierra de Juárez and onto the upper Papaloapan basin were the other important source of wild vanilla for export; this trade seems to have been well established, and its product was quite prestigious.[34] Of the vanilla gathered there, Humboldt wrote that "it seems that this variety was the first one introduced to Spain in the sixteenth century, because in Cádiz *Teutila vanilla* is preferred to all others even today," adding that "the town of Teutila in the Intendancy of Oaxaca is renowned for the excellent quality of the vanilla produced in the surrounding forests."[35] In fact, the mountain town of Teutila was only the buying and curing center for the region's vanilla; its actual provenance was probably the wooded hill ranges in the environs of rivers, perhaps the Santo Domingo, the Tonto, or the Valle Nacional.[36] In any case, there is no evidence to suggest that Oaxaca's vanilla was of the planted sort. Humboldt may have assumed so, but he was careful not to state it, and later sources indicate that Oaxaca's vanilla harvest was always in all likelihood predominantly of wild origin.[37] Widespread, regular planting was thus essentially a Veracruz phenomenon.

At the outset it may have been difficult to distinguish cultivated from wild fruits; perhaps once cured there was nothing in their appearance that obviously set them apart. The quality of the spice still depended primarily on proper maturation and curing, and no distinctions were made according to origin. It appears that meticulous care in the curing process earned Teutila its high reputation before the emergence of planted vanilla, and the same care succeeded in preserving it for some time after, even though cultivation was not significant there.[38] Where cultivation became prevalent, however, differences emerged, and these became the basis for a commercial taxonomy enforced by export merchants. As early as 1722, de Jussieu reported to the *Académie des Sciences* that the traders in Cadiz distinguished between three kinds of vanilla: *de Ley*, *Simarona*, and *Pompona*. In Humboldt's time, vanilla from Misantla and Colipa, then the main zones of cultivation, was already classified according to six categories: four classes of cultivated vanilla, each with its own selection criteria, wild vanilla (*cimarrona* or *silvestre*), and *pompona*.[39] The wild vanilla from these places was considered of poor quality, "very thin and almost devoid of juice," in Humboldt's words, surely the result of early picking prompted by competition.

Varied growth conditions probably account for the morphological differences between wild and cultivated vanilla. By the time of Fontecilla's treatise (1861), the wild vanilla plant called *cimarrona* or *silvestre* exhibited thinner vines, slightly more pointed leaves, and smaller, rougher fruits than those of its tamed counterpart, then appropriately called *mansa*.[40] Already in 1820 the German botanist Christian Julius Wilhelm Schiede had observed these marked differences while traveling around Misantla, mistakenly concluding that they corresponded to separate species. There were in fact several types of wild vanilla, the *cimarrona* being perhaps only the most common, all of which are now recognized as *Vanilla planifolia*, the species cultivated for commerce.[41] These varieties had names such as *mestiza*, *tarro*, *puerca*, and *mono*, and their value relative to the *mansa* depended on the extent to which their various features as finished products approximated or were made to resemble those of the current standard of trade.[42] Of the *mestiza*, for example, Fontecilla wrote that "after curing it blends in with the *mansa* to such an extent that few intelligent people are able to distinguish it."[43] The *puerca*, on the other hand, developed an unpleasant smell while being cured, and thus had no value. Regardless, many contrived a use for it, so it was not unusual for unwary buyers to discover disguised *puerca* in the middle of an otherwise fine bundle.[44]

The gradual adoption of commercial standards for vanilla reflects not only the recognition of diversity within the species—highlighted by the physiognomic effects of cultivation—but also, more significantly, an increase in production and exports made possible by the new method of procuring the vanilla fruit. Regardless of what caused the onset of cultivation, it is clear that a sharp increase in production was its most notable proximate consequence. Vanilla plants proliferated, and there is ample reason to believe that these cultivated vines yielded more—and better—fruit than their wild counterparts. Proper and assiduous care, as well as the provision of an adequate mixture of shade and sunlight, helped produce a more vigorous plant. Meanwhile, competition among gatherers of wild vanilla would become only more intense, and hasty picking, which was often careless and premature, resulted in damaged vines and deficient fruits, diminishing both long-term returns and product quality. Even in his day Fontecilla was able to witness this phenomenon: "Until a few years ago 150 to 200 thousand [*cimarrona* vanillas] were harvested in Papantla, but because while cutting it they would damage the vines very much, the harvest has shrunk down to 40 or 45 thousand today."[45] To a certain extent, vanilla planters were able to improve on these conditions, thereby securing more and better vanilla fruits. These social and cultural (in the botanical sense) factors, coupled with the sheer increase in the number of producing plants, help explain the likely multiplication in the supply of vanilla brought about by the introduction of planting. They also give a more precise historical meaning to Humboldt's secondhand observation that "wild or *cimarrona* vanilla, which grows on terrain covered by bushes and other climbing plants, bears very dry fruits in rather small quantities."[46]

Early figures on the production of exportable vanilla do not exist, but Humboldt's statistics are suggestive. His sources were "persons in Xalapa and Veracruz who for thirty years have been trading vanilla from Misantla, Colipa, and Papantla." They calculated that, on the average, Misantla and Colipa, where the practice of cultivation had spread most vigorously, produced seven times more vanilla than either Papantla or Teutila.[47] Papantla, destined to become the capital of Mexican vanilla, was a latecomer to the business; there, the vanilla economy was still in its infancy.[48] Teutila's production, on the other hand, was still bound to the limits and vagaries of wild-picking. These wide disparities are a measure of the extent to which the adoption of systematic planting transformed vanilla production and trade. Such practices enabled greater Misantla swiftly to emerge as the preeminent source of the world's vanilla. More broadly, planting and cultivation became in effect the foundation of a less uncertain and vastly more prosperous vanilla business.

The vanilla plant grows from fruit seeds as well as from vine cuttings. It is not known which was used when it was initially cultivated in Veracruz, but the relative ease of propagation from cuttings soon established it as the method of choice. Vanilla seeds are tiny and lie clustered in viscid matter, which makes them difficult to handle. Apparently, seeds also take much longer to develop and reach fruition.[49] Besides, well-developed fruits are too profitable to be kept for seed. There is little opportunity cost in cutting short vine segments, and these grow fast once inserted in suitable soils. Fontecilla notes that a cutting takes root very easily, "even leaving it lying on the ground, and other times fastening it to a tree, without touching the ground, as long as it has shade and humidity."[50] To plant it, two of the vine's nodes are placed underground and covered, and several more are left above to sprout. The cutting is then tied to its supporting tree until it develops aerial roots and can cling to the *tutor* unassisted. This usually happens within a few weeks. A plant bears fruit starting in the third year, and its productive life spans four to seven years, after which its low yield renders it uneconomical.

Since vanilla cuttings take root so readily, it is quite conceivable that in the beginning they were planted or simply placed at the base of supporting trees and left to grow and fructify virtually on their own. These planted vines augmented the harvest and made its gathering less peripatetic. In this scenario, labor requirements were still minimal, for it did not involve clearing a field or planting trees. Humboldt reconstructs it well: "This operation did not demand much care, because all it took was to clear the soil a bit and plant a couple of epidendrum cuttings at the feet of a tree, or else to tie the cut vines to the trunk of a liquid-amber tree, a candlewood or an arborescent piper."[51] Vanilla was planted, but not yet fully cultivated. The setting would have been communally owned forest hills and meadows controlled by Indian towns, as well as adjoining lands to which townspeople gained access customarily or through specific agreements, perhaps some of the very same hills on which vanilla grew wild. Growing demand, the accretion of differential individual usufructuary rights within communal lands, disputes over the putative ownership of vanilla plants, and the emergence of theft, all led to a gradual shift toward planting under more clearly demarcated land-use rights. Vanilla would then be increasingly grown on plots allocated or appropriated specifically for the agricultural use of individuals or family units, spaces for which certain exclusionary rights had been established, whether or not they lay in the commons.

Those who in addition to their subsistence plots of maize and chile could procure or lay claim to some virgin forest land were able to devote it to vanilla. Many who could not, on the other hand, incorporated vanilla into their *milpa* (corn field) rotation. In either case, the intensification of planting implied the onset of cultivation in the full sense of the word. In Mexico's vanilla region, thick vegetation had to be cleared in preparation for any kind of agriculture, and slash-and-burn tactics were deemed most efficient. In the *milpas*, field rotation was commonly practiced, a strategic response both to the Sisyphean task of keeping the brush in check and to the risk of soil exhaustion. Lands in need of rest from maize and threatened by creeping vegetation would be adapted for the growing of vanilla, which does not require weeding, and maize production would be shifted to a recently cleared area. In time, as those vines became less productive, the vanilla field would finally be surrendered to the brush. Another segment of the lot would undergo *tumba, roza y quema* for maize, vanilla would take over the vacated corn field, and the cycle would begin anew.[52] Out in the virgin forest, clearing would proceed in the same fashion and a similar cycle would ensue, except that maize did not usually partake in the rotation. In these ways, vanilla entered into full cultivation.

Land-clearing, selecting or planting supporting trees (*tutores*), trimming their foliage, and guarding the coveted fruits as they slowly matured—all became an intrinsic part of vanilla production both in the *milpa* and out in the forest. Growers bestowed many cares upon vanilla, and it appears that quality and yield improved as a result. Cultivation had indeed many rewards. Experience would yield a certain horticultural know-how: what kinds of trees made suitable *tutores*, how to slash and burn the *monte* while preserving those trees, how to select cuttings and optimal length, when and how to plant them and how many to allocate per *tutor*, what care young vines demanded, and how to determine when a plant had outlived its usefulness. By the middle of the nineteenth century a set of practices was well established; these found expression in Agapito Fontecilla's practical treatise of 1861.

Keeping a vanilla field is a labor-intensive endeavor, though not in the sense usually associated with agricultural work. It involves numerous tasks throughout the year, most of which call for finesse rather than physical strength or endurance. The term "horticulture," rather than "agriculture," best captures the kind of care and attention which vanilla production requires; after all, vanilla is an orchid. Certain operations, such as training the young vines or picking the fragile fruits at the point of maturity without damaging them or the vines, take delicacy and dexterity, and thus, even though performing them is not particularly strenuous, it consumes much time.

The adoption of planting increased vanilla production and at once rendered it plainly visible to Europeans. The provenance—geographic and botanical—of this precious flavoring would at last cease to be considered an enigma, as speculation, fueled by ignorance and scarcity, withered in the face of a familiar practice and a more bountiful supply. No more would it be said, as the Abbé Raynal had, that "all these circumstances are known only to the natives of the country." And the fantastic stories of how the Indians "have kept this source of wealth to themselves, by taking an oath, that they would never reveal to their tyrants anything respecting the cultivation of the vanilla, and would suffer the most cruel tortures rather than be perjured" would slowly give way to researches about the prospects for its propagation and transplantation.[53] In every sense, cultivation brought vanilla in from the wild.

Prominent among those who reflected upon these new possibilities was Humboldt. "Considering," he wrote, "the excessive price at which vanilla is constantly sold in Europe, one is astonished by the negligence of the inhabitants of Spanish America, who disregard the cultivation of a plant which nature produces spontaneously in the tropics, almost wherever there is heat, shade, and high humidity." He had in mind chiefly other regions of the Spanish Empire—for example, near the Orinoco, where Aimé Bonpland had collected excellent wild vanilla, or Cuba, where systematic cultivation might have been undertaken, and he acknowledged that Mexico was in part a notable exception, since "all the vanilla consumed in Europe comes from Mexico, by way of Veracruz."[54] If it made sense to lament that other regions where vanilla was also indigenous had not embraced cultivation, it was also right to wonder why tropical zones with suitable climates outside of the Americas had not yet taken it up either. After all, comparable ecological conditions existed elsewhere, and the profitability of the vanilla trade had already a long reputation. Besides, many other American plants had seen their way to Europe and beyond,[55] and the available facts about the cultivation of *V. planifolia* did not make it appear particularly daunting.

In fact, European botanists had shown interest in vanilla since the seventeenth century, initially for taxonomic purposes. Even though the French would excel in the exploration of vanilla's commercial and culinary potential—producing most of the early accounts of its botany and preparation—English gardeners and plant scientists were the first to attempt its transplantation.[56] An early edition of Philip Miller's *The Gardener's Dictionary* includes vanilla, from which a modern author has concluded that "the Mexican *Vanilla* had been introduced to cultivation [in Europe] prior to 1739." Miller, who was curator of the Chelsea Physic Garden, was well known for his interest in the propagation of exotic plants. The accomplishment was precarious, for vanilla "appears to have been again lost," only to be "re-introduced by the Marquis of Blandford and flowered in the collection of . . . Charles Greville, at Paddington," sometime around 1800.[57] During the next few decades, vanilla was transplanted to botanical gardens across Europe, and by 1840 *V. planifolia* was "as common in the gardens of the British Islands as in those of the continent."[58]

In these northern "hot and humid houses" vanilla flowered so rarely that those occasions were greeted with reports. Perhaps it was not properly cultivated, or adequate climatic conditions were not maintained. In despair, specimens were sent to Java in 1819, where they eventually bloomed but would not produce any fruit. Around that time, *V. planifolia* was also taken to the island of Réunion (Bourbon), with similar results. Meanwhile, at the Liége Botanical Gardens, Charles Morren devoted himself to improving on the culture of vanilla, and by the 1830s he had perfected the technique to such an extent that his plants bore many flowers annually.[59]

Morren also explored the anatomy of the vanilla flower, describing it in the now familiar terms cited above. In view of vanilla's inability to fertilize itself, he reasoned that in Java and in Europe flowering plants would not bear fruit due to "the absence of the species of insect which nature has doubtless given to the climate of Mexico to effect in this latter region a fecundation." Evidently, an effective agent was missing, and therein lay the explanation for the infertility of transplanted vanilla.[60] Aware that recent research on the reproductive physiology of orchids revealed the possibility of achieving fecundation through human intervention at the stage of pollination, Morren set out to apply to vanilla the principles of vegetable physiology underlying Charles-François Brisseau de Mirbel and Adolphe Brongniart's successful fecundation of other orchids at the Jardin du Roi's hothouses in Paris.[61] To that end, in 1836 he devised a simple horticultural treatment that would permanently revolutionize vanilla production and trade. Cutting or lifting the protruding rostellum, he gently pushed the anther into the stigma cavity with his finger, thus enabling the pollen to drop in and cling to the inner tissue. The flower reacted within hours, and soon thereafter the ovarium began to elongate, signifying that a fruit was in the making. He treated fifty-four flowers in this way, "which having been fecundated . . . produced the same number of pods; and in 1837 a fresh crop of about a hundred pods was obtained upon another plant by the same methods; so that now there is not the least doubt of the complete success of this new cultivation."[62]

Morren had induced self-pollination by hand. This "art of producing fruits in the *Orchideæ*," as he referred to his invention, would quickly transform the geography of vanilla. Of this he was keenly aware. The experiments proved, he wrote, "that in all the intertropical colonies vanilla might be cultivated and a great abundance of fruit obtained by the process of artificial fecundation," and also "that henceforth we may produce in Europe vanilla of as good a quality (if not better) than that which is exported from Mexico."[63] Only his first claim proved to be prophetic. While in Europe native vanilla remained a greenhouse curiosity, the fruits of *V. planifolia* soon became the most valuable crop produced by several French colonial islands in the Indian Ocean. Exports to France started—on a small scale—in the late 1840s. By 1890, the island of Réunion alone exported as much vanilla as all of Mexico, and Madagascar's production would yet surpass that of the rest of the world combined.[64] Artificial pollination made this geographic and productive expansion possible.

Morren's general method was undoubtedly effective, but it was also imprecise. His published descriptions of the process of hand fertilization were vague and did not facilitate replication by those untrained in plant physiology. In other words, they did not provide practical instruction in the "art of producing fruits in the *Orchidaceæ*." His English paper, for example, provided scant guidance, stating only that "it is thus necessary *either to raise the velamen or to cut it* when the plant is to be fecundated, and to place in direct contact the pollen and the stigmatic surface."[65] On a routine basis, should the rostellum be cut or merely lifted? What instrument should be employed? How should the flower be held in the hand? How should the fingers be moved, and in what sequence? These concrete questions still had no answer. Morren had discovered a method, but he had not developed a technique, and that was, in the end, what prospective planters would need, especially if cultivation was to rely on hired or slave labor.

During the following decade, a standard procedure for hand pollination was adopted in the new vanilla fields of Réunion. Arthur Delteil wrote that some advocated clipping the rostellum with small, sharp scissors, but this was regarded as being too slow and cumbersome, and in the end lifting it prevailed as the most practical method of fertilization. Edmond Albius, a black slave, devised a simple technique involving the use of a small, blunt stick made out of bamboo or palm stem. The left hand, facing upward, holds the flower between the index and middle fingers, while the right hand uses the wooden stick to lift the rostellum, gently pushing it against and under the anther. The resulting pressure lifts the anther, exposing its pollen mass directly above the cavity of the stigma, now open. The left thumb then lightly presses on the anther from behind, pushing the pollen against the stigma's inner membranes. After carefully withdrawing the stick and releasing the flower, hand pollination is complete.[66]

This procedure was precise, reliable, uncomplicated, and fast. It is not hard to see why it was so swiftly propagated. As English botanist Henry Ridley would later put it: "The operation is by no means so difficult as from the above account it might appear to be [since] with a very little practice it is easily and satisfactorily performed, and I have found no difficulty in teaching natives to perform it successfully." Indeed, according to a study cited by Ridley, "a quick worker with the vines close together and full of bloom can fertilize 3000 a day, and from 1500 to 2000 is a good average number."[67] Considering that the flowers remain open only for a few hours, this reveals the extent to which fertilization could become systematized. Thus, in more ways than one, hand pollination was the cornerstone of an expansive intertropical vanilla industry. Albius's technique became the standard in Réunion and in all other vanilla regions under French control. With slight modifications, it has been eventually adopted wherever vanilla is cultivated, though in Mexico it would take hold only very slowly.[68]

In order to comprehend the economic rationale behind these horticultural developments, it is necessary to examine the various uses of vanilla across the centuries, as well as the historical geography of its consumption. Even the briefest outline of these topics will serve to illuminate the series of factors that turned an obscure spice obtained from a wild fruit for the enjoyment of a conquered nobility into a highly valued—even coveted—crop subject to considerable international trade. Such an historical context will also place in bold relief the impetus behind Morren's search for a means to achieve the reproduction of vanilla, and it will make sense of the swift spread of cultivation across the French colonial tropics. All these considerations will in turn yield a more refined understanding of the evolution of Mexico's vanilla economy.

Out of Mexico: Uses and Markets

Nothing is known about the origins of cured vanilla in Mesoamerica, but by the early sixteenth century, prior to the arrival of the Spaniards, it was already well established as an ingredient in the medicinal and gastronomic practices of the Mayas, the Nahuas, and their Aztec rulers. A wide array of curative and protective properties were attributed to the vanilla fruit and flower, used alone or in combination with other plants. Martín de la Cruz's manual of herbal medicine, written in Nahuatl and dated 1552, contains a colored drawing of a vanilla plant bearing fruits, as well as a description of a "traveler's safeguard" prepared with various dried flowers, including *tlilxochitl*, vanilla.[69] Francisco Hernández's impressive *Rerum Medicarum Novae Hispaniae Thesaurus*, based on the observation of native medical practices and flora undertaken throughout seven years of residence in New Spain during the 1570s, lists the multiple uses to which vanilla fruits were put, from easing digestion and strengthening the mind to inducing abortion and facilitating urination.[70] Bernardino de Sahagún's *Historia general de las cosas de Nueva España* mentions yet other cures involving *tlilxochitl*.[71] In this respect, vanilla was not unlike hundreds of other plant products which underlay an herbal medicine that was quite sophisticated, as any of the works just cited amply demonstrates. In the great market of Tlatelolco, whose prodigality so impressed Cortés and Bernal Díaz, there was, in Francisco López de Gómara's words, "a wonderful variety of herbs and roots, leaves and seeds, which are sold for food as well as for medicines, the men, women and children being very wise in the use of herbs, [with which] they treat almost all diseases."[72]

Although many of these practices were met with disdain by the Spaniards and appear to have gradually fallen into disuse, the presumed pharmacological powers of vanilla—both therapeutic and toxic—were not altogether ignored. European doctors would prescribe it for assorted nervous and gastrointestinal maladies, and up until the 1910s a listing for vanilla appeared in the *United States Pharmacopoeia*. Moreover, during the eighteenth century vanilla was considered a highly effective aphrodisiac in parts of Europe.[73] On the toxic side, sometime in the late nineteenth century the French coined the term *vanillisme* to describe a peculiar nervous condition associated with the handling or ingestion of vanilla, and their texts on the plant henceforth invariably included a chapter on the illness.[74] Earlier, Humboldt had reported hearing rumors of similar symptoms: "They say quite gravely that vanilla stupefies people (*la vainilla da pasmo*)," noting that "in Mexico there is worry about the perception that this flavoring is harmful to the health, especially to those whose nervous system is very irritable."[75] Overall, however, the pharmacodynamic virtues and perils of vanilla for the human organism were never systematically exploited after the subjugation of the native cultures of Mesoamerica, and having since received only sporadic attention, interest in them withered in the course of the twentieth century.

The culinary fate of vanilla, on the other hand, could not have been more different. It was one of the many flavoring ingredients of a frothy native drink of the nobility called *cocoatl*, "cocoa water." Variously modified and refined, hot chocolate became a fashionable drink in many European countries, and this unforeseeable predilection of the well-to-do single-handedly assured vanilla of a highly lucrative outlet for nearly three hundred years. The vanilla trade would owe its development—indeed, its very existence—to the transculturation of chocolate. The presence of vanilla, wrote Jean Anthelme Brillat-Savarin, philosopher of gastronomy, enabled hot chocolate to "achieve the *ne plus ultra* of perfection to which such a concoction may be carried,"[76] and thus while its therapeutic uses became marginal and declined, the "delicious perfume of vanilla"—again Brillat-Savarin—conquered first the wealthiest and most punctilious palates of Europe, and then very gradually colonized all the rest. Improbable as it reveals itself to have been, this process would induce the emergence of two defining features of the modern vanilla economy: planting and artificial pollination; moreover, it would account for the geographical configuration of vanilla production and consumption at the dawn of the twentieth century. Its inception consequently merits examination.

The two original uses of vanilla were actually more closely connected than they now seem. Gastronomy and herbal medicine were not always as dissociated as they are today, and vanilla provides an excellent case in point. Both the chocolate drink and the healing potions made with vanilla contained many of the same combinations of grains and spices. Judging from the recipes, some of these remedies were in fact virtually identical to *cocoatl* in their composition, and what set them significantly apart was only the context and manner in which they were imbibed, that is, their social meaning. The common denominator, aside from vanilla, was the use of cacao beans as the principal ingredient. Sahagún's description of a remedy is typical: "Those who spit blood will get cured drinking the cacao made with those aromatic spices called *tlilxochitl*, *mecaxochitl*, and *ueinacaztli*, as well as with a certain kind of chile called *chiltecpin*, all well toasted and mixed in with *ulli*."[77] Indeed, all of these beverages, including chocolate, bore the generic name *el cacao*, usually followed by a reference to distinctive additional ingredients, as in the text just cited. Thus, when Bernal Díaz wrote about Moctezuma drinking chocolate from golden goblets, he described it simply as "a beverage made out of cacao."[78] What Moctezuma drank with great ceremony was a concoction radically unlike the one now known by that name.

Chocolate was originally not one but a family of hot drinks prepared with ground cacao beans toasted with assorted spices. Aside from vanilla, the mixture could include pepper, annato, numerous kinds of chile, various dried flowers, and multiple maize products, as well as several other spices. This oily paste—cacao beans are roughly 50 percent vegetable butter—was dissolved into plain hot water or into a thick corn flour drink called *atole*, then stirred vigorously until a thick head of foam appeared. Unless honey was added, chocolate was not a sweet beverage, and in fact most versions of it were rather bitter. Sahagún listed "many forms of cacao, exquisitely made, such as cacao made with fresh cacao pods, which is very tasty to drink, cacao made with honey, cacao made with *ueinacaztli*, cacao made with fresh *tlilxochitl*, cacao made red, cacao made vermilion, cacao made orange, cacao made black, cacao made white."[79] Perhaps they had differing properties and symbolic meanings. All these chocolate beverages were unctuous and thick, so much so that one of the earliest Spanish promoters of the brew advised "opening the mouth wide when drinking it, because as it is frothy it dissolves and goes down only little by little."[80] Thus described, these ancient chocolate potions reveal themselves to be less distant from their strictly curative counterparts.

The native elites drank *el cacao* copiously, relishing it in all its forms; Bernal Díaz wrote of seeing fifty large jars of frothy cacao being brought to Moctezuma's table, and noted that among beverages it was considered the best in the land.[81] Chocolate was prized at least as much for its perceived healthful and nutritive qualities as for its pleasing taste. It was usually served after dinner, both as a delicacy and a digestive, and Bernal Díaz reports that Moctezuma drank it at that time also as an aphrodisiac, perhaps mindful that cacao butter is a great source of energy.[82] Clearly, food and medicine were not mutually exclusive designations; in fact, they overlapped quite regularly. In other words, nourishment and health were internally related concepts. From this point of view, it makes sense to think of the curative brews described by Sahagún as specifically medicinal versions of chocolate, instead of as drugs.

In this analysis, the gap between the early medicinal and gastronomic applications of vanilla narrows considerably. Perhaps this is why in virtually every case on record vanilla is used in a similar way, namely, in combination with ground cacao beans. It is no wonder then to find in Sahagún's account of the organization of the native market (*tiánquez*) that spices such as *tlilxochitl* were located in the section designated exclusively for those who sold cacao.[83] For centuries to come, this link would persist unchanged. Throughout, it was the raison d'être of the vanilla economy.

The conquering Spaniards also attributed various nutritive and curative properties to chocolate, and this fact to a large extent explains its cultural survival and adaptation. The Franciscan Toribio de Motolinía said of it that "it is good, it is good [*sic*], and is considered a very substantial beverage," and the Jesuit José de Acosta wrote that it was said to help the heart, the stomach, and the prevention of colds.[84] The "anonymous conqueror" was more exuberant: "This drink is the healthiest and most substantial of all the foods known in the world, for he who drinks a cup of it can do without any more food for a whole day, even while on a journey."[85] Overcoming significant gustatory differences, chocolate remained a highly desirable drink even after the glamour conferred to it by Moctezuma's table rituals had long faded. The medical nomenclature and popular beliefs of the time—in which dietetics, health, and healing were closely intertwined—rendered chocolate a most virtuous liquid. In the tradition of the *Corpus Hippocraticum*, the causes and cures of disease were analyzed largely in terms of the interaction between natural elements, including alimentary resources, and the human body; in this complex calculus constructed around countervailing concepts such as *the hot, the cold, fire, water, wind,* and *earth,* cacao drinks fared quite favorably.[86] The elaborate endorsement of Juan de Cárdenas, a physician educated at the nascent University of Mexico, embodies this logic and language:

Again I say that nowhere in the world is chocolate more necessary than in the Indies, because as these lands are humid and slothful, bodies and stomachs fill up with
phlegm and superfluous humidity, and *the heat* of chocolate boils these and turns
them into blood, which wine can not accomplish because the phlegm renders it
acidic, usually making matters only worse.[87]

Thus, as warriors, priests, and doctors alike sang the praises of the noble
drink, a new colonial society proceeded hastily to make it its own.

As early as 1538 serving chocolate during meals was already de rigueur
for the Spanish elite in Mexico City. A dinner without *el cacao* had become
as unthinkable as one without wine. When news of the Treaty of Nice—ending the latest Italian war between Spain and France—reached New Spain,
Viceroy Mendoza, Hernán Cortés, and the Royal Audiencia were moved to
celebrate with lavish feasts lasting several days. In each of the many elaborate outdoor performances and gargantuan banquets that took place, *"cacao
con su espuma"* was served alongside assorted wines and *aloja*, a traditional
Spanish beverage made out of honey, water, and spices. It is quite telling that
the chronicler Bernal Díaz, who was there, did not consider the presence of
chocolate to be in any way remarkable.[88] A better indication of cultural as-
similation is hard to imagine. Although the range of potential ingredients
was broadened to include spices the Spaniards found more palatable, such as
sugar, cinnamon, cloves, aniseed, and sesame, *el cacao* continued to be prepared in the same manner, and vanilla remained a principal component.[89]

Within decades chocolate emerged as the social drink par excellence of
Spaniards and Criollos alike. Among them, women were said to be particularly fond of it; Acosta, who thought it was, in any case, "crazy how much
people like it," remarked that women "would die for it."[90] Thomas Gage,
who drank four or five cups a day to "strengthen the stomach," wrote enthusiastically that "with this custom I lived twelve years in those parts
healthy, without any obstructions or oppilations, not knowing what either
ague or fever was."[91] Chocolate became especially fashionable in the north-
western provinces of the kingdom of Guatemala, where most of the cacao
was grown, and according to Cárdenas it was there that chocolate paste
was first formed into tablets ready to be dissolved. Meanwhile, the surviving Indian nobility continued to drink *el cacao*, and the most ordinary version of it—prepared cold with *atole* or *pinole*—found its way into the
streets and markets of many cities, where it was bought for refreshment by
mestizos and Indians alike.[92]

Still, the Hispaniolization of chocolate—swift and far reaching as it
was—did not have any immediate effect on vanilla production. Before the
Conquest, vanilla was relatively unimportant in economic terms; the fact
that it does not appear in any of the surviving tribute lists provides a good
indication of this.[93] It had fairly limited uses and users, and the practice of

gathering fruits from the wild was probably adequate to meet these needs, its inherent uncertainties notwithstanding. Judging from the evidence, these conditions remained basically unchanged well into the seventeenth century. Despite appearances to the contrary, it is unlikely that the overall consumption of cacao drinks increased rapidly in the wake of the Conquest. While the size of the native population—including the ruling classes—dramatically declined, the number of Spaniards and Criollos in New Spain remained relatively small—well under a hundred thousand altogether at the close of the sixteenth century. Moreover, cacao beans continued to be used as a medium of exchange, and this surely detracted from their culinary employment.[94] Thus, the habit of chocolate had still a fairly limited constituency and, a fortiori, so did vanilla, especially considering that it was still only one among many suitable ingredients for chocolate—one which, however prized, could always be substituted. Indeed, as noted, there is virtually no mention of vanilla plants in early colonial sources, let alone any hint of changes in aggregate demand for the spice.

If the early vanilla economy remains entirely outside the scope of these sources, this is doubtless not only because its scale was extremely small and its product relatively unimportant, but also because it did not spring from a set of agricultural practices that could be readily described and brought under control.[95] In comparison, the exploitation of other native resources and activities—mineral, vegetable, and human—struck the Spaniards as being far more attractive, accessible, and remunerative, and to these their attention was devoted. This relative lack of interest on the part of the new rulers of the land helps explain why the transculturation of chocolate per se had no discernible impact on the organization of vanilla production. Both marginal and hidden from view, the myriad upheavals of the epoch left it fundamentally unaltered. Vanilla fruits continued to be gathered by Indians from wild plants in their native habitats, just as they had been before, and that peripatetic, unencumbered harvest remained their sole source.

A significant structural transformation of the vanilla economy would have to await the kind of surge in demand and trade profits that only exportation for overseas consumption could bring. The unlikely impetus for the development of such a state of affairs can be traced to a traditional form of religious observance reentrenched in Catholic practice during the Counter-Reformation of the sixteenth and seventeenth centuries, and to the creative response elicited in compliance across the Hispanic world. The Roman Church had long emphasized the importance of fasting for those aspiring to lead a true Christian life, and the obligation to do so was minutely defined in ecclesiastical legislation. The precise nature and meaning of this obligation were debated at the Council of Trent (1545–63), and although the bishops failed to agree whether or not it originated in divine law, they issued a decree reaffirming the stringency of the requirement and enjoining the faithful to fulfill it absolutely:

The holy Synod furthermore exhorts, and, by the most holy advent of our Lord and Saviour, conjures all pastors, that, like good soldiers, they sedulously recommend to all the faithful all those things which the holy Roman Church, the mother and mistress of all churches, has ordained, as also those things which, as well in this council as in the other œcumenical councils, have been ordained, and that they use all diligence, to the end that they be observant of all things thereof, *and especially of those which conduce to mortify the flesh, such as the choice of foods and fasts.*[96]

Controversial, selective, and at times self-interested as it was, Philip II's zealous implementation of many of the Tridentine decrees profoundly affected the religious practices and institutions of the Hispanic world, molding them into the best likeness there would be of the Church according to Trent.[97] Spain, "the light of Trent," became also its imperfect incarnation.[98] Among the traits of this reformed Catholicism was a renewed insistence on compliance with the law of fasting. Odd as it may seem, this was the driving force behind the dissemination of chocolate consumption throughout Hispanic Europe.

The penitential self-restraint embodied in fasting had two purposes: the mortification of the flesh and the instillment of temperance—*padecer dolor* and *reprimir el ardor*, in the words of Juan de Cárdenas. While some forms of fasting demanded absolute abstinence from food and drink, others—especially the fasting mandated during holy days and seasons—called only for the renunciation of nourishment, customarily interpreted to include food but not liquids. Calendric fasting—for example, all the days of Lent, the Fridays of Advent—was of the latter type, and the laity as well as the clergy had a serious obligation to observe it. In these instances, the dictum *liquidum non frangit jejunium*, liquids do not break the fast, applied.

Hence chocolate, by virtue of being a liquid, was allowable during regular fast days. However, as explained, chocolate was no ordinary beverage, since it was also "substantial" or nutritious and a stomachic balm. As such, drinking it considerably eased the burden of fasting without violating the Church's positive legislation on the matter. Given the religious climate of the age, this was no small attribute. On that account, chocolate's devotees would proliferate, initially among the Criollos and Spaniards of Guatemala and New Spain—already familiar with the drink—for whom chocolate became the indispensable companion to fasting. More significantly, in this novel role chocolate would decisively capture the attention—and palates—of the ecclesiastical and aristocratic worlds of Spain and its European domains. There, too, the observance of fasting would become inextricably associated with the *bebida indiana*. The Counter-Reformation thus granted chocolate—and vanilla—a permanent foothold in Europe.

Beginning in the late sixteenth century, theologians, physicians, popes, and aristocrats pondered over the permissibility of drinking chocolate—at once liquid and nutritious—during fast days. These protracted and animated theological debates—carried out in America as well as in Europe—bear witness to the swift spread of chocolate as a fasting aid. This habit must have been widespread in New Spain by the 1580s, for Juan de Cárdenas felt compelled to devote a whole chapter of his *Problemas y secretos maravillosos de las Indias* (1591) to showing why chocolate did break the fast, thereby refuting what "the majority of the people of this land believe." Against the prevailing opinion—and a fortiori, practice—Cárdenas argued that cacao was a buttery substance which afforded sustenance, and he reminded his opponents that "it is not the intention of our Holy Mother The Church that thirst be quenched [during fast days] with beverages giving so much sustenance . . . but instead with a most simple element, which is water."[99]

Although Cárdenas's logic was sound, Church authorities would not side with him. The book's censor, the Dominican friar Agustín Dávila Padilla, emphatically dissociated himself from these views, claiming that the chapter in question was not a part of Cárdenas's text at the time he approved it for publication. "I will not dare condemn those who drink chocolate by saying that it breaks the Church's fast," Dávila wrote, "because the clear truth is that beverages do not break the fast." Cárdenas's opinion, he added, was altogether rash.[100] However, Dávila also felt strongly that the faithful should consider whether it was appropriate to drink chocolate during fast days other than as medicine, given its nutritiousness. He echoed the views of Jordan de Santa Catalina, an ascetic Dominican friar from their convent in Oaxaca, who had long lamented that "the gluttony of the Indies turned this medicine into a treat," so that chocolate was "greatly abused" and "drunk . . . at all hours."[101] Dávila's general remarks give the impression that in those years the use of chocolate in this connection was common in New Spain and the adjoining provinces of Guatemala, but quite probably not yet so in Spain.

Nevertheless, the debate over the proper interpretation of the ecclesiastical laws on fasting for the case of chocolate had already managed to cross the Atlantic, engaging the highest echelons of the Roman Church. As Dávila points out in his *Historia* (1596), Pope Gregory XIII (1572–85) had "twice" responded to the "insistent" requests of the authorities in the Province of Chiapa—then apparently the capital of the habit—by declaring that chocolate did not break the fast.[102] It is not easy to find a better indication of the extent to which the controversial practice had become established in Mesoamerica.[103] Beginning in the early part of the seventeenth century, this custom would spread throughout Spain's clerical and aristocratic milieus and beyond them to the middle sectors of society, igniting similar debates, which for decades would continue unabated.[104] In the end, Gregory XIII's prescient decision would prevail, largely an expedient ecclesiastical acknowledgment of Catholicism's dogged affection for chocolate, appropriately sanctioned by the clever moral reasoning of Cardinal Francesco Maria Brancaccio and the notorious casuist Antonio Escobar y Mendoza.[105]

Given the religious and imperial context of chocolate's transatlantic expansion, its consumption within Europe was at first circumscribed to Spain and its territories in Italy and the Netherlands; however, monastic communities quickly introduced it into France and Germany.[106] More importantly, chocolate was taken up in aristocratic circles, where before long it was prized principally for its secular qualities. This aristocratic fashion soon spread beyond the domains of Spain and Catholicism, a process that gradually eroded the beverage's Tridentine aura.[107] These developments need not be examined here; for the present purposes it suffices to say that by the late seventeenth century chocolate was well known not just in Madrid or Rome, but in Paris and even in London, as Mme. de Sévigné's letters and Samuel Pepys's diary demonstrate. At the royal courts, inside monasteries, and in chocolate "houses" and shops, genteel Europe suddenly displayed an insatiable appetite for chocolate. The ensuing surge in demand for its ingredients transformed Mexico's vanilla economy.

Were it not for this intricate and unforeseeable chain of developments, vanilla might have remained an obscure and commercially insignificant plant, its fate perhaps no different from that of most other entries in Martín de la Cruz's now arcane *Indorum Herbis*. Instead, European consumption underlay the inception of a profitable transatlantic trade in vanilla, which in turn encouraged the emergence of systematic planting in suitable regions linked by mule trade to the port at Veracruz. Both the decisive shift from gathering to cultivation—of which there is already some evidence in the early eighteenth century—and the eventual ascendancy in vanilla production of Misantla and later Papantla can be traced back to the development of commercial exportation. Moreover, as will be explained shortly, the durable internal organization of Veracruz's vanilla business also took shape in the wake of overseas demand. Thus, in essence, the horticultural basis, geography, and structure of Mexico's modern vanilla industry originated in Europe's multifarious cravings for chocolate.

Likewise, the steady incorporation of chocolate into the alimentary customs of a growing segment of European society during the eighteenth century provides an explanatory context for Morren's experiments in the reproduction of vanilla and for the consequent spread of intertropical cultivation.[108] As noted, Morren was well aware that his discovery signified the impendent end of Mexico's long-standing vanilla monopoly, which had never succeeded in keeping up with the growing pace of demand. In the previous decades, moreover, the naval wars of Europe as well as the internal battles that culminated in the independence of Mexico (1821) had severely disrupted the vanilla trade, and its subsequent reorganization was slow and conflictive. Thus, the hope—expressed by Brillat-Savarin—that the disappearance of "the barriers erected by a suspicious nation" would facilitate the access to "the true treasures" of the Americas, including vanilla, did not materialize soon enough.[109] The French were by that time easily the most avid and ingenious users of vanilla, and had attempted on several occasions since 1819 to undertake its cultivation in Réunion with cuttings brought from Cayenne and Mexico; Morren's successful experiments with artificial pollination showed them how this might be finally accomplished. "It is a subject," he announced, "which well deserves attention in a commercial point of view." In this spirit, colonial cultivation was born, and within half a century French vanilla was supplying the expansive markets of Europe.[110]

Ironically, by the time France's colonial crops established their presence in the continent, the chocolate drink that had single-handedly driven vanilla trade for over two hundred years was fast falling out of favor. As explained, this chocolate was a very rich, oily beverage, due to the high fat content of cacao beans (roughly 50 percent).[111] While this had once been regarded as its chief virtue (a "nutritious drink"), nineteenth-century tastes found it too heavy. Thus, for a time, chocolate paste manufacturers had resorted to adding starchy substances to their mixtures in order to reduce its unctuousness, much in the way that sixteenth-century Nahuas made *el cacao* with *atole*. Then, in 1828, the Dutch chemist Van Houten patented a screw press that would separate some of the cacao butter, leaving a lighter, drier powder that came to be known as "cocoa." Although old-fashioned chocolate remained in use, for example, by the British Navy, Van Houten's method was adopted widely and cocoa soon eclipsed chocolate in popularity. The new drink did away not only with cacao butter, but also with vanilla.

However, during the second half of the nineteenth century this leftover butter became the source of a new kind of "edible" chocolate, in which vanilla would again figure prominently. Solidified cacao butter—unlike the unprocessed paste—remains moist and malleable; colored and flavored with chocolate paste, sugar, and vanilla, it becomes the confection now known simply as "chocolate." Variously modified and refined, solid chocolate was enthusiastically embraced across Europe and the United States, and thus the historic link between cacao and vanilla was preserved. Together, cocoa powder and solid chocolate formed the basis of a new, progressively mechanized manufacturing industry.[112] Meanwhile, vanilla also acquired other uses, particularly in perfumery and in the preparation of candies, pastries, cakes and—most significantly—ice cream. In the end, then, the demise of the old chocolate beverage did not have an adverse effect on vanilla consumption. In fact, the contemporaneous emergence of these new uses—some linked to industrial processes—notably invigorated the vanilla economy, judging from the tremendous growth of French colonial cultivation in the late 1800s.[113]

Among the nascent industrial uses of vanilla, the manufacturing of ice cream in the United States was to be of special importance for Mexico's trade. Although dairy-based frozen mixtures had already a long history as luxurious desserts, the wholesale production of ice cream in the United States began only in the 1850s. In the following half-century, steady improvements in freezing technology and in dairy processing made possible the mechanization of ice cream manufacturing: hand-cranked ice and salt tub freezers gave way to steam-powered ones, eventually to be replaced by brine freezers operating by means of compressors. As a result, commercial production rose from four thousand gallons in 1859 to over twelve million in 1904.[114] This remarkable increase had a profound effect on vanilla trade, since from early on vanilla was among the principal flavors. As an expanding and cheaper supply of French vanilla inexorably gained control over Europe's markets, the ice cream industry to the North became an important outlet for Mexico's production. By the 1880s, the United States was already the top destination for Mexico's vanilla, and ice cream manufacturing absorbed a sizable share of these exports.[115]

Thus, in the course of fifty years (1850–1900), Mexico's long-standing commercial hegemony abruptly crumbled and the traditional nature and geography of the international demand for Mexican vanilla were radically transformed. Soon thereafter the business would also be affected by the introduction of artificial vanilla flavorings. Vanillin—from which cured vanilla derives most of its aromatic qualities—was synthesized for commercial purposes in the 1870s. The German chemists Tiemann and Haarmann first extracted it from coniferin, a substance present in coniferous trees, and a few years later their French counterpart de Laire obtained it from eugenol, a constituent of the oil of cloves.[116] Until the 1940s, eugenol would remain the preferred source of synthetic vanillin. Although the flavor of this "artificial vanilla" has never measured up to that of the original, its relative inexpensiveness would secure it a prominent place in the market for vanilla flavor.[117] To a lesser extent, "imitation vanilla" would also attain commercial viability.[118]

This newly fragmented and competitive trading scenario reshaped a business that had always differed in a fundamental respect from most other agricultural export enterprises. Just as coffee, cotton, or sugarcane, vanilla is a processed vegetable commodity; unlike them, however, its preparation cannot be mechanized or even standardized. It also differs from most other spice crops (e.g., pepper or cloves), the drying of which is a routine, uniform procedure. Vanilla is thus as much an artisanal as a horticultural product. A delicate, intricate, and fairly individualized curing procedure turns the vanilla fruit into a spice, whose degree of quality and relative value depend upon the manner in which this lengthy manual transformation is carried out. In order to understand the economics of vanilla production it is therefore also imperative to examine the curing process itself.

Out of a Fruit: The Making of a Spice

Once picked, vanilla had to undergo a carefully monitored sweating and drying process lasting up to six months. Along the way, heat-induced fermentation caused the formation of vanillin, and the withering pods thereby acquired their characteristic aroma. The green fruits turned deep brown or black and slowly shed most of their moisture, becoming fragrant sticks at once dry and supple. Properly cured vanilla retained its appearance, odor, and flavor for years. In Mexico, this transformation was called the *beneficio*.

From a commercial point of view, three interrelated properties determined the degree of excellence—and the relative value—of cured vanilla: aroma, appearance, and weight. A sweet, penetrating aroma was clearly superior to a feeble one. Appearance consisted of various aspects: length, color, texture, and body. All things being equal, longer pods had higher value; dark, even coloration, supple and oily texture, and surfaces that were not scarred or split were also considered signs of quality. Finally, since vanilla was sold by weight as well as by class, heavier was obviously better.[119] In each instance, the goal of the *beneficio* was to bring out these features to the fullest extent possible, to maximize weight without sacrificing the rest. Curers spoke of aiming for a point of perfect equilibrium: any less dryness would expose the spice to mildew—which eventually destroyed the aroma—or to discoloration, while any more dryness would only make the product lighter, leathery, and less fragrant.

This was in practice an exceedingly complex task, for although large numbers of pods had to be processed together, individual fruits reacted quite differently to the same treatment. Thus, no single path led to a successful *beneficio*, and the challenge—and risk—lay in figuring out what a particular fruit required in order to attain optimal curing.

The stakes were very high, for the slightest miscalculation could lead to a severe loss in value; a fruit that showed any signs of excessive drying, for example, was worth as much as two-thirds less than it otherwise might have. According to Fontecilla, three or four minutes of overexposure to the sun is all it took for something like this to occur.[120]

Ideally, vanilla should be physiologically mature at the time of picking.

Upon reaching this stage, the fruit turned yellowish and its tip darkened. Further ripening was inadvisable, because the pod was then likely to split open. However, this was rarely a problem, since premature picking was in fact the norm. For various reasons—including the prevalence of theft, price speculation, and the need for quick revenue on the part of producers—vanilla was seldom allowed to attain full maturity. Early picking has been a characteristic of Mexican production since at least the early 1800s. Thus, at the *beneficio*, the *pinta*—as yellowish vanilla was called—was invariably outnumbered by the *verde*, that which was still green. In addition, since collection was usually staggered over four or five months, the *verde* itself encompassed fruits at various stages of maturation. This absence of uniformity in the vegetative development of harvested vanilla accounted for the intrinsic irregularity of the pace of fermentation and drying. Hence, the processing of vanilla did not always follow the same trajectory.

Another fundamental source of uncertainty in the course of the *beneficio* was the weather. Solar heat was the principal type of energy used in treating Mexican vanilla; both sweating and drying were based largely on a sequence of direct exposures to the sun.[121] This is why curing had to take place within the so-called dry season, normally between November and June. However, in Mexico's vanilla region, sporadic precipitation was not unknown during those months; haphazard rain spells interrupted the normal sunbathing cycles and could at times disarray the entire process. Moreover, until the end of April, these rains were often accompanied by strong northerly winds. Those *nortes* brought in waves of cool, humid air, which fostered the spread of fungus diseases among the fruits being dehydrated. In an attempt to counteract these climatic hazards, rudimentary wood-fired ovens were eventually introduced as supplemental sources of heat. Still, for the most part, the curing environment could not be controlled, and thus the exact duration of the *beneficio* could not be determined beforehand.

For all these reasons, the preparation of vanilla was at its best an artisanal undertaking. Each fruit had a certain potential for excellence, determined largely by its appearance and degree of maturity at the time of picking, and the job of the *beneficiador* was to identify and attempt to fulfill that potential. To that end, the fruits needed to be individually steered through a series of procedures that could not be mapped out or scheduled in advance. In practice, this meant that at every stage of the curing process the pods had to be reclassified according to their current condition in order to be given the specialized attention deemed appropriate. Knowing how to do this well was a skill not easily described, in part because it could not be systematized. Fontecilla spoke of the possibility of developing "a refined sense of touch" after many years of practice, but in the same breath he stated that costly errors were frequent, even among *maestros*.[122]

In essence, then, the making of vanilla was a slow, lengthy, and risk-laden manual enterprise requiring skill as well as constant and extreme care in the consideration of details. To a significant extent, this accounted for the remarkably high value of well-cured vanilla in international markets. Unlike most other processed agricultural goods, vanilla was in the end a meticulously hand-crafted product, and as long as it remained in strong demand, its intricate and laborious preparation guaranteed that it would command a very high price. The *beneficio* turned this fragile fruit into a durable and prized commodity, and as such it was the principal source of its value. In and of themselves, vanilla fruits had no use—commercial or otherwise. Hence, of the two phases of vanilla production, cultivation and curing, the latter— when carried out successfully—was by far the most profitable.

This disparity is important because since at least the late eighteenth century curing and cultivation have been largely in separate hands: Totonac Indians grew vanilla out in the hills and non-Indians—*criollos*, European immigrants, or *mestizos*—in the towns purchased it for the *beneficio*. The origins of this long-standing division—just as those of systematic planting—are linked to the development of a vigorous export commerce, analyzed earlier. Trade networks centered in Xalapa and in the port of Veracruz relied on merchants residing in the zones of vanilla collection and cultivation for deliveries of vanilla to send overseas. As this line of trade showed signs of sustained prosperity, these local merchants, as well as speculators and others with ties to exporters, made the *beneficio* a part of their business. They alone had the capital or—more often—the credit necessary to finance curing on an expanded scale, and their access to information about preparation and packing standards favored in Europe gave them a clear competitive advantage. By the time Humboldt traveled through Mexico, most of the vanilla cured for export in Misantla and Colipa was handled by *gente de razón*. "They are the only ones," he wrote, "who know the *beneficio de la vainilla*."[123] Ever since then, Mexico's raw vanilla harvest has been managed by non-Indian *beneficiadores*, who obtained the lion's share of the profits derived from exportation.

As this brief account implies, the original economic separation of the two stages of vanilla production occurred for commercial—not technological—reasons, Humboldt's statement notwithstanding. Clearly, many Indian cultivators knew perfectly well the essentials of curing vanilla: sweating and drying through controlled exposure to the sun. Moreover, their curing practices were not significantly different from the *beneficio* procedures carried out by *gente de razón*. Humboldt's descriptions reveal no innovations, and Fontecilla's elaborate instructions, written half a century later, show the enormous benefits derived from experience, but—with one exception—retain the original technical basis.[124] Even the use of wood-fired ovens during periods of rain is probably in origin a native practice; it is telling that the Spanish term for this procedure is *poscoyon* or *poscoyol*, a version of a Totonac word that means "light baking" (*soasar*).[125] Thus, there can be no technological explanation for this division simply because no technical change occurred. Instead, it is useful to think of the *beneficio* as the core of a new set of economic relations born in the wake of an expanding export trade and dominated since its inception by *gente de razón*. The emergent commercial interest in vanilla—explicated earlier—led gradually to the establishment of curing workshops, which in turn required hired labor and an adequate supply of fruits; in this context, new social relationships were forged. For reasons suggested above, the organizers of these enterprises were not themselves cultivators, but rather townspeople with mercantile connections. With few notable exceptions, Mexico's vanilla economy would remain structured in that way.

During the late nineteenth century, a few prominent curers became also the principal exporters of the spice. A combination of experience and resources enabled some of these businessmen to refine their *beneficio* procedures and improve the quality and reliability of their product, thereby earning a valuable international reputation. In artisanal fashion, their names reassured buyers of the quality of the vanilla prepared and exported under their supervision. In this way, the large-scale *beneficio* developed into an export business closely identified with the name of a person or family. Henceforth, the Mexican curing industry would remain structured along these lines. Since the workrooms and drying yards were invariably located in the owner's house, these family businesses were commonly referred to as Casas—for example, the Casa Tremari.

The best cured vanilla usually developed in time a silvery luster produced by the formation of vanillin crystals on the surface of the pods.[126] This argentine coating—which the French called *givre*—was considered the supreme sign of excellence. In becoming *plateada* or *givrée*, vanilla offered visible proof that it had at last been transformed into a precious, fragrant, and imperishable commodity. From the point of view of its remarkable history, this final trompe l'oeil effect seems only fitting. After all, for related botanic, commercial, and gustatory reasons, during centuries vanilla compared with silver, not just in appearance but in value.[127]

In the growing areas, it was this last quality that made vanilla unique. This "precious fruit," noted a Papantla district official in the early 1840s, "is a perennial source of profits."[128] On account of its high value and in the context of an ever-growing international market, vanilla would become a powerful agent of social transformation in nineteenth-century Papantla. The next chapter describes the land and society of Papantla prior to the ascendancy of the vanilla trade.

2 The Tecolutla River Basin

The Terrain

From above the clouds, the high volcanic ranges and valleys that take up much of Mexico's territory seem worlds apart from the torrid strip of lowland trapped between them and the gentle windward shores of the Gulf of Mexico. On the coast, looking inland, it is not easy to imagine that beyond the sea of hills on the horizon rises a jagged longitudinal rock mass reaching more than two kilometers into the sky. From below, the true magnitude of this mountain range is impossible to grasp. The broad highland plateau beyond its easterly escarpments is entirely out of sight, and the escarpments themselves are deep and recede into the distance, broken by broad valleys or precipitous ravines and shielded from view by clouds, fog, and the intricate vagaries of their rugged topography. It is true that long ago it was oftentimes possible for those sailing into Veracruz to catch a glimpse of lofty mountain tops—the white cone of the Citlaltépetl, or the craggy chest of the Naucampatépetl—floating in the air, but side by side with a tropical coastal foreground these must have seemed aloof, ethereal, merely decorative elements in the landscape. Standing at the seashore, the Sierra Madre Oriental seems no more than a vast liminal presence.

However, in assembling even a general description of the lowlands of northern Veracruz, it would be a grave mistake to relegate the adjacent mountain ranges to the status of mere boundary, for the distinctive features of lowland ecology and topography in this area owe their being precisely to the complex geological formations abutting to the west. As it turns out, it is impossible to describe the climate, vegetation, topography, and hydrography of the *tierra caliente* in the environment of Papantla without invoking the Sierra Madre Oriental. Moreover, the history of the patterns of human settlement and trade in this area has also been decisively influenced by the high volcanic range that rises on its fringes. Therefore, although the Sierra Madre may seem remote from and even irrelevant to the natural and economic habitat of the *tierra caliente*, this impression needs to be resisted, for these mountains are indeed the mother of much of what lies below them. They are thus an obligatory starting point.

The mountain range, or *cordillera*, known as the Sierra Madre Oriental runs in a general south-southeast to north-northwest direction, from the Cofre de Perote—along the border between the states of Puebla and Veracruz—across to the Sierra del Burro in northern Coahuila and the Big Bend in southwestern Texas. Just north of the Cofre, however, the range veers to the west and follows a more or less latitudinal course across the northern portion of the state of Puebla—Teziutlán, Tlatlauquitepec, Zacapoaxtla, Zacatlán, and the upper reaches of Huauchinango. Once in the environs of Tulancingo, Hidalgo, it recovers its north-northwest orientation.[1] With the exception of Huauchinango, these towns (c. 1,890–2,050 meters above sea level) sit on the high eastern slopes of the volcanic range. Due west of this line, across the summits, the highland plateau commences. Toward the east, on the other hand, the land mass breaks and falls precipitously toward the Gulf, forming labyrinthine canyons, abrupt ravines, narrow terraces, and nest-like valleys carved according to the abstruse blueprints of gravity and geology. Beyond this elaborately broken incline lies the *tierra caliente* of Papantla.

These jagged escarpments cover an ecologically diverse area of roughly 8,000 square kilometers, ranging in altitude from 1,600 down to 500 meters above sea level, and are collectively known as the Sierra de Puebla.[2] As historian Bernardo García Martínez explains, "When we speak of *sierra* in this sense we are not referring to a *cordillera* such as the Sierra Madre, but instead precisely to these abrupt areas, to the rough, terraced piedmont which is a part of the great bluffs of the highland plateau."[3] The broad definition allows for toponymic subdivisions within the Sierra Norte de Puebla itself, so that sets of mountainous branches, demarcated by custom, topography, or trade routes, are sometimes individually identified—for example, the Sierra de Huauchinango or the Sierra de Zacapoaxtla. This reflects in good measure the severe fragmentation and concomitant ecological variety of the *serrano* territory, as well as the isolation imposed by natural barriers on zones that border on each other and appear on any map to blend in harmoniously.

There are multiple ways in which the mountains of the Sierra Norte de Puebla molded nature and society in the lowlands around Papantla; the very shape and relief of the terrain are perhaps the fundamental ones. As it cascades toward the sea, the Sierra branches out in various directions, repeatedly rising and falling along the way. Overall, however, it is possible to conceive of it as a deep geological basin. A useful image in this connection is that of a semicircular Roman amphitheater—albeit a ruined one, for sure. The towns of the so-called *bocasierra*—Teziutlán, Zacapoaxtla, Tetela, Zacatlán, Huauchinango—are strung along the broad outer edge of this basin. Down below, past the vicinity of Tlaxcalantongo, Filomeno Mata (Santo Domingo), Mecatlán, Olinta, and Huehuetla at the narrow end of the basin, the converging escarpments turn into a series of dense hill ranges, low plateaus, and somewhat broader river valleys. Beneath, the succession of wide, often sudden altitudinal swings characteristic of the *sierra* moderates at last; though still highly irregular, the landscape is thereafter less rugged, comparatively open, and at places even gentle. Here, the Sierra gives way to what may be described as a piedmont which slopes downward from the southwest toward the coast, directly to the east-northeast. Together, the bottom of the Sierra proper and the upper reaches of its piedmont mark the beginning of the so-called *tierra caliente*.[4] This piedmont—roughly between 500 and 100 meters above sea level—falls largely inside the modern state of Veracruz. Between the seventeenth and the early twentieth centuries, those lowlands formed the western confines of the political jurisdiction of Papantla.[5]

Eastward, the piedmont declines onto what geographers refer to as the coastal plain. Here, however, the name misleads, for the terrain is mostly far from flat; rather, waves of low, dome-like hills sliced by river valleys narrow and wide spread in every direction, as if the piedmont had suddenly resurfaced in an attempt to reach the ocean. As anthropologists Isabel Kelly and Angel Palerm once observed, lying beneath the piedmont "there are no outstanding peaks, no great scarps, and no deep valleys, yet there is virtually no level land."[6] Strips of alluvial plain—chiefly along stretches of the Tecolutla and Cazones Rivers—constitute the exception. Among the hill ranges—called *lomeríos*—lies the town of Papantla. Only well into the seaboard does the landscape come to a more or less flat rest, most notably in the environs of Gutiérrez Zamora and across the Tecolutla River to the south and southeast, where the waters of the Chichicatzapa, the Solteros, and other minor streams traverse a broad expanse of *llanuras*, floodplains, estuaries, and marshlands. Yet even there the terrain undulates noticeably until the coastline is in close proximity. In effect, then, the topography of this *tierra caliente* historically ruled by Papantla—a somewhat brusque piedmont followed by chains of low hills resembling a rough sea, in the words of one observer[7]—is essentially derivative of that of the sierra.

Another way to see this is by considering the link between the drainage patterns of the sierra and the surface hydrology of the adjoining lowlands. The steep sierra is crisscrossed by numerous rivers and creeks tortuously negotiating a way down and out onto the distant ocean. The jagged contours of the land are made more so through the erosive labors of these bodies of water. They flow turbulently through serpentine gorges and deep ravines and cascade down the sides of mountains, often with impressive force. These currents can be grouped into six separate river systems, four of which—the Necaxa, Laxaxalpan, Tetela, and Apulco—come together at the base of the piedmont to form the Tecolutla River (formerly San Pedro y San Pablo), the spinal chord of the lowland territory of Papantla. Past where the meandering waters of the sierra join to form a single stream—near Comalteco, scarcely 100 meters above sea level—the new river flows fairly placidly across 100 kilometers, through valleys in Espinal and Papantla to the wavy plains of Gutiérrez Zamora and then sluggishly onto the sea through the river-mouth sandbar at Tecolutla. The shape of the landscape both in the piedmont and in the coastal hill-land owes much to this impressive congregation of highland currents. As with topography, so with hydrography: the distinctive features of the low hinterlands of Papantla come into being by way of the sierra.[8]

As it turns out, the old administrative domains of Papantla can be broadly defined as encompassing the lowland basin of the Tecolutla River system—that is, the country drained by the Tecolutla, its immediate sources, and its tributaries, from the edges of the sierra and the piedmont down to the Gulf coast. The overlap is not quite complete, since political divisions invariably reflect far more than physiography, but it is nonetheless remarkable.[9] The northern, southern, and southwestern borders of this basin territory are harder to delimit, either from a topographic or from an ecological point of view, but for centuries other rivers were used to give them a political definition. The Tecolutla is framed by two parallel river systems: the Cazones to the north and the Nautla to the south. Both of these currents can also be traced to sources high up above the Sierra de Puebla which, however, do not drain into the broad geological basin or amphitheater described above.[10] Historically, Papantla's administrative jurisdiction extended to the banks of these two rivers. This was the case during the colonial centuries, when Papantla was first an Alcaldía Mayor and later a *subdelegación* of the Intendancy of Veracruz.[11] After 1825, however, the Cantón or Partido of Papantla lost the left bank of the María de la Torre-Nautla basin and a wide strip of land to the north of it (now part of Martínez de la Torre) to Jalacingo, and its southern border became the Arroyo de Solteros, which flows into marshlands adjacent to an estuary (Estero Dulce) linked to the sandbars of the Nautla.[12] The Cazones and the Solteros remained the limits of the Cantón of Papantla until it was abolished by the Constitution of 1917. To the southwest, the Cantón ended at the edge of the lands of Acateno and Tenampulco, both belonging to the state of Puebla. The Arroyo de Solteros descends from the range above San José Acateno, a territory which was for centuries under the control of Teziutlán. Lower Tenampulco—where the *cabecera* is located—is topographically a part of the Tecolutla piedmont, for it lies at the foot of a spur of sierra that marks the southern margin of the mountain basin; over these lands, however, Jonotla and Tetela—not Papantla—maintained jurisdiction since colonial times.[13]

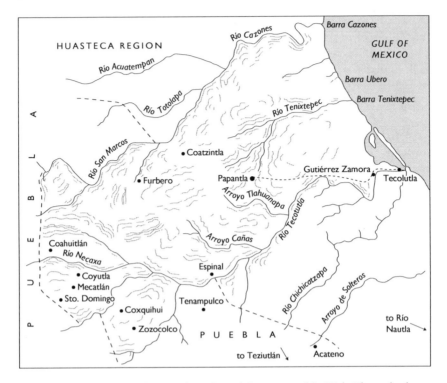

MAP 2.1 Old Cantón of Papantla. Adapted from Leopoldo Kiel, *El estado de Veracruz* (Mexico, D.F., 1924), p. 48.

Altogether, the old jurisdiction of Papantla comprised about 3,500 square kilometers (865,000 acres) of rumpled *tierra caliente*, and it included eleven colonial *pueblos*. It is presently divided into fourteen municipalities: Filomeno Mata and Mecatlán at the edge of the sierra; Zozocolco, Coxquihui, Chumatlán, Coyutla, Progreso (Coahuitlán), and Espinal down the piedmont; Papantla, Coatzintla, and Poza Rica among the rolling hills; and Gutiérrez Zamora, Cazones, and Tecolutla along the wavy coastal plains.[14]

Climate and Agriculture

It is generally recognized that cultivation cycles, crop geography, plant growth, and yield depend largely on climatic conditions, particularly in what Eric Wolf has called paleotechnic ecotypes—that is, systems of agricultural cultivation which depend exclusively on human and animal energy.[15] The history of essentially agricultural economies and societies is shaped in part by the climatic aspects of cultivation, and it cannot be understood without reference to them. The emphasis here is not so much on the history of climate per se—climate as a function of time, in the words of Le Roy Ladurie—nor on the impact of individual climatic disasters such as droughts or hurricanes, though both of these are indeed important to agricultural history, but rather, at a more fundamental level, on the incorporation of the particular climatic determinants of cultivation in a given area into historical explanations of the farming practices encountered there. Climate influences not only the output of agriculture but also the nature of cultivation itself. In Papantla, temperature and rainfall patterns have clearly shaped the character of agriculture, and hence also of human culture more generally.

Overall, temperatures in the Tecolutla basin are fairly warm all year long—the annual mean is around 72–79 degrees Fahrenheit—and relative humidity is always high. There is nonetheless a sensible seasonal oscillation; on the average, the difference between the mean temperatures for Papantla in the coolest and warmest months (December–January and June–August, respectively) is sixteen degrees Fahrenheit.[16] The swing is still fairly moderate. However, these averages fail to convey the short-term, intraseasonal variability that characterizes the area's temperature. Seasonal patterns notwithstanding, the temperature in Papantla—for instance—can rise above 90 degrees Fahrenheit in January or drop below 60 degrees Fahrenheit in May. Frosts are only extraordinarily a danger to be reckoned with here, but the biological cycle of various economic plants is sensitive to temperature swings, even within a more restricted range; for example, the flowering of vanilla orchids during the spring, on which the development of fruits depends, may be stunted by such shifts.

Irregular though they are, these short-term temperature fluctuations are not, strictly speaking, random. They do not happen in isolation from other environmental developments, but rather in concert with or as a consequence of them. In general, temperature and its behavior are shaped by physical geography as well as by other climatic factors, particularly atmospheric circulation and precipitation. Throughout the tropics, altitude plays a preeminent role in determining temperature; in the lowlands of the old Cantón of Papantla, however, its role is fairly marginal. Here, the proximity to the sea and the influence of the northeastern trade winds are far more important. These are broad, year-long wind currents that blow in from the east and the northeast over the seaboard and directly into the sierra.

Between May and October, when they are strongest, the trade winds gather considerable moisture from the warm seas beneath and transport it inland. The clouds and humidity associated with these warm winds contribute decisively to the makeup of the local climate—including temperature. Moreover, they are the source of the summer rains, the ancestral sine qua non of paleotechnic agriculture throughout Mesoamerica. Toward the end of this season, particularly in September, hurricanes are potentially an overwhelming climatic influence. From November through April, on the other hand, the trades are weaker and the Gulf waters colder, and altogether they bring in much less atmospheric humidity. Instead, a current of drier air flowing from the north largely takes over.[17]

Across the windward coast of Veracruz, however, these months are often hardly dry, for this is also the season of the *nortes*—cold, gusty wind fronts from the north made infamous by generations of fearful sea travelers caught in their midst upon approaching the port at Veracruz. The *nortes* are polar air masses that drift southward during the winter months. They warm up somewhat and pick up moisture as they cross the Gulf of Mexico, sowing high humidity, rain, and lower temperatures along their inland paths. Their might varies a great deal; some are powerful, even damaging storms, others just cool breezes and a constant drizzle. Throughout the Tecolutla River basin, the frequency and intensity of the *nortes* are the key to understanding the climatic profile of any given "dry" season. The repeated intrusions of these north winds explain to a considerable degree the sudden spells of cool weather and thus the wider fluctuations in temperature commonly experienced during these months. More importantly, without the associated rain and moisture, winter crops would not be possible across this area. Despite its destructive potential, the Janus-faced *norte* is in fact the basis of a particular rural economy and way of life.

Out of these winds, the mountains make rain. Once inland, the ocean-soaked trades quickly run up against dense hill and mountain ranges. Pushed up by the unruly sequence of ubiquitous slopes that lead up to and then constitute the sierra, the restive winds cool down and release their moisture in the form of rain. Here, the sierra shows anew its connectedness with the fate of what lies beneath. Across the lowlands, topography largely dictates the spatial distribution of rainfall and, a fortiori, the differential prospects of *temporal* agriculture. As this is essentially a landscape of nooks and crannies amidst dome-like hills and gently sloping surfaces, the rainfall is highly uneven; one town might get more abundant rain than another, even if they are in close proximity. Still, there are some trends in the spatial distribution of annual precipitation: it rains more at the upper end of the piedmont, close to the sierra, and less in the hills around Papantla and Coatzintla. On the average, the approximate total range is 1,100–3,000 millimeters (44–120 inches) per year, from 1,100–1,500 millimeters in the hills to 2,000–3,000 millimeters where the piedmont joins the sierra. In the lower piedmont, south of the Tecolutla River and along its valleys, as well as in the plains of Gutiérrez Zamora and Tecolutla, annual precipitation is in the neighborhood of 1,500–2,000 millimeters. In comparison, average rainfall in the highland Valley of Mexico is only 600–800 millimeters. Unlike much of the rest of Mexico, the Tecolutla basin is certainly not arid.[18]

Beyond that, what distinguishes these lands in regard to agriculture is the seasonal distribution of their precipitation. In most of highland Mexico the rainy season usually runs from May to October, when the trade winds muster the strength required to climb over the sierras and into the mountain valleys and plateaus. As a rule, the other half of the year is rather dry, often receiving well below 10 percent of the total annual rainfall. From the point of view of precipitation, therefore, the seasons there tend to be very well defined, and except where irrigation is available, this pattern dictates the rhythms of agriculture. Across the Tecolutla basin and in much of the rest of Veracruz, however, the successive waves of *nortes* produce a significantly different rainfall distribution. The bulk of the precipitation still comes between May and October, when the eastern trade winds and occasional hurricane formations dominate the atmosphere, but due to the influence of the *nortes* the rest of the year is by no means dry. Around Papantla, from a quarter to a third of the yearly rain generally falls between November and April.[19]

In a Mexican context, this pattern of rainfall distribution is indeed exceptional. Largely on account of it, two crops of maize a year can be obtained across the basin without the assistance of irrigation, and this faculty increases considerably the potential yearly yields of cultivated land. One planting normally takes place between late May and early July—*maíz de temporal*—and another between December and January—*maíz venturero*, or *de tonalmil*. Moreover, this relatively generous temporal distribution of precipitation has on the whole a beneficial effect on the development of a variety of tropical plants of commerce with longer vegetative cycles—for instance, vanilla or coffee.

This is not to say that rain supply is not a problem that local farmers have to contend with; sometimes it rains too much, other times too little. Both cumulative rainfall and its temporal distribution can fluctuate a great deal from year to year; indeed, compared to many highland areas, where rain patterns tend to be more or less stable, the interannual variability of monthly precipitation is very high, particularly during the summer months. As Kelly and Palerm noted during their stay in Papantla, "Precipitation is highly irregular," and thus "the Totonac farmer is mightily preoccupied with the rainfall," since "one year he may have abundant crops, the next, virtually none."[20] Variability is itself a serious hazard.

Still, the basin's climate provided a strong foundation for the development of a relatively prosperous indigenous agriculture. For the family economy of rural cultivators, the prospect of having two corn harvests a year made quite a difference.

Vegetation and Agriculture

In the lowland tropics of Mexico, the heavy influence of the geographic environment on the makeup of systems of cultivation manifests it-

self most clearly through the natural vegetation. Historically, the production of basic food crops—especially maize, chile, and squash—has been the
main object of agriculture throughout the Tecolutla basin; the slash-and-
burn and fallowing practices that are invariably associated with their cultivation may be seen essentially as adaptations to the multifaceted constraints imposed by the local forest cover. In a tangible way, the origin and
raison d'être of the Totonac farming system are to be found in the forests.

By all accounts, the Tecolutla River basin was once an area largely covered by high tropical forests. "All the lands of the Cantón of Papantla,"
reads a report from the early 1830s, "are so filled with trees of diverse
classes, producing wild fruits and timber, that they make the trails impassable."[21] Low altitudes, warm temperatures, and high atmospheric humidity
all year round favored the development of an exuberant flora of considerable diversity: several stories of trees and intricate networks of vines
crowned by a canopy more than twenty-five meters high. The Spanish word
selva—from the Latin *silvestris*—seems to convey more vividly the phys-
iognomy and internal complexity of this ensemble of floristic arrangements.
These original or virgin forests are commonly known as *monte alto*.

On the basis of structural characteristics—that is, environment and mor-
phology—scientists have classified the *monte alto* of the Tecolutla basin as
"tropical rain forest," albeit of the semi-evergreen variety. While "true"
rain forests—present across southern Veracruz, southeastern Mesoamerica,
and large sections of South America—are overwhelmingly evergreen, the
primary vegetation of northern Veracruz tends to be partially deciduous,
which means that a good number of tree species shed foliage—though
never completely—during the drier months. These forest formations are
primarily woody, and neither low herbaceous plants nor shrubs are abundant, as the high canopy prevents much sunlight from reaching the ground.
The tall *Brosimum alicastrum*—known in the area as *ojite*—is commonly
the dominant tree species.[22] Of the *monte alto* near Tajín, Kelly and Palerm
wrote that "the examples we have seen have a somber magnificence," noting that "undergrowth is not particularly heavy, perhaps because little sun
penetrates, but the tall trees are festooned with a great wealth of vines, and
sometimes with orchids and bromelia."[23]

While *monte alto* was far and away the predominant climax vegetation in
the old jurisdiction of Papantla, it does not appear to have been the only one.
In certain sites of very poor drainage and scarce relief, where soil conditions
were adverse to the growth of high forests, savanna woodlands—associations of shorter trees, shrubs, and a sea of tall bunch-grass—were probably
the original vegetation.[24] The coastal *llanuras*, stretching from the right bank
of the Tecolutla River to the Arroyo de Solteros on the southeastern end of
the canton, would have been the principal habitat of these primary savannas.

Perhaps because grasslands present special difficulties for cultivators relying upon slash-and-burn and fallowing techniques, the areas where this type of vegetation seems to have occurred naturally have not had—at least since the Spanish conquest—strong historical links with agriculture.[25] Instead, these lands were exploited primarily as cattle ranges, whereas the natural domains of the *monte alto*—both the piedmont and the hill country—have been the enduring heartland of paleotechnic agriculture in the basin.

Unfortunately, it is not possible to paint a more complete picture of the original forests of the Tecolutla basin; no analytic studies or comprehensive accounts of their internal composition exist, only scattered descriptions of particular stands.[26] This dearth of detailed information is already irremediable, since these forests have now virtually disappeared, casualties of the progressive development of cattle ranching, agriculture, and the oil business in the course of the last century.[27] However, even this rough portrait is enough to suggest how this type of forest shaped the basic conduct of agriculture in its midst.

"The first problem faced by cultivators," writes a student of Mesoamerican agriculture, "is getting enough sunshine," because in the forest most of the solar energy is absorbed by the canopy, and "most crops are low-growing heliophytes that require high levels of radiation and temperature to develop and produce."[28] Thus, before any planting can take place, most of the tree cover and the undergrowth need to be eliminated, in order to create a propitious environment for the development of crop plants. Indeed, as Kelly and Palerm have put it, maize fields must be "literally carved out of the forest."[29] Clearing a plot involves—to start with—slashing the low vegetation, felling all trees, and chopping the branches and trunks—steps referred to as *rozar*, *tumbar*, and *picar*, respectively. This is a long and arduous process. In the 1940s a cultivator in Tajín spent around twenty full days of work on the *roza* of one and a half hectares of thick secondary growth—and that with the aid of a steel machete; the subsequent felling and chopping of the larger trees in that area took him and eight or nine of his friends—all working with steel axes—at least another two weeks, often longer. Before these tools were available, successfully deforesting a field was probably an even more complicated and laborious endeavor.[30]

After completing these tasks, the emerging field is not yet ready for planting, as a thick tangle of fallen vegetation still covers the ground. The final step in the preparation process consists of burning this debris after it dries—clearly the most efficient removal method, in terms of both labor spent and results obtained. The prefatory chopping of protruding branches and trunks is essentially a way to improve the probability of a thorough burning. Once all useful timber has been hauled away, the remaining vegetation is allowed to dry over a period of weeks and a strip of land surrounding the clearing is swept clean to prevent the fire from spreading to the adjoining forests. Then, on a windless day, the lifeless remains of the forest are set on fire, and at last planting may proceed.[31]

Even after a successful burning, a new field retains many vestiges of its former cover. Its surface is "a bed of ashes, dotted with odds and ends of burned timber, and with charred stumps still standing."[32] Underneath, the roots of the *monte* vegetation remain. Such is the setting for the milpa, for neither the soil nor the surface require any further preparation for planting. The ashes produced by the *quema* will contribute to the fertility of the soil.[33] When the rains arrive, the maize seed—in some cases already germinating—is simply placed into rows of holes in the ground made by a long, pointed dibble (the *espeque*), where rainfall, sunlight, and soil nutrients will cause it to develop.[34] Chile, squash, and beans are planted either amidst the corn or by themselves, using essentially the same method. In many ways, then, crop agriculture rises on the ashes of the forest.

Deforestation and burning, however, do not mark the end of the natural vegetation's role in *roza* agriculture. This zero-sum link between farming and the *monte* captures only the first phase of a longer process, for the ecological modifications brought about by clearing produce in the milpa a microenvironment that fosters the growth not only of cultivated plants but of many others as well. Two kinds of secondary vegetation are worth distinguishing: herbaceous and woody. The first comprises a wide array of weeds and grasses unable to survive in the *monte alto*, all hardy, fast-growing, and in many cases perennial plants. The second consists of shrubs and trees, many from species found in the original *monte*, gradually recolonizing what were formerly their domains. Profuse and rapid, this successive renascence of vegetation is from the start a threat to the development of crop plants.

Soon after the clearing, weeds begin to sprout, sometimes even before the planted seeds do. They grow and spread rapidly under direct sunlight, and have adapted to compete very favorably with the food crops of the milpa; thus, if weeds are allowed to proliferate, they will invariably starve or choke the maize and its planted companions. Although grasses— *zacate*—also find their way into the milpa, the presence of weeds and roots from the felled forest usually keeps their propagation in check.[35] Weeds, then, are the main enemy; accordingly, cultivation consists almost entirely of weeding. The *escarda* or *limpia*, as this task is called, is truly a Sisyphean endeavor. Many weeds grow long roots, which cannot be pulled out without risking some damage to the young crop plants. Uprooting is also generally inadvisable since it clears the way for the establishment of grasses. Hence, the *escarda* for the most part involves cutting or breaking off the weeds at ground level while leaving their roots in place, enabling them to regenerate (and then to propagate) fairly quickly. The battle against weeds is thus a recurring one.

Assiduous cultivation is especially urgent during the early stages of development of the maize plant, when it is most susceptible to weed competition. "The owner of the field," noted Kelly and Palerm, "accompanied by assorted members of the household, works daily at this never-ending task." In addition, the entire milpa usually undergoes two systematic weed clearings within sixty days following the planting, this time with the help of others. *Tonalmil* maize has a longer growing cycle and usually requires further *limpias*. The cultivator's tools are the *coa*, the machete, the hoe, or the bare hands. The amount of labor invested in each of these sessions is by no means inconsiderable; for the first crop, when weed encroachment is bound to be less severe, it takes between eight and ten man-days of work to temporarily clear one hectare. On a rough calculation, this represents perhaps twice what planting requires and, more significantly, about a third of the labor time spent per hectare on the original felling of the *monte*.[36]

Altogether, then, the cultivation of fields carved out of the forest is a major undertaking, one which turns increasingly onerous as the milpa goes through successive harvests. The problem is not only that the number of systematic weedings per growing cycle increases, as each new maize planting— *tonalmil* and *temporal*—requires a preliminary *escarda*, but also—more importantly—that the process of weed-clearing becomes progressively more laborious. Weed propagation is the main cause; in spite of the sustained efforts of cultivators, weeds routinely manage to produce seed and thereby to spread their kind across the field. The *escarda* as practiced simply lacks the means to forestall this invasion. Inevitably, therefore, weed competition stiffens noticeably over time, and even a steep escalation of labor expenditures cannot curb the trend for very long, let alone reverse it. Meanwhile, shrubs and trees that once shaded the field also begin to grow back; some develop directly from stumps and roots left in place after the *desmonte*, and thus manage to regenerate rather quickly.[37] The incipient return of the forest intensifies the competition faced by the already embattled crop plants.

Largely because of this relentless sprouting of weeds and woods, but also because of a progressive reduction in soil fertility, both the productivity of land and of the labor spent cultivating it tend to decline rapidly from one cycle to the next; thus, the second *temporal* or *tonalmil* planting will normally yield less maize and require at least as much and often more cultivation work than the first one, and so on.[38] Rates of decline are bound to fluctuate considerably, because in every case they depend on an array of local and temporal conditions, but a 25 percent yearly reduction in crop yields does not appear to have been unusual in the 1940s, when iron and steel instruments were already widely used for cultivation.[39] Under such adverse circumstances, it makes no sense to insist on cropping the same field for very long, since there comes a point when it would be evidently more productive in terms of both labor and harvest yields to clear, burn, and plant another patch of forest instead. After all, a new *desmonte* takes only about as many man-days of work as the three *escarda* sessions required to obtain an additional *temporal* harvest, and the young field is likely to produce far more.[40]

Thus, agriculture shifts to a fresh clearing, and the old field is surrendered to the invading vegetation, which is free at last to take over grounds it had assailed from the beginning. When an abandoned milpa is overgrown with weeds, grass, and young shrubs, it is called an *acahual*. In Papantla, *acahuales* became the preferred setting for planting vanilla once it was turned into a cultivated fruit, and to that end, desirable supporting trees— for instance, *cojón de gato, laurel* or *capulín*—were usually allowed to grow alongside the crops while the milpa was still in production.[41] The *acahual* is the first in a succession of secondary vegetation formations that— unless it is interrupted—leads eventually to the full regeneration of the *monte* and to the restoration of the soil's lost fertility. The development of a dense cover of shrubs and relatively small trees marks a particularly important turning point in this process, because it creates an environment at ground level which is no longer suitable for weeds and grass; deprived of sunlight, they wither away. In the end, then, the establishment of a *monte bajo*, as this successor vegetation is sometimes called, gradually eliminates what assiduous cultivation could not.

The eventual return of forest vegetation completes a long cycle that commenced with the felling of the original *monte*. This secondary growth can then be slashed and burned to create a fresh milpa, whereupon the cycle begins anew. In the end, this traditional system of agriculture represents a shrewd adaptation on the part of maize cultivators in the Tecolutla basin to the unstinted growth of natural vegetation characteristic of their geographic environment. But while agroecologic circumstances constitute the raison d'être of field-rotation agriculture, socioeconomic conditions generally dictate its actual workings.[42] The duration of a cycle and the length of the cultivation and fallowing periods within it can vary sizably over time as well as space, depending largely on the availability of land—itself a function of demographic pressure, land-tenure arrangements, and the commercial value of local agricultural production.

Throughout the centuries of Spanish domination and well into the nineteenth century, the Tecolutla basin supported only a tiny and scattered population devoted largely to subsistence cultivation, hunting, and gathering organized around communal land holdings; trading was fairly limited all along, in scope as much as in scale. By the 1870s, however, a commercial revolution was clearly in the making, spearheaded by a flourishing vanilla economy. In its wake, social relations and land-tenure patterns would undergo profound change. The following pages examine the human and economic geography of old.

The People

Perhaps the most striking quality of the historical geography of human settlement in the Tecolutla basin is dispersion. With the still somewhat enigmatic exception of the urbanized ceremonial center at El Tajín, which was abandoned around the year 1100, the inhabitants of the basin did not form true cities or even sizable towns until well after 1900.[43] Since the sixteenth century, when the written record begins, and almost certainly before then as well, the vast majority of those who peopled this territory—largely Totonacs—have led rural lives. But unlike their rustic counterparts in much of Mesoamerica, most of the Totonacs of the Tecolutla lowlands did not generally reside in villages, preferring instead to live scattered across the land next to the fields they cultivated.

In the nineteenth century, the basin's villages functioned primarily as the administrative, judicial, religious, and commercial centers of extended, homonymous territorial jurisdictions which would later become municipalities; Chumatlán, for example, referred to the village of Santa María Chumatlán as well as to the lands belonging to a political community, and the term *el pueblo* (the people, or polity) *de Chumatlán* was meant to include all members of this community, whether or not they lived in the village of Chumatlán.[44] There were remarkably few of these colonial villages in the roughly 3,500 square kilometers that comprise the Tecolutla basin; a total of eleven at the time of Independence. Although villages were surely an important locus of communal culture, they were only sparsely populated, since most members of their respective *pueblos* did not dwell in them. "The majority of the Indians who belong to this parish," observed an official in 1830, referring to the *pueblo* of Papantla, "spend their entire lives in their milpas, and do not come [to the village] to attend mass except for the major feasts."[45]

In this respect, the villages in the Tecolutla basin were very different from the typically populous and compact ones of eighteenth- and nineteenth-century Oaxaca and the Valley of Mexico.[46] Papantla's skeletal villages possessed the emblematic Spanish plaza framed by a church and a government house, and perhaps a jail house, a cemetery, and an inn for passing muleteers, but were nevertheless not population centers worthy of note. The traditional grid pattern of Spanish urban design was largely absent from them, not due so much to the unevenness of the terrain, but rather to the fact that people chose not to settle in that fashion. Similarly, where the territorial jurisdiction of a village encompassed subordinate units, the administrative seat of those places (known as *rancherías* or *congregaciones*) consisted at best of a small cluster of rickety buildings and maybe a chapel, since here, too, most people tended to live spread amidst the fields, away from these hamlets.[47] Throughout, concentration was fairly minimal; scattered (*desparramada*), strewn (*esparcida*), spilled (*derramada*), and spread (*dilatada*)—these were some of the words used to describe the historic pattern of human occupancy in the basin.

Census figures display this diffuse form of settlement. The earliest count detailing the spatial distribution of the basin's population dates from 1871 (see Table 2.1).[48] At that time—thanks to vanilla—"Papantla" was already a common word in the lexicon of import merchants and spice retailers in Paris and Bordeaux, as well as one which the trading houses on William Street in lower Manhattan were fast beginning to recognize. Even so, Santa María Papantla, capital of Mexico's vanilla business, was then only a modest village of fewer than 2,500 people. Within the hierarchy of urban settlements in Mexico—*pueblo*, *villa*, and *ciudad*, in ascending order of importance—Papantla lay at the bottom; it still held the rank of *pueblo*, and not of *villa*, in spite of being the seat of the Cantón that bore its name and the sole municipality in that jurisdiction with an *ayuntamiento* (municipal council).[49]

The village proper consisted of a few hundred assorted buildings—mostly dwellings—nestled among hills; of these, well under a hundred were *cal y canto* (masonry) structures roofed with shingles or tiles—vaulted ceilings were extremely rare—and the rest were thatched huts made out of timber, bamboo, and mud. Only a handful of Papantla's buildings antedated the century. The church was large and sturdy, but wore also a humble shingle roof and looked truncated since it had no bell towers; instead, a lonely belfry sat high atop a nearby hill. The central plaza—which scarcely thirty years earlier had "a solitary, melancholy, somber, even lugubrious and terrifying air due to its contiguity to the cemetery"—was now partly framed by some houses with arcades, yet it remained uneven, unpaved, and bare. Urban symmetry was nowhere to be found: the masonry houses near the center as well as the thatched huts in the four Indian barrios were set haphazardly; the streets were few, rough, and narrow, and since not a single one was cobblestoned, heavy rain turned them into mud lanes.[50]

Over four-fifths (83 percent) of the inhabitants of the *municipio* of Papantla who were counted in 1871 made their homes outside the village, in *rancherías*. This term denotes both a scattered type of settlement and the political status generally assigned to localities of that type. As ecologist William T. Sanders has defined them, *rancherías* are agricultural communities "in which the population density of the residential area is the same as the area used for subsistence," that is, where nucleated or clustered dwellings are absent or at most very scarce.[51] Writing in 1845, José M. Bausa described one such settlement—the "beautiful and distended *ranchería* of Polutla," three leagues to the northeast of the head village of Papantla—as consisting of "fertile lands and an assortment of milpas, whose cultivators would form, if they were brought to live together, at least an important population cluster

TABLE 2.1

Cantón of Papantla in 1871

Municipio	Cabecera	Congregación or Ranchería	Population
Papantla	Papantla		2,380
		San Pablo	374
		Cazonera	320
		Mesa Chica	163
		Cuespalápam	148
		Coyuxquihui	196
		Pueblillo	201
		Joloápam	280
		Puxtla	155
		Rincón	157
		Cazones	200
		Pagüita	121
		Mesillas	176
		Aguadulce	284
		Cerro del Carbón	331
		Poza Larga	526
		Cazuelas	201
		Aguacate	188
		Totomoxtle	356
		Palmar	340
		Cedro	509
		Tepetate	133
		Boca de Lima	35
		Tenixtepec	190
		Polutla	507
		Tornacuan	475
		Loma de la Cruz	197
		La Concha	184
		Arroyo Colorado	215
		Carrizal	208
		Volador	243
		Santa Agueda	342
		Aguacate	292
		Talaxca	300

(Continued on next page)

TABLE 2.1 *(Continued)*

Municipio	Cabecera	Congregación or Ranchería	Population
		Sombrerete	367
		Mozutla	322
		Pital	340
		Cerro Grande de C.	437
		Hojital	317
		Tajín	247
		San Miguel	181
		Tlahuanapa	280
		Calera	274
		Mascapan	49
		Isla de Juan Rosas	109
		Estero	119
		Paso del Correo	56
		Sabaneta	33
Espinal	Espinal		834
		San Pedro	112
		Entabladero	185
Zozocolco	Zozocolco		377
		Temesostepec	96
		Zozocolco el Viejo	111
Coxquihui	Coxquihui		245
		Talostoque	31
		Comalteco	44
Chicualoque	Chicualoque		208
		Paso	41
		Isla	51
Coatzintla	Coatzintla		587
		Llano de Vega	28
Tecolutla	Tecolutla		430
		Cristo	150
		Cabezas	432
Mecatlán	Mecatlán		518
Santo Domingo	Santo Domingo		620
Coyutla	Coyutla		858
Chumatlán	Chumatlán		174
Coahuitlán	Coahuitlán		412

SOURCE: See note 48 to Chapter 2.

in its own right, with the means to build a church, etc."[52] Dispersion was clearly its defining element.

In effect, then, *rancherías* were administrative subdivisions within municipalities encompassing a certain dispersed population and—by implication—the lands it occupied or laid claim to. By 1871, forty-seven such localities were recognized within the municipality of Papantla. Some, like Polutla (507 members), Poza Larga (526), and Cedro (509) contained more people—albeit scattered—than many of the *cabecera* villages elsewhere in the Cantón; others, like Paso del Correo (56 members), consisted merely of perhaps a dozen families, each living by the lands it cultivated. New settlements were generally spawned through migration; some of these would subsequently disappear, be absorbed into other entities, or—in many cases—gain recognition as *rancherías* in their own right.

Between 1862 and 1874, all of Papantla's established *rancherías* were gradually renamed *congregaciones*. Despite their name, it is clear that these new sub-units of municipal administration had no discernible relation to the civil congregations formed by the Spanish authorities in the sixteenth and early seventeenth centuries, which had no lasting importance in and around Papantla.[53] *Congregación* was simply a new legal name given to the old *rancherías*.[54] While many of these newly designated *congregaciones* would in time develop a core hamlet—perhaps with a chapel and a store—which would serve as a gathering place and where local authorities would be stationed, overall they retained the non-nucleated residential structure of *rancherías*. Thus, at bottom, these were human congregations only in a political sense and not in terms of a pattern of settlement. Dispersion remained the rule.

A similar distribution of human population prevailed in the basin's other municipalities, albeit on a reduced scale. The head villages were tiny, and since their jurisdictions were in many cases rather small in extension, they contained few, if any, administrative subdivisions; where there were some, these were *rancherías* or *congregaciones* of the type just described. The majority of the minute *municipios* of the piedmont—that is, Santo Domingo, Chumatlán, Mecatlán, and Coahuitlán—had none, but in these places, too, many residents were in all likelihood country—and not village—dwellers.[55] Altogether, then, probably fewer than a third of the nearly twenty-one thousand inhabitants of the Cantón who were counted in 1871 lived in a village—or, as the Totonacs eloquently refer to them, a *cachikin* or *lugar de casas* ("where there are houses").[56]

This diffuse form of settlement practiced in the nineteenth century appears to have been of long standing. In 1581 Juan de Carrión, Alcalde Mayor of Hueytlalpan, reported that Papantla—then under his jurisdiction—was "a *pueblo* [people] with nothing to yoke it together, whose Indians live far from each other on hill slopes," and various documents from earlier decades reveal that Papantla, as well as some of the *pueblos* of the piedmont, were made up of numerous scattered clusters of dwellings.[57] Likewise, Fray Juan de Torquemada—a Franciscan who lived in Zacatlán and traveled through Totonac country at the turn of the sixteenth century— explained in his *Monarquía Indiana* (1615) that, among the Totonacs,

the villages which were the capital [*cabeza*] or metropolis of a Nation or Province were somewhat more ordered than the rest of the *sujeto* settlements belonging to that Señoría or Kingdom. In this capital they had their temples and cults . . . ; here would live the Lord and King and here he had his houses . . . along with others belonging to nobles; and although these did not line up to form streets, at least they kept to some order, which depended on what the terrain would allow. Such a settlement (in a certain way confused and scattered) would consist of a hundred or two hundred houses, sometimes more, sometimes less. The other *pueblo* [people]—I mean the rest of the Nation or Señoría—who belonged to this capital lived scattered over hills and mountain ranges, through valleys and ravines; they were many, by far the majority, and they settled down wherever it suited them best.[58]

To be sure, the degree of dispersion varied somewhat over time. In the second half of the eighteenth century, for instance, many Totonacs kept adobe houses in the immediate environs of the village of Papantla, partly at the insistence of the parish priest and of royal officials. For administrative purposes, these dwelling areas were subdivided into eight so-called Indian barrios. In 1767 about eight hundred heads of family (a total of 3,134 individuals) were said to reside in these areas. Still, many of them had their milpas far out in the *montes*, where they spent much of their time, often long periods.[59] Yet others lived full-time in *rancherías*.[60] By 1830, only four of the barrios remained and the village's Indian population had declined considerably, as many had resettled permanently in new and old *rancherías*. Insurgent warfare, the demise of colonial rule, and persistent political discord among Totonacs helped to bring about this shift. These specific historical developments are examined below. More broadly, however, it seems clear that certain general factors shaped the enduring historical character of the basin's human geography. These involve the relationship between agricultural practices and population dispersal, density, and spatial distribution, respectively. Each aspect will be briefly treated in turn.

Unquestionably, the remarkable predominance of non-nucleated settlements throughout the Cantón of Papantla reflects to a large extent the powerful centrifugal influence of *roza* agriculture. In order to function adequately, this system of agriculture requires a fair amount of land per family, most of which is not under cultivation at any given time. As explained, fields are abandoned every few years and allowed to rest until the rebirth of forest vegetation has eradicated weeds and replenished the soil. Since the period of regeneration is invariably much longer than the useful life of a milpa, cultivators must have access to several times as much land as they wish to plant on a yearly basis. How much so will depend on local conditions, but a factor of four or five seems usual. Thus, for instance, assuming that one needs to plant 1.5 hectares (3.71 acres) of maize, etc., twice every year to feed a family, that an average field can last, say, three years (six harvests), and that it must then lay fallow for some twelve years, one would require at least 7.5 hectares (18.53 acres) of cultivable land to accomplish this. Where the *acahual* is subsequently devoted to vanilla, such a cycle takes much longer to complete and—according to Kelly and Palerm's calculation—no less than 12 hectares (29.6 acres) are then needed.[61]

The relatively large land-area-per-family requirement underlying this system of agriculture makes sizable concentrated settlements rather impractical, because even if cropland is held communally and families can initially plant where they please, sooner or later some will be forced to travel great distances in search of new spots on which to carve out and cultivate a milpa; indeed, the larger the residential nucleus, the more acute the predicament. The ruggedness of the terrain only compounds this problem. Where land is used more intensively over time, as is the rule in the central highlands of Mexico, agricultural practices do not penalize concentration so severely. In Papantla, living close to the fields made better sense, and there were abundant sources of water for domestic use throughout the forest areas inhabited by *roza* agriculturalists—hence, in large measure, the overwhelming preference shown in the basin for the *ranchería* type of settlement. In general, population growth tended to generate further dispersion, as young men sought lands from which to support their own families; perhaps this dynamic explains in part the routinary sprouting of new *rancherías*, of which there is notice particularly during the nineteenth century. In the last analysis, both active dispersion and the very low incidence of residential clustering among these full-time cultivators must be viewed as cultural traits, themselves the product of a host of evolving circumstances, some ecological, others—as will be seen—social or political.[62] Still, it seems clear that the material demands of the *roza* system must have played a decisive role in molding these practical choices.

From a broader demographic perspective, the sustainability of paleotechnic *roza* agriculture rests on the possibility of keeping population density in check. As explained, the system's cropland-per-family ratio tends to be high, and this imposes a tight limit on the number of people a given amount of land can reasonably support on a permanent basis. To preserve a balance, population growth beyond this limit must be accompanied by a corresponding increase in the total land area susceptible of being cultivated via the *roza*. For as long as this outlet is available, whether by expanding the perime-

ter of a *ranchería* or through outright migration, this system of agriculture
can function in a stable manner. Otherwise, the only alternative is to intensify land use, which—in the absence of a new technology—effectively means
shortening the fallow period and thereby inviting increased weed infestation,
poorer yields, and a lower productivity of labor—in a word, breakdown.

In the decades between Independence and 1870, and indeed throughout
the colonial centuries, *roza* agriculture faced no such pressure. Across the
Tecolutla basin the people were not only mostly scattered, but few, and forest land was comparatively plentiful. Unfortunately, population estimates
for the period are extremely scarce and in many ways deficient; the few that
exist for 1743–1873 are reproduced in Table 2.2.[63] While they are probably
untrustworthy as indicators of demographic growth trends, these figures do
unanimously suggest that population density overall must have been consistently very low. Taken at face value, they point to an average of 3.3 to 7.5
people per square kilometer, even fewer (around 5.0 for 1871) if village-
dwellers are excluded. It is true that with the exception of the 1804 count,
which is perhaps even exaggerated, these tallies—especially those prior to
1870—are almost certainly too low, on account of both the difficulty of surveying dispersed settlements and the listlessness of local public officials entrusted with this task. Nevertheless, even allowing for the likelihood of pervasive undercounting in the more remote locations, it is fair to conclude that
this was historically a sparsely populated area. Indeed, even if the reported
figures for 1871 turned out to be as much as 50 percent lower than the real
ones, which is highly improbable, the overall rural density would still have
been around 10.0 people—that is, two families—per square kilometer.[64]
Thus, judging from the cropland-per-family ratios discussed above, it appears that there was more than enough available land, and that any demographic threshold was far from being reached. From this point of view, then,
the *roza* was an eminently workable system of agriculture.

Of course, Totonac agriculturalists did not deem all areas of the Tecolutla basin to be equally attractive or even worth cultivating under the *roza*,
and the spatial distribution of human settlement therein seems to reflect
these considerations. Not surprisingly, a strong historical correlation between the location of settlements and vegetation zones is evident; while
agricultural communities dotted much of the landscape where high tropical
forests were the climax vegetation, they were largely absent from large areas in which soil conditions appear to have favored the development of savanna woodlands. As explained earlier, *roza* cultivators found the latter environment comparatively intractable.

The pattern that emerges is both striking and enduring. The grassy *llanuras* and floodplains in the southeastern portion of the Cantón, below the
Tecolutla River, were largely unpopulated in 1871, as they had been in the
sixteenth century and perhaps earlier as well. A similar expanse lay west-

TABLE 2.2

Population Figures, 1743–1873

Jurisdiction[a]	1743[b]	1804	1826	1830	1837	1868	1871	1873
Papantla	3,000	—	—	5,471[c]	7,108[d]	9,908	14,058	14,267
Espinal	280	—	—	828	794	1,223	1,131	1,295
Coatzintla	100	—	—	109	113	329	615	373
Zozocolco	1,280	—	—	211	274	560	584	673
Coxquihui	732	—	—	242	419	211	320	317
Chumatlán	732	—	—	110	118	132	174	146
Mecatlán	280	—	—	164	117	593	518	594
Sto. Domingo	440	—	—	602	502	555	620	763
Coahuitlán	324	—	—	244	281	178	412	344
Coyutla	100	—	—	272	101	863	858	1,122
Chicualoque	48	—	—	75	68	170	300	279
Tecolutla	—[e]	—	—	176	134	887	1,012	986
Total	7,316	26,028	7,981	8,504	10,029	15,609	20,602	21,159

SOURCE: See note 63 to Chapter 2.

[a] Generally called *pueblo* before the 1850s and *municipio* thereafter.

[b] Villaseñor's unit is the family; his figures have been multiplied by six.

[c] Includes the *rancherías* of Boca de Lima, Tenestepec, Boquilla, and Cazones, the ranchos of Cazonera and Zepillos, as well as Estero, a small settlement on the right bank of the Tecolutla River which held—albeit briefly—the status of *pueblo*. The census lists all these separately.

[d] Includes the short-lived *pueblo* of Estero, which the census lists separately.

[e] Tecolutla was not yet a *pueblo* in 1743.

southwest of Papantla and Coatzintla and due north of the Coyutla-Espinal River. As will be seen, these were to become almost exclusively the domains of cattle. In 1871, just as three hundred years before, people settled and farmed primarily in three zones: the forested hill country surrounding Papantla and stretching north and east, the piedmont woods in the southwestern corner of the Cantón, and the rich meadows of the Tecolutla River and its tributaries.

Inasmuch as this spatial settlement pattern reflects the zonal distribution of agroecologic conditions most favorable for the practice of the *roza*, it provides graphic evidence of the extent to which the livelihood of the basin's inhabitants was tied to the kind of milpa agriculture described in these pages. Indeed, in a census of skills and occupations carried out in 1871, 87.7 percent of the working males surveyed (children were not considered) were described as *labradores*, meaning, literally, "he who works the land," a term commonly used to identify those who farmed for themselves. Another 4.7 percent appeared as *jornaleros*, which referred to those who labored on the land for others; and less than 8 percent of the working men of the Cantón were listed under nonagricultural occupations—merchants, carpenters, butchers, priests, soldiers, etc.[65] Late in the nineteenth century, this was still almost exclusively a land of scattered independent farmers. The main outlines of the basin's economic geography prior to the 1870s suggest why this would be so.

Colonial Geography and Economy

The nature of the topography and subsoil of the Tecolutla River basin, as well as the character of its indigenous human settlements and agricultural methods, rendered it on the whole unappealing to Spanish colonization and enterprise throughout the colonial centuries. For Spaniards—and later, mestizos—eager to turn the fruits of local land and labor into tangible riches, power, and prestige, the combined wealth of natural and human resources found in Papantla's territory must have seemed both relatively meager and, above all, persistently intractable. Hence, by and large, they sought fortunes and found livelihoods not in this verdant country, but elsewhere in their New World. Their strong urban culture, with its associated trades and industries, failed to take root here, and a largely autarkic, family-based milpa agriculture was to constitute the mainstay of local economic life. Well into the 1800s, this area remained in virtual geographic and commercial isolation, practically absent from the regional and international networks of trade and transportation that developed across much of Mexico in the wake of Spanish rule.

As a rule, the conquering Spaniards and their descendants were drawn to places where they could find either deposits of precious metals or relatively populous native settlements; for them, these were the two principal indigenous springs of wealth. Silver mining would create towns, roads, and trade where none had existed before, as well as a demand for labor, farm produce, and meat that was to engender migrations and transform land use and ownership in places both near and distant. Yet neither the industrial, commercial, and demographic developments associated with colonial mining, nor their ripple effect on the conduct of agriculture and ranching, ever reached the confines of greater Papantla. The basin possessed no valuable metal ores, and—isolated by the ragged escarpments of the sierra—it was too remote and inaccessible from the mining centers of the highlands to compete in supplying them with foodstuffs. What riches it lacked in silver and gold, the basin's subsoil would make up in oil; but not until the close of the nineteenth century, when its vast petroleum deposits started to be exploited commercially, would industrial activity come to influence the area's grain and meat economy.

In the absence of mines, Spaniards on the whole preferred to settle where there were already many Indians, in order to live off and profit from their labor. In this regard, too, greater Papantla was found to be wanting. The basin's small and scattered surviving population was a feeble and unmanageable source of labor, whether forced or free. Whatever tribute and labor services could be exacted were bound to be relatively scanty; moreover, since forest land and water were abundant, flight was always an option.[66] Hence, not surprisingly, Spanish settlement was a slow and precarious process. When Bishop de la Mota y Escobar visited the *pueblo* of Papantla in 1610, he found only five Spaniards living there, and by his own account there were almost none elsewhere in the basin, then part of the diocese of Tlaxcala; indeed, just two Spaniards inhabited Chumatlán a decade earlier, when a royal officer made an inspection tour of that *pueblo*. Almost a hundred and fifty years later, a total of fifteen Spanish families were said to reside in Papantla, and still fewer—in many cases, none—in the other villages of the jurisdiction. Two hundred *pardo* militiamen stationed in Papantla, along with their relatives, were the only other non-Indians listed in the area.[67] Across the Tecolutla basin, then, the Spanish presence was tenuous for centuries.

The undistinguished record of Catholic evangelization and institutional life in greater Papantla provides yet another indication of the relative half-heartedness of the colonization process. Although Franciscan and Augustinian missionaries—including the notable Fray Andrés de Olmos—were active in the Totonac sierras during the sixteenth century, their proselytizing incursions into the lowlands appear to have been very limited. Later on, the secular clergy would also neglect the area, and resident priests remained a scarce commodity throughout the colonial centuries. By the middle of the eighteenth century there were only three parishes—Papantla, Zozocolco, and Mecatlán—and a handful of priests operating in the whole basin, a situation not unlike that which Bishop de la Mota had recorded back in 1610. The "weakness of colonial religious architecture in most of Totonacapan," to which Angel Palerm has called attention, is graphic evidence of this historic pattern of neglect. Papantla's church, as noted, was altogether a very modest and unremarkable edifice, and a few decades into the nineteenth century some of the village churches (e.g., in Coatzintla) were still no more than thatched timber and mud huts without a priest of their own.[68]

As it was, though, the lack of mines and the paucity of indigenous laborers—while crucial—were not the only disincentives to colonization; in the case of Papantla, climate, topography, and geography also conspired to keep Spaniards away. From early on, Spaniards by and large came to regard the *tierra caliente*—especially the lowlands along the Gulf coast—as intrinsically unhealthy and inhospitable, and tended to flock instead to more temperate and familiar climates. This widespread aversion, it appears, stemmed at least in part from the notorious insalubrity of the port of Veracruz and its swampy surroundings, where virtually all travelers made their first acquaintance with New Spain. Deserved or not, it contributed to the unattractiveness of the Tecolutla basin.

Difficulty of access was yet another hindrance. Since pre-Conquest times, getting in and out of the basin has generally involved traversing the sierras that rise to its west and southwest; as will be explained below, coastal routes from the south and southeast were not really developed or widely used until the twentieth century.[69] The rugged topography and complex hydrography of these sierras, already described, has never made for easy journeys. Travelers had to negotiate narrow mountain passes, ravines, thick forest vegetation, long series of arduous climbs and precipitous descents through winding trails, often mud-laden, as well as countless river crossings. Swollen streams made fording perilous, and bridges were scarce and mostly flimsy.

Early travel accounts by Spaniards convey a sense of these hardships. "To reach all these *pueblos*," wrote Juan de Carrión after visiting Papantla in 1581, "one must make many dangerous river crossings." Between April and September it rains so much, he added, "that the rivers and streams rise greatly, uprooting trees and blocking passes and roads."[70] Likewise, during his lengthy journey through the sierra and down to the basin, Bishop de la Mota complained bitterly and regularly about the sorry condition of the paths; the five-league stretch between Chila and Coahuitlán, for instance, he described as "perverse." For centuries, many a traveler would echo these sentiments. Of course, the very presence of well-established indigenous communities across the basin—as well as the archeological evidence of its ancient urban splendors—clearly demonstrate that the topographic obstacles presented by the sierras were far from insurmountable; it does seem, however, that they made greater Papantla, *ceteris paribus*, less inviting than other more open areas.

Geography begot isolation in other ways as well. Midway through the sixteenth century colonial trade and transportation routes linking the population centers of the central highlands with the Gulf coast and the world beyond were already more or less established, and all bypassed greater Papantla altogether. Well to the southeast, the town and port of Veracruz emerged as the official gateway to New Spain, and a sinuous *camino real* through La Antigua, Xalapa, Las Vigas, and Perote quickly became the principal Sierra Madre crossing leading to Mexico City, with a rival pass further south near Orizaba gaining in importance as the centuries wore on.[71] These vital roads—which carried the bulk of the people and goods moving in and

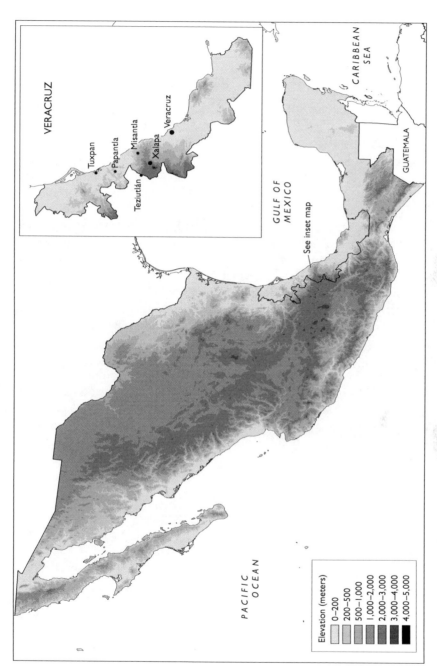

MAP 2.2 Topography of Mexico and Veracruz.

out of the entire viceroyalty—gave a great impetus to Spanish colonization and agricultural enterprise in many neighboring areas along the way. In more ways than one, roads created markets. These developments, however, did not extend to the Tecolutla basin. Distance was—as with respect to mining centers—a serious obstacle; although maps might give the impression that Papantla and the Xalapa route are not too far apart, in fact the broad Sierra de Chiconquiaco—a ragged spur of the Sierra Madre that stretches latitudinally toward the ocean—stands between them like a wall.

To the north, the Spaniards adopted an old route that went from Tulancingo at the upper rim of the sierra through Huauchinango and Xicotepec and down to Tuxpan; it also branched out to Pánuco and other *pueblos* of the Huasteca.[72] This trail—far poorer and of scant economic importance when compared with its southern counterparts—was nevertheless the main regional link to the altiplano, yet it skirted the basin's piedmont and approached the coast well to the north of Papantla. The Tecolutla basin, it turns out, was not on the way to anywhere.

It is only against this elaborate backdrop of colonial neglect and physical isolation—itself the product, as explained, of diverse factors—that the basic characteristics of greater Papantla's old economic life can be properly understood. The nature and social organization of agriculture and commerce, as well as the patterns of land use and tenure prevailing throughout the colonial centuries, clearly reflect the preponderant influence of these conditions. In particular, three defining aspects of the socioeconomic organization of the basin are worth pointing out: first, the unrivaled predominance of indigenous, family-oriented milpa agriculture; second, the relative insignificance of trade, both local and long-distance; and third, the absence of chronic conflicts over land. Each will be examined in turn.

THE UNRIVALED MILPA

For reasons that should by now be apparent, the institution of the hacienda did not take root in colonial Papantla. Those few Spaniards who made their way down to the basin would quickly come to understand that manorial agriculture, however desirable, was altogether impracticable in that setting. Native labor was scarce and, since good land was abundant, coercion would not work. Beyond this, the larger problem was that agriculture was bound to be a bad business. Even in the unlikely event that labor could be secured, virtually none of the land-based enterprises that might have been founded on the exploitation of this labor would have readily generated profits, since there were no viable commercial outlets for their products. Given the weakness of Spanish colonization, internal markets were nonexistent; elsewhere, the mines and towns were all too far, and the terrain made the cost and burden of transporting foodstuffs or almost anything else prohibitive. Owing to demography and geography, then, there was simply no way to make farming estates function, or pay.

Under these circumstances, Spanish residents for the most part did not—and could not—do much to modify the prevailing organization of agriculture in the basin. The means of production in agriculture—land, labor-power, and technology—remained almost exclusively under the control of Totonacs, who went on farming just as they had before. Clearly, Totonac cultivators had to operate under the same geo-economic constraints faced by prospective *hacendados*, but for them agriculture was not primarily a business, and this made all the difference. Since the chief aim of milpa cultivation was to provide nourishment for a family, the lack of market outlets did not present a serious problem; likewise, given the scale of cultivation, family labor was often sufficient to maintain a milpa, and cooperative arrangements could provide for gaps. Conquest or not, the subsistence-oriented milpa continued to reign unchallenged.

Self-sufficiency, it would appear, was the organizing principle of the lowland Totonac family economy. A goal of self-sufficiency is sometimes taken to imply a broader cultural philosophy of willful isolationism, but this is not what it meant in Papantla. There, subsistence-oriented agriculture was primarily a strategic economic adaptation to local circumstances. Throughout the colonial centuries, the conditions that made this a successful survival strategy remained essentially constant. As described, the *roza* is an eminently sustainable and labor-efficient system of cultivation, provided that there is an abundance of land, which was then undoubtedly the case in the basin. Thus, barring climatic disasters, these milpas generally yielded whatever maize, beans, chile, and other crops were deemed necessary to feed the family and meet any other obligations—ceremonial, tributary, etc.—until the next harvest. It is important to see that, on the whole, producing more (for instance, by increasing the area under cultivation) made no economic sense for any given family, not only because there were no markets for these extra goods, but also because the humid climate would quickly spoil the grain, making long-term storage for later consumption impracticable. The next corn harvest, moreover, was only six months away. These considerations—and not native indolence—explain the central historical paradox of traditional agriculture in the lowlands, namely, that although land was comparatively abundant and more fertile in the short-run vis-à-vis the highlands, the typical lowland milpa field was actually much smaller.[73]

While the family milpa was the main source of their livelihood, the Totonacs of greater Papantla also relied extensively on gathering, fishing, and hunting to supplement their domestic economy. The vast forests of this lush land were home to countless birds, mammals, and other animals, as well as a wide variety of fruits, nuts, roots, flowers, barks, leaves, fibers, and wood. These were sources of food, medicine, fuel, and raw materials for housing and tools. Fishing was an important activity for those who lived near the Tecolutla (then, San Pedro y San Pablo) and other waterways. In addition, it appears that many raised fowl (especially turkeys) near their houses, and cultivated some cotton to make their clothes. Juan de Carrión, Papantla's earliest chronicler, marveled at the prodigality of these lands, where "foods grow in such abundance that there are not enough people to enjoy and eat them, and so the birds eat them."[74]

Considered as a whole, the economic history of greater Papantla in the colonial period is, at heart, that of these self-sufficient domestic production and consumption units. They generated or collected practically the entire pool of locally available goods, allocating them largely in accordance with their own priorities. Since all could cultivate the same foodstuffs and had access to a similar range of natural resources, there was in fact little basis for local economic exchange. Not surprisingly, therefore, there is no evidence of the existence of a local indigenous market system in greater Papantla before or after the Spanish Conquest, or for that matter in the nineteenth and early twentieth centuries. In this respect, as in many others, the Totonac of the Tecolutla basin resembled the Maya of the Yucatan peninsula.[75]

In a colonial context, this more or less autarkic form of economic organization, however simple, can also be regarded as an expression of relative strength. Indeed, the wholesale survival of the self-sufficient Totonac household as the sole significant form of agricultural production in the area epitomizes the shallow impact of Spanish colonization therein. Despite the Conquest, Papantla's remained a thoroughly Totonac-dominated economy, one in which there was little opportunity for Spaniards to interfere and exercise any kind of proprietary control over production. For the conquered, colonial backwaters can be preserves of relative autonomy; isolation and neglect, it turns out, have a bright side as well.

TRADE AND THE SPANISH ECONOMY

Powerless to command Indian labor or overcome the barriers of geography, Spanish entrepreneurship was confined to the interstices of the Totonac economy. In most cases, it involved simple and very modest long-distance commercial transactions, the few that local circumstances would allow. Perhaps the earliest and most important was the salt trade. Both the basin and the sierras above it lacked salt deposits and obtained supplies either from Tehuacán or—in the case of the entire Tecolutla basin—by sea from Campeche in the Yucatan peninsula.[76] This coasting trade was already well established long before the Conquest, but by the time of Carrión's *Relación* (1581) it was operated by Spaniards. He relates that small ships would bring salt and wine to the mouth of the Tecolutla, where these were bartered for timber, maize, and fowl to sell in San Juan de Ulúa and Veracruz. At the same time, it is clear that Spaniards also took over the management of the inland salt trade, introducing mule trains for its distribution all the way up the sierra; according to Bishop Mota, the few Spaniards who lived in Papantla in 1610 were all devoted to this business.[77] In all likelihood, this salt trade gave birth to the *arriería* (mule trade) networks that were until not long ago the main commercial link between Papantla, the sierra, and the rest of Mexico.

In the course of the sixteenth and seventeenth centuries, the banks at the eastern end of the Tecolutla River (near the ocean) sprouted tiny enclaves of Spanish, mulatto, and mestizo activity. A few fisheries were founded, of which a settlement at the mouth of the river, called Tecolutla, became the most important. These waters were rich in many species of fish, and a dried-fish trade developed in close association with the salt business. In addition, certain kinds of wood were regularly shipped to Veracruz for house- and shipbuilding and repair.[78] Meanwhile, packs of mules occasionally made their way down the sierra and up from the river to supply Spaniards in Papantla and a few other clusters of *gente de razón* with commodities essential for maintaining government and a pretense of "civilized" life. Bishop Mota, for instance, observed dryly that the bread available in the environs of Papantla came from twenty leagues away. By and large, all these early transactions had little connection with or impact on the economic life of Totonacs.

Inland, the mule trade in salt and trinkets gradually managed to incorporate certain extractive activities of the Totonacs—many traditional, others new—into the world of colonial commerce. From the forests the Totonacs obtained beeswax, rubber, chicle, copal, pepper, pita fiber for cordage, and the medicinal sarsaparilla root, which they sold or bartered to non-Indian middlemen for sale in Veracruz or up the sierra. These lightweight products bore tolerably well the high costs of transportation through and out of the basin, thus providing Papantla's would-be merchants a rare opportunity to turn a profit. By the eighteenth century, vanilla was among these forest commodities. This was, however, a relatively petty trade, subject to the vicissitudes of collecting from nature and hindered by the basin's precarious routes and means of transportation.[79] Significantly, participating in this trade allowed the Totonacs to secure some money or extra goods without modifying their basic economic organization. These exchanges represented an unusual opportunity to supplement the domestic economy, and as such were surely relished by many.

In time, these long-distance mercantile networks expanded to include a few agricultural goods. Chief among them was tobacco, for which many parts of the basin provided excellent growing conditions. The royal monopoly established in 1765 outlawed its cultivation in this area but did not succeed in suppressing it.[80] Dried chile—largely from Espinal—and cultivated vanilla joined the trade in the course of the eighteenth century. The chile went up the sierra, while the vanilla was sent to Veracruz en route to Europe. The Totonacs also took up growing sugarcane to make *piloncillo* sugar and cane alcohol, partly for their own consumption. Again, a high value–weight ratio is the common denominator for these commodities. A handful of merchants from Papantla—along with their counterparts in Teziutlán and other *serrano* towns—orchestrated this trade, sometimes providing cash advances to growers. Where it developed, this incipient commercial agriculture and horticulture did so in the context of traditional small-scale milpa production and did not entail significant organizational changes; the Totonac system of land use was well equipped to embrace new crops or to expand somewhat the cultivation of old ones. Here, subsistence and commercial agriculture were not at odds or in competition with each other.

Maize was also the subject of some trade, generally local but under certain circumstances long-distance as well. The local trade supplied corn mainly to those who were not themselves from farming families. This population grew only very slowly in the course of the colonial centuries; still, the assorted non-Indians residing in the village of Papantla and its hinterland—bureaucrats, merchants, priests, artisans if there were any, fishermen, petty traders, and their families—needed food, and local merchants would have to procure from the Totonacs whatever the various prescribed colonial exactions would not provide. To a much lesser extent, the same occurred in other villages. There were, as noted, no Indian markets in the basin. The historical evolution of arrangements to supply Papantla with food is hard to trace, but by the late eighteenth century a simple system of contracts involving cash advances or *repartimientos de mercancía* to neighboring Indian growers was firmly in place.[81] *Pardo* militiamen often grew their own corn, which they also sold or bartered. In 1785 some ten merchants—apparently all Spaniards—were devoted to this business. These storekeepers—the same few who operated the trade in forest goods and other agricultural commodities—also handled the local sale and distribution of the maize they purchased from producers.

Judging from a correspondence generated during the severe agricultural crisis of 1785–86, it seems clear that in the late eighteenth century the Spanish merchants of Papantla also shipped some of the extra grain for sale in Veracruz. In those documents, a number of these traders come across as well-established businessmen, with extensive local knowledge, links, and influence, and with their own ships to boot; Juan Vidal Villamil, for instance, stated that "some *vecinos* of this jurisdiction, including myself, have given money to Indians for the planting of maize, and [we] own ships with which to bring it ourselves to [Veracruz]."[82] Still, a quick examination of a few cost and price figures suggests that this trade was only a worthwhile business in years when maize was otherwise very scarce in Veracruz; at other times, high transport costs got in the way of profits.

According to these letters, the normal cost of placing a fanega (55.5 liters) of maize at the docks in Veracruz was two pesos—one peso for the grain itself, two reales for taxes, and six reales for shipping. This meant that freight alone increased the cost of Papantla's maize by 75 percent. Meanwhile, contemporaneous sources suggest that in years of good harvests the retail price of corn around Veracruz was more or less two pesos; under these circumstances, wholesalers from Papantla might actually lose money. In contrast, during times of scarcity near Veracruz corn prices could rise to as much as four or five pesos. In those cases, there was room for gain, assuming that harvests were any better back in Papantla. Overall, though, the long-distance maize trade from Papantla faced severe restrictions, and thus, despite the enormous productive potential of the basin, it was a fairly modest affair. The prospect of windfall profits—and not the expectation of steady returns on investment—is probably what kept it alive. Ordinarily, merchants probably fared better in lines of trade for which freight costs were less punishing. Still, in terms of total value, the basin's Spanish business did not amount to much. Late colonial treasury records show that Papantla's *alcabala* (sales tax) receipts were consistently rather meager.[83]

This rough outline of the basic characteristics of colonial Papantla's economic organization reveals a clear divide: production remained overwhelmingly the domain of Totonacs, while a subordinate sphere of petty commerce developed in the hands of *gente de razón*, for the most part Spaniards. That does not imply that Totonacs were alien to the realm of commerce, for without their active participation there would have been little to trade; rather, the point is that those in control of production were not themselves merchants, and vice versa. Two different economies and societies coexisted uneasily in the basin; dependent and quite limited, the Spanish commercial economy was clearly the weaker one. Spanish Papantla's very faint urbanity is possibly the most perspicuous sign of this debility; trade—it has been said—is a great builder of towns.

There was, however, one notable exception to this historic pattern of economic organization: livestock raising. Here was, at last, a land-based productive undertaking that the conquering Spaniards did find practicable; unlike agriculture, ranching required little labor and could be managed with the help of a few mulatto or mestizo cowhands. In the course of the sixteenth century, a few Spaniards introduced cattle, horses, donkeys, pigs, and mules into the grassy *llanuras* and floodplains of the basin, where these animals could graze freely and reproduce. As explained, these ranges were not usually devoted to agriculture, since Indian farmers preferred to live and work in the forested hills; hence, while the Totonac milpa flourished in the *monte*, Spanish-owned ranches found a foothold in the grasslands.

Even in this one major enclave of Spanish-organized production, however, prosperity proved to be elusive. Despite the abundance of local pas-

ture land, livestock raising in colonial Papantla remained uniformly a
picayune enterprise. Over time, mule raising would survive mainly in more
temperate regions of the Mexican countryside, including parts of the sierra,
which offered better conditions—commercially and environmentally—for
the business of breeding these animals for sale. Horse raising, on the other
hand, clearly did endure in Papantla, but always on a petty scale. As for
cattle raising, the absence of markets was yet again the main obstacle to
growth. Due to the size, composition, and distribution of the basin's population, the internal demand for beef, milk, and hides was rather feeble.
Meanwhile, long-distance transactions involving cattle on the hoof were
not a viable option. Herding them for sale up the sierra was not only very
difficult, since the narrow and rugged trails were unsuited for cattle, but
also uneconomic, given the considerable loss in weight and value which this
long trek entailed. These adverse circumstances effectively prevented the development of an expansive cattle-raising economy in greater Papantla. The
basin's *llanuras* would not go the way of Pánuco or the Llanos de Almería
(near Nautla), cattle-rich coastal areas neighboring to the north and south.
Papantla's colonial cattle ranches, it seems, were always few and poorly
stocked, marginal operations, economically as well as geographically.

Although Spanish ranching played a fairly insignificant role in the economic life of Papantla, it nonetheless had a profound impact on the historical development of a land-tenure pattern across the basin's plains. There,
cattle ranching paved the way for the creation of large private holdings. In
the aftermath of the Conquest, most of those more or less vacant lands
were deemed not to belong to Indian communities; hence, Spaniards wishing to raise livestock were able to obtain title to *estancias* (estates) in these
parts by means of royal grants. Juan de Carrión provides a good account of
this process:

The *pueblo* of Papantla has much land, and many *llanos* that are *tierras baldías*,
where the Viceroys of New Spain have granted lands for livestock *estancias*, now
stocked with cows, for the raising of which these are very good lands. A certain
Diego de Cepeda, resident of Mexico, has an *estancia* fifteen leagues east of Papantla, and there is another one nearby that belongs to a certain Diego Larios, also
a resident of Mexico; to reach these two *estancias* from Papantla one must cross a
large river called San Pedro y San Pablo.[84]

By 1610 there were already several *estancias de españoles* in Papantla;
Bishop Mota lists them along with the names of their owners and the kinds
of livestock kept, usually some combination of cattle, mares, and mules.
These first estates appear to have been located in the two areas of the basin
where grasslands were abundant: the southeastern *llanuras* below the Tecolutla River, and a broad expanse that lay west-southwest of Papantla and
Coatzintla and due north of the Coyutla–Espinal River.[85] Significantly, some

of these early sites mentioned by Mota—for example, Larios, Jamaya, and San Miguel—would retain both their original names and a connection with ranching well into the twentieth century.

Scarcely populated or productive, the basin's vast idle lands gradually became the domain of a few Spanish estates. Some of them grew extremely large over time, a stagnant cattle economy notwithstanding. Larios, for instance, probably encompassed nearly one hundred thousand hectares at the time of Independence. By then, a dozen or so large estates, their boundaries largely undefined, laid claim to the greater part of the *llanuras*.[86] These were merely units of property, and not—aside from the small-scale ranching operations therein—economic and social organizations or institutions. Despite their size, "*ranchos*" was the term generally used to describe these holdings during the eighteenth and early nineteenth centuries.[87] In 1800, as in the 1500s, most of this territory was still comprised of idle lands, only now these belonged to a number of absentee landowners.

THE ABSENCE OF CHRONIC CONFLICTS OVER LAND

The foregoing overview of Papantla's colonial economic geography suggests why land itself would not have been a likely source of social conflict, either within Indian communities or between communities and *gente de razón*. In the absence of demographic pressures on forested lands, the Totonacs' *roza* system of agriculture could function optimally, free from the tensions generated by scarcity.[88] Moreover, native agriculture did not have to face much outside competition over the use of potentially cultivable lands, and this helped to preserve the integrity of the communal properties of the Totonac *pueblos*. Avid encroachment of Spanish haciendas upon Indian communal lands—evident in other parts of New Spain—was not even a possibility here, simply because there were no haciendas to begin with. From the start, a dearth of markets and labor for hire had made manorial farming wholly impracticable, so when it came to agricultural production, there were no likely alternatives to the milpa. Under these circumstances, Spanish-controlled land use was largely restricted to livestock raising, which for the most part occupied pastures and savanna woodlands well removed from the heartlands of agriculture. Spanish ranching and Totonac farming each had their primary spaces and thus rarely found themselves struggling over the use of land. This radical separation of cattle ranching and agriculture explains in part why the plough was not adopted by the basin's farmers; the Spaniards were not involved in agriculture, and the Totonacs did not on the whole keep cattle. The *roza* system of cultivation did not require turning up the soil.[89]

Disputes between Totonacs and Spaniards over the legal status of particular territory did arise occasionally, but these were prompted by naked greed and not land scarcity. The few of which there is notice date from the late eighteenth century, when Papantla's emergent merchant nucleus intensified its efforts to develop profitable lines of business. Perhaps the most notorious of these disputes involved a corrupt 1787 scheme by prominent local merchants Juan Vidal and Joaquín Suárez to claim ownership of lands that had traditionally belonged to the Totonacs of Coatzintla. They argued that the lands in question were *realengas* (of the crown) and idle, and on that basis sought to obtain legal title to them. It is telling that the contested territory consisted mainly of pasturelands, and that the merchants wanted it to graze their cattle. In the end, however, the ploy was unsuccessful, and the Indians' property rights were duly confirmed.[90] For the Totonacs, it seems, economic independence was a source of great political leverage, even in a colonial context.

There were other, more serious social conflicts in late colonial Papantla, but land had nothing to do with them. Historian Michael Ducey's careful analysis of a number of local riots and revolts in the 1760s and 1780s suggests that issues of commerce and its regulation were often at the root of these violent clashes. A 1762 riot was linked to the efforts of a powerful merchant to have the Alcalde Mayor removed. A few years later, the Alcalde confiscated some of the Indians' tobacco crop, provoking another riot. In both cases, the town hall was burned down. In October 1767 a dissident faction of Indians rebelled against Alcalde Mayor Alonso de la Varga, who abused his powers in an attempt to monopolize the local trade. Along with a business associate, the rapacious de la Varga conspired to drive away competing merchants, forced Indians to buy his wares, and pressured them to sell their products—including vanilla and maize—at unfair prices. The dissidents' wrath extended also to the Indian officials of the *pueblo*, whom they regarded as accomplices of de la Varga. The motives behind a 1787 rebellion appear far less clear, but the enforcement of the tobacco monopoly, as well as the rival dealings of unscrupulous merchant–bureaucrats and their respective Indian allies, seem to have played a significant role.[91] Not surprisingly, all these uprisings occurred in the village of Papantla, the political and commercial capital of the basin. As Spanish merchants and bureaucrats jockeyed for the control of commerce, the latter routinely abused the powers of their office for the sake of personal gain, giving rise to myriad grievances. Indian officers frequently took sides or participated in these crude struggles over the conduct of commerce, creating or accentuating divisions inside the Totonac community.

Tax collections and the organization of communal finances in general were also a source of conflict among Totonacs. Since Indian officers were in charge of enforcing fiscal obligations, disputes and accusations regarding power and money often flared up during the annual elections, revealing the deep factionalism and entrenched animosities that seem to have characterized Papantla's communal relations in the decades prior to Independence. Indeed, as Michael Ducey has noted, Papantla's eighteenth-century Indian politics reflected very little "communal solidarity."[92] Beyond personal enmities and specific allegations of malfeasance, the peculiar structure of Totonac economic life helps to account for these incohesive propensities. This was a society of independent farmers, and while some Indians were surely more prosperous and influential than others, in the end most had free access to the resources necessary to make it on their own. Hence, unlike in other Indian communities operating under different ecological and external social pressures, here the individual benefits of subordination—or, for that matter, of cooperation—were not always obvious or compelling. Thus, the same set of circumstances that thwarted Spanish attempts to control Indian labor in Papantla also lent communal governance (in the broadest sense) an unruly and fragmented quality.

Papantla's Bourbon-era village frays underscore the established bipolar nature of the basin's economic order: Indian agriculturalists and gatherers settled around their milpas and Spanish traders operating out of the villages. Independence from Spain—for which many in the basin fought ardently—brought some changes, particularly in the political arena, but the old economic organization remained essentially intact. Independence per se did not loosen the grip of those circumstances—geographic, demographic, and social—that had long shaped the basin's economic life. The vanilla business, however, would in time manage to accomplish just that.

New Country, Old Patterns

After 1810, in the wake of a generalized political crisis, the persistent tensions over authority, autonomy, and exploitative commerce that characterized social relations in late colonial Papantla burst into open warfare. In and around Papantla, but also in other parts of the basin, the fighting was protracted and at times intense. Two names, Olarte (for Serafín and Mariano Olarte, insurgent Totonac leaders) and Coyusquihui (the impregnable rebel camp in a hilly area south of Papantla), have come to symbolize Papantla's active participation in the struggle for independence from Spain. Many Totonacs as well as non-Indians rebelled against taxes, arbitrary local rule, and entrenched privilege, seeking to overturn the established political order; this meant challenging not only Spanish authorities but also their Indian allies. The insurgents' grievances were old, and in many cases probably very concrete as well.

Not surprisingly, many insurgents saw Spanish merchants cum public officials as the embodiment of oppression. In Papantla, the Vidal family was singled out for attack. Juan Vidal, who was perhaps the most powerful and prominent of the basin's merchants, had also held diverse official positions, including administrator of the tobacco monopoly, collector of the *alcabala*, postal administrator, and captain of the local militia. One of his sons became Papantla's loyalist military commander in early 1821.[93] This was, moreover, the same Juan Vidal who had once tried to usurp lands from the *pueblo* of Coatzintla. The influence and interests of the Vidal family were far-reaching, and they knew well how to protect them. For the insurgents, to do away with men like Juan Vidal was to strike a blow at the heart of the old political order. That, it seems, was for them the tangible meaning of "independence."

In the end, though, Papantla's insurgents had to settle for much less than they had hoped for. Independence did come, but not without an ironic twist. An expedient alliance of loyalist and insurgent military commanders—based on Iturbide's clever Plan de Iguala of February 24, 1821—paved the way for an essentially conservative political transition, which achieved independence from Spain while preserving the privileged standing of many who had long fought to prevent it. Thus, former foes of an independent Mexico ended up successfully claiming a prominent role in the management of the new country.

The Spanish merchant elite managed to survive the rocky transition to a republican form of government relatively unscathed; in politics, as well as in business, this small group retained an overwhelming influence. The Vidal family, for instance, did not see its local prominence diminish in the wake of Independence. In 1830, Papantla's Alcalde was none other than José María Vidal, the former loyalist commander.[94] Later, with Centralism on the rise, Juan Vidal *hijo* would hold various high posts in the administration of Papantla; that the Vidals were able to follow in the footsteps of their father—the intervening defeat of royalism notwithstanding—is indicative of the limited impact of the coming of Independence on the political fortunes of the ruling merchants of the basin. As for business, it is telling that twenty-five years after the signing of the Treaty of Córdoba twenty-odd Spaniards (including Juan Vidal) still controlled virtually all of the basin's commerce and capital.[95] This was not exactly the kind of "independence" that the Indian rebels of Coyusquihui had fought for.

Among Papantla's Totonacs, the war deepened already grievous divisions, abetting the centrifugal forces that were already at work. Historian Michael Ducey has characterized this period as one of "civil war within the pueblos." When the royalists took Papantla "after 18 months of insurgent rule," he writes, the Indian community "literally split in two, as large numbers of villagers took refuge in the hills, while loyalist Indians enlisted in government militias."[96] As will be seen, many never returned. Here, it seems, Independence abolished the República de Indios in more ways than one. At the same time, guerilla warfare gave rise to a new generation of Totonac leaders, men with a new authority earned on the battlefields. They managed to retain a prominent local role in the years after Independence, even though many of the freedoms they had fought for failed to materialize.

To be sure, the rules of politics were never the same once the colonial order was effectively dismantled. The awkward truce that led to Independence soon gave way to half a century of internecine disputes over national laws, governing institutions, and forms of administration. In Papantla, however, the sources of social friction seem not to have changed appreciably. Many of the conflicts—political as well as social—that had animated years of guerrilla warfare across the basin were left essentially unresolved, and would resurface with a vengeance amid the chronic political instability of the early republican decades. Thus, when former insurgent Mariano Olarte rebelled once more in late 1836, he and his many followers would still be fighting largely over the old local issues of authority, autonomy, and commercial practices. The rhetoric and factional intricacies of national political contestation were new, but Papantla's basic social conflicts and protagonists had remained substantially the same.[97]

To the extent that these social struggles were rooted in the peculiar form of economic organization that had long prevailed across the basin, their recurrence points directly to the fact that Independence did not significantly alter the rules of economic life. In effect, the radical division between agricultural producers and traders—largely along ethnic lines—persisted, and with it, inevitably, the tangle of conflicts and alliances over terms of trade between them.[98] Looking past the daring of battles fought, the high hopes of political pronouncements, and the local freedoms imagined in constitutional articles, it is possible to see that the defining aspects—demographic, geographic, and commercial—of Papantla's colonial economy were not affected by the dramatic political upheavals of the early nineteenth century. In fact, these would not begin to change for another half century. In the last analysis circa 1870, just as a hundred years earlier, dispersed settlement, faint urbanity, labor scarcity, geographic isolation, poor communications, subsistence-oriented Totonac agriculture, a lack of internal markets, sluggish ranching, and limited long-distance commerce were still to characterize the basin's economic order. These are striking continuities, worth documenting and analyzing in some detail.

The historic sparsity and overwhelming rurality of the basin's population have already been discussed; it is worth noting, however, that the geographic dispersion of human settlements actually increased in the wake of the wars of Independence. In those years, the Olartes, their followers, and

their families abandoned their dwellings in the barrios at the outskirts of
the village of Papantla and established permanent rebel camps in Coyusquihui and other points south of the Tecolutla River. By some accounts, over
two thousand people came to live in these thickly forested areas; after the
war, a number of these sites remained as *rancherías* in their own right, since
many opted to stay away from the village. Considering contemporary population figures, it is clear that the struggle for Independence led to a significant spatial redistribution of Papantla's population.[99]

Totonacs still constituted the vast majority of the basin's inhabitants. "All
of the *pueblos* of the Cantón," reads a report from 1830, "are for the most
part made up of *indígenas*, with the exception of the *pueblo* of Tecolutla,
which is all *gente de razón*, and the *cabecera* (Papantla), where one fourth
are of that class and the rest are *indígenas*." In 1845, Bausa estimated that
one-third of those in the *cabecera*, one-twelfth of those in Espinal, and all of
Tecolutla and Chicualoque's inhabitants were *de razón*. "All the other *pueblos* of the Partido," he added with typical disdain, "are made up of *puros indígenas incultos*, lacking entirely in civilization."[100] Using the demographic
figures provided by these authors (see Table 2.2), one would conclude that
80 to 85 percent of the basin's people were Totonacs, but considering that
many who lived scattered in remote locations were not likely to be counted,
it seems fair to think that the actual percentage of Totonacs was even higher.
The census of occupations of 1871 confirms this impression; more than 90
percent of the working males surveyed were *labradores* or *jornaleros*, and it
is safe to presume that nearly all of them were Totonacs.

Very low overall population density and widespread availability of land
for family farming—communal or otherwise—meant that the historic
shortage of labor for hire continued; moreover, the governmental disarray
that followed the collapse of Spanish rule rendered institutionalized forms
of labor coercion even less effective than they had once been. In 1870, as in
1780 or 1700, there was no local supply of labor with which to undertake
large-scale manorial agriculture. José María Bausa complained bitterly,
about *la falta de brazos*, which "kept agriculture in a complete state of
ruin." The cause of this calamity, he wrote, was "the abundance amidst
which the Indians are accustomed to living." "For the mule trade," he
noted, "we have had to make use of people from the sierra, who do this
service out of need and are thus not ashamed of it."[101]

It is telling that even domestic servants were hard to find, control, and
keep. Bausa's lengthy and graphic lamentations on this subject make up
perhaps the most engrossing part of his *Bosquejo*; "Papantla," he explained, "suffers extraordinarily because of the lack of domestic servants."
Although he grumbled chiefly about what he considered to be routine bad
manners, irreverence, absence of subservience, immorality, and poor serv-

ice on the part of these workers, it seems clear that what he really deplored was their extraordinary bargaining power. Of cooks, for instance, he wrote:

One can hardly find them; they hire themselves out only after imposing a thousand advantageous conditions; they dislike being directed by the lady of the house; they get offended by the slightest suggestion, which they regard as scolding rather than something to be grateful for; they damage the reputation of the house and in the end do as they please. The poor masters suffer but can't say a word for fear that the women will leave; the families have to resign themselves to eating the badly seasoned food that they are given, and have to put up with the whims of the cooks. Should any displeasure be expressed, they leave without warning, and if perchance the master of the house has guests, he will be embarrassed by a disobedience that ought to be punished. . . . In sum, the masters have to live at the mercy of their cooks, and have to take their meals whenever the cooks decide to serve them, whether or not they are hungry, because what matters to those women is to serve at certain hours so they can take off.

The behavior of other domestic employees—nursemaids, servants, handymen—he described in similar terms. Bausa's proposed remedies for this "opprobrious" situation—which he insisted was of long standing—included imprisonment and "correctional" forced domestic service for "dissolute female vagabonds."[102] It is hard to imagine a more eloquent indication of the elite's frustration with the chronically depressed state of the labor supply in Papantla.

Meanwhile, difficulty of access and prohibitive freight costs continued to hinder the development of agricultural and commercial enterprises, since Independence did not lead to any investments in new or improved means of communication and transportation for the basin. For the most part, people and goods moving to or from Papantla had still to negotiate the tortuous and narrow trails of the Sierra de Puebla, and the hardships this involved remained a salient aspect of local life, including business. Not surprisingly, contemporary evaluations of the basin's trails by travelers and public officials echo—sometimes word by word—those of their colonial predecessors. Writing in 1830, the *jefe político* of Papantla observed: "It is worth noting that all of the Cantón's trails cross very arduous terrain; they are dangerous during most seasons because the *pueblos* are located in a *serranía*, and [also] there are no bridges whatsoever over the rivers."[103] Fifteen years later, Bausa was unable to report any improvement: "In the summer, [the trails] are terrible, and in the winter and the rainy season they become impassable, due to mud, quagmires, slippery ascents and descents, ditches, swamps, swollen rivers and streams, and the lack of canoes with which to traverse the latter."[104] Needless to say, even in the best of times, only pedestrians, mules, and—in some cases—horses could make use of these trails; stagecoaches, mule-drawn wheeled carts, or litters were entirely out of the question.

Midway through the nineteenth century, the main *serrano* routes out of Papantla took the traveler through Teziutlán and on to Perote, through Zacapoaxtla toward San Juan de los Llanos (Libres), or through Huauchinango in the direction of Otumba. The choice depended on the final destination as well as on the season: Huauchinango–Otumba was taken to reach Mexico City directly, Zacapoaxtla–San Juan for Puebla and Mexico City, and Teziutlán–Perote for Xalapa, Veracruz, Puebla, or Mexico City. There were also other minor upland routes and branches. Inside the lowlands, aside from the paths linking the *pueblos* of the basin, a northern trail connected Papantla to Tuxpan and the Huasteca, and two southern ones—much less traveled—led to Misantla inland and to Veracruz along the coast. In addition, the old cabotage between Tecolutla, Veracruz, and other Gulf ports continued.[105]

In the course of the nineteenth century, the Camino de Teziutlán gradually emerged as the principal artery linking the Tecolutla basin with the centers of Mexican government and business. It was often the quickest and always the least unreliable route to Xalapa and Veracruz, both state capitals at various times, and as such it also offered the most direct access to the all-important former Camino Real connecting the port at Veracruz with Mexico City. The swampy coastal route to Veracruz, though less circuitous, was very poorly maintained, lacked convenient stopovers, and involved too many difficult river crossings. The Misantla road had similar disadvantages, and once there, the trek from Misantla on to Xalapa over the rugged Sierra de Chiconquiaco was by all accounts famously dangerous.[106] Thus, for instance, regular mail bound for Veracruz, Xalapa, Puebla, and Mexico City came to be sent through Teziutlán; the route taken was probably Papantla–Paso del Correo–Pueblillo–La Laja–Acateno–Tlapacoyan–Teziutlán. The last stretch—a series of very steep, slippery slopes long known as the *cuesta* of Teziutlán—was particularly arduous. At the time of Bausa's writing, it took the postman on this route three full days to travel some twenty-four leagues (c. seventy-one miles) on foot.[107] Even so, there was no easier way up from Papantla.

Still, it would be a mistake to interpret the ascendancy of the Teziutlán route merely as a direct consequence of topography; other *serrano* towns could have conceivably played this role as well. In fact, Teziutlán's long-standing importance as a gateway for Papantla's traffic also reflects the expansive influence of its merchant class. Midway through the nineteenth century Teziutlán's merchant families developed an active interest in the commercial possibilities of the adjoining coastal lowlands, not only around the Tecolutla basin, but also—perhaps even more aggressively—throughout the neighboring Nautla (Bobos) basin. They had a prominent hand in the organization and development of modern long-distance trade patterns in the lowlands, both bringing in assorted manufactures and—more importantly—extracting some spices, tobacco, and vanilla for resale above or abroad. By means of credit and transportation arrangements, often cemented by kinship ties with local merchants, Teziutlán gradually arose as the financial and commercial hub of the lowlands. A detailed chronology of this rise is hard to provide, but by the 1870s Teziutlán's position appears well established. While other *serrano* towns also fostered trade links with the Tecolutla basin (e.g., Huauchinango with some of the piedmont *pueblos*), none managed to achieve the stature of Teziutlán. Traffic patterns would naturally reflect these disparities.

All in all, these long-distance commercial transactions remained rather modest, in scale as well as in scope. Exports from the basin were still confined to those few selected commodities that had traditionally borne well the high costs of transport, and imports—manufactured or otherwise—had a very limited market, given the thin, scattered, and largely self-sufficient local population. As during colonial times, there is no evidence of public market gatherings or marketplaces—permanent, hebdomadal, or seasonal—anywhere in the basin for the first half-century after Independence. In an unusual effort, a *plaza del mercado* (marketplace) was established in Papantla toward the end of 1837, but it was closed after only seven months; *"no es costumbre"* (it is not customary), a despondent Bausa wrote by way of explanation. Not until well into the twentieth century, it appears, would Papantla have a regular market.[108]

In the absence of public markets, commerce was centered around general stores owned by Spanish or other *de razón* merchants and located in the principal villages. Commercial transactions were, in a sense, private affairs, often carried out in family homes, which doubled as stores. Village merchants and their roving agents handled much of the buying and selling; they were at once exporters of vanilla, chile, pepper, tobacco, timber, and other agricultural and forest commodities, importers of assorted manufactures and sumptuary goods, and top middlemen for all types of local products traded for consumption inside the basin.

As before, production and commercial exchange were still largely separate realms. The means of agricultural production remained almost exclusively in the hands of subsistence-oriented Totonac families. Together, the labor and marketing conditions prevailing across the basin continued to render large-scale manorial farming fairly impracticable. If the term "hacienda" is used to denote the practice of manorial agriculture in any of its forms (demesne, sharecropping, or tenancy), then there were no haciendas to speak of in post-Independence Papantla. This is a point worth emphasizing, because imprecise terminology is often the cause of confusion. During the early and mid-nineteenth century, some of the basin's large estates were occasionally—though not usually—referred to as haciendas; but in fact none was devoted to manorial farming. The Larios estate, for instance, was described in 1830 as an "uninhabited hacienda."[109] The term was probably used to highlight the impressive size of this estate (perhaps as many as 100,000 hectares), and not its function, or maybe it simply reflected the dreamy designs of former Mexican President Guadalupe Victoria, who obtained title to most of the lands south of the Tecolutla River (including Larios) in the aftermath of Independence and hoped in vain to make them productive. In any case, all evidence suggests that, except for cattle ranching, these lands—which Bausa would subsequently describe as "beautiful and deserted"—had always been mostly idle.

Indeed, to the extent that they were exploited at all by those who held title to them, the basin's private estates—generally and more appropriately called *fincas rústicas* (rural estates)—were devoted to cattle ranching for much of the nineteenth century, as they had been during the colonial past. However, greater Papantla's geographical isolation and peculiar demographics kept the ranching economy sluggish. The herds, which were not large to begin with, appear to have diminished in size during the years of upheaval that preceded Independence, and would remain rather puny for decades afterwards. In 1830, the *jefe político* (the chief executive official in each political district, appointed by the State Governor) of the newly established Cantón of Papantla estimated that there were roughly 130 horses, 100 mares, 31 donkeys, and 1,500 head of cattle in the entire territory under his jurisdiction; most of the *ranchos* he cared to mention had at best "some" or "a few heads of cattle," and others were simply "altogether unproductive." Fifteen years later, Bausa painted a similar picture of widespread underdevelopment, neglect, and inactivity. Despite the "abundance of grass and watering holes, and the extensive grasslands," he noted, "it is a well known fact that with the exception of Rincón, Jamapa, and Cacahuatal, which are well stocked, the *fincas rurales* have very little or no cattle."[110]

These enormous, largely idle, and ill-defined private properties may have comprised as much as 50 percent of the Cantón's territory, the rest being lands of the *pueblos*. Map 2.3 displays the approximate location of the basin's historic estates.[111] The Tecolutla River was the southern boundary of Papantla's communal holdings, and the entire expanse below the river was claimed by fewer than ten huge estates: Larios, Malpica, Cacahuatal, Masacapa, Mesa Grande, Cuespalapa, Mesa Chica, and Puxtla. In addition, El Rincón straddled the river.

Another set of properties was found north of the river and its piedmont affluents. San Miguel, San Lorenzo, and Texquitipan were located west-southwest of Papantla; the Tulapilla estate lay between Coahuitlán, Coyutla, and Chicualoque; and the old estate of Jamapa (Jamaya), visited by Bishop Mota in the early 1600s, bordered on Tulapilla and the communal lands of

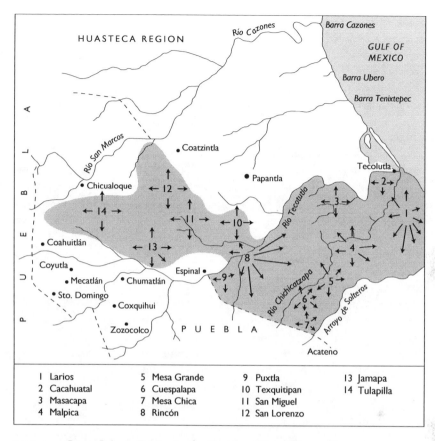

MAP 2.3 Large Private Estates in the Cantón of Papantla, c. 1845

Espinal. These were the principal private estates of the Canton at the dawn of the Republic, but there were probably a few other minor ones as well. By the middle of the nineteenth century, there were also several *fincas rústicas* on the so-called *terrenos propios* of the municipality of Papantla.[112]

Although most of the basin's inhabitants lived on lands belonging to the *pueblos*, either out by their milpas or in the villages, not all did. The private properties of the Cantón were home not only to the relatively few cowboys, ranch hands, and others associated with the cattle-ranching enterprises, but also—more importantly—to a number of independent agricultural settlements. This was especially true of the southern estates; the *rancherías* of Coyusquihui, Pueblillo, Paso del Correo, Mesa Chica, and Cuespalapa, for instance, were all located there. Vast, virtually unpopulated, and practically unrestricted, these territories of exuberant forests, ample pastures, and ubiquitous streams were Papantla's enduring frontier. As noted, the Olartes and their followers chose to set up their rebel camps out there, and at least some of the aforementioned *rancherías* trace their development—if not their origins—back to those years of intermittent warfare. Before, as well as after, other farmers must have surely followed the same path.[113]

Though nominally private, much of the deserted hill territory within these southern estates was effectively open to small-scale agricultural colonization. In the absence of land surveys, boundaries remained fuzzy, and it is not clear that private property rights were vigorously enforced in any case. There is, for instance, no firm evidence of rent payments before the last decades of the nineteenth century.[114] Until then, the southern *rancherías* of the Cantón do not appear to have been much different from those established on communal lands; perhaps absentee landowners were simply unable to exercise control over every idle nook of their properties.[115] For the most part, they did not even try, and when they did, they were not likely to succeed. The case of Jamaya is suggestive. Around 1841, farmers from the *pueblo* of Espinal took over lands claimed by the estate of Jamaya; the landowners eventually took notice and then spent close to half a century trying by all means to get them out. Property rights notwithstanding, it was all in vain; in the end, the owners had to settle for a cheap sale.[116] As a rule, however, squatting went uncontested.

Historian John Tutino has suggested that the decades between 1810 and 1880 should be regarded as a period of "agrarian decompression" in Mexico, and recent rural scholarship has generally concurred. Citing evidence from central and northern Mexico, Tutino argues that the political chaos and economic malaise that followed Independence hurt both mercantile and landed elites, paving the way for an "expansion of peasant and ranchero production," mostly at the expense of haciendas.[117] Greater Papantla, however, witnessed no such process, as should be evident by now. It is difficult to speak of a "decompression" across the Tecolutla basin when there was no "compression" to begin with. Before and after Independence, this remained a land of subsistence-oriented farmers, no hacienda agriculture, stagnant cattle ranching, very low population density, and an accessible *monte* frontier. Halfway through the nineteenth century, manorial agriculture had yet to gain a foothold here, and milpa farmers still faced little outside competition for the use of forest lands. To the extent that the total acreage controlled by Totonac agriculturalists increased in the wake of Independence (through internal migrations, etc.), the cause must be sought not in a decline of rival private estates, but rather, it would seem, in the political and demographic history of communal social relations and land-use rights. After all, these communities were still the only institutional actors on the agricultural scene.

In regard to economic organization and social relations of production, then, a remarkable continuity marks the onset of republican life in greater

Papantla. Independence or no, most of the basin's inhabitants still made their living much as their forebears once had. Most Totonacs grew or plucked from the forests what they ordinarily needed to feed and clothe themselves, as well as whatever someone showed an interest in buying; a few others, mainly Spaniards and other *gente de razón*, busied themselves buying, selling, and exporting anything and everything they thought would turn a profit. Bouts of political instability notwithstanding, this was still the Papantla of old. Meanwhile, the foundations were being laid for a quieter yet more profound revolution which would take shape after 1870; this time, merchants, not soldiers, would be the vanguard of change. What follows now is an account of the early growth of Papantla's vanilla business (c. 1760–1870).

3 *The Vanilla Economy*

On the night of February 9, 1880, a Spaniard named Francisco Naveda was murdered in Papantla. At the time of his death, he was one of perhaps a dozen important vanilla merchants operating in the area—not the most prominent, the biggest, or the wealthiest, but certainly a prosperous businessman. As Naveda died intestate, Papantla's judicial authorities were required to make an inventory of his assets; on Monday the 29th of March of that year, the court secretary, Naveda's widow, and various other interested parties convened at a large, sturdy house facing the main plaza of the Villa, which served as the Naveda family residence, warehouse, and curing workshop. The record shows that during the next few days they found a total of 384,822 vanilla pods stored in the house and also that Naveda had purchased an additional 156,626 beans from three other local merchants.[1] Although he was killed in early February, when the buying season was not yet halfway over, Naveda had already managed to accumulate a private stock that would yield approximately 2,200 kilograms of cured vanilla. Remarkably, eight or even five decades earlier the amount of vanilla in Naveda's possession alone might have constituted a year's exports for all of Mexico; on the average, moreover, such a year would not have been considered a bad one for the entire business. By the 1870s, however, it was not unusual in the midst of a good harvest for a single merchant who was both affluent and diligent to have gathered over half a million vanilla beans well before the ides of March. In the course of a few decades, vanilla had become big business.

The story of the early rise of vanilla in Papantla is neither spellbinding nor particularly glamorous. In it there are no daring exploits, no heroic figures, and no spectacular breakthroughs. It is nonetheless worth telling, for the vanilla business was arguably the single most important source of social and economic change in nineteenth- and early-twentieth-century Papantla. In a space characterized by the striking durability of old forms of economic activity and of social organization, the exponential increase in vanilla production and exports that began in the middle decades of the nineteenth century set the stage for an epoch of great turmoil and transformation. After

1870, in the wake of a remarkable business boom, the basin's historic patterns of land tenure, land use, labor, and human geography would face a level of disruption unprecedented in local memory, and the enduring Papantla of old would gradually cease to be. In order to understand how the vanilla business spearheaded such broad social changes, it is first necessary to examine how the trade took root and flourished across the basin.

Vanilla, 1760–1830

Records show that when the Spanish royal fleet bound for Havana and Cadiz sailed from Veracruz in mid-1761, its merchant ships were carrying roughly half a million vanilla beans on board. Estimating an average weight of 4 kilograms per thousand vanillas, this cargo would have amounted to some 2,150 kilograms.[2] In 1763 the next fleet took close to 2,600 kilograms, probably the product of two harvests.[3] Twenty-five years later, the volume of exports had not changed appreciably; by Humboldt's account, vanilla shipments for 1787–90 totaled 1,103,295 beans (4,413 kilograms), an average of 1,103 kilograms per year. These figures give some idea of the size of New Spain's vanilla exports.[4] On this basis, it seems fair to estimate average annual exports for the mid- to late eighteenth century of around 1,000–1,300 kilograms. By 1800, vanilla had been a more or less established article of trade for more than a hundred years; during the second half of the eighteenth century, the practice of cultivating it (as opposed to just gathering it from the wild) had begun to spread, a development that both reflected and enhanced its commercial potential.[5] Still, as the numbers show, this remained a very tiny business.

On the whole, the next three decades (1800–30) saw a moderate increase in the volume of annual vanilla exports, in spite of the imperial wars and the secessionist upheavals that marked those years. Mexican figures for 1802–28 indicate average annual exports of 2,067 kilograms, and French import records paint a similar picture. Already, France was far and away the main consumer of vanilla in Europe; the Spaniards, as Humboldt had noted, no longer used vanilla for their chocolate.[6] French demand single-handedly drove the market for the aromatic, and merchants in Bordeaux and Marseilles channeled the bulk of the European trade. French imports are thus good indicators of the general scale of New Spain's—and later Mexico's—exports for this period. For 1818–30, the French average was 1,938 kilograms (see Appendix Table A.3).

This was still a very modest amount, but percentage-wise it represented a significant increase from the baseline of the late eighteenth century. Judging from the export volumes for some of the better years in this period, it seems fair to conclude that overall productive capacity had expanded.[7] As

before, wide fluctuations from year to year are in evidence; wars, protracted insurrections, and, finally, the conflict with Spain over the fort of
San Juan de Ulúa are part of the reason, since these disrupted commerce at
various times. Ultimately, however, the fickleness of vanilla harvests and the
error-prone quality of early curing methods are probably the main explanations. By its very nature, vanilla trading was—and would always be—an
unstable business. In any case, it is clear that at the dawn of the Republic
Mexico's vanilla trade remained a very small-scale enterprise. In these
times, the vanilla stocks that Francisco Naveda left behind in 1880 would
have indeed made up a good year's exports for all of Mexico.

Throughout these seven decades (1760–1830), most of the vanilla
shipped to Europe came from the area of Misantla, southeast of Papantla
and north of Xalapa. Papantla's share then was diminutive. Until at least
the 1820s, Misantla was the undisputed world capital of vanilla, although
this was indeed an accomplishment of rather modest proportions. By 1800,
the Totonacs of Misantla and Colipa already cultivated a few hundred
thousand fruits, in addition to which they continued to extract the *cimarrona* (wild vanilla) from the forests of Quilate. Quite appropriately, therefore, when the young town councils of these *pueblos* designed their coats of
arms around the time of Independence, it was Misantla's—and not Papantla's—that displayed vanilla vines forming a prominent orle.[8]

According to Humboldt, only about 10 percent of an average yearly harvest then came from Papantla. He wrote that "the district of Papantla . . .
produces very little vanilla, which is also badly dried, although it is very
aromatic," adding that "the Indians of Papantla and Nautla are accused of
introducing themselves furtively in the forests of Quilate to pick the fruit of
the *epidendrum* planted by those of Misantla."[9] Using Humboldt's high figures, Papantla's annual exports at the turn of the century would have averaged roughly 365 kilograms; assuming that Papantla's share remained constant, the average for the years leading up to 1830—based on the available
export series—would have been only about half that much. In either case,
it is evident that Papantla's vanilla economy was then extremely small, both
in absolute terms and relative to the rest of the business.

Tiny, however, was not the same as insignificant. In the context of Papantla's peculiar geographic situation and historic economic organization,
vanilla's qualities made for a truly unique commodity. As noted, the difficulties in transportation and a scarcity of labor that had restricted the commercial outflow of agricultural and forestal products to a minimum kept
the Tecolutla basin a land of subsistence-oriented Totonac farmers and a
few petty *de razón* merchants, cowhands, bureaucrats, and part-time soldiers. The handful of goods from Papantla which did find an external market—wax, skins, chile, assorted forest products, and under certain circum-

stances timber, tobacco, and maize—were unlikely to create, let alone sustain, significant wealth. Some of these commodities had only a limited or sporadic demand (tobacco had promise, but its cultivation was long forbidden), and in all cases, given the high costs of transportation, low value-to-weight ratios severely affected the profitability of their trade. Economies of scale might have made some a better business, but a chronic scarcity of labor precluded the implementation of manorial forms of agricultural organization. Vanilla, on the other hand, faced no such difficulties.

Ever since French high society took to drinking chocolate, Mexico's vanilla was in strong demand overseas. Mexico's meager exports were still—and would be, until the late 1840s—the only source of vanilla for Europe, and supply, it seems, perennially lagged, keeping prices very high. Given the lightness of cured vanilla, this commercial state of affairs made for an extraordinarily high value-to-weight ratio, unmatched by any other product exported from Mexico, including silver. Compared by weight to the basin's pepper, wax, hides, or chile, let alone its maize or timber, vanilla was much more valuable. In 1826, for instance, a kilogram of vanilla was worth nearly thirty times more than a kilogram of dried chile, and twelve times more than the equivalent amount of cured tobacco. Remarkably, that was a year in which vanilla sold relatively cheaply; at other times, the value gap might have been twice as wide. In light of the tight economics of commercial transportation in and out of the basin, this was no small advantage.

A comparison with other high-value export goods highlights vanilla's special status. Around the turn of the century, few Mesoamerican commodities were as coveted and expensive (per kilogram) as cochineal and indigo, the latter often from Guatemala; in fact, throughout the early republican decades, *grana fina* was Mexico's most important vegetable export (in total value). In unit terms, however, vanilla was far more valuable than either, as the data in Table 3.1 clearly show.[10] The margin of difference, moreover, was often very substantial—up to more than five times the price of cochineal and as much as nine times that of indigo. Vanilla, it turns out, was the diamond of Mexico's plant economy.

This invisible quality is the key to understanding vanilla's salient importance in the economic and social life of nineteenth century Papantla. Given the basin's geographic isolation, poor communications, and household-centered productive organization, vanilla was an ideal commodity—light, expensive, and cultivable on a small scale with relatively modest labor expenditures. Vanilla represented a rare and seemingly happy combination of the new and the very old. On the one hand, nothing quite like it had arisen before in these lands; salt, a leading commodity in earlier centuries, was neither local nor nearly as valuable. Historically, vanilla's economic potential was truly unprecedented. On the other hand, the successful development of

TABLE 3.1

Value-to-Weight Ratios of Mexican Export Commodities

Year	Indigo (pesos/kg)	Cochineal (pesos/kg)	All vanilla (pesos/kg)	1st vanilla (pesos/kg)
1787–1790	2.7	7.4	11.2	
1802	4.8	6.6	9.1	
1803	3.9	6.9	8.2	
1804	4.3	9.0	27.4	
1805	n/a	7.4		10.0
1806	3.9	8.7	20.3	
1807	4.4	8.7	22.5–25.0	
1808	4.7	8.7	17.5–18.8	
1809	4.1	10.4		22.5
1810	4.4	10.4		n/a
1811	3.9	9.4		22.5
1812	3.3	8.7	15.0	
1816	3.8	11.2		15.2
1817	n/a	11.3		15.0
1819	3.3	9.8	20.9	
1823	4.4	6.7	37.5	
1824	3.9	6.9–8.0		30–37.5
1825	1.9	5.2	10.0	
1826	2.0	5.2	10.0	
1828	3.3	5.6	22.0	

SOURCE: See note 10 to Chapter 3.

the trade and of cultivation in Papantla resulted in large measure precisely from the fact that growing vanilla did not call for any major changes in the established social patterns of economic activity. Whether picked from the wild or cultivated in the *acahuales*, vanilla production followed the old rhythms of Totonac gathering and farming. This was the central paradox of vanilla, a crop at once traditional and potentially revolutionary.

Not surprisingly, Papantla's incipient vanilla economy mirrored the structure of the larger society: Indian producers and non-Indian long-distance merchants. The latter would encourage *acahual* cultivation and forest gathering by advancing goods and—more importantly—by paying money in exchange for these orchid pods. Initially, these must have been very modest operations, but they signaled to all that vanilla—fruit of the *montes*—had become something of value. Local merchants would also strive through trial and error to understand and master the exacting art of the *beneficio*, which turned their fragile, perishable purchases into shiny "silvery sticks" worth a small fortune in Veracruz and abroad. In the late eighteenth century, these were men like Juan Vidal, Joaquín Suárez, and a handful of other Spaniards and *criollos*—the petty merchants, storekeepers, and part-time bureaucrats who handled the basin's modest long-distance trade. A number of these traders and their heirs survived Independence and held on to their businesses, of which vanilla was already by far the most promising.

In the last analysis, then, what set vanilla apart from the rest of the basin's products was the potential for large profits. Although until the late 1820s Papantla's vanilla exports were evidently very small (probably well under 350 kilograms a year), the knowledge that vanilla was indeed something special had already been around for perhaps a century; the trade in wild vanilla—described in an earlier chapter—was at least as old. Why the business had not grown faster is a very complex question for which there is no precise answer. The chronology of the growth of overseas demand—examined in an earlier chapter—is surely a key factor. In addition, the spread of cultivation was apparently a slow process, and this kept harvests small and uncertain. At the other end of the local business, the processing capacity and know-how of the budding *beneficios* was still both limited and erratic, as were the resources (capital, credit, transport, information) of the town merchants, who were then by most standards small-time entrepreneurs.

Direct evidence of the kinds of profit margins associated with the early vanilla trade is unavailable, but there are clear indications that they could not have been inconsiderable. A long history of voracious competition among town buyers and an equally long record of complaints about endemic vanilla thievery out in the fields suggest strongly that vanilla's high value-to-weight ratio often did translate into handsome profits, for local sellers as well as buyers. As early as 1743, Papantla's Alcalde was being accused by a rival buyer of trying to corner the market by dictating when vanilla could be cut and sold. As the town merchants fought over the green vanilla, thieves roamed the forests and *acahuales* looking for unguarded vines; often, it was sometimes said, they actually worked in unison. For merchants as well as for thieves, vanilla was simply the best deal in town.

In a vain attempt to prevent premature picking, curtail theft, and bring some order into the business, it became customary by the second half of the eighteenth century for the authorities to issue a yearly edict announcing when harvesting was allowed to begin and threatening all those who would jump the gun—buyers and sellers—with stiff punishment. The rewards must have far outweighed the risks, however, because early picking remained a widespread practice. José María Quirós, a member of Veracruz's merchant guild (Consulado) was among those who bemoaned at length the famously chaotic conduct of the local vanilla trade and the proven ineffectuality of the law. His arguments are telling, and thus worth citing:

In order to curtail these excesses an edict is published every year banning any harvesting until the fruit is ready, which is by the middle of March but might be earlier, when the fruit has already ripened, the storms have ended, and the sunny days essential for the *beneficio* have arrived. But so extreme is the greed caused by its high value, and so feeble the zeal to prosecute violators, and so great the ease with which they move it from one *pueblo* to another or hide it in the hills of other jurisdictions, that the chaos gets worse every day. Rest assured that it is possible to prevent the theft of anything except for vanilla. Despite the letdown experienced by those who buy it before it is ripe, because a lot of it rots away and even the fruit that does survive is not as fine as when cured at the right time, they will not desist; instead, they do even more of the same, providing incentives for theft and wickedness.[11]

"Rest assured," Quirós concluded, "that it is possible to prevent the theft of anything except for vanilla." It is hard to imagine a more eloquent characterization of vanilla's unique commercial status. Following Independence, the new State government and the local town councils continued issuing such edicts, with equally unimpressive results. A few decades later, these yearly ordinances setting the start of vanilla harvesting had become so universally ignored that the Veracruz legislature decided simply to repeal the law.[12]

Regulating the vanilla business—small as it was—had proven utterly impracticable. Why? Although the quality and volume of Papantla's early exports would have probably been higher had the harvesting process been managed in a more orderly fashion, all the parties involved were caught in a classic "prisoner's dilemma." A merchant worried about competitors surreptitiously hoarding vanilla, and knowing that the supply was always tight, had to decide whether to do it himself. A grower worried about thieves raiding the family *acahual*, and knowing that buyers could already be found, had to decide whether to cut early. A gatherer worried about others beating him to a favored stand deep in the forest and hence faced the same dilemma. Under these circumstances, collective actions were exceedingly hard to bring about. Ripe vanilla would command much higher prices, but all found the wait very risky. Notwithstanding the consequent damage to the crop, the high stakes involved incited many to flout the laws, often including those who were entrusted with enforcing them. There is little doubt, then, that the early vanilla trade must have been very lucrative indeed.

In an area traditionally rich in natural resources but poor in terms of commodities, vanilla came to represent a different kind of wealth: capital. Before, the prospects for capital accumulation had never been very good: subsistence-oriented farming, petty commerce, and ranching did not make many fortunes. The growth of vanilla would change all that. For Papantla, the vanilla trade was to be the great engine of capital formation and, a fortiori, of economic and social change. Without it, it is impossible to understand the course of Papantla's modern history. As the business slowly developed, several fundamental issues would begin to loom large: Whose capital was it to be? How would it be used? What effects would this new money have on the economic organization of land use and tenure, and indeed, on the entire social fabric of the old Papantla? In 1830, it was still too soon to tell.

Vanilla, 1830–1870

Over the next forty years, Mexico's vanilla exports grew considerably, as did Papantla's market share. Statistics showing export volumes are lacking for the entire period, but fortunately there are enough foreign import figures and contemporary narrative accounts to give a fair idea of the evolution of the business through these middle years.[13] France remained the principal destination and entrepôt for vanilla in Europe, with the United States becoming a consumer worthy of note toward the late 1860s. Writing around 1860, Papantla merchant Agapito Fontecilla observed that "France is the main market for vanilla: that is where most of the perfumes, chocolate, ice creams, etc. are consumed."[14] Although French Customs classified vanilla imports by country of shipment, and not by country of origin, it is usually possible to identify their real provenance, since prior to the late 1840s there were no important producers aside from Mexico, and later only a selected few.

An analysis of these French records yields the following yearly averages: for the 1830s, 6,219 kilograms; for the 1840s, 10,966 kilograms; for the 1850s, 8,715 kilograms; and for the 1860s, 8,839 kilograms (see Appendix Tables A.4 and A.5). Clearly, the Mexican business had become much larger; whereas during the first three decades of the century, average annual exports scarcely surpassed 2,000 kilograms, for the years 1831–59 the figure for French imports alone is close to 9,000 kilograms. Since until the early 1860s French imports and Mexican exports were probably roughly equivalent, these import statistics are a very good reflection of the scale of exports during the years in question. Evidence of another sort confirms this judgment. Fontecilla estimated that "taking the average of these last twenty years (1840–1860), the number of vanillas picked per harvest is no less than two million and a half." Using his own conversion rate of 4 kilograms per thousand, this would be about 10,000 kilograms.[15] Allowing for spoilage and for exports to countries other than France, the numbers are essentially in agreement. They suggest that in a matter of thirty years Mexican exports had increased more than fourfold.

Calculating export volumes for the 1860s is somewhat more complicated, because in those years France ceased to be the only important importing country. Long a re-exporter of Mexican vanilla, the United States first appears as a significant consumer market at this time. On the basis of trade statistics and consular reports, it is possible to estimate average U.S. imports of Mexican vanilla for 1860–69 at nearly 2,900 kilograms per year (see Appendix Table A.6). Combined with French import data for those years, average annual exports from Mexico for the 1860s would come to around 11,700 kilograms. Despite all the troubles and wars of those years, the vanilla business continued to grow.

To a significant degree, the overall growth of the trade during these four middle decades reflects the emergence of Papantla as an important vanilla center. Whereas around the turn of the century the Tecolutla basin supplied merely one-tenth of Mexico's vanilla exports, by 1860 its share was already roughly one-half, and growing. In absolute terms, this represented an increase—in averages—from around 200 kilograms to as many as 6,000 kilograms per year.[16] Papantla's vanilla economy was at last coming of age. No longer could it be rumored, as Humboldt had once reported, that the vanilla sold in Papantla was mostly stolen from the Quilate forests to the south, or that its curing establishments turned out a shoddy product. While the name "Papantla" was not yet synonymous with "Mexican vanilla," the basin had indeed become—in a matter of decades—a production zone to be reckoned with.

It remains somewhat unclear why the town of Misantla—long considered the capital of the trade—failed to keep pace. Although in 1860 its district still produced more or less half of what Mexico exported, the rate of growth here had been comparatively less impressive. Moreover, beginning in the 1850s, a growing percentage of this region's crop came to be cultivated and/or processed in Jicaltepec—a remote French colony founded in late 1833 on the banks of the Nautla River—and did not go through Misantla. These French settlers grew, cured, and exported their own vanilla, and also bought some from the Totonacs in the area.[17] Without Jicaltepec, greater Misantla's share of the total exports for this period would have surely decreased even more.

Once the rise of Jicaltepec is taken into consideration, it becomes apparent that the relative importance of the town of Misantla as a trading and curing center diminished sharply in these years. Whether the volume of vanilla handled by its merchants actually declined or merely stagnated is hard to say with any certainty, but the available evidence does suggest that the transition to Independence in Misantla was both violent and disruptive, and that—unlike in Papantla—the fighting severely affected its commercial establishment. It is well known that this rebellious town was burned down twice by royalist forces, once in 1815 and again in 1817. Some years later, its *jefe político* remarked that the wars "left in misery a town that once rivaled any of its coastal counterparts in terms of work and resources," explaining that "for this reason the vanilla trade has decayed so much that harvests now are not one third of what was once handled." Town commerce, he lamented, "has been reduced to two stores." Other contemporary sources convey the same sense of business languor in the aftermath of Independence.[18]

In contrast, Papantla's vanilla merchants prospered as a class during these years. Crop failures and recurrent political upheavals notwithstanding, their business expanded considerably. Although their combined annual output of 5,000 or 6,000 kilograms was still far from huge, it was nevertheless twenty-five times what their predecessors would have normally handled half a century earlier. Now, vanilla's presence was impossible to overlook. On the average, the town merchants of 1860 were successfully processing at least 27,500 kilograms of green fruit every year (using Fontecilla's 5.5:1 raw-to-dry weight rate), and much more than that was in fact being bought and sold, since the spoilage rate was still fairly high. Between January and May, if not earlier, vanilla could be seen and smelled all over the *pueblo*.

Significantly, Papantla's merchants began to experiment with different curing techniques during these decades. Juan Pérez adapted an oven for sweating green vanilla, a delicate and time-sensitive process that otherwise had to be entrusted to the vagaries of solar heat. During winter wet spells (e.g., because of *nortes*), much vanilla was lost for lack of sun. Pérez's method (named *poxcoyon*, after the Totonac word for "baking") made it possible to save at least some of that vanilla. By mid-century, the *poxcoyon* was widely employed among Papantla traders. Around that time, Agapito Fontecilla introduced the use of thermometers to regulate oven temperatures and endeavored to determine adequate time and temperature ranges. In this way, he sought to minimize the risk of over-baking, which could reduce vanilla's value by one-half or even more. "Given that a full oven frequently contains $1,500 or even $2,000 pesos worth of vanilla," he wrote, "it is easy to calculate the importance of having a safe way of doing this." Still, judging from his convoluted description of the process, it is clear that curing continued to be an unsystematic and risk-laden enterprise where hands-on experience and a bit of luck mattered at least as much as science. Losses, moreover, remained considerable. There is little doubt, however, that these technical modifications made the *beneficio* somewhat less unpredictable, and as such contributed to an increase in exports and profits.[19]

Out in the countryside, too, vanilla was increasingly visible. Wild stands suffered due to reckless competition, and their yields diminished considerably. Overall, this source was fast becoming unimportant, in relative as well as in absolute terms; by 1860, writes Fontecilla, less than 5 percent of an average harvest consisted of wild vanilla.[20] It is clear, then, that Indian cultivation was the mechanism of growth. In *acahuales* and freshly cleared fields, vanilla vines became a more common sight. It is impossible to know precisely how much land was brought under vanilla cultivation in these years because of the diversity of planting techniques and the high variability of fruit yields. However, extrapolating from production averages, it would seem that by the 1860s around a thousand hectares were devoted to growing vanilla.[21] Considering that the basin had then a fairly small population and that family plots were still the norm, this estimate suggests a high degree of involvement with the crop on the part of Totonac farmers. Vanilla was becoming everyone's business.

Thus, in the course of these middle decades, vanilla swiftly developed into the driving force of Papantla's commercial economy. It brought fresh capital not only to merchants, but also to *milpa* farmers, petty brokers, *beneficio* workers, and others indirectly associated with the growing trade. It also turned Papantla, at least for six months at a time, into a town full of activity, with sellers streaming in, myriad negotiations carried out in broken Totonac or Spanish, silver coins changing hands, open yards and alleyways carpeted with vanilla drying in the sun, and enough intrigue, suspicion, speculation, and gossip to keep everyone's lunch conversations lively. Old people knew that the *pueblo* had not always been like that, and to them these changes must have seemed profound, which they were. Yet in terms of the social organization of production, vanilla represented continuity. It was not grown in manorial plantations, as would be the case in Réunion, nor did it give rise to a new class of specialized farmers. Rather, its cultivation simply became a part of the lowland Totonac agricultural cycle. Indian farmers planted it, tended it, and—if they were lucky—also harvested it themselves. Then they sold it to local intermediaries, or brought it into town directly to the merchant stores. Like pepper, chile, or tobacco, vanilla was for them a supplementary cash crop, albeit—no doubt—a very special one. A shared enthusiasm for vanilla notwithstanding, the basin was still a divided world. While producers and long-distance traders now interacted much more frequently, their respective domains remained largely separate. All things considered, the old Papantla was very much alive.

Perhaps the best way to understand the complex interplay of these ultimately contradictory developments—new money, old patterns—is to examine now in some detail the participation of merchants and producers in the business of these years—that is, the social aspects of Papantla's evolving vanilla economy.

Vanilla Economy and Society
Circa 1830–1870: The Merchants

Of the people who dominated the vanilla trade in Papantla, most had not been born in Mexico; this was a business largely managed by immigrants and by the children of immigrants. That was true in 1830 and—with a somewhat different cast of characters—also in 1870. Among the traders, three broad groups may be identified: heirs of the old Spanish merchants, with local roots going back to the years before Independence; new Spanish-born merchants, who arrived in the area during these decades; and Italian merchants, recent migrants who joined the trade toward the close of this period. This classification is useful mainly for analytic purposes; marriage links, especially among Spaniards, would often end up blurring these distinctions.

In 1830 there were ten resident merchants operating in the Tecolutla basin. Of these, six remained Spanish subjects. The rest were now Mexican nationals, all non-Indians and some probably born in Spain.[22] For the most part, they seem to have been people who had weathered the turn to Independence successfully. The Vidal clan was perhaps the most notable example of these surviving merchant lineages. It is hard to know what became of these early traders, since many of their names have been lost. In any case, by 1845 the number of Spanish merchants in the basin had grown to twenty-one. The vanilla business was on the rise, and the town of Papantla—where most of the merchants resided—was already a much busier place. "They pretty much own the trading business," Bausa wrote of them, adding that they were also the wealthiest men in the area.[23] This group included both old and new families, such as Vidal, Bustillo, Fuente, and Danini. Among them was also a young Agapito Fontecilla.

Fontecilla, whose *Tratado* remains the best source on Mexican vanilla in the nineteenth century, arrived from Spain when he was a young man, perhaps sometime in the 1830s. According to his own recollections, already by the early 1840s he was involved in the trade and *beneficio* of vanilla.[24] He must have done very well, because over the next two decades his name appears in numerous notarized transactions, in which he is acting as guarantor for other people, buying urban real estate and shares in rural properties, or bidding for expropriated Church lands.[25] In time, he would establish himself as one of Papantla's foremost notables—businessman, investor, curing expert, promoter of culture and education, man of letters, and crafty politician. Fontecilla belongs to the first generation of Papantla merchants to have made a fortune largely as a broker, on the basis of buying and selling vanilla. Significantly, he was married to Rosalía Vidal, a member of one of Papantla's oldest ruling families. Rosalía's money and social ties surely helped Fontecilla to establish himself in business. Their son, Agapito Fontecilla y Vidal, would, in turn, also become a prominent vanilla merchant.

Marriage was clearly how another immigrant trader of this time, the ill-fated Francisco Naveda, got his start-up capital. Younger than Fontecilla, Naveda was born in 1832 in the Spanish province of Santander. His business career took off after 1860, when he wedded twenty-year-old Josefa Silvera in Teziutlán. The Silveras were then an established, well-to-do merchant family from Papantla and Teziutlán; Josefa's brother, Román, traded in vanilla, and their father had perhaps done so as well. Josefa's inherited assets suggest that her family was indeed prosperous; they included many valuable properties, among them two of the best residences then standing in Papantla as well as another house in Veracruz. These Silveras were also related to the Zorrilla family (Josefa's sister, Rosalía, was married to Lorenzo Zorrilla), one of the ascendant trading clans of Teziutlán, whose business interests would become far reaching. There is little doubt that Josefa's ample personal resources and family connections underwrote Francisco Naveda's business career.[26]

Besides suggesting that marriage alliances played a key role in the formation of Papantla's early vanilla elite, Naveda's personal trajectory is interesting because it highlights the capital importance of the strong Teziutlán–Papantla link being forged during these years (c. 1850s–60s). Although Papantla's vanilla generally traveled by mule to Tecolutla or Tuxpan, from where it was shipped to Veracruz and occasionally Tampico, Papantla's financial transactions and most of its other commercial exchanges were by this time often channeled through Teziutlán. These merchants supplied their counterparts in the basin with dry goods, groceries, toiletries, tools, and most other outside products sold in town stores, which involved providing credit. They also had business ties and better communications with the export-import houses that received the coastal vanilla shipments in Veracruz. Thus, vanilla was paid for in Veracruz, and these credits (as financial instruments) made their way back to the basin through Teziutlán, whose merchants acted as a kind of clearing-house for Papantla. Once they were already playing this role, it became relatively easy for them to assist also in financing the purchase and processing of vanilla. Good connections in Teziutlán would clearly afford a significant business advantage.

Up until about 1870 the overwhelming majority of Papantla's important vanilla merchants remained Spanish-born. Age-wise, they were a diverse group; Fontecilla, for instance, was probably born in the 1820s, Francisco Naveda in 1832, and Matías Collado around 1842, which suggests a more or less continual trickle of arrivals from Spain. In this respect, Papantla's commercial situation was not unique; young Spanish-born would-be merchants were a fixture in many other Mexican *pueblos* as well.[27] Italian immigration, on the other hand, was a different story altogether.

Papantla's Italians arrived in large groups, as part of a government colonization scheme. In the aftermath of the Ayutla revolution (1855), the Liberal government actively promoted subsidized agricultural colonies that would attract foreign settlers, who were seen as instruments of progress and civilization. An original proposal calling for the establishment of four colonies between Xalapa and Veracruz was considered and quickly discarded; instead, by mid-1856 a decision had been made to create a single "model" colony, which was to be located—of all places—in the Tecolutla basin. The selected site was an estate (they called it a hacienda) named Tesquetipam or Texquitipan, a large expanse of forest and grasslands three leagues to the south of Papantla, bounded on the southeast by the Tecolutla River (Texquitipan is identified as no. 10 on Map 2.3). According to the enabling legislation, the colony was to encompass a total of 21,000 acres (8,500 hectares), with hundreds of farming lots of up to 100 acres each surrounding a spacious grid-patterned central town. Every family would receive—and agree to pay for—a plough and a team of oxen. With four plazas, five churches, two markets, a hospital, and scores of perfectly straight streets, this planned agricultural town would have made nearby Papantla look like a relic from a primitive past.[28]

Hard to reach, difficult to farm, and devoid of markets, Texquitipan was —to put it mildly—an unlikely setting for a "model" colony. It is safe to say that it would not have even been considered, let alone selected, had it not been for the decisive influence of Xalapa-born statesman José María Mata. The son-in-law of Melchor Ocampo, Mata was an accomplished soldier, an avid promoter of foreign colonization, a distinguished orator, legislator, and politician, as well as a prominent member of the Constitutionalist Congress of 1856–57. He happened also to be the newest owner of Texquitipan. It is not entirely clear how Mata had acquired these lands, but it appears that he had done so by means of the recently enacted Lerdo Law (June 25, 1856), which mandated the sale of disentailed church property.[29] Mata was keenly interested in—and stood to benefit from—the development of commercial agriculture in the area, and was then in an excellent position to influence the simultaneous implementation of the new disentailment and colonization policies. In February 1857, he agreed to sell Texquitipan to the federal government, and less than two months later, as plans to establish the colony moved forward, Mata himself was named director, a post that involved taking charge of the day-to-day administration of this ambitious project. Soon thereafter, the government signed an elaborate contract with an Italian colonel to have two hundred "sober, hard-working, and intelligent" farmers—with or without family—shipped from Genoa to Tecolutla.[30]

Mata's plans to oversee the settlement were soon derailed by the outbreak of civil war; in February 1858, an embattled President Juárez named him Minister to Washington, and he quickly exited the scene. Now the model colony—an ill-conceived project from the start—was more than ever condemned to failure. In the meantime, Luigi Masi—the Italian colonel— had managed to enlist a group of colonists, apparently Piedmontese and Lombards, and had them sent to Mexico. A first group (118 colonists and 114 family members) reached Tecolutla in April 1858, with a second group (32 colonists and 98 family members) following several months later.[31] According to the stories told by their descendants, the forsaken colonists made their way to the promised lands of Texquitipan, which they found inhospitable and insalubrious. Left largely to their own devices, they struggled to survive. A number of them fell ill—probably with malaria—and died, and the rest eventually dispersed. Some moved to the town of Papantla, others returned to Italy, and still others eventually resettled downstream at El Cristo, near Tecolutla and the sea. Less than three years after the arrival of the first Italians, the federal government rescinded the purchase contract it had signed with Mata, who then sold most of the lands in question to a wealthy local merchant.[32] With that, the whole sorry episode came to an end. For the time being, Texquitipan would remain a place of forests and savannas, untouched by ploughs that were meant to break open not just a piece of land but an entire society.

The colony may have not amounted to anything, but not so the surviving colonists. Despite an inauspicious beginning, many of these Italian migrants went on to become prosperous merchants and farmers in the basin. A number of those who moved to Papantla in the wake of the debacle of Texquitipan eventually joined the vanilla trade, whereby they managed in a relatively short time to attain both wealth and social standing. Unlike the Spaniards, most—if not all—of the Italian settlers became Mexican nationals. Already by the mid-1880s, Papantla's merchant establishment was no longer exclusively Spanish; a listing of the surnames of the leading traders for that time would have had to include not only Fuente, Fontecilla, and de la Sierra, but also Curti and Tremari, among others.

Of the Papantla Italians, by far the most successful would be Pedro Tremari. He was to become Mexico's most prominent vanilla exporter, and also one of the basin's top fin de siècle landowners and businessmen. English oilman and entrepreneur Percy Furber wrote of him that "he had been brought to Papantla by his Italian parents when he was a child," adding that "they had settled in Papantla and Tremari had made a fortune trading in vanilla beans."[33] But while Tremari may have started out in Texquitipan, this is not to say—as it turns out—that he was the son of farmers. It appears that a good number of the *modelo* colonists recruited by Colonel Masi were in fact not land-tillers, as the contract had stipulated, but rather urban folk—artisans, professionals, performers, clerks, etc.—eager to try their fortune abroad.[34] This would in part account for the colony's swift collapse—after all, the French colonists of Jicaltepec had successfully adapted to a similar environment—and also for the relative ease with which Tremari and others like him seem to have found their way into the vanilla trade.

As noted, another group of the wandering Italians—perhaps including some of those with a real interest in agriculture—ended up settling down in the lowland coastal plains of El Cristo. Little is known about the early years spent there, except that many got involved in commerce, at first trading mainly in processed agricultural goods such as cane alcohol and vanilla, which they often also produced. Much like their French counterparts at Jicaltepec, they cured their own vanilla as well as that which they bought from nearby native growers. Trade soon eclipsed farming as their principal occupation, as the proximity to Tecolutla and its cabotage gave them a certain competitive advantage. Largely through their entrepreneurship, the coast began to develop a strong commercial establishment of its own. Many Italian families eventually resettled in Cabezas del Carmen, a strategic roadside and riverfront *ranchería* not too far from El Cristo, which had for some time functioned as a kind of entrepôt; in 1877, Cabezas was renamed Gutiérrez Zamora. These first Italian merchants of Gutiérrez Zamora had surnames such as Montessoro, Arzani, Romagnoli, Gudini, Saqui, Montini, Casasa, and Tassinari. A separate group of Italian migrants—including the Gaya and Bayardini families—arrived around 1880; after living for some time at El Negro, in the old lands of Larios, they also established a presence in Gutiérrez Zamora.[35] By the turn of the century, Gutiérrez Zamora had become a thriving commercial town; vanilla was its main business, and the Italian-Mexicans its main businessmen. In all of Mexico, only nearby Papantla then concentrated more vanilla. This was not quite the *colonia modelo* that José María Mata had once envisioned, but it is nevertheless hard to imagine that he would not have been impressed.

The success of many Italian migrants in the vanilla trade suggests that while family capital and connections may have afforded some a clear business advantage, not having these to begin with was not an insurmountable barrier to entry. This was true for Spaniards as well as for Italians. In fact, during these decades of rapid growth and generally escalating demand, vanilla was a more or less open field of enterprise, with ample opportunities—and risks—awaiting anyone able and inclined to gamble. To a large extent, a peculiar characteristic of the business accounted for this. As Fontecilla explained, "Vanilla, a luxury item, has been and remains susceptible to extreme swings; it has gone through periods of very high value, and others of depression: a rumor of war in Europe or any simple crisis will lower its price, just as well-being in that part of the world or a small harvest here will increase it; but in either case it has been for many years one of the most valuable products exported by the Republic."[36] Despite this well known volatility, traders—big and small—faced great obstacles in trying to assess the condition of their market, because during much of this period—probably until at least the 1850s—the central, defining feature of the local vanilla business was precisely the lack of timely and reliable information.

Because cultivation was highly decentralized, it was very difficult for anyone to know with any certainty how large or how good a harvest was likely to be. Up in remote Papantla, it was also difficult to learn about market conditions in Europe, and thus about effective demand at any time. News took days to arrive, and then it was not always easy to decide whether the information was trustworthy or spurious. To differing degrees, prices in Papantla, Veracruz, and France were all quite variable, and it did not take much personal miscalculation to be caught by a sudden downturn or to miss a potential bonanza.[37] The problem was not only that the market was fickle, but also that it was hard for any given individual trader to figure out what signals it was sending.

This climate of uncertainty, however, was clearly also one of widespread opportunity. Cornering the local market was well near impossible, because of the scattered character of vanilla production, and in fact there was plenty of room for intermediaries and freelance speculators to maneuver. In the end, big merchants did have certain advantages, since they could afford to acquire more vanilla as well as to undertake the *beneficio*, which is where the big profits were to be made. However, with a bit of luck and cunning, even a small-time speculator could wind up reaping windfall earnings and rising from the ranks. After that, mastering the *beneficio* or hiring someone who did—neither of which was easy—were the keys to sustained prosperity. This is presumably how Pedro Tremari and others like him got their start, and in general what made trafficking in vanilla attractive to so many.

Given this state of affairs, it is no wonder that all sorts of schemes, rumors, gossip, misinformation, and disinformation were rife in Papantla, and that theft and deceit ran rampant. These were the weapons of the trade. By far the most vivid description of the character of vanilla trading during these early years comes—not surprisingly—from José María Bausa, whose *Bosquejo* shows him to have been a man obsessed with order. At that time (1845), the basin's leading merchants were still all Spanish. There were a total of seven main general stores in the area, as well as several smaller ones. In addition to the year-round or professional merchants, whom Bausa referred to as "regulars" (*rutineros*), there was also a small army of occasional vanilla dealers, speculators who resold their holdings to local or traveling merchants. These middlemen were Totonac as well as non-Indian. All of them scrambled for vanilla, aptly described as a "precious fruit, a perennial source of profits."

Bausa wrote of the regular traders that they "spend all year just lying in wait for the vanilla harvest, which . . . makes for a highly lucrative business because of the disorderly manner in which it is carried out; some buy and sell at very advantageous prices, while others, on the contrary, get it for more and sell with less profit." Uninformed about outside market prices, he added, these merchants "all buy and sell everything without much forethought, just hoping for the best; they are always filled with uncertainty and distrust . . . ; they live isolated, surreptitiously waging a war with each other, especially in the disastrous and wild vanilla trade, where infamy has taken the place of reason and justice." Among the speculators, meanwhile, there was a "monstrous imbalance" of profit and loss, which "elevates some while sinking others—suddenly or gradually—into a tomb of misery."[38]

The net outcome, in terms of the conduct of business, was chaos. Buyers, he went on, "rush to the hills like a swarm long before the law permits honest commerce, to victimize hapless or unwary Indians through fraud and deceit." Remarkably, even though the legal opening of the harvest season—which half a century earlier was normally in March or even April—had been gradually brought forward to January 1st, these edicts (which would soon be formally eliminated) were still observed mostly in the breach. When it comes to local commerce, Bausa complained, "the rules that would make it lawful are barely followed."[39]

In the end, Bausa observed, the source of this pervasive behavior was not just greed ("the disorders ushered in by greed"), but also ignorance, in particular a lack of current knowledge about the situation of markets beyond Papantla. This was a problem not only in the vanilla trade but as well with other commodities. The solution, he suggested, was for local merchants to work with brokers (*corredores*), who could "keep [them] abreast of current prices, supply them with the articles they need, sell on their behalf whatever they want to dispose of, obtain money for them when they urgently need it, arrange for the exchange of payment notes in the ports or places of their choice, keep them informed about commercial relations, etc." This was precisely the role that some merchants in Teziutlán would soon begin to play in earnest. However, at the time of Bausa's *Bosquejo*, Papantla's established merchants did not yet do business that way, at least not on a regular basis. In terms of access to networks of credit, information, or trade, the basin's commercial life at mid-century was not a very sophisticated affair. That was the direct legacy of centuries of commercial feebleness and relative isolation, a long era which was only then coming to an end.

However, in spite of all these shortcomings and uncertainties (and often because of them), it is evident that trading in vanilla was potentially an extraordinarily profitable enterprise. This was the bottom line, the promise that fueled all the furor. Vanilla's unique status was an open secret; everyone knew it, but no one talked about it much. Although Bausa and Fontecilla frequently alluded to vanilla's unmatched profitability, they chose not to discuss it in any detail; instead, they simply resorted to an old comparison, stating that vanilla was "worth more than silver."[40] To a large extent, such reserve reflects the fact that Papantla's business culture was obsessed with secrecy. It is telling that Fontecilla, who provided a meticulous description of every aspect of the business, was silent on the topic of returns on investment. He may have been willing to explain the intricacies of vanilla growing and preparation, but he was first and foremost a businessman, and no businessman likes to call attention to his profits, especially when they are incomparably high.

In the absence of detailed business records and price series, it is impossible to obtain a precise idea of contemporary profit margins. However, as shown below, there is some evidence to suggest that merchants who did their own *beneficio* could achieve annual rates of return of between 50 and 100 percent. Of course, this is not to say that every top trader generally earned this much, only that some could and probably did, at least sometimes. Balancing good years with bad years, however, average long-term returns were in all likelihood lower. Still, in a broader business context, these profit levels were clearly extraordinary, and for the Tecolutla basin they were just short of miraculous.

According to Fontecilla's figures for 1840–60, the price of vanilla sold in Veracruz fluctuated between 5.5 and 35 pesos per kilogram, with an average of close to 19 pesos per kilogram. For most of these years, Papantla's merchants were not themselves involved in exportation, so Veracruz was generally their point of sale. The cost of the *beneficio*, mostly labor, was approximately 1 peso per kilogram. Packaging—placing around 3 millares (12 kilograms) in a tin and putting the tins into wooden crates—was extra, but the cost per kilogram appears to have been relatively negligible.[41] Freight costs for vanilla—by mule to the environs of Tecolutla and then by ship on to Veracruz—are unfortunately not listed anywhere, but using maize as a rough guide it would seem—to err on the side of caution—that 0.5 pesos per kilogram constitutes a very generous estimate. All this adds up to a fixed cost of roughly 1.5 pesos per kilogram for everything except the raw material, green vanilla.

Naturally, the price that merchants paid for green vanilla was highly variable. It generally depended on factors such as quality, time of the year, size of the harvest, whether the vanilla was stolen or not, whether it was part of a previous credit arrangement (*habilitación*), and whether it was bought directly from the producers or through one or more speculators. Information—or the lack thereof—clearly played an important role in determining the local price structure. As it turns out, learning about these prices is now exceedingly difficult. Largely due to the fragmentary nature of this market, as well as to a widespread habit of secrecy, green vanilla transactions are virtually and significantly absent from historical documents, public and private alike. For instance, even though it was not uncommon to provide cash to growers in exchange for future deliveries at a prearranged price, these advance payments were almost never notarized. Likewise, Fontecilla casually neglected to say anything about the purchase of green vanilla.

Nonetheless, it is possible to form some idea of the likely range of local prices during these years. Later sources (for the 1880s) suggest prices for green fruit fluctuating from 30 to 60 pesos per millar (equivalent to about 22 kilograms of green and 4 kilograms of cured vanilla).[42] This would mean paying between 1.4 and 2.7 pesos per kilogram of the green, which translates into 7.5 to 15 pesos per kilogram of the dry. Perhaps prices during this earlier period were on the average somewhat lower than these. In any case, even at these higher prices the potential profits were considerable. Using an average of 11.25 pesos per kilogram for the green vanilla, the total cost of placing one kilogram of cured vanilla at the port of Veracruz would have been 12.75 pesos, while the average selling price was 19 pesos. On the basis of these numbers, the return on investment is nearly 50 percent, while at the high end—15 pesos per kilogram for the green and 35 pesos per kilogram selling price—it exceeds 120 percent. If average green prices during these years were indeed lower, then the potential profit margins were correspondingly higher. Moreover, since the local market was so convoluted, there were additional ways of maximizing earnings; purchasing stolen vanilla, for instance, could reduce overall costs significantly. Clearly, vanilla could build fortunes.

Exporting vanilla was also potentially a very remunerative enterprise. Fontecilla's figures indicate that between 1840 and 1860 the price of vanilla in France was, on the average, nearly 30 percent higher than in Veracruz, and that the range of prices—6.4–52 pesos per kilogram in France versus 5.5–35 pesos per kilogram in Veracruz—was much wider there, particularly at the high end.[43] In other words, export earnings alone could conceivably be nearly as sizable as those derived just from the local trade. Until at least the 1850s profits from the exportation of Papantla's vanilla remained exclusively in the hands of export-import trading concerns in Veracruz and—to a much lesser extent—Tampico and Tuxpan. As Bausa had noted, the basin's merchants lacked the organizational capacity needed to undertake this aspect of the business. Over time, however, this would change, and local merchants would begin to claim a stake in the exporting business, thereby enhancing their earning potential. By the turn of the century, most big merchants were also exporters. Judging from the familiarity with price differentials and fluctuations exhibited in his *Breve tratado* (1861), it is likely that Agapito Fontecilla was already then starting to explore this path.

Vanilla Economy and Society
Circa 1830–1870: The Producers

If the town merchants did not profit even more handsomely, it was because raw vanilla did not generally come cheap. Relative to other vegetable commodities, vanilla's cost per unit was extraordinarily high, not only as a dry aromatic but also as a horticultural product. This had less to do with production costs—which were not insignificant but consisted mostly of family labor—than with the forces of demand. With town merchants so eager to get it, selling green vanilla was also bound to be a good money-making opportunity, as the basin's farmers were quick to find out.

As it turned out, others also had the same idea—hence, the emergence of a stratum of roaming speculators, who jostled with producers for a share of the profits to be derived from these transactions. Sometimes these intermediaries worked for themselves, and sometimes they acted as agents of the big traders. Here, the potential earnings may not have been nearly as large but they were certainly attractive enough to have made theft, trickery, and fraud an integral part of doing business.

Despite the many abuses endemic to the trade, growing vanilla was more often than not a profitable undertaking. From the perspective of the producers, virtually all Totonacs, fierce competition among all sorts of buyers had a paradoxical effect: on the one hand it made good, ripe vanilla an extremely valuable commodity, enticing many to undertake cultivation; on the other hand, it fostered widespread theft and—consequently—preemptive premature picking, which in effect greatly diminished the worth of their harvest. According to Fontecilla, fruits cut in October and part of November generally sold for a third of the price of those left on the vines until after the new year.[44] Still, judging from the swift expansion of production in the course of these decades, it seems clear that many Totonac farmers found vanilla cultivation well worth the effort and the risk.

There is no evidence to suggest that growers were on the whole less savvy than dealers; in fact, according to Bausa, advance contracts were frequently breached by the growers, who did not think twice about selling to the highest bidder even if it meant betraying someone they were close to.[45] If anything, their business disadvantage was that they had less information and were in a more vulnerable position than other parties, and were thus more likely to end up being victimized. However, those who managed to hold on to their ripe fruit generally found themselves in relatively strong bargaining positions, and were able to make what for them were fairly large sums of money, especially if they sidestepped the local speculators. In the end, of all the cash crops or marketable forest products known to the Totonacs, vanilla was still far and away the most promising. For cultivators, it seems, vanilla was seldom a fair business, but it was nevertheless often a good one.

Compared to other native peoples of Mexico, the Totonacs of mid-nineteenth-century Papantla were on the whole very prosperous and remarkably independent agriculturalists. Most had access to land and water, the possibility of two maize crops a year, and now, increasingly, cash earnings from the sale of vanilla. In their own peculiar and typically prejudiced ways, those who wrote about them during this period recognized this relative collective well-being. Bausa remarked that "travelers who pass through this town coming from all directions admire and praise without exception the cleanliness of the natives, because in effect people here are very tidy, and both Indians and non-Indians make sure to appear in public neatly attired in their respective dresses." When it came to describing Indians, "cleanliness" was—and still is—a common and often racist way of alluding to a lack of visible signs of poverty and squalor. "Those who are dirty, in rags, and forlorn," Bausa added, "one can tell right away that they are not from around here."[46] Some years later, Fontecilla characterized the prosperity of vanilla cultivators as "very uncommon," insisting that "almost certainly there are no people on earth who are as comfortably off as those of Papantla, not only because of the fertility of its soil and the generosity of the harvests obtained from its cultivation, but also because its forests produce spontaneously many valuable goods."[47]

By all accounts, vanilla growers liked making money as much as anybody else, and were keenly aware of the business potential of their crop. However, despite—or perhaps because of—the clear benefits afforded by this new source of liquid wealth, the overwhelming majority of the basin's Totonacs chose to remain first and foremost milpa farmers. They did not give up their old ways in order to concentrate on vanilla. Instead, they seem to have adapted those ways—making vanilla an integral part of their agricultural cycle—to render them more reliable, secure, and productive, and thereby to increase their general welfare.

A related question is why these farmers on the whole did not cure and market their own vanilla, as did the French of Jicaltepec and the Italians of the coastal zone. According to Fontecilla, Totonac cultivators "usually don't know how to cure vanilla, and for that reason they sell it green." However, this is not an entirely satisfactory answer, because they could have learned had they chosen to, as others did. Indeed, many of those who worked in the village *beneficios*—probably including some *maestros*—were also Totonac. One answer, simple and perhaps also compelling, would be that they did not need to. Green vanilla generally made them good money, which in combination with the fruits of the milpa and the forest already provided families a more or less secure, even comfortable existence. A complementary explanation would be that lowland Totonacs lacked a strong mercantile tradition; theirs was not a culture of traders, of produce markets, or of commercial artisanal production. The colonists of Jicaltepec and Gutiérrez Zamora, on the other hand, had other backgrounds, different expectations, and ultimately a different understanding of progress and self-advancement.

Far from disrupting the Totonacs' deeply rooted subsistence-oriented family economy, the expansion of vanilla cultivation—in *acahuales* or in newly cleared plots—served in fact to strengthen it. Earnings from the sale of raw vanilla—which could at times be substantial—made it easier for families to purchase articles they could not or did not themselves make, such as certain tools, animals, cotton for clothing, or, in some cases, *chichique*, a local flavored cane alcohol. Vanilla money often paid for weddings, funerals, feasts, and other familial and communal ceremonies; it also enabled families to save for emergencies, such as food-crop failures, serious illness, and other catastrophic situations. Thus, growing vanilla was, in effect, a new means of bolstering up an old and entrenched form of life. In this respect, vanilla was no different from pepper, tobacco, wax, chile, timber, pita, sarsaparilla, or any of the other products the Totonacs of the Tecolutla basin had produced or extracted and sold for centuries as part of a cultural and economic strategy for survival. Only it was better, because it was much more lucrative.

The essentially conservative family use of vanilla earnings among Totonac farmers is best illustrated by a custom which contemporary observers consistently misunderstood: burying money. In 1830, Papantla's *jefe político* commented wryly:

> The Indians in general are in the habit of hiding the money they get from selling their crops, burying it no one knows where, and not revealing the secret location to anyone in or out of the family, not even when they are about to die; for this reason all is lost instead of being put to good use, because if they spend anything at all it is in order to buy a mule or a horse, or for a wedding, since the few articles that they do buy—such as soap, salt, etc.—they get in exchange for firewood, which they cut by the outskirts of the villages.[48]

Aside from reflecting a mixture of ignorance and perplexity, this statement suggests that saving was a widespread practice among native farmers, and that much of their crop earnings were routinely withdrawn from circulation, at least for a while. In the logic of their form of economic organization, this made perfectly good sense. After all, when the milpa was bountiful and the forests were generous, not much had to be bought. Besides, out by the fields and even in Papantla there were not many things one could buy anyway. Evidently, there were some who invested their earnings, buying animals, setting up small distilling and lumbering operations, or becoming vanilla speculators, but it appears that in many cases the choice was simply to save them. To be sure, burying money may have struck some as a strange custom, but it was certainly not an unreasonable one, since there were then no safer alternatives. As a matter of fact, Papantla's non-Indian town residents did it as well.[49]

Fifteen years later, José María Bausa complained about the same native practices, both the real and the imagined ones. Vanilla profits were not reinvested, he explained, because people—especially those he contemptuously called "*la indiada*"—kept them buried. Bausa then repeated the story about how once money was secretly hidden underground it was usually lost forever, because its owners would die without telling anyone where they had put it. It is telling that exactly the same argument was made by other contemporary writers, which suggests that this myth had a certain currency among non-Indians.[50] Why did it have such appeal? Why would anyone believe that Totonac farmers routinely threw away their money? It is hard to know for sure, but, in a way, the story expresses a very revealing worry. For many outside observers, much of the money earned by Totonac vanilla growers was as good as lost, since they could not see—literally, as well as figuratively—where it went, how it was used, and why it failed to generate more consumption and investment. In their eyes, the economic behavior of these farmers was not only strange but also irrational, since it betrayed a fundamental lack of interest in what they understood human "progress" and "civilization" to be all about.[51]

In the course of these decades, vanilla energized Papantla's economy, bringing the basin's two worlds somewhat closer together. Each side, however, had a very different idea of what the vanilla trade should and would ultimately accomplish. Among the local Spaniards, Italians, *criollos*, and mestizos, vanilla created wealth where little or none had existed before. It gave rise to a new class of immigrant merchants, more ambitious, less provincial, and perhaps also more ruthless. It spurred dreams of what they liked to call progress—more trade, better roads and communications, productive agricultural estates and cattle ranches, busy local marketplaces, better buildings, and high culture, all of which essentially meant more business. For them, vanilla was the key to a new Papantla. For many Totonac farmers, on the other hand, vanilla cultivation was first and foremost a tool for self-preservation. By offering them money without sacrificing their independence, it served to buttress their milpa-based family economy, which was the social foundation of the old Papantla. To these families, that was clearly progress. This budding divergence notwithstanding, around 1870 the old pattern of social organization still had the upper hand. As census figures show, the overwhelming majority of the basin's population clung to the milpa, and almost all cultivated farmland retained the legal status of communal property. Thus, as Mexico returned to republican rule, the revolutionary dreams of Papantla's emerging bourgeoisie remained just that.

This deep social divide, however, was not the only significant one. Along with tensions between Totonac farmers and town merchants, frictions within the Indian community were an old fact of life in Papantla. Some had to do with communal governance and taxation, others with the conduct and control of commerce. In an economic environment that did not punish those with a flair for independence, the enforcement of collective discipline (and especially of unpopular dictates) was bound to be a contentious matter. As noted, the *pueblo* of Papantla was plagued by such internal conflicts during the late colonial and early republican years. There, the struggle to end Spanish rule sharpened many long-standing political divisions, effectively tearing apart the República de Indios. Thus, when the coming of Independence abolished separate Indian governments (replacing them with municipalities), Papantla's Indians—unlike others elsewhere in Mexico—did not mourn, resist, or ignore this institutional transformation. The colonial *caja de comunidad* (communal treasury chest), the old embodiment of the fiscal and social ties that kept Papantla's Totonacs united as one body, simply ceased to function (if it had not already done so). In a political sense, the single community was no more.

Political office would now be held through the new Ayuntamiento, which in theory represented the interests of all citizens, Indian and non-Indian alike. In fact, town merchants soon came to control the workings of this body, despite the effort of some Totonacs to make it more broadly representative. It is telling that when Mariano Olarte and his followers rebelled in 1836, one of his grievances concerned irregularities and abuses in the conduct of local elections.[52] Effectively shut out of the town government, the locus of post-Independence Indian politics shifted decisively to the *rancherías*, yielding to the centrifugal tendencies that had long characterized the socioeconomic life of Totonac Papantla. For most practical purposes, there would be not one but several Indian communities in this *pueblo*, each of which had (or would develop) its own local leadership. To the extent that there were still Indian figures whose sphere of influence transcended this blooming localism, these would be mainly military men, whose exploits had earned them a larger following—people like Mariano Olarte in the 1820s and 1830s, or Simón Tiburcio, Pablo Hernández Olmedo, and Antonio Jiménez after the 1860s. In some cases, entrepreneurial middlemen would attain this status as well. On the whole, though, fragmentation was to be the dominant feature of Totonac political and social organization in nineteenth-century Papantla.

In regard to social relations, moreover, the development of the vanilla business seems to have abetted this trend, particularly within communities. Just as the fast growth in vanilla production and trade of these middle decades pitted producers against town merchants in a battle of unprecedented intensity, it is very likely that the rise of vanilla also exacerbated differences within and among members of the Totonac communities, creating new divisions and accentuating old ones. The vanilla trade may have strengthened the family economy of individual Totonac cultivators, but it also created conditions that on the whole conspired to make communal cohesion a less likely prospect.

Unfortunately, this is a subject about which there is very little direct information. In documentary sources, nineteenth-century communal social relations and economic arrangements do not easily render themselves visible. In the past, the problem has been compounded by certain ideological predispositions. Following Mora, the liberals of the time rejected in principle the idea of communal property relations, which they considered to be an integral part of Mexico's inherited "Indian problem," and hence did not see the need to understand how these social regimes—the Indian commons—may have functioned in practice.[53] Thus, despite the prominence given by intellectuals during this epoch to the supposedly retrograde economic and social effects of this type of land-holding, the changing realities of communal life remained largely unexamined. More recently, in a different intellectual climate, historians have sometimes filled this void by assuming—tacitly or openly—that in economic and social terms communities were islands of relative harmony, homogeneity, and consensual egalitarianism. Accordingly, deviations from this norm were to be interpreted as isolated and regrettable instances of individual corruption or exceptional greed. Then and now, such a priori notions have forestalled a more complex and nuanced contextual analysis.

In spite of a lack of sources which would address questions of communal discord more explicitly, there is strong indirect evidence to suggest that the expansion of the vanilla business produced serious tensions in the basin's Totonac communities—particularly in Papantla, where vanilla cultivation was widespread. The prevalence of theft, for instance, was clearly both a reflection and a persistent cause of conflict among Totonacs. Evidently, communal solidarity did not inhibit many from pilfering their neighbors' fruit. As traders of all sorts scrambled for vanilla, the lure of easy money sometimes proved irresistible. It is easy to imagine how this unstoppable practice would have fostered a general climate of suspicion and apprehension which tore at the social fabric of the communities.

Along with vanilla theft, the emergence of a group of Indian speculators probably gave rise as well to new kinds of internal social friction. These entrepreneurs advanced money to other growers and often acted as middlemen for the big town merchants. The disagreements and inequities common in such commercial relationships—including quarrels over the terms and fulfillment of advance contracts, disputes over weights and measures of quality, fraudulent and deceitful practices, and rivalries among traders—could not have done much to foment cohesion. Bausa's elaborate remarks about the frequency with which traditionally strong *compadrazgo* bonds between Indians were strained by conflicts over vanilla transactions suggest that already by the mid-1840s the growth of the vanilla business was affecting communal social relations.[54] In addition, it would not be surprising if as a result of this mid-level local trading wealth disparities among Totonacs had increased considerably.

Likewise, the swift and profitable expansion of vanilla cultivation raised the stakes involved in the allocation of communal farmland, which in all likelihood made that process more conflict-ridden. Little is known about how farmland (*tierras de común repartimiento*) was distributed among families in these (or any other) Indian communities, but distribution probably reflected traditional patterns of occupation and inheritance as well as current political clout. In general, some lands were clearly better than or at least preferable to others—for example, lands that were more fertile, sunnier, or less prone to flooding, and perhaps also closer to town, to the road, or to water sources. This had always been the case, although the criteria of desirability may have changed somewhat over time. However, for as long as agriculture consisted largely of growing maize, beans, squash, and—to a lesser extent—cotton, sugarcane, etc., all predominantly for domestic use, land allocation—that is, who got to use which piece of land—was not bound to have very significant economic consequences. This is not to say that it did not matter, nor to suggest that it could not have been the subject of internal disputes; rather, the point is that the economic potential of farmland remained more or less uniformly limited. Provided that every family of cultivators had at least enough land to carve out a decent milpa, the scope of any differences arising from the use of specific plots of land also remained somewhat narrow.

Vanilla changed this situation. Some lands were better suited than others for the cultivation of vanilla and hence became far more valuable. In addition, whereas the traditional milpa was abandoned after a few years of cultivation, vanilla stands tied up lands for much longer, usually ten years or so. Whether in the *acahual* or in fields cleared expressly in order to plant it, vanilla represented a more long-term investment in a particular piece of land. These changes in land use and value probably made use rights a more contentious issue. The incentives to control, protect, obtain, challenge, or retain—as the case might be—access to particularly well-suited lands were now very high. It is hard to imagine that this did not have a divisive effect on at least some of these communities.

Overall, then, the early development of Papantla's vanilla economy had paradoxical consequences for the area's native agriculturalists. On the one hand, it strengthened their household economies, while on the other it strained the bonds of community, fostering dissensions born of opportunity. Meanwhile, the basin's emboldened town merchants pursued their own separate business dreams. The Papantla of old still held up, but it also showed signs of great stress. Around 1870, as the growth of vanilla exports accelerated, spreading wealth and continuing to sow the seeds of change, a reconstituted state government renewed its old legal crusade against communal landholding. Embattled as well as internally weakened, some of the communities would then begin to crumble. Turmoil and transformation would quickly follow. Fruit of the old Papantla, vanilla was to end up destroying it.

4 The End of Communal Landholding

On December 16, 1875, as Porfirio Díaz and his allies plotted the revolt that would overthrow President Lerdo de Tejada, five men assembled at the eastern *ranchería* of El Cristo—near the Tecolutla river and the coast—to start dividing up Papantla's communal lands. They were Cecilio Rodríguez, the trustee in charge of Indian community affairs in Papantla's municipal government; Antonio Pascoli, a local topographer hired to conduct the land surveys; and the three members of a Junta de Indígenas (Indian Commission)—Simón Tiburcio, Pablo Hernández Olmedo, and Antonio Jiménez—appointed by the municipal authorities to carry out the division. They worked quietly and very quickly, placing wooden crosses at various selected spots—for example, under an "ancient *zapote mamey* tree" and next to an "impassable swampy pool"—to mark the boundaries of this *congregación*, and did not face any interference from local farmers, Totonacs or Italians. By the end of the day, the rough outlines of El Cristo had been demarcated; a crude map showed a scalene triangle covering about half a square league of farmland.[1] It was agreed that two days later the group would meet again to survey neighboring Palo Hueco and Cabezas.

This first laying of boundary crosses, unceremonious and seemingly inoffensive, marks the beginning of an epoch of great upheaval in Papantla. In the previous hundred or so years, the Tecolutla basin had been the scenario of numerous rebellions, riots, and even military battles. Some of these episodes of open conflict and warfare reflected social struggles peculiar to the area, others were tied to the convulsed political history of nineteenth-century Mexico, and many combined the two. In the end, however, none had a particularly profound or lasting effect on the basic structures of local society. Lives were lost, fortunes changed, political alliances were forged or fractured, concrete grievances persisted, subsided, or got resolved, and while all of this surely mattered considerably, greater Papantla's social organization nevertheless emerged from these episodes essentially unchanged. In 1870, as in 1770, the basin was still largely a world of independent family farmers.

In contrast, the social conflicts and confrontations of the late nineteenth century were to have deeper consequences. In the course of the previous decades, the vanilla economy had for the first time enabled the formation and accumulation of local capital, creating a small class of wealthy rival merchants as well as a prosperous middle layer of diverse petty traders and entrepreneurs. Not surprisingly, the conduct of business sharpened social divisions, both between Indians and non-Indians and within the Totonac *pueblos*. After 1870, as markets and opportunities in the vanilla trade continued to expand and as new land-based investment possibilities began to appear, land tenure became a prominent bone of contention, especially among business-minded people inside and outside the communities. For them, controlling land meant eliminating competition over the supply of valuable agricultural commodities, principally vanilla, but also—among others—tobacco and timber, which would reduce costs and boost profits.

At least initially, then, the communal land question—that is, whether and how use rights would be redistributed and made legally exclusive—presented itself in Papantla primarily as a commercial issue, the extension onto a new arena of a heated business race fueled by vanilla. At the same time, with the return of peace, the state government began anew to press for the dissolution of communal forms of property, prompted by a combination of ideological and fiscal considerations. Together, these different pressures would shatter the old land-use arrangements, putting an end to collective land tenure. This process of disintegration—or "extinction," as the bureaucrats of the day liked to call it—was long, tortuous, and conflict-ridden because much more than the legal transformation of an old land-holding pattern—inspired by liberal ideas—was clearly at stake.

In greater Papantla myriad conflicting business interests were the driving force behind the land division. This competition involved many and affected all; merchants, traders, and politicians jockeyed for power, profits, and graft, while farmers sought to protect and enhance their economic independence and prosperity. Some benefited from current communal arrangements, whether fair or unfair, and opposed any changes; others saw a division as a golden opportunity to achieve (or craft) a more advantageous distribution of land-use rights; and yet others hoped that a new property regime would enable them to make their de facto possessions de jure. The bitter conflicts over business—including the control of land—coupled with the iniquities, the scams, and the new burdens of legal ownership engendered in the process of parceling out the lands, would provoke a number of notable Indian uprisings and rebellions among the former *comuneros* of Papantla, particularly in the 1890s.

When it was all over, some thirty years after the first crude survey at El Cristo, trade, investment, and land speculation had visibly reshaped the socioeconomic life of the basin. In addition to the pattern of land tenure, Papantla's human geography and land use, as well as the scope of its business enterprises and its old economic organization, had changed significantly. By

1905, not only vanilla but also cattle ranching, tobacco, and oil wells competed with the milpas for a piece of the land. Wealthy merchants—often the original vanilla barons or their children—were by then also big landowners in the formerly communal territories, as well as beyond, and across the basin the dispossessed Indian *jornalero* had become a far more common figure.

In terms of both economic and social developments, it makes sense to distinguish four stages in this process of transformation: the demise of communal tenure (c. 1870–79); the era of *condueñazgo* (c. 1880–90); land subdivisions and rebellions (c. 1891–98); and the new property regime (after 1898). They are the subject of the following chapters. Since the vanilla economy paved the way for these social changes, the first step must be to examine the evolution of the business after 1870.

The Vanilla Boom, 1870–1890

By the late 1860s, Mexico's average annual exports of vanilla had risen to almost 12,000 kilograms, roughly half of which then came from Papantla. For the nation as a whole, this represented a sixfold increase in exports since the time of Independence; as for Papantla, its output was then probably between twenty and thirty times larger than it had been a half century earlier. Overall, this was a period of solid growth; in absolute terms, however, the scale of Mexico's vanilla economy remained somewhat small. As long as Mexico retained a virtual monopoly in the production of vanilla for export, there was nothing to compare it with, but this had changed quickly—beginning in the late 1840s—with the commercial development of artificially pollinated Bourbon vanilla. The early growth of exports from French colonial plantations was nothing short of spectacular, and from 1861 on—a mere fifteen years after the onset of commercial cultivation on the island—the yearly volume of Réunion shipments to France would regularly surpass Mexico's aggregate annual exports (see Appendix Table A.4). Figure 4.1 compares average yearly exports by decade for the period between 1840 and 1869.

As shown, the rate of growth as well as the average annual output of Mexico's vanilla economy leading up to the year 1870 paled in comparison to those of its upstart Bourbon competitor. Already by 1860 at least some of the principal Mexican dealers were aware of this trend, as Fontecilla's *Tratado* shows. He wrote then that vanilla from Bourbon and Java was a "fearsome competitor," capable of conquering Mexico's markets, and he predicted—as it turns out, far too optimistically—that in the course of a few years those islands would probably be producing as much as Mexico.[2] The causes of this remarkable growth disparity are complex, but they can be summarized as follows: the scale of productive units (large capitalist

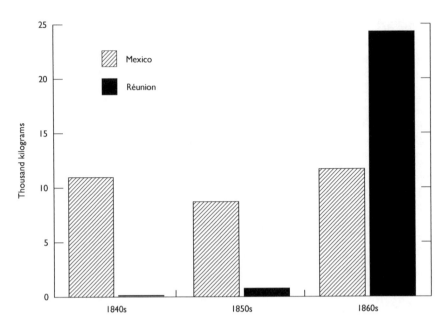

FIGURE 4.1 Average yearly exports, Mexico and Réunion

plantations versus small plots); the nature of labor systems (slave versus family); and technology (artificial versus natural pollination). Relying on plantation-style horticulture, a number of small islands off the southeast coast of Africa would swiftly develop into tropical vanilla factories. It is particularly worth noting that artificial pollination increased enormously the productivity of vanilla cultivation, and that it would not become widely practiced in Mexico until much later. In the meantime, however, Mexican producers—especially those in the Cantón of Papantla—found other ways of increasing the size of harvests, for after 1870 Mexican vanilla exports started to grow at a much faster rate than during the previous fifty years.

Indeed, judging from a combination of export and import statistics, between 1870 and 1890 Mexico's productive capacity expanded greatly. Prior to 1870, a truly excellent year for the business would have meant shipping 15,000 or perhaps 16,000 kilograms abroad, and those years—as the averages suggest—came around very seldom. By 1890, Mexico's vanilla economy was able to grow and process as many as 70,000 kilograms in one season, and annual exports of over 50,000 kilograms were by then not at all unusual. As will be seen, much of this growth took place around Papantla. A significant shift in markets spurred this development.

In the course of these decades, French imports—and through them the European market—became thoroughly dominated by French colonial vanilla (Appendix Tables A.4 and A.7). Although Mexico's share of the rapidly expanding French import market decreased dramatically after the rise of French colonial plantations (100 percent up to 1846, 26 percent in 1866, and 6 percent in 1886–88), the volume of Mexican vanilla shipments to France actually remained more or less stable. Whereas through the 1860s France's annual imports of Mexican fruit averaged 8,839 kilograms, for the 1870s and 1880s the averages were 7,984 kilograms and 10,066 kilograms per year, respectively. The original vanilla of commerce was no longer predominant in France, but its aromatic qualities were still considered superior, and thus Mexico's best classes continued to be held in very high esteem.[3] Still, it is clear that after more than a century of monopolistic supremacy, Mexico had been effectively relegated to a small corner of the booming French—and European—vanilla market. France now had its own. In years to come, new industrial and domestic uses would multiply European demand for the spice, but colonial vanilla would continue to own the lion's share of these markets.

However, just as Mexico was becoming progressively less and less significant a source of vanilla for France, France was also losing importance as an export destination in Mexico. In the course of the 1870s and 1880s, while the trade with France vacillated between stagnation and slight growth, the United States rapidly took over as the principal consumer of Mexican vanilla. For the most part, these new Mexican exports would represent net growth and not a simple switch of destinations. As Mexican and U.S. trade statistics clearly indicate, the emergence of the United States as an important vanilla market in the years following its Civil War coincided with a period of great productive and commercial expansion for Mexico's vanilla economy (Appendix Tables A.8 and A.9). Prior to the mid-1860s, the United States imported very little vanilla and American participation in the trade was chiefly restricted to the shipping and reexporting businesses. Between 1870 and 1890, however, the importation of vanilla for internal consumption increased approximately twelvefold, from an annual average of around 4,000 kilograms during the late 1860s, to more than 11,000 kilograms per year for the 1870s, to over 50,000 kilograms during the prosperous 1880s, in large measure as a result of growing demand from the budding ice cream and confectionery industries. By 1890, the United States had swiftly emerged as the second largest vanilla market in the world, still only about half as large—in terms of trade volume—as France, but growing at a faster pace. Most of this new vanilla—perhaps five times what Mexico had normally exported to all its markets in the 1860s—came to be grown in the state of Veracruz, and above all, in Papantla.

In fact, as these trade figures suggest, underlying the very rapid growth of vanilla consumption in the United States during these two decades was an equally extraordinary increase in vanilla cultivation and trade inside Mexico. In the process, Mexico's vanilla economy quadrupled in size. While the overall volume of exports to France remained more or less constant, new vanilla fields sprouted all over the countryside to meet this newly arisen, boundless demand from the North. The trend started midway through the 1860s, when the first sizable shipments of Mexican vanilla made their way to the U.S. market, and was fully in evidence by the early 1870s. Already in 1872–73, more than 50 percent of Mexico's vanilla exports were destined for the United States, and by the second half of the 1880s the norm was over 90 percent. By 1890, Mexico's vanilla trade was once again virtually a single-market business, though more than just shipping routes had changed.

Given the moderate and gradual growth—in absolute terms—of Veracruz's vanilla economy over the previous five decades, the almost sudden multiplication of annual production and exports that characterized this period is truly a remarkable development. In this shift, the 1870s were surely the key years, for it was then that a vast and unprecedented expansion of cultivation, a concomitant increase in processing capacity, and the forging of new business links locally and abroad all got underway. Because new vines do not usually bear fruit before the third year and do not generally reach peak yield levels until the fifth, the full commercial impact of those processes was not visible right away. However, the changes set in motion during the 1870s paved the way for a great export boom during the 1880s.

Extrapolating from incomplete or partial Mexican, U.S., and French vanilla trade records, a reasonable estimate would be that Mexico's average annual exports for the 1870s were between 16,000 and 18,000 kilograms, with a pattern of progressive growth exhibited in the course of the decade. This is only an educated guess, but for the present purposes it will suffice.[4] The data series for the 1880s are more complete, and the picture that emerges is correspondingly clearer. Mexican sources indicate average annual exports of 48,296 kilograms, and import statistics—which are perhaps more reliable—suggest an even larger volume of trade, approximately 50,000 kilograms per year. Here the numbers speak for themselves. Within these ten years, Mexico had more than doubled its vanilla output.

There is little doubt that this enormous jump in production was largely the result of a huge expansion of the area under cultivation, because artificial pollination (which increased yields but also required additional labor expenditures) was then barely practiced in the state of Veracruz. In fact, the method of hand-pollination had just been introduced to Mexico by the French colonists of Jicaltepec–San Rafael. According to local recollection, a number of the colonists traveled back to France in the mid- to late 1870s, saw the blooming *planifolia* in the greenhouses of Paris's Natural History Museum, and learned Albius's thirty-year-old technique. Back in Mexico, they began to apply it in their own vanilla fields, probably in the course of the 1880s.[5]

However, despite widespread assumptions to the contrary, it is not clear that the practice spread quickly beyond the margins of the Nautla River.[6]

Writing to the Minister of Fomento in October 1887, Agapito Fontecilla observed that "in these last few years some in the Cantón of Misantla have started to fertilize vanilla flowers," noting that he could not say for sure whether this was a good idea—although he was inclined to think that it was—because he knew very little about it. Moreover, in an earlier report on the state of the vanilla business (November 1883), Fontecilla made no mention whatever of fertilization by hand. These texts, as well as later sources, suggest strongly that through the 1880s artificial pollination was not widely practiced or even particularly well known around Papantla, where the bulk of the nation's vanilla was then cultivated.[7] There, increased output was simply the product of expanded cultivation. As will be seen, changes in the legal status of communal lands directly assisted this trend.

Significantly, it is in these years that the district, or canton, of Papantla finally emerged as the leading producer of Mexican vanilla. As the United States developed a voracious appetite for this aromatic, the new Villa of Papantla became the undisputed national capital of the vanilla business, while nearby Gutiérrez Zamora grew into a noteworthy curing center. Indeed, as it turns out, the spectacular growth in Mexican exports during this period was principally Papantla's. Whereas in the 1860s Papantla generally produced approximately half of Mexico's total vanilla exports, by the late 1880s its share had grown to at least two-thirds.[8] In absolute terms, that meant a vast expansion in production, from around 6,000 kilograms to perhaps 33,000 kilograms per year on average. This represented a 550 percent increase in output over two decades. Production also rose noticeably in Misantla (and particularly around Jicaltepec–San Rafael) during these years, but it is clear that Mexico's vanilla boom was above all Papantla's.[9]

In the area of processing, greater Papantla's ascendancy was even more pronounced. By 1890, the *beneficiadores* of Papantla and Gutiérrez Zamora were handling not only the basin's voluminous harvests but also much of what was cultivated in neighboring Misantla. Although San Rafael remained a significant curing center, especially for the crops grown by the French colonists themselves, the rest of the green vanilla grown in that canton increasingly gravitated toward the markets of Papantla. As Fontecilla then put it, "The vanilla harvested in [the Canton of Misantla] is sold—most of it green but also half-cured—to the merchants of [the Canton of Papantla]."[10]

In sum, three interrelated developments characterized Mexico's vanilla trade in this period. First and foremost, over the course of these twenty years Papantla's vanilla economy tapped the newly vibrant flavoring market in the nearby United States and proceeded to grow by leaps and bounds. Second, France declined in importance as an export destination, its Mexican imports dwarfed by those of the United States; in Europe, meanwhile, colonial vanilla swiftly took over the market. Third, "Papantla" became almost synonymous with "Mexican vanilla." Local cultivation spread in a truly unprecedented fashion, and the basin's curing establishments developed into clearing-houses for the bulk of Mexico's exports. In the process, the character of local business changed as well.

The Evolution of Business

"France," boasted the U.S. consul for Tuxpan in 1874, "was formerly the great market for vanilla, but the enterprise of some of our American merchants has diverted the trade; so that New York has become the great depot for vanilla."[11] As it turns out, this historic shift in the local vanilla trade would involve much more than a mere change of destination. The rise of U.S. demand came at a time when improved means of transportation and access to new forms of communication were transforming the pace and the organization of Mexican commerce. Commodity price information could suddenly travel long distances much more quickly, shipping became more frequent and regular, and contacts between top buyers and sellers across national borders—even in remote places like Papantla—began to be more commonplace. Up and down the Gulf coast, the growing avidity of U.S. traders surely abetted this process. By 1890, Mexico's vanilla economy had turned largely into an appendage of the enormous New York–centered natural flavoring import trade. For Papantla's big town merchants, this meant better market information and closer trade and credit links with New York, which made their transactions less unpredictable and speculative. As production grew, a number of them expanded the range of their operations, becoming successful exporters. Theirs was no longer the primitive and petty—if often absurdly lucrative—brokering of the 1840s and 1850s; in these years, their business soared, in scope as well as in scale.

Improvements in commercial navigation between the United States and Mexico were key to the development of the binational vanilla trade. Even though steamers were already crossing the oceans by the late 1830s, prior to 1850 the U.S.–Mexico sea trade was conducted by less capacious sailboats. By the early to mid-1840s, there was a regular packet-boat service between New York and Veracruz—run by Hargous & Co. The first steam line connecting the two countries began operations in 1850; it went from New Orleans to Veracruz and back and was principally devoted to the cotton trade. These trips ended with the outbreak of the U.S. Civil War. It was not until the late 1860s that steamers finally linked the ports of New York and Veracruz; beginning in 1868, F. Alexandre & Sons—a New York shipping concern—contracted with the Mexican government to run a regular round-trip service (every twenty days), including stopovers at Havana and Sisal (Progreso). The company received a very generous subsidy for every trip completed, as well as fee and export-duty exemptions. By the late 1870s, the voyages had become biweekly, and these steamers called at other southern Mexican ports. These were precisely the years during which U.S. vanilla imports began to climb. In all likelihood, Alexandre's Veracruz line quickly became an important channel for these shipments.

Around the same time, "to provide for the needs of the budding commerce between Mexico and the United States," the federal government contracted F. Alexandre to start another steam line, this one between New Orleans and Veracruz, with a similar set of subsidies and privileges. These steamers did roundtrips every two (and later three) weeks, calling also at Tampico, Tuxpan, and later Matamoros or nearby Bagdad. The New Orleans–Veracruz line began its operations in mid-1873.[12] Regular steamboat service spurred an impressive commercial renaissance in Tuxpan, an old coastal trading town 22 leagues distant by mule path from Papantla. Between October 1876 and September 1877, for instance, twenty-eight steamers called at Tuxpan, all from the United States. Timber, skins, hides, sugar, coffee, chicle, rubber, honey, and spices from Tuxpan's rich hinterlands now had better access to foreign markets.[13] With this new direct connection to U.S. markets, the port at Tuxpan also became an attractive alternative for some Papanteco traders looking to export their vanilla. Instead of shipping it by mule train to Tecolutla and then by sailboat to Veracruz, they could now send their vanilla straight to Tuxpan, embarking it there for the United States.

Indeed, after 1874, Tuxpan's importance in the vanilla trade increased dramatically. Up until the early 1870s, Veracruz accounted for nearly 100 percent of shipments, but by the end of that decade Tuxpan was already channeling between 15 and 40 percent of the merchandise. During the 1880s—key years of growth for the business—Tuxpan managed to surpass old Veracruz as a gateway for vanilla exports, first in 1881–82 and then consistently between 1885 and 1892 (Appendix Table A.10). This was a remarkable achievement, especially considering that its port facilities were very rudimentary and that a sandbar at the mouth of the Tuxpan River often prevented ships from docking at the wharves, forcing them to load and unload offshore by means of rafts and lighters.[14] Vanilla sent to France continued to go via Veracruz, as did part of the increasingly voluminous shipments destined for the United States, but most of the new U.S.-bound vanilla—grown largely in the Tecolutla basin—came to be exported by way of Tuxpan. In effect, then, the rise of Tuxpan as a steamer port facilitated—or perhaps even accelerated—the expansive reorientation of Papantla's vanilla economy toward the United States.

Significant improvements in means of communication also transformed the nature of the local vanilla business, at least for the ruling class of merchant–curers. A privately owned telegraph line began to make its way across northern Veracruz in the early 1870s, and by 1873 the town of Papantla was already connected and had an office. This cable went from Teziutlán down to Jalacingo and Tlapacoyan, entering the Cantón of Papantla at La Laja, just below San José Acateno, Puebla. The line was probably laid directly parallel to the old trail down from Teziutlán. After La Laja, it ran through the *ranchería* at Joloapan and across the Tecolutla River to Papantla, past which it continued north to Tuxpan and on to Tampico.[15] The telegraph effectively put an end to certain aspects of Papantla's historic isolation. The town was still hard to reach, but not anymore to communicate with. Receiving news from Teziutlán, Tuxpan, Veracruz, Mexico City, or even New York was all of a sudden much easier and quicker, and written contacts could become more frequent and reliable. It was no longer necessary to wait a few days for the post to deliver a message up over the rugged sierras, and the ninety or so often muddy miles separating Tuxpan from Papantla could now also be bridged in just minutes. The telegraph defied the old barriers of topography.

For a volatile commodity trade like that of vanilla, these changes were nothing short of revolutionary. Previously, a lack of timely and trustworthy information had almost single-handedly shaped the conduct of business. Uncertainty and speculation were rife, in part because merchants could not know what the markets would bear, and periodic boom-and-bust cases involving dealers of all ranks were not uncommon, since guessing was necessarily a big component of any trading strategy.[16] The arrival of the telegraph enabled an increased flow of information, and with it, gradually, a more regular operation of market forces. Now it would be possible for curers in Papantla to learn quickly about current prices in New York, as well as about the evolving seasonal patterns of demand—mainly from vanilla extract manufacturers and buyers—in the United States. This allowed them to develop more elaborate business strategies—to adjust their price offers for raw vanilla, to time their shipments so as to maximize bargaining power, and in general to calculate potential or expected earnings somewhat more confidently. Likewise, New York dealers could now obtain prompt information about weather conditions and the estimated size of harvests back in Papantla so as to modify their expectations accordingly. Vanilla remained a tricky sort of business, largely because it was still based on scattered, small-scale, and independent horticultural production, but the telegraph—as well as steam navigation—did much to modernize its conduct.

In a context of rapidly rising U.S. demand, these new avenues of communication and transportation served to forge close business ties between the basin's top dealers and New York importing concerns. Traditionally, Papantla's town merchants had sold their vanilla stocks to trading houses in Veracruz. These establishments, predominantly German- and Spanish-owned, would then make their own arrangements to send the spice abroad.[17] This pattern of trade remained strong during the 1870s and—albeit less so—the 1880s; shipments to France continued to be made exclusively from Veracruz and through its trading houses and a share of the growing U.S. exports was channeled through them as well. The new Tuxpan trade, however, was to be something significantly different. Suddenly able to develop more direct links with trading houses in the United States, some of the basin's dealers began to export their own vanilla through Tuxpan, bypassing the commercial companies of Veracruz. Prior to the 1870s, the export merchant had been a rare figure; Agapito Fontecilla was possibly one. Now, with the rise of New York and Tuxpan, more ventured in that direction. These new exporters placed their vanilla stocks in consignment with New York importing houses, which sold them on their behalf. This marked the beginning of a new era for Papantla's vanilla business.

When Francisco Fontecilla died in 1877, this shift was underway. A postmortem review of the business records he left behind showed that he had 852 pounds of vanilla on consignment with P. Harmony & Nephew in New York City; another 625 pounds he had sent directly to a trading house in Bordeaux. Three years later, when the Spanish merchant Francisco Naveda was killed in Papantla, his account with Martínez Hermanos of Veracruz had a credit of $18,640.87 pesos from vanilla sales, indicating that he was still sending much of his vanilla to Veracruz companies. However, by then he also had an account with Gavino Gutiérrez y Cía. of New York—with a small credit balance of $381.11 pesos—which reflected his incipient association with the exporting business.[18] Direct transactions of this sort became commonplace in the course of the 1880s, and by 1890 the basin's leading merchants were themselves involved in exporting—often through Tuxpan— most of the nation's vanilla production. The port at Veracruz would yet regain its former preeminence as a vanilla depot, but by then its trading houses had been effectively displaced from the central position they once held in managing vanilla exports. The future belonged to Papantla's merchants, and to their new business partners in the lower end of Manhattan.

The pages of the leading spice trade journal in the United States reflect well this momentous transition. Published in New York and founded in late 1871, the *Oil, Paint, and Drug Reporter* followed domestic and international developments in the "chemicals" market, which included a wide variety of flavorings and food additives. The vanilla "bean" was among the "drugs" covered by the *Reporter*; chopped and processed with alcohol, vanilla was turned into an extract sold to the ice cream, soda water, confectionery, and baking industries. Already in the 1870s, a small weekly column tracked vanilla prices and market trends. After 1880, longer articles about Mexican vanilla began to appear on a more or less regular basis. Time and again, the *Re-*

porter described the vanilla plant and fruit and explained to its readers how it was cultivated and cured down in Mexico. An early piece (June 1881) entitled "Vanilla Beans" announced the new trade status of Mexico's aromatic:

The use of this article in this country has largely increased in the last few years and is constantly growing, with the increase in population and in the demand for flavoring extracts, confectionery, syrups, perfumery and the like, for which purposes the vanilla has no rival. As a consequence the price, though varying considerably with the size and quality of the crop, is always high. In the last six years it has been as high as $28–$30, and as low as $8 per pound for a prime article. There are several varieties of the plant which produces the bean—or rather pod—of commerce, and they are found in several parts of the world, but the best quality of beans come from Mexico, of which country the plant is a native, and those from the province of Papantla, are most esteemed.[19]

Likewise in these years Papantla's weather became a news subject, and crop forecasts began to receive prominent coverage. New York dealers were now in tune with the rhythms of Papantla's harvest and curing cycles, and followed them closely and with great interest. In mid-1886, for instance, the *Reporter* noted "unusual activity" and "excitement in the market," with prices rapidly rising because of "reports of a short crop, which from rumors grew into an established fact and there is no doubt that the yield will not be more than fifty to sixty percent of last year's crop." This shortage, the article explained, "is due to the bad weather which prevailed during the curing season this year, when a large portion of the crop became mouldy, and the beans were found to be infested with a species of lice, which feed upon the vanilla plant."[20] Clearly, vanilla interests in New York and Papantla already had their own information networks.

Advertisements for Mexican vanilla—which start to appear more regularly in the course of the 1880s—reveal the emerging business ties between curers and importers. In these years, the firm Dodge & Olcott became the leading U.S. importer of the basin's vanilla. By 1886, they had associated with one or more of Papantla's top traders, investing in expanded curing facilities and assuring themselves of a steady supply. Their large stocks were shipped out of Tuxpan. As shown, these were years of extraordinary growth in vanilla production and exports; through this direct business arrangement, Dodge & Olcott and their Mexican partners fostered this process and managed to capture a large share of the market. At that time, Dodge & Olcott offered extract manufacturers "an assortment of fine OLD AND MATURED BEANS, and in addition a FULL LINE of the NEW CROP ranging in quality from ORDINARY to PRIME." Their advantage, the advertisement stated, was that, "as we obtain our supplies direct through our establishment at the place of growth in Mexico, and we have no intermediate expenses to pay, we are in a position to offer excellent bargains in all qualities, including cuts."[21]

In a June 1887 news note, the *Reporter* commented on this new development in the business:

The increase in the demand for vanilla beans is remarkable. The popular taste is rapidly changing in favor of this pleasant flavor, while the demand for fruit flavors such as strawberry, raspberry, pineapple and even the old reliable lemon is dying out. This largely increased demand is no doubt influenced in a considerable degree by the care and attention paid the article by Messrs. Dodge & Olcott. They have materially increased their facilities for transacting their vanilla bean business in Mexico by adding another large building and the adjoining grounds to their already extensive establishment in the curing districts of that country, and are at present actively engaged in curing the crop of beans. The opportunity offered large consumers to purchase direct from curers in this way should prove a most attractive feature. Messrs. Dodge & Olcott have the honor of being the first American house which has established a branch of this kind in Mexico.[22]

An 1888 advertisement (Figure 4.2) boasts of these direct links between curing and importing.

It is not known how long this particular partnership between Dodge & Olcott and their Papantla counterparts lasted, but the fact that it was established shows that the basin's merchants were now dealing directly with New York. Other local merchants also developed connections with New York trading houses; also in 1888, for instance, the importing firm of Tyler & Finch was offering "choice selections from the best stocks of the best curers in Mexico, including every quality from the cheapest to the finest of the crop."[23] On the whole, consignment—and not direct investment—would become the prevailing form of business relationship between Mexican curers and U.S. houses.[24] Still, it is clear that Papantla's trade now had a distinctly new character and orientation.

The progressive Americanization of Papantla's vanilla exports manifested itself in other ways as well. Slowly but surely, the pound displaced the kilogram as the dominant unit of the export trade, since that is how prices were quoted in New York. At the local level, however, the millar (one thousand units) remained the basis of most transactions. More significantly, a new classification system was adopted. Until about the 1850s, vanilla was divided into various categories, according to length, appearance, and other such considerations—*primera*, *segunda*, *zacate*, and *rezacate* were the usual classes. By the time of Fontecilla's *Tratado* (1861), these divisions had been abandoned and mixed beans were bundled and sold together, except for the *rezacate* and the *cimarrona*, which were of inferior quality.[25] With the rise of U.S. demand, vanilla came to be reclassified into "whole" and "cuts." This shift reflected the new industrial uses of vanilla. The main criterion for selection was now whether the pods were split or not. Split or otherwise imperfect vanilla began to be separated and cut into little pieces (*picadura*),

FIGURE 4.2 Dodge & Olcott advertisement. From *OPDR* 34 (July 25, 1888).

which made it much easier and faster to cure.[26] By the middle of the 1880s, the *Reporter* was already quoting "cuts" prices in New York. Although these "cuts" would not produce the same quality of flavor and aroma, many of the large manufacturers who purchased vanilla did not always need anything better, and *picadura* was initially much cheaper than whole beans. The new market dictated the shape of the product.

In effect, then, the vanilla trade was undergoing not only a quantitative transformation but also a qualitative one. A variety of industrial processes linked to mass consumption—and not elite culinary practices or small-scale manufacturing of luxury goods—were now to be the main sources of demand. This was generally true in France as well as in the United States, except that in Europe Mexican vanilla was largely confined to the narrow luxury sector, with Bourbon steadily taking over the rest. The United States, on the other hand, quickly developed an expansive industrial market for Mexican vanilla, where fine and not so fine whole beans—and even the new, lowly *picadura*—would readily find takers. Vanilla's commercial image and status were evolving; no longer a scarce, mysterious, and exclusive silvery icon of aromatic perfection, vanilla was fast becoming a popular and ubiquitous mass-produced flavor.

Together, all these changes in the character of the product and the business, as well as the resulting boom in production and exports, led over time to a significant reduction in prices. The record for these years is unfortunately spotty and often difficult to interpret, but it does exhibit a distinct overall trend. Two types of prices for Mexican vanilla were normally quoted in New York, according to quality and class: price ranges for whole vanilla, including top prices for the finest beans, and price ranges for cuts (from 1886 on). Quotations fluctuated constantly, and thus it is hard to estimate average prices without a complete data series, but the notable decline in top prices is nevertheless suggestive. Between 1875 and 1880, the very best vanilla sold for as much as US$30 per pound, whereas in 1880 the highest quote was US$20, in 1886, US$18, and by 1890, US$10.[27] The pattern is not as simple as these figures would imply, however; top prices in New York generally declined through 1881–85, when exports grew dramatically, then rose for the next two or three years, only to decrease again in 1889–90. On the whole, though, a downward trend seems evident during these years, not only in top prices, but also for vanilla of lesser quality.[28] "For some time past," noted the *Reporter* in April 1891, "vanilla beans have been selling at very low prices; in fact we cannot remember when the article has been as cheap as it is at present."[29] Although a combination of short crops and growing demand would lead to considerable price increases in the course of the 1890s and early 1900s, the long-term pattern is unmistakably one of decline; after 1880, vanilla never reached US$20 per pound again, a sum seemingly not uncommon back in the 1870s.

For the basin's town merchants, this was probably in principle a distressing trend. This is not to say, however, that these were lean years for them; in fact, quite the opposite seems to have been the case. In the absence of detailed account books, it is impossible to provide a precise picture of how this new trade environment affected the historically high potential for profits of Papantla's vanilla business. Still, a number of observations are worth making. It seems reasonable to suppose that rates of return on investment generally declined during these years. Before, the local vanilla trade was chaotic and highly speculative; disjointed markets and small harvests created many opportunities for windfall earnings. After 1870, new means of communication and transportation as well as direct trade ties with importers helped to create a more integrated market in which prices could keep close track of changing conditions. This made the business much less irregular and unpredictable, making success less a matter of gambling than of hard bargaining and shrewd calculation. As production soared and prices came down, potential rates of return were bound to become, in the language of the business world, "more reasonable."

Still, this new state of affairs was on the whole highly beneficial for Papantla's merchants, who were in fact instrumental in bringing it about. Order, too, had many advantages. To begin with, in spite of the overall decline of the 1880s, vanilla still commanded a very high price abroad, as much as $26.4 pesos per kilogram (US$10/pound) in 1890, perhaps the low point for this period. In 1880, when New York prices were still considerably higher, Francisco Naveda was paying $50 pesos per millar of raw vanilla, or roughly $12.5 pesos per kilogram once cured. After adding labor, packing, and transport expenses (discussed in the previous chapter), as well as dealers' fees, there was still, it appears, an ample margin for profits. By cutting out intermediaries in the export trade, those local merchants who became themselves exporters in these years got to keep a larger share of earnings; for them, New York's prices—and not Veracruz's—were now the ones that mattered.[30] As exporters, they also benefited from a process of gradual currency depreciation (peso vs. dollar), which started to pick up pace after 1870 (0.958:1 in 1870, 1.097:1 in 1880, 1.2:1 in 1890, and 2.062:1 in 1900).[31] This progressive decline in the value of the peso would give an added boost to their business.

It would seem, then, that although unit prices and hence unit profits tended to decline, market conditions as well as the new organization of the trade continued to allow merchants to obtain generous earnings. Vanilla was still very expensive, and the business remained a lucrative one. Moreover, whatever local town merchants may have lost in terms of potential returns on investment, they more than made up through increases in the volume of trade. Indeed, surely the most significant new aspect of the vanilla business in these years was its size. As noted, between the 1860s and the 1880s Papantla's average annual exports rose by about 550 percent. In addition, the basin's dealers also processed and exported vanilla grown in Misantla. Even as profits per unit shrank, this massive increase in the size of Papantla's vanilla economy in all likelihood meant a net gain in the rate of local capital formation.

Judging from their growing investments in other types of enterprises (which are discussed below)—urban and rural real estate, cattle ranching, timber, financing, and marketing other crops—it is apparent that in these years the basin's merchant elite was getting wealthier. Without a doubt, this money came largely from the vanilla trade. International price decreases notwithstanding, the transformation of the business was for them clearly a beneficial one. No wonder, then, that at this time it is hard to find complaints from merchants about the terms of trade; for instance, Fontecilla's *Informes* of 1883 and 1887 comment on many recent developments in the business, negative as well as positive, but the decline in prices is notably not among them. Interestingly, he was more concerned with the general decline in the quality of the curing. Good *maestros*, he explained, were scarce. The problem, he wrote, was that "the skilled *maestros* who were around when I published my treatise (1861) have already died, and the new ones have not reached their level of expertise, and since vanilla crops have increased so notably, [the merchants] have had to turn the job over to many who in other times would have been considered mere apprentices."[32]

Nonetheless, it seems clear that in these years volume was becoming an increasingly important element in the profit structure of Papantla's vanilla business. As unit prices and profits declined, scale was to be the key to sustained capital accumulation. This made merchants ever more eager to control larger vanilla stocks and thus also to find new ways to promote or procure the expansion of production. Other sectors of the local trade—that is, growers and middlemen—probably reacted in a similar fashion. Around this time, it became increasingly common for farmers to arm themselves and guard their plantings during harvest time. If vanilla theft could not be eliminated, it would at least be made more hazardous. As will be seen, the net effect was to make land-use rights the object of unprecedented covetousness and conflict. Since vanilla cultivation was then—as it had always been—overwhelmingly in the hands of Totonac farming families, and since the basin's choice croplands were legally held by Indians in community, this competitive business drive would manifest itself most prominently in protracted struggles over the legal standing and de facto reorganization of communal land-tenure arrangements.

One early manifestation of this emerging state of affairs was the mortgaging and selling of vanilla fields, which begins to appear in legal records over the course of the 1870s. These practices were probably not altogether new, but now they became more frequent and at times also more formal in character. Farmers would pledge their vanilla plants as guarantee for their debts, in some cases agreeing to pay back with vanilla at a set price, or they would sell them outright to settle outstanding loans. The *pueblo* lands on which these vines had been planted were not part of the transactions, since the farmers in question did not themselves own them and could not offer them as security.[33] Migrants and young men starting out on their own were more likely to find themselves in these situations, as they borrowed money in order to finance their initial expenses. In this way, offering cash advances to growers sometimes gave merchants and moneyed middlemen the opportunity to gain some measure of control over future vanilla stocks.

At the same time, other land-based investments were becoming very attractive as well. After about 1870, the end of the civil wars, the amelioration of Papantla's historic isolation, and, in particular, the increased circulation of capital generated by the booming vanilla trade created the conditions for a generalized business awakening. Although vanilla would remain the backbone (and the driving force) of the basin's commercial economy, a certain diversification is also evident. For the most part, this involved developing or invigorating old branches of the local economy, such as cattle ranching, logging, and the production of cane alcohol, tobacco, and chile; in addition, a few new lines of business also appeared for the first time in these years—for example, coffee and, notably, petroleum. In all cases, land—communal or private—was a principal factor of production.

In these years, tobacco developed into an important commercial crop in the basin, probably second only to vanilla in terms of its aggregate value. In 1873 the basin's total production was estimated at 16,000 arrobas (about 184,000 kilograms), in 1889 at 10,609 arrobas (122,000 kilograms), and by 1893–94—when a more detailed survey was carried out—at around 30,000 arrobas. Much of this tobacco was cultivated by smallholders in Papantla, Coyutla, and Espinal. These figures are not particularly trustworthy (especially for 1873), but they do give a general sense of the scale of production. Compared to Los Tuxtlas or Córdoba (68,160 and 52,172 arrobas in 1889, respectively), the basin's tobacco crop was still modest, but it would in time become among the largest in the state.[34] Teziutlán was the main entrepôt for the region's tobacco, not only from Papantla but also from the neighboring Cantón of Jalacingo (especially Tlapacoyan and Martínez de la Torre), which also became a notable *Nicotiana tabacum* producing zone at this time.

The principal merchants of Teziutlán—among them Manuel Zorrilla, the Lapuente brothers, and Agapito Fontecilla senior, who had permanently resettled in this cooler *serrano* town by the early 1880s—orchestrated much of the lowland trade, sending down a wide array of imported and domestic manufactures on credit and receiving farm and forest products in return. Their basin counterparts, many of them also vanilla traders, fomented the expansion of local tobacco planting by lending money to native farmers— directly or through intermediaries—expressly for that purpose. Papantla growers generally sold the green leaves to the merchants, leaving the curing to others, much as they did with vanilla.[35] The traditional cultivation and preparation of *chilpotle* (dried chile), which also appears to have grown in these years, seems to have followed a similar credit pattern.[36] These kinds of financial relationships were not new, but their magnitude was. At the same time, some local merchants and potentates began to grow more to-bacco, chile, and other commercial crops in their own private estates, usu-ally along the fringes of the communal territories, using mainly laborers and colonists who had migrated from the sierras.

Notarial and property records provide good examples of these tiered business networks. In 1878 the Sociedad Pérez Hermanos of Espinal was forced to mortgage its assets to guarantee debts totaling $17,121.21 pesos. On top of that, they also owed $15,641.82 pesos not covered by the agree-ment. Ricardo and Avelino Pérez, general merchants, had a large house and store facing the main plaza of Espinal. They came from a well-known fam-ily of military officers, landowners, and businessmen, with interests both in the piedmont of Papantla and the adjoining Sierra de Puebla. General Hi-lario Pérez Olazo had been *jefe político* of Papantla at the time of the U.S. invasion, and their father, General Miguel Pérez Olazo, had since come to own the huge Jamaya estate nearby. Aside from the retail trade, Pérez Hermanos of Espinal produced cane alcohol, raised cattle, owned a couple of vanilla fields, and brokered local crops. A list of their creditors suggests the range of their transactions. They owed money to Manuel Zorrilla, Mariano Olazo, Juan B. Diez, Ignacio Lapuente y Hno., and Proal y Manuel, all of Teziutlán, as well as to Düring & Co., Germán Kroncke & Co., Sucs., and A. Gutheil & Co., which were then some of the leading merchant houses of Veracruz. The largest single debt covered by the bankruptcy agreement was with J. J. Puigdengolas & Co. of Tuxpan. The largest overall debt was with their father, who grew, bought, and processed tobacco, chile, and vanilla in Jamaya and at a ranch in Tenampulco, Puebla, all of which were presumably marketed by the sons. During these years, two other well-known army generals— Jesús Lalanne and Pedro Hinojosa—acquired and began to exploit some of the area's private estates in similar fashion.[37]

In another promissory document, this time from 1880, Luis Vega acknowledged an overdue debt of $728.96 pesos to Agapito Fontecilla of Teziutlán for "merchandise" sent to him on a four-to-six-month credit basis. Fontecilla's lawyer, Antonio Maldonado, stated that his client wanted to be paid in cash, tobacco, or *chilpotle*. Also in the same year, Mariano Olazo's successors agreed to settle an $18,388.42 peso debt to Manuel Zorrilla with proceeds and credits from the sale of vanilla, tobacco, and cattle, as well as with rents from Olazo's estate at Joloapan, located south of the Tecolutla River along the route between Papantla and Teziutlán.[38]

As these and other records indicate, investments in cattle and commercial alcohol distillation also expanded in these years. It is impossible to quantify the growth of cattle ranching, but a number of developments are suggestive. In early 1869, only 12 different cattle brands were used in all of Papantla, versus 614 in Tuxpan, 509 in Tampico, and 69 in Misantla. Tax evasion may have played a role, but, in general, sizable operations registered their brands to protect themselves against rustlers. By all accounts, Papantla's ranching economy was small and relegated to grassy pockets of private lands; an 1873 report lists 3,000 pigs, 2,000 horses, and only 2,000 head of cattle for the whole Cantón, perhaps a generous estimate. Local meat and milk consumption were very limited, and although there was a hides trade, many of the other animal byproducts had no reliable outlets. Over the next twenty years, stock raising became a larger and more visible enterprise; in particular, a new *ganadería de engorda*—specializing in fattening up feeder calves for sale on the hoof in distant markets—started to develop. Young beef cattle slowly began to fill Papantla's abundant natural pasture lands, mainly in privately owned ranges west and south of the town, where they were fed and turned into prime slaughter stock. The fattened animals were then herded and sold upland, where demand and prices were high. In a typical contract, Teziutlán merchant Manuel Zorrilla agreed in 1879 to send two hundred young bulls and heifers to San Miguel del Rincón for the *en-gorda*. The owner of the estate, Papantla's Ignacio Danini, agreed in turn to provide the necessary pasture lands and to pay all related expenses. Once the cattle were sold, profits (or losses) would be divided equally. As part of the deal, Zorrilla lent Danini $2,000 pesos, for which Danini offered San Miguel as collateral security. Significantly, selected feeder grasses also began to be planted in those years. In 1888, soon after a state law was passed requiring *engorda* businesses to pay a head tax, only two such establishments were registered in Papantla; by 1890, the number of tax-paying ranches had risen to thirty, with over six thousand head of cattle declared. Later, with the arrival of the railroad to the sierra and Tampico, Papantla and the Huasteca would become Mexico's preeminent *engorda* regions.[39]

In the meantime, the manufacture of commercial *aguardientes* was also increasing. Sugarcane was the base ingredient, but fruit flavors were sometimes added. Although the making of spirits had a long history in the basin (for example, *chichique*), in general the technology used had been very rudimentary, the quality of the drink was in consequence notoriously erratic, and the volume of production had remained small. It is telling that until at least the late 1840s the spiral still was not used in Papantla.[40] By 1878, there were six registered *aguardiente* factories in the basin, producing about 580 barrels of cane alcohol per year. Each had a *trapiche* (animal-powered sugarcane press) and also a still. Twelve years later, greater Papantla's commercial distilling capacity had doubled; in 1890, there were sixteen such factories producing about 1,250 barrels a year, as well as nearly 90,000 kilograms of *panocha* (crude brown sugar cones).[41] Although these industries were still fairly small and comparatively primitive (other Veracruz factories were already using water- and steam-powered machinery), the local spirits business was clearly growing, and, among other things, this meant that sugarcane cultivation had to increase as well.

Other industries also developing in these decades were timber and oil. Commercial logging, which was an old activity in the basin, began to intensify notably at this time, thanks to investments in better sawing equipment and to improved maritime transportation. Initially, the forested banks of the lower Cazones and Tecolutla Rivers were the main logging areas, since the timber could be floated downriver and exported through Tuxpan or Tecolutla; by the 1880s, however, inland territories, including old communal forest areas around the town of Papantla, were being harvested as well. Precious woods, particularly cedar and mahogany, were the timber of choice. In 1873, for instance, General Jesús Lalanne teamed up with Julio Leví & Co. of Veracruz to cut down and export 1,500 tons of cedar and 300 tons of tinctorial woods from Larios y Malpica; Lalanne—who had acquired a part of Larios in 1871, while he served as military commander of the Huasteca—put up the land and labor, and Leví the capital. By 1878, José de la Luz Silvera was operating a steam-powered sawmill in the vicinity of Gutiérrez Zamora. Silvera, who was a vanilla dealer from a distinguished merchant family (Francisco Naveda's in-laws), was instrumental in the creation of Gutiérrez Zamora as a separate municipality in 1877 and served as its first mayor.[42] Almost certainly it was vanilla money that financed his logging enterprise.

Oil mining, by contrast, was then a new and uncertain business. In the late 1860s, when U.S. physician Adolfo Autrey traveled to Tuxpan and Papantla to prospect for oil, he quickly discovered that the hard part was not finding it but figuring out how to make it pay. Indeed, there were many well-known oil pools and tar pits—some fairly large—in the area; people referred to the thick, dark substance variously as *chapapote, petróleo,* or *asfalto,* and had a number of local uses for it. As oil derivates started to become important industrial and household commodities in the United States, many—Autrey among them—hoped to turn Mexico's heavy crude oil into quick wealth. In particular, lamp oil (kerosene) seemed to have a potentially promising market in Mexico at that time. Already in 1870, Veracruz's governor reported numerous "discoveries" and mining claims, nine in Papantla alone. These surface deposits were, in his words, "springs of abundance" which would soon bring great prosperity to the state.[43]

In the short run, however, problems with technology and ground transportation, a weak local market, and cheaper U.S. kerosene would keep these pits from being worked. The governor's optimism was at least premature, if not also naive. As the U.S. Consul in Tuxpan wrote in September 1874,

While kerosene, & c., can be brought from the United States at such low rates, it will not pay to work these springs. Some of the asphaltum has been shipped to the United States, but the result was not very favorable. One company was formed to work some rich springs near Papantla, and machinery was brought out for the purpose; but the kerosene was very inferior and could not compete with that brought here. . . . There is no doubt but these springs will all be valuable some day.[44]

Only after 1900—and in a very different international oil business context—would northern Veracruz's oil fields begin to be exploited in earnest, and it was not until July 1905 that Papantla's first well—at El Cuguas, twenty-five or so miles due west of the town—was actually drilled.[45]

The Papantla company described by the Consul was in fact Autrey's.[46] Although he soon found out that he was not about to become Mexico's Rockefeller, Autrey nevertheless stayed in Papantla, where he practiced medicine and got involved in various businesses. By 1878, he ran one of the basin's largest *aguardiente* factories. Evidently, he also continued distilling small quantities of kerosene, which he must have sold in Papantla; the crude oil was transported on mule-back from the pits to his still. It is a

telling detail that his company's name was La Constancia (Perseverance). In
1882 this "petroleum factory" was listed in a state census of industrial establishments as having three employees; that same year, Autrey won a prize
at Querétaro's Industrial Exhibition for the quality of his lamp oil.[47] By
1881, Papantla's principal streets were already furnished with public lamps,
perhaps in part lit with Autrey's kerosene, and the town's well-to-do homes
also had their own oil lamps.[48] Whether they used some of Autrey's artisanal illuminant, or—as elsewhere—had to rely on Waters-Pierce's mass-
produced import, is not in the end very important. Thanks to Autrey, however, Papantla's merchant elite learned early on about the potential value of
the numerous oil deposits spread across the basin's northwest. Once again,
land was suddenly showing itself to be a likely spring of wealth. Particularly after 1884, when a new federal mining code for the first time granted
landowners exclusive subsoil rights, local entrepreneurs would develop an
active interest in these territories, in large measure for speculative purposes.

All in all, then, the commercial economy of the basin grew very substantially in the course of the 1870s and 1880s, not only in scale but also in
scope. Most remarkable was the boom in vanilla production and exports,
which in turn gave great impetus to many other land-based enterprises.
Along the way, a somewhat larger, more prosperous, self-assured, and
openly ambitious local business class emerged. With access to information,
direct links to foreign markets, as well as full-fledged networks of trade and
credit relations, they came to see their own possibilities in a new light. The
names were both old and new: Tremari, Fuente, Curti, Fontecilla, Zorrilla,
Silvera, Contreras, Bauza, Arenal, Garmilla, Patiño, Collado, etc.; all along,
a trickle of immigrants continued to nourish their ranks. As their business
expanded, some no longer fit the image of the petty backwoods merchant.
In this respect, the inventory of Josefa Silvera and Francisco Naveda's
household belongings is suggestive. It included cedar and marble furniture,
an old grand piano (inherited from her mother), lithographs, porcelain, a
number of oil lamps, two pistols and a Remington rifle, a very large set of
dishes, kitchenware, German silver-plated tableware, the first eleven volumes of the *Diccionario universal enciclopédico* (the rest had yet to be published), and a nine-volume *Catecismo de perseverancia* by the Abbé Gaumé.
The total value of their assets was calculated at $88,574 pesos, a re-
spectable sum at that time.[49]

Even more so than their predecessors, these merchants sought to play a
prominent role in the political life of Papantla, serving as *jefes políticos*,
mayors, and aldermen, and also volunteering for the town's new Charity
Commission. Together and on their own turf, they were increasingly a powerful group. It is revealing that when the state government imposed a tax on
the vanilla trade at the end of 1874 (one peso per millar, to be used for road

improvement), the vanilla merchants chose to fight it openly, arguing that prices and profits were in sharp decline; less than three years later, the legislature bowed to their wishes and repealed the tax.[50] An incipient urbanization reflected this fresh assertiveness; as their aspirations changed, so did the appearance of the town. In these years, its core streets and plaza were at last paved with brick and stone, the old church finally got a belfry, and a few public lights were installed.[51] Papantla was now their Villa.

Although the development of new markets, communications, maritime transportation, and financial relationships clearly enabled the extraordinary growth of the vanilla business in these years, these changes alone do not tell the whole story of Papantla's social and economic transformation. After all, the vanilla boom was obviously not only a commercial phenomenon, but also an agricultural one. For the business to grow and prosper, vanilla cultivation had to increase, but since farming and trading had long been largely separate endeavors, such an expansion process was bound to be complicated and conflict-ridden. As merchants and middlemen avidly sought to augment their vanilla stocks, some basic questions arose: Who would grow the new vanilla? On which lands? Who would own it? Who would get to buy it? How would thievery be curtailed? In effect, this meant sorting out property relations. For Totonac farmers and petty dealers, as well as for town merchants, the issues were ultimately ones of right, might, and profit. Essentially, vanilla now made land worth controlling. The ensuing competition would gradually eliminate communal land rights, ushering in an era marked by both unprecedented agricultural growth and overt social strife.

The Demise of Communal Property

Although competition over potentially lucrative crops and fields was the driving force behind land-tenure reform in the basin, other factors contributed as well. The disentailment of communal landholdings was an old dream of liberal intellectuals and politicians, a lineage with strong roots in the state of Veracruz. Already in 1826 the state congress had mandated the elimination of collective land tenure, decreeing that "all Indian communal lands, wooded or not, will be converted into individual property, distributing them equitably among all the people . . . who make up the community." Outside of the legislative chamber, few seem to have taken notice. Again, in 1856, more than two months before the federal Lerdo Law was issued (June 25), Governor Ignacio de la Llave sought to apply the law of 1826 (modified), setting up detailed disentailment procedures and calendars. Indian communities, he argued, were not only illegal, but also prejudicial to the well-being of the nation. Once more the results were mostly negligible, as the wars that soon followed precluded any enforcement. Thus, although in a strict sense the communities were no longer legal entities, in fact they continued to be recognized—and in some places also to function—as such. In the *pueblo* of Papantla, the "Indian community" in an organized and unified political sense had long expired, but native Indians retained control of—and rights over—much of their ancestral territory. Legal extensions, new calendars, and additional exhortations were issued in 1861 and 1867, but their practical effect was equally insignificant. Over four decades of legislative pronouncements notwithstanding, the liberal dream remained just that.[52]

With the defeat of the Imperialists in 1867, a relative peace returned and the triumphant Liberals in the Veracruz state government made a fresh attempt to enforce the laws on communal landholding. Unlike previous decrees, the new one (No. 152, 17 March 1869) did not simply set new deadlines for the division of collective landholdings into individual plots, but also modified the disentailment procedures in significant ways. To begin with, the municipal governments were now to be exclusively in charge of organizing and carrying out the land distributions, since the Indian communities as such no longer had legal status (Article 2).[53] Disputes, however, were still to be settled by the courts. In addition, all local heads of family were now eligible to receive land, whether or not they were *indígenas* (Article 4); whereas the law of 1826 had specified that the intended beneficiaries were Indians (however that was defined), its 1869 counterpart did not. In effect, this significant omission—deliberate or otherwise—allowed non-Indians to participate in the division. Finally, this new law imposed severe penalties for noncompliance; after the deadline, undivided territories would be declared "public lands" and thus be open to colonization claims (Article 3).

Once again, enforcement was another matter altogether. More than a year after the publication of the decree, only a handful of the affected municipalities had carried out the mandated subdivision, despite the fact that the original grace period (six months) had expired. Governor Hernández's annual address expressed frustration and even some despondency; the threat of penalties, he said, had accomplished nothing. Still, as will be seen, his administration had every reason not to give up; sooner or later, the Governor vowed, the law would prevail and private property rights would rule over the entire land, even if this required using force and spilling some blood. Meanwhile, perhaps sensing that the times were changing, many of the remaining landholding communities were at last beginning to pay attention to the new legislation; in the Cantón of Papantla, for instance, all of the *pueblos* drafted a joint letter to the state congress asking to be allowed to retain communal ownership.[54]

Ideology aside, the Veracruz state governments of the Restored Republic had powerful fiscal motives to press for land-tenure reform. They inherited severe budget deficits, a deficient tax system, as well as inefficient and cumbersome collection mechanisms. Without adequate income, it was hard to maintain a bureaucracy, let alone to rule effectively; as was said then, "Treasury receipts are the blood of the body politic."[55] The governors' *Memorias* for these years attest to the sorry state of Veracruz's treasury; suffice it to say that in 1872 the state's financial situation was so unpromising that the telegraph company refused to send Governor Hernández's official telegrams unless they were paid for in cash. Thus, fiscal reorganization soon became a top priority, since it would lay the foundations for strong and stable government. This involved replacing indirect taxes—mainly the sales taxes (*alcabalas*), which in the late 1860s were still the single largest source of revenue—with direct ones—such as property taxes, head taxes, agricultural production taxes, and business licensing fees.[56] The idea was to eliminate the old consumption and traffic levies, which had an admittedly deleterious effect on economic activity; as a consequence, production and trade would increase, as would property values, incomes, and business in general, thereby creating a much larger direct tax base. The transition was complex and tortuous, and it took some twenty years to complete.[57] However, one immediate consequence of this developing fiscal strategy was to focus attention on augmenting property tax revenues, particularly in the countryside. Communal lands became a prime target.

Although Veracruz was an overwhelmingly rural state with a predominantly agricultural economy, rural property tax receipts had always lagged far behind urban ones. As the authorities recognized, this made no sense, and efforts were made to address the shortfall. The lack of a land registry (*catastro*), inadequate methods for assessing value, and limited collection capabilities were mostly to blame, but these problems had no quick or easy solutions. The assessments were finally modified in the late 1880s, collection mechanisms improved only very gradually, and a *catastro* was never formed. At the same time, one obvious way to tackle this situation was to expand the tax rolls by incorporating former communal lands. Once registered—which involved paying a title transfer fee—the many small private farms into which communal territories were to be turned would be subject to the annual property tax. Thus, the breakup of the communities would produce urgently needed revenues. For the governments of these years, doing away with communal land tenure was not only an ideological obsession, but also, more concretely, a way to create a new class of propertied taxpayers.[58]

It was in this context of fiscal pressure and incipient state assertiveness that the Cantón of Papantla faced the question of land-tenure reform. There, as elsewhere, some regarded the new legislation with suspicion and fear, while others saw it as a golden opportunity. In the end, as will be seen, local conditions—in particular, the balance of social forces and economic inter-

ests—decisively shaped the implementation and outcome of the state mandate. That is why disentailment was a relatively uncontested process in some
pueblos, whereas in others it became an exceedingly troublesome, protracted, and even violent affair. Perhaps nowhere in Veracruz was the division of communal lands more openly conflictive than in the *pueblo* of Papantla. There, a rapacious entrepreneurial class (which included Indians) and
strong but deeply divided groups of Totonac farmers fought with each other
and among themselves, not so much over whether the land should be privatized, but rather over how it would be divided and who would get to own it.

Local demographic patterns would play an important role as well. According to the available population figures, between 1870 and 1880 greater
Papantla's population appears to have grown by 50 percent, from 20,000
to about 30,000. By 1895, when the first federal census was conducted, the
basin's population was calculated at over 44,000, more than twice what it
had been at the conclusion of the war against the empire of Maximilian.
Actual growth rates were probably somewhat lower, since the data series is
not entirely reliable, but there is little doubt that the basin's population increased significantly during these years. Although natural reproduction was
surely an important contributing factor, migration—particularly from the
neighboring Sierra de Puebla—accounted for a good part of this growth. In
the 1895 census, nearly 10 percent of the basin's inhabitants were listed as
having been born in the state of Puebla, but the actual percentage was in all
likelihood higher. These were family farmers, laborers, and ranch hands
from the piedmont and highlands who had been resettling in the private estates of Papantla, Coyutla, and Espinal, either working for the latest absentee landlords, renting land from them to plant for themselves, or both.[59]
Yet others came to farm not in those privately held areas, but in the extensive communal *montes* of Papantla, Tecolutla, and Gutiérrez Zamora,
where they became known as *fincados* (settlers). In addition, there were the
Italian colonists, whose numbers continued to increase during these
decades. Table 4.1 displays the available data.[60]

Within the communal territories, this rapid demographic growth altered
the more or less generous family-to-cropland ratio that had long characterized the basin's milpa agriculture. Finding an adequate expanse of *monte* to
farm was no longer as easy. Given its high acreage requirement, the *roza*
system is particularly susceptible to population increases, which can quickly
disrupt the optimal rhythms of fallowing and field rotation. In the absence
of more detailed figures, it is hard to know just how severe a problem this
became. Nevertheless, it is fair to assume that rapid population growth
could only strain social relations, making satisfactory land use arrangements ever harder to sustain. The incentive to increase vanilla cultivation
complicated matters even further. In effect, more and more people wanted

TABLE 4.1

Population of Papantla, 1871–1900

Municipality	1871	1873	1878	1882	1885	1895	1900
Papantla	14,058	14,267	18,439		14,598		23,643
Espinal	1,131	1,295	1,451		2,250		4,124
Coatzintla	615	373	523		855		1,167
Zozocolco	584	673	1,031		2,135		3,049
Coxquihui	320	317	401		1,148		3,259
Chumatlán	174	146	269		381		—[a]
Mecatlán	518	594	432		774		1,293
Santo Domingo	620	763	962		761		1,521
Coahuitlán	412	344	332		879		1,691
Coyutla	858	1,122	1,580		2,039		4,042
Chicualoque	300	279	319		567		—[b]
Tecolutla	1,012	986	—[c]		955[d]		1,462
Gutiérrez Zamora	—	—	2,095		1,670		4,598
Total	20,602	21,159	27,834	31,846	29,012	44,282	50,756

SOURCE: See note 60 to Chapter 4.

[a] In June 1890 Chumatlán lost municipal status, becoming a *congregación* in the municipality of Coxquihui.

[b] In January 1894 Chicualoque lost municipal status, becoming a *congregación* in the municipality of Coyutla.

[c] In July 1877 the old jurisdiction of Tecolutla and two of Papantla's *congregaciones*—Cazonera and Boca de Lima—became the municipality of Gutiérrez Zamora.

[d] In December 1879 Tecolutla became a municipality once again. Aside from the pueblo of Tecolutla, it comprised the *congregaciones* of Boca de Lima and El Cristo, as well as a number of private estates.

to use communal farm and forest lands precisely at a time when the commercial possibilities of some native crops and natural resources were also expanding very quickly. Communal land-use rights, moreover, were not equally distributed—not even nominally, as they may have once been. Migrants, in particular, had no such right, having instead to negotiate their access, and among local farmers there were some who managed to exercise their prerogatives more vigorously or aggressively than others. In this increasingly competitive context, those who already possessed or controlled good farmland were likely to welcome the opportunity to formalize these rights, making them legally exclusive. Thus, demographic factors would also contribute to the demise of communal land tenure.

Perhaps the best way to understand how these various pressures—com-

mercial, demographic, fiscal, and legal—combined to transform property
relations in the Tecolutla basin is to examine closely the case of one municipality. Because of its size and economic preeminence, Papantla is the obvious choice. The bulk of the canton's Indian population resided in Papantla,
as did most merchants, including almost all of the prominent and powerful
vanilla traders. Moreover, it was only in the *pueblo* of Papantla that conflicts over business and land led to a series of uprisings and rebellions,
which are often mentioned as examples of agrarian discontent in the Porfiriato but have yet to be adequately explained. What follows is essentially
an account—along the lines of the argument thus far presented—of how
and why in the course of the 1870s Papantla's old landholding community
ceased to be. Whenever possible, reference will also be made to parallel developments in the neighboring *pueblos*.

According to Decree No. 152 (1869), town governments had up to six
months to divide the communal territories in their jurisdictions into as
many individual fractions as there were qualified heads of family. Municipal authorities were asked to decide who was qualified, to survey the available lands marking the boundaries of every fraction, and to distribute these
plots among the new owners, issuing each of them a property title. If there
were any ownership or boundary disputes with private estates, among Indian communities, or between the community and the town itself, the
courts were to adjudicate them swiftly. The law's tight timetable made this
sound exceedingly simple, but in a place like the Tecolutla basin such a
process was in fact virtually impracticable, at least in a short period of time.
Aside from an old dispute between the *pueblo* of Espinal and the estate of
Jamaya, these communities had no outstanding land litigation; even so, the
obstacles to the kind of division envisioned by the law were enormous.

Because of the highly irregular topography of the basin's communal territories, conducting a detailed survey was bound to be a very slow and
costly undertaking, one that few local governments could afford. In those
years, municipal finances were often as precarious—if not more so—than
those of the state government. Parceling out these lands was difficult for
other reasons, too. The *tierras de común repartimiento*—as communal
farmland was often labeled—were actually many types of land, ecologically
as well as in terms of their economic and social uses. Thus, dividing them
was not like allocating units of some sort of uniform commodity: certain
areas were not well suited for agriculture, and some croplands were definitely better than others, especially when it came to growing vanilla, tobacco, or chile. In addition, *roza* cultivation made for elaborate land-use

patterns (fallowing, field rotation, etc.), and collecting forest products was an entrenched aspect of the Totonac family economy, around which local rules of access to woodlands had developed. Here, the individual *milpas* were carved out of the forests and dispersed settlement was the norm; thus, unlike in many nucleated *pueblos* of the highlands, there was no single, separate *ejido* or *monte* area designated for communal forest gathering or grazing. In the basin, the *tierras de común repartimiento* and the forests were usually one and the same, making land-use practices—and the customary rights associated with them—especially complex. All of these thorny issues would have to be sorted out before a land subdivision could proceed, and it is unclear that anyone—let alone a partisan municipal government—was then capable of accomplishing this.

Beyond that, the distribution of communal land—who used or claimed rights to which lands—could not be ignored, and by all accounts tenure patterns were not uniformly equitable. Because all lands were not the same, it followed that some people possessed better plots than others, and often, as it turns out, much larger ones as well. When the first crude survey of the lands of Papantla was conducted in 1875–76, the official deeds fixing the boundaries of each *congregación* noted the existence not only of regular farming fields—milpas, *milcahuales*, and *sementeras*—but also of a good number of *ranchos*, a term used in that context to denote certain land areas—apparently more substantial ones—held by particular individuals and their families. In describing the borders of Polutla, Taracuán, and Poza Verde, for instance, the disentailment commission mentioned the ranchos of Juan Pérez, Julián Olmedo, Guadalupe Almora, and Víctor Santo, as well as the milpa of Lucio Hernández.[61] Throughout the survey, such ranchos—evidently well known and easily identified—frequently served as reference points. This suggests that there was a class of communal farmers who, in effect, already had exclusive control over good-sized plots of land, even though they did not—and could not—have private title to them. For all practical purposes, it seems, the ranchos were theirs, and any attempt at disentailment would have to take that into account.

Unlike what students of Papantla's late-nineteenth-century history have often supposed, the allocation of communal land was not the product of exercises in collective decision-making, and the actual distribution of land was not especially egalitarian.[62] Collective ownership, it is clear, did not preclude internal socioeconomic differentiation. These communal *rancheros* (in the special sense just described) were Papantla's most prosperous farmers, the ones who had effectively parlayed the basin's small-scale economic opportunities into a life of independence, security, and relative wealth. They had good and abundant land for their rotating milpas and to keep their animals, as well as easy access to water and forest products. In addition, the expanding trade in vanilla and other agricultural commodities provided them with considerable cash earnings, which they could spend, invest, or save. As the vanilla economy grew in importance, some became middlemen and petty lenders. José de la Cruz Avila was perhaps a typical communal *ranchero* of the 1870s: his rancho contained sugarcane, coffee, and vanilla fields, a sugar-mill and a still, and two houses; on a nearby spot he had planted more vanilla and a good amount of maize.[63] Not surprisingly, many of these Totonac *rancheros* were influential figures in their *rancherías*, often serving as local municipal agents. As prominent members of their small communities, and also due to their business dealings, they had more frequent contact with townspeople. Hence, many spoke—or at least understood—some Spanish, a skill that afforded them an additional degree of local power.

Some historians have observed that a strong agrarian middle class was forming or growing in parts of Mexico around this time, and perhaps these Totonac *rancheros* fit that description.[64] From an economic perspective, as well as in terms of social hierarchy, they had gradually established themselves as the dominant group among Papantla's rural cultivators, though they rarely acted as one since they lived dispersed out in the *rancherías* and were concerned mainly with their own local affairs. Those who were less fortunate, less audacious, or simply young and without influential relatives composed a lower echelon of Totonac communal farmers. They also had milpas and vanilla fields of their own, but lacked the standing, the resources, and some of the security enjoyed by *rancheros*. Perhaps these evolving socioeconomic differences did not matter much as long as there was sufficient land for everyone, and as long as the commercial possibilities of agriculture remained limited. By the early 1870s, however, those circumstances were starting to change. The so-called *rancheros* would then seek to protect and even expand their holdings, and the idea of a government-orchestrated land division in which all heads of family would receive "equal parts, in quantity or quality" (Article 4) probably filled many with apprehension. A *reparto* that could be managed by them, however, was another matter altogether, and soon some would begin to see that as a splendid opportunity to do business.

A further complication was that native Totonac farmers were not the only people with a direct interest in the lands of the *pueblo* of Papantla. A number of non-Indian town dwellers used communal lands, mainly for pasture, but perhaps also for some agriculture. Presumably, they would have paid rent, but it is hard to know for sure. The outskirts of the Villa were a favored area, but some held land out in the *congregaciones* as well. In addition, as noted, there were settlers from the sierra and from Italy. A good number of the Italian colonists farmed the communal lands of El Cristo; one Antonio Jamolo, for instance, had planted not only the usual crops but also an orange grove. Many of these *fincados* grew vanilla with money provided by merchants from the towns of Cabezas and Papantla, who regarded that vanilla (the plants and the fruits) as their own, even though the land itself was not.[65] As the selling and mortgaging of vanilla plantings suggest, all of these investments in the land granted "outsiders" certain acknowledged rights, and a land division would have to take them into consideration. All in all, then, several groups of people with diverse and potentially conflicting interests—the Totonac *rancheros* and *milperos*, the various *fincados*, the town residents—claimed certain differential rights, legal and customary, in regard to the disposition of Papantla's communal property. Clearly, reconciling such disparate claims would not be an easy matter.

In light of all of these prospective difficulties, it is not surprising that Decree No. 152 was not well received in Papantla, and that leading Totonacs would initially look for a way to avoid a land division altogether. After the new law became known in Papantla, a group of Indians gathered in the town's main plaza and burned a copy of it in protest.[66] Afterward—sometime between mid-1869 and mid-1870—a petition was sent to the state congress requesting permission to retain communal landholding, not just in the municipality of Papantla but in the rest of the canton as well. Unfortunately, the text of this letter has not been found, so it remains unclear who drafted and signed it. Without it, one can only speculate about the precise nature of the arguments marshaled in support of the request. In all likelihood, it was the work of Totonac notables, but it is telling that neither the municipal authorities nor the *jefe político* seem to have actively objected. Clearly, each had their own reasons—practical, principled, or self-interested—to avoid pushing through or participating in an individual land division.

In Papantla, the town government lacked the political strength and the resources needed to grapple with the many tangled issues that would inevitably arise. On the side of the Totonacs, the so-called *rancheros* who dominated the political life of the dispersed *congregaciones* could not have agreed with the virtually absolute authority over land distribution which the law bestowed on the Ayuntamiento (municipal council), especially since it was a body heavily influenced by Papantla's merchant establishment. Moreover, these rural community leaders had their own interests to consider, as did the *indios ladinos* (Hispanized Indians) of the town—petty merchants, military officers, and artisans, including vanilla workers—who also had a strong voice in Totonac affairs. Had a decision been made to proceed with an individual land distribution as prescribed by Decree No. 152, the likelihood of serious conflict was high. In these circumstances, the only wise choice was to respect the status quo, and that is what the Ayuntamiento would initially do.

During the next few years, no effort seems to have been made to enforce the disentailment decree in the basin. In October 1871 Papantla's petition was still being reviewed by the state government.[67] Phasing out communal land tenure was a genuinely complex and often contentious undertaking, and despite the threat of expropriation written into the law, progress was very slow or negligible in many other parts of the state as well. Faced with widespread noncompliance, the authorities in Xalapa had no choice but to prolong the grace period. One-year extensions were granted in December of 1873, 1874, and 1875.[68] Along the way, the government was also forced to reconsider its strategy. As the case of Papantla clearly showed, there were places in which it was simply unrealistic to expect that a more or less peaceful individual division could be implemented in the foreseeable future. The problems connected with parceling out the lands were often truly intractable, and the government's capacity to mediate effectively or to impose settlements was decidedly limited. Evidently, some sort of legal accommodation had to be made on this issue, or else Veracruz's latest push to eliminate communal landholding might also end in failure. Governor Landero y Cos's reluctant solution was to permit the provisional establishment of *condueñazgos*.

In July 1874 the state legislature decreed that "in places where there are serious problems associated with the division of communal lands into as many fractions as there are individuals entitled to them, the Executive . . . may authorize their division into lots assigned to a certain number of owners."[69] This was the legislature's response to Papantla's petition. The law of 1869 was still in effect, but the government acknowledged that it could not always be applied. In such cases, a partial privatization would be better than none. The *condueñazgos* were private landholding associations or companies in which each member, or *condueño* (co-proprietor), owned a share of the lands in question. These shares, or stocks (*acciones*), only represented percentages of ownership, and did not entail exclusive rights to specific plots of land. Thus, the internal allocation of land would be left up to the *condueños*. This was not a new type of institution; there had been *condueñazgos* in the Huastecas since at least the beginning of the century. In Papantla, a number of private estates—for example, Cacahuatal—had long been held in *condueñazgo*, so the concept was not entirely unfamiliar.[70] Now the state government hoped that some of the communities that were not complying with the individual land distributions contemplated in Decree No. 152 could at least be divided up into *condueñazgos*.

Although these landowning associations fell short of the ideal regime of individual private property espoused by the ruling liberals of Veracruz, in their eyes, *condueñazgos* were nevertheless an improvement vis-à-vis communal ownership. Significantly, the new *condueño* shares could be legally bought and sold. In addition, the *condueñazgos* would be subject to property taxes, since for legal and fiscal purposes they were considered to be private estates. For state officials, these were definitely steps in the right direction. Still, Decree No. 68 represented a kind of capitulation, albeit one that state officials regarded as merely temporary. Individual private property remained the ultimate goal, and the establishment of *condueñazgos* was seen as a conjunctural concession to the agrarian realities of some *pueblos*.[71]

In the end, though, only a small minority of Veracruz's landholding *pueblos* took advantage of this option. Many eventually managed to carry out individual divisions directly, and others had land-related problems that the formation of *conduenazgos* could not resolve. In the cantons of Acayucan, Minatitlán, and Tantoyuca, a number of *pueblos* did divide their lands into *grandes lotes* (as *condueñazgos* were often called), but it took them until the mid-1880s to do so.[72] In the *pueblo* of Papantla, however, Decree No. 68 paved the way for a comparatively rapid division. In July 1875—barely a year after the publication of the enabling decree—the Ayuntamiento proceeded to form a disentailment commission, which included three prominent Totonac representatives. This joint commission agreed that Papantla's communal lands would be divided into twenty-three *conduenazgos*, three *fundos legales*—those of Papantla, Cabezas, and San Pablo—and one *ejido*. The boundaries of these *grandes lotes* were surveyed between December 1875 and February 1876, preliminary *conduen̄o* lists were completed by April 1877, and the *conduen̄os* were given formal possession of their lands in November 1878. In just three years, Papantla's communal territories had been peacefully disentailed. By October 1880, the state government had officially approved this subdivision.[73]

Other Tecolutla basin *pueblos* would also turn their communal territories into *condueñazgos*: Coatzintla beginning in 1875, Coahuitlán between 1879 and 1882, Coxquihui around 1880, and Chicualoque by 1887.[74] It is worth noting that there were more ex-communal *condueñazgos* formed in the Cantón of Papantla than in any other Veracruz district; nowhere else was the *grandes lotes* provision in Decree No. 68 nearly as effective, and no large *pueblo* adopted this landholding arrangement as swiftly as did Papantla. This is a curious pattern, suggesting perhaps that the *condueñazgo* legislation was enacted with Papantla's petition specifically in mind. In any case, it is clear that the decision to form *condueñazgos* was everywhere ultimately a local one; the state government allowed their creation but could not compel it. The establishment of *condueñazgos* was evidently far from inevitable, and cannot be understood as an external imposition. If a land division based on *grandes lotes* prospered in Papantla, it was because none of the local groups powerful enough to oppose and disrupt it did so. In fact, most of Papantla's Totonac leaders—including many of the so-called *rancheros* in the various *congregaciones*—as well as the town merchants, the Ayuntamiento, and the *jefe político*, all appear to have embraced this new type of land distribution.

It is possible to imagine why this would have been so. For the various reasons cited above, many Totonacs with considerable local influence were opposed to the demarcation and distribution of individual parcels of land. However, once the allocation of individual plots was no longer an immediate requirement, disentailment acquired a very different meaning for them. Dividing the land into *grandes lotes*, it seemed, offered certain definite advantages. In principle, the establishment of private *condueñazgos* allowed the current patterns of land use in the *congregaciones* to remain unaltered. This meant not only that *roza* cultivation could continue without important modifications, but also—even more significantly—that an equitable distribution of land would not have to be undertaken.[75] Forming *condueñazgos* did not involve meddling with the ranchos, and this the *rancheros* surely appreciated. As a contemporary state government report on Papantla's proposed *condueñazgos* acutely observed, there were those "for whom a division of the communal lands into individual lots was not convenient, because they already possessed a good part of them."[76] In addition, the formation of *grandes lotes* promised *congregaciones* a great deal of local autonomy in the management of their lands, which were henceforth to be considered private estates. This meant that the Ayuntamiento would no longer have any jurisdiction over the internal administration of the former communal territories, a prerogative which it had obtained when communities formally lost their standing as legal corporations.[77] Each group of *condueños* would elect their own land administrators—a manager (*apoderado*) and a treasurer, or sometimes a larger board of directors—to regulate and supervise the affairs of the estate. In this way, community notables could retain and even hope to increase their local influence.

To understand what these concessions would have meant to them, it is important to recall the economic situation of Papantla in the early 1870s. As shown, these were times of incipient commercial ferment. Prompted by new markets and improved facilities for trade, a generalized drive to expand vanilla cultivation was already underway. Other land-based business ventures were also on the increase. In these circumstances, the ability to control access to land was fast becoming a great asset, and this the *condueñazgo* seemed to provide. Under this new property regime, the *condueños* were empowered to decide what to do with unoccupied lands (e.g., who could use them, or whether to rent them, and to whom), and how to regulate access to timber and other forest goods (setting fees, issuing permits and concessions, etc.) within the boundaries of their *grandes lotes*. For those who could expect to play a leading role in the management and exploitation of these spaces, this was no petty prerogative. With the approval of *condueñazgo* authorities, moreover, shares of ownership could even be bought and sold. Given the opportunity to exercise this kind of exclusive land control, it is no wonder that most community representatives quickly agreed to the formation of *grandes lotes*. The appeal of *condueñazgo* was thus paradoxical: it would preserve certain key aspects of communal land-holding, and doing so would also enable some to advance their own particular business interests. Evidently, not everyone had reason to regard the adoption of these new land-tenure rules with such optimism, but it is not clear that Totonac farmers on the whole understood (or were made to understand) what this transformation would entail. In any case, these were the points of view that ultimately prevailed.

With the backing of many Totonac notables, Papantla's land division could at last commence. For a number of them, this meant not just acquiescence, but active participation and support. In fact, three Indian bosses—Simón Tiburcio, Pablo Hernández Olmedo, and Antonio Jiménez—were commissioned by the Ayuntamiento to carry out the division. Along with a succession of municipal trustees (who were perhaps also Totonac), they personally directed every aspect of the process, from the initial land surveys to the formation of *condueño* lists, the hearing of all claims, and the formal transfer of property rights. The trustees came and went, but from beginning to end, Tiburcio, Hernández, and Jiménez were intimately involved with the myriad details of the division. Simón Tiburcio's Papantla home functioned as the Commission's headquarters. In effect, the members of this Junta de Indígenas—as it was called—were to be the architects of Papantla's *grandes lotes*. The provisions of Decree No. 152 notwithstanding, the Ayuntamiento would act less as a direct executor than as an overseer, allowing the Indian Commission to orchestrate the land division and ratifying most of its decisions.[78]

Who were these powerful men, the Totonacs who shaped Papantla's *condueñazgos*? Significantly, all of them were military officers who had recently led local troops in battle; as a result, they were known, respected, and trusted well beyond their home *rancherías*, something that few other Totonac leaders could boast of at the time. Of the three, by far the most prominent was Simón Tiburcio. Born in Poza Larga sometime between 1840 and 1844, Tiburcio had an early and distinguished career as a Liberal military officer. After a stint as a corporal in the local National Guard, Tiburcio joined the Liberal war effort against the Conservatives in 1858–60, fighting in Cruz Blanca, Tuxpan, and Veracruz. Between 1864 and 1867, he battled the forces and partisans of Maximilian's Empire, first helping to organize the resistance to the Austrians around Papantla and later joining General Ignacio Alatorre in the successful sieges and occupations of Teziutlán, Xalapa, Puebla, and Mexico City. By the conclusion of these wars, Tiburcio had become a renowned figure in Papantla and was undisputedly the most powerful Totonac leader of all. In 1869 he was briefly appointed as the canton's *jefe político*, and then sat as Papantla's district judge in 1871 and 1874. In

1876, when Porfirio Díaz rose in Tuxtepec to unseat President Lerdo, Papantla's land division was just getting underway. Tiburcio promptly joined Díaz's side, serving in the Huasteca under the orders of Generals Hinojosa and Pérez Olazo, who happened also to be two of the basin's newest entrepreneurial *hacendados*. When he returned, he was more visible and well connected than ever. It was at this time that he claimed to have been awarded the rank of Colonel, even though an army review fifteen years later could not confirm this appointment and instead ranked him as a Major in the Infantry reserves. In Papantla, however, he would be known as a Colonel for the rest of his life, a grand title that reflected well not just his pervasive local influence but also his high personal ambitions.

Unlike the vast majority of Papantla's Totonacs, Simón Tiburcio knew how to read and write and expressed himself very well in Spanish. Around 1904, he penned a short memoir of his early military years that revealed much about his self-perception. Significantly, although he stated at the outset that he had been "born of the *raza indígena pura*," the text makes it clear that he did not think of himself as an Indian. Immediately after describing his racial origins, Tiburcio added that he was "educated by a noble family," presumably non-Indian, "under the auspices of freedom and progress." He frequently referred to other Totonacs as "them," and at one point explained how he tried to recruit soldiers among the *indios totonacos* "by using *their* language or dialect" (emphasis added) to persuade them that the foreign interlopers had to be expelled. Although he prized himself on his position of leadership among Totonacs and on his ability to speak their language, he nevertheless did not regard himself as just another one of them. Evidently, the Indians who followed him did not feel the same way, but neither did many of the non-Indian townspeople, who—despite his military stature—still considered him first and foremost a Totonac Indian.[79]

The background of Pablo Hernandez Olmedo and Antonio Jiménez was roughly similar to Tiburcio's, but the range of their military experience was much narrower, as it was for the most part confined to service in Papantla's National Guard. Hernández was probably born in the mid-1840s, Jiménez in the late 1830s; Hernández fought against the Austrians in 1866 and for Porfirio Díaz—under Tiburcio's command—in 1876. Unlike Tiburcio, their reading and writing skills were somewhat limited, and their Spanish was rudimentary. They were in many ways more akin to the other *rancheros* whose outlook they represented, except that their military standing effectively gave them a broader authority.[80] In the end, however, the difference between Simon Tiburcio's socioeconomic aspirations and cultural hybridization, on the one hand, and those of Hernández, Jiménez, and many other Totonac *rancheros*, traders, artisans, and soldiers, on the other, was mainly one of degree. They all were developing new interests and allegiances that transcended the strict confines of traditional Totonac society. Their consent and collaboration made *condueñazgos* possible.

The lands that Tiburcio, Hernández Olmedo, Jiménez, and the municipal trustee set out to divide first had to be clearly demarcated. According to the law of 1826, the disentailment would include all lands obtained through royal grants, as well as any other areas subsequently purchased and held communally (Article 1). At the outset, the Junta decided that the boundaries of Papantla's communal territories were already more or less clear, and therefore did not bother to look for the *pueblo*'s original land titles to confirm and legitimize their assumptions. As it turns out, these titles no longer existed, neither in Papantla nor at the National Archive, but this initial oversight—whether innocent or malicious—would in time become a source of great controversy. Instead, the commissioners simply ratified the current boundary lines. To the north, the historic lands of Papantla's community extended up to the Cazones River; to the south, they bordered the Tecolutla River and the arroyo of Tlahuanapa. Due east, they reached the ocean between the mouth of the Cazones River and the sandbar of Boca de Lima, beyond which they skirted the Lagartos estuary down to the Tecolutla River. To the northwest they adjoined the lands of Coatzintla (a range of hills served as the dividing line), and to the southwest the arroyo of Tlahuanapa separated them from the private estate of San Miguel and San Lorenzo.[81] The easternmost part of these lands belonged by this time to the municipality of Tecolutla, but by law Papantla retained jurisdiction over their disentailment. In all, these communal territories comprised more than half of the total area covered by the modern municipality of Papantla.

Although none of these boundaries were in dispute at the time, questions would soon be raised about the provenance of the estate of San Miguel and San Lorenzo, immediately to the southwest of the communal area. The legal origin of this property was certainly murky. According to Bausa, General Guadalupe Victoria had acquired title to these and many other adjoining territories (all largely unexploited and wholly unsurveyed) in the aftermath of Independence, and in the mid-1840s they remained in the hands of his estate, which was trying to sell them. When José María Mata obtained Texquitipan in late 1856, probably by means of the Lerdo Law, he simultaneously became the owner of San Miguel and San Lorenzo, as well as of other neighboring properties (e.g., Agua Dulce), all of which had once been claimed by Victoria. After his colonization scheme failed, Mata sold Texquitipan to a local businessman (1861) and San Miguel and San Lorenzo to a group of Italian entrepreneurs who had been involved in the organization of the immigrant colony (1866). Perhaps Victoria had never been the rightful owner of the specific territories in question, which had instead belonged all along to the *pueblo* of Papantla. In that case, all subsequent transactions would have been null and void. This is what some of Papantla's farmers would come to believe. Suspicions were raised by the fact that as soon as the disentailment commission determined that San Miguel and San Lorenzo lay beyond the communal boundaries, Simón Tiburcio rushed to collect money from farmers all over Papantla and then bought the estate as a private *condueñazgo* which he alone would control and profit from. This would in time suggest to many that Tiburcio had knowingly appropriated lands that should have been considered communal. Regardless of who was ultimately in the right, this was a grievance that would fester for years.[82]

Before dividing the demarcated lands into *grandes lotes*, the Commission set aside two zones that would remain under the jurisdiction of the Ayuntamiento. One was Papantla's *fundo legal*, the lands for the town proper. Following the formula of the old Spanish grants, 600 varas measured from the central plaza in the direction of each cardinal point were reserved for the Villa of Papantla. Another 850 hectares surrounding this *fundo legal* were designated as the *ejido* of Papantla and excluded from the land area to be divided into *condueñazgos*. This was a curious decision, because although both state and federal law exempted *ejidos* from disentailment, the aim of those legal provisions was clearly to preserve existing *ejidos* and not to create new ones.[83] Because of its traditional patterns of settlement and land use, Papantla does not seem to have had an *ejido* prior to 1875, and now 850 hectares were being set aside ostensibly for that purpose. This had the appearance of legality, because the law simply stated that Ayuntamientos had to ensure that *ejido* lands were spared disentailment, but was in reality a clever distortion of the spirit of those laws. In theory, *ejido* lands were reserved for public use, but, in fact, the Ayuntamiento quickly rented them out. Given their proximity to the town, these were prized lands (especially as pastures), and prominent local figures—Indian and non-Indian alike—wound up being tenants. Perhaps this is why no one seems to have complained.[84]

After this inauspicious beginning (or auspicious, depending on one's perspective), the Commission proceeded to form the *grandes lotes*. It was December of 1875. Conducting a thorough survey of Papantla's vast communal territories was apparently never seriously considered, probably because of the great expense and delay this would have involved. Instead, the Commission decided to rely on the "jurisdictional boundaries of the *congregaciones* and *rancherías*" in the communal zones of the municipality as the basis for the new *condueñazgos*. As the Junta de Indígenas later stated, this policy was adopted primarily to avoid "affecting the properties of the residents," which otherwise might have ended up being fragmented in the course of the division. This scheme surely pleased the *rancheros*; their holdings would remain intact and they could expect to assume an equally prominent position in the management of the new coterminous *condueñazgos*. This approach also made the Commission's job easier from a technical point of view, since the boundaries of the *congregaciones* were often known and generally recognized. In a number of cases, though, two or more *congregaciones* would be joined in a single *condueñazgo*, but always respecting their boundaries and—as the Junta stressed—only with the approval of all "interested parties."[85]

With the assistance of Antonio Pascoli, a local Italian resident contracted by the Ayuntamiento, the subdivision of communal land into individual *lotes* was completed very quickly. Pascoli claimed to have been trained as a land surveyor, but the mapping work he performed would strongly suggest otherwise. The process began at El Cristo on December 15 and concluded sixty-eight days later at Santa Agueda. In practice, these demarcations basically involved walking the outskirts of the *congregaciones* or *rancherías* in question, defining in writing their boundary lines by reference to a series of visual landmarks, and placing wooden crosses at selected spots to mark the corners of the new estates. Whenever possible, the borders were made to coincide with established roads and footpaths or with natural features of the landscape, such as rivers, streams, big trees, and marshes. This made progress easier and faster. In some places, narrow trails were opened to create a dividing line, but where the terrain was particularly difficult to traverse (e.g., over certain mountains and ravines), Pascoli appears to have simply traced an imaginary geometrical line, placing boundary crosses at each end.[86] Maps 4.1 and 4.2 are directly based on Pascoli's original topographic drawings.

Pascoli's peculiar method of surveying land accounts for the speed with which the initial phase of the division was completed. In most cases, it seems to have taken only one day to determine and mark the boundaries of an entire *lote*, and on three occasions two *lotes* were demarcated in a single day. It is not impossible that some work may have been done in advance, but the language of the official documents certifying the completion of each setting of boundaries suggests that this was not so. In any case, it is clear from these records that the "Measurement Commission"—as the Ayuntamiento would refer to the Junta, the trustee, and the surveyor—did not actually measure any land. Although their final report included figures for the total area of each *lote*, these were merely gross estimates and not the product of any sort of calculation. Table 4.2 lists these figures.[87] Considering the sinuosity of Papantla's terrain, it is no surprise that many of the Commission's estimates would prove to be wildly inaccurate. Lot 22, for instance, was said to comprise 3,500 hectares, when in fact it had more than 10,000; the estimate for Lot 17 was nearly 4,000 hectares, but its surface area was actually over 11,000 hectares. In some cases, the inverse was

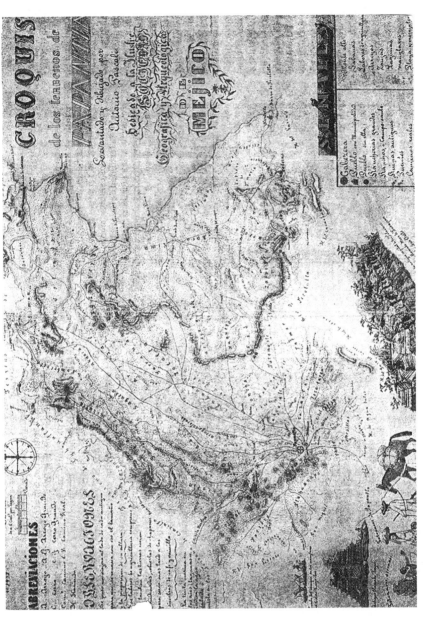

MAP 4.1 Antonio Pascoli's Map of Papantla. Courtesy of Mapoteca Antonio García Cubas, Sociedad Mexicana de Geografía y Estadística. Photo: Pedro Hiriart.

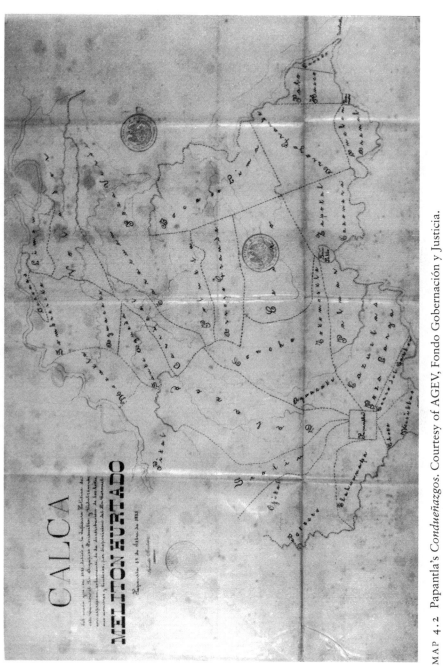

MAP 4.2 Papantla's *Condueñazgos*. Courtesy of AGEV, Fondo Gobernación y Justicia.

TABLE 4.2

Condueñazgos of Papantla

Lot	Congregaciones	Survey date	No. of shareholders	Estimated area (sgm/ha)
1	El Cristo	16 Dec 1875	44	0.5 sgm = 878 ha
2	Palo Hueco	18 Dec 1875	91	1 sgm = 1,756 ha
3	Cabezas (*fundo legal*)	18 Dec 1875	—	—
4	Anclón y Arenal	19 Dec 1875	87	1 sgm = 1,756 ha
5	Zapotal y Cazonera	20 Dec 1875	241	1 sgm = 1,756 ha
6	Arroyo Grande de Boca de Lima	20 Dec 1875	155	1.5 sgm = 2,634 ha
7	Arroyo Grande de Cabezas	4 Jan 1876	174	4 sgm = 7,024 ha
8	Cedro	7 Jan 1876	189	3 sgm = 5,268 ha
9	Boca de Lima	12 Jan 1876	224	3.25 sgm = 5,707 ha
10	Polutla, Taracuán y Poza Verde	15 Jan 1876	486	5.5 sgm = 9,658 ha
11	Cerro del Carbón	17 Jan 1876	104	1 sgm = 1,756 ha
12	Cazuelas y Poza Larga	17/23 Jan 1876	246	2 sgm = 3,512 ha
13	Tlahuanapa	23 Jan 1876	122	1.5 sgm = 2,634 ha
14	San Pablo (*fundo legal*)	25 Jan 1876	—	—
15	Chote y Mesillas	28 Jan 1876	179	1 sgm = 1,756 ha
16	El Palmar	3 Feb 1876	92	1.75 sgm = 3,073 ha
17	Carrizal y Volador	3 Feb 1876	245	2.25 sgm = 3,951 ha
18	Concha, Aguacate y Totomoxtle	5 Feb 1876	255	4 sgm = 7,024 ha
19	Ojital y Potrero	8 Feb 1876	205	2 sgm = 3,512 ha
20	Escolín	12 Feb 1876	115	1.5 sgm = 2,634 ha
21	Talaxca Arroyo Colorado	12 Feb 1876	319	4 sgm = 7,024 ha
22	Pital y Mozutla	14 Feb 1876	278	2 sgm = 3,512 ha
23	Cazones y Limón	15 Feb 1876	146	1 sgm = 1,756 ha
24	Sombrerete, Caristay y Aguacate	18 Feb 1876	274	2.25 sgm = 3,951 ha
25	Santa Agueda	20 Feb 1876	99	1 sgm = 1,756 ha
	Total		4,370	48 sgm = 84,288 ha

SOURCE: See note 87 to Chapter 4.

true: Lot 18 was assumed to cover some 7,000 hectares, but in reality had no more than 3,150, while Lot 8 was recorded at around 5,250 hectares when it had only about 3,600. Overall, though, underestimates prevailed; taking as a whole the seventeen *condueñazgos* that remained a part of Papantla after the creation of Gutiérrez Zamora (1877), the Commission's figures turn out to have been nearly 15,000 hectares too low.[88]

Of course, the Commission was well aware of these shortcomings. When Tiburcio, Hernández, and Jiménez presented a record of the tasks performed for the approval of the Ayuntamiento, they prefaced their report with a caveat. "The Commission," they stated, "does not believe that its work has any scientific merit whatsoever, because the limited skills of its members preclude achieving such perfection, but it has nevertheless tried as much as possible to carry out this assignment conscientiously."[89] At this point, however, no one seems to have been overly concerned with these serious technical deficiencies. After all, the aim of this land division was merely to demarcate some *grandes lotes*, and this the Commission had more or less managed to accomplish. For this type of distribution to proceed, boundary lines were all that was required. In due course, though, the evident inaccuracy of many of the area estimates would give rise to serious conflicts.

Once that stage was finished, in late February of 1876, the Commission set out to prepare the lists of *condueños*. The Revolution of Tuxtepec disrupted the process and preliminary rolls did not come up for approval until April of 1877. At this stage of the disentailment the central question was that of eligibility. Decree No. 152 (1869) simply stated that "all heads of family" were to be included in the land division, and the Ayuntamiento had to decide how to interpret this phrase. At issue was "the spirit of the law": were these to be considered "Indian community lands," to which presumably only Indians should have a right, or were they instead "lands of the municipality," to be distributed among all the sons and daughters of Papantla, whether or not they were Indian? The original law of 1826 explicitly endorsed the first definition, but Decree No. 152—which superseded earlier legislation—was ambiguous, in part because Indian communities were no longer legal entities. Historians have generally ignored this crucial question, assuming that the land privatizations prescribed by post-Reforma laws were in principle clearly limited to members of the extinguished communities, but at least in Veracruz this was not the case.[90] Not surprisingly, Papantla's Ayuntamiento adopted and enforced the second definition, thus enabling many of the local non-Indians to participate in the division as legitimate *condueños*. Judging from the available evidence, the Junta de Indígenas did not object.

According to the criteria established by the Ayuntamiento in April 1877, shares would be awarded to "all residents who were born in the municipality" and were heads of family, whether male or female. In 1878, orphans were also included. Birthplace—and not race or ethnicity—became the basis of eligibility. "Those who have been born in this municipality," explained Papantla's mayor, "have legitimate property rights over the territory that is now being divided," because these lands "were purchased by their ancestors."[91] The logic of this argument was clearly fallacious, but it does not appear to have been challenged.

Regarding allocation, it was agreed that farmers would receive shares of the *lotes* in which they had established their plantings; in effect, the residents of the ex-communal *congregaciones* would become their owners. The rest of the eligible municipal residents could join as *condueños* in the *lote* of their choice. All those who believed they had rights to a land share and had not been included in the preliminary lists were at this time invited to submit their names to the Junta. Presumably, these would have included not only the native residents of the town, but also those of the non-communal territories of the municipality. There were more than ten established *rancherías*—including Pueblillo, Coyuxquihui, Joloapan, San Miguel, and Mesa Chica—in the private lands south and west of the Villa, and many of these farmers were surely natives of Papantla. In 1871, no less than 15 percent (more than two thousand) of the inhabitants of the municipality resided outside the communal zone.[92] Remarkably, however, these settlements were never mentioned in the documents detailing the establishment of *condueñazgos*. Perhaps some did claim their rights before Tiburcio's Junta and were awarded shares of ownership, but there was no special provision made for the incorporation of these people as a whole. Thus, it appears that a good number of Papantla's Totonacs may have been left out of the land division, while at the same time town merchants such as Agapito Fontecilla y Vidal—who had grown up and gone to school in Spain—became legitimate part-owners of the former territories of the Indian community.[93] For this, the Junta de Indígenas' connivance was at least partly responsible. The "spirit of the law," often invoked throughout these proceedings, proved to be quite malleable.

The status of the *fincados* (settlers) also had to be resolved. These were the "many families of foreign origin who farm the lands of this municipality," a group that included Italian colonists as well as Indians and mestizos born elsewhere. According to Papantla's mayor, "Most of the families occupying the *lotes* of El Cristo, Palo Hueco, *fundo legal* de Cabezas, Arenales y Anclón, and Arroyo Grande de Cabezas in the Municipality of Tecolutla" belonged to this category. Long a sparsely populated area, the eastern end of Papantla's historic communal territories had recently attracted a fair number of migrant farmers. The Italians, in particular, had become avid vanilla cultivators, and Papantla's authorities regarded the activities of these business-minded colonists "as an important factor in the development and increase of the population and general wealth of the municipality." Although they were not a large group, the economic potential of their agricultural enterprises was already evident. The Ayuntamiento and the commercial interests it represented did not want to see these settlers dispossessed or even disturbed, but by the Ayuntamiento's own rules of eligibility these people clearly had no *condueñazgo* rights.

As a solution, Papantla's mayor, Abraham Bauza, proposed the creation of a special class of shares to be held by the Ayuntamiento on behalf of these families. In each lot they would set aside as many municipal shares (*acciones concejiles*) as there were settler families, and these shares of ownership would guarantee the rights of the *fincados* to the lands they were already cultivating. In time, the Mayor suggested, these certificates could be sold to the colonists. He cited public interest and progress as reasons, but he added that in any case it was the Ayuntamiento's prerogative to dictate the conduct of the land division.[94] In effect, he was attempting to retain partial ownership of these new *lotes* in order to protect the interests of a certain group of farmers who had no land rights of their own. In more ways than one, this was evidently illegal. Aside from *fundos* and *ejidos*, municipalities were not allowed to own or administer land. Moreover, nowhere in Veracruz's land legislation was such a maneuver contemplated; even if the shares were immediately sold to the *fincados*, the invention of municipal shares was a clear violation of the law. Still, the Ayuntamiento approved the creation of these shares and ordered that a separate list of eligible families be formed. It also resolved to refer the matter to state authorities, hoping to obtain support for this controversial plan.

In this case, the Junta de Indígenas actively opposed the usurpatory pretensions of the Ayuntamiento. The "spirit of the law" had its limits, and the imposition of *acciones concejiles* went too far. At this point, in mid-1877, the land division came to a stop. The problem was not simply that the creation of these shares was illegal, but also that allowing them would have serious repercussions. The Ayuntamiento was attempting to carve out a role for itself in the management of some of the *lotes*, and this threatened the rights and interests of many legitimate *condueños*. At issue was not so much whether the *fincados* would be permitted to stay, but rather who would control the lands they now occupied—that is, who would set and collect rents, impose tenancy conditions, etc. This was a business matter as well as an administrative one. Town merchants like Pedro Tremari (who was himself ineligible to become a *condueño*) had a direct stake in the unhindered survival and prosperity of the many settler-owned *vainillales* of eastern Papantla, and they relied on the authority of the Ayuntamiento for continued favorable access to those lands. The *acciones concejiles* would protect these profitable arrangements, effectively removing them from the jurisdiction of the Indian-dominated *condueñazgos*.

For more than a year, the disentailment process remained at a standstill. A new state government was preoccupied with more urgent political matters, so Papantla's request for guidance did not receive prompt attention. In addition, the law enabling *pueblos* to divide communal lands in the form of *grandes lotes* had expired at the end of 1876 and the state legislature—then in the midst of serious internal conflicts—had yet to pass an extension.[95] Among certain Totonacs, these unforeseen delays provoked considerable uneasiness since the final composition of their new *condueñazgos* hung in suspense. In April 1878, Tiburcio, Hernández, and Jiménez appealed directly to the governor, asking him to deny the pretensions of the Ayuntamiento and to speed up the conclusion of the land distribution in its current form. In a letter signed by well over one hundred prospective *condueños*, including many *ranchería* officials, the Junta warned that while "the Indian Community" had embraced the opportunity to subdivide its lands, it "does not accept and will never allow" municipal shares. As Tiburcio would later argue, the law did not empower municipal councils to keep land, let alone to give it to those who had no right to it; moreover, the proposed shares deprived legitimate owners of their private property, and there was barely enough land to satisfy the needs of all those who had a clear right to it. In early July, the *jefe político* weighed in on the side of the Indians, advising against the creation of municipal shares and for an expeditious ratification of the Junta's labors.[96]

As it turns out, a few days later the state legislature issued a decree that dealt directly with the dispute over the fate of *fincados* that had temporarily paralyzed the land division in Papantla. Besides extending the disentailment period for an additional two years, Decree No. 39 of July 12, 1878 established that "those individuals who were settled (*fincados*) beforehand in communal territories that have been or should be divided, and do not have rights to them, will be granted a share equal to that of the rest," provided they paid an annual fee to the municipality (Article 4). At that time, the president of the Veracruz state legislature was none other than Abraham Bauza, who as mayor of Papantla had first pushed the idea of the *acciones concejiles*. In this way, Bauza and his allies back in Papantla hoped to resolve the impasse; in essence, their will was now written into law. Since the law did not suit their interests, they simply changed it. Still, Tiburcio and his people would not budge, and in the end their position prevailed, at least in principle.

Meeting with the Ayuntamiento on October 16, 1878, Simón Tiburcio argued at length that Decree No. 39 could not be applied retroactively. Papantla's land division had been undertaken in accordance with Decree No. 152, which did not provide for the *fincados*. He acknowledged that by law the Ayuntamiento had the last word, but he also reminded them that the division was already a fait accompli, and that any changes would severely harm the interests of the legitimate *condueños*. Tiburcio's exposition was forceful and comprehensive, and he displayed a detailed command of all the relevant legislation. The new law should be respected, he told them, but not enforced. That same day, the Ayuntamiento reluctantly acquiesced, voting to exclude from the land distribution all heads of family not covered by "the spirit" of the law of 1869.[97] There would be no municipal shares in the *condueñazgos*.

Tiburcio's rhetorical or jurisprudential skills aside, this retreat was not ultimately a concession to the power of reason, but to the local balance of power. If Papantla's communal lands were being peacefully divided, it was only because the Totonacs—and, in particular, their leaders—had agreed to it. This was something municipal officials could not ignore. Although they were legally in charge of the process, their coercive powers were in fact quite limited. The Ayuntamiento was in no position to dictate the terms of the disentailment and could at best only hope to negotiate them. At bottom, this was the Junta de Indígenas' land division. If birthplace became the basis of eligibility, it was not without the Junta's consent; if many of the residents of Papantla's non-communal *rancherías* were left out of the *condueñazgos*, it was because the Junta did not target them for inclusion. Now, Tiburcio and his cohort rejected both the establishment of municipal shares as well as the retroactive application of Decree No. 39, Article 4, and the Ayuntamiento was forced to yield. Papantla's *fincados* would have to negotiate their status with the new private authorities of the *condueñazgos*.[98]

Once this dispute was resolved, the land division could at last reach its conclusion. In late 1878 the *condueño* lists were declared closed. The preliminary registers presented in 1877 had been amended to include many new names, and each of these new *condueños* had selected (or been assigned to) a lot. Originally, the Commission had proposed limiting the number of shares in each *lote* to sixty-six per *sitio de ganado mayor* (which translates into no fewer than 26.6 hectares per share). Enforcing this ratio, they argued, would ensure an equitable distribution of land.[99] In reality, however, this was an impossible idea and no effort was made to implement it. Farmers wanted shares in the lots where they lived, and those who had no *fincas* were allowed to pick the *condueñazgo* of their choice. Inevitably, some lots were bound to end up with more *condueños* per *sitio de ganado mayor* than others, and shifting people around would not have been an easy task. Moreover, the area estimates for many of the lots were acknowledged to be highly impressionistic (and were, in fact, notably inaccurate), and this made the distribution plan impracticable ab initio. Instead, the *condueño* lists seem to have been formed without much regard for the size of the *lotes*, and each *condueñazgo* was provided with as many shares as there were names in the final register.

In all, there would be 4,370 certified *condueños* assigned to twenty-three *lotes* estimated to cover a total of forty-eight *sitios de ganado mayor*, or about 84,000 hectares. The figures for each *lote* are reproduced in Table 4.2. Some associations were tiny—El Cristo only had 44 members—and others were very large, none more than Polutla, Taracuán, and Poza Verde, which had nearly 500 members. Most had between 150 and 300 *condueños*. Lot sizes (as estimated) also ranged very widely, from half a *sitio* (± 878 hectares) to five and a half *sitios* (± 9,658 hectares). Considering the manner in which the *condueñazgos* were formed, it is not surprising that the results were very uneven.

Moreover, the quality of the lands varied substantially across and within *lotes*. Cazuelas y Poza Larga was crisscrossed by hill ranges, and only a third of its area was considered cultivable; Carrizal y Volador, meanwhile, was said to consist largely of good farmland, while Pital y Mozutla was characterized as being mostly "hills and gullies." Elsewhere, there were long stretches of swampland and grassland, as well as fertile valleys and meadows. *Roza* agriculture was remarkably adaptable, but it clearly had its limits. At this point, however, none of these many differences—in lot sizes, potential share values, and land quality—seemed to matter too much. The shares were just abstract units of ownership, not attached to any particular piece of land. It was thus hard for anyone to know what their share might amount to, which fostered the illusion of equity and kept potential turf conflicts at bay. The emphasis now was on becoming a *condueño*, and those who had a right to obtain paper shares for the most part did so.

Population figures offer a comparative perspective. In the state census for 1878 the municipality of Papantla was listed as having 18,439 inhabitants, of which 9,443 were females and 8,996 males. Table 4.3 presents the complete data.[100] Judging from these numbers, the 4,370 shares that were distributed probably covered the vast majority of Papantla's eligible inhabitants—married couples, widows, widowers, some single adults, and orphans. Even if these census figures turned out to be as much as 10 percent too low, which is not unlikely, the inference would be the same: with the possible exception of non-communal *ranchería* residents, all those who were entitled to receive shares seem to have been included in the land division. There is no evidence—for instance, complaints of exclusion—to suggest otherwise. At the same time, the census shows a very young population—11,482 persons (62 percent of the total) under the age of eighteen. Most of them were not made *condueños*, and in time they would want land, too.

Just who were these new shareholders? The registers compiled by the Junta de Indígenas and approved by the Ayuntamiento provide a revealing glimpse of the people who inherited Papantla's old communal lands. Not surprisingly, most were men, but a substantial number of shareholders turn out

TABLE 4.3

Population of the Municipio of Papantla, 1878

Sex	Under 18 years	18–50 years	50+ years	Single	Married	Widowed	Total
Female	5,543	3,425	475	6,084	3,002	357	9,443
Male	5,939	2,782	275	5,954	2,830	212	8,996
Total	11,482	6,207	750	12,038	5,832	569	18,439

SOURCE: See note 100 to Chapter 4.

to have been women—for example, 12 of 44 (27 percent) in El Cristo, 27 of 91 (30 percent) in Palo Hueco, 18 of 87 (21 percent) in Anclón y Arenal, and 52 of 241 (22 percent) in Zapotal y Cazonera.[101] Quite a few children—presumably orphans—were also included; some are listed by name and labeled as "minors," while others are included simply as someone's heirs, as in "heirs of Agustina Capitanachi" (incidentally, of Italian origin). In some lots, as many as 10 percent of the *condueños* belonged in this category.

In addition, the shareholder registers exhibited some very curious irregularities. All of the lists contained several names marked variously as "not born here," "has no land rights," "deceased," "moved to another lot," or "appears twice in the list." In no case, however, were the rolls amended; in determining the total number of shares to be awarded in each *lote*, these names were not excluded. In El Cristo, for instance, six of the forty-four names listed had one of these disqualifying annotations, but the land was nevertheless divided into forty-four *acciones*. The same occurred in the other *lotes*. It is hard to tell whether or not some of these people actually received the shares in question; at least the dead surely did not. In any case, these anomalies suggest that perhaps the land division was not entirely free from fraud. Considering what was at stake, this should not surprise.

In November 1878, the shareholders were given formal possession of their *grandes lotes*. Accompanied by Simón Tiburcio, Pablo Hernández, and Antonio Jiménez, Papantla's Mayor and lands trustee visited each lot, gathering with many of the soon-to-be *condueños* in the house or rancho of a prominent local resident. There, the trustee declared that those whose names appeared in the respective registers would from then on be considered "absolute owners, without restriction or reserve of any sort." His statement is worth quoting at length. In accordance with the provisions of Decree No. 152, he said, the Ayuntamiento granted them "without objection from any party, the real, pure, sole, perfect, and irrevocable possession of the aforementioned estate, with the limits and boundaries that have been stated." In consequence, he continued, the Ayuntamiento "ceases to hold and surren-

ders the rights of administration that the law had conferred upon municipalities with regard to communal territories, these lands having been turned
into private property." The new *condueños*, the trustee then explained,
would henceforth have to pay all the taxes levied on rural estates.[102] With
these words, at once grandiose and ominous, the historic lands of Papantla's
community were turned into private *condueñazgos*.

The preceding analysis highlights three generally ignored aspects of Papantla's initial land division: the Junta de Indígenas essentially managed the
process, local non-Indians were included as beneficiaries, and the land surveys had no scientific merit whatsoever. The first two directly contradict the
typical assumptions that have guided the study of communal disentailment
in Papantla and elsewhere. At least for Totonac leaders, the preservation or
defense of communal lands along ethnic lines was not a priority. It is also
clear that the creation of *condueñazgos* should not be regarded simply as an
external imposition. In fact, as explained, many *rancheros* seem to have
seen this as a grand opportunity; in a time of incipient economic ferment,
the ability to control land was increasingly a coveted asset. It is hard to
imagine that the Junta would have been able to operate as it did without
the support of these people. As for the third aspect, how the land was actually divided, its importance would become apparent only afterward, in
the conflicts that erupted during the 1880s and 1890s.

Ultimately, it is clear that Papantla's peaceful transition from communal
landholding to *condueñazgo* cannot be understood without reference to developments in the vanilla economy. The push to reform land tenure came at
a time when production and exports were beginning to increase considerably; the ensuing race to grow and hoard vanilla—which engulfed many
farmers as well as merchants—gave land rights a fresh meaning. Although
Papantla's influential Totonacs opposed individual parceling, they embraced a division into *condueñazgos* as an attractive alternative. Under this
new arrangement, vanilla cultivation and exports underwent a remarkable
expansion—the vanilla boom of the late 1870s and of the 1880s. In the
process, the *condueñazgos* also became hotbeds of serious business and social conflicts, which eventually led to a full-scale privatization of landed
property. What follows now is an analysis of the short but eventful life of
Papantla's ex-communal *condueñazgos*.

5 The Experience of Condueñazgo

In October 1880, when state authorities at last gave formal sanction to the *condueñazgos* distributed back in 1878, the governor urged Papantla's *jefe político* to foster among shareholders a "spirit of association," encouraging them to establish rules for the administration of their properties and ensuring that any agreed-upon procedures gave every *condueño* "equal benefits and responsibilities." At the same time, he cautioned public officials to exercise the outmost prudence and tact in promoting the internal organization of these *condueñazgos*, "because these are private properties, in which the authorities cannot and should not give orders, only recommendations." Veracruz's bureaucrats suggested forming "agricultural associations" named after patriotic heroes, each with a board of administrators in charge of running the affairs of the estate, an idea that the *jefe político* duly communicated to the political officers of the various *rancherías*.[1]

These instructions display the deep ambivalence that would characterize the state government's stance with respect to Papantla's ex-communal *condueñazgos*. Legally, the mandate to disentail village lands had been fulfilled; these were now regular—that is, taxpaying—rural properties, and their management was therefore a private matter. Moreover, joint-stock holdings were clearly not objectionable in and of themselves, since many other kinds of property—including real estate—were then held in that fashion. Yet, despite their seemingly unassailable legal and fiscal standing, these *condueñazgos* were from the start viewed with some suspicion, as potential new incarnations of an ancient Indian communalism doggedly resistant to modern notions of citizenship, individual rights, and progress. To government officials, the *condueñazgos*—at least those composed of Indians—were retrograde institutions because among the poor and the ignorant collective land tenure led inevitably to abuse and usurpation, by powerful insiders as well as wealthy outsiders. Individual land parcels were really the only way to safeguard the interests of an ignorant majority.[2] Thus, the desire to bring about the fragmentation of these joint holdings would remain alive and in abeyance, despite the absence of any legal imperative.

In the end, however, government attitudes and policies regarding ex-communal *condueñazgos* played only a secondary role in determining how these new landowning associations would operate. To understand what happened in Papantla after 1880 it is imperative to look beyond official designs and pronouncements, whose local influence was often evanescent or at most tangential, and instead to examine the interplay of growing commercial, demographic, fiscal, and political pressures during these years. Papantla's land division had not been driven mainly by government pressure, but by a host of local interests and transnational circumstances. These would now dictate the functioning of *condueñazgos*.

For several decades already, a growing vanilla business had been progressively invigorating the basin's long-stagnant agri-commercial economy, opening up possibilities never available before. Slow and steady at first, this historic transformation began to pick up speed toward the late 1860s, fueled by the swift expansion of a previously insignificant U.S. consumer market nearby. In retrospect, the 1870s were clearly a crucial moment of transition, the beginning of Papantla's vanilla boom. In those years, cultivation spread considerably; export data show that Mexico's—and, in particular, Papantla's—vanilla production soared, with record total volumes of 25,370 kilograms in 1877–78 and 40,986 kilograms in 1879–80, of which maybe two-thirds came from Papantla. This business awakening entailed changes not only in the pace and range of economic activities, but also in the character of the social relations and institutions through which those activities were carried out. Among the latter, landholding arrangements acquired a new importance; as fields and forests turned into more valuable resources, the idea of modifying communal tenure rules became appealing to many. In effect, the creation of *condueñazgos* during the 1870s was a tangible reflection of a new economic outlook and its concomitant social realignments.

In light of this, it is not surprising to discover that Papantla's vanilla production and exports grew at an unprecedented rate under the *condueñazgo*. Whereas in the 1870s the basin's average annual exports were probably around 12,000 kilograms, during the 1880s they climbed to about 33,000 kilograms, an increase of 175 percent. As noted, this growth was largely the result of expanded cultivation, and not of improved yields, since artificial pollination was not yet widely practiced in Mexico. In the absence of effective policing, the proliferation of firearms in the hands of growers helped to keep vanilla theft in check. Most of this new vanilla was planted in Papantla's ample ex-communal territories, where the majority of farmers lived and where the best lands were to be found. The export figures for 1881–85 are particularly suggestive; thanks to Papantla's booming output, Mexico's shipments surpassed 50,000 kilograms during each of these years (Appendix Table A.9). Never before had the country produced nearly as much vanilla. Significantly, the volume of exports jumped dramatically just four years after the establishment of the *condueñazgos*, which is about as long as it takes for new vanilla plants to reach full maturity. By 1888–89, a mere decade after the constitution of these private landholding associations, Papantla alone was producing some 50,000 kilograms per year, an extraordinary development. There can be little doubt that this process of agricultural and commercial expansion was the defining feature of Papantla's economic life during these years.

Although a boom in business was already underway before the old communal land-tenure arrangements were modified, helping as it did to bring that about, the new institutional framework decisively boosted this trend, accelerating the rate of growth in cultivation and trade. It was above all the prospect of a malleable administrative autonomy in a time of unprecedented economic buoyancy that had made the idea of *condueñazgo* landholding appealing to many. At least from this perspective, the *condueñazgo* did not disappoint. As will be seen, the proprietary organization and management of *condueñazgo* associations enabled influential stockholders and allied commercial interests to extend their control over productive resources and thereby to benefit from increased economic activity. Wielding the suitably vague legal prerogatives afforded by the new regime of ownership to claim exclusive rights over specific areas or products, groups of prominent *condueños*—resident and absentee alike—greatly expanded their investments in land-based enterprises. Many *condueñazgos* quickly enacted policies and imposed fees designed to regulate access to fields and woodlands, in effect formalizing an emergent set of power relations shaped by fresh business opportunities.

In social terms, too, the transition to *condueñazgo* was both the product of and a catalyst for significant transformations. But whereas the intensification of business activity that followed the shift to joint-stock land ownership was in many respects predictable, some of the fiscal burdens and exclusionary provisions of this new organization of land tenure were unforeseen, at least by those who stood to lose the most as a result. That is why no one seems to have fought against the formation of *grandes lotes*. However, as soon as the new land managers moved to impose a restrictive—and in some cases venal—interpretation of property rights and responsibilities, the broad practical implications of *condueñazgo* landholding became evident. For many, access to milpa–forest lands—the long-standing basis of independent farmer life in Papantla—would no longer be what it once was. This belated realization gave rise—in the course of the 1880s—to widespread distress and disillusionment, increased communal strife and factionalism, tense confrontations, and even rebellion. The darker side of the vanilla boom was now in plain view; among those whom this did not please or favor, some would strive to turn back the clock. Years of fierce local conflict lay ahead.

Even though it manifested itself fairly suddenly, the undoing of Papantla's traditional social order was long in the making. For at least half a century the developing vanilla economy had constituted a powerful force for change. Because of its heterogeneous social bases—Indian growers and middlemen, non-Indian curers and exporters—as well as its capital importance in the context of the basin's economy, the growth of the vanilla business involved and affected every segment of local society. Back in the 1840s José María Bausa was already drawing attention to "the disorders ushered in by greed" of vanilla, not just in the conduct of business, but in social relations more generally. Over time, the continual growth of vanilla cultivation and trade generated new wealth, jarring ambitions, unfamiliar pressures, and fresh distrust; these "disorders," in turn, began—imperceptibly, at first—to unhinge the social conventions and practices regarding land use which had been the enduring foundation of the old Papantla. Out of that divisive process came the *condueñazgos*, on which a multitude of competing interests would abruptly converge.

The Meaning of Condueñazgo

The internal administration of the *grandes lotes* was a private, largely informal affair; not surprisingly, it generated few written records, and only a small number of these appear to have been preserved. Still, analyzing the available documents in the context of the socioeconomic developments just described, it is not hard to perceive the general outlines and dominant goals of *condueñazgo* organization. As soon as shareholders were given formal possession of their territories, late in 1878, groups of influential *condueños* began to take advantage of their broad yet undefined prerogatives. Mainly, this involved a proactive, de facto extension of use rights—laying claim to additional lands or appropriating particular forest products, for instance. Something like this had already been going on for some time, but the establishment of the *condueñazgo* afforded these groups new kinds of leverage because it provided a legal basis for exercising peremptory powers of exclusion. Now, these leading figures could seek to limit or tax others' access to productive resources, profiting not only from reduced competition but also from the discretionary administration of such regulations.

In principle, all *condueñazgos* required a certain governance, if only to ensure that property taxes got paid. Local circumstances would dictate what form this would take. In *lotes* where business opportunities were clearly on the rise, and where a more or less consolidated group of powerful new *condueños* already existed, the appointment of a single representative or proxy with broad powers of attorney was often sufficient. This *apoderado* could manage (or mismanage) the distribution of rights and obligations within his *lote*, imposing fees, collecting taxes, and awarding contracts in accordance with the wishes of his ruling faction. As long as his authority remained effectively undisputed, a formal system of checks and balances was unnecessary. This simple type of arrangement worked also in another kind of setting, in *condueñazgos* where there was not yet much competition for resources, where land remained plentiful, the local population was relatively low, and the commercial drive was comparatively subdued. Some of the more remote, inaccessible, and sparsely settled *lotes* were also the largest, much more so in fact than what Antonio Pascoli had originally estimated them to be. In such places, the push to restrict land use was both weaker and less conflictive, at least initially. There, too, formal *condueñazgo* administration would be minimal: a representative—perhaps even one per *ranchería*—in charge of fiscal matters, and *apoderados* appointed to carry out specific transactions. In contrast, where land-based resources were increasingly valuable and coveted, and where no one group of *condueños* was dominant, a more elaborate form of governance had to be put in place. Here, the operation of the *condueñazgo* was nominally entrusted to a board of directors, with a president, a treasurer, and other officials elected by the shareholders.

This variety in forms of administration was not insignificant, reflecting as it did a range of economic, demographic, and sociopolitical conditions among the ex-communal *condueñazgos*. Some had richer lands, were more densely peopled, contained more *rancherías*, or had stronger commercial links to the towns than did others. In spite of those organizational differences, however, the practical aim of *condueñazgo* management was everywhere more or less the same: to assert and enforce an exclusive definition of land-use rights, regulating access by means of membership, fees, and contracts. Such designs found clear expression in the detailed regulations issued by *lote* administrators, which gave concrete meaning to an otherwise ambiguous property regime. An examination of the rules imposed in two very different *lotes* serves to illustrate the general trend.

In August 1879 a number of the *condueños* of lot 24, Sombrerete, Caristay y Aguacate, appointed one of their own—a well-known *ranchero* named Narciso Salas—as their *apoderado*, empowering him to promote, manage, and oversee the use and business of their lands. Gathered before Sombrerete's municipal agent, they stated that if every shareholder were simply allowed to do as he or she pleased, utter confusion would inevitably result and "nothing good" would be accomplished. For this reason, and in order to advance their common interests, they had decided to give Salas "ample, effective, and sufficient" powers to act on their behalf and to enforce a series of regulations. The surviving document contains few names and no signatures, which is very unusual; thus, it is hard to know if all or even most of the 274 *condueños* in fact subscribed to it. But whether or not these rules were truly the product of the shareholders' collective will, they nevertheless reveal much about the kind of economic organization that was taking root inside the *grandes lotes*.[3]

The principal duties and powers of the *apoderado* were of three types: legal, fiscal, and economic. The first two—which involved representing the association in its dealings with local and state authorities, for example, over taxes—are mentioned only in passing, however. Virtually the entire document is devoted to economic questions, and, in particular, to establishing rules of access to the *lote*'s natural resources—especially land, timber, and wild forest products—through a system of contracts and fees. Evidently, this is what truly mattered to the interested parties. To understand what was at stake here, it is important to note that this large *lote* was on the road from Papantla to Cazones and Tuxpan, and that it still had much unoccupied land. Most of it was good for something potentially lucrative: farming, cattle ranching, logging, or forest gathering. The shareholders now owned all of these territories, and they intended to benefit from their sole right to them. That was, in essence, the *apoderado*'s mission.

Narciso Salas was given broad powers to regulate key aspects of land use across the *lote*. At his discretion, he could issue permits for the establishment of cattle ranches and coffee plantations, as well as for timber extraction in general. Commercial logging would be allowed only on a contract basis; Salas was free to negotiate and award these concessions, provided that certain terms—prices, types of wood, quantities, and duration—were all clearly stipulated in writing. Perhaps most importantly, he was placed in charge of admitting *colonos* into the *lote*. Here, the term *colono* was used to refer not only to the *fincados*, but, in effect, to anyone and everyone who was not a legitimate *condueño*. As will be seen, this was a crucial distinction, with especially serious consequences for the younger generations of Totonac farmers. From a legal point of view, shareholder rights were held individually (by heads of family) and could therefore be passed down only to a single heir. Hence, if a family had more than one offspring, which was almost always the case, the remaining sons and daughters would possess no land rights of their own. According to the bylaws that were being put into effect, these people would have to be considered *colonos*.

In lot 24, *colono* land use would be allowed only on a strict permit and fee basis, and only as long as it did not affect the interests of the *condueños*. For regular milpa plantings, the rent per harvest cycle would be as follows: for up to six almudes, one peso; for between six almudes and one fanega, two pesos and a half; and one peso for every additional fanega or fraction thereof. For vanilla stands, the land rent was generally higher, especially once the plants reached maturity and began to produce good fruit: for up to six almudes, one peso annually for the first three years and five pesos annually thereafter; for more than six almudes, five pesos annually per fanega or fraction thereof. The *condueños* were exempt from these fees for the use of farmland and were free to plant what and where they wanted. This was a considerable privilege, not only for those who had already established ranchos, but for shareholding merchants and townspeople who were not themselves farmers. The consequences were—to say the least—paradoxical. While someone like Agapito Fontecilla y Vidal could freely exercise or delegate his (new) right to farm (in his case, on lot 5), many young Totonac farmers would soon find themselves disfranchised, forced to pay for access to lands which a few years earlier would have been considered their own. Clearly, this was not the kind of arrangement that would foster or preserve communal cohesion.

The exploitation of forest products was heavily regulated as well. Access to timber and other materials used to build houses or for "public service" within the boundaries of the *lote* remained free, even for *colonos*. However, everything taken from the *monte* for commercial purposes would now have to be paid for, even by the *condueños*. The list of fees was exhaustive: the *apoderado* would charge for trees made into charcoal (four reales apiece); for the lianas used to build fences (four reales per thousand); for ordinary timber from the *monte bajo*—for instance, laurel (two reales per hundred); and for building materials such as bamboo and liana (two pesos per hundred and thousand, respectively), whenever these were destined for houses located outside the *lote*. In addition, hule, chicle, pepper, sarsaparilla, and wax extracted from the *lote*'s forests would be subject to a fee equivalent to 10 percent of their market value. Finally, the cost of taking precious woods—chiefly, mahogany or cedar—was set at one peso per log. As noted, this last forest enterprise—potentially the most profitable one—also required obtaining a concession directly from the *apoderado*.

The vanilla trade was also taxed, albeit indirectly. During the harvest months, the town merchants, their associates, and competing petty traders would set up small stores (*changarros*) out in the *congregaciones* in order to attract vanilla sellers interested in dry goods, alcohol, tools, or trinkets. According to the new regulations, these seasonal establishments would now be charged three pesos per month. Permanent stores, on the other hand, would pay only six pesos a year, provided that their capital did not exceed five hundred pesos.

Above all, the establishment of such an elaborate fee schedule points to the thoroughly commercial orientation of *condueñazgo* management. In lot 24, the *monte*'s abundant resources were no longer free, not even for all of those who were supposed to own them. Less than a year after taking possession of these territories, the *condueños* (probably a dominant group of them) had enacted a new set of land-use rules that profoundly redefined an older—and already eroded—meaning of joint ownership. At least for some of these shareholders, the main business of their *condueñazgo* was business.

Notwithstanding differences in local conditions and in structures of governance, other *grandes lotes* adopted strikingly similar policies around this time. Lot 15, Chote y Mesillas, is a case in point. Located directly to the south of Papantla's new *ejido*, Chote's land area was significantly smaller and more densely populated than Sombrerete's. In proportion to its size, moreover, Chote y Mesillas had a much higher number of *condueños*. As elsewhere, the quality of the terrain varied considerably within the *lote*; high hill ranges covered the north and west, while rich alluvial farmland stretched to the south and east.[4] Proximity to the town of Papantla made this territory especially valuable, and the desire to exploit it was correspondingly keen. Here, the task of regulating land access was complicated not only by the usual consuetudinary claims, but also by the fact that no one group of shareholders was dominant. In December 1880, 45 of the 179 *condueños* gathered in Papantla to form the Sociedad Agrícola de Benito Juárez, ostensibly to represent the interests of all shareholders. The association's members would elect a five-person board of directors in charge of managing the *lote*'s business—issuing permits, collecting fees, paying taxes, and—it was hoped—distributing annual dividends. The effort was led by Vicente Pérez, who had obtained power of attorney for around one hundred stockholders from both Chote and Mesillas, including all those who accompanied him. Pérez laid out a detailed set of land-use and tax rules that was nearly identical to the one imposed on lot 24 the previous year: contracts for commercial logging, land rentals for *colonos*, and universal fees for the extraction of forest goods. The main difference was in the rates charged; given its size and location, Chote's tariffs were generally higher. Those present at the meeting agreed that these rules would be binding on all shareholders, whether or not they had consented. For one reason or another, more than seventy of the lot's *condueños* had not participated in the formation of this governing association. As for the many *fincados* and new *colonos*, they plainly had no say in the matter.

Unlike *colonos*, the *condueños* remained at liberty to make plantings or graze cattle as they pleased. Although it was evident that the unfettered exercise of these individual rights could (and would) give rise to problems, very little was done to delimit them. The association's charter simply asked certificate holders not to abuse this prerogative by occupying much more land than what might correspond to their share of ownership; in the event of conflicts between *condueños*, the board would endeavor to resolve them amicably. There was, however, no enforcement mechanism, in part because reliable estimates of the *condueñazgo*'s land area were lacking. In practice, therefore, this was a meaningless injunction; among shareholders, might was free to make right.

A number of other clauses in Chote y Mesillas' administrative charter reaffirmed the proprietary and extractive character of *conduenazgo* organization. Two, in particular, are worth highlighting. First, as payment for his services, the board's treasurer would keep 20 percent of all fees collected. This would encourage zealousness—but not probity or equity—in the enforcement of the lot's regulations. Second, anyone—including shareholders—found to be violating the aforementioned rules would be considered a thief and was therefore subject to arrest and prosecution by the appropriate authorities.[5] These lands were now private property, and some among those who had become owners intended to treat them strictly as such.

This profit-driven model of land and forest management was adopted in ex-communal *conduenazgos* not only within the municipality of Papantla, but also in some other *pueblos* of the Cantón.[6] The remarkable uniformity of these regulatory documents—in aim as well as in language—suggests a probable common origin or inspiration. Much older *conduenazgos* located in historically private territories are a likely source; the nearby Cacahuatal estate, for instance, had long been run along entrepreneurial lines by a host of investors and farmers—including many town merchants—who held it in *conduenazgo*. In any case, at this time a standard set of land-use procedures was being implemented in many ex-communal and non-communal *conduenazgos* alike. The shareholders of San Miguel y San Lorenzo—the purportedly private estate that Simón Tiburcio and his associates had managed to acquire in the midst of Papantla's recent land division—introduced a permit and tariff system in the last days of November 1880.[7] A mere five days later, neighboring Chote y Mesillas followed suit. The two lists of regulations are virtually identical. These parallels point to a critical aspect of this push to redefine property rights: the visible hand of town merchants and their allies, who promoted the adoption of these regulations behind the scenes. Some were themselves shareholders, while others just had personal connections or credit investments out in the *grandes lotes*. What they had in common was a desire to take advantage of the new business possibilities afforded by the *conduenazgo*. In this regard, it is telling that the two men who bore legal witness to the creation of Chote's governing association were Angel Martínez and Abraham Bauza, both well-known vanilla traders.

A brief but interesting firsthand account of *conduenazgo* organization comes from Modesto González, who was Isabel Kelly and Angel Palerm's chief informant when these two anthropologists conducted field work in the settlement of Tajín (1947–48). Tajín was originally part of lot 19, Ojital y Potrero, and González grew up there in the 1880s. There is no sense of nostalgia in Modesto González's words. Over half a century later, what he remembered about the *grandes lotes* were the conflicts, the rents, and the commercial regulations:

When I was a boy I lived with my mother on land which is a little beyond the parcel . . . which Pablo González now has. But in these days there were no parcels; they had not yet divided the land. Everyone built his house wherever he liked, and he planted wherever he wanted. For that reason, there were many squabbles. In those days, there were no authorities in Ojital y Potrero, but there were in Papantla. In Ojital y Potrero—it still was not called Tajín—there were only two *apoderados*. They watched that the people did not cut the sapote trees and that they took the chicle [to Papantla?]. They charged rent for the fields and the houses; I think they delivered the money to the treasury in Papantla.[8]

Some might be tempted to interpret the enactment of *condueño* regulations as an attempt on behalf of the collectivity to defend and protect the *lote*'s valuable natural resources from the rapacity of non-Indian outsiders. As it turns out, scholars of Papantla's history have long portrayed the ex-communal *condueñazgo* as a refuge of communal cohesion, the product of a collective ethnic impulse or decision to protect and conserve a traditional form of social organization. In this view, the Totonacs embraced the *grandes lotes* in order to preserve "the principles of community and reciprocity that had characterized the relationship between Indians and land in the *común* of Papantla."[9] But the evidence tells a very different story. This entrenched interpretation rests on three related premises: first, that the *condueños* were exclusively Totonacs; second, that the Totonacs as a whole resisted the very idea of a *reparto*; and third, that a shared ethnicity automatically generated recognizable common interests and a strong sense of solidarity. In fact, the first two assumptions are demonstrably incorrect, and the third one is questionable and surely at least simplistic. For one, the land division of the late 1870s had changed the definition of "outsider," since non-Indians from the towns were awarded shares in the *lotes* whereas young Totonacs who resided in them were not. In addition, merchants and *colonos* could buy their way into the *condueñazgos*, and did. Indeed, a much less clear-cut pattern of allegiances, motivations, and interests is already evident in the process that led to the establishment of *condueñazgos*. Hence, to analyze these social upheavals and transformations merely in terms of Indian resistance versus outside aggression is to distort the true nature of the conflicts that tore at Papantla's social fabric in the course of these years. These struggles were intra-ethnic as well as inter-ethnic, and the dividing lines were not primarily ethnic ones. The forces of change—the promoters of increased cultivation and commercialization, of new business rackets and mercenary dealings—were to be found inside the landholding associations, not just outside. These Totonac *rancheros*, *indios ladinos*, and non-Indian merchants formed the new ruling elite of the *condueñazgos*. Individually or in groups, allied or in open competition with others, they sought to reap the benefits of *condueñazgo* autonomy, scrambling for control of the *lotes'* resources. Their deals and enterprises wrought great changes, boosting vanilla production while undermining the long-standing bases of communal life.

Pressured by so many competing economic interests, it is not surprising that some *condueñazgos* simply fell apart. In one case, the pursuit of territorial control—defensive and offensive, direct and indirect—quickly led to the de facto partition of a *lote*. Unable or unwilling to agree on or abide by a set of land-use rules, groups of shareholders seceded from the *condueñazgo*, claiming for themselves a section of the *lote* and denying others any rights of usufruct over it. The results were balkanization, exclusion, and strife. This is what happened in lot 23, Cazones y Limón. In October 1880, twenty or so *condueños* filed papers seeking the transfer of a large land area around the *congregación* of Cazones and the *ranchería* of Limón from lot 23 to neighboring lot 24. Half of them lived in Cazones, and the other half were residents of Papantla. Among them were various town merchants from the Patiño and Bauza families; they were accompanied by Narciso Salas, *apoderado* of lot 24, who welcomed them into his newly expanded *condueñazgo*. They claimed that another two dozen shareholders had agreed to join them; if so, almost 50 of the original 146 grantees were quitting *condueñazgo* no. 23, taking with them a sizable piece of the lot.[10] Less than a month later, another 25 shareholders—all of them inhabitants of the *ranchería* Los Migueles—withdrew from lot 23 to join lot 17, Carrizal y Volador. These *condueños*, too, took the liberty of attaching the lands they regarded as theirs to the adjoining *lote*. Miguel Contreras, a Papantla resident who served as the *apoderado* for lot 17 would henceforth represent them as well.[11] By this point, about half of lot 23's shareholders had disassociated themselves from it; worse still, the rest of the *condueños* appear to have been left with relatively little land.

As a legal entity, however, lot 23 continued to exist, its original boundaries—and corresponding tax levies—unaltered. In March 1885 Papantla's municipal treasurer took the remaining *condueños* to court because they had fallen in arrears with the property taxes; according to his records, lot 23 owed some taxes going back several years. Evidently, partial payments had been made, but for tax purposes the *lote* was still considered a single property, so the owners as a whole could be held responsible for the entire amount. The treasurer had been unable to collect this debt because it was not clear who was the "legitimate representative" for this lot; unless those listed as *condueños* resolved to address this matter promptly, everyone would be made liable. Faced with this ultimatum, a "considerable number" of these shareholders named Joaquín Palacios of Cazones as their *apoderado*. Palacios then wrote to the Ayuntamiento describing his party's situation. His letter has not been preserved, but some of his statements are paraphrased elsewhere in the case record. Palacios argued that he and the other *condueños* he represented were not "in possession" of the *lote*, since it had been effectively "dismembered" or "partitioned" in the aftermath of the original 1878 *reparto*; these lands, he explained, were now in the hands of others. On behalf of his group, Palacios requested more time to pay the back taxes, as well as assistance from municipal authorities in recovering the lost territories. After all, they were supposed to be owners, too. The Ayuntamiento nevertheless refused to become involved in the dispute, on the grounds that it had no jurisdiction over the internal affairs of the *condueñazgos*. As far as the government was concerned, they had in fact been given legal "possession" of their *lote* back in 1878, and any subsequent claims involving disagreements among the *condueños* could only be heard and adjudicated by the courts.[12] For these people, "co-ownership" had become nothing more than a burdensome legal fiction.

As these records suggest, Papantla's ex-communal *condueñazgos* proved to be highly malleable—and manipulable—landholding institutions. Symbols of new times and ways, the Indian *apoderados* of many *grandes lotes* swiftly emerged as powerful local bosses. More often than not, they became controversial figures, not just because of the conflict-prone nature of their undertaking, but also because their enforcement of *lote* regulations was selective and sometimes even crooked. A state treasury special agent sent to Papantla in 1889 to investigate allegations of fiscal malfeasance described in telling detail the notoriously arbitrary powers wielded by one *apoderado*:

The administrator of one *lote* in which there are many *condueños* has become a cacique. He manipulates the shareholders at will and does what he likes with their property; he awards manifestly and unfairly one-sided contracts for the extraction of precious woods, chicle, rubber, etc. etc., taking for himself as much as two-thirds of the profits, and he speculates with commodities in association with other people who are in turn exploiting him. He also regularly collects the property taxes due to the state and the municipality, but he makes the payments when he feels like it.[13]

Simón Tiburcio's management of San Miguel and San Lorenzo was equally rapacious. In 1886 he sold the property's entire stock of mature cedar and mahogany trees (about 2,500 trees in total) to Teziutlán merchant Diego Ramos; the decision, as well as the proceeds, appear to have been mainly his. By then, Papantla's Totonac war hero and a few Indian associates ran a thriving business, negotiating outside contracts for the sale of standing timber in other *condueñazgo* estates effectively controlled by them.[14] These were perhaps extreme cases, but similar issues—concerning logging contracts, taxes, membership rights, and business practices—framed the conduct of *condueñazgo* governance everywhere. The difference, it seems, was mainly one of degree.

On the whole, three general developments associated with the establishment and operation of the *condueñazgos* deserve special mention: first, the eventual disfranchisement of many young Totonacs and their families; second, an increase in direct taxes of various kinds; and third, a growing and often heavy-handed intervention on the part of town merchants in matters concerning land use and agriculture across the former communal territories. These trends combined to produce new and deep social conflicts out in Papantla's countryside, which soon led to episodes of organized dissension and outright rebellion. Each will be briefly discussed in turn.

The "inheritance" issue has already been mentioned; in short, the rising generations of young Totonac farmers would not automatically become shareholders in the *grandes lotes*. This problem was intrinsic to the *condueñazgo* system but did not necessarily condemn it to failure. Under certain circumstances, accommodations could be—and were—made to ensure continued access on reasonable terms for all; witness, for instance, the longevity of some Huastecan *condueñazgos*.[15] In the end, the meaning of property rights—concretely, who is entitled to benefit from a share of ownership—is always subject to social interpretation. In the case of Papantla during the late nineteenth century, what turned membership rights into an immediate source of conflict was the climate of relentless economic competition, fueled primarily by the vanilla trade. As shown, many *condueñazgos* quickly imposed restrictions and rents on all resident non-shareholders. Meanwhile, town merchants and other non-farmers got to enjoy—and exploit—the redefined privileges of land ownership. This situation could produce nothing but widespread resentment.

An examination of the age structure of Papantla's cantonal population during the age of the *grandes lotes* suggests the likely magnitude of this problem. Rough figures are available for 1878 and 1885, the birth year of the *condueñazgo* and the year of the first well-known rebellion, respectively (see Table 5.1).[16] Papantla—the municipality as well as the Cantón—had then a remarkably young population; those under eighteen years of age represented 61 percent of the total in 1878, and 47 percent in 1885. From a demographic perspective, disfranchisement was therefore a very serious issue, potentially affecting a great many new families. Furthermore, it appears that the number of adults—in particular, unmarried adult males—actually increased during this period, in relative as well as in absolute terms. A trickle of migrant workers coming down from the sierra contributed to this trend. Although the total counts provided by these censuses are not entirely reliable, the age distributions—as a percentage of the total population—are probably fairly accurate. Thus, it seems fair to assume that Papantla's population was somewhat less young as a whole in 1885 than it had been in 1878. All of this presumably translated into more demand for land, precisely at a time when the

TABLE 5.1

Age Structure, Cantón of Papantla, 1878 and 1885

	1878	1885
Total population	27,834	29,012
Females under 18	8,177	6,627
Males under 18	8,710	7,120
Total under 18	16,887	13,748
Percentage under 18	61%	47%
Single females	9,147	8,425
Single males	8,905	9,191
Married females	4,537	4,161
Married males	4,338	4,907
Widowed females	558	1,302
Widowed males	349	1,214

SOURCE: See note 16 to Chapter 5.

NOTE: As usual, the numbers provided do not add up. Cantonal figures are used because municipal data are not available for 1885, but any differences in age ratios would be minimal. In 1878, for instance, 62 percent of Papantla's municipal population was under eighteen years of age, whereas the average for the canton was 61 percent. It should also be noted that the census figures for 1885 are probably on the low side.

old communal territories were for the most part no longer freely available. Essentially, for many of those coming of age in the *grandes lotes* the alternatives were three: to pay rent and accept a subordinate status, to protest and fight to reverse the recent course of events, or simply to move away. Some appear to have exercised this last option. According to census data, the population of Papantla's non-communal *rancherías*—chiefly those south of the Tecolutla River—increased in these years, in both relative and absolute terms; whereas in 1871 these settlements accounted for 15 percent of municipal inhabitants, by 1885 their share (of a much larger total) had grown to 22 percent. Perhaps this was in part the result of internal migrations linked to the land-tenure changes taking place north of the river. As for those who stayed put, they faced an unenviable choice.

Late in 1894, in the midst of the longest and bloodiest period of civil unrest seen in Papantla since the days of Mariano Olarte's guerrilla, the state government asked Ignacio Muñoz to prepare a report describing the state of land tenure in the ex-communal areas of the basin. Muñoz, a state legislator and an engineer, would be subsequently sent to Papantla as the head of a military commission charged with surveying and parceling out several *grandes lotes.* Ever since the *conduenazgos* were established, he wrote, this type of automatic disfranchisement had been a persistent source of discord and upheaval:

As one would expect, most of the *conduenos* of each *lote* had a family, and their children were still little at the time when the *reparto* was carried out; for that reason they did not get shares in the *reparto* of those *lotes*. Today, those children have become adults, and now most of them lack lands of their own, and do not have land-use rights in the *lotes*, and thus they believe—or pretend to believe—that they have been dispossessed of a land which they consider to be their own, because their parents had received a share.[17]

The imposition of a wide array of direct taxes in the course of the 1880s was another source of grave concern and broad disaffection. As noted, charging for commercial access to forest resources which used to be free appears to have become a common practice in the *grandes lotes*. Even shareholders were expected to pay these fees, and farmers who were not *conduenos* had also to pay for the cropland. In effect, these were new internal taxes. At the same time, Veracruz's tax system was being thoroughly reorganized. This process of fiscal reform culminated in late 1886 and early 1887, when—as part of an agreement at the federal level—the *alcabalas* and other indirect taxes were for the most part abolished. Various direct levies replaced them: some of the old ones—for example, property taxes—were restructured, and a number of new ones—such as business license fees and personal taxes—were imposed. Simultaneously, state and municipal authorities stepped up their efforts at collection. As a result of all these changes, state—and in some cases municipal—revenues increased dramatically.[18] Many Totonac farmers resented these taxes, which affected them in ways the old *alcabalas* had not. Three were felt to be particularly burdensome: the property tax, the personal tax, and the coffee and tobacco tax.

The rural property tax was of course not new, but communal lands had not been subject to it. With the establishment of the *grandes lotes*, the shareholders had become landowners and as such also taxpayers. With *apoderados* and municipal authorities pressing for payment, the *conduenos* quickly discovered the paradoxical consequences of ownership. That things should be so was neither self-evident nor commonsensical, and this made some long for the exemptions of the old regime. It also did not help that the method for assessing rural property values was apparently modified in these years, generally resulting in higher tax bills.[19] Furthermore, it was tempting and easy for *lote* administrators to inflate the amounts due, pocketing the difference; they kept their own accounts and dealt directly with local treasury officials who were not always known for their rectitude. To make matters even worse, the *conduenazgo*'s property tax burden was not distributed equitably among the shareholders. With the connivance of the *apoderados*, non-resident *condueños*—including town merchants—often did not pay their share, forcing local farmers to contribute more.[20] The bitter irony of this was not lost on everyone.

The personal tax was a levy on salaries and other forms of individual income, part of what was then called "moral capital." It was first established in June 1875, as a one and a half percent tax on personal earnings. Other than civil servants, who had no choice, most people seem to have ignored it, although it appears that in some cantons—including Zongolica, Chicontepec, Tantoyuca, Pueblo Viejo, and Papantla—Indians were often made to pay it. On the whole, however, this tax initiative was a failure; already in 1878, Governor Mier y Terán acknowledged that the law as it stood was "truly unenforceable." The revenues it produced were rather meager.[21]

After years of discussion, the personal tax was completely revamped in May 1885. Law No. 12 imposed a head tax on males between the ages of eighteen and sixty. In place of the old percentage of earnings formula, the new tax rate would be based on a man's occupation. Four broad classes of "trades and professions" were established, with a flat rate assigned to each category: from twelve and a half cents a month at the lowest end to between one and three pesos a month at the highest. This type of personal tax was much easier to assess, since it involved no individual calculations. Moreover, municipal treasurers were placed in charge of collecting it, and as an incentive the state government agreed to cede 20 percent of those revenues to the Ayuntamientos.[22]

This time, the results were very gratifying, at least from a fiscal point of view. By 1887, personal taxes had already become the second largest source of revenue for the state of Veracruz. Only business license fees produced more tax income statewide. Significantly, between 1887 and 1889 revenues from the new head tax exceeded those from urban and rural property taxes combined.[23] In Papantla, the growth of personal tax collections was also notable, even considering that it was one of the few cantons where the old one-and-a-half percent tax seems to have been paid. Table 5.2 shows the available fiscal data.[24]

As these numbers indicate, Papantla's personal tax revenues increased more or less fivefold in a very brief period of time. This meant not only that more people were being charged, but also that those who had paid the old tax—largely Totonacs—were being asked to contribute more as well as more often (monthly). As will be seen, this immediately became a source of great discontent.

A third conflictive levy was the coffee and tobacco tax. It was first imposed back in 1871 as a special *alcabala* to fund local public education. Every load of coffee or tobacco shipping out of towns in Veracruz would be subject to a toll. From the beginning, disputes over collection and alloca-

TABLE 5.2

Personal Tax Revenues from the Cantón of Papantla

Period	Old or New Law	State revenue	State revenue as percent of total revenue	Total revenue
1881				
(2nd semester)	Old	$1,199.23		$ 1,199.23
1882				
(1st semester)	Old	$ 834.38		$ 834.38
1885				
(1st semester)	Old	$1,084.85		$ 1,084.85
1885				
(2nd semester)	New	$2,385.25	80%	$ 2,981.56
1886	New			
		$6,146.04	80%	$ 7,682.55
1887	New			
		$6,947.69	80%	$ 8,684.61
1888	New			
		$5,332.93	80%	$ 6,666.16
1889	New			
		$7,165.78	80%	$ 8,957.23
1890	New			
		$8,032.62	80%	$10,040.78

SOURCE: See note 24 to Chapter 5.

NOTE: Date of Old Law is 28 June 1875; date of New Law is 30 May 1885.

tion methods diminished its effectiveness, but in time it did produce a considerable income. At that point, however, it was essentially a consumption tax, and Treasury records in fact labeled it as such. In Papantla, where producers were rarely involved in marketing their own crops, this tax affected Indian tobacco growers only indirectly. A new law tightening the collection mechanisms was enacted in mid-1884, but the tax remained a kind of *alcabala*. As the coffee and tobacco trades expanded, so did this revenue.[25]

The situation changed abruptly in late 1886, as Congress moved to amend Article 124 of the Constitution, forbidding the collection of transit fees. In Veracruz, the legislature rushed to comply by passing Decree No. 66, which among other things transformed the basis of the coffee and tobacco tax from shipments to plantings. Effective January 1, 1887, coffee and tobacco farmers would be taxed directly according to how much land they had placed under cultivation. These acreage-based payments were due before harvest time and irrespective of actual yields. In good years and bad, a new levy was all of a sudden part of the cost of planting. Not surprisingly, farmers saw this tax as unjust and oppressive. Protest took many forms, and during 1887 statewide revenues from coffee and tobacco showed a dramatic decline, in excess of $98,000 pesos.

The government was thus forced to reconsider its strategy, and late that same year the tax basis was once again modified. Producers, however, remained the target. Beginning on January 1, 1888, crops—and not cropland—would be subject to a tax, forty cents per quintal of coffee and thirty cents per quintal of tobacco. These fees were payable after the harvest, either by the growers or—if agreed upon—by those who financed and purchased their crops. In any case, the tax came out of the farmer's earnings. Municipal treasurers could keep 8 percent of all such revenues as honorariums, and the rest was to be divided as follows: 80 percent would go to the Ayuntamientos (for local primary schools) and the remaining 20 percent to the state treasury. This new fiscal arrangement gave local authorities a powerful incentive to enforce the law. Overall, though, direct coffee and tobacco taxes would end up yielding much less total revenue than the old *alcabala*. In Governor Juan Enríquez's eyes, this meant that the shift had benefited taxpayers. For farmers, however, especially small-scale growers who did not process and market their crops, the net effect of this change was an increased tax burden.[26]

Along with disfranchisement and direct taxes, a third development tied to the establishment and operation of *condueñazgos* was the growing intervention of town merchants in land and agriculture-related affairs inside the *grandes lotes*. In part, this was simply the product of increased business activity. With more market-oriented cultivation, more cash advances for producers, more mortgages and sales of vanilla plantings, and more forest-based enterprises, the tiered networks of commercial relations and financial obligations spreading out from Papantla and Gutiérrez Zamora became both wider and more visible.[27] Moreover, many of the town merchants became *condueños* in their own right, some thanks to the original *reparto* and others by purchasing shares of ownership. Foreign *colonos* and ambitious local entrepreneurs began to buy ex-communal stocks as well.[28] This allowed them a more direct access to the *lotes'* land and resources. Given their disproportionate economic and political influence, they were thus able to establish a strong presence in the *condueñazgos*, often at the expense of—but at times also in alliance with—some of their fellow owners. For those not directly favored or with rival business interests, as well as for the many who became disfranchised in the course of the 1880s, this relatively swift and perplexing turn of events must have felt like an invasion, Trojan-horse style.

Thus, against the background of Papantla's late colonial and early re-publican history, these years of *condueñazgo* reveal themselves as an epoch of profound and rapid change. Life in the old lands of the *pueblo* was no longer what it used to be; all of a sudden—or so it must have seemed—there were more taxes, highly restrictive and exclusionary land-use rules, covetous non-Indian *condueños*, and powerful *apoderados*. Business deals—in farming, logging, forest extraction, ranching, and credit—were everywhere, brusquely reshaping both social relationships and the natural landscape. Some embraced these changes, many did not, but only a relative few had readily anticipated them. Ironically, the agreement to create *con-dueñazgos* had appeared on the surface to represent a victory for continu-ity and tradition, the introduction of seemingly cosmetic legal modifications designed to truncate government attempts to implement a radical transfor-mation of communal land tenure by means of an individual land division. Shortsighted though it was, this widespread perception helped to ensure a remarkably trouble-free transition to joint-stock ownership. But as the true significance of the transition to *condueñazgo* made itself evident, surprise quickly gave way to discontent, and in some cases also to active opposition.

Two uprisings—one quashed, the other aborted—shook Papantla in the course of the 1880s. Despite obvious differences in strategy, rhetoric, and fate, these movements had much in common: a repudiation of specific re-cent changes, a desire to reconstitute the past, and probably also a core group of supporters, for whom the ex-communal *condueñazgos* embodied all that had gone wrong of late. Together, they shed light on the nature of the bitter social conflicts that arose during these years. The first rebellion broke out at the close of 1885, led by a charismatic preacher named Anto-nio Díaz Manfort. Many were killed or arrested. During 1887, a second dissident movement took shape in and around the ex-communal *rancherías* of Chote y Mesillas, this one organized by Antonio Vásquez and Miguel Herrera. Thanks to last-minute negotiations, a violent clash with local au-thorities was narrowly averted, but deep feelings of injustice would persist. What follows is a brief examination of these events.

The Lure of the Past

Antonio Díaz Manfort was a religious healer, a *curandero*, a man known across the lowlands of the old Totonacapan as the Médico Santo. The rebellion led by him gave voice to a wide range of grievances. His ser-monic manifestos denounced the establishment of church fees (for baptism, marriage, and burial) and the idea of civil matrimony; the growing power and influence of foreigners, especially merchants; the imposition of assorted taxes and permit fees; the division of communal territory; the erosion of

Catholic belief and authority; and the regulation of religious processions. The rhymes he composed—perhaps meant to be sung—bemoaned the dissolution of traditional social bonds and kinship obligations, the sudden rise of jealousy and rivalries even among members of the same family: "Good manners are no longer found / among the youth of the family / today envy reigns supreme / along with discord and wickedness / this is certainly the truth." Everywhere he looked, there were signs of dislocation: "When a son gets married / he quickly abandons his parents / neglecting the care of his mother / proclaiming with great disgust / I no longer want to obey."[29] The world as he knew it—and as he thought it should be—was being turned upside down. Undermined by recent changes, the old local social order was collapsing. Díaz Manfort's ill-fated movement was a last-ditch messianic effort to resurrect a disappearing past.

The rebellion began in late 1885. After an initial skirmish in the neighboring municipality of Martínez de la Torre, Díaz Manfort and a band of supporters made their way north to "the outskirts of Papantla," where on December 30, 1885, he declared war on the government, decrying "the injustice of the laws of Porfirio Díaz" and calling for an armed revolution to usher in an era of social and moral restoration. His *proclama* stated that he had already gathered 7,000 men, but this was merely propaganda; Díaz Manfort was in fact trying to recruit armed volunteers, offering to pay them at the rate of four reales per day. An itinerant preacher, Díaz Manfort had small groups of committed followers in several lowland *pueblos* belonging to the cantons of Misantla, Jalacingo, and Papantla. Most of them, however, were not from Papantla. All in all, the rebels probably numbered no more than 125, and it is unlikely that they were ever together in one place.[30] According to government sources, Díaz Manfort and a cluster of rebels managed to hide out in the hills surrounding Papantla until April 1886; during these months, their ranks were said to have increased somewhat. At least some of these local supporters came from Chote y Mesillas.

Papantla's government was then in the hands of merchant Agapito Fontecilla y Vidal, a Spanish national who was both *jefe político* and municipal mayor. Fearing an attack on the town, Fontecilla ordered the national guard to pursue Díaz Manfort. These local security forces were commanded by Captain Pablo Hernández Olmedo, one of the Totonac architects of the *condueñazgos*. In late April, Hernández Olmedo's men captured fifteen rebels, chasing away the rest. Among those arrested was Francisco Pérez Zepeta, a resident of Las Mesillas and one of the original *condueños* of lot 15.[31] By then, Díaz Manfort had moved down to the Cantón of Misantla, where he tried to organize other military actions. On May 2, local militia forces managed to track down the Médico Santo. In the ensuing shootout, Díaz Manfort was killed. His Misantla followers were then gradually arrested and the rebellion was at last suppressed.[32]

Aside from the Chote connection, which is very suggestive, very little is known about the Papantla phase of the movement. Díaz Manfort's core supporters came mainly from Misantla, and only a few documents connected with events in Papantla have survived the ravages of time. Still, analyzed in context, Díaz Manfort's rambling manifestos are revealing. Beyond their messianic and redemptive rhetorical style, they in fact give voice to many of the concrete and mundane local grievances generated by the social, economic, and fiscal developments of the early to mid-1880s. A few examples will suffice.

When Díaz Manfort calls for the abolition of all taxes ("We reject the levies and all of the taxes of the government of Porfirio Díaz"), one has to recall that a burdensome personal tax had just come into effect (June 1885), and that municipal authorities had every incentive to enforce its collection. Likewise, only recently had Totonac farmers become liable for the dreaded property tax. Elsewhere in Veracruz, new taxes had aroused protest as well. In nearby Tuxpan, anger over the personal tax fueled an armed uprising in which the *jefe político* was killed (July 1885).[33]

When Díaz Manfort declares that small-scale butchers should no longer pay duties of any sort, one has to bear in mind that slaughterhouse fees had recently been increased substantially. On top of the old butchering fee, for which new rates had been established in 1883 and 1884, an additional tax—equivalent to 20 percent of the basic levy—was imposed in May 1885. This new *derecho de matanza* was meant to fund public education. As it turns out, one of the Médico Santo's followers in Colipa (Misantla) was precisely a disgruntled butcher.[34]

When Díaz Manfort attacks the privileges currently enjoyed by foreigners, protesting that it is they who should be paying rent, he is addressing a situation increasingly prevalent in the new *grandes lotes* and other ex-communal territories, in which "Mexicans" (he never uses the word "Totonacs") were in many cases forced to pay for land that until recently had been considered theirs, while "foreigners" and "*gachupines*" (a derogatory name for Spaniards) had gained greater access to it.[35] And when Díaz Manfort vows to revert the land divisions ("We reject the breakup of communal lands, and we vow to make these lands entirely free, like they used to be"), his words call attention to a paradoxical—and upsetting—consequence of *condueñazgo* landholding; namely, that with the *reparto* came taxes, fees, regulations, and *colonos*, and the land was no longer free, not even for the so-called owners. If private property meant taxes, exclusion, and privileges for the few, then the whole idea was nothing but an evil trick. Hence his resolve to undo these developments: "The lands are declared free; no man should meddle with them, no matter how rich he may be, nor should the government intervene in this, because only God has the right to get involved in the land."

Judging from the manifestos, these were some of the specific issues that animated Díaz Manfort's revolt. Religious matters—church fees, processions, piety—also featured prominently in these texts. Considered as a whole, two main themes underlay Díaz Manfort's diverse grievances: the right to freedom (from exactions) and the necessity of returning to the moral traditions of the past. "Freedom, Rights, and Religion" ("Livertad Fueros y Religion") is how he entitled the second of his *proclamas*. Unjust laws, widespread greed, and selfishness had undermined the foundations of the good society of old, and Díaz Manfort was taking up arms to rebuild them. Thus, his crusade was less a defense than a reconquest of what had been lost. The enemy, he recognized, was also within: the evils to be eradicated were internal (the strained bonds of family and community) as well as external (the despotism of the government and of the rich). Viewed in this way, the land *reparto* was both a symptom and an agent of injustice and social decay. These were years of rapid socioeconomic change and growing government intrusiveness; those two wrenching processes were, at bottom, the object of Díaz Manfort's attacks. Pulled asunder by this confluence of forces, the old ways of Papantla were now unraveling. El Médico Santo rose to stop this, but he could not.

Tax grievances would also play a central role in the unrest that surfaced around Chote y Mesillas during 1887 and early 1888.[36] In Papantla, as elsewhere, the new tax on coffee and tobacco plantings (effective January 1, 1887) was not well received. Many refused to pay it and were fined. In addition, as the tax assessments were based on the surface area placed under cultivation, treasury officials had the plantings measured, billing farmers for the cost of this procedure. These exactions produced much disaffection. To complicate matters, in October of that year torrential rains caused damage to many crops, yet this brought no tax relief, since acreage planted was the only factor that collectors were supposed to consider. By December, the acrimony produced by the new tax had become a serious concern, and state authorities sent an inspector general—one Sr. Malpica—to investigate and deal with the situation.

At the same time, there were other signs of rising discontent, not just with taxes in general but with the basic organization and governance of land tenure under the *condueñazgo*. In practice, the regulations implemented by Chote y Mesillas' board of directors had favored a privileged group of residents and town merchants, generally at the expense of other *condueños* and of numerous disfranchised farmers. New taxes and fees proliferated, but few shareholders seemed to obtain any benefits. Where was all this money going? Moreover, the shift from communal to private property had promised to deliver a degree of freedom from municipal intrusion in landholding and use questions, but—if anything—the fiscal arm of the government now reached further and deeper than it ever had before.

To some, this turn of events simply did not make sense. Then there was the troubling matter of San Miguel and San Lorenzo, the supposedly non-communal *condu'eñazgo* on the western border of Chote y Mesillas. Ten years earlier Simón Tiburcio—one of the prime engineers of the *grandes lotes*—had bought this territory with money collected from farmers all over Papantla, and now he ran it as his fiefdom, selling its best trees to the highest bidder. There, being a shareholder was worth nothing. Was the *condu'eñazgo* perhaps an inherently corrupt legal scheme, a thinly disguised form of usurpation? More disturbing still, had not those lands once belonged to the *pueblo* of Papantla? There were some in Chote y Mesillas and other nearby *rancherías* who believed that both San Miguel and neighboring Agua Dulce used to be communal property. If so, why had they been excluded from consideration at the time of the *reparto*? In and around Chote y Mesillas, these vexing developments prompted a variety of desperate responses. Some, like *condueño* Francisco Pérez Zepeta, joined Díaz Manfort in a fight to overthrow this dreadful new system. When that failed, a new plan quickly emerged, using the law as a means of deliverance.

The general idea was to obtain copies of Papantla's original land-grant titles—ideally the *mercedes reales*—from the National Archive in Mexico City, in order to show that the *reparto* of the 1870s had not been lawful. If the communal land boundaries set during disentailment did not match those found in the archives, as some suspected, then the *pueblo* had been robbed and the whole legal basis of the *condu'eñazgos* could—or should—be called into question. Before long, many other lofty hopes would also be pinned on these titles. They would prove that these lands rightfully belonged to Papantla's natives, paving the way for a reversion of the *grandes lotes* to communal status. And once this had been accomplished, a number of oppressive levies—in particular, the property tax—would, of course, disappear. If only these historic documents could be located, a radical restoration of land-tenure rules and fiscal exemptions might be brought about. Or so many were led to believe.

The drive to find Papantla's property titles appears to have been led initially by Antonio Vásquez, a Spanish-speaking Totonac from Las Mesillas who was *condueño* of lot 15. With donations from local supporters, Vásquez traveled to Mexico City in late March 1887, visiting the National Archive to request a search for all documents pertaining to the lands of his *pueblo*.[37] It is not clear exactly what Vásquez himself hoped to do once he got them. The search was duly ordered, but the results would be long in coming. In the meantime, Vásquez became acquainted with a retired army captain named Miguel W. Herrera, who proposed to assist the Papantla dissidents in their effort to locate the titles and overturn the prevailing order. Herrera lived in Papantla and knew the Tecolutla basin well; he had served as an aide to General Pedro Hinojosa, currently the Minister of Defense, who had been military commander for northern Veracruz during the Tuxtepec revolution and who now owned the huge Tulapilla estate, just west of Papantla.[38] Touting his connections, Herrera offered to use his influence in Mexico City in order to resolve the Indians' problems. With him now apparently in charge, local expectations quickly soared, as did the sums of money collected around Chote y Mesillas, ostensibly to cover travel and other expenses. Herrera was most probably a swindler, preying on desperate country people whose scant knowledge of the law and lack of political patrons made them easy victims. In due course, some of his erstwhile followers would regard him as such.[39] At the time, however, his willingness to become involved must have seemed like a stroke of good fortune. It was not all that clear how the legal case would be made and won, but the sketchiness of the whole enterprise was lost or obscured in translation, and Herrera's alleged influence inspired confidence. Given the growing burden of taxation, it is not surprising that at least some farmers would have found the plan appealing and worth supporting; they knew that the property tax was a byproduct of the *condueñazgo*, and they surely relished the prospect of returning to a system of tax-free land tenure. Their participation reflected not simply a degree of ignorance, but—more significantly—mounting exasperation. In late August, five months after Vásquez's first trip to the capital, Herrera made his own request for information regarding Papantla's communal land boundaries. To show off his connections, he got Ignacio Mariscal, the Minister of Foreign Relations, to write a brief note to the archive's director ordering a search for the documents in question.[40] This was really unnecessary, but it served to impress his clients. Despite Mariscal's intervention, the land titles were not produced because none had yet been found. And so the wait continued. Meanwhile, the weather turned sour and tax pressures mounted.

Local political jockeying would add kindling to the fire. Papantla's government was then largely in the hands of vanilla traders; their deals, alliances, and rivalries were frequently the source of Byzantine political intrigues. Among Papantla's brash elite, politics was an extension of business, and this was a time of fierce competition. Agapito Fontecilla y Vidal was still the town's mayor, and also the district's *jefe político*; his detractors had tried unsuccessfully to drive him out of office, arguing that Spaniards could not hold elected municipal positions.[41] Like a number of his counterparts, he was also a *condueño*, an investor, and a moneylender. As a merchant, he was free to pursue his own considerable business interests, in and out of the *condueñazgos*, while as a government official, he was charged with administering the affairs of his domain, maintaining public order, and enforcing the law, which included overseeing the collection of taxes. These were supposed to be two separate endeavors, but often it was hard for anyone to tell them apart, and a little malicious rumor-mongering could make it even harder.

When Fontecilla learned of the land titles scheme, he moved to stop the fundraising and detain the organizers, but Herrera and Vásquez eluded capture. In early October, back in Mexico City, Vásquez and his associates complained to Porfirio Díaz that the *jefe político* was jailing their followers in an attempt to thwart efforts to claim lands that were legitimately theirs. Fontecilla, they said, wanted those lands for himself. Governor Enríquez reported to Díaz that this was all part of a scam dreamed up by Herrera, Vásquez, and a Mexico City partner, and he denied that any arrests had taken place.[42] Still, the tax grievances driving the whole endeavor were very real, and they would not simply go away. As soon as the inspector general arrived in Papantla, probably around the middle of December, "a multitude of Indians," many from Chote y Mesillas, gathered to tell Malpica that the payments, fees, and fines demanded were both "excessive" and "unjust." By Fontecilla's own account, they held the *jefe político* personally responsible for those exactions, saying that he had imposed them in order to harm their interests. Malpica proceeded to contradict every one of these claims, explaining that those were now the laws of the land. The Totonacs left empty-handed. Fontecilla's report blamed the secret Machiavellianism of his enemies, who were spreading falsehoods to "excite the passions" and "exploit the ignorance" of the Indians. Perhaps this was in part the case, but much more than political intrigue was surely at play. Merchant encroachment and high taxes had come hand in hand after the establishment of *condueñazgos*, and Fontecilla—big businessman and top politician—was the clearest embodiment of both. It is not hard to imagine how some might have reached the conclusion—with or without outside help—that through him the two were directly connected. Significantly, he even owned some land in the vicinity of Chote y Mesillas, either in the *lote* or adjacent to it, which lent plausibility to the accusation that he had a personal stake in blocking the title search.[43] A few days later, rumors began circulating that Malpica had deposed Fontecilla and the political heads of the *congregaciones*; according to reports, some people were refusing to pay the personal tax. All that Fontecilla could think of (or would say) was that Malpica's prudent words had been deliberately mistranslated. There was, certainly, a lack of understanding.

Back in Chote y Mesillas, a tax revolt was brewing. Herrera and Vásquez had just returned from Mexico City and were quick to seize the opportunity. Sought by the authorities and unable to deliver on their promise, they apparently persuaded the locals that Fontecilla was acting against them to prevent the re-communalization of the *lotes* (and perhaps also of San Miguel), and with it the abolition of taxes. According to Governor Enríquez, they further claimed that Fontecilla's ultimate aim was to usurp the Totonacs' lands. Soon thereafter, an armed mobilization got underway. On December 30, two years to the date of Díaz Manfort's *proclama* in Papantla, Fontecilla received the first report of impending trouble.[44] The following day he heard that about two hundred men had congregated at El Chote; the leaders were Herrera, Vásquez, and José M. Salazar. Fontecilla hurriedly organized his forces, asking Captain Pablo Hernández Olmedo to raise an army of Indian volunteers to protect the town, and then sent an urgent telegram to the governor. "The apparent pretext" of this revolt, he wrote, "is the payment of taxes, but one can detect aspects of a caste war, because the ringleaders are saying that they will bring down the authorities and then only the Indians will govern."[45] The message was an exercise in obfuscation: at that point, Herrera and Vásquez wanted mainly to get rid of Fontecilla, and while the push to reject taxes was certainly cause for grave concern, this was by no means a caste war.

Herrera quickly realized that a bloody confrontation was imminent, and this was certainly not what he had bargained for. The next day, January 1, 1888, he sent Fontecilla a message offering to call off the uprising and recognize his authority in exchange for a general amnesty. After consulting with Xalapa, Fontecilla agreed, and following an exchange of letters a meeting was set for January 3. Herrera's letter stated that the main aim of the would-be rebels from Chote y Mesillas—or at least his—had been to unseat the *jefe político*. He did not even mention taxes. At the meeting, he said that they had been misled to believe that their lives were in danger, which is why they had rebelled. Vásquez and Salazar, however, did bring up the subject of taxes. According to Fontecilla, they pointedly wanted to know which levies would be eliminated, and when they were told that this could not be done, they tried at least to negotiate some reductions. The *jefe político* then lectured them on the social benefits of taxation, but evidently they were not impressed. As Fontecilla tells it, Herrera declared that his followers had been instructed to "kill all the *gachupines* and burn down the houses of the *de razón*" if they heard a shot, since that would signal that their leaders had been killed. The Indians, Herrera added, were upset that the *gachupines* were enriching themselves at their expense. The situation outside was clearly very delicate; face to face with Hernández Olmedo's loyalist forces, a throng of rebels waited by the plaza expecting to see some concrete results. For them, the rebellion was, finally, about taxes.

The outcome was hence an extremely awkward one; the rebels were offered amnesty, but the taxes would remain. Herrera was then faced with the unenviable task of demobilizing his clients. Not surprisingly, this was not easy, for having gone this far, many refused to give up their high hopes. An angry standoff ensued, but Herrera eventually prevailed on them to return to El Chote. According to Fontecilla, the "seditious chiefs" apparently had assured their followers that some taxes would indeed come to an end. At any rate, the tax revolt had been effectively aborted. Wisely, Herrera and Vásquez soon departed for Mexico City, where they sought out General Hinojosa's protection.[46]

Around Chote y Mesillas, however, tensions continued to run high. Pressured by Porfirio Díaz's inquiries and alarmed by vague rumors of a broader Indian conspiracy in the making, Governor Enríquez personally intervened to defuse the crisis. He immediately removed Agapito Fontecilla from the post of *jefe político*, and then ordered the new *jefe* and the local treasury administrator to reduce the property taxes paid by Papantla's Indians. At the same time, the reform of the coffee and tobacco tax basis had come into effect with the new year, eliminating one conspicuous source of vocal discontent. Perhaps these steps would help to ease the situation. In case they did not, Enríquez took additional precautions. He had forty national guardsmen and twenty state *rurales* posted in the town, and he asked President Díaz to send federal troops. On February 21, 1888, one hundred infantrymen from General Rosalino Martínez's Veracruz battalion arrived in Papantla, where they remained stationed for at least one month. Furthermore, the governor issued arrest warrants against Herrera, Vásquez, and Salazar, even though they had been promised amnesty. Putting them on trial in Papantla would show the Indians that the government's response to their demands was not motivated by fear.[47] No one was immediately detained and no trials were held, but sometime later Antonio Vásquez was reportedly apprehended and summarily shot.[48]

In the short run, these measures stifled the opposition movement, but before the end of the year the search for land titles was underway once again. After fruitless inquiries at the National Archive, Herrera, Vásquez, and a number of other Totonac *condueños* from Papantla turned to Fomento. In mid-August, they wrote to the minister in charge, requesting any original documents that would show the pueblo's "true boundaries." They argued that in the *reparto* of the *condueñazgos* carried out on the basis of Pascoli's 1876 map, "a sizable extension of land was taken from us in order to benefit certain individuals." This map was spurious, they said, since it was drawn without consulting any property records, and yet Papantla's authorities continued to rely on it.[49] But Fomento swiftly refused to get involved, claiming a lack of jurisdiction. At this point, a discredited Miguel Herrera faded away, having failed to deliver on his many promises.

His Totonac associates pressed on, however. The root causes of these farmers' discontent remained unaltered: the *condueñazgo* system, its taxes, fees, illegitimate design, venal governance, and exclusionary practices. And regardless of Miguel Herrera's self-interested and possibly fraudulent representations, some would interpret the local government's interference with their plan as an indication that they were on to something promising. Why else would Fontecilla and his kind have opposed it so vehemently? Perhaps the law did offer a way to undo the current state of affairs, to regain certain rights to the land, to restrain the covetous pretensions of the newly powerful.

In early November, yet another group of Papantla Totonacs traveled to the National Archive; some had been there previously, with Herrera and Vásquez. This time their leader was Francisco Pérez Zepeta, a well-known veteran of Díaz Manfort's rebellion. Once more they asked to see any and all "documents showing the limits and boundaries of the lands of our community," requesting also certified copies or excerpts that could be used as evidence in the courts. This time they were shown what little had been found: four documents from Tierras and one from Mercedes, but no ancient village titles or vice-regal land grants, and only a few scattered late-eighteenth-century references to boundaries.[50] Most of them could not read those old papers, which in fact contained nothing of great value. Still, they wanted copies, but to obtain them they needed power of attorney from their community or municipality, and this they did not have. On someone's advice, Pérez Zepeta and his companions appealed directly to the Minister of Foreign Relations, explaining that those copies could help decide the fate of *pueblo* lands which were "currently at risk of being lost for lack of titles and document showing ownership." Their request was immediately granted, and the certified copies were finally issued four months later, in March 1889.[51] The title search—lengthy, expensive, controversial—had at last been completed. It is not clear how many understood or were made to understand this at the time, but—whatever they had thought these records could accomplish—the results were decidedly disappointing. Papantla's communal land titles did not exist.

Hope was not all lost, however. Before long, Pérez Zepeta would find another self-assured Mexico City advocate, who would sell him and his fellow dissidents on a new plan to challenge the legality of the 1870s *reparto* and the resultant *condueñazgo* regime. Law was still the weapon of choice. This time their agent was Severiano Galicia Chimalpopoca, a wily and pugnacious young agronomist and would-be politician from Amecameca who would come to play a prominent role in Papantla's impending land troubles.

In the course of the 1870s and 1880s, a booming vanilla business, progressive disfranchisement, increased taxation, and the growing involvement of town merchants in ex-communal land matters transformed the face of Papantla. The uprisings just analyzed reflect the conflicts and dislocations born of these rapid changes. By the mid-1880s, the socioeconomic organization of the countryside was no longer what it had been for hundreds of years prior to 1870; Papantla's historic pattern of social relations in agriculture was beginning to give ground. Occupational statistics provide clear evidence of this shift. Between 1871 and 1885 the number of men categorized as *jornaleros* (day laborers) in the Cantón of Papantla increased enormously (see Table 5.3).[52]

TABLE 5.3

Jornaleros *and* Labradores *in the Cantón of Papantla, 1871 and 1885*

Census Category	1871	1885
Males with listed jobs	5,119	7,531
Listed as *jornaleros*	242	2,571
Listed as *labradores*	4,487	4,061
Males under 18	5,269	7,121
Males 18–50	4,514	6,393
Males 50+	479	1,007
Total number of males	10,262	14,521

SOURCE: See note 52 to Chapter 5.

It seems unwise to draw too many elaborate conclusions from these figures because the 1885 census figures are almost certainly too low. In particular, Papantla's municipal population appears to have been under-
counted (see Table 4.1); perhaps the introduction of the revamped personal
tax in mid-1885 is part of the reason. The actual number of *labradores* (independent farmers) in the basin was probably higher. Still, the tenfold increase in the number of *jornaleros* stands out as a profoundly significant
development. The definition of *"jornalero,"* in the case of the basin, is not
entirely clear; this was merely a general census category and its meaning
and application varied from place to place. Some were private estate workers, like the hired hands who grew tobacco and chile in the ranchos or haciendas of Espinal. In 1871, 200 of the 242 *jornaleros* listed resided in Espinal. By 1885, there were more of these people, many of them migrant
workers from the Sierra de Puebla, but certainly not 2,500. In all likelihood, most of the men labeled as *"jornaleros"* were those who did not have
ownership rights over the land they farmed, among them—most notably—
the disfranchised youth of the *condueñazgos*. This is probably the new social phenomenon that the census of 1885 is obliquely denoting; all those
who were not *condueños* fell in this broad category: *colonos*, renters,
squatters, and dependent laborers of all kinds. Their numbers had mush-
roomed under the *condueñazgo* property regime. This was not anymore the
Papantla of 1870, the old Papantla; while family-based agriculture continued to be the norm, independent farmers no longer comprised the overwhelming majority of the basin's population.

The 1885 census of occupations reflects other notable social changes.
Whereas back in 1871 a total of 101 persons were described (or described
themselves) as merchants, by 1885 their number had risen to 246. There
were also by then many more "store clerks" and "employees." Significantly,

agricultores—mainly merchants and senior military officers with growing farming interests, in historically private as well as ex-communal territories—appear for the first time. In all, perhaps the most revealing development is the emergence of a sizable class of part- and full-time domestic service workers, largely women: 95 cooks, 271 laundresses, 40 pressers, and a startling 939 domestic servants.[53] José María Bausa would have been extremely pleased. What a difference forty years had made!

Much, of course, remained unaltered. Subsistence-oriented milpa agriculture was still the core of Papantla's economic life, and the dispersed form of settlement that had long defined the basin's social organization showed few signs of weakening. An 1890 report from the *jefe político* bemoaned the absence of population centers in the *congregaciones*, noting that people "generally place their dwellings very far apart from each other, so much so that a *congregación* with 300 or 400 residents takes up an area of four to six leagues."[54] But despite the endurance of these ancient practices, the rural landscape, too, reflected the emergence of newly viable profit-making enterprises. The expansion of cattle ranching and the acceleration of unregulated commercial logging during these years began to eat away at the *monte alto*. The traditional agro-ecologic management of woodland resources associated with slash-and-burn clearings, field rotations, vanilla *acahuales*, and the selective extraction of forest products now had to compete with much more destructive forms of land use. This marked the beginning of Papantla's gradual deforestation.

Scarcely a decade after their establishment, Papantla's *condueñazgos* had become breeding grounds of business and social conflict. In spite of their name, these joint-stock associations of landowners had not displayed much solidarity. There were some who tried hard to bring back the past, or at least to mitigate the burdens of the present, but they did not succeed. Again and again, they would try. Then, in the late 1880s, local groups and state authorities made a fresh effort to carry out an individual *reparto*. But who would get what? And who was to decide? The abolition of communal landholding was in the end a relatively simple and deceptively peaceful process; dissolving the *condueñazgos*, however, would require considerable bloodshed.

6 *Division and Rebellion*

In the course of the 1890s Papantla's troubled ex-communal *con-dueñazgos* were partitioned, as were the *grandes lotes* that had been formed in the rest of the Tecolutla basin's municipalities. Why were these land-holding institutions so short-lived? A zealous and overbearing government commitment to the idea of individual private property has often been cited as the prime cause. This was surely a significant factor, but land tenure policies cannot fully explain the demise of joint ownership in and around Papantla. Otherwise, there would have been no *condueñazgos* to start with and individual plots would have been allocated directly, as was done in many other parts of the state. What state authorities wanted and what they finally accomplished were often two very different things. Elsewhere in Veracruz the *condueñazgo* managed to survive well into the twentieth century. Why not also in Papantla?

The preceding chapter described the kinds of conflict that arose either as a result of or concurrent with the establishment of *condueñazgos* in Papantla. During the 1880s, taxation, land-access rights, *condueñazgo* management practices, the uses and abuses of the law, and merchant encroachment became sources of persistent internal discord. Among the aggrieved, who were numerous, there were some who organized to fight back. Firearms were plentiful, part and parcel of vanilla-growing in Papantla. At the same time, many others had clearly benefited from such trends: merchants as a whole, local power brokers, new and old, and a sizable group of *rancheros* and *labradores* out in the *rancherías*. They had come to dominate the *condueñazgos*, reaping the fruits of the business boom. When the opportunity presented itself, most of them—but not all—would embrace the individual *repartos*. Some—for instance, the town merchants—had favored a land sub-division all along, and from their seats on the Ayuntamiento they became its most ardent promoters. Others, in particular shareholding *labradores*, were more recent—and sometimes reluctant—converts. Caught between twin threats, the plight of the legally dispossessed and the might of commercial interests, they came to see individual *repartos* as a way to safeguard their legal rights to the land.

Before examining the tortuous dissolution of the *grandes lotes*, it will be useful to sketch the development of the vanilla economy after 1890. As shown, in the history of the Tecolutla basin business and land issues have been inextricably intertwined, and this latest period is no exception.

The Ups and Downs of Vanilla, 1890–1910

During the 1880s, Mexico's vanilla production and exports boomed. Average annual exports for this decade were around 50,000 kilograms, of which at least two-thirds came from the basin. In 1888–89 Mexican exports exceeded 70,000 kilograms for the first time ever, and the feat was repeated the following season. Scarcely ten years earlier, a mere 25,000 kilograms was considered a very good annual output. Under the *condueñazgo* regime, Papantla's productive capacity grew at a prodigious rate. Back in 1883, Agapito Fontecilla senior had observed:

As for production in the state of Veracruz, it can be increased at will [*cuanto se quiera*], because the cantons of Papantla and Misantla alone can produce many millions, since both have vast lands that are very good for the cultivation of this product, lands which until recently have been held communally and are now being divided.[1]

Ten years later, Mexico's vanilla exports had doubled, due largely to a phenomenal spread of cultivation across Papantla. With the area under cultivation continually on the increase and with a corresponding expansion of curing facilities, there was every expectation that the 1890s would turn out to be another record decade.

The weather, however, would not do its part. Between 1892 and 1899, a series of droughts, frosts, and even snowstorms descended on large areas of northern Veracruz, repeatedly damaging many crops and perennial plants, among them the delicate vines that produced vanilla. The summer and early fall of 1892 were dry, as were the fall of 1894 and long stretches of the years 1895, 1896, and 1897. In addition, early 1895 brought a serious frost and some snow, and in February 1899 a severe storm left Papantla, Misantla, Chicontepec, Tantoyuca, and a vast area of the Sierra de Puebla covered in snow.[2] As a result, vanilla production and shipments dropped markedly from 1894 through the first few years of the new century. Food and other commercial crops suffered considerably as well. As these natural calamities befell Papantla's farmers, a concerted land subdivision drive was already underway.

The 1890s began promisingly for the vanilla business, and exports surpassed 90,000 kilograms in both 1891–92 and 1892–93, this despite the drought of 1892, which apparently affected the quality of the crop—that is, the percentage of harvested beans turned into cuts—but not its overall volume.[3] The 1893–94 season saw a slight decline in shipments, but the totals were nevertheless quite high. Then disaster struck. New York's *Oil, Paint and Drug Reporter* described it thus:

As to the crop of 1894–95, reports early in the Autumn of drought have since been fully confirmed, and at least one-half of the crop, which is a small one, is "cuts," the balance of whole beans not being as sightly as usual. Reports of recent date state also that such extreme weather as they have lately experienced around Papantla has never been known. Heavy frost and snow have killed the plants, and for the next two years no crops are expected.[4]

Although their dire forecast turned out to be somewhat exaggerated, the impact of drought and frost were nevertheless quite severe. Figure 6.1 shows yearly vanilla exports for the period 1890–1910.[5]

Mexican statistics show total exports amounting to less than 26,000 kilograms for 1894–95, a fifteen-year low. However, the actual harvest was probably not as short as this figure would suggest; as prices shot up, merchants in Papantla opted to hold on to their stock, delaying deliveries to take advantage of a strengthening export market. Shortly before the start of the 1895–96 cycle, the *Reporter* observed:

It is an open secret that the Mexicans have made the most of their opportunity. They have sent their goods forward in driblets, instead of in round lots, as has been their custom in times past. There is an impression that a considerable quantity of beans has been held back to be shipped whenever the holders think the market here will take at high prices what is offered.[6]

This might explain why exports for 1895–96 climbed back up to around 80,000 kilograms, a volume that was more or less normal for the early 1890s; these included part of the 1894–95 crop. In terms of production, however, the figure is deceiving; the damage was real, and output would remain low for several years. To make matters even worse, long periods of drought followed the frosts of early 1895, making it impossible to replant much of what had been lost. The years 1896 and 1897 were also fairly dry. In consequence, exports plummeted again in 1896–97 and 1897–98 (34,710 and 18,887 kilograms, respectively). In an 1898 open letter sent to New York, Papantla's most prominent vanilla traders explained that "it will take some time to replace them [the lost vines], and then three or four years must elapse before they begin to yield crop."[7] The recovery was slow, and the astonishing blizzard of 1899 dealt the business a further setback. The U.S. Consul in Tuxpan estimated that only 60 percent of the vanilla vines (and half of the tobacco plants) survived the cold weather of that year.[8] The 1898–99 and 1899–1900 seasons were decidedly lackluster, and 1900–01/1901–02 were both remarkably lean years. All in all, Mexico's average annual exports between 1894–95 and 1901–02 were a mere 39,120 kilograms. Unusually bad weather had left its mark. Needless to say, vanilla was not the only crop affected.

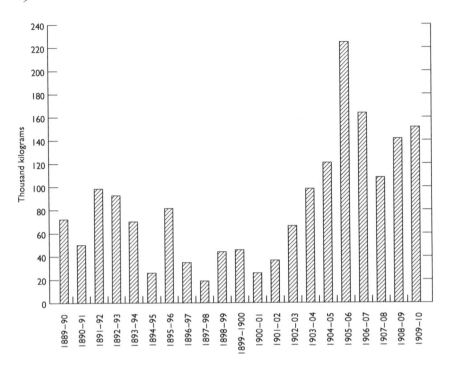

FIGURE 6.1 Mexico's vanilla exports, 1889–1910

Beginning in 1902, vanilla production began to grow once more, return-ing at last to its previous course. By 1902–03, exports had regained the magnitude of the early 1890s, upwards of 90,000 kilograms. The following season, Mexican exports surpassed 100,000 kilograms for the first time, and just one year later (1905–06) recorded shipments jumped to an amaz-ing 224,710 kilograms. All of a sudden, Papantla was awash with vanilla. Henceforth and until the 1960s, harvests would normally yield well over 100,000 kilograms of cured beans.

In general terms, this second boom of the 1900s can be seen as the cul-mination of a process of fast growth that began in earnest back in the 1870s. Figure 6.2 displays average annual exports by decade from the 1820s through the 1900s. It illustrates the evolution of Mexico's vanilla economy from Independence to the eve of the Revolution.

As shown, the average annual rate of growth in output was notably rapid for the 1880s and the 1900s. During the 1900s, two specific developments seem to have assisted this trend. First, the scarcity and the high prices gener-ated by the climatic disturbances of the mid- to late 1890s appear to have triggered a significant expansion of cultivation, a process that bore fruit in the years after 1901, when many new plants reached maturity. Second, hand

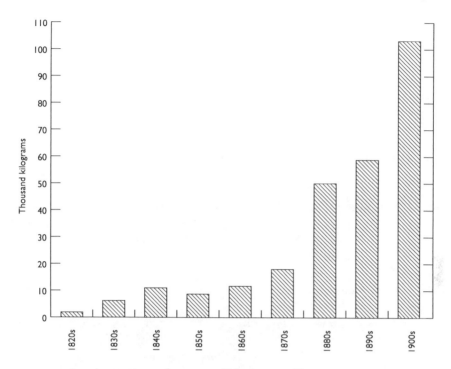

FIGURE 6.2 Average annual exports of Mexican vanilla, 1820s–1900s

pollination began to be practiced in the area of Papantla around this time. The immigrant growers of Gutiérrez Zamora were apparently the earliest converts to this more labor-intensive form of cultivation. In 1910 artificial fertilization was not yet common—let alone widespread—in the Cantón of Papantla, but its incipient adoption probably accounts for part of the growth witnessed in that decade. In Karl Kaerger's estimation, based on a visit to the French colony at San Rafael, artificial pollination normally increased yields by a factor of ten.[9] In Papantla, the transformations in land tenure and use brought about through the establishment, management, and eventual dissolution of the *condueñazgos* produced a large pool of farmhands: the disenfranchised, the dispossessed, and sierra migrants. These recent social changes made hand pollination economically feasible. For those who could afford the necessary labor power, the rewards were bound to be abundant.

Throughout this period, the United States remained by far the principal destination of Mexican vanilla (see Appendix Table A.9). At the same time, the U.S. market expanded at a much faster rate than Mexico's vanilla economy. Average annual imports—which were 11,300 kilograms for the 1870s and 51,300 kilograms for the 1880s—rose to 83,770 kilograms during the 1890s, to 176,246 kilograms for 1900–04, and to 374,849 kilograms for

1905–09 (see Appendix Table A.8). Virtually all of this vanilla was for internal consumption. Mexican beans had thoroughly dominated this market since the 1860s, when vanilla first attracted the attention of U.S. manufacturers. This favorable situation changed abruptly in the late 1890s when Mexico proved unable to satisfy the ever growing U.S. industrial demand for vanilla. The turning points were the 1896–97 and 1897–98 seasons, the nadir of Mexico's climate-induced production crisis. Faced with recurrent shortages, U.S. importers and extract manufacturers started to turn to colonial vanilla (e.g., Bourbon, Tahiti, Seychelles), beans of lower quality—and cost—which had been previously shunned by the majority of industrial consumers.[10] As will be seen, price differentials also played a large role in this shift. Beginning in 1886–97 and until the 1940s, colonial vanilla imports would always exceed those from Mexico. Figure 6.3 illustrates the transition.

By the time Mexico's vanilla economy returned to a path of growth, the market had changed and the use of Bourbons had become well established. As the *Reporter* noted in late 1910, "Value for value, Mexican beans are supposed to retain a prestige over their rivals as imparting a more delicate bouquet to the extract, but so firmly have Bourbons become established in the formulas of manufacturers throughout the country that minor and occasional shifts in the market, whereby Bourbons might fail temporarily to hold their selling advantage, have seldom resulted in any marked change in the character of buying."[11] The days of near-monopoly were over; even in the United States, Papantla's vanilla now had to compete.

In France, Mexican vanilla retained its luxury status, and with it a tiny— and shrinking—share of the market (see Appendix Tables A.7 and A.9). Mexican vanilla shipments declined in the course of the 1890s, in both relative and absolute terms; whereas in the late 1880s Mexico generally accounted for roughly 6 percent of all French imports, by 1900 the figure was under 1.5 percent. During the lean 1890s, average annual Mexican imports were only 3,762 kilograms; not since the decade of the 1820s had France received so little Mexican vanilla. The vanilla trade with France improved slightly in the 1900s; direct shipments averaged 4,393 kilograms per year, while reexportation from the United States—which resumed after a long hiatus—added on the average another 14,473 kilograms annually. Overall, however, Mexican beans rarely captured more than 5 percent of the huge French business in any of these years. By 1910, French vanilla was flooding the world's markets, Papantla's impressive second boom notwithstanding. Mexico's export trade had become almost exclusively confined to the United States, but even there the "original vanilla of commerce" no longer reigned supreme.

Another way to trace the evolution of Mexico's vanilla business in these years is through prices. Price histories shed light on the meaning of broad,

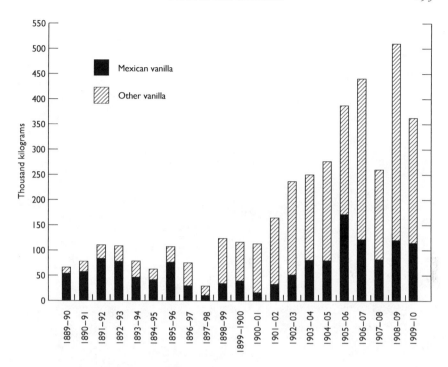

FIGURE 6.3 U.S. vanilla imports, 1889–1910

seemingly impersonal export volume trends for merchants and producers involved in the local trade. As such, they can help to integrate economic data into social analysis. In the case of vanilla, only wholesale New York prices are available as a more or less complete series, but these do provide a very good indication of the likely fluctuation of prices down the entire chain of commercial transactions that culminated in the shipment of vanilla cases for consignment in lower Manhattan.

Not surprisingly, the figures show a good inverse correlation between export volumes and prices. As noted, the boom of the 1880s had led to a gradual yet significant decline in prices; the days of US$30 or even US$20 per pound of fine Mexican vanilla were gone, never to return. Ordinary grades of whole vanilla, which had sold for US$6–8 per pound in 1886, fetched only around US$4 per pound in late 1891, when it was becoming apparent that a record harvest (98,000 kilograms) was in the works. As will be seen, complaints about a continual drop in the prices Papantla merchants paid for green vanilla surfaced during that year's violent revolt. On the whole, the bountiful early 1890s represented a historic low point for vanilla prices. "We cannot remember," noted the *Reporter* in April 1891,

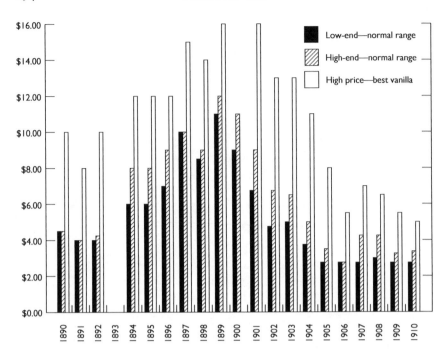

FIGURE 6.4 Mexican whole beans, New York prices, 1890–1910 (U.S. dollars per pound)

"when the article has been as cheap as it is at present."[12] However, another decade would pass before prices would resume their downward spiral. In the meantime, severe shortages sharply reversed this trend. Figures 6.4 and 6.5 show the range of whole and cut bean prices in New York for the period 1890–1910.[13] "High price" represents the top asking price for the best whole vanilla in any given year. Not very many beans qualified for such consideration, but the fluctuations in this category are nevertheless significant. Prices rose from US$8 per pound in 1891 to a formidable US$16 per pound in 1899 and 1901, then dropped back to US$8 per pound by 1905 and down to US$5 per pound by 1910. The "normal range" is more important, because the vast majority of whole beans sold at those prices. The same fluctuations are observed: from US$4 per pound in 1891 up to US$10 per pound in 1897, and peaking at US$11–$12 per pound in 1899, then dropping to US$4.75–$6.75 per pound by 1902 and settling at between US$2.75 and US$4.25 per pound from 1905 to 1910. The market for cuts (*picadura*) follows a similar pattern.

Two periods, in particular, deserve attention: the late 1890s and the late 1900s. Already in 1894–95, the first season of relative scarcity, industrial

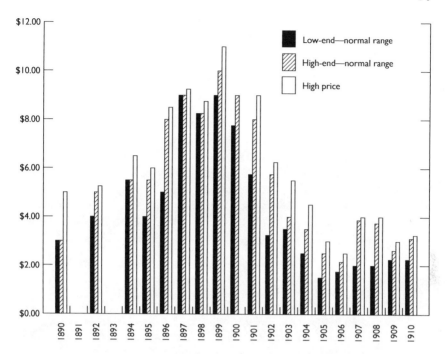

FIGURE 6.5 Mexican cuts, New York prices, 1890–1910 (U.S. dollars per pound)

consumers in the United States began to complain about the high price of Mexican vanilla; vanillin was then a fairly new and infinitely cheaper substitute, and some manufacturers were becoming interested in it. Still, as the *Reporter* noted, "Certain manufacturers must have vanilla beans."[14] Papantla's merchants took full advantage of this situation, driving a hard bargain in order to increase their profits. "During the past year [1895]," explained the *Reporter*, "they [the basin's merchants] have, with one or two exceptions, worked in harmony, and have consigned the bulk of their cut beans to one firm here; the whole beans have likewise been confined pretty closely within the limits of one channel." Pedro Tremari was apparently the mastermind of this strategy. As a result, "high prices [US$6–$8 per pound for the ordinary grades of whole beans] have been obtained for the stock, as dealers were obliged to make purchases to supply their customers." Looking ahead, the *Reporter* cautioned:

There is a possibility that higher prices may be realized for beans, but how much of an advance will take place may depend in some measure on the consumers. They may be willing to pay ten dollars per pound for whole beans, but should the market go above that figure, they might be tempted to turn to substitutes, such as vanilline.[15]

By the late 1890s, ordinary whole Mexican prices had reached US$12, and the best beans were being offered at US$16 per pound. Even the lowly cuts were very expensive—US$9–$10 per pound, three times what they had sold for at the start of the decade. Faced with skyrocketing prices, industrial consumers began to turn away from Mexican vanilla, substituting it with Bourbon beans or synthetic vanillin.

Trade statistics show that U.S. imports of French vanilla increased abruptly in 1898–99 and expanded progressively thereafter (see Appendix Table A.8). A price analysis suggests why. Between 1898 and 1900, the gap between Mexican and Bourbon prices widened considerably (see Figure 6.6). Whereas Bourbon whole beans and Mexican cuts had once sold at a similar range of prices, by 1899 the Mexican *picadura* had become twice as expensive as colonial vanilla. The shift was already in evidence by early 1898. The *Reporter*'s observations are worth quoting at length:

The superiority of [Mexican beans] is unquestioned . . . [but] dealers were compelled to handle the poorer varieties of Bourbon . . . quite against their wills, as the consumers refused to pay . . . the extreme figures demanded by the holders of the stocks of Mexican. There is a limit beyond which people will not go, and that limit has been reached by the Mexican variety. . . . With cheaper varieties of beans and an increasing supply of vanillin, consumers are in a position to refrain from buying Mexican beans until the price is satisfactory to them. The curers have overlooked the fact that vanillin has made heavy inroads on their business since it dropped from $5.50 per ounce to $1.70 or less. Its sale has increased enormously at the lower figures, and they may as well quickly convince themselves it has come to stay. "Necessity is the mother of invention," and extract makers have ascertained that a mixture of vanillin extract with that made from the cheaper varieties of beans answers the purpose of a successful substitute for Mexican beans at $15 to $16 a pound in first hands, or almost $20 by the time they would reach the consumer.

These ominous remarks, part of a scathing article blaming curers for "the trouble between the two branches of the trade," were published in response to an open letter—dated January 22, 1898—drafted by Papantla's leading merchants in defense of their market stance. "It is well known," they wrote, "that the Mexican vanilla has the most delicate flavor, and its worth in every market is double or three times greater than that of other vanillas," since "the active principle of Mexican vanilla is not only the most delicate, but also . . . yields a greater percentage of essential oil." "The rise in prices," they went on, "is due to the insignificance of the last crops and the coming ones, economical reasons that regulate the supply and demand." "The value set by Mexican exporters on their vanilla," they concluded, "is not above the market, but is based on sales made in the markets and taking into consideration the relative prices obtained from sales of vanilla and from other sources and the cost of the article in the producing districts, owing to the small crops." The letter was signed by Tremari, Curti, Fuente, Arenal,

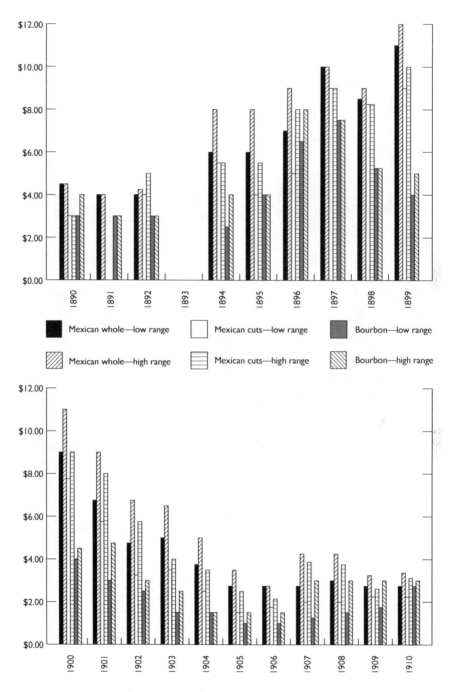

FIGURE 6.6 Normal price ranges for Mexican whole, cuts, and Bourbon vanilla, 1890–1910 (U.S. dollars per pound)

Fontecilla, and seven other top Papantla merchants. In the end, New York would have the last word. Speaking for the dealers, the *Reporter* warned that "the Mexicans may as well make up their minds that if they do not accept lower prices their trade will be beyond recovery in another year or two, and that it is not a question of antipathy to them on the part of dealers and consumers, but is one of business, pure and simple."[16]

The nature of the business was indeed changing. Over the next decade, the value of Mexican vanilla declined considerably, and the price gap vis-à-vis Bourbons nearly disappeared (see Figure 6.6). By 1906, a record year for exports, ordinary Mexican whole beans had dropped to US$2.75 per pound. Never before had Mexican vanilla sold for less in New York. Prices improved somewhat during the following years, thanks in part to the passage of the United States Pure Food and Drug Act of 1906 (effective January 1907), which defined the term "vanilla extract" to include only flavoring products containing a certain minimum quantity of vanilla-bean oil.[17] Still, by the close of 1910, whole beans from Mexico were fetching under US$3.50 per pound. Overall, vastly increased production, the growing popularity of Bourbons (particularly in the newer western U.S. markets), and the latent threat of vanillin accounted for these pricing trends. Mexican vanilla was still far more prestigious and exquisite, but prestige was no longer worth what it used to be.

As a result, Papantla's vanilla trade became increasingly a volume business, not only for town merchants, but also—albeit to a lesser extent—for producers, whose prices must have declined considerably as well. Throughout the 1890s and until 1903, merchant exporters benefited from the progressive devaluation of the peso against the U.S. dollar (1.2:1 in 1890, 2.062:1 in 1900, and 2.375:1 in 1903), but between 1904 and 1910 the peso appreciated slightly (1.991:1–2.008:1) just as New York vanilla prices were tumbling.[18] With the possible exception of the late 1890s, profit margins almost certainly shrank in the course of these decades. Scale thus became a key aspect of the curing and export business.

For the basin's town merchants, this turn of events made financing the vanilla trade more complicated than ever. In order to augment their export volumes, more capital had to be placed in circulation. As vanilla production increased, so did the customary cash advances—*habilitaciones*—extended to cultivators, and also the amount of liquid capital required to purchase green beans at harvest time, since Totonac farmers demanded immediate payment in silver coins. At the same time, unit profits—and hence the rate of capital formation—were probably not any longer what they once had been. With lower returns on investment and higher up-front expenditures, it became increasingly necessary—even urgent—for merchants to find additional sources of capital. Without a hefty cash flow, it was now much harder to compete.

In this context, broader business strategies evolved. On the whole, Papantla's big dealers seem to have reacted to these circumstances in three ways: first, by redoubling their efforts to control—but not necessarily to take over—vanilla production; second, by diversifying their local investments; and third, by developing a more extensive network of credit relations with commercial and banking interests in Teziutlán, Veracruz, and Mexico City. In and of themselves, none of these steps were particularly new, but the intensity with which they were pursued would be, as well as the means. In all three endeavors, land ownership would come to figure prominently.

First, acquiring title to a farmer's cropland became a very effective way of ensuring a steadier—and possibly cheaper—vanilla supply; the farmer would still bear the risks, while the landowning merchant secured the right to purchase the harvest. Second, land became both a speculative and—indirectly— a productive investment. With the advent of petroleum exploration and mining at the turn of the century, potentially oil-rich fields turned into coveted commodities. Papantla's merchants were quick to seize this new opportunity. In addition, logging, cattle ranching—principally the *engorda*—and tobacco farming were three particularly promising emerging lines of business. Third, and perhaps most importantly, land became the principal source of collateral security in credit transactions both within and beyond the confines of the Tecolutla basin. Land mortgages gave merchants access to pools of capital with which to finance—and even expand—their operations.

In these ways, the evolution of Papantla's vanilla economy would spur the dissolution of the already troubled *condueñazgos*. As will be seen, town merchants would be among the most avid architects—and shameless beneficiaries—of a tortuous and often usurpatory process of land parcelization. They were not, however, the sole promoters of full-fledged privatization. Many Indians would also support the idea of an individual *reparto*, though not all for the same reasons. Indeed, the *condueñazgos* were not just dismembered; in many cases, they also crumbled from within.

The End of Condueñazgo

After General Juan de la Luz Enríquez assumed office in December 1884, the government of Veracruz gradually stepped up its efforts to reorganize the legal structure of land tenure across the state. Enríquez sought not only to parcel out the remaining formerly communal territories, but also to sort out the legal status of property in *fundos legales*, *ejidos*, and *censo* or emphyteutic land leases. In all cases, the goal was to privatize the holdings of Ayuntamientos and legally extinguished Indian communities. Addressing the state congress in September 1888, the governor spoke of the need to enact "clear, precise, and equitable" legislation to tackle once and for all the "transcendental task of subdividing the land."[19] His motives were fiscal as much as ideological:

It is well known that two-thirds of the state's territory is composed of lands that belonged to the extinguished communities, lands rented out or leased by municipalities, *ejidos* and *fundos legales* without buildings on them. On the whole, none of these lands figure in our property registers, nor, therefore, are they taxed, gravely diminishing our public revenues.[20]

As the 1880s drew to a close, the revenues produced by Enríquez's earlier tax reforms began to afford his government a somewhat broader scope of action. A relative political and military stability contributed as well. In Mexico City, General Porfirio Díaz had returned to the presidency, this time to stay.

Less than a year later, the state congress complied, approving a new Ley sobre Subdivisión de la Propiedad Territorial (Law No. 26, 4 July 1889), followed by detailed enabling regulations. The law stipulated that all undivided communal territories and—with a few exceptions—all Ayuntamiento lands (the *fundo*, the *ejido*, any *propios*) would have to be promptly turned into individual private properties. The grace period was one year for *ejidos* and two years for the former *tierras de repartimiento*. The penalties for noncompliance were severe: in *ejidos*, lands not properly adjudicated would become public, to be claimed by anyone; in communal areas, the holders would forfeit their rights of ownership and any undivided territories would be put up for sale by the respective Ayuntamiento. Similar punitive clauses had been routinely included in earlier land legislation, but now—more than ever before—the state government had the capacity to enforce or uphold the enactment of these drastic provisions. This time around, the threat was at least credible.

Over the next ten years, the vast majority of Veracruz's remaining communal landholdings were finally parceled out into individual plots, most of the state's ex-communal *condueñazgos* were dissolved, and scores of village *ejidos* became private property.[21] Passage of the state law of 1889—and pressure from state authorities—surely facilitated these developments. It is easy, however, to overstate their explanatory importance. The same can be said of the federal regulations regarding disentailment issued soon thereafter.[22] In the case of Papantla, it has been generally assumed that the law of 1889 was directly responsible for the fragmentation of the *grandes lotes*. In this view, the dissolution of the *condueñazgos* was essentially the making of a state government bent on enforcing an unpopular law.[23]

In fact, the law in question did not apply to *condueñazgos*, which had been legally constituted as private estates. It merely prohibited the establishment of more *grandes lotes*, stipulating that communal territories had to be divided into individual plots (Article 19 of the regulations). Papantla's *con-

dueñazgos, however, were no longer communal, and neither the state government nor the Ayuntamientos had—strictly speaking—any jurisdiction over them. The formal possession deeds signed back in November of 1878 made this very clear: the *lotes* were henceforth to be considered *propiedad particular*. It is no secret that state leaders had never liked the *condueñazgo*, which they regarded as a pseudo-communal form of landholding. As the Governor's *Memoria* for 1894 expressed it, "The division into *grandes lotes* preserves to some extent the community, with all of its problems."[24] Thus, Veracruz officials would make every effort to bring about the division of the *grandes lotes*, initially supporting local initiatives in favor of the *repartos*, offering tax incentives and financial aid, mediating land disputes among *condueños*, and supplying technical assistance, including teams of topographers. As will be seen, these were all weighty influences. There were, however, no legal means simply to compel the dissolution of the *condueñazgos*. Over time, the proliferation and deepening of local conflicts would bring about more overt kinds of pressure by Veracruz and federal authorities; after 1895, as civil strife once again spun inexorably out of control, armed state agents would completely take over the process of parcelization in many of the *grandes lotes*. This was not law enforcement, however, but rather a heavy-handed political intervention devoid of legal foundations.

Even in those tracts of land unquestionably covered by the law of 1889, the desired results were not necessarily—let alone immediately—forthcoming. Papantla's municipal *ejido* is an excellent case in point. Notwithstanding the clear wording of the law, two successive attempts to privatize these lands in the early 1890s failed to yield results. Meanwhile, the tenants—mostly town notables—continued paying rent to the Ayuntamiento. The prescribed subdivision of the so-called *ejido* into individual plots did not begin until late 1898, almost nine years after it was supposed to have been completed, and the legal status of those five hundred hectares surrounding Papantla's *fundo legal* would not be finally settled until after the Revolution.[25] Elsewhere in the state, a number of compulsory land divisions dragged on for years, mired in a tangle of disputes; throughout much of the 1890s, the deadlines imposed by the law of 1889 had to be extended annually.[26] Although the government's coercive powers had increased considerably since the 1870s, their sphere of operation was still fairly limited. In the end, the *repartos* remained by and large municipal affairs, their pace and conduct determined chiefly by local conditions.

Even though the enactment of the Ley sobre Subdivisión did not cause—and does not explain—the demise of Papantla's *condueñazgos*, it nevertheless had a certain influence. This latest official crusade to do away with communal and municipal landownership in favor of individual private property created a climate in which it became easier for interested parties within Papantla to press for the breakup of the *condueñazgos*. For one, the law contained rough procedural guidelines for carrying out land divisions. Although it was not devised with the *grandes lotes* expressly in mind, it required only minor adjustments in order to serve this new purpose. As such, it provided a new framework of reference for local organizing efforts, alliances, and rhetorical strategies. In addition, the law was misused to confer a false air of special authority and legitimacy on those who advocated parcelization. Obfuscation and ignorance played a large role: it is evident that many did not understand that *condueñazgos* were exempt from the provisions of the new law, and most government officials systematically refused to make that clear. If there were shareholders who believed—or were made to believe—that the *reparto* was not a matter of choice, so much the better; "encouragement" was to take many forms.

Still, the initial push for a subdivision of the *grandes lotes* had to come principally from the *condueños*, or at least from some of them. Back in 1869, when the state government mounted the first serious effort to disentail communal lands, the balance of social forces in Papantla had precluded carrying out an individual *reparto*. The communal *rancheros* and other leading Totonacs seem to have mistrusted the Ayuntamiento's intentions; moreover, some of them had reason to fear the prospect of an equitable division. The town merchants liked the idea of a *reparto* but could not exert a decisive influence, since they did not control the lands in question. The means of production—in particular, land and labor—were overwhelmingly in the hands of Totonacs. Furthermore, marking out the boundaries of individual parcels would be expensive as well as complicated, and it was not clear who would pay for that. With the vanilla trade on the increase, an enticing compromise was eventually reached, and the *condueñazgos* were established instead. By the late 1880s, however, the situation was substantially different.

The previous chapter described how the commercial and agricultural boom of the 1880s reshaped socioeconomic relations in and around the *grandes lotes*. Out of the myriad new conflicts, the social displacements, and the voracious business competition that characterized those years, the forces of privatization emerged stronger and more determined than ever. First and foremost came the town merchants, a compact yet quarrelsome bunch, eager to gain more control over the basin's natural and human resources. Most had become legitimate co-owners in one or more *lotes*, either as beneficiaries of the original *reparto* or as buyers of other people's shares, and often as both. Now they had a voice in the management of those *lotes*. But this was not enough for them; property titles were far more desirable than share certificates, not least because they could be used to borrow money. And unlike before, these merchants now had some company. Totonac speculators, whose ranks had swelled during the rush of the 1880s, readily welcomed additional lines of business. Parcelization would offer many fresh opportunities, particularly in share sales and influence peddling, where local knowledge offered comparative advantages. Other Totonac *rancheros* and *labradores*, especially shareholders in *lotes* with thriving agricultural and commercial economies, would also come to favor—or at least accept—the idea of a land subdivision. Their reasons were probably as diverse and shifting as their interests. A few had prospered tremendously with the boom and wished to consolidate their gains. Others feared losing what they had and wanted to protect their land rights. Demographic growth, internecine competition, and merchant encroachment had eroded the traditional independence of numerous basin farmers: the disfranchised were now everywhere. After a decade of fractious *condueñazgo*, individual *repartos* would become an appealing alternative for them.

These farmers' newfound support for privatization is best characterized as circumstantial and contingent, as opposed to principled or ideological. If the process of division somehow turned out not to yield precisely the results that each expected (i.e., receiving whatever lands they felt entitled to), these *rancheros* and *labradores* might just as easily oppose it. Still, by the early 1890s, groups of shareholders in at least a handful of Papantla's *grandes lotes* appear to have been ready—and in some cases eager—to bring about the formal dissolution of their *condueñazgos*. Yet this was anything but a united front.

At the same time, there were many Totonacs with strong reasons to oppose the distribution of *condueñazgo* land among shareholders. The largest group was composed of the disfranchised, mostly young people who did not receive certificates of ownership during the original *repartos* of the 1870s. They were now mere *fincados* on the lands of their forebears, and not all had simply resigned themselves to that fate. Many of those who did not have the fortune of inheriting land-use rights had become *jornaleros*, picking other farmers' vanilla or tobacco and paying rent on their own milpas. Parcelization would formalize a state of dispossession which they had motive to regard as unjust. Given the opportunity, at least some would attempt to prevent or obstruct the subdivisions.

Others who were not automatically disfranchised had sold their certificates of ownership, and faced the possibility of losing their lands in the new *repartos*. Some had done so involuntarily, unwittingly, or out of need, often for a few pesos. Women—especially widows—fell disproportionately into this category. Then there were those who had sold their shares for profit but who continued to exert—or abuse—the rights of *condueñazgo*. Ignacio Muñoz's account makes reference to "the many who have sold their stocks and—taking advantage of communal tenure—are still exploiting their *compañeros*, who are forced to indulge their whims to avoid being mistreated and constantly bothered."[27] As long as the *condueñazgo* persisted, they could have it both ways, but a subdivision based on shares threatened to leave these de facto landowners with nothing.

Numerous as they were, the disfranchised were not the only—nor the most formidable—potential source of opposition to parcelization. Whereas the disfranchised were likely to object to the *repartos* in principle, there were others—mainly shareholders—who were averse to the idea for other reasons. Totonac *condueños* in the more remote, less commercially developed *lotes* on the whole had little interest in a process that was at once costly and prone to controversy. They did not see the practical point or benefit of such an undertaking, and were justifiably afraid of what it might in the end produce. This is not to say that there were no advocates of privatization in those places, only that they tended to be fewer and—at least initially—relatively less powerful. But even in *lotes* where the competition over resources, rights, and privileges was far fiercer, more than a few shareholders were reluctant to carry out a *reparto*. Some *apoderados*—especially the more abusive ones— seem at first to have opposed the idea, fearful that they would lose their broad discretionary powers.[28] Likewise, other *condueños* surmised that they had nothing to gain from a division of land into equal parts, since that might entail having to surrender some territory currently under their control. Still others worried about the unlikeliness of a fair process; parceling out these lands was bound to be an exceedingly complex affair, providing ample room for contentiousness, manipulation, or even fraud. Who would survey and demarcate the plots? How would that be paid for? How would the individual parcels be allocated? What if the surface area of the *lotes* turned out to be much smaller—or larger—than assumed? Here, the conflicts would be not about the (in)justice of a *reparto* limited to shareholders, but over who among them was to get what, and at what cost. In this zero-sum game, merchants, *rancheros*, and *labradores* jockeyed for position, their stance ever contingent on the next turn of events. Rivalries, envies, alliances, negotiation strategies, a sense of grievance, or fear of losing out could turn wary supporters into critics, foes, or surreptitious saboteurs of a *lote*'s subdivision. But the reverse was also true. Today's skeptic could be tomorrow's booster, and vice versa. It was all a matter of detail and circumstance.

Among Totonacs, opposition would also take a more ideological air. Two distressing developments had followed the establishment of the *grandes lotes*: tax increases and merchant encroachment. *Lotes* close to the *pueblo* of Papantla generally bore the greatest brunt; a whirlwind of agricultural expansion, commercial competition, and fiscal pressures had turned some of these landholding associations into caldrons of social strife. There, some residents organized to protest and resist those changes. For them, this odious trend of affairs was no mere coincidence, but rather a direct affront: the *conducñazgo* was nothing but a vast scheme of plunder perpetrated by venal public officials, greedy town merchants, and ambitious Totonac bosses. Since the mid-1880s, a series of closely related dissident movements—including one rebellion, and nearly a second one—sought to reverse course by attacking the institutional legitimacy of the *conducñazgos*, promising instead a return to a lost world of communal sovereignty that would entail the abolition of taxes, the end of disfranchisement, the exclusion of town merchants, and through these, the rebirth of more traditional social relations. Various plans all failed to bear fruit, yet the grievances persisted, as did the radical idea that the privatization of land tenure was ultimately a trick on the people. When the parcelization of the first *grandes lotes* got underway, dissenters—both old and new—would denounce this as a further step toward legitimizing fiscal oppression and shameless usurpation. Fresh oppositional strategies soon emerged, but the logic of the argument remained the same, as did its appeal.

In sum, by 1890 Papantla's had become a deeply divided society, not simply along ethnic lines, as had long been the case, but within and across them as well. And unlike twenty-five, fifty, or a hundred years before, the business of the land was now the principal bone of contention. This unprecedented situation was the product of a recent wave of unsettling changes—in the economic potential of agriculture and ranching, in patterns of social relations, in business practices, and in legal norms, all of which made land tenure the prime arena of civil strife. As Totonac shareholders and town merchants set in motion the dissolution of some *conducñazgos*, the bitter conflicts engendered in the course of the 1880s quickly intensified. As parcelization progressed, another set of conflicts would arise, these concerning thorny distributive and procedural issues. The ensuing struggles plagued Papantla for nearly a decade; some would be finally settled only through violence and naked repression.

What follows is a brief account of the subdivision of Papantla's ex-communal *conducñazgos*. The story unfolds in three stages: 1889–91, 1892–94, and 1895–1900. Told in full detail, each would fill up a small book. Here, the aim is simply to provide a broad overview—along the lines of the argument just elaborated—of how a regime of individual private property became implanted in the historic lands of Papantla, and of what this meant.

1889–1891

As the 1880s drew to a close, signs of the growing strength and prosperity of Papantla's merchant establishment were not hard to find. The vanilla harvests of 1888–89 and 1889–90 were the largest ever, and although

New York prices were not what they used to be, the potential for substantial profits was—it seems—still ample. Business opportunity, political clout, and civic pride combined to produce a new wave of public and private investments, particularly in communications and transportation. On November 4, 1889, a federal telegraph office opened in Tecolutla, linking the port with the Villa of Papantla. A few months later, a group of merchants proposed building another line, this one between Nautla, San Rafael, and Gutiérrez Zamora. In 1890, the *vapor* "San Rafael" began calling at Tuxpan, Tecolutla, Nautla, and Veracruz; previously, the port of Tecolutla had lacked regular steamship service. Inland, new roads were built, one between Papantla and Coyutla with a shortcut to Espinal, and another from the river south to San Rafael; in addition, the long and arduous trek to Teziutlán was rerouted, making it seven leagues shorter. All of these roads were completed by 1890.

Moreover, in July of that year a company controlled by Manuel Romero Rubio—Porfirio Díaz's father-in-law—began constructing a railroad from Tecolutla to Espinal. By April 1891, four kilometers of track had been laid. Although the company's immediate aim was to exploit some asphalt mines near Espinal, this venture excited the imagination of many local merchants and landowners. It was said that the line would one day connect with the Ferrocarril Interoceánico; a branch line from San Marcos to Teziutlán—which had recently resumed construction—was projected to continue down to Nautla. Closer to home, meanwhile, mercantile Papantla took further steps in the direction of modern urbanization. In December 1891, work got underway to provide the *cabecera* with a steady supply of potable water. The town government also decided that Papantla should have a public clock; it would be placed on the church tower, which had finally been completed in 1879.[29] It was in this climate of optimism and assertiveness that the town merchants and other prominent shareholders turned their attention to the privatization of the *condueñazgos*.

In the meantime, state officials were taking steps in the same direction. In May 1889, as the Ley sobre Subdivisión was being drafted, Governor Enríquez asked the *jefe político* in Papantla about the status of communal disentailment in the canton, explaining that he had no information regarding the current situation, since Xalapa's records had been lost. In his reply, Marcelino Sánchez—who had replaced Agapito Fontecilla—made a strong plea for the enactment of a new law that would "make those little communities (i.e., the *condueñazgos*) disappear," touting the fiscal benefits of such a move. Although he acknowledged that these *lotes* had been constituted legally, he nevertheless believed that if the government were willing to pay for the parcelization, the shareholders—mainly Indians—could be made to go along. Five months later, a Treasury agent sent to Papantla issued a report echoing Sánchez's sentiments. "This is a most propitious moment," he wrote, "to carry out the subdivision of the *lotes*," thereby putting an end to the fraudulent practices of exploitative *apoderados* and their associates. He recommended starting with one of the "easier *lotes*," where most shareholders were already in favor of individual parcels. Enríquez apparently liked the plan, referring it to his staff for a legal opinion. He was then duly reminded that the government lacked jurisdiction to undertake a *reparto* in properties that were legally private. The *condueños*, however, were free to do it themselves "whenever they please, in the same way that one distributes an inheritance or divides the assets of a corporation."[30] This tempered Xalapa's drive, at least for a while. But in Papantla, the *jefe político* was undeterred.

After the passage of Law No. 26, Sánchez took it upon himself to promote *lote* subdivisions. Although the law was not what he had lobbied for, it did offer a handy set of rules that could be adopted to organize the *repartos*; given the source, it was relatively easy to confer on these guidelines a veneer of officiality. Finding willing participants would not be hard, either. By the end of the year, a few *condueñazgos* had formed divisory boards, a first step toward the partition of their lands. Not surprisingly, most of those *grandes lotes* were at the eastern end of the basin, in the municipalities of Gutiérrez Zamora and Tecolutla. Six of Papantla's twenty-three ex-communal *lotes*—El Cristo (lot 1), Palo Hueco (lot 2), Anclón y Arenal (lot 4), Zapotal y Cazonera (lot 5), Arroyo Grande Cabezas (lot 7), and Boca de Lima (lot 9)—now belonged to those two jurisdictions. On the whole, these easternmost *condueñazgos* were significantly different from the ones surrounding the town of Papantla. With the possible exception of Boca de Lima, this was a zone of relatively recent—and fast—agricultural development, largely the product of migration. There was plenty of good farm and pasture land, and—with the opening of cabotage routes—proximity to the Tecolutla River and the sea afforded new commercial possibilities. Although the practice of agriculture was very old in these parts, many of the native population settlements were not, and the roots of communal land tenure arrangements were therefore not as deep.

Over the previous twenty-five years, moreover, much of the area had been colonized—in more ways than one—by Italian immigrants. By the 1880s, they were the most prosperous farmers and the principal merchants in the eastern Tecolutla basin; in the process, they had come to dominate the young municipal politics of Gutiérrez Zamora, where four of those six *lotes* were located. In the early 1880s, another group of colonists—French-Americans from New Orleans—acquired a part of the estate of Mesacapa, just south of the river, which was renamed "Colonia Americana" and later "Colonia San Antonio." They, too, invested heavily in the lands and crops of the neighboring *condueñazgos*. Even though very few of these immigrants had received shares in the original *repartos*, many purchased them in the late 1870s and throughout the 1880s, especially in Palo Hueco, Anclón y Arenal, and El Cristo, as well as in Cacahuatal, a non-communal *conduenazgo* across the river, where cattle ranching was then thriving. In July 1883, for instance, the Italian merchant Bartolo Casasa bought ten of Palo Hueco's ninety-one shares of ownership, paying between ten and twenty-five pesos for each. Around the same time, Joseph Delahoussaye and Alcibiades Decuir—both from New Orleans—acquired their own shares in the same *lote*; one paid fifty pesos, the other one hundred, but Decuir's purchase included milpas and vanilla fields as well. Two years later, the Decuir family bought stock in El Cristo, and the following year Casasa obtained five more certificates from Palo Hueco. Numerous other transactions could be cited; during those years, recording share sales was a regular part of the local notarial business. In this way, families with names like Tremari, Gudini, Chena, Capitanachi, Montini, Montessoro, Bayardini, Romagnoli, Garelli, and Bocardi became *conduenos* in the bustling eastern *lotes*. Totonac *rancheros* purchased shares as well, although to a lesser extent. Prices ranged from four to five hundred pesos, depending on who bought and sold, and on whether other assets—such as vanilla plants or feeder grasses—were included or not. In most cases, single shares fetched ten to fifty pesos.[31]

It is not clear why so many of the original recipients parted with their certificates; sometimes debt or a death in the family appear to have played a role, but plain ignorance was in all likelihood the leading cause. It is hard to imagine that the potential value of these legal documents was widely understood, especially in *conduenazgos* where the average shareholder saw little current value in them—where the dividends of ownership went exclusively to *lote* managers and other potentates, or where improper tax apportionment made nominal ownership unreasonably burdensome. In such situations, the cost of signing away unspecified and unrealized property rights might well have been perceived as negligible, at least in the short run, particularly if one could continue farming more or less as before. At any rate, these sellers seem not to have attached much value to their certificates, and nobody disabused them of that notion. This is what the prevalence of low prices in sales involving original shareholders or their immediate relatives would indicate. But for the buyers, of course, those papers had an altogether different meaning and value, looking forward to the day when possession of these shares would give them exclusive entitlement to a piece of land. Notarized transactions generally spelled out these expectations quite clearly, but most sellers—commonly referred to as the "primitive owners"—could not understand Spanish, let alone read it.

Thus, in the twelve years since the establishment of the *grandes lotes*, a good many Italian colonists had gone from being mere *fincados* to owning a large number of *conduenazgo* shares. In Palo Hueco and El Cristo, their dominance was overwhelming; when the *jefe político* approached them with his plan for parcelization, they readily embraced it, forming the first *reparto* boards. Arroyo Grande Cabezas and Anclón y Arenal soon followed suit. These settler families had preferred private landholding all along; that was ostensibly why they had journeyed to Mexico in the first place. At last their chance had come to get clear title to the properties they effectively controlled. Two surveyors, Víctor M. Assenato—born and trained in Italy—and Salvador Martínez, were hired for this purpose.

Before the process could unfold, however, two legal questions had to be settled. The first concerned responsibility for the issuance of individual property titles. Veracruz's disentailment laws conferred those powers on the Ayuntamientos, but recent federal directives envisioned otherwise. Governor Enríquez wrote to Díaz extensively on that topic, and in the end prevailed on him to sanction the titling role of municipal governments.[32] Although *condueñazgo* lands were already private, they were treated de facto in the same fashion. In time, a special decree would remedy this legal defect, explicitly enabling municipalities to issue individual title-deeds for *conduenazgos*. A second question related specifically to the *conduenazgos*, where stock certificates were to be exchanged for ownership titles. By law, real estate sales had to be registered, with the seller paying a title transfer fee (2.5 percent of the assessed value to the State Treasury, plus one-quarter of that amount to the federation). But many share purchases had gone completely unrecorded, and others, though notarized, had failed to fulfill that fiscal obligation. The sellers—mostly Indians—could hardly be expected to pay at this point, and although buyers might be persuaded to do so in order to regularize their holdings, they now faced overdue fines. Left unresolved, this situation threatened to paralyze the legal subdivision of the *lotes*. Alarmed, *jefe político* Sánchez asked the state congress to condone the fines; the lawmakers promptly complied, granting a grace period to all those currently in arrears (Decree No. 58, 14 December 1889).[33] With these procedural obstacles seemingly out of the way, the drive to break up the *conduenazgos* of Gutiérrez Zamora and Tecolutla took center stage.

In the course of 1890, Palo Hueco carried out the first subdivision, following guidelines borrowed from the recent law. The board signed a detailed contract with topographer Martínez, specifying wages and fees, the provision of laborers to cut through the undergrowth, the number of plots to be demarcated, the location of pathways, the drawing of boundary maps, and a timeline for completion. The cost of the entire operation was to be prorated among the beneficiaries. Board members then compiled an updated register of *conduenos* in order to organize the distribution of the lots. With a *reparto* now imminent, a flurry in stock transactions ensued. Latecomers tracked down several of the original shareholders, persuading them to sell their certificates. Vanilla plantings and pasturelands also changed hands at this time, as merchants sought to consolidate their position.[34]

Once surveyed, Palo Hueco was found to measure 773 hectares, close to the original estimate of half a *sitio de ganado mayor* (878 hectares). However, the perimeter lines marked by Martínez elicited strong protests from neighbors in El Cristo, who felt they were being robbed.[35] This was the first of many instances in which the expedient vagueness of the boundaries set in the original *reparto* of the *lotes* would give rise to problems. In this case, the conflict was soon resolved. The *lote* consisted of two broad types of land, 442 hectares of "very fertile" soil and 331 hectares of swampy terrain, which the *jefe político* described as being "potentially productive, with some effort." How were these disparate lands to be "equitably" divided? According to the law, individual plots were supposed to be allocated by means of a lottery, though shareholders were allowed to retain the lands they already held, provided that the area in question did not exceed the size of a single parcel. The idea was to balance fairness and equity in the distribution of land, but local realities would dictate otherwise. Several merchants owned multiple shares, as well as crop- and grasslands. They wanted to pair their shares with their holdings, and—wherever it was feasible—to turn them into adjoining parcels, thereby constituting much larger estates. As a result, parcel assignation would be the product not of a lottery, but of prior claims, hurried negotiations, and backroom deals.

The *reparto* of 1878 had awarded a total of ninety-one shares in Palo Hueco, but apparently only eighty of these turned up when the divisory board summoned all holders. It is not clear what happened with the other eleven; perhaps they were lost, or their owners had moved away or died. By law, the *lote* was nevertheless supposed to be divided into ninety-one parts, since each share was worth only a fixed percentage of ownership regardless of what happened to the rest. Unclaimed plots might then—under certain conditions—be declared vacant, or *baldíos*, after which the Ayuntamiento could auction them off or adjudicate them to interested parties. Anything else was tantamount to illegal expropriation. All the same, the *condueños* in charge of the subdivision opted to award land only to the eighty who had presented their shares. The 442 hectares of fertile soil were divided into fifty-eight plots (7.62 hectares each), and the 331 hectares of swampy land into an additional twenty-two (15 hectares each). According to the *jefe político*, the larger—but poorer—properties were distributed among those who did not have previous holdings, and the good land went mainly to the *condueños* who were already farming it.[36] But the process of laying out and allocating parcels was in all likelihood a bit more complex than that. Even within the same category, some lands were simply better than others (especially for ranching), and location (access to water sources, or to the road) was nothing to be indifferent about. This gave the surveyor—as well as those who had the means to influence him—considerable room for maneuver. Still, the owners of Palo Hueco—at least the ones whose opinions mattered—were by now a rather compact group, so they managed to resolve any differences and carve out the *lote* without much difficulty. If there was opposition, either from participants or from the disfranchised, it was not serious.

When it was all over, by the end of the year, a tiny corner of the old communal lands of the *pueblo* of Papantla had been turned into individual private plots. Gratified, the *jefe político* informed Xalapa. "This first fractionalization," he wrote, is an accomplishment "of great transcendence in this canton, because having vanquished the resistance of Indians to individual *repartos*, I trust that the subdivision of other *lotes* will soon follow, and this will further increase our agricultural wealth."[37] During 1891 and early 1892, El Cristo, Arroyo Grande Cabezas, and Anclón y Arenal carried out their *repartos* much in the same way. Of the six *grandes lotes* in Gutiérrez Zamora and Tecolutla, only Boca de Lima and Zapotal y Cazonera failed to produce quick subdivisions; Boca de Lima, in particular, had many Totonac shareholders who were adamantly opposed to parcelization. Both of these *lotes* remained in *condueñazgo* for the time being.[38] All across the basin, people took notice. Some were alarmed, others delighted.

A final step, the titling and registration of these land parcels, would take much longer, partly for lack of clear jurisdiction and procedures, partly due to foot-dragging on the part of proprietors hoping to avoid paying taxes. The Ayuntamientos were slow to issue new titles of ownership, and the recipients were even slower to present them at the Registro Público. The outbreak of fighting around Papantla in June 1891 would cause further delays. This made it hard for Treasury officials to assess and collect the appropriate property taxes. Palo Hueco's titles began to trickle in only in November 1891, nearly a year after the subdivision had been declared completed, and it would be several more months before the tax roster was finally ready. The new fiscal registers offered a graphic précis of what privatization had thus far wrought. Palo Hueco's eighty shares had been converted into twenty-one separate properties owned by twenty individuals or firms. Of these, at least eight and possibly as many as ten were town merchants or merchant-farmers, six of whom had Italian names. Of the three female proprietors, two were the widows of merchants. The remaining landowners—between eight and ten—were Totonac farmers, a few clearly with more land than others. Property values (land and cattle) provided further indication of the lopsided distribution of Palo Hueco's former assets. No less than 76 percent of the total cadastral value corresponded to merchant properties, of which 61 percent represented Italian holdings. Indeed, the new estates of Pedro Tremari and of the Casasa brothers alone accounted for more than half of the tax due.

Neighboring El Cristo exhibited the same pattern, only more pronounced. Forty-four shares were turned into seventeen parcels held by fifteen people or firms—thirteen of Italian origin, one French-American, and one Mexican. Here Romagnoli, Casasa, Decuir, and Montini were the principal proprietors.[39] As these tax lists showed, the lands of Palo Hueco and El Cristo had become the domain of a few rich men, none of them farmers; this was the culmination of a transformation in social and economic relations that had been taking place since the 1870s. There were still Totonac *rancheros* and *labradores* in these places, but not many.

Elsewhere, groups of *condueños* in two of Papantla's landholding associations—Cedro (lot 8) and Sombrerete, Caristay, y Aguacate (lot 24)—had expressed interest in a division as early as 1890. Like-minded people in other *lotes* surely harbored the same designs. However, Palo Hueco's "success story"—orchestrating a speedy and orderly *reparto*—would not repeat itself in Papantla. There, a series of storms were brewing at the start of the decade. A persistent discontent about taxes, the progressive decline of vanilla prices, the new anxieties and machinations generated by the prospect of new *repartos*, and the meddlesome role assumed by the Ayuntamiento—behind which it was easy to see the hand of some merchants—combined to create a climate of unrest. As it turns out, the experience of Palo Hueco, El Cristo, and a few other "easy" *lotes* would be exceptional, as was the acute imbalance of power that characterized social relations in those settler-ruled *condueñazgos*.

State tax revenues from the Cantón of Papantla rose considerably in 1889 and 1890, a reflection of both heightened enforcement and increased economic activity. As the annual figures for various types of tax demonstrate, the fiscal reforms of the mid-1880s were already paying off (see Table 6.1).[40] The shift to more direct taxes raised more revenue for the state and perhaps added vigor to the economy, but it also placed a heavier burden on the basin's subsistence-oriented rural producers, whose limited reliance on market transactions had probably shielded them from the worst excesses of the old *alcabalas*. Now they had the personal tax and the property tax—among others—to contend with, and the government's expanding bureaucratic control made paying up much harder to avoid.

As enforcement increased, so did the fines, and, in some cases, also the resentment. "Taxes have increased considerably, causing much uneasiness in society," read a news brief from Papantla published in February 1890. "Many Indians," it went on, "are no longer planting tobacco because of the fines levied on them for failing to inform the Treasury about the tobacco fields they had previously planted."[41] Judging from municipal receipts and population figures, the municipality of Papantla alone produced as much as three-quarters of the state revenues obtained from the canton as a whole.[42] Papantla was the agricultural, commercial, demographic, and political center of the basin, and the government's fiscal encroachment was

TABLE 6.1

Selected State Tax Revenues, Cantón of Papantla, 1887–1890
(in pesos)

Tax	1887	1888	1889	1890
Title transfer	$ 469.92	$ 390.20	$1,000.46	
Cattle, consumption	2,296.12	2,081.95	2,710.53	$3,471.75
Cattle, additional	460.54	416.25	541.48	694.21
Coffee and tobacco (consumption)	103.26	—	—	—
Coffee and tobacco (20% production)	—	46.17	175.76	272.42
Coffee and tobacco (total production)	1,186.63	250.92	955.22	1,480.54
Urban property	1,365.96	1,170.27	1,586.18	2,110.83
Urban property, arrears	83.10	35.35	380.01	467.28
Rural property	1,192.14	968.48	1,637.44	3,636.71
Rural property, arrears	322.43	248.94	2,139.73	694.55
Personal, Law No. 12	6,947.69	5,332.93	7,165.78	8,032.62
Business license and *engorda*	6,576.18	6,509.71	8,818.55	12,199.16
Surcharges and fines— overdue direct taxes	119.04	181.98	434.89	1,125.71
Total, all revenues	$32,990.82	$25,663.48	$39,587.20	$52,995.71

SOURCE: See note 40 to Chapter 6.

felt there more strongly. Resistance to these pressures—and to the land policies they were associated with—had led to uprisings twice in the previous five years, and it would do so yet again.

At the same time, by 1890 vanilla prices were the lowest that anyone could remember. Vanilla was often the main source of cash income for farmers, and this depressing trend caused widespread distress. In New York, the *Reporter* noted dryly that "the low prices which importers were obliged to pay in the primary market [during 1890] were not at all satisfactory to the shippers or gatherers."[43] Although the local price slump was ultimately a reflection of international market developments, many growers and middlemen blamed it on the greed of the town merchants, who were certainly doing all they could to reduce their costs and protect their profits. In the course of the 1890–91 season, Papantla's principal dealers took an unprecedented step, agreeing among themselves to fix the price of green vanilla. The cartel would impose a fine of $300 pesos to any member caught paying more. The list of participants read like a Who's Who of Papantla's merchant elite: Tremari, Fuente, Arenal, Zorrilla, Silvera, Garmilla, Sierra, Patiño, and Vaquero, among others.[44] Not surprisingly, the pact did not last long. Still, their brash attempt to impose even lower prices added strain to Papantla's already fractious social relations.

It was in the midst of this social malaise that word of a possible land-tenure reform spread through the *grandes lotes* of Papantla. In a few *condueñazgos*, factions talked of forming divisory boards, wishing to get the process underway. In the town, the advocates of privatization began stirring things up. To set the example, the Ayuntamiento hired Salvador Martínez to survey and map the town's *fundo legal* and *ejido*, a first step toward the subdivision of the latter.[45] Overall, a sense of uncertainty prevailed. Although parcelization was by no means compulsory, not everyone knew or would say this. The fact that a new land law had come into effect was well publicized, but the scope of its provisions was often ill-understood and deliberately distorted. In consequence, rumors and speculation proliferated and the air filled with contradictory expectations of change. Meanwhile, skeptics and opponents of various stripes began to warn shareholders against selling their certificates. In light of what was then occurring in Palo Hueco, this was probably prudent advice, any ulterior motives notwithstanding. Vexed, the *jefe político* asked Xalapa to weigh in, and so, in August 1890, Governor Enríquez sent out a most peculiar circular, informing all former *comuneros* that they were, in fact, free to sell their shares whenever, however, and to whomever they decided to.[46] The Ayuntamiento joined the fray, too, actively supporting *lote* subdivision. For those who had reason already to fear the effects of government initiatives on their lives (e.g., taxes, the previous *reparto*), this was a bad omen. The intervention of Ayuntamiento members also meant that the prerogatives of public office were likely to be abused in pursuit of private agendas, since merchant-politicians meddling in the *repartos* were bound to have particular business interests to promote. This would turn municipal politics into an extension of the scramble for *condueñazgo* land. At the outset, however, the net result of all this flurry of activity was confusion. As 1890 drew to a close, the parcelization of Papantla's *grandes lotes* was still just talk.

As part of its effort to spur—or at least ease—these *repartos*, Xalapa also offered a series of legal and fiscal incentives to *condueños* who turned their holdings into individual plots. Decree No. 50 of November 20, 1890, acknowledged explicitly for the first time that the hoped-for subdivision of the *grandes lotes* was not obligatory. To encourage it, the government would issue title-deeds and waive payment of the title transfer fee for parcels created within the following two years. It would also exempt the titles of new properties valued at under one hundred pesos from having to be inscribed at the Registro Público. Those who opted to remain in *condueñazgo* would face tightened fiscal regulation. These incentives were an implicit recognition that cost would be a big concern for some shareholders, and that taxes and fees were a persistent source of popular discontent. The concessions were modest, however, and unlikely to sway many. The law did not address surveying costs, which were by far the most expensive part of the whole operation. In Papantla, moreover, full-scale privatization faced far more formidable difficulties, the signs of which were not hard to find.

Barely four months after triumphantly announcing the parcelization of Palo Hueco, the *jefe político*'s euphoria had given way to wariness and apprehension. Sánchez now grudgingly recognized that land-tenure reform was a profoundly divisive issue, and that—at least in Papantla—the potential for violent conflict was consequently very high. His new assessment, bitter as well as pompous, is worth quoting in full:

The first steps toward establishing dispositions of transcendental importance are always difficult, above all when such dispositions are opposed by inveterate habits. If, in a land of enlightened masses, efforts were to be made to make true property-owners, with all of the prerogatives inherent in that station, out of those who are now *condueños* of *grandes terrenos*, and yet cannot dispose of the parts that correspond to them, but are instead at the mercy of exploiters, hymns of gratitude would be sung to the Administration that managed to accomplish such a thing, because with this act doors that are now wide open to all types of abuses would be closed. But here, where it is necessary to struggle with many difficulties, where the astuteness and evil intentions of the exploiters go as far as to incite the Indians to armed opposition to the individual division of the *lotes*, it is only little by little and with the utmost prudence that it is possible to advance the visionary intentions of your honor [i.e., the Governor], which strive to foster the development of our agricultural riches and the well-being of a race which is for us venerable and—for its many merits—deserving of our utmost consideration.[47]

Sánchez's diagnosis of the social situation was simplistic, incomplete, and prejudiced, though perhaps not entirely mistaken. There was indeed a strong undercurrent of opposition, but it was not merely the product of manipulation. His prognosis, however, would prove essentially correct, though in ways and for reasons he could scarcely imagine, and partly as a consequence of his own actions. As he composed this report, in late March 1891, trouble was already in the air. The various social grievances that led to the 1887–88 insurrection had not subsequently disappeared; if anything, they had grown more intense, festering into new rancors. The prospect of another land-tenure reform brought them out into the open, as old and new dissenters in a handful of Totonac *congregaciones* rushed to contest the direction of change. Taxes, land, and the abuse of authority would again be the bones of contention, but by 1891 the stakes were higher and the battles would hence be fiercer.

As word of an imminent privatizing drive spread through the countryside,

Francisco Pérez Zepeta and a few associates searched anxiously for a new strategy of opposition. The long and tortuous effort to locate Papantla's ancestral titles in the Mexico City archives had ended in failure, but finding a way to reclaim and retain the *pueblo*'s communal patrimony was now more urgent than ever. The advocates of a new order had made their intentions clear: the shareholders would become landowners. Share purchases in Papantla, once fairly infrequent, had increased markedly of late. In Tlahua-napa, for instance, where only 4 of the 122 original certificates had been sold in the previous decade, 5 changed hands in the first half of 1890 alone. And that was just the beginning. But were these documents really valid? Could they truly confer land rights? Would they? Pérez Zepeta, for one, did not think so. He had parted with his own stock in Chote y Mesillas back in June 1887, in the midst of the first title search, and had then sold it again—this time in notarized fashion—to the same buyer in April 1890 (see Figure 6.7).[48] For him, that piece of paper had—or ought to have—no legal value, though it was good, why not, as a source of quick cash. Time was running out, however, and so were his options. If Papantla's old titles were missing, how else could these lands be claimed? By July 1890, Pérez Zepeta's group had found a man in Mexico City who said he knew just how to do it.

Severiano Galicia was born around 1860 in Amecameca de Juárez (Mexico State) to a liberal family of relatively modest means. Most of the 1880s he spent at the National School of Agriculture training to become an agronomist. As a student, Galicia worked with a local political club, the Sociedad Mutualista de Ocampo, which once sought to get him nominated for Chalco's seat in the federal Congress. Young Severiano, they wrote, was "the only popular candidate," a man with a "natural talent for speaking and writing elegantly." After his father died in 1882, he was left the sole supporter of his mother and younger siblings; money worries would plague him for years. Thanks in part to the backing of Ignacio Mariscal, whom he referred to as his "protector," Galicia completed his degree in 1887, at which point he secured a post as topographer in the "Scientific Commission" sent by Fomento to survey and divide the lands of the Yaqui in Sonora. Unhappy with what he saw there, he complained, made some enemies, and two years later finally quit. He stayed in Sonora and got into business, hoping to cash in on some silver and gold ore deposits he had come across as a surveyor, but rivals with much better political connections snatched them away. He filed a lawsuit, complained directly to Porfirio Díaz, and got Congressman Benito Juárez Maza to intercede on his behalf, all to no avail. By mid-1890, Galicia was back in Mexico City, embittered as well as unemployed. It was then that he offered his services to the Totonacs from Papantla, who were quick to accept. Calling himself their *apoderado*, he contacted the National Archive in early July, requesting a title search yet again.[49]

n.º 1.

El C Alcalde Municipal que suscribe en nombre

del H. Ayuntamiento de esta Cabecera y en cumplimiento del art° 5° de la
Ley del Estado Numero 159, de 17 de Marzo de 1869.

Abril 20 de 1877

CERTIFICO: que el Ciudadano *Fran.º Perez Zepeta*

de este origen y vecindad, está comprendido como dueño en el reparto de terrenos
de esta MUNICIPALIDAD practicado conforme á la ley espresada y sus concordan-
tes encontrandose como tal su nombre inscrito tanto en el acta general de division como en la escritura de adjudicacion del LOTE numero quince que lo componen las ranche-
rias de CHOTE Y MECILLAS en el cual le fue determinada su accion de terreno.

Y para que sirva de titulo de propiedad al interesado; y haga de él el uso que
le convenga, se le espide el presente con el timbre correspondiente y sello de la Municipalidad en Papantla á *veinte* de Abril de mil ochocientos setenta y siete

A. Barra

J. M. Romero García

Vendo y traspaso mi acción que represento por el
presente certificado al C. Juan Vicente perez
en la cantidad de 10 p pesos diez que recibí á mi sa-
tisfaccion traspasandole todos los derechos que á el
tenia para que lo disfrute como tuyo adquirido
con justo Titulo renunciando todos sus derechos
á él en fee de lo cual lo firmo el presente en
presencia de dos testigos en las Mesillas Junio. 17 de
Jesus Garcia   *Fran.co P. Zepeta* 1881

FIGURE 6.7 Share certificate of Francisco Pérez Zepeta. From DRTP, Chote
y Mesillas.

Around the same time, Galicia got involved with a land fight affecting his native Amecameca, where he still had a certain political following. An old boundary conflict between the village and the hacienda of San Juan de Guadalupe had recently been rekindled, when the hacienda owners moved to survey and claim the disputed area as theirs. A large group of disgruntled villagers countered by forming the Junta Reivindicadora de Terrenos y Montes de Amecameca to carry out their own land survey, for which they hired Galicia in early 1891. They would try to beat the hacienda at its own game. Following federal public lands law, Galicia would draw boundary lines in accordance with the old colonial deeds; any territory not covered in these titles would then be registered as *excedencias* in the Junta's name (which had been constituted as a "sociedad agrícola").[50] This is also what Galicia proposed to do in Papantla, but with a twist.

To Pérez Zepeta and his companions, finding Galicia must have seemed a true godsend. He was smart, eloquent, self-confident, sympathetic to their cause as he understood it, and apparently well connected. More importantly, he told them what they wanted to hear, namely, that there was indeed a way to get Papantla's lands back. According to Galicia, the federal public lands laws of July 20, 1863 and December 15, 1883, enabled his clients to appropriate the *excedencias* and *demasías* of Papantla's *grandes lotes* and *ejido*. By definition, *excedencias* were untitled—that is, public—lands occupied by individuals who owned or had legal rights to an immediately adjacent territory. *Demasías*, meanwhile, represented the difference between the actual and the legal size of a particular landed property; if a plot in fact measured 100 hectares but the title of ownership—for whatever reason—declared it to be only 75 hectares, the remaining 25 hectares would be considered *demasías*.[51] By law, individuals working such lands could—under certain circumstances—file a claim of ownership (*denuncia*), conduct a survey, and obtain a property title.

A conventional reading of these legal provisions appeared to offer the Totonacs at least two promising lines of action; first, they could ask to carry out their own land surveys; and second, they could seek to exploit the fact that Papantla's *lotes* had been poorly demarcated and inaccurately measured. Implemented together, they were bound to have a tremendous local impact, potentially subverting recently entrenched landholding and power arrangements. But this was not all, for a much more radical and controversial interpretation of the law was also possible. If Papantla's colonial titles did not exist, and Galicia had verified that this was indeed the case, the argument could be made that these lands were all legally public, since there were no original titles covering them. The *condueñazgos* were therefore invalid and the share certificates worthless. The claimants could then seek ownership of the entire ex-communal territory, not just the *grandes lotes* but also San

Miguel y San Lorenzo and other adjoining estates believed to have been un-lawfully parceled off. This was a bolder proposition, and a much riskier one also. To Papantla's dissidents, it was far more enticing as well.

Thus, Galicia's initial proposal was both ambitious and ambiguous. It did not dampen the Totonacs' desire for sweeping legal and social change, however. The basic idea was clear enough, and quite ingenious: a public lands law that had often been applied in detriment of the *pueblos* would now serve to empower them instead. Beyond that, the details were fuzzy, perhaps deliberately so. It is hard to know whether Galicia believed that a broad *baldíos* claim could work, or whether he was simply trying to earn his keep. It was far from certain that this type of legal procedure—the more expansive *denuncia*—was applicable in the case of Papantla, but Galicia nevertheless raised the possibility, even though he was thoroughly unfamil-iar with the history of the ex-communal *condueñazgos* and with the evolv-ing complexities of Papantla's socioeconomic situation. Moreover, he was not a lawyer, but then neither were his desperate clients, who were prima-rily concerned with the rightness of the end, not with the means.

Down in Papantla, word of Galicia's plan breathed new life into a strug-gling dissident movement, for which this represented a last chance to pre-vent permanent disfranchisement and expropriation. Money collections be-gan again, particularly around Chote y Mesillas, Cerro del Carbón, Palmar, and Poza Larga y Cazuelas, *grandes lotes* immediately to the south and east of the town, where opposition leaders like Pérez Zepeta bore some sway. There, groups of aggrieved *condueños* and *fincados* joined in support of this latest venture. To them, the idea of conducting their own land surveys and thereby advancing—or, at the very least, safeguarding—their interests was evidently attractive, especially if the alternative was a share-based *reparto* managed by others, which could very well leave them with nothing. Ironi-cally, though, the proposed public lands claims effectively recognized the extension of a private property regime over territories that had for centuries been held communally, precisely the opposite of what the assiduous fund-raising and the title-searching pilgrimages to Mexico City had ostensibly in-tended to accomplish, at least originally. A combination of pragmatism, urgency, self-interest, and confusion about the exact nature of Galicia's de-ceptively simple scheme probably accounts for this sudden—and perhaps unwitting—shift in stance. The circumstances had changed, and so had the dissidents' strategy.

From another perspective, moreover, it is possible to see a certain degree of continuity. Underlying the appeal of a kind of communal restoration was a desire to wrestle control away from abusive and dishonest authorities—be they tax collectors, the *jefe político*, vanilla merchants, or *condueñazgo* ad-ministrators. For those who pinned their hopes to it, Galicia's plan promised

to deliver some of that lost independence: they would claim Papantla's land
for themselves, and this would enable them to undo the many wretched legacies of *condueñazgo*. Such a step, they believed, would also put an end to the
current fiscal regime, source of so many woes. Land and tax issues remained
inextricably intertwined. The means may have been new (and somewhat
vague), but the goals were essentially the same. Thus linked, a host of disparate aspirations swiftly coalesced around Galicia's proposal.

Not surprisingly, local authorities were quick to label this incipient challenge as subversive. The pervading mood in Papantla was already one of ten-
sion; survey engineers Salvador Martínez and Víctor Assenato were doing
the rounds looking for contracts, and the possibility of conflictive *lote* subdivisions loomed large on the horizon. Fresh talk of eliminating taxes made
government officials very nervous, knowing that not long ago this had escalated into a serious confrontation. The rumored land *denuncias* were perceived as an even graver peril. It is unlikely that the *jefe político* understood
Galicia's scheme (after all, even the participants had differing notions of it);
all he knew for certain was that some malcontents had apparently hired an
engineer to claim and measure lands on their own, and this he deemed unac-
ceptable. To Marcelino Sánchez, this was nothing but a shameless scam, the
latest episode in a long-running racket organized by professional thieves and
agitators. He would crack down hard on them, determined to bring an end
to these ventures once and for all. But although he would portray this simply
as an issue of law enforcement, it is clear that his reaction was guided by a
different kind of reasoning. At bottom, this was a question of political and
economic power and not merely a matter of contrasting legal interpretations.
The *denuncia* movement challenged the authority of state and local officials
(and of the *condueñazgo* associations) and at the same time threatened many
well-established economic interests. Such audacity would not be tolerated.
Even the more narrowly conceived *denuncias* were bound to open a Pan-
dora's box of conflicts, for the issue of *excedencias* and *demasías* was potentially an explosive one. Neither the *grandes lotes* nor the village *ejido* had
ever been precisely demarcated, and the rough surveys that had preceded the
1878 *repartos* had in many cases produced wildly inaccurate size estimates
of the territories that were turned into *condueñazgos*. If the application of
public land laws were to be permitted in these parts of Papantla, such gross
ambiguities in the definition of the legal boundaries and surface areas of the
lands covered by the original *reparto* would inevitably trigger an avalanche
of ownership claims and counterclaims, upsetting the prevailing order. For
many, this was a deeply unsettling prospect, but for others—including Galicia's clients—it was perhaps a final opportunity for redress. Legality aside,
the new claims were indeed subversive, and deliberately so. More immediately, the emergence of this movement raised yet another volatile issue: Who

would get to organize the land surveys, and on what terms? Francisco Pérez Zepeta and his fellow dissenters claimed for themselves the right to do their own, and for this they would be persecuted.

Early in 1891 Galicia informed his associates that he had obtained authorization from the Ministry of Fomento to undertake the proposed land surveys. They took this as definitive proof of his seriousness, and also—more importantly—as a clear indication of federal approval for the plan in question. Soon thereafter, preparations for his arrival got underway. In fact, Galicia's "license" or "concession" meant very little. As historian Robert Holden has shown, these permits were routinely issued and very easy to get. "Fomento," he notes, "used a preprinted form to accept the applications for authorization, merely filling in a few blanks to indicate the name of the contractor, the area to be surveyed, and the dates."[52] This was simply a kind of registration for would-be surveyors of public lands, and not—as Papantla's dissidents were led and led others to believe—an endorsement of Galicia's plan. Still, growing rumors of an imminent federal intervention spread through a handful of southern and eastern *rancherías* and into the town, sowing confusion, igniting hopes, and provoking alarm.

Back in Amecameca, meanwhile, Galicia began his controversial survey of the *pueblo*'s boundaries, intent on claiming any *excedencias*. The hacienda owners, municipal authorities, and the *jefe político* all strongly opposed these proceedings. As the mapping progressed, villagers and other interested parties congregated to follow Galicia's defiant work. Determined to stop him, Galicia's powerful foes cunningly accused him of leading a seditious conspiracy, pointing to those large gatherings as evidence. His real aim, they claimed, was to spark a socialist uprising. The charge was clearly unfounded, but its import was not lost on anyone, evoking as it did the memory of Chalco's agrarian rebellion of 1868, which had been ruthlessly suppressed. Severiano Galicia was far from being (or wanting to be) another Julio López, but such malicious imputations were not to be taken lightly. Threatened, Galicia quickly sought the protection of Ignacio Mariscal, who got Porfirio Díaz to intervene in the conflict and save him from prosecution or worse.[53] Once again denied, Galicia was forced to leave Amecameca, whereupon he turned his attention to the pending land surveys in Papantla.

Following some negotiations regarding payment, his trip was scheduled for late May. Pérez Zepeta then made final arrangements for Galicia's arrival and got his supporters ready. Their lands were at last about to be measured and recovered. Sometime after mid-May, Pérez Zepeta, Gregorio Santiago, Pedro Salazar, Esteban Pérez, and Hilario Jiménez rode up the sierra toward the San Juan de los Llanos station, where they had agreed to meet the surveyor's party. They brought money for Galicia, as well as horses. As soon as *jefe político* Sánchez heard of it, he issued an urgent order for their arrest. Upon reaching Libres, the Totonacs were detained and escorted back to Teziutlán, where a detachment of national guards and state *rurales* from Papantla picked them up. Commanding these forces was none other than Simón Tiburcio, Papantla's mightiest and most feared Indian cacique, who personified better than anyone else the kinds of land management scams, betrayals, and abuses that the dissidents had long rallied against. Tiburcio and Pérez Zepeta represented opposite poles of a sharply divided Totonac society, and they had clashed repeatedly since at least 1885. Their enmity ran deep; Pérez Zepeta accused Tiburcio of having personally stolen the lands of San Miguel y San Lorenzo during the first *reparto*, and he had sought since then to find a way of getting them back. Galicia's public lands claim aimed to do just that, so Tiburcio had a personal stake in preventing it. The prisoners were marched down to the basin; once they had made it back into the Cantón of Papantla, in Joloapan, Tiburcio had Pérez Zepeta killed. Whether or not the *jefe político* had authorized Pérez Zepeta's murder, he undoubtedly saw it as a good thing; like Antonio Vásquez, Pérez Zepeta was an incorrigible troublemaker, and that was the fate they both deserved. The next day, Tiburcio brought the remaining captives into the town, placing them in the custody of a company of soldiers from the 23rd Infantry battalion, who had been stationed there for months. Precisely what the prisoners stood accused of, nobody knew.

When word of Tiburcio's actions reached the expectant *rancherías*, other dissident leaders gathered their people to decide how to proceed. The meeting took place on the Thursday of Corpus Christi (May 28, 1891), one of Papantla's most important feast days. Tensions were already high, because the *jefe político*—a man well known for his imperious disposition—had denied permission for a religious procession. Marcelino Sánchez learned of the gathering and sent a squad of local guardsmen to break it up; as the *Periódico Oficial* would later put it, he was convinced that a seditious conspiracy was underway. Inevitably, a shootout ensued; when it was all over, one man was dead and several people had been injured on both sides. Fearing reprisals, many of the assembled men, women, and children fled to the hills. The *jefe político* then sent the Guard—led by Simón Tiburcio and Pablo Hernández Olmedo—after them, and the dissidents, now declared rebels, responded with guerrilla attacks, demanding the immediate destitution and prosecution of the *jefe político*, the municipal treasurer, and the local State Treasury agent. By mid-June, there was a small war going on in Chote y Mesillas, Cerro del Carbón, El Palmar, Poza Larga y Cazuelas, and other neighboring *lotes*.[54]

Led by Totonac *rancheros* Agustín García Silva and Abraham Santos, the dissidents initially succeeded in fighting off Sánchez's forces and even managed to stage a number of offensive operations. They seized control of some of the roads leading into the town but did not attempt to take it, since there were federal soldiers there. Believing that Galicia's trampled mission had federal approval, they were disappointed to discover that the troops were not coming to their aid.[55] Unable to subdue his numerous opponents and fearing for the safety of town dwellers, the *jefe político* appealed for help from the state government. Governor Enríquez quickly asked President Díaz for military support, and around the sixteenth of June the warships *Independencia* and *Libertad* sailed from Veracruz toward Tecolutla with some three hundred soldiers from the 4th Infantry battalion on board. Men from the 3rd Cavalry battalion were also dispatched. Meanwhile, the rebels were also trying to get Díaz's attention and intervention, sending urgent letters to Mexico City. It was as a result of the sudden troop movements that the press first learned that there was trouble in Papantla; information was scarce, since the telegraph lines had been cut. On June 20, *El Monitor Republicano* ran its first story, citing "rumors of an uprising in Papantla." It concluded by noting that people in Veracruz were saying that the army was being sent to quell "a revolutionary movement of the Indians of Papantla." This was no doubt exactly what the *jefe político* had wanted everyone to believe.[56]

Before long, the troops had landed in Tecolutla, marching inland to track down the "revolutionaries." In retrospect, this marked the beginning of nearly a decade during which Papantla's social conflicts would be settled by military means. Colonel Melitón Hurtado was placed in charge of the "pacification" operation, displacing the disgraced *jefe político*. Right away he recruited Tiburcio and Hernández Olmedo to aid in these efforts, asking them to raise and lead a large auxiliary force of "loyal" Totonac farmers. Unlike the soldiers, they knew the terrain and the locals and could help the army to identify and track down the rebels and their supporters. For Tiburcio and his allies, this was to be a splendid opportunity to settle old scores; the time had come to take sides. A short but intense spate of persecutions and bloodshed ensued, pushing many residents in the besieged *rancherías* to seek refuge deep in the forests. Many decades later, Modesto González recalled those terrible days:

The people of Tajín were afraid. The Federal troops took the men to fight against the rebels. Only the old men, and the women, and the children were left. Nobody wanted to sleep in his house; at night, the people gathered and went to the *monte* to sleep.[57]

By some accounts, the rebels went out of their way to avoid antagonizing the *federales*; their quarrel was not with the army, but with a *jefe político* and a rival Totonac faction bent on eliminating them. Their leaders soon realized the precariousness of their situation, and within a week of Hurtado's arrival sought to negotiate a surrender. On June 26, one month after the killing of Pérez Zepeta and the initial skirmish of Corpus Christi, a delegation of Totonac dissidents from the affected *lotes* met with the Colonel to negotiate an end to the violence; according to the *Periódico Oficial*, they represented about three hundred *sublevados*. An agreement was reached "to surrender unconditionally" in exchange for "clemency" and Hurtado's promise that the government would hear and consider their grievances. Soon thereafter, *jefe político* Marcelino Sánchez was dismissed; Congressman Teodoro G. Lecuona—sent to conduct a special investigation—took his place on an interim basis. As far as Xalapa was concerned, the uprising was "completely over."[58] Among Papantla's Totonacs, however, the social rift was now deeper than ever; "loyals" and "rebels"—as they came to be called—would eye each other warily for a long time to come. As that bloody June drew to a close, the fighting had stopped, but the issues that had ignited the conflict remained unaddressed.

Meanwhile, a war of words was just beginning. News of the fighting in Papantla must have startled Galicia, who had not foreseen that his plan would elicit such a violent reaction. For that, he was partly to blame. There is evidence to suggest that he brazenly inflated his clients' expectations about his trip, saying or implying that it had the full backing of the federal government and would thus override any local opposition. Out in the *rancherías*, this message played out all too well, a floating quilt of deliverance wishes to which fanciful patches could be added as needed. One account, often repeated, had Galicia promising that Díaz himself and the Minister of War would come with him to Papantla, bringing federal troops to carry out the land surveys. With this mighty show of force, victory over corrupt officials, tyrannical bosses, and oppressive levies was all but assured.[59] Tales like this one may not have come directly from Galicia, but they were spun in part from his own yarn. They helped drive the resurgence of the dissidents' movement (boosting money collections), and then fueled their anger after the *jefe político* blocked Galicia's arrival. They also exacerbated Sánchez's sense of alarm and outrage, prompting him to take drastic measures against the *denunciantes*. Whether or not he acknowledged it, Galicia's self-serving braggadocio—well meaning as it may have been— helped to precipitate these clashes. To his credit, he then rushed to publicize his clients' plight and motives, hoping to win them (and himself) some sympathy and perhaps also a measure of protection. He took a letter he claimed to have just received from Papantla to *El Monitor Republicano*, where it was published on June 25. Although it was signed by dissident leader Abraham Santos, it is evident that Galicia had a hand in composing it. In an editorial preface, the paper noted that there was no insurrection or rebellion in Papantla; some law-abiding Totonac citizens had tried to exercise the right to survey their lands and a vengeful *jefe político* had responded with violence and repression. The letter then told the story of the Fomento concession, explaining how political and fiscal tyranny were at the root of the conflict. It denounced "the large contributions and fines that are imposed on us," protesting that "given the maltreatment we suffer, it would seem that we are the slaves of the *jefe político*." Even Porfirio Díaz took notice.[60]

The following week, Enríquez's government published a lengthy rebuttal. The uprising that had just ended, said the *Periódico Oficial*, was the outcome of a long history of organized deceit and manipulation regarding the distribution of Papantla's ex-communal lands. The real culprits—a gang of confidence tricksters and shameless agitators—were to be found in Mexico City:

The lands of Papantla that used to belong to the extinguished Indian community . . . were divided into *grandes lotes* . . . many years ago. . . . Some time ago the government enacted a law granting incentives to *condueños* who subdivided their lands into small individual plots. In some *pueblos* this provision is producing good results, for the treasury as well as for individuals. In Papantla, it has not been possible to put this beneficial measure into practice all across the canton, because lately some individuals in the capital of the Republic who live off exploiting the ignorance of our Indian people persuaded those who led the recent uprising that all of the lands in the canton belong to the Indians; that they would be able to parcel them out among themselves if they obtained the original titles from the National Archive; that they did not have to pay taxes on what was rightfully theirs; and that the Minister of War and other officials would go to Papantla with federal troops to give them possession of their lands. Despite the ridiculousness of this propaganda, not only on this occasion but on many others have the Indians been exploited by those swindlers who live it up in Mexico thanks to the fees they periodically collect through their agents. Since the *jefe político* is bound to combat this exploitation, the Indians who have been duped interpret his actions as opposition to their wishes. . . . It is a well known fact that when it comes to land, the fears and ambitions of Indians are aroused, and like soft wax they lend themselves to the machinations of those who know how to take advantage of those feelings.

To make matters even worse, continued the *Periódico Oficial*, Papantla's vanilla dealers were in the habit of spreading all sorts of absurd stories about goings-on in the town—new taxes, fines, a military levy—in order to get growers to sell at low prices out by the fields. These false rumors generated additional animosity against the authorities. This constituted an implicit acknowledgement that fiscal pressures were a significant source of discontent; still, the government's stance remained firm: "The Indians of Papantla are obliged to pay the property tax." As for the controversial *baldíos* surveys, they "have nothing to ask or expect from the Ministry of Fomento, because the lands are already theirs and no one in the state disputes it; they can either keep them in *grandes lotes* or subdivide them, taking advantage of the incentives offered by our legislature."[61]

Several days later, Galicia counterattacked. This time, the letter printed in *El Monitor* was signed by Mateo Xochihua and Arcadio Malpica, both

Totonacs from Papantla, but Galicia was almost certainly the author.[62] In it, the so-called swindlers—as Xalapa's letter had described Galicia and company—were portrayed instead as "people we consider honorable, because they have not yet charged anything for their work." But despite self-serving and deceitful remarks such as these (he had been paid), the letter did present a series of arguments and complaints that Pérez Zepeta's companions down in Papantla would have certainly recognized as their own. Galicia may have written this text, but he did not simply invent most of what it said; all in all, it was an ingenious combination of disguised self-defense and forceful advocacy.[63]

In response to the *Periódico Oficial*, Xochihua and Malpica's letter noted that the group's aim was to obtain *excedencias* and *demasías*, explaining that the state congress had jurisdiction "over the *fundos legales* and the *egidos*, but not over their *excedencias*, which belong to the nation."[64] That is why they had applied to the Ministry of Fomento, and why they still hoped to carry out the surveys. This was followed by a litany of complaints about the oppressive character of daily life in Papantla, in which taxes and fees were the common denominator. Some were linked to the *condueñazgos*: they had to pay for access to land and timber, and the property tax rate was excessively high. How could the government say that they already owned these lands? Others had to do with specific levies: they paid a monthly school tax, but there were no schools outside of the town; they also had to worry about the personal tax and buy permits to plant tobacco, sugarcane, and coffee; and the civil registry fees were onerous: birth certificates were $3 pesos for boys and $1.50 pesos for girls, marriage licenses were $7 pesos, death certificates (or, as they put it, "to report the death of a person") cost $1.50 pesos, and burial rights cost another $3 pesos. Then they had heavy fines to contend with. Especially galling—they said—were those connected with the enforcement of a new dress code recently imposed by Marcelino Sánchez; while in town, men had to wear pants and women cotton skirts and blouses or else they were sanctioned. Moreover, payment receipts were seldom provided. Finally, they complained about the progressive decline in green vanilla prices, which they blamed on the *jefe político*: "Before, the price of vanilla used to be 15 to 20 pesos per hundred, then it went down to 5, and recently the *jefe político* ordered that we should be paid between $2.50 and $3, so we don't get rich (those were his words)." Exaggerated or unbelievable though it may sound, the letter concluded, this was the true plight of Papantla.[65]

Galicia's aim was to show that this had been a clash generated by the abuse of political authority—that is, by disregard for the law, unjust taxes, dictatorial propensities, and racism. But in many ways (though without meaning to), this text also captured the essence of the social and economic developments that had transformed Papantla during the course of the 1880s, the era of *condueñazgo*: lower vanilla prices, more taxes, competition for land and other natural resources, and merchant domination. These were the deep springs of the conflict. Beyond that (again unwittingly), the letter illustrated how a segment of Papantla's Totonac population made sense of some of these wrenching developments. Green vanilla prices are a case in point. Their long-term decline resulted from complex market changes, and their sudden drop in 1891 was the product of a local buyers' cartel. Nevertheless, people blamed the *jefe político*, who may have liked—or even benefited from—the lower prices but who certainly did not bring them about. Likewise, land-use and timber-extraction fees were imposed by *condueñazgo* managers, yet many assumed—or were told and believed—that the orders came from the top. Beneath these grievances about the conduct of government lay the strife born of socioeconomic change and competition. State officials would try to refute Galicia's specific allegations, but they were unprepared—and disinclined—to address the larger implications.[66]

Revealing as it was, though, this war of words would not settle any social conflicts. Following the formal end of hostilities arranged by Colonel Hurtado during the last week of June, the situation in Papantla remained tense. At that time, Governor Enríquez sent up Teodoro Lecuona on a fact-finding mission; his confidential report would acknowledge that Pérez Zepeta's extrajudicial killing had triggered the violence. In early July, a Totonac delegation was brought to Xalapa to present their grievances directly to the governor. However, none of the surviving dissident leaders made the trip; despite Hurtado's assurances, the murderous prosecution of private vendettas continued out in the countryside. The visitors petitioned in vain for relief from so many taxes and fees and for the re-opening of primary schools in the *congregaciones*, but as far as the government was concerned there was absolutely nothing to negotiate. "The Indians," reported the *Periódico Oficial*, "have brought every document they thought would be useful, but they have not been able to prove that there have been any tax extortions or land usurpations." They were told instead that "the *lote* administrators elected by the *condueños*—that is, by themselves—are the ones who have exploited them with levies of various sorts, making them believe (taking advantage of their ignorance) that these exactions were ordered by state and municipal authorities."[67]

Enríquez tried to persuade them that an individual *reparto* was now their best course of action, and they all agreed that Galicia should do the land surveys, since he had already received about $1,000 pesos for that purpose. Afterward, Enríquez and the Totonac delegates wrote separately to Porfirio Díaz requesting that he summon Galicia to pay off his debts in Papantla. Replying to the governor, Díaz offered to interview Galicia,

. . . and if I find him docile and reasonable, I will send him to speak with you. But if, on the contrary, in studying his character I decide that his presence there would be counterproductive—which is likely, because he is a very *ladino* Indian [meaning "mestizo," also "cunning"] who has also upset things in some *pueblos* in the State of Mexico, fancying himself the savior of all those of his class—then it will be preferable to leave him in this Capital, where we can keep him under control.[68]

The meeting between Díaz and Galicia took place in early August. There is no record of their conversation, but it is clear that Galicia told the president what he wanted to hear. Díaz wrote to Enríquez saying that Galicia had pledged to use all his influence to resolve Papantla's land troubles and to inculcate in his followers the respect and obedience owed to the government. Although Galicia had warned him that there were many obstacles to overcome, he would nonetheless try. Gone, then, was his search for *excedencias* and *demasías* to claim; the engineer of the *baldíos* plan had now agreed to convince his clients to subdivide their *lotes* into individual parcels. At least this time he really did have the president's backing. A week or so later, Galicia left Mexico City for Xalapa, where he met with Enríquez to receive instructions regarding his mission in Papantla; traveling with him was a *licenciado* by the name of Jesús Serrano, on leave from the Ministry of Foreign Relations. While in Xalapa, Galicia got to see for the first time a map of Papantla's ex-communal *lotes*, which he was allowed to borrow. It was the only one the government had, a copy of Pascoli's 1876 drawing made by Agapito Fontecilla y Vidal back in 1881. Map, tools, and superior orders in hand, Galicia set out once again for Papantla. It was late August. He was accompanied not only by Licenciado Serrano, but also by Agustín García Silva and a group of his followers, who had journeyed there to meet him.[69]

Since the events of June, a precarious truce had held in Papantla; Hurtado's troops still occupied the town and patrolled the countryside, with the assistance of "loyal" Indian militias. Among Totonacs in the affected *rancherías*, an increasing polarization was evident, and the potential for more widespread violence remained high. Guns were everywhere, not just in the hands of soldiers and militiamen; in the wake of the vanilla boom, Papantla's had become a heavily armed rural society, as farmers acquired muskets, carbines, and rifles to protect their precious fruit. This was especially evident at harvest time, when many stayed out at night by their fields, periodically shooting into the air to ward off any intruders. Both sides clearly had the means to fight. Upon arrival in Papantla, Galicia was supposed to present himself before Colonel Hurtado and the new *jefe político*, who would organize and supervise the *repartos*. But Galicia had a different idea. Instead, his party bypassed the town and went straight to El Palmar, a stronghold of the dissident movement, setting up headquarters in García Silva's rancho. Along the way, numerous supporters came out to greet them. Galicia's presence instantly rekindled broad hopes and fears.[70]

At first, a tense calm prevailed. In early September, Galicia and García Silva invited the authorities in Papantla to meet at Palmar. According to a report published in *El Monitor*, "The Indians who had rebelled, led by Mr. Severiano Galicia and Agustín Silva, held a banquet at Silva's rancho in honor of Colonel Hurtado, the military commander, and Mr. Lecuona, the *jefe político*; around two thousand Indians—almost all of them armed—attended the banquet, but it was a very cordial affair, with many toasts to peace, etc." It must have been a grand event; more than half a century later, Modesto González had not forgotten it, telling anthropologist Angel Palerm about it. At the time, its symbolism was not lost on anyone: there were the young surveyor and the fearless Totonac *ranchero* meeting with the *jefe político* and the military commander as equals, on their terms and on their turf.[71]

Having publicly established his independence from these high officials, Galicia began to work out the details of a land *reparto* with his hosts. Throughout, he kept Díaz informed by telegraph. In retrospect, it seems clear that he did not know how dangerous a terrain he was stepping into; a bold naiveté coupled with the knowledge that President Díaz supported his mission propelled him into action. As it turns out, there were at least four competing interpretations of what Galicia's project meant to accomplish, and the differences between them were irreconcilable, making a clash all but inevitable. First was Galicia's own plan; although never fully articulated, it appeared to involve individual land *repartos* among shareholding farmers, free from meddling by town merchants, politicians, and allied Totonac strongmen. Borrowing an idea he had first developed during his time with the Yaqui, he also envisioned the creation of nucleated population centers in the *rancherías*. In these new town zones, every resident—even those who were not shareholders—could claim a small plot of land in order to build a house. These civilizing hamlets, each with its own primary school, might then grow into residential and commercial hubs, giving the Indians a degree of control over local trade, politics, and community life. A brief description of this project appeared in a Mexico City daily:

Ing. Severiano Galicia and Lic. Jesús Serrano arrived some time ago; they were sent by the President of the Republic—at the request of some *vecinos* from around here—in order to settle the land issues that have for some time agitated the Cantón. The petitioners had agreed with Galicia's proposed way of resolving the matter, [which included] forming some *pueblos* or *barrios* in the *rancherías* of the Municipality and then establishing primary schools in them, as General Díaz had recommended.[72]

These so-called petitioners, however, had their own ideas, and they went much further than Galicia's. For García Silva, Santos, and their followers, the proposed *repartos* held a bigger promise. As they saw it, the new land-tenure reform would pave the way for a full restoration of a lost territorial, political, and fiscal autonomy: no more taxes and fees, no more share certificates, no more venal *lote* administrators, no more rapacious bosses like Simón Tiburcio, no more merchant encroachment, and no more overbearing *jefes políticos*. That is what many of them had been seeking since the days of Díaz Manfort, and what a number of their companions had died fighting for. Their moment had at last come; Galicia's land divisions would serve to usher in a radical transfer of local powers and a different structure of social relations. Whether or not Galicia understood this was in the end not all that important. The fact that his mandate was said to come from the president himself boosted their confidence; not long before, they were persecuted, but now they appeared to have the upper hand.

From another perspective, though, Galicia's project represented a very grave danger. For those who had benefited the most from the *condueñazgo*—*apoderados*, town merchants, Totonac speculators and brokers, some shareholding farmers—these *repartos* threatened to wipe away their gains, undermining the legal foundations on which these property-holding associations had been built. And it was not just the rich who reacted this way; many farmers—shareholders and *fincados*—who for one reason or another had sided with the "loyals" during the recent conflicts feared reprisals and exclusion should Galicia's clients gain control of the *lotes*. Finally, there were the authorities in Papantla, whom Galicia had chosen to defy, betraying Xalapa's trust. Lecuona and Hurtado would not let this stand. As far as they were concerned, these people were in effect trying to wrestle control of the land issue away from the government and various local vested interests. They also harbored a deep hostility toward taxes, questioning one of the chief prerogatives of legitimate authority. Thus, it did not matter that the lands in question were private, and hence outside the direct jurisdiction of the government; to these officials, what Galicia and his armed friends were promoting smacked of sedition. On this, they had the support—open or tacit—of more compliant sectors of the local population. Some—for example, certain *apoderados*—simply did not want the land subdivided, preferring to keep the current arrangement; others—many town merchants and *condueños*—did favor a *reparto*, but only one they might have a better chance of controlling.

After the banquet, Galicia held large meetings with farmers from many *rancherías*, where he explained his plans for a *reparto* and obtained their written consent. He spoke in Spanish and dissident leaders translated his words into Totonac; in fact, however, they were not always saying the same things. To confuse matters further, as the enhanced message of Galicia's licentiously translated speeches traveled hurriedly beyond Palmar, the project's foes made sure to twist its meaning yet again. Meanwhile, money collections to pay for the surveys resumed; with the dissidents momentarily free to exercise their muscle, many were persuaded to contribute and sign

up. Some even took advantage to settle their own scores. Sitting in Papantla, Colonel Hurtado and the *jefe político* watched and waited. Around
mid-month, a decision to intervene was finally made; alarmed by reports of
widening insubordination and upset by what he would later describe as
Galicia's "bad faith," Enríquez ordered the ringleaders' immediate capture.
Apparently unaware of all these developments, Galicia proudly informed
both Díaz and Enríquez that he had succeeded in persuading the Indians to
accept a land *reparto*. García Silva, Santos, Serrano, and Galicia then prepared to travel up to Mexico City, bringing a document signed by all those
who agreed with the plan (as each understood it) along with papers detailing the alleged wrongdoing of the previous *jefe político*. On the eve of their
departure, Colonel Hurtado lured the group into Papantla with the pretext
of signing some documents giving Galicia power of attorney. Once there, he
had them arrested; Agustín García Silva, Abraham Santos, and a few other
dissident Totonacs were jailed, never to be heard from again, while Galicia
and Serrano were held in detention. The date was probably September 21.[73]
With that, the truce was broken. Two days later, fearing an attack, Hurtado
ordered Pablo Hernández Olmedo to gather up as many "loyals" as possible and bring them to defend the town. That same week, a worried Governor Enríquez announced that he was going to Papantla to settle the conflict
in person; he left Xalapa on the 28th. Troop reinforcements were also sent.
Never before had a sitting governor of Veracruz traveled to the Tecolutla
basin. As the *Periódico Oficial* put it, Enríquez would face up to "the con-
trarious interests of some individuals in the Cantón who exploit the ignorance of the Indians with respect to the complex and troublesome business
of the land," as well as to "the demands made by these same Indians once
they become associated with those who prosper at the expense of their ignorance." In short, his would not be a conciliatory trip.[74]

Governor Enríquez remained in Papantla for nearly three weeks; this
pueblo's long-running unrest was quickly becoming a source of political
embarrassment, so he was determined to reestablish order once and for all.
Assuming that most "rebels" had simply been duped into subversion, Enríquez believed that his presence—and that of new federal troops—would
effectively unmask the deception. What he heard from town merchants, local officials, and Colonel Hurtado served only to strengthen his punitive resolve. His first step was to call on García Silva's followers to lay down their
weapons, pay taxes, and pledge obedience to the government. Many did so
without delay, but others fled instead to the *monte*. These he would deal
with very harshly. A few Totonac dissidents managed to slip away to the
capital, where they sought help from Ignacio Mariscal and Porfirio Díaz.
As for Galicia, he was placed in jail, to be prosecuted for organizing a seditious conspiracy. Licenciado Serrano, meanwhile, was set free; he promptly

returned to Mexico City. Having taken charge of the situation, Enríquez wrote a long letter to Porfirio Díaz outlining the troubled history of Papantla's communal disentailment and highlighting what he regarded as the main causes of the current turmoil. The original *reparto*, he acknowledged, was partly to blame. Those in charge had not seen the original property titles, relying instead on what they knew and on what they were told by some interested parties, and the man who drew the maps had no qualifications to do so. This is what had given rise to the *baldíos* plan, but the lands the petitioners hoped to claim were now in fact private estates. Then, he went on, there were the many abuses committed by *apoderados* and *ladino* bosses, coupled with the Indians' natural aversion to taxes. These factors, too, contributed to create a climate of opposition to land-tenure reforms, which was assiduously manipulated by the very same exploiters and agitators. Despite these difficulties, progress was being made toward parcelization, but the previous *jefe político*'s lack of tact had brought that to a sudden halt. The principal culprit, however, was Severiano Galicia, whose duplicitous behavior, the Governor had concluded, was directly responsible for the recent disturbances. As Enríquez explained it to Díaz:

Galicia and his partner offered to survey the lands of the Cantón and give the Indians what belonged to them; they would group them into a *pueblo*, creating a new municipality that would be governed by the Indians alone, independent from the *jefe político* or anyone else, in which they would not have to pay any taxes. In order to achieve this, they would have to agree to subdivide the lands, which did not mean that they could not then keep them as one great community, a subterfuge employed by Galicia so that he could tell you and me that the Indians had consented to the subdivision.[75]

Distorted as it was, the charge was nevertheless revealing, a seamless webbing of contradictory meanings: Galicia's proposal, his clients' own designs, and their enemies' worst fears. What held them together was the unspoken recognition that this latest wrangle over the *repartos* reflected a much larger battle for political control and economic domination in the countryside. At stake was the Totonac farmer's historic independence, which had been rapidly eroding for the past two decades as part of a grating reconfiguration of rural social relations. Some liked to call this progress, the spread of business, reason, and the rule of law, but others considered it an onslaught of thievery, despotism, and betrayal. Governor Enríquez chose to blame the whole episode on Galicia, but he was merely a convenient scapegoat. In fact, the problem ran much deeper; Papantla was in the throes of a lopsided civil war driven by social conflicts Galicia had nothing to do with and did not really understand. It is not clear that the Governor understood them either, but he was nevertheless made keenly aware that the more recalcitrant Totonac dissidents represented a threat, which he moved decisively to eliminate.

During his last week in Papantla, Enríquez ordered a series of military operations against García Silva's collaborators. This time, Hurtado's men were merciless. "Loyal" Totonac squads commanded by Tiburcio and Hernández Olmedo once again joined the fray, lending invaluable assistance. "I am confident that precious few will manage to escape," Enríquez told Díaz, "persecuted as they are by local people." He strongly recommended that captured dissident leaders be sent to Yucatán as conscripts. "The Indians from these places," he argued, "fear banishment more than death." The soldiers and their auxiliaries fanned out across the countryside, hunting down those suspected of being rebels. These raids met with resistance, and there were skirmishes for nearly a month, but in the end the military's superior organization and firepower would prevail. Following the governor's return to Xalapa on October 18, the *Periódico Oficial* announced merely that Papantla's problem was "on the way to being resolved favorably and definitively."[76]

Ten days later, *El Monitor* began reporting on the new "disturbances" in Papantla. "We are told," read an article, "that the Indians have fled to the Sierra, and that their families have done the same, to escape the outrages; of those who have been captured by federal forces, the least worse off have been taken as recruits."[77] Others, it is hard to know how many, were presumably killed. Epidemics were taking a toll as well; smallpox had run rampant for most of the year, and yellow fever struck in October, following the arrival of military reinforcements from Veracruz. These new troops would be deadly in more ways than one. In the course of two months, 115 people died from yellow fever in the town alone; out in the fields, many other such deaths went unrecorded. Among the hardest hit were soldiers, who were garrisoned all over town. But for this outbreak of *vómito negro*, Colonel Hurtado's campaign to root out the dissident movement would have been even fiercer. *El Monitor Republicano* described the situation:

From letters that have been received in this capital city, we know that the disturbances in Papantla have not yet come to an end. The forces that were sent there are being decimated by the *vómito*. It seems that right now there are many soldiers afflicted by that terrible disease, which has already killed many of them. There are also some wounded soldiers. The 21st Battalion, which is searching out the rebels, has suffered casualties because of that disease.[78]

By the middle of November Hurtado's men had captured or killed many of those who had been identified as rebels. At Enríquez's express request, nearly two hundred prisoners would be exiled as military conscripts or forced laborers. The first group, a roped-gang of ninety Totonac captives, was reported to have left Papantla for Veracruz on the 16th; many ended up in Yucatán. Some three weeks later, another seventy-six Indian prisoners were being conducted on foot to Tehuacán, presumably to work in the salt mines. Upon reaching Tlacotepec, two of them died, and fourteen others were reported to be ill.[79] As the military campaign drew to a close, the yellow fever epidemic in Papantla began at last to subside, but the many ravages of 1891 would not soon be forgotten.

Meantime, Severiano Galicia sat in Papantla's municipal jail awaiting the prosecution of his case. Since October, he had sent a dozen letters and telegrams to Porfirio Díaz, steadfastly protesting his innocence and pleading for help. "My ignorance of the Totonac language," he wrote, "forced me to rely on interpreters to persuade the Indians to subdivide their lands; many of them, acting in bad faith and with premeditation, and a few others for lack of understanding, told the common masses things that were different from or distortions of what I was trying to say, which was inspired by the instructions that I received from you in person and by telegram." For his present predicament he blamed "not so much the blundering of the Indians, but the malevolence of their exploiters, their timidity in voicing grievances before the state government, and the bad faith of some who intimidate them, persecuting even innocent children and defenseless women." Given "the conflicting interests of expert schemers, the hollow pretensions, and the ancient customs" surrounding Papantla's land issues, he had feared from the start that his mission might end in failure. He had told Díaz as much back in August, and the president had nevertheless urged him on, pledging to assist him. Now he was imprisoned, "the innocent victim of a powerful intrigue," all for trying to carry out Díaz's orders. To make matters even worse, the *jefe político* in Chalco had just decided to reopen the sedition case pending against him. Unless the president stepped in, his prospects looked dismal.[80] In response, Díaz pressed Enríquez for information on the charges, urging him repeatedly to bring the trial to a speedy conclusion, even recommending a little leniency. But the governor had other ideas, determined as he was to make an example out of Galicia. As the year came to an end, the legal proceedings were at a standstill, and the president's envoy remained locked up.[81]

In Xalapa, the *Periódico Oficial* said nothing about the military operations in Papantla; this was no longer a war of words. When it was all over, the newspaper published a short, triumphalist note stating that due to "the efforts of the Governor" and "the prudence and tact of the current authorities in the Cantón," the Indians of Papantla "have come to understand the benefits of individual *repartos*; many of the *lotes* have already been subdivided, and the rest will soon be as well."[82] This prevarication was, of course, for public consumption; in fact, Papantla's subdivisions had barely started and the brutal repression of the previous months had left the entire process in disarray. The dissidents appeared to have been crushed, but the sources of their discontent had not gone away. Pérez Zepeta, García Silva, and Santos may have been killed, but others would soon replace them.

The events of 1891 would shape the conduct of future *repartos* in at

least three tangible ways: the feud between so-called rebel and loyal Totonacs would remain a defining aspect of the process in several *lotes*, military officers would be brought in to take charge of the land surveys, and—
the legal autonomy of the *condueños* notwithstanding—both the *jefe
político* and the Ayuntamiento would play a direct role in the management
of the subdivisions. In short, Papantla's land-tenure reform became inextricably contentious, openly politicized, and increasingly militarized, the battleground of a rural society bound in strife.

1892–1894

By many accounts, Juan Manuel Vidal was a swindler, a liar, a thief,
and a despot, an old fox who would do and say anything in order to get
ahead. During 1891 and 1892, he was also the mayor of Papantla. Heir to
a prominent family name, he lacked the wealth and the social standing of
his influential forbears. Of Juan M. Vidal it was said that if after he told
you something he closed his mouth, it was all a lie, but if he kept his mouth
open, then it was probably not true. Already a rogue of long experience, his
sordid behavior while in office would only enhance this reputation. His de-
vious land schemes and authoritarian manner injected more poison into a
convulsed social situation.[83] Following the routing of García Silva's movement, Vidal pushed for a quick subdivision of Papantla's *grandes lotes*, beginning with two—Cerro del Carbón and Chote y Mesillas—where the dissidents had been especially active and in which he and a few associates had
interests of their own. In both Chote y Mesillas and Cerro del Carbón, Vidal was himself the president of the divisory board. He worked closely with
Simón Tiburcio; both had the backing of Colonel Hurtado, who remained
in Papantla until the last days of 1891. At Vidal's behest, divisory boards
from several *condueñazgos* signed surveying and parceling contracts with
Ing. Salvador Martínez, collecting funds from shareholders to pay him in
advance. Soon thereafter, the mapping of Cerro del Carbón got underway.

From Xalapa, Governor Enríquez actively assisted this process. As Hurtado prepared his departure, a newly appointed *jefe político*—Manuel
Maraboto—arrived in Papantla with orders to speed along the *repartos*.
Right away he summoned the *apoderados* and *regidores* in the remaining
condueñazgos, telling them to organize their people for the task at hand
and to begin clearing the underbrush along their *lote*'s boundaries. Less
than two weeks later, Enríquez wrote to the president requesting military
engineers to divide Papantla's lands. Now that order had been reestab-
lished, he argued, the time was ripe for a concerted drive. His plan was to
parcel out eight to ten *condueñazgos* in two or three months, but for that

he needed more surveyors, and a team of military officers could work faster and charge less than their civilian counterparts. Díaz consented, and the following month the Ministry of War dispatched a commission of engineers headed by Colonel Victoriano Huerta; one of its six members was the president's nephew, a young officer named Félix Díaz. They reached Papantla on February 25, bringing new topographic equipment purchased with a loan from the state government. In late March, when their work commenced, Huerta's squad had signed contracts with six *conduetñazgos*. Five more would soon follow suit. On paper, nearly every *conduetñazgo*—El Palmar being the most notable exception—now seemed to be moving decisively in the direction of parcelization.[84]

The appearance of progress was mostly deceiving, however. The earliest *repartos*—conducted by Ing. Martínez and orchestrated by Vidal—were troubled and troubling from the start. In a bold act of skullduggery, the mayor forced shareholders in Chote, Cerro del Carbón, and Tlahuanapa to give him their certificates for registration; some were then sold off, reported as lost, or simply duplicated, much of this with the connivance of the town's notary public. In this shuffle, Vidal and his partners came out big winners. At the same time, the sale of shares from these *lotes* increased abruptly. Misinformation, trickery, intimidation, and misfortune played a large role. One ruse involved spreading the rumor that as a consequence of the recent turmoil the government had given up altogether on the idea of carrying out subdivisions, making stock certificates useless. More than a few Totonacs were apparently fooled in this way, agreeing to sign away their papers in return for a little money. This kind of deception had only a small chance of succeeding in more or less unified communities, where neighbors were more likely to protect each other, but these were places fraught with discord, where loyalties were far from assured and betrayal had its own rewards. In addition, the conflicts of 1891 had left many families vulnerable and even destitute, and there was no shortage of people willing to take advantage of them. In Chote y Mesillas, where 179 certificates had been issued, more than fifty share sales took place during 1892, the vast majority between January and August. Three individuals were the principal beneficiaries: Juan M. Vidal, Simón Tiburcio, and Antonio Chena, the last a merchant who became Chote's single largest stockholder in a matter of months. Something similar happened in Cerro del Carbón and Tlahuanapa; in the latter, merchant Melquíades Patiño ended up buying one-third of the *lote*'s 122 shares of ownership. In more discreet fashion, a select group of farmers augmented their shares as well. A good many others simply held on to theirs; considering the scale and provenance of the grabbing, that was no small achievement.

Moreover, new rackets arose as soon as Salvador Martínez began to demarcate individual parcels in each of these *grandes lotes*. Under Vidal's ad hoc rules, shareholders who wanted to ensure that their assigned parcels would coincide with their farmlands had to pay for the privilege; otherwise those lands might well be handed over (or sold) to somebody else, forcing the current user to buy back the plot, pay rent, or sell the plantings to the new landowner. Disfranchised farmers already faced this prospect, but *condueños* were supposed to have a first claim to their fields. Once that guarantee was removed, the opportunities for graft were endless. Holders of more than one share could negotiate with Martínez to get them joined into a larger unit, even if this involved displacing others. In Chote y Mesillas, for instance, Antonio Chena would obtain a single parcel measuring 168 hectares, the equivalent of eleven shares; Juan M. Vidal was similarly favored, receiving 96 adjoining hectares for his six shares of ownership. Deals such as these—along with other displays of venality—soon gained Martínez an unsavory reputation.[85] Many who had cautiously welcomed these *repartos* soured on them as a result; for the remaining dissidents, meanwhile, these high-handed maneuvers were a bitter confirmation of long-standing fears. But with organized opposition in the affected *lotes* weakened by death and exile, and with the memory of a brutal repression still very fresh, vocal protests were slow in coming. Besides, who was there to complain to? The mayor? The *jefe político*? Simón Tiburcio?

Word of these developments nevertheless spread quickly to other *rancherías*, complicating the *jefe político*'s campaign to arrange *repartos* in the rest of Papantla's *lotes*. Soon enough, expressions of dissension began to pour in. In late January, the *apoderado* and the *regidor* of Poza Larga (lot 12) told Maraboto that while their people remained willing to undertake a land subdivision, they would not agree to do it with Salvador Martínez, who was known to be victimizing their neighbors in Cerro del Carbón. In response, they were invited to choose another surveyor. *Condueños* in other *lotes* also complained about Martínez, asking to rescind their contracts. Two weeks later, the *apoderado* of Boca de Lima (lot 9) wrote to Governor Enríquez saying that a number of *condueños* "want to remain in community, leaving the *lote* the way it is now." He had heard that there were now laws mandating individual *repartos*, which he personally favored, but the shareholders wanted to know if it was nonetheless possible to keep the *condueñazgo*. Not long thereafter, the *apoderado* of nearby Arroyo Grande Boca de Lima (lot 6) followed suit, echoing Boca de Lima's request for guidance. In each case, the reply was the same: while not exactly obligatory, the *repartos* were convenient as well as necessary, since individual private property would afford former shareholders many benefits. Both *condueñazgos* would end up reluctantly signing contracts with Huerta's commission.

Yet another letter came from more than two hundred farmers in Polutla, Taracuán, y Poza Verde (lot 10). In this one there was no ambivalence. "It is not in our interest to proceed with a subdivision of the *lote*," the farmers wrote, "because we are accustomed to living in community." For that reason, they respectfully requested an exemption. We the farmers, they went on to tell Enríquez, are the only ones who have been paying taxes here, implying that regardless of who held the stock certificates, they were in justice the true owners of those lands. This was a direct rebuff of Xalapa's plans, sent out on the eve of Huerta's arrival in Papantla. The reply was accordingly curt and legalistic: before any decision could be made on their case, they would have to get power of attorney from a majority of shareholders or constitute themselves into a *sociedad agrícola*, as stipulated in the Commercial Code. This was, in fact, a legal option, but not one that the authorities were now prepared to countenance. Against the petitioners' manifest objections, the *jefe político* found other shareholders willing to form a divisory board and Polutla joined the long list of *condueñazgos* under contract to be parceled out by Huerta. To avoid further delays, Maraboto thereafter "discouraged" the drafting of petitions like Polutla's; otherwise, he told Enríquez, "the majority of the shareholders in the *lotes* would have sent them."[86]

By mid-March, it was already evident that the military *repartos* ordered by Xalapa would face considerable obstacles, this despite the recent "pacification" of the countryside. The subdivisions sponsored by Juan M. Vidal continued to move forward, their sinister management casting a shadow on the entire enterprise. Remarkably, the *jefe político* could not or would not interfere. But this was only part of the problem. Opposition to the impending military surveys was on the rise, and not just from the expected quarters. Maraboto had anticipated some initial resistance coming from erstwhile "rebels" and their sympathizers, which he got, but he soon discovered—to his bewilderment—that not all "loyals" wanted these subdivisions either, even though they claimed they did. Some of those for whom the *condueñazgo* had been a good business were loath to see it go, at least for now, and while in public they embraced the *repartos*, in private they counseled against them. Like many of the dissidents, these people favored joint-stock ownership, though for altogether different reasons. Thus, the path to parcelization would be far more tortuous than Maraboto and his superiors had originally supposed, blocked as it was by a gamut of contradictory interests and opaque agendas. Although the new *jefe* had succeeded in getting most *condueñazgos*—or factions thereof—to sign up with Huerta's commission, it was doubtful that the divisory boards—many of them hastily convened—would have the clout, the will, or the resources to make the rest of the shareholders and *lote* residents follow along. Still, Maraboto kept up the pressure, believing he could ultimately compel wayward shareholders into submission. Persuading the Indians, he told the governor, would require "the patience of Job," but there were moments when it was simply necessary "TO GIVE ORDERS so as to be obeyed." He was not the first—nor would he be the last—of Papantla's *jefes políticos* to overestimate the effective powers of his office.[87]

Those powers, such as they were, derived primarily from the governor's direct involvement in the affairs of Papantla. Since his visit back in October, Juan de la Luz Enríquez had made the subdivision of the *grandes lotes* one of the priorities of his administration; the Galicia episode had made him look foolish, and he had staked his reputation on the prompt resolution of Papantla's land disputes. He had jailed Galicia, authorized Hurtado's repression, ordered the banishment of the dissidents, requested the military commission, and appointed Maraboto. Juan M. Vidal and Simón Tiburcio were his political allies, and other local authorities—including judges—were also Enríquez loyalists. This was the context in which the *repartos* were being pushed through. Enríquez's sudden death on the afternoon of March 17, at the age of 55, left Vidal's clan, Maraboto, and the project in general without a patron. Teodoro Dehesa, director of Customs in Veracruz, was the chosen successor; although he did not formally assume office until December, he was effectively in charge already in April. In ways no one could have foretold, this fortuitous transition was to have tremendous repercussions in Papantla.

In the short run, however, nothing appeared to change. Victoriano Huerta's commission began measuring several *lotes* at once, Salvador Martínez was kept busy demarcating individual parcels, and Manuel Maraboto continued in his post. For Juan M. Vidal and Simón Tiburcio, these were the best of times. Traffickers in *condueñazgo* land rights, their respective businesses were flourishing. By hook and by crook, they took what had belonged to farmers and communities; sometimes they kept it, but more often than not they sold it to other merchants, the final beneficiaries of this pillage. Moreover, their field of action was not limited to Papantla's ex-communal *condueñazgos*. Vidal made himself the *apoderado* for various *lotes* in Chicualoque, on the western end of the canton, and then sold off El Brinco's lands and Paso de Chicualoque's fine timber. Tiburcio exploited the disputed *lote* of San Miguel and San Lorenzo for sixteen years (1876–92) before selling it to Pedro Tremari. In both cases, the shareholders got nothing. Then there were Palma Sola and Nextlalpan, a vast expanse of forest and grassland between San Miguel y San Lorenzo and El Brinco. These adjoining estates, too, were held in *condueñazgo*. Tiburcio and a few associates purchased shares in these *lotes* using money collected from local residents misled into thinking that they were buying their own land rights; by the mid-1880s, Tiburcio and company already controlled the properties and ran them as their own, selling cedar and mahogany to various commercial houses. Over time, Tiburcio bought or edged out his various business partners; by 1892, two-thirds of the shares were in his name. Papantla's Totonac war hero was now one of its biggest landowners.[88] For the mayor and the cacique, the future looked then very bright; more lucrative deals were in the making, and no challenge to their power was anywhere in sight.

Meantime, Severiano Galicia remained in prison, his fate still uncertain. In the months since his arrest, the prosecution had barely moved forward. Informed of this by Galicia's friends, Díaz telegraphed Enríquez on March 2, demanding a prompt resolution of the case. "As you will recall," he wrote, "I have taken the liberty of recommending this to you because his situation is especially saddening to me, given that he was my commissioner." Fifteen days later, Enríquez died; soon thereafter, Díaz sent a similar request to Dehesa, noting that he did not understand why Enríquez had repeatedly refused his plea. "I am neither for nor against this Señor," he said, "but I do want this matter to conclude as soon as possible." Dehesa did comply; after 261 days in jail, Galicia was set free on bail in July and the charges against him were effectively dropped. He was lucky to have walked out alive. His remaining followers in Papantla rejoiced, and were soon seeking his help once again.[89]

That same month, Manuel Maraboto took a leave of absence, never to return. In his place, Dehesa had Angel Lucido Cambas appointed; he would stay on as Papantla's *jefe político* for the next four years. Fifty-eight years old, Lucido Cambas had previously held a number of official posts and had earned Dehesa's undying trust while serving as Customs Administrator in the port of Nautla. A native of Xalapa, he had resided in Papantla for some time already, so he knew the local situation fairly well.[90] Lucido Cambas's appointment heralded a sharp political turnaround. He was no friend of the Enríquez loyalists who controlled most public offices in town, many of whom he regarded as criminals. Immediately, he took steps to begin dislodging them from positions of power. He also disagreed with Maraboto's policy of pushing through the *repartos* at any cost, ignoring the objections of many shareholders. Since the *lotes* were private properties, he argued, their parcelization was strictly voluntary. "Even though laws—in my humble opinion—can not be applied retroactively," he told Xalapa, "the previous authority got directly involved in the subdivisions, following—mistakenly, in fact—the spirit of Law No. 26."[91] As a result, the *jefe político* would no longer act as the *repartos*' unconditional enforcer, leaving the surveyors and the divisory boards to sort out difficulties on their own. Furthermore, in an effort to defuse lingering tensions, Lucido Cambas adopted a more conciliatory attitude toward the dissidents, listening to their complaints and offering them a measure of protection. These shifts were all closely intertwined; in Papantla, *reparto* disputes had become political ones, and vice versa. Before long, Vidal, Tiburcio, and company were on the defensive, the dissidents were on the move yet again, and most of the *repartos* had gotten quagmired. Suddenly, civil conflicts that appeared to have been settled by force resurfaced with a new intensity. Papantla's social wars were not yet over after all.

Barely a few weeks after Lucido Cambas had taken charge, Victoriano Huerta was already complaining about him to the president. The new *jefe político*, he said, was obstructing the *repartos*. In fact, Huerta's problem was that he had made deals with small groups of *condueños* and Lucido Cambas was refusing to use his authority to compel the other shareholders to cooperate with the surveys, as Maraboto had tried to do. Lucido Cambas did not block the subdivisions, he was just not pushing them, and coming from a *jefe político* that alone sent a strong message. Díaz referred the matter to Dehesa, adding that if the military engineers were not wanted, he was prepared to recall them. In response, Dehesa defended Lucido Cambas's integrity, as he would do over and over again, calling him an honest man and a loyal friend. Still, he would make inquiries. At about the same time, a new crop of dissident leaders made contact with Severiano Galicia, apprising him of the latest developments and asking for his help in obtaining the release of some conscripts. Chief among them were Mateo Morales from Cerro del Carbón, Francisco Ramírez from El Palmar, and Nicolás Atzin from Poza Larga. "They keep doing the land *reparto* against our will," the group told Galicia, "and all they do is steal from us, taking the best lands from the poor to give them to their friends." There was now a *jefe político* who appeared to be their friend, they added, but they were not really sure of this and did not know how to react to him.[92] Given the grim treatment they had received from previous *jefes*, their skepticism was fully warranted, but they would soon discover that such an improbable realignment of forces was indeed underway.

In August, Lucido Cambas sent Dehesa a confidential letter describing the political situation in Papantla. "The Enriquista party is united," he wrote, "and afraid of losing the immunity it enjoyed even when committing crimes." The main culprits were Manuel Espinosa, State Treasury agent, Enrique Consejo, municipal secretary and stamp tax administrator, Mayor Juan M. Vidal, Simón Tiburcio, and Francisco Patiño Ramírez, one of Tiburcio's business associates. A judge and the town's notary public were also part of the ring. Vidal, he said, was "a man without training, profession, or occupation, whose life is a problem, because he has always lived without working, extorting from the proletariat and the Indians." He worked in tandem with Tiburcio, Consejo, and Patiño Ramírez, "a fearsome group, who will even order the assassination of those who oppose them" and whose businesses had grown at the expense of the Indians' lands. Tiburcio, he explained, "used to be the cacique of these Indians, but he lost the prestige he once had by exploiting them over and over, and he tries to recover it by means of terror." After the last uprising, Lucido Cambas went on, they had continued jailing, robbing, and murdering their adversaries, all with the help of a friendly judge. Another judge had indicted Vidal and Patiño for theft, but the process was going nowhere. "It is imperative," the *jefe político* concluded, "to clip the wings" of this criminal association. The first steps were taken right away: the judge in question was soon removed by administrative means and a thorough audit of Papantla's Treasury office was ordered, as a result of which Espinosa was eventually indicted for the embezzlement of thousands of pesos in tax monies.[93] Vidal and Tiburcio would be next.

During the rest of 1892, the *repartos* would advance very little. Cerro del Carbón's individual parcels had been mapped and allocated since mid-summer, but a tangle of procedural disputes kept the subdivision from being completed. Chote y Mesillas would reach that stage in late October, only to face the same difficulties. Vidal and company had managed to steer them this far, but the final steps were proving to be the hardest, especially now that their monopoly of power was being challenged. Under Vidal's rules, the Ayuntamiento would only issue property titles to shareholders who presented individual parcel maps, for which Salvador Martínez charged five pesos apiece. Many were resisting this final extortion, and thus most parcels remained in a legal and fiscal limbo, no longer part of a *condueñazgo* and not yet registered as separates properties.

Elsewhere, progress was minimal. Ing. Martínez had another two contracts left in Papantla, one for Cedro (lot 8) and the other for the village *ejido*. Almost nothing had been done on either. His contracts with Tlahuanapa (lot 13) and with the combined *lotes* of Cazones and Sombrerete (lots 23 and 24) had been rescinded, and Huerta now had them. Meanwhile, the military engineers were simultaneously working in eleven of Papantla's *condueñazgos*, plus others in neighboring municipalities, still mostly making basic perimeter calculations (e.g., Map 6.1). By year's end, only a few *lote* surveys had moved beyond this first stage. Huerta had probably chosen to undertake all of them at once—instead of concentrating on one or two at a time—because in that way he could collect much more money in advance. But with his men spread so thinly, the mapping proceeded extremely slowly. It did not help that Huerta spent weeks at a time away in Mexico City, and in his absence the pace of work slackened even further. Moreover, some divisory boards—for example, those in Polutla (lot 10) and Carrizal (lot 17)— were refusing to cooperate, while others could not always come up with the

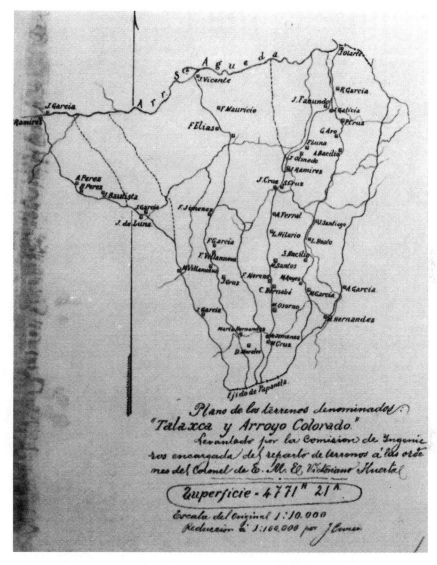

MAP 6.1 Huerta's Map of Lot 21. Courtesy of AGEV, Fondo Gobernación y Justicia.

jornaleros needed to assist with the surveys. Papantla was then in the midst of a drought, the harvests had not been good, and maize was scarce, so many farmers—including *reparto* supporters—had more urgent things to worry about. Finally, and perhaps most importantly, a power struggle between the *jefe político* and the mayor's clan engulfed these budding *repartos*, and as the jostle for local political control intensified through the autumn and early winter months, the parcelization drive was effectively held in suspense.[94]

Lucido Cambas finally confronted the mayor in mid-October, after Vidal tried to pull off another dubious business deal. Without the knowledge of the Ayuntamiento, he had given Huerta a contract to subdivide the village *ejido*, even though Salvador Martínez had previously been paid $2,000 pesos for the same purpose. Huerta would charge tenants a flat fee, regardless of how much land each held, and Vidal would compel selected residents to serve as peons free of charge. This was not only illegal and inequitable, but also detrimental to the interests of the municipality, which would get nothing for the sale of its assets at a time when its treasury funds had been unaccountably depleted. The *jefe político* moved swiftly to nullify the contract, privately accusing Vidal of maladministration, corruption, and abuse of office in this and many other land matters. "One could make a long list," he informed Xalapa, "of the arbitrary and abusive actions that have been committed since January." Several weeks later, Vidal was removed from office. Depriving him of power, however, would prove far more difficult.

Their interests threatened, the mayor and his associates launched a covert offensive designed to get rid of Lucido Cambas. The strategy was to rally their supporters, promote and provoke agitation in the *rancherías*, and bog down the *lote* land surveys, all in order to show that the *jefe político* was dangerously inept and thus had to be removed. Soon, Simón Tiburcio and his men were sowing intrigues, confusion, and fear across the countryside; seeking to spark new clashes, they went after the dissidents, harassing and persecuting them once more. At the same time, longtime promoters of the *repartos*—Simón Tiburcio among them—began to instruct farmers to obstruct them, telling them that the government was trying to take away their lands. With that, what little progress had been taking place came almost entirely to a halt. Huerta, Tiburcio, and Patiño Ramírez then journeyed to Mexico City to meet with Minister of War Hinojosa, urging him to press the president for the dismissal of Lucido Cambas, whose opposition to the parcelization of the *lotes*—they claimed—was fostering a climate of unrest. In late November, Huerta complained directly to Díaz, blaming the *jefe*'s "bad will" and "decided opposition" for the lack of results, and accusing him of serving the interests of powerful vanilla merchants who did not want the *repartos*. Díaz asked Dehesa to investigate and take action, but Dehesa—who became governor on December 1—sided with Lucido Cambas and the *jefe* remained in office. Shortly thereafter, Vidal was formally unseated.

For Vidal and Tiburcio, this left only one course of action: if Xalapa would not oust Lucido Cambas, they would do it themselves. On December 15, Tiburcio gathered his men in the *ranchería* of El Cedro; rumor had it that they were planning to storm the town and assassinate Lucido Cambas later that night. A group of armed dissidents led by Francisco Ramírez and Nicolás Atzin rushed to the *jefe político*'s house, offering to defend him; fearing for his life, Lucido Cambas agreed. At this point, two separate yet related conflicts—one between the *jefe político* and the former mayor's gang, the other between rival Totonac factions—converged into one. The attack did not take place that night, and over the next few days Vidal as well as Tiburcio went out of their way to deny that there was a conspiracy against the *jefe*. Still, tensions continued to mount and the dissidents maintained their nightly rounds in the central plaza. The "loyals" and the "rebels" faced each other once again, only now their roles had been reversed. The vanilla harvest had already begun, and the scramble for business compounded the turmoil; vanilla traders never minded a little seasonal chaos, for nervous farmers often made for better bargains. Lucido Cambas asked Dehesa to ensure that the federal troops stationed in Papantla were not removed; Tiburcio had friends high up in the military—General Hinojosa and Colonel Hurtado among them—and there were ominous rumors of an impending transfer up to Teziutlán. The current standoff, it was clear, would not last long. "It is a fact," the embattled *jefe* wrote, "that they are trying to rouse up the Indians." Exactly what Tiburcio and the rest had in mind was not yet known, but a clash of one sort or another was now nearly inevitable. "Where is cholera," he told Dehesa, "now that I need it!"[95]

Lucido Cambas had not planned on joining forces with the dissidents. Unlike them, he was a committed advocate of parcelization, although like them he rejected the abuses and the corruption that had thus far plagued the *repartos*. He had not resorted to the haughty authoritarianism typical of previous *jefes políticos*, he had abandoned the policy of ostracizing dissident sympathizers, and—most significantly—he had challenged the unbridled rule of their bitter enemies. For this, they had come to respect him. Still, their respective views concerning the resolution of Papantla's land-tenure conflicts were radically different, and hence any alliance was bound to be a precarious one. Severiano Galicia's reappearance made this evident. Since July, the dissidents had resumed their dealings with Galicia, hoping to revive the drive to stop the *repartos* and to bring back some of their exiled companions. After his release, the Ingeniero had obtained a post—with Díaz's help—as inspector of the Hidalgo Railroad, from where he kept in regular communication with his clients. His money worries remained unabated, and representing Papantla's Totonacs offered him supplemental income as well as the chance to rejoin an unfinished battle. Although he now operated more circumspectly than ever, his renewed involvement with the dissidents did not stay secret for long. On December 13, just two days before Tiburcio's threat of revolt, Lucido Cambas sent Dehesa a confidential memo detailing Galicia's activities and warning that they could spell trouble. Five days prior, Nicolás Atzin had been jailed overnight for public drunkenness; while in detention, he had bragged about giving money to Galicia, stating that the Ingeniero "was soon coming to lead the Indians in opposing the land *repartos* at all costs, that they were preparing to receive him, that they would never consent to the *repartos*, and that this time around things would come out differently." The *jefe* also reported having been shown letters written by Galicia asking for money and giving instructions regarding new *baldíos* claims. Galicia, he wrote, "had saved his life miraculously, because everyone who was imprisoned with him passed on to the next life"; now these Indians saw him "as a martyr for their cause" and thus trusted him blindly. He would have to be closely watched. Despite these grave concerns, Lucido Cambas had no choice but to accept the dissidents' protection, even though this could—and would—be seen as a tacit legitimization of their positions and pretensions. His foes' rivals had become allies, at least for now.[96]

As 1892 came to an end, the dissidents' town patrols continued, and fears of an attack persisted from one day to the next. With a factional insurrection looming, Governor Dehesa sprang into action. On the second week of January, Juan M. Vidal was indicted for embezzlement and summarily jailed; Treasurer Manuel Espinosa and surveyor Salvador Martínez were detained as well. Simón Tiburcio went into hiding, and rumors of an imminent attack intensified. On January 11, Francisco Ramírez, Mateo Morales, and three other dissident leaders wrote to Galicia with news of the latest developments. Forty of them were now guarding the *jefe político* every night. Lucido Cambas, they said, "cares about and defends us." They were thankful that justice was finally being done, but there would not be peace until Simón Tiburcio was caught. "We are lawful and working men," they continued, "not like Hurtado's pals, who are thieves and extortionists who want to live lazily off our labor." The president needed to know, they told Galicia, that these people were "parceling out our lands unfairly and deceitfully, without consideration for the poor man, destroying his vanilla or coffee plantings and taking away his lands to give them to friends who ply them with food or presents." Governor Dehesa had in fact tried to remove Tiburcio from the scene, asking Porfirio Díaz to summon him to Mexico City and keep him there for a while, but Díaz had demurred, suggesting instead that Tiburcio be arrested if there was evidence that he had committed any crimes. This did not happen, and so for the next several weeks he remained absconded in the countryside, still plotting riot and revenge.

In early February, Papantla's own *Eco Popular* reported that "a certain colonel—leader of the Indians—is on the run, and he is getting people together to harass the authorities." Word that another Totonac uprising was in the making soon made its way into various regional and national newspapers; some stories blamed Lucido Cambas for the ongoing unrest, one speculated that he had been wounded in an attack, another described the alarming presence of armed columns of Indians all over town, and still others pointed out that it was Tiburcio who was inciting the Indians to violence. Municipal elections were being held in late February, and these dueling snippets of information and partisan propaganda were part of the fight to influence the results. A slate amenable to Lucido Cambas was awarded the Ayuntamiento, and Tiburcio's challenge then fizzled out. At the beginning of March, a despondent Simón Tiburcio abandoned Papantla and sought refuge in Mexico City. The basin's most fearsome cacique had been forced into exile.[97]

"I fear an attempt on my life or my liberty," Tiburcio told Díaz later that month, "so I have come to the capital to implore your protection." His patriotic credentials, he noted, bore witness to his loyalty; he had fought for the Republic since 1864, he had supported the Plan of La Noria in 1871 and the Plan of Tuxtepec in 1876, and he had most recently assisted Colonel Hurtado in the suppression of Papantla's uprisings. "Now that the rebels from that time are being favored," he wrote, "I am being persecuted" and "slandered with accusations of conspiracy." Tiburcio was left alone, but it would be a few years before he could go back to Papantla. Anticipating a long absence, he had sold his ill-gotten share of ownership (67 percent) in Palma Sola and Nextlalpan just prior to his departure. The buyer, merchant Pedro Tremari, had agreed to pay him $15,000 pesos for these rich lands, which included large timber stands, pastures, and a cluster of oil pits known as El Cuguas. Tiburcio would, in turn, negotiate with the resident farmers whose money he had used to buy the shares, and who argued—rightly so—that those lands were in part theirs. Once Tiburcio had settled in Mexico City, fellow Papantla native General Abraham Bandala helped him to apply for and join the army officers' reserve corps, in which he received a salary. However, he was unable to demonstrate that he had attained the rank of Colonel and was appointed only as a Major. To him, this was yet another humiliating demotion. He would spend years trying in vain to climb back up the ladder.[98]

The removal of Vidal and Tiburcio from positions of direct influence was a stunning victory for Lucido Cambas and—for somewhat different reasons—for the dissidents. A year earlier, this turn of events had seemed utterly unthinkable. García Silva's movement had been bloodily suppressed, the new *jefe político* was a staunch supporter of the "loyals," and Huerta's commission had just arrived to conduct a rapid breakup of the ex-communal *condueñazgos*. The battle for Papantla's land and political control appeared won. However, the promise of speedy *repartos* had failed to materialize. Instead, the "rebels" had become allies of another *jefe político*, the "loyals" had lost some of their chief protectors, and another cast of characters had taken charge of local government. Any jubilation, however, was bound to be short-lived. Although the threat of revolt had subsided, the new ruling alliances were neither strong nor stable; if anything, Papantla's politics became more complicated and uncertain than before. On the most contentious issues—land-use rights, taxation, local autonomies, and the conduct of commerce—the social fissures remained as deep as ever, only now, unlike during the previous three years, no faction, figure, or coalition seemed strong enough to attempt imposing its own solutions. This was true in the town as well as in many *rancherías*. Most big merchants were wary of Lucido Cambas's intentions, and his association with the dissidents made them more so. They would vie with him for control over municipal affairs. Out in the *lotes* surrounding the village, Tiburcio's sudden absence produced a vacuum of power, which a variety of Totonac factions competed fiercely to fill. The colonel's friends and followers remained strong, though they now lacked the backing of most political authorities. The dissidents, no longer persecuted, lost their fear, raised their profile, and expanded their activity. Overall, neither group could decisively gain the upper hand, and so for the time being a hostile, often murderous stalemate ensued. Nowhere was this sense of impasse more evident than in the land *repartos*. Huerta was still commissioned in Papantla, but he and Lucido Cambas were barely on speaking terms, and neither had the means to pursue this alone. Meanwhile, farmers who were unsure about or opposed to parcelization felt freer to express their concerns and to refuse participation, while those who had championed it were now for the most part powerless simply to push it through. As a result, the land subdivisions progressed slowly and tortuously, if at all. That pleased the dissidents, but it troubled Lucido Cambas, and this divergence of interests would eventually pull them apart.

In April 1893, Governor Dehesa appointed a special agent to oversee the subdivision of Papantla's *condueñazgos*. Guillermo Vélez's mission was to coordinate the work of the various parties involved, to investigate all complaints and violations of the law, to make sure that the land rights of exiled dissidents were respected, and to resolve any disputes preventing the progress of parcelization. It was an impossible job. His weekly reports, filed over the course of five months, document the near-paralysis that had befallen the whole enterprise. The two *condueñazgos* subdivided by Salvador Martínez in 1892—Chote y Mesillas (lot 15) and Cerro del Carbón (lot 11)—had yet to be dissolved because the Ayuntamiento (the new one) would not issue the individual property titles, arguing variously that it lacked the authority to do so or that the proper procedures had not been followed. Tax officials and divisory board members were protesting, each for their own reasons and all to no avail. Ing. Martínez, who had been set free, was trying to enforce his survey contract with Cedro (lot 8), but this *lote* now had a new *apoderado* who refused to recognize its validity, saying that he had not signed it and that in any case the *condueños* no longer wanted a *reparto*. Poza Larga (lot 12) had not one, but two contracts, the first one with Martínez and a later one with Huerta. Despite Martínez's prior claim, Huerta's contract finally prevailed, in part because the board did not want to work with Martínez anymore. Both *lotes* had long been strongholds of Tiburcio supporters; with the Colonel—a native of Poza Larga—now gone, the local balance of forces had shifted and his topographer friend was running into difficulties. Huerta's party was not faring much better.

One year after their arrival in Papantla, the military engineers had at last completed the mapping of individual plots in one *condueñazgo*, Cazones y Migueles and Sombrerete, Caristay y Aguacate (lots 23 and 24, combined). The scandalous manner in which land parcels were allocated in this enormous *lote* would cast widespread doubt on the military commission's equanimity, stiffening opposition to its survey works elsewhere in the municipality. The small village of Cazones—and not Papantla—served as the primary commercial and social hub for many of these distant territories, which were largely unaffected by the sociopolitical disturbances surrounding the *cabecera*. The dissident movement had not had a strong presence in these *rancherías*, and neither had Simón Tiburcio's henchmen, so while most other *repartos* were tangled in those conflicts, this one managed to lumber on. Cazones and Sombrerete's divisory board represented an alliance of ambitious town merchants and Totonac *rancheros*. It was headed by Joaquín Patiño, scion of a large and prominent business family with interests all over the basin. Patiño, the two indigenous *apoderados* of the combined *lotes*, and a few other local Totonac potentates worked with Huerta's men to parcel out some 10,800 hectares of land into 418 plots— each measuring 25.77 hectares (63.65 acres)—and into *fundos legales* for each of the *rancherías*. Joaquín's brother Manuel, also a merchant, got fifty-eight parcels, and Manuel's mistress, Piedad Muñoz, another twenty-eight; ten additional plots of land went to other members of the Patiño clan, for a grand total of ninety-six (2,474 hectares). Furthermore, all but a few of these parcels were joined together, forming a fairly large estate. Another vanilla trader, Rafael Vaquero, received twenty plots (515 hectares), and several influential *rancheros* did very well also: Juan Hernández Mata, divisory board member, got seventeen parcels (438 hectares); Miguel Pérez Olmedo, fourteen (361 hectares); José Merced Pérez, nine (232 hectares); Severo Moncayo, board treasurer, seven (180 hectares); and Antonio Pérez Trujillo, *apoderado*, five (129 hectares). Many of their parcels were allocated in clusters as well. In all, this compact group of *condueños* claimed exclusive legal rights over 40 percent of the *lote*'s lands. Although a good number of the shares they now held had been purchased from the original own-

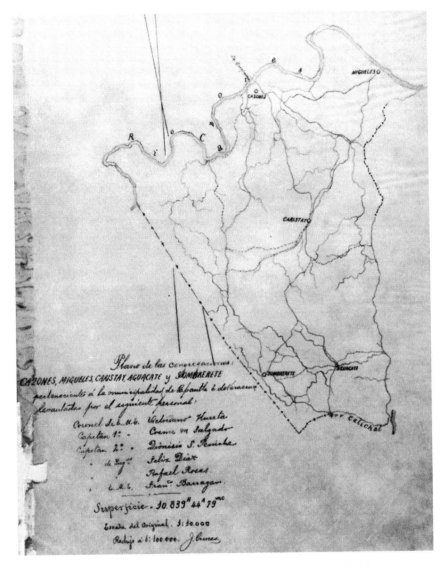

MAP 6.2 Huerta's Map of Lots 23 and 24. Courtesy of AGEV, Fondo
Gobernación y Justicia.

ers, close to half of them represented stock certificates that had been declared vacant and sold by the divisory board after their current holders
could not be found, failed to present them, or refused to pay the survey
fees. Not surprisingly, most of these confiscated shares ended up in the
hands of Manuel Patiño and Piedad Muñoz, though this is also how

Guadalupe Hernández Zamudio, the sister of Papantla's new State Treasury agent, acquired her fifteen shares (387 hectares). The remaining 234 parcels (56 percent of the total area, or 6,030 hectares) were distributed among nearly two hundred Totonac farmers and a dozen or so non-residents, mainly Papantla merchants and politicians like Bartolo Zardoni and Juan M. Vidal, most of whom possessed no more than one share.

In order to accommodate the territorial designs of the powerful, many shareholding farmers were allocated lands that did not include their plantings, forcing them to move out and start anew. Protesting these expropriations, sixteen Totonac shareholders refused to accept their assigned parcels. Guillermo Vélez asked the *jefe político* to intervene, and he reluctantly persuaded them to give in. In early July, the subdivision maps and *condueño* lists were forwarded to Papantla for final approval and individual titling. The Ayuntamiento, however, was still ignoring these requests, and Lucido Cambas, who knew how this *reparto* had been conducted, did not immediately push the matter, asking instead for guidance from Xalapa. Thus, as in Chote y Mesillas and Cerro del Carbón, the dissolution of Cazones and Sombrerete remained unfinished.[99]

By then, relations between Huerta and state authorities had completely broken down. Since April, Huerta had abandoned Papantla, directing his officers' work from Mexico City. Both Vélez and Lucido Cambas blamed Huerta's indifference for the lack of significant results, and Huerta continued to accuse Lucido Cambas of obstructing the progress of his *repartos*. Dehesa and Huerta took these complaints directly to Porfirio Díaz, asking him to take sides in this increasingly acrimonious dispute. The governor urged that Huerta be pressured to speed up the surveys, while Huerta insisted that Lucido Cambas and other local officials had to be removed. Around this time, the State Treasury sued Huerta to force repayment of the loan he had received back in February 1892; the courts ruled against Huerta, but he simply ignored the verdict. The government of Veracruz would spend years trying to get paid.

During May, June, July, and August, the military commission's field work was reduced to a minimum: Ing. Dionisio Sierra Peniche concluded the controversial subdivision of Cazones and Sombrerete, and Ing. Cosme M. Salgado concentrated on finishing the protracted parcelization of tiny Tlahuanapa (lot 13), which was finally completed in mid-August. Here—once again—the disparities were glaring. An area of 846 hectares was divided into 121 parts, nearly 7 hectares each. Another Patiño merchant, this time Melquíades, turned forty-one shares into one contiguous estate encompassing 284 hectares, while nine Totonac *rancheros* and town merchants received triple, quadruple, or quintuple parcels (21–35 hectares). Finally, forty shareholders—twenty-one men, eight women, and eleven families, most of whom were Totonac farmers—got single plots of land (7 hectares), and the four remaining parcels were declared vacant for the time being. With *repartos* such as these, it is no wonder that resistance to the land surveys became wider and more vociferous. As Tlahuanapa was being finished, Ing. Cosme Salgado proposed concentrating on Talaxca (lot 21) for the next parcelization. Lucido Cambas was absent, so Guillermo Vélez called in the members of the divisory board, who said that although they were entirely in favor of the *reparto*, they could not pledge the cooperation of the other *condueños*, for many—led by the local municipal delegate—were against it. Furthermore, they noted, every divisory board member had been threatened with death, and the board president had recently been shot at while walking on a county trail. When questioned, the delegate was defiant; he informed Vélez in no uncertain terms that he would not have anything to do with the land subdivision because he was opposed to it. Warned that he could be sanctioned for refusing to obey orders, the delegate asked for time to consult with the others. Lucido Cambas, he said, "had assured them that their lands did not have to be subdivided," so they would wait for him to return from Xalapa to see what he had to say. Vélez termed this "a kind of rebellion," and so it was; if the parcelization of Tlahuanapa and Cazones—marked by inequity, expropriation, and dislocation—reflected the true meaning of the *repartos*, then the common farmer's best bet was probably to avoid them. The many *fincados* had nothing to gain from subdivision, and single shareholders had developed a well-founded fear of displacement. Faced with mounting discontent from below as well as from above, the military commission's days in Papantla were numbered.[100]

Late in September, Porfirio Díaz stepped in with an ultimatum. For nearly three years, Papantla's intricate land disputes had produced one upheaval after another, forcing the president to intervene time and again. "I have been informed," he told Dehesa, "that the subdivision of Papantla's lands is a very difficult thing, and that it is provoking much irritation." If Dehesa believed that the *repartos* should not be carried out after all, he would recall the military engineers, "even though the Indians will remain slaves of the merchants, *gachupines* for the most part." However, if the governor wanted to continue the subdivisions, he would support him vigorously, but Dehesa would have to remove Lucido Cambas and Papantla's new mayor from their posts, at least temporarily. These two, Díaz wrote, "have solemnly sworn not to allow these *repartos*, and they seem determined to keep their word." The final decision was Dehesa's, he said: "The *reparto* can be done or not, it is all the same to me." As for the Indians, "if they do not understand the benefits of private property, they do not deserve them either, and nothing would be lost by letting them remain for now in the conditions in which they have always lived." Three weeks later, Dehesa recommended the removal of the military commission. Lucido Cambas, he affirmed, "is not opposed to the land *reparto*, quite the contrary; he uses persuasion and reason to convince the Indians to accept it." He would thus continue as *jefe político*. Papantla was by then in the midst of another political crisis, so the governor asked that the federal troops be kept in place. Dehesa's letter arrived on October 18; that same day, Díaz ordered the commission's immediate withdrawal. Within days—and without warning— the surveyors abandoned Papantla. There would be no more *repartos*, at least for the time being.[101]

In the course of nineteen months, the military commission had managed to subdivide only two of Papantla's sixteen *condueñazgos*. Salvador Martínez, whose surveys also stopped definitively at this time, had finished two subdivisions on his own. Of the remaining twelve, Huerta had signed contracts with nine, and in nearly all of these he had collected partial payments in advance. When the surveyors left, those fees were not returned, even though the promised work had not been done. According to Lucido Cambas, Huerta walked away with $3,761.25 pesos paid by shareholders from several of these *lotes*, as well as with $2,000 pesos taken from the *conshueños* of Santo Domingo, in the basin's piedmont. These losses would not soon be forgotten, adding to the long list of grievances plaguing Papantla's land-tenure reform. Three years after a motley group of government officials, merchants, and Totonac bosses first set its sights on the dissolution of the *condueñazgos*, the push for parcelization had yielded abundant strife and meager results. The four completed *repartos* encompassed only 20 percent of the *pueblo*'s ex-communal lands, and none of those subdivisions had yet been legally implemented, which meant that all of Papantla's *grandes lotes* remained—fiscally as well as juridically—in *condueñazgo*.[102] Governor Enríquez's blinkered drive to produce quick *repartos* had ended in failure. It had outlived him, but not for very long.

For the old dissident groups, the sudden departure of Huerta's commission represented yet another improbable triumph, the culmination of a year marked by dramatic reversals of fortune. The shift in political winds had enabled them to operate more freely, and the gross inequity of the few *repartos* that managed to carry on broadened the social appeal of their cause. Thwarting the land subdivisions now seemed an attainable goal, though their ultimate aim—to undo the corrosive socioeconomic legacies of the *condueñazgo* regime—remained as elusive as ever. Still, thanks in part to Lucido Cambas's calculated forbearance, a renewed—and often violent—assertiveness coupled with a guarded optimism are evident at this time. Between the dissidents and the *jefe político*, an unlikely marriage of necessity, convenience, and principle held fast. In this favorable political climate, the dissidents' pleas for the return of those who had been exiled in

1891 were finally heard. In May, Governor Dehesa asked the Minister of War to release the conscripts from Papantla, providing him a long list of names. How many of them were able to go back home, it is not clear, but the governor's recommendation was nevertheless significant, given that it was his predecessor in office who had sent them away.

Working for the dissidents behind the scenes, Severiano Galicia had helped to gather and put forward the numerous individual petitions that accompanied Dehesa's discharge request. Since December, when Lucido Cambas had accused him of abetting the dissidents' subversive ambitions anew, Galicia had kept a low profile in regard to the affairs of Papantla. At that time, the president had called him to account for his actions; as in the past, he resolutely denied any wrongdoing, and he gave Díaz a stack of documents—letters, receipts, and a lengthy memo—intended to prove his innocence. There the matter rested, but Galicia understood that he was being watched, and that henceforth he would have to operate more discreetly. Aside from lobbying on behalf of the conscripts, his involvement with the dissidents was then reduced to a minimum, a disengagement made easier by the fact that the *repartos* were faltering on their own, lessening the demand for his services. But he would not let go of Papantla. When he left prison, Galicia apparently believed that the president should—and would—make amends by appointing him to some official position of influence. These delusive hopes were quickly dashed; although Díaz did get him a job (as a railroad inspector), Galicia complained that the pay was woefully insufficient and kept asking for a bigger and better reward. A plea to be nominated for a seat in the Mexico State legislature was followed by a fawningly sycophantic letter celebrating the start of Díaz's new presidential term and later by a request for the directorship of the National School of Agriculture. In each case, he was politely turned down. Bitterly disappointed, Galicia maintained his ties with Papantla's dissidents, partly out of conviction, partly for the money, and perhaps also out of spite. And when the opportunity presented itself, he would furtively lead them into another grave confrontation with the authorities.[103]

At the moment, however, his assistance was not especially needed. The festering social strife that precipitated the surveyors' withdrawal had taken center stage and guns were now doing much of the talking. Since late 1891, an intermittent, low-intensity civil war had been fought in Papantla. The combatants were mainly Totonacs, as were the victims, and murder was the tactic of choice. Following Tiburcio's exile, the violence had flared up again, with the dissidents now leading the attack. Hardly a week passed by without a killing or at least a shooting; dead bodies were found in the hills, by the milpas, and on the roads. In a rural society torn by deepening disputes over land rights, governance, and business, this is how political differences had come to be resolved. Clearly, these struggles involved not only Totonacs, but also town merchants, local officials, and various outside parties, all of whom—as shown—took sides and weighed in to pursue their own particular interests. The sharp factional alignments that characterized Papantla's political and social life at this time were not defined by ethnicity, but by the confluence—often adventitious—of ambitions, beliefs, sympathies, and enmities. Indeed, town politics had also been polarized by those larger conflicts regarding the distribution of power and profits, and were thus not immune to the violence that haunted broad swaths of the countryside. Nine months after Juan M. Vidal's forcible removal from office, Papantla's Ayuntamiento was again mired in scandal. In early October, shortly before the military commission was recalled, Mayor Pastor Pimentel and several close associates—some with well-known ties to the dissidents—were implicated in the assassination of Abel Mercado, a lawyer linked to a series of shady business deals and a close collaborator of Simón Tiburcio, many of whose land scams he had brazenly legalized. Given the victim's notoriety, the fact that he was not Indian, and the identity of the culprits, Mercado's killing attracted tremendous attention. But in the end he was just one more casualty of a social war neither side had yet found the means to win.

This state of effective parity among the contending parties—precarious and hostile though it was—would not have been possible without the intervention of Lucido Cambas. Following his appointment as *jefe político*, he had withdrawn the government's unconditional support for the "loyals" and their business patrons, removing them from positions of power in the Ayuntamiento. At the same time, he had put an end to the government's harassment of the dissidents, leaving them free to organize and mobilize. His purpose was to combat official corruption and abuse, to forestall another dissident uprising, and thereby to create a climate conducive to cleaner land subdivisions. Things did not turn out as he had hoped, however. Lucido Cambas envisioned his role as that of a powerful mediator, balancing opposing social forces of unequal strength and steering them into a settlement, but few others saw him that way. The dissidents considered him an outright ally, the "loyals" despised him, and the big merchants disapproved of his efforts at conciliation, which they blamed for the new rounds of violence and the stalling of the *repartos*. Moreover, all sides came to regard him as being uncommitted to parcelization, though this was by no means the case. In the midst of this grinding stalemate, Pimentel's arrest dealt a severe blow to Lucido Cambas's already troubled strategy. The whole affair was a profound embarrassment for the *jefe político*, who had supported the mayor's election and who now faced fresh accusations of maladministration, duplicity, and worse. For Totonac cacique Pablo Hernández Olmedo, Mercado's murder exposed the criminal complicity of Lucido Cambas, Pimentel, and the dissidents, all of whom were hell-bent on annihilating Simón Tiburcio's people and power. For the town merchants, it was further indication that the *jefe político*'s policies were dangerously misguided. If they could not get him to rectify, or get rid of him, they would at least try to gain back the Ayuntamiento. In spite of this onslaught, Lucido Cambas stuck to his position, but he would find it increasingly difficult to rein in the violence and the plotting, let alone to break the impasse regarding the land question.[104]

Lucido Cambas believed in the kind of *repartos* vaguely imagined in a Liberal land legislation—the Ley Lerdo, Article 27 in the Constitution of 1857, the disentailment laws of Veracruz—inspired by a republican understanding of individual private property as the foundation of citizenship, liberty, and social progress. In this view, collective landholdings would be parceled out among community members in a more or less egalitarian distribution of small lots, producing a class of propertied family farmers. *Repartos* like these, however, could not take place in Papantla, because the social and legal changes introduced with the establishment of *condueñazgos* essentially precluded them. The problem was not only that land rights were now limited to shareholders, but also that the distribution of those shares had become highly uneven, and the largest shareholders tended to dominate their associations. For them, the point of parcelization was to consummate these gains. This was not a sociopolitical reality in which the Liberal landtenure reform laws could be expected to produce the desired results. There was relatively little that any government could do to roll back these local developments, although that is precisely what the dissidents kept hoping for. Moreover, municipal authorities had more often than not a personal stake—as *condueños*, business brokers, or influence peddlers—in the outcome of land subdivisions, and the original spirit of the laws did not enter into their calculations. To such people, Lucido Cambas's qualms about a lack of fairness, negotiation, and due process were entirely alien, and a provocation.

Standard accounts of *pueblo* land privatization in Mexico generally highlight "the role of the state" in the breakup of communal landholdings, implying that this is something apt to be described in unitary fashion. In fact, this notion obscures more than it illuminates. In Papantla, the involvement of government functionaries in the *repartos* is best portrayed as complex, circumstantial, and frequently contradictory; in short, as anything but coherent. Far from speaking with one voice, it was not uncommon for public officials—from the president down to the *jefe político* and the mayor—to have divergent understandings of (and interests in) parcelization. Lucido Cambas fought with Vidal and with Huerta, and Dehesa rejected Díaz's persistent recommendations; with regard to Papantla's land subdivision, each had his own pragmatic agenda. Much like the other parties in this grievous and winding process, state authorities sometimes acted in concert, and other times at cross-purposes. It thus makes sense to conceive of multiple—often clashing and shifting—government influences, as opposed to a single one, and then to see them as part of a larger web of social forces striving to shape property relations. For although these influences could undoubtedly be powerful, and in the end even decisive, local interests—not state mandates—were the main engine of village land-tenure change. Tired of the endless agitation, the constant bickering, and the recurrent upheavals, the president himself was prepared to give up altogether on Papantla's *repartos*, if that was what it took to restore social order. But it would not be. Parcelization had an impetus of its own, as did the resistance to it. These conflicts over land rights were rooted in the rapid transformation of Papantla's economic and social organization, and it would take much more to extinguish them.

With the surveyors gone, Veracruz officials focused their attention on the legal situation of the four subdivided *condueñazgos*. There was uncertainty concerning the Ayuntamiento's capacity to issue individual title-deeds; it had been established by decree during Enríquez's years, but that special provision appeared to have expired in late 1892 (Decree No. 50, 20 November 1890), and titling had since then been suspended. At stake was the municipal government's role in the *repartos*, long a subject of considerable political controversy. Chote y Mesillas's divisory board had asked for clarification of the law: Did the Ayuntamiento have the authority—and the obligation—to produce these documents, or could the *condueños* simply notarize and register the subdivision of their property, much like in any inheritance proceeding? Was Decree No. 50 still valid? Governor Dehesa referred the matter to the legislature, noting that he did not think municipalities should have been involved in these transactions between private parties. Meanwhile, Papantla's new mayor had agreed to process the backlog of applications for formal dissolution. The Ayuntamiento reviewed and endorsed Chote's subdivision in late January, and Tlahuanapa's in late March, but further action would have to await the lawmakers' decision. In July, the state legislature ratified the issuance of Ayuntamiento titles for subdivided ex-communal *condueñazgo* lands, and by the end of 1894 a slightly modified version of the old provisions had been reenacted into law. At that point, Xalapa began granting final approval to the *repartos* that had been completed.[105]

By then, Papantla's sociopolitical conflicts had taken yet another unexpected twist. Back in March, the federal government had promulgated a new public-lands law providing much clearer administrative guidelines for the privatization of *terrenos baldíos*, *demasías*, and *excedencias*. The law caught the eye of Severiano Galicia, who saw in it a fresh opportunity to promote the controversial land *denuncias* he had first tried to carry out—with disastrous results—three years earlier. If Papantla's old communal territories lacked property titles, then they were legally public, and anyone had the right to claim them—or so the argument went. Emboldened by their recent successes and perhaps also blinded by their faith in Galicia, the Totonac dissidents quickly embraced the plan, apparently convinced that this time they had the means to prevail. As they would eventually discover, this was a terrible miscalculation. On August 4, eighteen separate *baldíos* claims were filed in the Ministry of Fomento's Xalapa office. More may have been submitted soon thereafter. The main dissident leaders figured prominently in these applications—Francisco Ramírez for El Palmar, Mateo Morales and Cayetano Santiago for Cerro del Carbón, Paulino and José F. Atzin for Poza Larga, and Fernando Vicente for Polutla. Although these *denuncias* were Galicia's business, he knew better than to handle them directly, so Ing. Sixto Sandoval, a resident of Mexico City, was listed as the chosen surveyor. In all, the lands of fourteen *congregaciones* in eleven of Papantla's *grandes lotes* were included in these first *denuncias*; in addition, two ex-communal *lotes* in Gutiérrez Zamora, one in Tecolutla, and a noncommunal area south of the river were claimed as public lands. None of these *lotes* had yet been formally subdivided. By law, the claimants had three months to conduct their surveys, consult with the abutters, address any opposition, and submit a detailed report, including maps.

Some two weeks later, Ing. Sandoval showed up unannounced in Papantla, holding a surveying permit from Fomento and a very long list of *baldíos* claims. Startled, Lucido Cambas notified Xalapa, explaining that the lands in question were not public and that the claimants were themselves shareholders. He had heard rumors that Galicia was preparing to return, but these had made no sense to him. Now he understood what the Indians had been talking about; they had been made to believe—once again—that the president would give them property titles, and that afterward "nobody would bother them or force them to subdivide the lands." The government had to act quickly, Lucido Cambas warned, to avoid a repetition of what had happened in 1891. For the next several weeks, the *baldíos* process continued its prescribed course, although Sandoval was not able to do any field work. On September 13, the *Periódico Oficial* printed the *denuncia* notices required by the law, making public the dissidents' extensive land claims. Tensions inevitably escalated, and the protests soon reached Díaz and Dehesa. Interestingly, the president at first misunderstood the nature of this latest wrangle, assuming that non-Indians were using *baldíos* laws to claim the old lands of the *pueblo*. It was hard for him to imagine that Indians might do so as well. "I will give orders," he told Dehesa upon hearing about the *denuncias*, "that no land be awarded to anyone who is not an Indian resident of the township in which that land is located, because giving it to outsiders is not only unjust, but also tantamount to activating a landmine that might explode any day, justifiably so on the part of the Indians." Ironically, this was precisely the kind of land policy that the dissidents had wanted all along, but now they had assumed the role of claimants and the president would not be sympathetic to their cause.[106]

Closer to home, the dissidents' gamble had far-reaching political consequences. To Lucido Cambas's foes, the *denuncias* exposed the calamitous wrong-headedness of the *jefe*'s stance toward the malcontents. Sensing an opening, they swiftly mobilized to seek his ouster. In early October, Simón Tiburcio wrote to Porfirio Díaz; still exiled, he complained of being persecuted and ruined, and he accused Lucido Cambas of working with Galicia and the dissidents of 1891 to exploit and terrorize the Indians who had shown their loyalty to the government. Later that month, Juan M. Vidal rejoined the fray, meeting with the president to plead against the *denuncias*. His sly performance made a deep impression on Díaz, who promptly sent a five-page letter to Dehesa recounting the details of their conversation. "Juan Manuel Vidal," wrote the president, "is a very important and influential man in Papantla," a selfless person of "noble and distinguished character." Asked to explain why Papantla's Indians opposed the *repartos*, Vidal replied that only a few did, and that they were led by *jefe político* Angel Lucido Cambas, "Papantla's most terrible scourge," a corrupt public official who had obstructed the land subdivisions, who had armed a group of Indians responsible for the assassination of honest farmers, and who had himself ordered many killings. As Díaz tells it, Vidal would frequently interrupt his tale, saying that he was afraid to speak these awful truths, that he had come simply to express his opposition to the *baldíos* claims, that he had no personal problems with Lucido Cambas and nothing to gain from this, and that he was only talking out of respect for the president's queries and out of pity for the poor Indians. Still, he spoke at length, finally suggesting that everything could be solved by removing Lucido Cambas and replacing him with Guillermo Vélez. Díaz was completely duped. He strongly urged Dehesa to get rid of Lucido Cambas, "otherwise it is almost certain that we will have an explosion over there," and he asked Vidal to speak with the governor, assuring him that Dehesa had been lied to and did not know what was really going on in Papantla. Vidal did not want to, but he reluctantly acquiesced, and Díaz reciprocated by offering to halt the *denuncias* process until Dehesa could sort everything out.[107]

The governor was not fooled, however. He spoke briefly with Vidal, who gave short and evasive replies to Dehesa's questions, asking that the meeting be postponed because he needed to be back in Papantla. Dehesa remembered a few things about Vidal's past, and he made further inquiries which produced much damning information. Vidal, he told Díaz, was not trustworthy. To clarify matters, Dehesa then commissioned Ing. Ignacio Muñoz to conduct a detailed investigation of the situation in Papantla. The choice of Muñoz was a carefully considered one; a military surveyor in the Comisión Gráfico-Exploradora and a newly elected Veracruz state congressman, he was also Porfirio Díaz's nephew. Dehesa's promotion of the young man's business and political career had helped to cement the governor's ties with the president, and Muñoz was fast becoming an important conduit between the two. With conflicts between the governor and various powerful federal cabinet ministers with personal business interests in Veracruz fast on the rise, it was essential for Dehesa's political prosperity to cultivate the president's goodwill. Muñoz was someone in whom Díaz could trust, and Dehesa hoped that his report on Papantla's troubles would put an end to the persistent disagreements regarding Lucido Cambas's actions.

Muñoz arrived in Papantla around November 25. By then the contested *baldíos* applications had moved into litigation at the district court, where they sat for a few months, eventually to disappear; unbeknownst to the petitioners, the president had already ordered them buried. Dehesa and Vidal did not meet again, but the campaign against Lucido Cambas continued nonetheless. "Let me emphasize," Vidal wrote to Díaz from Papantla, "that as long as the current *jefe político* is not removed from this *pueblo*, there will not be complete peace and public trust, nor will it be possible to address the issue of the individual land *repartos*." Muñoz, however, came to exactly the opposite conclusion. After spending just two weeks in Papantla, he produced a lengthy report outlining the history of the *pueblo*'s land disentailment, the causes of the present turmoil, and his proposed solution to those problems. Lucido Cambas, Muñoz wrote, "is an honorable man, whose honesty is beyond reproach." He knew the locals and their conflicts better than anyone else and should therefore remain in his post. In a separate letter, Muñoz explained to his uncle that Juan Vidal's accusations were not to be believed; he had an old grudge against the *jefe*, who had put him in prison when he was mayor. Although Lucido Cambas was "not much loved there, and had almost no close collaborators or even friends to help him," he was nevertheless "the only person possibly capable of carrying out the *repartos* in peace."

Muñoz's report described a society at war with itself, in which the authorities were unable to stop the killings routinely perpetrated by both sides; at the time of his visit, more than 250 men were being held in Papantla's jail. His report pointed to disfranchisement as the main source of social friction. To this he might have added taxation, merchant encroachment, a history of heavy-handed meddling and partisanship on the part of local officials, and, finally, the vexatory spirit of enterprise surrounding the vanilla trade. Muñoz identified Galicia as the mastermind of the *baldíos* scheme, and he depicted the dissidents—with whom he did not speak—as a small group of disfranchised, disgruntled, and perhaps deluded Indians attempting to appropriate what rightfully belonged to others. The first claim was correct, not so the second; the dissidents were not so few, and a number of them, including several leaders, were in fact *condueños*. Muñoz simply assumed—or was led to believe—that this was a conflict between a majority of the Totonacs who had *condueñazgo* land rights, and a minority who did not. But numerous Totonac farmers owned no shares, and many shares were no longer in the hands of Totonacs. This was a reality that Muñoz ignored. Not surprisingly, his report was silent about the lopsided distribution of landownership in those *lotes* that had already been subdivided, which violated the spirit—and the letter—of the laws he was so keen to uphold. On the basis of such faulty suppositions, Muñoz formulated four concrete recommendations. First, the *repartos* should be finished as soon as possible, for only then would peace be restored; second, a federal battalion should be sent in to maintain order and—if necessary—to enforce orders; third, military engineers should be commissioned to do the land surveys and subdivisions; and fourth, Angel Lucido Cambas should be left in charge of the whole operation. In essence, Muñoz was advocating a return to the policies of 1892, with one major difference. Back then, Lucido Cambas had sought to appease the dissidents, as Muñoz put it, "so that he could gradually neutralize the pernicious influence of the ringleaders who did not want the *reparto*, and also in order to persuade the malcontents into compliance and avoid any further alteration of public order, which he undoubtedly achieved, albeit only to a small degree." However, Muñoz concluded, the time for conciliation was now over. The governor and the president would have to make this clear to Lucido Cambas, personally instructing him to end "the agreements or any other ties he might have had with the dissident leaders" and ordering him to concentrate on completing the *repartos*.[108]

Díaz and Dehesa both praised Muñoz's report, which became the blueprint for yet another drive to subdivide Papantla's *condueñazgos*. After two years of polite discord, they now had a common Papantla policy. For this they had Galicia and the dissident leaders to thank. The incendiary *baldíos* claims had forced the state government to focus once more on the land question, and had also given local *reparto* boosters a powerful new argument to bolster their case. More specifically, the *denuncias* had undermined the political viability of Lucido Cambas's mediatory stance, which had enabled the dissidents to survive and recover from the repression of 1891–92. To the *jefe político*, the *denuncias* represented not only a personal betrayal but also a political turning point: the dissidents could no longer be supported. Faced with new pressures to push through the *repartos*, he would comply, keeping his own reservations well out of the way. The dissidents and their sympathizers did not know it yet, but the land *denuncias* has produced a momentous change, and it was not the one they had hoped for.

They would soon find themselves standing again on the defensive, and this time there would be no reprieve.

1895–1900

In these times of open hostility, the weather contributed its own unforgiving harshness. The autumn had been dry, and 1895 came in with a frost. It would be a poor season for vanilla. When summer arrived, the rains did not, and the drought extended into the fall. Maize got scarce, and as the streams dried up, so did water. The cattle suffered along with the crops. In the town, potable water became an expensive commodity. The people's insistent prayers for rain were not being answered, and the image of the Santo de Joloapan—venerated for its ability to break open the clouds—had steadfastly refused to cooperate. Out by the fields, the assassinations continued, an endless settling of accounts. In January, a judge freed several "loyal" Totonacs who had been imprisoned in 1892 for the killing of "rebel" leaders the previous year. Three days later, one of them was dead, his upper body riddled with eleven bullets. Murders like his had ceased to be noteworthy. The *baldíos* claims were still tied up in court, and the dissidents remained expectant, their hopes kept alive by Galicia's assurances. Meanwhile, some of the subdivided *condueñazgos* moved toward dissolution. In late January, Xalapa approved Tlahuanapa's parcelization, requiring only that a majority of the shareholders record their consent before the Ayuntamiento. With that, the *gran lote* of Tlahuanapa ceased to be. It would be the first of many.

In late May, Dehesa sent Lucido Cambas to speak with the president; the *jefe político* returned committed to speeding up the *repartos*. By then, the big merchants had regained control of the Ayuntamiento, and Pedro Tremari himself was mayor. He was among the richest, shrewdest, and most ambitious vanilla traders in the basin, and also—having purchased Nextlalpan, Palma Sola, and San Miguel from Simón Tiburcio—one of its largest landowners. He had just bought a large house on the corner of Papantla's main plaza, which he would quickly transform into the town's very best. Oil prospector Percy Furber, who met him in 1897 and to whom Tremari would sell the pits at El Cuguas, described him as "a small man with the energy of a dynamo," and his house as a "palatial home . . . built of white Italian marble imported by him from Italy." With Tremari in charge, the Ayuntamiento soon became an active promoter of the *repartos*, and slowly but surely it began to issue individual title-deeds. In early July, the *condueñazgos* of Chote y Mesillas and Cazones and Sombrerete moved one step closer to dissolution; summoned by Tremari, the dominant shareholders gave formal consent to the subdivision of their *lotes*, and the files were then sent to Xalapa for final review.[109] Now three of the four *repartos* carried out by Huerta and Martínez were effectively finished, and the stage was set for the resumption of parcelization in other *lotes*. Only the surveyors were missing.

Lucido Cambas's new stance was clearly expressed in his report evaluating the 1892 subdivision of Cazones and Sombrerete (lots 23 and 24). He duly pointed out that the land-grabbing Patiño clan "committed very serious misdeeds, which have given rise to great discontent among the Indians." They had taken the *condueñazgo*'s best lands to form a large estate, dispossessing many Indian farmers. Still, he wrote:

The fact that a long time has passed, the difficulty of carrying out a new distribution of parcels, and the need to conclude these *repartos* so that the residents of the other *lotes* cannot have a pretext to oppose the *reparto*, lead me to propose that the irregularities that were committed in those *lotes*—as well as in Tlahuanapa—be overlooked, but making sure that from now on there are no grounds for such grievances in the remaining *lote* subdivisions.[110]

Tremari's manifest zeal, Lucido Cambas's new standoffishness, and the ominous lack of progress in the *denuncias* all rattled the dissidents. What if the *baldíos* claims were denied? Why was the Ayuntamiento stirring things up? Perhaps their position was not as strong as they had been led to imagine. In a letter dated July 13, sixty-four dissidents, including several of the *denunciantes*—among them Mateo Morales, Fernando Vicente, Agustín Bautista, Cayetano Santiago, Paulino and José F. Atzin, Juan Valles, and Tiburcio Pérez—tried appealing directly to Dehesa. Speaking, they said, for "the majority of the Indians and residents in the *congregaciones* of the municipality of Papantla," they made their case against the *repartos*:

We beg you Mr. Governor, we who are poor Indians and are asking for your favor, we do not want the division to happen, because the water springs are not just anywhere, and people prefer to live near where they are found, and also our farms are in two or three separate parts, please present this petition of ours before the State Legislature so the Diputados may address it in accordance with justice.

Asked to comment on the merits of this petition, a hardened Lucido Cambas dismissed it altogether, calling it the work of Galicia's misguided followers. Galicia, he wrote, "advises them to oppose the land *repartos* and everything else, he is the one who made them file the *baldíos* claims, and the one who keeps these poor wretches agitated, making them believe that by doing so they will not have to pay taxes and the *repartos* will not take place." Xalapa's reply to the dissidents was chilling: the governor would soon be sending surveyors to carry out the *repartos*, and any concerns should in due course be brought to their attention.[111] At this point the dissidents began to understand that their *denuncias* had little chance of succeeding and that government officials in Papantla and in Xalapa would no longer uphold them in this social conflict over land rights.

By then, Governor Dehesa had begun to implement Muñoz's recommendations. On July 4, he had sent the Minister of War a request for troops and a list of five officers he wanted commissioned in Papantla to finish the subdivisions. Two of them, Dionisio Sierra Peniche and Rafael Rosas, had been members of Huerta's team. To ensure a tight chain of command, Muñoz himself was appointed to lead the whole operation. The plan was to sign new survey contracts with the divisory boards of the remaining *condueñazgos*, starting with those *lotes* where Huerta's men had already done some work. In each case, the military engineers would demarcate and allocate the parcels, draw the maps, and prepare the property titles. The Ayuntamiento would then certify the shareholders' consent and—following Xalapa's approval—sign the individual titles free of charge. Finally, Muñoz, the *jefe político*, and the divisory board would formally dissolve the *condueñazgo*, gathering in situ to distribute the individual titles and maps. Lucido Cambas's instructions were explicit: he was to employ the powers of his office to facilitate every aspect of the process. In early August, a company of soldiers from the 13th Infantry battalion arrived in town; a month later, Muñoz and his officers made their way to Papantla, and the subdivisions resumed soon thereafter.[112]

Neighboring Ojital y Potrero (lot 19) and Escolín (lot 20) came first; developments there were indicative of the new alignment of forces driving the *repartos*. Both divisory boards were presided by Benigno Rivera, a member of the Ayuntamiento. Parcelization got underway as soon as Rivera signed the contracts; by concentrating on one or two *lotes* at a time, this military commission made fairly fast progress. The problems began when Rivera tried to collect the survey dues, which many shareholders refused to pay. Some argued that they had already paid Huerta and that those monies should now be taken into account. Others said that they lacked the funds or that they did not believe the *reparto* would actually happen. All of them clearly had a point: Huerta had taken $590 pesos from Escolín and $1,000 pesos from Ojital y Potrero, the economies of family farmers were suffering the effects of a prolonged drought, and the land subdivision process had dragged on fruitlessly for a number of years. At a rate of 75 centavos per hectare, thousands of pesos were at stake. Then there were those who opposed parcelization per se and who advised their fellow farmers against it. Chief among them was Agustín Bautista, a dissident shareholding *ranchero* from Escolín, who had signed the *denuncia* application claiming his own *lote* as *baldío*. Bautista had publicly denounced the surveys, saying that he was represented by Severiano Galicia and that they would not allow this *reparto* to take place. In late October, the surveyors complained that their fees were not being paid in full, and Lucido Cambas had promised to intervene. Nearly a month later, the conflict persisted. Benigno Rivera then wrote to Ignacio Muñoz apologizing for the delay and asking for outside help. He and a group of *condueños* were trying hard to fulfill their contractual obligations, he explained, but they lacked the means to compel the rest to do the same. "I have no authority, I am simply the president of the *lotes*," he wrote, "and with a bunch of Indians as stupid and rebellious as these, I am in need of energetic support and assistance in order to make them understand that the *reparto* has to be carried out whether they want it or not." This was, in a nutshell, the newly dominant philosophy of parcelization. Muñoz referred the matter to Dehesa, who ordered the *jefe político* to enforce the contracts by any means necessary. Lucido Cambas acknowledged that some of the shareholders' objections were not unreasonable, but he nevertheless pressured them to comply, which most did. By the end of January 1896, the *condueñazgos* of Ojital y Potrero and Escolín had been dissolved.[113]

In comparison with the *lotes* fractioned by Huerta and Martínez, the distribution of parcels in Escolín and Ojital y Potrero was less unequal. Of Escolín's 115 plots (30 hectares each), 3 were left vacant and 78 (68 percent) went to individuals or families—mainly Totonacs—holding a single share. Nine people received two parcels each, and 3 others got eight, five, and three, respectively. Several of them were non-Indian townspeople, but most were local farmers. In Ojital y Potrero, about half of the 205 new plots (31 hectares each) were claimed by single shareholders, 8 were unassigned, and the rest went to owners of between two and eight *condueñazgo* certificates. Numerous *rancheros* got multiple parcels, but the vanilla merchants once again fared best: Papantla Mayor Pedro Tremari took 5; Espinal Mayor Natividad Cámara, 8; Adolfo de la Sierra, 7; and Melquíades Patiño, 4. Although many of these plots were allocated in blocks, such favoritism was a bit more restrained than in previous subdivisions; in both *lotes*, the largest estate comprised 5 land shares (150 hectares).[114] These differences notwithstanding, all of the *repartos* had a common denominator: most resident farmers, the disfranchised, got nothing.

As the dissolution of these two *condueñazgos* came to a close, Muñoz and Lucido Cambas set their sights on another group of *lotes* to the north and west of the village. In February, work began in Talaxca y Arroyo Colorado (lot 21) and Pital y Mozutla (lot 22), with Santa Agueda (lot 25) following soon thereafter. Surveys also got underway in two *lotes* from neighboring Coatzintla. Meanwhile, Lucido Cambas was trying to conclude the crooked *reparto* of Cerro del Carbón, where most property titles had yet to be distributed. The process had long been paralyzed by the opposition of dissident *condueños* led by Mateo Morales, as well as by a dispute with Salvador Martínez. Demanding extra payments, Ing. Martínez had walked away with the individual parcel maps, without which the Ayuntamiento would not issue the title-deeds. Lucido Cambas sought and received permission to produce a new set of parcel maps, eliminating the need to negotiate with Martínez. As soon as these copies were ready, Cerro del Carbón would be finally dissolved, with or without Morales's consent. As March drew to a close, Muñoz advised Dehesa to obtain a federal edict declaring that the *lotes* just fractioned—and hence the individual parcels—did not contain any *baldíos*, *excedencias*, or *demasías*. This was necessary, he noted, in order to avoid the possibility of any subsequent *denuncias*, given that the lands in question lacked primordial titles. It was an implicit acknowledgement that the dissidents' *baldíos* claims had not been prima facie frivolous, and that their alleged transgression was essentially political, not juridical. Dehesa agreed, and a request was sent to the president.[115]

For the dissidents, this sudden *reparto* offensive was both disconcerting and distressing. Soon after the arrival of Muñoz's commission, they had been summoned to Xalapa "to arrange their participation" in the subdivision of the lotes they had claimed as *baldíos*. The meeting, however, apparently did not take place. Instead, they found themselves increasingly monitored, intimidated, and harassed. Their old friend Lucido Cambas, who knew them well, was now policing their movements and contacts, intent on neutralizing their influence. Galicia, too, began to feel the pressure, as he was taken to task for orchestrating the *denuncias*. To protect himself, he prompted the dissident leaders to write an implausible letter clearing him of any involvement and denying that they had paid him $3,000 pesos, but no one was fooled by it.[116] As the *repartos* progressed, the government's hard line would only intensify. The local advocates of parcelization—in the Ayuntamiento, among the Totonac *rancheros*, and within the respective shareholder associations—had clearly regained the upper hand. The dissidents were alone again, much like they had been a decade earlier, when the social conflicts shaped by the *condueñazgo* had first broken into the open.

As a last resort, they appealed directly to President Porfirio Díaz. Their letter, seven pages long, was written on the last day of March. Mateo Morales, Fernando Vicente, and thirty-two other men signed it, adding in a postscript that countless others would have done so, too, had they known how to write. Their patriotic credentials, they duly noted, were beyond reproach, having always fought on the right side of history: for the Constitution and the Reforma, for the plans of Tuxtepec and Palo Blanco. This was the standard rhetorical opening of many a presidential supplication. The president's "faithful Indians" were now imploring for his help. "For centuries," they wrote, "our forbears owned all of the lands in this municipality," which had been passed from generation to generation until recently. In 1877–78, these lands were divided into *grandes lotes* owned by shareholders, and "to this day we still do not know why" certain estates—now private—were not included in the *lotes*. Be that as it may, they were willing to forego any rights to those territories, for they were now more directly concerned with the fate of the rest.

Ever since that first *reparto*, the letter continued, "greed has driven many of the local capitalists to acquire almost all of our lands," taking advantage of the Indians' ignorance to buy their share certificates at extremely low prices. In 1892, a team of surveyors came in to subdivide the *lotes*; in Cazones, they catered to the wishes of the Patiño family, "stripping the Indians of their possessions to give those *señores* all of the best lands, where they now graze their feeder cattle." The current military commission was no better: "The rich, who have bought their shares, are receiving them together and where they want, placing ours wherever they please." They had been told that the government wanted these land *repartos* in order to augment tax receipts, because the *grandes lotes* did not yield enough revenue. Let us keep them, they said, and rest assured that we will work together diligently to make the *lotes* produce for the nation, developing their agriculture and paying all taxes on time. They, too, were "supporters of progress." "It would be very sad," they concluded, "if for lack of support from our republican and democratic government we found ourselves reduced to a state of slavery akin to that which our ancestors lived under during three hundred years of Spanish domination in the fatherland."

On the basis of these arguments, the dissidents made six concrete requests: first, the suspension—"for now"—of Papantla's land *repartos*; second, official advice on which crops yielded the highest revenues for the national and state treasuries, so they could grow them; third, the return of the share certificates "that the rich of this *pueblo* have purchased with lies," sold back for what they were bought; fourth, the legal reconstitution of the *grandes lotes* as rural estates held by joint-stock agricultural associations; fifth, the expedition and registration of new property titles for these *sociedades*; and sixth, the granting of formal and actual possession of the *grandes lotes* to their Indian owners. This course of action was "founded on the principles of equity and justice," and so they begged the president kindly to adopt it.[117]

Composed at a time of desperation, the dissidents' petition made important strategic concessions. Gone was the challenge to the legitimacy of Papantla's established communal land boundaries, and gone also were their longstanding objections to taxation. The *baldíos* claims, moreover, went unmentioned. Appealing to Díaz's paternalism, the letter portrayed the conflict exclusively as one between poor, ignorant Indians and greedy, non-Indian capitalists, even though many of the dissidents' fiercest opponents were in fact other Totonacs. This was a clever—and perhaps necessary—

omission; intra-ethnic struggles are much harder to categorize and moralize, and hence less likely to elicit the kind of sympathetic reaction the dissidents were hoping for. In other respects, the letter was more transparent, a damning digest of the flagrant abuses committed in the establishment, management, and dissolution of the ex-communal *condueñazgos*. Deprived of options, the dissidents were reduced to calling for the preservation of these landholding institutions; having spent years trying to undermine them, they now simply wanted the *condueñazgos* restored to their original state in order to give Indians another chance to run them. It was a last-ditch attempt to be heard and considered. And it failed.

On the advice of Muñoz and Dehesa, Porfirio Díaz disregarded the petition altogether. "I recommend speeding up the work," he told the governor. In doing so, local authorities stepped up their intimidation campaign. Lucido Cambas summoned potential troublemakers in the *lotes* undergoing parcelization, warning them sternly not to interfere with the process. Some went into hiding, others were pressured to move and stay away, and several were apparently jailed. In May, Muñoz reported that the subdivisions were moving forward without major difficulties. He expected them to continue in the same fashion "as long as we keep cleansing from each *lote* the rebellious Indians who try to disturb the others." Lucido Cambas, he noted, had recently been dealing with a local *tinterillo* (pettifogger) named Pedro Carranza, who was advising the dissidents at Galicia's behest. The *jefe político* wanted him detained and had asked Dehesa for instructions. "Send me the malcontents and the *tinterillo* who incites them" had been the governor's reply. Before long, Carranza had fled Papantla, seeking refuge in Teziutlán. Hostility had turned into persecution.[118]

Thanks in good measure to Lucido Cambas's steadfast enforcement of Xalapa's intransigent policy toward the dissidents, the *repartos* continued to make fast progress. Muñoz called on him constantly to intervene, reporting back to Díaz and Dehesa on his performance. To harden Lucido Cambas's resolve, and to reward his continued cooperation, the president had apparently promised him a seat in the Congress. As his job grew nastier and more repressive, Lucido Cambas sought renewed assurances. "Please do not forget the offer made to Don Angel Lucido Cambas," Muñoz telegraphed his uncle in mid-June, to which Díaz responded, "I do not forget my offer; I trust he will not forget his commitment either." By then, the subdivision of Talaxca y Arroyo Colorado and Pital y Mozutla was nearly finished, Santa Agueda's was very advanced, and Cerro del Carbón's was again proceeding. Soon, ten of Papantla's seventeen *grandes lotes* would have been fractioned, slightly more than half of the 83,000 ex-communal hectares once held in *condueñazgo* (see Map 6.3). Anticipating the prompt conclusion of these *repartos*, the surveyors had already started to organize the next round. Muñoz kept asking that the *lotes* be declared *baldío*-free, since a lingering

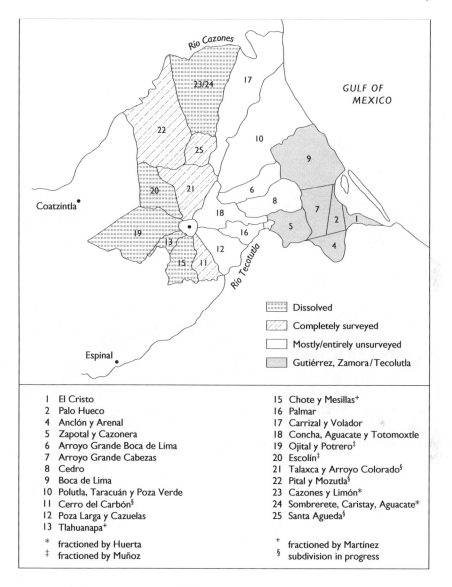

MAP 6.3 Dissolution of Papantla's *Condueñazgos*, June 1896

uncertainty regarding the outcome of the *denuncias* was making many farmers nervous. The weather worried them also. May had come and gone and the rains were not in sight. Another dry summer loomed, the second in a row. As June began, Lucido Cambas ordered the reluctant *condueños* of Arroyo Grande Boca de Lima (lot 6) to prepare for parcelization. A divisory board was appointed on June 8, and on June 11 this Junta signed a new subdivision contract. The neighboring *lotes* would be next.[119] For dissidents and *reparto* supporters alike, the signs could not be any clearer: the spread of parcelization was now inexorable. Two weeks later, a massive rebellion broke out, and Papantla was once more engulfed in fighting.

On the day of St. John the Baptist, June 24, a large group of armed rebels—in some reports, as many as nine hundred, though this seems improbable—descended upon the town of Papantla. Along the way, they captured and executed several opponents. Most came from northeastern, eastern, and southeastern *rancherías*, men from Polutla, Arroyo Grande Boca de Lima, Cedro, Palmar, and Cerro del Carbón, whose lands had yet to be subdivided. Some dissidents from other places also joined. The rebels cut the telegraph line, knocked down a few posts, and blocked all access roads into the town. For six days and five nights, they camped out on the outskirts of Papantla, clashing during their incursions with a hastily organized contingent of government forces. On a few occasions, they almost reached the central plaza, but were repelled after brief yet bloody gun-battles. By all accounts, these skirmishes—some of them said to have involved as many as a hundred men—left many dead and wounded on both sides. When the siege began, there were only fifty federal soldiers stationed in town, as the rest of the company was out by the fields protecting the surveyors. With Muñoz away in Xalapa, Lucido Cambas quickly took charge; he declared a state of emergency, drafting townspeople and the "loyal" Totonac militias to serve as auxiliaries. Although these forces managed to keep the rebels at bay, an overwhelming sense of panic nevertheless gripped the town.[120]

It does not appear that the dissidents issued a manifesto, but if they did it has not survived. On the whole, both official and journalistic accounts attributed to them a similar set of motives. On June 25, Ignacio Muñoz told Díaz that the rebels were upset because the Ministry of Fomento had not acted on their *denuncias*, and that Galicia's agent Pedro Carranza had warned them that the president was about to give away their lands. That is why they had revolted. The next day, Fomento provisionally ruled that Escolín and Ojital y Potrero had no *baldíos*. Governor Dehesa later wrote that the movement's only aim had been "to impede the continuation of the land divisions that were then being undertaken." Mexico City's *El Universal* reported that the uprising was triggered by "the presence of some engineers who were going to measure some lands," since "the Indians believed that their properties were going to be taken away." A letter from Papantla sent to *El Hijo del Ahuizote* (dated June 28) claimed that the Indians had rebelled because the *jefe político* had told them "that the *repartos* would not take place" and had then reneged on his promise. Lucido Cambas's fate was the subject of sustained speculation. Two city newspapers reported that the dissidents had killed him, and another noted that they had tried and failed. A local paper told a different story. According to *El Oriente*, anonymous notes were left at the *jefe político*'s house saying that the rebels wanted to kill the stamp tax administrator, Mayor Pedro Tremari, merchant Rafael Vaquero, the local judge, and a few others, while assuring Lucido Cambas that he was held in high esteem and would not be harmed.[121]

Four or five days into the siege of Papantla, a group of rebels attacked Cazones, the riverine village along the road to Tuxpan which had in recent years emerged as a satellite commercial center for some of Papantla's northern *rancherías*. There, the fighting was also fierce. The dissidents tried to take the town on at least two separate occasions; and while they did not succeed, the battles were protracted and the casualties numerous. The rebels angrily demanded to know where Manuel Patiño—the new *latifundista*—could be found, because they wanted "to chop off his head." They did not get him, but others were not so lucky. "Many dead and wounded," Patiño telegraphed Díaz on June 30, "businesses and families are threatened, we are under siege." There were reports of looted stores and shootouts in Gutiérrez Zamora, another important mercantile town. The attackers were said to have ransacked the house of the mayor, killed a few people, and thrown open the jailhouse doors; most residents had fled in advance, taking refuge on the other side of the river. Out in the countryside, the rebels struck as well, raiding various *rancherías* in pursuit of specific antagonists. The time had come to even out the scores. For a few days of rage, the dissidents terrorized Papantla.[122]

The insurrection would not last long, however. As the rebels approached Papantla on June 24, Lucido Cambas hurriedly asked caciques Pablo Hernández Olmedo and Antonio Jiménez to gather their followers and defend the town. Although they intensely disliked the *jefe político*, who had long restrained them, the dissidents were their bitter enemies, and since much more than the *jefe*'s survival was now at stake, they eagerly complied. In yet another reversal of roles, the old "loyals" were once again fighting for the authorities. Lucido Cambas also managed to telegraph Dehesa that afternoon, reporting the uprising and asking for federal troops. The governor requested Díaz's assistance and within hours the president had ordered a massive deployment of soldiers to Papantla. Two days later, the warships *Independencia* and *Libertad* were once more sailing from Veracruz toward Tecolutla. Brigadier General Rosalino Martínez—who had ruthlessly fought the Maya in Yucatán—was put in charge of military operations. He brought aboard five hundred soldiers from the 23rd and the 7th battalion, as well as some heavy artillery. In addition, forces from the 16th and the 4th Infantry battalions were dispatched from Mexico City.[123] This time, only the guns would speak.

Rosalino Martínez's troops reached Tecolutla on the 27th and Papantla

on the 29th of June. As the army approached, the rebels scattered to the
hills. Pablo Hernández Olmedo, Antonio Jiménez, and their "loyal" squads
were immediately placed under General Martínez's command; their collaboration would prove invaluable. Martínez encamped in Papantla and
promptly sent out a large detachment of soldiers to Cazones. Two days later,
Muñoz arrived from nearby Espinal, leading a "volunteer force" organized
by Mayor Natividad Cámara. By then, many rebels had been captured and
some were turning themselves in. In his first on-site report to Díaz, Muñoz
wrote that the uprising had not been as large as feared, adding that the
rebels were all from *lotes* "that have yet to benefit from the current *reparto*,
where the ringleaders are very wicked and cruel." He thus urged that
Martínez be instructed to deal harshly with the dissident leadership, because
"this is the only way to root out the evil." Over the next few weeks, the soldiers and their Totonac auxiliaries combed the countryside, hunting down
the rebels and arresting anyone suspected of being a sympathizer. The troops
needed local partners who knew the terrain and could identify the dissidents.
The participation of the Totonac "loyals" was therefore essential to the success of the operation, and by all accounts it was unstinting, even enthusias-
tic. These military raids were characterized by wanton acts of violence and
destruction. Many—the exact number will never be known—were killed,
sometimes in cold blood, and hundreds were imprisoned. "It is said," reads
a memoir of these times, "that for many years there were places where one
would find heaps of skulls and human remains, which in time the earth pi-
ously covered." Midway through July, the prisoner count stood at four hundred, with new captives coming in every day. General Martínez told the
president that the movement's leaders as well as "those directly involved in
crimes" were being pulled aside, "and we have been applying to them the
severest of punishments." Díaz knew well what this meant.[124]

By then, many dissident leaders had been killed, some during combat
and others following their apprehension, but Francisco Ramírez, Mateo
Morales, and Nicolás Atzin were still on the run. General Martínez believed that they might have fled to Mexico City, where Severiano Galicia
could offer them protection. He recommended that Simón Tiburcio—who
was there and knew them well—be asked to find them. But that would not
be necessary. A few days later, on July 17, Pablo Hernández Olmedo and
fifty of his men captured Francisco Ramírez somewhere in the hills of Papantla. "The *jefe* of the rebellion," a proud Martínez notified Díaz, "is now
in my power." Under interrogation, Ramírez declared that Mateo Morales
had all the documents concerning the *repartos* and the rebellion—including
Galicia's letters—in his possession. After the questioning was over, Francisco Ramírez was hanged on an ancient ceiba tree near Xilitlaco, along the
road from Papantla to Agua Dulce. There was no trial, no defense, no room

for appeal; his public execution was purely and simply a gruesome display of power. There is no record of what happened to Morales and Atzin, but the fact that their land shares were claimed by family members—together with frequent allusions to the complete suppression of the rebel movement—would indicate that they did not survive either.[125]

On the same day that Francisco Ramírez was apprehended, Ignacio Muñoz met with Porfirio Díaz—at Dehesa's request—to decide what the next steps should be. General Martínez and his troops would soon return to Veracruz, but Díaz agreed to keep an infantry company in Papantla. Together with the Totonac militias, they would protect the military surveyors, who were to resume the land *repartos* right away. In addition, Severiano Galicia and Pedro Carranza would be prosecuted for their alleged role in the Indian uprising; Dehesa and Muñoz wanted them punished, and the president did not object. Díaz and his nephew also considered Lucido Cambas's situation. Despite his recently hardened stance, many merchants and *rancheros* thought he was partly to blame for the rebellion; he had allowed the dissidence to flourish in the first place, and for that they would never forgive him. Rosalino Martínez had become their latest spokesman. "In order to bring peace to this canton," he told Díaz, "it is absolutely indispensable not only to substitute the current *jefe político*, but also to send him out of here." The old man "lacked the prestige and respectability needed for his post," Martínez wrote, and on top of that he was "completely demoralized" by the recent turn of events. This time, Dehesa left the decision up to Díaz: Lucido Cambas could stay on as *jefe político*, or he could be replaced and then promoted to the Congress. The president opted for the latter, but the change would not take place immediately. For the time being, Lucido Cambas remained in office.[126]

Following this meeting, Galicia and Carranza were both arrested. According to *El Nacional*, Carranza was accused of being the chief instigator and Galicia the mastermind of Papantla's latest rebellion. The government of Veracruz formally charged them with seditious conspiracy, and within days they were sent down to the military prison in Veracruz, where they would await trial. Yet again, Governor Dehesa would argue, the Indians had been "seduced by men without conscience who maliciously exploit their ignorance, inciting them to avenge alleged grievances or defend imaginary rights." Back in Papantla, meanwhile, Hernández Olmedo and Jiménez continued the persecution of the dissidents. The sweeps would go on for months. As a reward for these services, both men received commissions as Cavalry Captains on active duty in the army reserve. The *jefes* of the "loyals" were now federal military officers; their faction had become the law. Shortly thereafter, Rosalino Martínez and most of his troops left Papantla. On the morning of July 30, the warship *Independencia* docked in Veracruz with the General and some three hundred Totonac prisoners aboard. Writing to Porfirio Díaz, Martínez reflected on the events of the previous five weeks. "In my estimation," he said, "this will never happen again, because this time the lesson has been harsh." The president congratulated him warmly. After a few days of captivity in Veracruz, the prisoners were returned to the cramped cellars of the *Independencia* and sent to "the coasts of Tehuantepec." Five of them died during a stopover in Coatzacoalcos, and the rest probably never got to see their homeland again.[127] This drastic punishment—in more ways than one a *destierro*—was a terrible epilogue to the bloodiest period of social conflict in Papantla's modern history. Most of the dissidents had been—or would soon be—killed, exiled, or jailed, paving the way for the completion of the contentious land subdivisions.

Just hours after Rosalino Martínez disembarked in Veracruz, Ignacio Muñoz arrived in Papantla to oversee the resumption of parcelization. A week later, his officers were back at work in Pital and Mozutla and Talaxca y Arroyo Colorado. Elsewhere, Muñoz began to "reorganize" the divisory boards, placing friendly *condueños* in charge. These *repartos* would commence as soon as the Totonac militias captured the few dissident leaders with "small guerrillas" still at large in the *montes*. During the first half of August, Hernández Olmedo and his men conducted raids in Cerro del Carbón, Tenixtepec, Polutla, and Palmar. On most of these expeditions, they carried lists of names and arrest orders issued by Lucido Cambas. Toward the end of the month, these mopping-up operations shifted to the area around Cazones. By then, the *condueñazgos* of Pital and Talaxca had been finally extinguished. Of Pital's 280 land parcels (36 hectares each), around 10 percent were claimed by town merchants, 34 were declared vacant, and the rest went mainly to Totonacs. Among the latter, a sizable sub-group—notably the Jiménez and San Martín families—fared especially well, receiving multiple parcels. These *rancheros*—led by Captain Antonio Jiménez—were the ones who managed the *reparto*. In Talaxca, the distribution of plots was somewhat more skewed. Of the 319 parcels (16 hectares each), about one-quarter were claimed by town merchants and other non-Indians, 16 were left vacant, and the remainder were assigned among Totonacs. Individual ownership of multiple plots—by *rancheros* as well as merchants—was again not uncommon, but clustering was relatively minimal.[128]

August would be the last of Angel Lucido Cambas's fifty months as *jefe político*. When he left, just like when he came, a brutally imposed peace reigned in Papantla. Then, and now once again, "loyal" militias terrorized the countryside as the powerful enforced their land *repartos*. In between, Lucido Cambas had tried long and hard to restrain them, only to find himself eventually—and no doubt reluctantly—on their side. The sad irony of this outcome surely did not escape him; he had ended up leading his former antagonists—who despised him still—in a crushing battle against those who had once placed their trust in him. Merchant and former Espinal mayor Natividad Cámara—who had profited handsomely from the land *reparto* in that *pueblo*—took over the post, and Lucido Cambas moved on to Congress, representing Sinaloa until his death two years later, at the age of sixty-four. Not long after he departed, Simón Tiburcio returned to Papantla, his first visit in nearly four years. He stayed for a month, ordering his affairs in preparation for the upcoming *repartos*. When he left, in early December, a handful of subdivisions were quickly moving forward. Lengthier visits followed, and in mid-1899 the Army granted his request to relocate permanently. The old *jefe* was back.

Four months after their arrest, Severiano Galicia and Pedro Carranza remained imprisoned. The government found it very hard to prove its accusations against Galicia, since the rebels who were interrogated as part of his trial did not know who he was and the few who had dealt directly with him had all been killed. Extralegal punishments of the sort administered to the rebels were not an easy option in his case; he had advocates in high places, including Ignacio Mariscal, and the press had taken note of his situation. In his letters to the president, Galicia proclaimed his innocence over and over, demanding to see any inculpatory evidence. Fortunately for him, none could be found. With Lucido Cambas gone and Muñoz concentrating on the *repartos*, the case against him languished and eventually collapsed. In mid-December, Galicia walked free. Pedro Carranza's fate, however, remains unclear.[129]

Between March and May of 1897, five more *condueñazgos* were dissolved. The first was Arroyo Grande Boca de Lima (2,861 hectares), many of whose shareholders had joined the rebellion and since been killed or exiled. The *lote* was divided into 155 parcels (18 hectares each), of which more than a third (55) were declared vacant. The distribution of the other 98 followed a more or less established pattern: one merchant took 8, and assorted townspeople, *rancheros*, and *labradores* got the rest. At the final subdivision ceremony, *jefe político* Natividad Cámara lectured the assembled Indians, speaking through interpreters:

This *reparto* has now been satisfactorily concluded, and here, as in the other *lotes*, the *condueños* are happy with the results of a process that caused them so much fear at the beginning. You were ignorant of the inestimable good that the government through its wise laws wanted to do you, and, advised in bad faith by people who exploited your ignorance, you were led to embrace those fears and induced to commit the gravest crime of all, which is to rebel against a legitimate government. You have seen the deplorable consequences that ensued for those who ill-advisedly revolted against the government in defiance of a law that has since been enforced, and that, far from taking anything away has instead guaranteed your property, giving each of you a piece of land which—as soon as you all plant it with vanilla, coffee, or sugarcane—will make you the richest inhabitants of the Republic. Work honestly and trust that the government which you loyally support will help you through its laws to change the very sad conditions in which unfortunately you still live. Stay close to the government and you will never again have family tragedies or material losses to lament.[130]

Santa Agueda, El Palmar, and El Cedro were fractioned in March as well. Of Santa Agueda's 99 parcels (20 hectares each), 15 were left vacant and around 20 went to various townspeople, one of whom got 7, and another 6. El Palmar, Francisco Ramírez's *lote*, also had a high proportion of vacant plots, 13 out of 93 (18 hectares each). Here, Adolfo de la Sierra and Agapito Fontecilla y Vidal received 8 and 3 parcels, respectively, and two Totonac *rancheros* each got 4. In El Cedro, by contrast, the *rancheros*—notably Manuel Malpica (7 shares) and his closest relatives (6 shares)—fared best, but ownership of the *lote*'s 189 plots (29 hectares each) was widely distributed, and only 5 remained vacant. Remarkably, town merchants were largely absent from the list of beneficiaries; Adolfo de la Sierra, with 3 joint parcels, was the main exception.

Next was Concha, Aguacate, y Totomoxtle, parceled out in April. An area of 3,146 hectares was turned into 255 plots (12 hectares each), of which 28 were unclaimed. Businessman Rafael Vaquero received 37 parcels (15 percent of the total), 17 of them together, with a dozen more going to other merchants. Simón Tiburcio obtained 3, as did several more well-positioned Totonacs. Still, single shareholders held on to the vast majority of the land plots, as in most of the other *repartos*. A few weeks later, it was Poza Larga's turn. This was Simón Tiburcio's home turf, and also Nicolás Atzin's. A few of Nicolás's kinfolk had participated in the revolt, but many others had not, and one had even served as divisory board treasurer. Like El Cedro's, this *reparto* was thoroughly dominated by Totonac *rancheros*; in fact, the only non-Indian *condueño* was the *jefe político*, who presented two stock certificates. Of the *lote*'s 244 parcels (13 hectares each), 45 percent (110) went to holders of multiple shares: the board president took 7, Agustín Tiburcio got 6, two *rancheros* received 5, four others—including Manuel Atzin—claimed 4, nine more—among them Pablo Hernández Olmedo—obtained 3, and nearly two dozen farmers each took 2 shares. Only 4 parcels were left without an owner. On May 12, the *condueñazgo* was formally extinguished and the proprietors received their assigned plots and individual land titles. The next day, a group of aggrieved shareholders—most of them from the Hernández family—rose up in arms. The *jefe político* sent Pablo Hernández Olmedo and fifty of his men to arrest them, with instructions to "make use of your weapons if needed, and if you encounter resistance and are fired upon." The uprising was soon quashed, and Papantla's militarized parcelizations continued.[131]

A few months would pass before another *lote* was ready. Two of the three that remained in *condueñazgo* were Papantla's largest, and as summer approached, the farmers turned to planting their milpas, reducing the manpower available to the surveyors. For two and a half years, the heavens had afforded little kindness; these were stingy times, in more ways than one. Autumn had already arrived when the subdivision of Polutla, once a stronghold of dissent, was finally carried out. This enormous *lote* (12,636 hectares) was fractioned into 486 parcels (26 hectares each), all but 4 of which were assigned. Pablo Hernández Olmedo was president of the divisory board. A group of merchants and village functionaries took around 15 percent of the plots; prominent among them were Rafael Vaquero (21 shares, 11 of them adjoined), Antonio Garmilla (13, 8 adjoined), Diego Ramos (10, 7 adjoined), and Lino Domínguez (8). In addition, Simón and Teodoro Tiburcio got 5, and Pablo Hernández Olmedo, chief enforcer of the new order, 13. By then, Natividad Cámara had passed away, and one of the military engineers—Rafael Rosas—was serving as *jefe político*. Formerly a member of Huerta's commission, Rosas had returned to work under Muñoz, who had recommended him for the post. Now that governing Papantla had been reduced to carving out the *condueñazgos*, a military surveyor seemed the most expedient choice. Later that year, the lands of Carrizal y Volador were subdivided. Pablo Hernández Olmedo once again presided over the *reparto* board. This was another vast *lote* (11,192 hectares), and its 245 parcels were by far Papantla's largest (46 hectares each). By hook or by crook, over 40 percent (105) of the plots went to merchants and *rancheros*, nearly all owners of multiple shares. Rafael Vaquero and Antonio Garmilla took 23 and 27, respectively (2,300 hectares in all), Pablo Hernández Olmedo got 6, and several others received between 3 and 6. A total of 28 plots (1,288 hectares) were declared vacant.[132]

By the end of 1897, Cerro del Carbón was the only *condueñazgo* left in the municipality of Papantla. A first subdivision—begun in the wake of the 1891 rebellion—had been practically complete before getting quagmired in late 1892. Three years later, Lucido Cambas had pushed to conclude it, but the rebellion of 1896 got in the way. The tortuous drama of this abortive *reparto*—featuring Ing. Martínez's venality, Juan M. Vidal's mayoral scams, relentless shareholder opposition, and deep factional hostilities—epitomized the social, political, and procedural conflicts that had plagued Papantla's land-tenure reform. The final act would be a fitting one. In April 1897 the *jefe político* ruled that Salvador Martínez's parcelization "suffered from vices and deficiencies" that could not be remedied, and he ordered a whole new land subdivision. Remarkably, the divisory board appointed for this purpose was headed yet again by Juan M. Vidal, whose unbridled corruption had poisoned the first *reparto*. Not surprisingly, Pablo Hernández

Olmedo was also in the Junta, and when the military surveyors at last began the field work, in late December, it was his militiamen who served as crew members. At the beginning of March 1898, the long and strife-laden partition of Cerro del Carbón came to an end. Predictably, a small group of merchants, Totonac bosses, speculators, and *rancheros* took a sizable portion of the *lote*. Out of 103 parcels (18 hectares each), almost a third went either to outsiders or to farmers in possession of at least three shares. Among them were Antonio Garmilla (10), Pablo Hernández Olmedo (3), Juan M. Vidal (2), and Simón Tiburcio (1). Nearly another quarter went to farmers holding two shares, 8 were left vacant, and the rest were assigned to owners of a single certificate. At the final gathering of the shareholders, Hernández Olmedo translated as the *jefe político* declared the last of Papantla's ex-communal *condueñazgos* abolished.[133]

After nearly a decade of uncertainty and conflict, and despite two large rebellions that sought in vain to modify the terms and conduct of the land distributions, Papantla's seventeen *grandes lotes* had now been divided up into approximately 3,500 private parcels (see Table 6.2).[134] Of these, around 235 (6.7 percent, 5,629 hectares) had been declared vacant. Some were subsequently claimed by the shareholders, and the rest were supposed to be auctioned off by the Ayuntamiento. At Muñoz's request, the State Treasury loaned funds to the divisory boards in order to cover the survey fees associated with these parcels. This ensured that the engineers got paid in full. The Treasury would hold the title-deeds as security until the plots were sold. In fact, numerous vacant land shares never made it into public auction, disappearing instead into the hands of divisory board members, government officials, and their business friends. This back-room scramble for extra parcels generated its own acrimonious disputes, with land-brokers in high places—e.g., Pablo Hernández Olmedo and Rafael Rosas—trading accusations of partiality, venality, and outright foul play. Several years later, when the Ayuntamiento finally auctioned the remaining shares of the extinguished *condueñazgos*, vanilla merchants, Totonac *rancheros*, and local officeholders took many. This was the sordid aftermath of the *repartos*.[135]

Parcelization had reorganized and redistributed land rights in the *pueblo* of Papantla. Overall, between a quarter and a third of the old communal territory in the municipality now belonged to townspeople—mainly the top merchants—and to a variegated Totonac elite. A relatively small class of Indian *rancheros*, bosses, and speculators owned roughly two-fifths of those lands (10 to 13 percent of the total), and an even smaller group of non-Indians held the rest (15 to 20 percent). In absolute terms, these were sizable conquests: 8,000–11,000 hectares for the former, and 12,500–16,500 hectares for the latter, including—particularly among the merchants—some very large estates. Still, at least two-thirds of the ex-communal *condueñazgo*

TABLE 6.2
Subdivision of Papantla's Municipal Condueñazgos

Lot	Congregaciones	Estimated area (hectares)	Actual area (approx. hectares)	Number of shares	Vacant shares	Approx. number of hectares per share
6	Arroyo Grande de Boca de Lima	c. 2,634	2,861	155	55	18
8	Cedro	c. 5,268	5,668	189	5	29
10	Polutla, Taracuán y Poza Verde	c. 9,658	12,636	486	4	26
11	Cerro del Carbón	c. 1,756	1,903	103	8	18
12	Poza Larga y Cazuelas	c. 3,512	3,198	244	4	13
13	Tlahuanapa	c. 2,634	846	121	4	7
15	Chote y Mesillas	c. 1,756	2,354	179	6	15
16	El Palmar	c. 3,073	1,689	93	13	18
17	Carrizal y Volador	c. 3,951	11,192	245	28	46
18	Concha, Aguacate y Totomoxtle	c. 7,024	3,146	255	28	12
19	Ojital y Potrero	c. 3,512	6,355	205	8	31
20	Escolín	c. 2,634	3,313	115	3	30
21	Talaxca Arroyo Colorado	c. 7,024	4,483	319	16	16
22	Pital y Mozutla	c. 3,512	10,239	280	34	36
23	Cazones y Limón	c. 1,756 ⎤	10,839	418	4	25
24	Sombrerete, Caristay y Aguacate	c. 3,951 ⎦				
25	Santa Agueda	c. 1,756	2,065	100	15	20

SOURCE: See note 134 to Chapter 6.

lands (55,550 hectares) remained the property of Totonac family farmers, mostly holders of single parcels. Despite the rapacity that so often characterized this land-tenure reform, more than two thousand individuals and families whose primary occupation was subsistence-oriented agriculture had managed to emerge as landowners. At the end of the nineteenth century, like a hundred years before, Papantla's ancestral village lands were overwhelmingly in the hands of Totonacs. Considering how the economic potential of land-based enterprises had grown during that century, this is not an insignificant continuity.

The differences, however, are also striking. Both the legal basis and the

allocation of land rights had shifted, giving town merchants and local Totonac potentates exclusive control over some of the best ranch and farm
lands north of the river. In the process, more than half of the Totonac
households in the *pueblo* were left propertyless. They were native sons and
daughters disfranchised by the *conolueñazgo*, and also migrants from the
sierra. When there were fewer people and before vanilla became big business, free land for the milpas was a birthright. There were clear inequalities
in wealth and power, but proprietary access to land was not a measure of
these. Now most farmers paid rent, or else they worked for others. This
was an historic change, fast as it was deep, the product of three decades
marked by divisive economic growth, inter-ethnic political realignments,
and internecine social strife. As the twentieth century commenced, the
wrenching reordering of Papantla's rural property relations was essentially
complete. Where independent farmers once dominated, a four-tiered social
hierarchy had now taken root: a compact group of non-resident landlords—Totonac caciques as well as Euro-Mexican merchants—with substantial holdings in several locations; the *ranchero* clans who ruled each of
the *congregaciones*; a hefty class of landowning *labradores*; and a bulging
stratum of tenants, *jornaleros*, and ranch hands.

Many had fought and died trying to oppose this outcome. They had
trusted the law to do them justice, but it did not, and taking up arms to
undo the present had served only to seal their defeat. How grievously the
law had failed them, they would never know. As the end of the *repartos*
grew near, Ignacio Muñoz pressed the federal government to certify that the
grandes lotes were *baldío*-free. But when the Ministry of Fomento finally
studied the matter, it concluded that Papantla's *lote* lands were, in fact,
legally public, since they lacked primordial property titles. In December
1897, Minister Manuel Fernández Leal informed Governor Dehesa that the
lotes—now nearly all parceled—would have to be privatized by positive pre-
scription as "possessed *baldíos*," in accordance with the public lands law of
1894. Applications for each *lote* were filed and approved beginning in
1898.[136] Muñoz, the divisory boards, and the Ayuntamiento were now doing precisely what the dissidents and Galicia had been ostracized for trying.
But for all those who had been killed, exiled, imprisoned, or disfranchised,
there would be no poetic justice here, only this retrospective academic vin-
dication. The old Papantla had passed away, and so had its consuetudinary
land rights.

Epilogue

Between 1900 and 1910, numerous ex-communal land parcels changed owners, often more than once. Papantla's Registro Público de la Propiedad recorded scores of purchase-and-sale agreements every year, the majority of which involved town merchants or Totonac entrepreneurs on at least one end of the deal. The motives behind these transactions were probably as diverse as the participants, but financial considerations—as opposed to productive ones—clearly predominated. For the town merchants, land became the collateral security of choice, both for loans made among themselves and for those given to Indian farmers. They habitually obtained land titles in lieu of the money owed to them, and in turn used these titles to secure loans of their own. Mortgaging these lands gave merchant financiers access to larger pools of capital, which was increasingly necessary at a time when investments in the vanilla business were increasing—along with the volume of exports—and the returns on those investments were diminishing. As for the land itself, more often than not it remained devoted to family agriculture: the Totonac milpa, the *vainillales* in the *acahual*, the *tareas* of tobacco. For many of these new urban-based proprietors, landownership was attractive primarily as a financial instrument and as a source of leverage with farmers, and only secondarily as a means of production. Ranching and logging—both demesne enterprises—were the common exceptions. Despite the new concentration of landed property, there was no rush to organize large-scale, centrally managed vanilla plantations. On the whole, landowning merchants clearly preferred an updated version of the old production arrangements; family farmers would continue to bear the risks and costs of cultivation, only now landlords (who were often creditors as well) could expect to acquire their tenants' green fruit at harvest time.

This general pattern of land tenure and use was also evident in the basin's old non-communal territories, which at this time became almost entirely the property of merchants. Papantla's haciendas were mainly devoted to raising feeder cattle, horses, and mules, leaving agriculture largely in the hands of

tenant families. After the turn of the century, expanding business and financing options led to a rapid concentration of landownership west and
south of the town. Two immigrant merchant-capitalists, Papantla's Pedro
Tremari and Teziutlán's Manuel Zorrilla, were the main beneficiaries. Building on Simón Tiburcio's previous land plunder, Tremari assembled—in a very
short span of years—a colossal *latifundio.* English oilman Percy Furber put
it more delicately: "His large hacienda had been built up gradually through
the steady acquisition of land from the native Indians and at this time [1897]
he had cleared and put into grass about 20,000 acres and owned about
15,000 head of cattle as well as many horses and mules." Tremari, Furber
explained, "shipped all his [vanilla] beans to the American Trading Company in New York and I understand that one year they sold over a million
dollars' worth of beans for his account." Vanilla exports financed land ac-
quisitions, and vice versa. Like many of his counterparts, Tremari had little
attachment to his young haciendas; he treated real estate first and foremost
as a speculative investment and did not hesitate to cash in when the opportunity arose. In 1897 he sold the oil pits at El Cuguas (later renamed
Furbero) to the Englishman; twelve years later, Furber's Oil Fields of Mexico
Company purchased the whole hacienda. Modestly referred to as "Palma
Sola y Anexas," it was an amalgamation of non- and ex-communal lands
comprising the estates of Nextlalpan, Palma Sola, San Miguel y San Lorenzo,
El Brinco, Chicualoque, Corrralillo, and Troncones y Potrerillo, more than
50,000 hectares in all. The price, $658,250 pesos, included various struc-
tures, fenced-in pastures, feeder cattle herds, and 150,000 vanilla plants.[1] To
their list of wares in high demand, the merchants had now added land.

Among *labradores,* most managed to hold on to their new properties,
but a good number of them did not. Some of those who lost their land titles were perhaps the victims of trickery or deceit, but in the majority of
cases indebtedness was probably the main cause. The huge increase in vanilla cultivation during the first decade of the twentieth century—when average annual exports reached 100,000 kilograms—was for the most part financed through cash advances to farmers, and the basin's small-scale
producers quickly found out that their vanilla was no longer worth what it
used to be. In addition, they still had many taxes to pay. The unfortunate
ones who found themselves unable to meet these fiscal and commercial obligations were forced to sell or hand over their property. Losing title to the
land, however, would not entail losing access to it. These ex-owners were
turned into tenants, but they remained family farmers, although now they
were practically—and sometimes contractually—obligated to deliver their
cash crops to the new landlords. In this respect, they became no different
from the disfranchised of the 1880s and 1890s, many of whom continued
working ex-communal lands as tenants cum *jornaleros.*

Thus, although privatization and parcelization had transformed the distribution of landownership, land-use patterns and the organization of agricultural production changed far less profoundly. At least in this corner of Porfirian Mexico, the concentration of landed property was not synonymous with widespread lack of access to land. After a quarter-century of jarring economic expansion and tremendous social upheaval, the historic lands of the *pueblo* of Papantla remained by and large a preserve of family farming. The ancient *roza*, the routines of milpa cultivation, the two crops of maize that the winter rains made possible—these were for most Totonacs still the foundations of daily existence. Except for the ubiquitousness of vanilla, the seeded pastures enclosed with barbed wire, the shrinking *monte alto*, and the trails of wooden stakes left behind by the military surveyors, a casual observer from the distant past might have said that this was still the rural Papantla of old. But it was not. By the time Mexico had a Revolution, Papantla had already finished one of its own. The great-grandparents of the *pueblo*'s indigenous farmers would have recognized the most basic rhythms of their lives, but not the circumstances in which they were lived. Town merchants and Totonac bosses now reigned supreme, many Indian agriculturalists were now anything but independent, and the old bonds of community—whatever they once were—had long since frayed. This was the world that vanilla had made.

REFERENCE MATTER

Appendix: Mexican, U.S., and French Vanilla Trade Data

TABLE A.I

Fleet Exports of New Spanish Vanilla

Date Departed	Captain	Number of vanilla beans	Kilograms
1761	Carlos Regio	537,027	2,148
1763	Francisco Espínola	651,115	2,604
1766	Agustín de Idiaquez	451,822	1,807
1770	Marqués de Casa-Tilly	449,550	1,798
1778	Antonio de Ulloa	367,765	1,471

SOURCES: Lerdo de Tejada, *Comercio exterior de México*, docs. 2–7 (for the years 1761, 1763, 1766, and 1770); and Humboldt, *Ensayo político sobre el Reino de la Nueva España*, 498 (for 1778).

TABLE A.2

Vanilla Exports, 1802–1828

Year	Number of vanilla beans	Kilograms
1802	1,793,000	8,069
1803	968,500	4,358
1804	1,014,000	4,563
1805	74,000	404
1806	676,317	3,043
1807	177,000	797
1808	729,000	3,281
1809	460,000	2,309
1810	418,941	2,061
1811	404,875	2,002
1812	118,000	545
1816	245,000	1,276
1817	644,000	3,034
1818	0	0
1819	202,000	862
1823	156,000	702
1824	144,700	767
1825	679,000	3,056
1826	848,900	3,820
1827	—[a]	—[a]
1828	581,000	2,615

SOURCE: Lerdo de Tejada, *Comercio exterior de México*, docs. 15–35 (at 4 kilograms/ millar). For some years, vanilla is listed by class. A discussion of the effects of war on the unusually high volume of trade registered during 1802 can be found in notes 3 and 8, following Lerdo's account lists; for 1805, see notes 1, 2, and 6.

[a] According to the trade lists compiled by Lerdo de Tejada, Mexico exported 15,264,000 vanillas (61,056 kilograms) in 1827 (doc. 34). Since this is clearly a mistake, the figure has been excluded from consideration. Mexico would not reach that level of production and exports for another sixty years, and there are no unusual circumstances that might explain such an extraordinary accumulation of vanilla (equivalent to more than twenty years of better-than-average harvests for that time) prior to 1827. The fort of San Juan de Ulúa had been surrendered to Mexican authorities in November 1825, and trade through the port at Veracruz returned to normalcy in 1826; during the years of conflict around Ulúa, moreover, Alvarado, Tampico, and other Gulf ports were able to channel Mexico's trade. The years 1825 and 1826 were in fact good ones for the vanilla export business, so it is unlikely that there was any significant backlog awaiting shipment in 1827 (see Lerdo de Tejada, *Comercio exterior de México*, docs. 30–34, especially the notes; also, on Ulúa, Trens, *Historia de Veracruz*, vol. 4, chs. 3–4). Likewise, as Harold Sims has shown, the laws decreeing the expulsion of Spaniards from Mexican territory had little impact on Veracruz merchants as a whole, and in any case were not passed by the legislature until December 1827. The expulsion order did contribute to considerable bullion flight, but only in 1828 and 1829, and there is no evidence that it had the same effect on vanilla, even assuming—to begin with—that there were sizable stocks of vanilla in the hands of fleeing Spanish merchants (see Sims, *La expulsión de los españoles de México*, especially chs. 8–10). This error has crept into—and mildly distorted—general accounts of the evolution of Mexico's foreign trade in the nineteenth century (see, e.g., Herrera Canales, *El comercio exterior de México*, 59, 67).

TABLE A.3

Mexican Vanilla Imported by France

Year	Kilograms
1818	685
1819	854
1820	837
1821	1,177
1822	1,001
1823	1,141
1824	1,405
1825	2,299
1826	2,633
1827	3,870
1828	2,286
1829	2,423
1830	4,582

SOURCES: France, Direction Générale des Douanes, *Tableau des marchandises étrangères importées en France...*, for the years 1818–24; and France, Direction Générale des Douanes, *Tableau général du commerce de la France...*, for the years 1825–30. The figures given are for "commerce général," defined as "tout ce qui est arrivé par mer ou par terre, par navires français ou par navires étrangers, sans égard à la destination ultérieure des marchandises, soit pour la consommation, soit pour le transit, soit pour l'entrepôt."

TABLE A.4

Vanilla Shipments to France, 1831–1870
(in kilograms)

Year	Mexico	USA	Cuba/ Puerto Rico	Others	Réunion	Total
1831	5,810	298	0	348	0	6,456
1832	4,637	529	0	145	0	5,311
1833	4,564	351	0	180	0	5,095
1834	4,659	182	0	291	0	5,132
1835	4,709	1,053	0	412	0	6,174
1836	5,260	1,741	0	2,550	0	9,551
1837	5,090	751	0	572	0	6,413
1838	1,262	3,329	1,240	364	0	6,195
1839	2,556	1,162	675	1,253	0	5,646
1840	3,937	407	0	2,623	0	6,967
1841	4,817	2,905	0	3,199	0	10,921
1842	4,995	1,311	145	272	0	6,723
1843	4,319	600	1,375	735	0	7,029
1844	7,096	111	35	546	0	7,788
1845	5,851	0	0	1,552	0	7,403
1846	5,344	399	276	10,370	0	16,389
1847	293	4,036	139	7,345	10	11,823
1848	8,898	4,555	383	6,116	39	19,991
1849	12,378	1,494	138	1,029	74	15,113
1850	10,816	40	0	415	84	11,355
1851	4,188	20	0	1,021	48	5,277
1852	7,755	1,497	0	3,088	274	12,614
1853	7,480	386	0	996	394	9,256
1854	6,728	205	0	1,320	458	8,711
1855	4,040	0	0	486	140	4,666
1856	7,331	0	0	1,817	816	9,964
1857	7,690	0	0	4,344	780	12,814
1858	4,448	0	0	2,290	1,917	8,655
1859	323	0	0	8,426	2,841	11,590
1860	1,817	0	0	9,036	6,764	17,607
1861	221	0	0	8,175	16,209	24,605
1862	4,517	0	0	5,040	40,572	50,129
1863	5,212	0	0	4,252	29,351	38,815

TABLE A.4 *(Continued)*

Year	Mexico	USA	Cuba/ Puerto Rico	Others	Réunion	Total
1864	6,228	0	0	933	13,774	20,935
1865	6,870	0	0	3,583	34,901	45,354
1866	5,848	0	5,846	2,696	34,751	49,141
1867	6,523	0	0	3,373	23,726	33,622
1868	3,826	0	0	5,285	27,181	36,292
1869	4,447	0	0	5,350	15,948	25,745
1870	6,402	0	0	23,983	10,323	40,708

SOURCES: Direction Générale des Douanes, *Tableau général du commerce de la France*, for the years 1831–1870. See also Kapp, "Les relations économiques extérieures du Mexique," 73–75.

NOTE: Mexico's nineteenth-century maritime commerce relied heavily on foreign vessels, and vanilla followed many routes on its way to Europe. More often than not, as the table shows, direct shipments remained the norm, but there were always important exceptions. French imports from the United States and from the Spanish colonial outposts of Cuba and Puerto Rico are easily identified as originating in Mexico. Until the mid-1850s, U.S. ships regularly transported vanilla from Veracruz and Tampico to New Orleans and New York, from where it was re-exported to Europe. During the military occupation of Veracruz (March 1847–July 1848), these U.S. shipments increased substantially. The category "Others" includes a variety of nations and trading posts from which France received vanilla, among them England, St. Thomas, Martinique, the Philippines, Spain, Sardinia, the Low Countries, Venezuela, and Austria. With the possible exception of a few small shipments—for example, from Brazil in 1844 and from British possessions in East Africa in the late 1860s—all this vanilla was grown in Mexico. Morren's greenhouse experiments with artificial pollination did not bear fruit until 1837, and this ingenious practice did not take root in Réunion until the late 1840s, at which time—as shown—small quantities of colonial vanilla were exported to the metropolis for the first time. This French vanilla is listed separately. Highly portable and lucrative, vanilla was evidently a commodity that changed flags with great ease; prior to 1870, however, it is fairly safe to assume that shipments by "others" to France involved mostly Mexican vanilla.

TABLE A.5

Mexican Vanilla Imported into France (Directly and Indirectly), 1831–1869

Year	Kilograms	Year	Kilograms
1831	6,456	1851	5,229
1832	5,311	1852	12,340
1833	5,095	1853	8,862
1834	5,132	1854	8,253
1835	6,174	1855	4,526
1836	9,551	1856	9,148
1837	6,413	1857	12,034
1838	6,195	1858	6,738
1839	5,646	1859	8,749
1840	6,967	1860	10,853
1841	10,921	1861	8,396
1842	6,723	1862	9,557
1843	7,029	1863	9,464
1844	7,788	1864	7,161
1845	7,043	1865	8,827*
1846	16,389	1866	12,707*
1847	11,813	1867	7,605*
1848	19,952	1868	5,865*
1849	15,039	1869	7,955*
1850	11,271		

NOTE: In order to get a more graphic sense of the scale of French imports for this period, all the categories from Table A.4 comprising vanilla presumably of Mexican origin have been joined into a single one. To err on the side of caution, imports from British East African possessions have been excluded from these calculations. Listed under "Others" in Table A.4, such imports were registered from 1865 to 1869. The aggregate figures for these years are marked with an asterisk (*).

TABLE A.6

Vanilla Imported by the United States, 1863–1870

Year [a]	Mexico (kilograms)	Others (kilograms)	France (kilograms)	Total (kilograms)
1863	255	695	35	985
1864	2,198	1,064	0	3,261
1865	2,529	415	0	2,944
1866	4,201	1,795	313	6,309
1867	1,949	322	42	2,313
1868	5,355	2,189	111	7,655
1869	—	—	—	4,652
1870	—	—	—	5,289

SOURCES: U.S. Department of the Treasury, *Report of the Secretary of the Treasury...*, for the years 1862–63, 1863–64, 1864–65, and 1865–66; U.S. Bureau of the Census, *Foreign Commerce and Navigation of the United States...*, for the years 1866–67 through 1869–70.

NOTE: Most of this vanilla was probably destined for internal consumption; beginning with the year 1867, the U.S. Bureau of Statistics in fact labeled it as such. Again, as in the case of French import records shown in Table A.5, shipments by "Others" (e.g., Cuba, Puerto Rico, England, and Hamburg) consisted mostly of Mexican vanilla. Midway through the 1850s, vanilla shipments from the United States to France come to an end (see Table A.4) and U.S. import records begin to include vanilla. Until 1863, however, vanilla appears only in consular reports from Veracruz and Tampico; the amounts in question, moreover, seem to have been fairly small, probably well under 1,000 kilograms. For these commercial reports see, e.g., U.S. Congress, House, *Report of the Secretary of State...for the Year Ending September 30, 1856*, 34th Cong., 3rd sess., 1857, H. Doc. 60, 200–202; U.S. Congress, House, *Letter of the Secretary of State....for the Year ending September 30, 1858*, 35th Cong., 2nd sess., 1859, H. Doc. 85, 626-27; U.S. Congress, House, Letter of the Secretary of State...for the Year ending September 30, 1859, 36th Cong., 1st sess., 1860, H. Doc. 4, 398, 403; U.S. Congress, House, *Letter of the Secretary of State...for the Year ending September 30, 1861*, 37th Cong., 2nd sess., 1862, H. Doc. 45, 386-87; and U.S. Congress, House, *Letter of the Secretary of State...for the Year ended September 30, 1862*, 37th Cong., 3rd sess., 1863, H. Doc. 63, 258–59. Usually, only a dollar amount is provided in these reports, but the one for 1859 does list the shipment's weight, a mere 436 kilograms.

[a] These figures refer to fiscal years.

TABLE A.7

Vanilla Imported by France, 1870–1910

Year	Mexico (kilograms)	USA (kilograms)	Réunion (kilograms)	Others (kilograms)	Total (kilograms)
1870	6,402	0	10,323	23,983	40,708
1871	6,893	940	18,261	3,307	29,401
1872	1,938	0	15,506	9,231	26,675
1873	6,690	0	13,773	8,514	28,977
1874	2,229	0	22,770	9,907	34,906
1875	13,320	1,599	18,478	9,028	42,425
1876	7,957	2,554	39,882	24,887	75,280
1877	7,670	0	37,949	17,448	63,067
1878	11,988	3,564	42,151	22,423	80,126
1879	6,096	0	73,464	21,521	101,081
1880	11,866	0	46,189	32,047	90,102
1881	11,072	0	28,266	32,801	72,139
1882	12,524	0	41,037	34,833	88,394
1883	9,195	0	38,342	30,504	78,041
1884	13,879	0	34,085	23,913	71,877
1885	3,426	0	55,713	34,125	93,264
1886	2,456	4,410	73,610	39,540	120,016
1887	3,785	2,612	79,728	26,464	112,589
1888	7,164	3,298	105,307	64,117	179,886
1889	12,166	2,806	72,781	29,783	117,536
1890	6,293	0	63,148	32,093	101,534
1891	6,172	0	117,976	44,065	168,213
1892	6,918	0	97,719	69,843	174,480
1893	3,929	0	106,329	27,680	137,938
1894	2,627	0	90,658	52,681	145,966
1895	3,257	0	100,334	32,527	136,118
1896	2,178	0	62,723	31,071	95,972
1897	1,060	0	83,669	38,859	123,588
1898	2,886	0	119,705	41,100	163,691
1899	2,300	0	85,814	68,213	156,327
1900	2,200	0	105,231	60,036	167,467
1901	2,100	6,155	70,442	126,140	204,837
1902	1,800	12,868	111,541	132,696	258,905
1903	2,800	51,162	57,486	157,499	268,947

TABLE A.7 *(Continued)*

Year	Mexico (kilograms)	USA (kilograms)	Réunion (kilograms)	Others (kilograms)	Total (kilograms)
1904	1,900	12,111	133,308	136,747	284,066
1905	3,669	24,459	97,616	245,736	371,480
1906	8,261	6,082	70,449	227,947	312,739
1907	8,929	13,090	68,902	218,430	309,351
1908	2,600	5,059	45,569	198,796	252,024
1909	9,670	13,748	111,051	179,198	313,667
1910	7,707	6,872	44,984	152,848	212,411

SOURCES: France, Direction Générale des Douanes, *Tableau général du commerce de la France...,* for the years 1870–1910; and France, Direction Générale des Douanes, *Tableau général du commerce et de la navigation...* for the years 1896–1910.

NOTES: For the years 1870–90, as in earlier years, imports from the United States can be safely assumed to have been re-exported from Mexico. However, the category of "Others" is no longer mostly Mexican vanilla. Now, it includes primarily shipments from British East African territories, from Guadeloupe and Martinique, and from French possessions in the Indian Ocean (aside from Réunion), where vanilla was by then also grown. Perhaps a tiny and fairly insignificant percentage of the assorted imports grouped in this column originated in Mexico, but not more. In this table, "Others" includes principally British East African possessions, Guadeloupe, Martinique, Mayotte, and Madagascar. After 1895 the bulk of the shipments grouped in this category came from Mayotte and Madagascar, both of which were French colonies at the time. Over the course of the twentieth century, Madagascar would emerge as the world's largest producer of vanilla.

TABLE A.8

U.S. Vanilla Imports, 1869–1910

Fiscal Year	Mexico (kilograms)	France (kilograms)	French Oceania (kilograms)	Other (kilograms)	Total (kilograms)
1869–1870	—	—	—	—	5,289
1870–1871	—	—	—	—	6,711
1871–1872	—	—	—	—	6,190
1872–1873	—	—	—	—	16,398
1873–1874	—	—	—	—	5,507
1874–1875	—	—	—	—	16,486
1875–1876	—	—	—	—	16,609
1876–1877	—	—	—	—	7,532
1877–1878	—	—	—	—	13,572
1878–1879	—	—	—	—	19,042
1879–1880	—	—	—	—	24,889
1880–1881	—	—	—	—	16,916
1881–1882	—	—	—	—	45,780
1882–1883	—	—	—	—	31,015
1883–1884	31,628	682	1,974	89	34,373
1884–1885	39,735	290	3,156	953	44,134
1885–1886	38,657	0	2,991	3,593	45,240
1886–1887	46,105	8,007	3,004	5,375	62,490
1887–1888	43,045	11,205	6,027	5,805	66,081
1888–1889	63,809	3,402	5,044	4,468	76,723
1889–1890	53,771	2,647	4,505	4,926	65,850
1890–1891	57,340	7,794	10,167	2,390	77,691
1891–1892	83,513	8,122	8,290	10,365	110,290
1892–1893	77,555	11,013	12,540	7,408	108,516
1893–1894	45,960	15,505	9,964	6,551	77,980
1894–1895	41,251	9,054	7,021	5,081	62,407
1895–1896	76,102	7,001	17,304	6,758	107,165
1896–1897	29,717	18,102	14,632	12,549	75,000
1897–1898	10,375	5,400	10,754	2,561	29,090
1898–1899	34,221	38,411	39,669	11,415	123,716
1899–1900	39,337	30,866	33,987	12,158	116,348
1900–1901	16,238	40,845	48,734	7,360	113,177
1901–1902	32,720	40,775	80,482	10,450	164,427
1902–1903	51,508	60,291	110,980	14,352	237,131

TABLE A.8 *(Continued)*

Fiscal Year	Mexico (kilograms)	France (kilograms)	French Oceania (kilograms)	Other (kilograms)	Total (kilograms)
1903–1904	80,591	61,081	92,793	15,684	250,149
1904–1905	79,604	57,580	121,175	18,058	276,417
1905–1906	171,438	86,952	110,876	18,235	387,501
1906–1907	121,858	170,377	120,867	27,466	440,568
1907–1908	81,978	53,860	95,755	28,397	259,990
1908–1909	120,242	150,232	202,668	36,625	509,767
1909–1910	114,514	46,343	185,365	16,236	362,458

SOURCE: U.S. Bureau of the Census, *Foreign Commerce and Navigation of the United States...*, annually, for the years 1869–70 through 1909–1910.

NOTES: In this table, "Others" includes primarily England, the French and British West Indies, and Germany, some as producers and others as re-exporters. For 1870–79 the figures provided refer to vanilla "entered for immediate consumption." For 1880–90 the data refer to total imports, but a comparison between "total imports" and "immediate consumption imports" figures shows them to be basically equivalent, which is to say that virtually all vanilla imports were by then destined for domestic consumption. Beginning in 1873 vanilla shipments were admitted free of duty, eliminating a steep US$3.00/pound tariff imposed previously.

Mexican Vanilla Exports, 1872–1910

Fiscal Year	USA (kilograms)	France (kilograms)	Others (kilograms)	Total (kilograms)
1872–1873	56%	39%	5%	—
1873–1874	71%	21%	8%	—
1874–1875	61%	32%	7%	—
1875–1876	—	—	—	—
1876–1877	—	—	—	—
1877–1878	11,518	9,779	4,073	25,370
1878–1879	12,024	4,996	760	17,780
1879–1880	24,935	14,719	1,332	40,986
1880–1881	61%	36%	3%	35,732
1881–1882	83%	11%	6%	59,212
1882–1883	88%	12%	0%	51,827
1883–1884	71%	28%	1%	53,532
1884–1885	82%	17%	1%	52,165
1885–1886	96%	4%	0%	43,878
1886–1887	94%	6%	0%	43,515
1887–1888	28,432	—	—	28,965
1888–1889	66,672	5,351	1,121	73,144
1889–1890	66,748	5,333	19	72,100
1890–1891	39,648	9,834	500	49,982
1891–1892	94,633	2,665	1,142	98,440
1892–1893	87,984	3,445	1,148	92,577
1893–1894	64,657	3,328	2,056	70,041
1894–1895	24,605	1,100	0	25,705
1895–1896	80,857	—	—	81,504
1896–1897	33,984	721	5	34,710
1897–1898	11,319	7,552	16	18,887
1898–1899	42,798	1,279	43	44,120
1899–1900	43,748	2,050	0	45,798
1900–1901	—	—	—	25,588
1901–1902	—	—	—	36,644
1902–1903	58,945	6,782	537	66,264
1903–1904	97,103	1,168	63	98,334
1904–1905	117,406	2,762	486	120,654
1905–1906	220,387	3,947	376	224,710
1906–1907	156,929	5,667	1,148	163,744

TABLE A.9 *(Continued)*

Fiscal Year	USA (kilograms)	France (kilograms)	Others (kilograms)	Total (kilograms)
1907–1908	95,581	12,168	322	108,071
1908–1909	132,669	8,650	212	141,531
1909–1910	136,644	12,902	1,837	151,383

SOURCES: Secretaría de Estado y del Despacho de Hacienda y Crédito Público, *Noticia de la importación y exportación de mercancías...de 1872 a 1873, 1873 a 1874 y 1874 a 1875*; Secretaría de Estado y del Despacho de Hacienda y Crédito Público, *Noticia de la exportación de mercancías...*, for the years 1877–78, 1878–79, 1879–80, 1880–81, 1881–82, 1882–83, 1883–84, 1884–85, 1885–86, 1886–87, 1887–88, and 1888–89; Secretaría de Estado y del Despacho de Hacienda y Crédito Público, *Exportaciones...*, for the years 1889–90, 1890–91, 1891–92, and 1892–93; Secretaría de Estado y del Despacho de Hacienda y Crédito Público, *Estadística fiscal*, for the years 1893–94, 1894–95, and 1895–96; Secretaría de Estado y del Despacho de Hacienda y Crédito Público, *Comercio exterior...*, for the years 1896–97, and 1897–98; Secretaría de Estado y del Despacho de Hacienda y Crédito Público, *Comercio exterior y navegación...*, for the years 1898–99 and 1899–1900; Secretaría de Estado y del Despacho de Hacienda y Crédito Público, *Boletín de estadística fiscal...*, for the years 1900–01, 1901–02, 1902–03, 1903–04, 1904–05, 1905–06, 1906–07, 1907–08, 1908–09, and 1909–10. The figures for 1877–78 through 1879–80 appear in the 1879–80 volume of Secretaría de Estado y del Despacho de Hacienda y Crédito Público, *Noticia de la exportación de mercancías....* Some of this data can also be consulted in Colegio de México, *Estadísticas económicas del Porfiriato*, 358–59.

NOTE: The percentages included in this table are based on value figures, since export volumes by country of destination were not recorded for these years. Judging from the statistics for the years in which both weight and value data were provided, there is a very close correlation (usually between 1 and 5 percent) between a country's weight-share and its value-share of total exports for that year. Thus, value figures give a good approximate idea of how many kilograms, as a percentage of the total, were shipped to each country in any given year.

TABLE A.10

Shipments of Mexican Vanilla by Port, 1872–1900
(in kilograms)

Years	Veracruz	Tuxpan	Other ports	Total
1872–73	99%	<1%	<1%	—
1873–74	98%	2%	0%	—
1874–75	72%	28%	0%	—
1875–76	—	—	—	—
1876–77	—	—	—	—
1877–78	85%	15%	0%	25,370
1878–79	58%	42%	0%	17,780
1879–80	72%	28%	0%	40,986
1880–81	25,173	9,930	629	35,732
1881–82	26,995	32,138	79	59,212
1882–83	39,172	12,636	19	51,827
1883–84	47,825	5,696	11	53,532
1884–85	31,374	20,791	0	52,165
1885–86	12,479	31,368	31	43,878
1886–87	8,556	34,950	9	43,515
1887–88	8,646	20,192	127	28,965
1888–89	29,979	43,038	127	73,144
1889–90	16,028	56,054	18	72,100
1890–91	20,315	29,665	2	49,982
1891–92	45,491	52,198	751	98,440
1892–93	60,558	31,961	58	92,577
1893–94	51,434	18,597	10	70,041
1894–95	21,562	3,609	534	25,705
1895–96	56,221	25,247	36	81,504
1896–97	16,538	17,379	793	34,710
1897–98	11,470	5,705	1,712	18,887
1898–99	29,689	12,437	1,994	44,120
1899–1900	20,282	21,556	3,960	45,798

SOURCES: Secretaría de Estado y del Despacho de Hacienda y Crédito Público, *Noticia de la importación y exportación de mercancías...* for the years 1872–73, 1873–74, and 1874–75; Secretaría de Estado y del Despacho de Hacienda y Crédito Público, *Noticia de la exportación de mercancías...*, for the years 1877–78, 1878–79, 1879–80, 1880–81, 1881–82, 1882–83, 1883–84, 1884–85, 1885–86, 1886–87, 1887–88, and 1888–89; Secretaría de Estado y del Despacho de Hacienda y Crédito Público, *Exportaciones...*, for the years 1889–90, 1890–91, 1891–92, and 1892–93; Secretaría de Estado y del Despacho de Hacienda y Crédito Público, *Estadística fiscal ...*, for the years 1893–94, 1894–95, and 1895–96; Secretaría de Estado y del Despacho de Hacienda y Crédito Público, *Comercio exterior...*, for the years (1896–97, and 1897–98); Secretaría de Estado y del Despacho de Hacienda y Crédito Público, *Comercio exterior y navegación...*, for the years 1898–99, and 1899–1900.

NOTE: Percentage figures are based on export value data and are approximate.

Notes

ABBREVIATIONS

ACAM   Archivo de la Comisión Agraria Mixta, Xalapa
ANGZ   Archivo de Notarías de Gutiérrez Zamora
ANP   Archivo de Notarías de Papantla, Papantla
AGA   Archivo General Agrario, Mexico City
AGN   Archivo General de la Nación, Mexico City
AGEV   Archivo General del Estado de Veracruz, Xalapa
AHSDN   Archivo Histórico, Secretaría de la Defensa Nacional,
        Mexico City
AJP   Archivo del Juzgado de Papantla, Papantla
BAGN   *Boletín del Archivo General de la Nación*
CPD   Colección Porfirio Díaz, Universidad Iberoamericana,
        Mexico City
DRTP   Documentos sobre el reparto de tierras del pueblo de
        Papantla, Papantla
MR   *El Monitor Republicano* (Mexico City)
OPDR   *Oil, Paint, and Drug Reporter* (New York)
PO   *Periódico Oficial del Gobierno del Estado de Veracruz*
RPP   Registro Público de la Propiedad, Papantla
SMGE   Mapoteca Ing. Antonio García Cubas, Sociedad Mexicana
        de Geografía y Estadística, Mexico City

INTRODUCTION

1. For a detailed discussion, see Kourí, "Interpreting the Expropriation of Indian Pueblo Lands in Porfirian Mexico."

CHAPTER ONE

1. According to Humboldt, "*All* of the vanilla consumed in Europe comes from Mexico" (*Ensayo político sobre el Reino de la Nueva España*, IV:10:292, emphasis added). Humboldt visited New Spain in 1803, and his Essay was first published in 1811.

2. Raynal, *A Philosophical and Political History*, II:6:405. For an interpretation of the emphasis on commerce in Raynal's *Histoire*, see Pagden, *European Encounters with the New World*, 169–72.

3. Humboldt, *Ensayo político sobre el Reino de la Nueva España*, 293; Raynal, *A Philosophical and Political History*, 405.

4. See, e.g., a recent essay on vanilla in Foster and Cordell, *Chilies to Chocolate*, 35–45. Its errors, as well as its tales, are representative of the genre.

5. On the botany and cultivation of vanilla, see Correll, "Vanilla: Its History, Cultivation and Importance"; a revised and enlarged version appears as "Vanilla—Its Botany, History, Cultivation, and Economic Import." See also Bouriquet, *Le vanillier et la vanille dans le monde*. Four older texts, still very useful, are Lecomte, *Le vanillier*; Delteil, *La vanille*; Chalot, *Culture et préparation de la vanille*; and Ridley, *Spices* (esp. ch. 2). Bouriquet and Correll provide extensive bibliographies. In addition, see Feldkamp, "Vanilla."

6. See Joseph Burnett Company, *Vanilla and Other Flavoring Extracts*.

7. Correll, "Vanilla: Its History, Cultivation and Importance," 237–38. In Mexico *V. pompona* was called "vainillón," "vainilla boba," or, borrowing the Totonac name, "plátano vainilla." It is an edible fruit with a certain resemblance to the banana. *V. tahitiensis* was bred out of *V. planifolia*, probably in the twentieth century.

8. Correll, "Vanilla—Its Botany, History, Cultivation, and Economic Import," 292. In English, it is common to speak of the "vanilla bean" because of its resemblance to a bean pod. The Spanish word *vainilla* in fact means "little pod," or "little sheath," from the Latin *vagina*. For a brief history of the word, see Bruman, "The Culture History of Mexican Vanilla," 365–66.

9. It should be pointed out that there is agreement, but no certainty, that *V. planifolia* is actually "the principal plant cultivated throughout the world." For a discussion, see Correll, "Vanilla—Its Botany, History, Cultivation, and Economic Import," 295–99. Correll writes that "the nomenclatural status of the vanilla of commerce has never been definitely settled to the satisfaction of all botanists." To make matters more complex, at different times Mexicans distinguished among the various kinds of "legitimate" vanilla for the trade, presumably all of them *V. planifolia*, each of which had its own name, e.g., "*mansa*," "*cimarrona*," "*mestiza*," and "*tarro*."

10. See, e.g., Desvaux, "Quelques notions nouvelles," 119–21.

11. For a detailed taxonomic history of vanilla, see Rolfe, "A Revision of the Genus *Vanilla*." *V. planifolia* was sometimes also referred to as *V. fragrans* Salisbury. Salisbury described it in 1807 and Andrews in 1808. Incidentally, both men failed to recognize it at the time as the "true Mexican vanilla of commerce" (ibid., 440–41).

12. There is disagreement as to whether *V. planifolia* is indigenous to the Caribbean. Correll states that it is ("Vanilla—Its Botany, History, Cultivation, and Economic Import," 293), whereas Bruman argues that "it probably represents an escape from cultivation of vines introduced during the colonial period" ("The Culture History of Mexican Vanilla," 361).

13. Correll suggests a range of temperatures between 70 and 90 degrees Fahrenheit, and 80–100 inches of annual rainfall ("Vanilla—Its Botany, History, Cultivation, and Economic Import," 320). The preceding description of *V. planifolia* is based on ibid., 292–93. See also Bouriquet, *Le vanillier et la vanille dans le monde*, chs. 3 and 5.

14. Kelly and Palerm, *The Tajin Totonac*, 123.

15. Morren, "On the Production of Vanilla in Europe," 8. See also Morren,

"Sur la fructification de la vanille," 489–92. The previous description draws on the works of Correll, Lecomte, and Bouriquet.

16. Delteil, *La vanille*, 13. On this question of insect fertilization in Mexico, Rolfe remarked, "I have not succeeded in finding any other records on the subject, and it would be interesting if this point could be cleared up" ("A Revision of the Genus *Vanilla*," 442). Darwin's observations appear in *The Effects of Cross and Self Fertilization*, 404 n. 55. Also see Darwin, *The Various Contrivances by which Orchids are Fertilized by Insects*, 266.

17. López y Parra, *La vainilla*, 47. The wording is reminiscent of Delteil's, whose work is cited extensively beginning on p. 48. On hummingbirds as means of cross-fertilization in other parts of the world, see Darwin, *The Effects of Cross and Self-Fertlization*, 371 n. 2. Since López y Parra's time, Mexican growers have overwhelmingly adopted hand pollination as their method of fertilization, and thus this issue is no longer studied.

18. Rolfe, "A Revision of the Genus *Vanilla*," 442. Also see Darwin's own explanation in *The Various Contrivances by which Orchids are Fertilized by Insects*, 90–91, as well as Morren's original account in "Sur la fructification de la vanille," 491–92.

19. Correll, "Vanilla—Its Botany, History, Cultivation, and Economic Import," 327–28. Also see Darwin, *The Effects of Cross and Self-Fertilization in the Vegetable Kingdom*, ch. 9.

20. The earliest known reference to the planting of vanilla appears in Fuentes y Guzmán, *Recordación florida*. The book mentions the existence of planted vanilla in the *corregimientos* of Yzquintepeque (Escuintla) and Cazabastlán (Zacapa), describing briefly the "curious and uncommon method of planting" employed in Yzquintepeque. The Indians would place vine cuttings at the feet of cacao trees, using string to fasten them to the tree trunks a few inches above the soil. The cuttings would gradually take root and develop into fully grown plants. Fontecilla would also later describe this method of propagation. In these parts of Guatemala, vanilla was planted under cacao trees and its commerce seems to have been closely tied to that of the cacao bean, from which chocolate drinks were prepared. These exceptionally early instances of planting remained marginal, and there is no further notice of them. At the time of Fuentes y Guzmán's writing, Cazabastlán's vanilla production appears to have been already in decline (see *Recordación florida*, vol. II, bk. 2, ch. 8, p. 100; and vol. II, bk. 5, ch. 7, p. 260).

21. See, e.g., Rossignon, *Manual del cultivo del café, cacao, vainilla y tabaco*, 226–27.

22. Bruman lists the evidence ("The Culture History of Mexican Vanilla," 363–64, 368–70). On Soconusco and Guatemala, see Thompson, *Thomas Gage's Travels in the New World*, 192, 196. López y Parra adds Michoacán, Guerrero, Jalisco, and Hidalgo, but does not show that the harvesting of wild vanilla is an ancient custom in these areas (*La vainilla*, 4). For Michoacán, see also León, *Manual para el cultivo y beneficio de la vainilla*. Only the geography of collection is of historical significance, since the plant is indigenous to much of Mesoamerica.

23. AGN, Ramo General de Partes, vol. 34 (1744). The entire document is reproduced in Bruman, "The Culture History of Mexican Vanilla," 373–75.

24. Clavijero, *Historia antigua de México*, 14. Clavijero's *History*, written in Spanish, was first published in Italian in 1780–81.

25. Fontecilla, *Breve tratado sobre el cultivo y beneficio de la vainilla*, 7. Fontecilla, prominent vanilla curer and merchant, was for a time Papantla's *jefe político* as well. His treatise was extremely influential in Mexico and abroad; originally published in 1861, it was reprinted in 1887 and 1898.

26. Tabasco—where cacao was also grown—would be another case in point.

27. For early evidence of a plausible instance of this, see Dampier's *The Campeachy Voyages*, in *Dampier's Voyages*, 2:216–17. Dampier traveled through the "bay of Campeachy . . . and parts adjacent" in 1676.

28. AGN, Ramo de Tierras, vol. 921, exp. 2 (1767); also reproduced in Bruman, "The Culture History of Mexican Vanilla," 375–76. The plots are referred to as "nuestros Bainillares."

29. Fontecilla, *Breve tratado sobre el cultivo y beneficio de la vainilla*, 8.

30. AGN, Ramo de Tierras, vol. 921, exp. 2 (1767).

31. Humboldt, *Ensayo político sobre el Reino de la Nueva España*, 293.

32. Fontecilla, *Breve tratado sobre el cultivo y beneficio de la vainilla*, 7.

33. See Humboldt, *Ensayo político sobre el Reino de la Nueva España* , 293.

34. See Bruman, "The Culture History of Mexican Vanilla," 369 nn. 41–42.

35. Humboldt, *Ensayo político sobre el Reino de la Nueva España*, 295. As Bruman points out, Humboldt's historical claim seems, prima facie, unwarranted ("The Culture History of Mexican Vanilla," 369 n. 42). Interestingly, as late as 1873 French commercial manuals were still extolling the virtues of vanilla from Teutila, singling it out as the best (*Dictionnaire universel théorique et pratique du commerce et de la navigation*, 2:1734).

36. For a geographical description of the Alcaldía Mayor of Teutila, see Gerhard, *A Guide to the Historical Geography of New Spain*, sec. 97. It is telling that in 1911 López y Parra cited Ojitlán, near the Santo Domingo River, as the principal vanilla-producing area in Oaxaca (*La vainilla*, 4).

37. Consider Fontecilla's statement, previously cited, that Veracruz was perhaps the only state in which vanilla had been planted. Oaxaca's harvest, he wrote, was mainly of wild origin (*Breve tratado sobre el cultivo y beneficio de la vainilla*, 8). Moreover, in an 1887 survey of vanilla production, only two municipalities in Oaxaca—Ojitlán and Ixcatlán—reported having any cultivated vanilla. Many municipalities also formerly in the jurisdiction of Teutila, e.g., Usila, Tuxtepec, Jalapa, Valle Nacional, Santa María Zapotitlán, and San Antonio Jicaltepec, reported the existence of wild vanilla in abundance (see "Datos sobre la producción de vainilla," 27:119–40 [dated September 1887], and 28:201–8 [dated October 1887]). More directly, López y Parra described the 1911 geography of vanilla as follows: "[It is] cultivated by the Totonacs of the windward coast or picked wild in the fertile and virgin forests of the Sierra de Oaxaca by Zapotecs and Popolocs" (*La vainilla*, 57). The windward coast (*costa de Barlovento*) refers in this case to a wide strip of land in the state of Veracruz that includes both Papantla and Misantla.

38. On Teutila's curing, see Humboldt, *Ensayo político sobre el Reino de la Nueva España*, 295.

39. De Jussieu's report appears in *Histoire de l'Académie des Sciences* (1722),

published in Paris in 1724. See also Lecomte, *Le vanillier*, 4; and Humboldt, *Ensayo político sobre el Reino de la Nueva España*, 294.

40. Fontecilla, *Breve tratado sobre el cultivo y beneficio de la vainilla*, 112–13.

41. In 1820 Schiede traveled to Misantla and Papantla and described one of these varieties of *V. planifolia* as a new species, *V. sylvestris* (see Schiede, "Botanische Berichte aus Mexico," 573–76). Charles Morren cast doubt on this classification, suggesting that *V. planifolia* Andrews and *V. sylvestris* Schiede were probably one and the same species (see Morren, "On the Production of Vanilla," 2–4). Rolfe settled the question in 1896, concluding that the two plants were "evidently forms of the same species, differing only a little in the length of the fruit, the former being a cultivated race and the latter the wild original" (Rolfe, "A Revision of the Genus *Vanilla*," 441, 464).

42. Fontecilla, *Breve tratado sobre el cultivo y beneficio de la vainilla*, 112–15. A similar categorization appears in Charles Young's report from the 1840s, presented in Desvaux, "Quelques notions nouvelles," 118–23. Many of these varieties quite probably antedate the *mansa*, a fact obscured by the tortuous taxonomic history of vanilla.

43. Fontecilla, *Breve tratado sobre el cultivo y beneficio de la vainilla*, 113.

44. See, e.g., Desvaux, "Quelques notions nouvelles," 121.

45. Fontecilla, *Breve tratado sobre el cultivo y beneficio de la vainilla*, 113.

46. Humboldt, *Ensayo político sobre el Reino de la Nueva España*, 293.

47. Ibid., 293–95.

48. Humboldt's brief remarks on Papantla are revealing: "The district of Papantla . . . produces very little vanilla, which is also badly dried, although it is very aromatic. The Indians of Papantla and Nautla are accused of introducing themselves furtively in the forests of Quilate to pick the fruit of the *epidendrum* planted by those of Misantla" (*Ensayo político sobre el Reino de la Nueva España*, 295). *Epidendrum* is the old Linnean classification for vanilla. So perhaps Papantla's actual production at the time was even smaller. Kelly and Palerm's review of documentary evidence led them to conclude that "there is no indication that the Papantla zone was an early source of supply. Vanilla is not mentioned among the tribute exacted by the Mexicans from the Tuxpan-Papantla area . . . and, in fact, there seems to be no mention of vanilla at Papantla until close to the middle of the eighteenth century" (*The Tajin Totonac*, 122–23).

49. Fontecilla, *Breve tratado sobre el cultivo y beneficio de la vainilla*, 25; see also Delteil, *La vanille*, 10–11.

50. Fontecilla, *Breve tratado sobre el cultivo y beneficio de la vainilla*, 25.

51. Humboldt, *Ensayo político sobre el Reino de la Nueva España*, 293.

52. Kelly and Palerm describe and analyze in detail a modern version of the maize–vanilla–*monte* rotation; see *The Tajin Totonac*, 100–2, 123–24. Fontecilla also mentions the maize–vanilla combination; see *Breve tratado sobre el cultivo y beneficio de la vainilla*, 21.

53. Raynal, *A Philosophical and Political History* II:6:405. Raynal tells this story, apparently well known, only to reject it.

54. Humboldt, *Ensayo político sobre el Reino de la Nueva España*, 292.

55. See Vavilov, *The Origin, Variation, Immunity and Breeding of Cultivated*

Plants; Sauer, *Agricultural Origins and Dispersals*; and Crosby, *The Columbian Exchange*. On specific crops, see Salaman, *The History and Social Influence of the Potato*; and Warman, *La historia de un bastardo*.

56. For a chronology, see Lecomte, *Le vanillier*, 1–7.

57. Rolfe, "A Revision of the Genus *Vanilla*," 440; also Miller, *The Gardener's Dictionary*. On the dates of the introduction of *V. planifolia*, see also Morren, "Sur la fructification de la vanille," 490. On Philip Miller and the Chelsea Physic Garden, see Jellicoe et al., *The Oxford Companion to Gardens*.

58. Morren, "Sur la fructification de la vanille," 490; also, Morren, "On the Production of Vanilla," 4–5, 7. From Paddington it was taken to Antwerp in 1812, and from there across Belgium and France.

59. Morren, "Sur la fructification de la vanille"; also, Morren, "On the Production of Vanilla." On Réunion, see Delteil, *La vanille*, 11–12; and Lecomte, *Le Vanillier*, 190–96.

60. See Morren, "Sur la fructification de la vanille"; and Morren, "On the Production of Vanilla," 5. Years later, Darwin explained that "the large tubular flowers of *Vanilla aromatica* are manifestly adapted to be fertilized by insects; and it is known that when this plant is cultivated in foreign countries, for instance in Bourbon, Tahiti, and the East Indies, it fails to produce its aromatic pods unless artificially fertilized. This fact shows that some insect in its American home is specially adapted for the work; and that the insects of the above-named tropical regions, where the Vanilla flourishes, either do not visit the flowers, though they secrete an abundance of nectar, or do not visit them in the proper manner" (*The Various Contrivances by which Orchids are Fertilized by Insects*, 90–91).

61. Morren, "Sur la fructification de la vanille," 489. "Without an exact knowledge of the organs and their functions, the fruit of this plant could never have been obtained" (Morren, "On the Production of Vanilla," 1).

62. Morren, "On the Production of Vanilla," 6. Also see Morren, Research Report.

63. Morren, "On the Production of Vanilla," 4, 9, 1.

64. E.g., Ridley, *Spices*, 66–81.

65. Morren, "On the Production of Vanilla," 8 [emphasis added].

66. Delteil, *La vanille*, 13, 25–27. Delteil is the source of most subsequent accounts and descriptions, both in English and Spanish. The anatomical drawings made for his text were widely reproduced.

67. Ridley, *Spices*, 51 and 49, respectively.

68. Ridley describes a slightly different operation, in which the wooden instrument, now sharp, is also made to pick the sticky pollen and place it in the stigma. The principle is the same as in Albius's technique. This modification, according to Ridley, makes the procedure more reliable (see *Spices*, 49–50). The introduction of artificial pollination to Mexico is considered in a later chapter.

69. *Tlilxochitl*, "black flower," is the Nahuatl word for the vanilla vine, flower, and fruit. The flower itself is not black, but yellowish; this name, the source of much confusion, probably derives from the dark color of the cured fruit. De la Cruz's manuscript was translated into Latin by Juan Badiano, who entitled it *Libel-*

lus de Medicinalibus Indorum Herbis; it has come to be known as the Codex Badianus (see Emily W. Emmart, *The Badianus Manuscript*, 188, 314–15).

70. See Bruman, "The Culture History of Mexican Vanilla," 362–63; and Hernández, *Rerum medicarum Novae Hispaniae thesaurus*, 38. A reproduction of Hernández's remarks on vanilla appears in Correll, "Vanilla—Its Botany, History, Cultivation, and Economic Import," 297 (fig. 3). For a modern edition, see Hernández, *Historia natural de Nueva España*, vol. 3, *Obras Completas*, 2:10:161.

71. Sahagún, *Historia general de las cosas de Nueva España*, 591, 626. Bruman notes these remedies, but his bibliographical references are incorrect (see "The Culture History of Mexican Vanilla," 362 nn. 4, 5; see also Alcocer, "Consideraciones sobre la medicina azteca," 3:375–82).

72. López de Gómara, *Historia de la conquista de México*, 127–28. The translation is by Leslie Byrd Simpson.

73. Swahn, *The Lore of Spices*, 164. Swahn cites a 1762 article by a German physician, B. Zimmermann, which described the extraordinary effects of vanilla on hundreds of impotent men. With similar aims in mind, the Comtesse du Barry, Louis XV's final mistress, was said to have served her lovers a chocolate drink flavored with vanilla (see Morton and Morton, *Chocolate*, 36–39).

74. See, e.g., Lecomte, *Le vanillier*, 155–63; or Bouriquet, *Le vanillier et la vanille dans le monde*, 647–62.

75. Humboldt, *Ensayo político sobre el Reino de la Nueva España*, 292.

76. Brillat-Savarin, *The Physiology of Taste*, 109.

77. Sahagún, *Historia general de las cosas de Nueva España*, 591.

78. Díaz del Castillo, *Historia verdadera de la conquista de la Nueva España*, 187. Motolinía also refers to the drink as "cacao" (*Historia de los indios de la Nueva España*, pt. 3, ch. 8, sec. 353, p. 154).

79. Sahagún, *Historia general de las cosas de Nueva España*, 465. Various other recipes for cacao taken from Sahagún's *Memoriales* appear in Ignacio Alcocer, "Las comidas de los antiguos mexicanos," 3:368–69.

80. *El conquistador anónimo*, 31.

81. Díaz del Castillo, *Historia verdadera de la conquista de la Nueva España*, 187, 100.

82. See Sahagún, *Historia general de las cosas de Nueva España*, 251, 465; and Díaz del Castillo, *Historia verdadera de la conquista de la Nueva España*, 187. On cacao's nutritional value, see, e.g., Knapp, *Cocoa and Chocolate*, 165–78; or West, "A Brief History and Botany of Cacao," 117–18.

83. Sahagún, *Historia general de las cosas de Nueva España*, 475.

84. Motolinía, *Historia de los indios de la Nueva España*, pt. 3, ch. 8, sec. 353, p. 154; Acosta, *Historia natural y moral de las Indias*, 4:22:180.

85. *El conquistador anónimo*, 31.

86. About the Corpus, Hippocratic scholar Ludwig Edelstein writes that "explanations of the causes of illness ranged from the air inhaled to the food and drink taken in," adding that "treatment consistent predominantly in changes in regimen" (see Edelstein, "Hippocrates of Cos," 4:6–7). Compare these views with those of Cárdenas or Gage, e.g., cited below.

This subject can be pursued from various angles. On late medieval medicine, see Thorndike, *Science and Thought in the Fifteenth Century*, chs. 1, 2, and 5; on Greek medicine, see Lloyd, *Magic, Reason, and Experience*, 146–69, 37–49. For the Hippocratic Corpus, see *Hippocrates*; or Precope, *Hippocrates on Diet and Hygiene*, chs. 9 and 11. On the translation of works by Hippocrates, Galen, and Avicenna, see Haskins, *The Renaissance of the Twelfth Century*, ch. 10.

For the case of chocolate, compelling evidence of this connection is offered by Dr. Juan de Cárdenas's detailed discourse on the dietetic properties of the cacao bean and drinks, in which he proposes to clarify matters by applying the teachings of "the divine Hippocrates" (see Cárdenas, *Problemas y secretos maravillosos de las Indias*, 97–113). Cárdenas also discusses specifically medicinal uses (107–8). A similar analysis of chocolate appears in Thomas Gage's account of his experiences in Chiapas and Guatemala. Of the cacao bean, he says that "it contains the quality of the four elements, yet in the common opinion of most physicians, it is held to be cold and dry *a praedominio*" (see Thompson, *Thomas Gage's Travels in the New World*, 151–59); Gage relied on Antonio Colmenero de Ledesma's influential *Tratado de la naturaleza y calidades del chocolate*.

87. Cárdenas, *Problemas y secretos maravillosos de las Indias*, 107 (emphasis added). He also employs these categories to analyze the properties and effects of every potential ingredient and combination in chocolate.

88. Díaz del Castillo, *Historia verdadera de la conquista de la Nueva España*, 568–69.

89. Cárdenas, *Problemas y secretos maravillosos de las Indias*, 101. For a list of ingredients and combinations, see also Thompson, *Thomas Gage's Travels in the New World*, 154.

90. Acosta, *Historia natural y moral de las Indias*, 4:22:180; see also Thompson, *Thomas Gage's Travels in the New World*, 143–45. Acosta notes that guests were always offered a cup of chocolate.

91. Thompson, *Thomas Gage's Travels in the New World*, 157.

92. Cárdenas, *Problemas y secretos maravillosos de las Indias*, 105; Thompson, *Thomas Gage's Travels in the New World*, 156–57.

93. Bruman, "The Culture History of Mexican Vanilla," 363.

94. On cacao's use as money, see, e.g., Mártir de Anglería, *Décadas del nuevo mundo*, 2:477–78, 675–76. Mártir de Anglería, who referred to cacao trees as "money trees," wrote of cacao: "Oh, blessed money, which provides humankind a delicious and useful potion and exempts its possessors from the infernal plague of avarice, since it can not be hidden underground, nor hoarded for very long!" (ibid., 477–78).

95. Bruman's research shows that references to vanilla in the *Relaciones Geográficas* of the 1570s and 1580s are remarkably scant (see "The Culture History of Mexican Vanilla," 363 n. 8). He provides other evidence of "the unimportance of vanilla in the middle of the sixteenth century" (e.g., 365 n. 20).

96. *De delectu ciborum, jejuniis, et diebus festis*, decreed in Session XXV, 4 December 1563 (see Council of Trent, *The Canons and Decrees of the Council of Trent*, 253; Council of Trent, *El sacrosanto y ecuménico Concilio de Trento*, 422; see also, e.g., Bungener, *History of the Council of Trent*, 530–31).

97. See Elliot, *Imperial Spain*, ch. 6; and Elliot, *Europe Divided*, ch. 5. See also Lynch, *Spain under the Habsburgs*, ch. 8.

98. The phrase is Menéndez y Pelayo's. In his view, Trent was "as Spanish as it was ecumenical" (see *Historia de los heterodoxos españoles*, 4:406).

99. Cárdenas, *Problemas y secretos maravillosos de las Indias*, 108–12.

100. Dávila Padilla, *Historia de la fundación y discurso de la provincia de Santiago de México*, 626–27. A collective work, it was completed by Dávila between 1589 and 1592 and published in Madrid in 1596.

101. Ibid., 626.

102. Ibid., 626–27. Significantly, Gregory (Ugo Boncompagni) was one of the canon lawyers who played a prominent role in drafting the Tridentine decrees; thereafter, Cardinal Boncompagni took charge of the papal legation in Spain, where he spent two years. Perhaps then he became acquainted with chocolate, already present in Philip II's Court life. Boncompagni's good relations with the Spanish monarch enabled him to accede to the papacy, chiefly through the efforts of Cardinal Granvelle, Philip II's influential counselor (see Kelly, *The Oxford Dictionary of Popes*, 269–71; and Ott, "Gregory XIII," 7:2).

103. But see Thomas Gage's account of life in Chiapa (Ciudad Real, now San Cristóbal de las Casas) in the early seventeenth century, which provides a vivid example of the extreme forms this habit was soon to adopt (Thompson, *Thomas Gage's Travels in the New World*, 143–45).

104. On chocolate in Spain, see Vicens Vives, *Historia social y económica de España y América*, 3:192, 307, 309. In all likelihood, the religious orders established in Spanish America played a crucial role in the dissemination of chocolate through their networks of convents and residences on both sides of the Atlantic. Clerical enthusiasm for chocolate lay at the heart of the debate on fasting.

105. The Neapolitan Francesco Maria Brancaccio (1591–1675) wrote an influential dissertation on whether or nor drinking chocolate violated the fast (see Weber, "Brancaccio"). Antonio Escobar y Mendoza (1589–1669), a prominent Jesuit theologian from Valladolid, defended the use of chocolate in his "Manual de casos de conciencia." In Brillat-Savarin's words, when it came to chocolate, Father Escobar's "spiritual reasoning was as subtle as his moral doctrine was accommodating" (see O'Neill, "Escobar y Mendoza"; and Brillat-Savarin, *The Physiology of Taste*, 109–10).

106. Colmenero de Ledesma's *Tratado de la naturaleza y calidades del chocolate* states that chocolate was consumed in Spain, Italy, and Flanders. See also Bruman, "The Culture History of Mexican Vanilla," 367.

107. See, e.g., Schivelbusch, *Tastes of Paradise*, 85–94. The marriages of Louis XIII to Anna of Austria—daughter of Spain's Philip III—and of Louis XIV to María Teresa of Spain—daughter of Philip IV—are often cited as the sources of chocolate's popularity in the royal court of France.

108. The timing of Morren's discovery, however, should be understood primarily in terms of the historical development of experimental plant physiology.

109. Brillat-Savarin, *The Physiology of Taste*, 108–9.

110. Morren, "On the Production of Vanilla in Europe," 9.

111. Whymper, *Cocoa and Chocolate*, 64 (Table 6).

112. On the making of "eating chocolate" and the establishment of chocolate factories throughout Europe and the United States, see Morton and Morton, *Chocolate*, chs. 5, 7, and 8; also Wickizer, *Coffee, Tea and Cocoa*, 301–11.

113. For various export statistics, see Lecomte, *Le vanillier*, 179–205; and Ridley, *Spices*, 66–81. A detailed discussion follows in Chapter 4.

114. Turnbow, Tracy, and Rappetto, *The Ice Cream Industry*, 1–7; "50 Years of Ice Cream Freezing"; "A Half-Century of Ice Cream Technology"; Buzell, "Origin and Development of the Ice Cream Industry."

115. See Lecomte, *Le vanillier*, 218–20; Whitmore, "Vanilla-Bean Production and Trade," 12–13.

116. Vanillin was first identified as the principal odoriferous and flavoring component of vanilla in 1858 (see Lecomte, *Le vanillier*, 134–38; Correll, "Vanilla—Its Botany, History, Cultivation, and Economic Import," 346–47).

117. Vanillin became commercially important at the turn of the century (see Ridley, *Spices*, 92). On imports of vanillin into the United States, see Whitmore, "Vanilla-Bean Production," 13–14.

118. Coumarin—found in tonka beans—was often the source of these imitation extracts (see Turnbow, Tracy, and Rappetto, *The Ice Cream Industry*, 241–42).

119. See, e.g., Bouriquet, *Le vanillier*, 675–80.

120. Fontecilla, *Breve tratado sobre el cultivo y beneficio de la vainilla*, 28.

121. Boiling water was used in French curing (see Delteil, *La vanille*, 34–41; and Bouriquet, *Le vanillier*, 521–28).

122. Fontecilla, *Breve tratado sobre el cultivo y beneficio de la vainilla*, 45–46.

123. Humboldt, *Ensayo político sobre el Reino de la Nueva España*, 294. His remarks give the impression that this was by then a well-established practice.

124. Ibid., 294. Fontecilla pioneered the use of thermometers to regulate the performance of ovens (*Breve tratado sobre el cultivo y beneficio de la vainilla*, 37–41). Compare these descriptions with early accounts of curing cited in Chalot, *Culture et préparation*, 85–86.

125. Fontecilla, *Breve tratado sobre el cultivo y beneficio de la vainilla*, 33. He claims that the use of ovens for curing vanilla originated in Papantla; however, Humboldt gives a detailed account of the *beneficio de poscoyol* practiced in Misantla and Colipa at a time when Papantla was not yet an important curing center.

126. See e.g., Bouriquet, *Le vanillier*, 679.

127. See, e.g., Fontecilla, *Breve tratado sobre el cultivo y beneficio de la vainilla*, 50.

128. Bausa, "Bosquejo geográfico y estadístico del Partido de Papantla," 407.

CHAPTER TWO

1. Tamayo, *Geografía general de México*, 1:359–68; see also Palacios, *Puebla*, 11, 44; and Secretaría de Agricultura y Fomento, *Regiones económico agrícolas* 2:731–33.

2. See García Martínez, *Los pueblos de la sierra*, 26–28. This excellent study provides the best analysis of the physical geography and changing human geography of the so-called Sierra de Puebla in the early colonial period. It is also quite helpful for understanding the early economic geography of the adjoining lowlands.

3. García Martínez, "Consideraciones corográficas," 39–40. The higher elevations of the sierra, already close to the highland plateau—e.g., where Zacatlán, Zacapoaxtla, and Teziutlán are located—are referred to as the *bocasierra*, the mouth of the sierra (see García Martínez, *Los pueblos de la sierra*, 147 [map 5]).

4. Ecologically, the *tierra caliente* extends up to the lower escarpments of the sierra (600–800 meters above the sea). The towns of Mecatlán and Filomeno Mata (c. 700–750 meters), e.g., are located in *tierra caliente* that is topographically still a part of the sierra.

5. Gerhard, *Geografía histórica de la Nueva España*, 224–26.

6. Kelly and Palerm, *The Tajin Totonac*, 47.

7. De la Peña, *Veracruz económico*, 1:97.

8. See Palacios, *Puebla*, 96–109; Tamayo, *Datos para la hidrología de la República Mexicana*, 160–62; Kiel, *El estado de Veracruz*, 48–53; Pérez Milicua, *Compendio de geografía física, política y económica*, 101–3; Secretaría de Agricultura y Fomento, *Regiones económico agrícolas*, 2:733–35.

9. On the complications associated with the concepts of "natural region" and "physiographic area," see the discussion and bibliographic references in West, "The Natural Regions of Middle America," 364ff. On regions as historical entities, see Markusen, *Regions*, 16–48ff.

10. Palacios, *Puebla*, 104–5, 109–10; also Tamayo, *Geografía general*, 2:190–92, 195. Both the San Marcos–Cazones and the María de la Torre–Bobos–Nautla drain the backside of the geological basin's watershed.

11. On the extension of the Alcaldía Mayor of Papantla, see Gerhard, *Geografía histórica de la Nueva España*, 224–26, 382–87.

12. On nineteenth-century boundaries, see Estado de Veracruz, *Estadística del estado libre y soberano de Veracruz*, pt. 1, 107–9, and pt. 2, 86–87. See also the map of Veracruz prepared by the Comisión Geográfico-Exploradora in 1905; and Pérez Milicua, *Compendio de geografía*, 116 and folded map. Two general studies of the state's political divisions are Florescano, "Las divisiones políticas del estado de Veracruz"; and Belmonte Guzmán, *La organización territorial de Veracruz*. On the Arroyo de Solteros, see Tamayo, *Datos para la hidrología de la República Mexicana*, 162–63.

13. Gerhard, *Geografía histórica de la Nueva España*, 264–65, 398–400.

14. Ten of these—Papantla, Espinal, Coatzintla, Zozocolco, Coxquihui, Chumatlán, Coyutla, Coahuitlán, Mecatlán, and Santo Domingo—were originally colonial *pueblos*. Also a colonial *pueblo*, Chicualoque had municipal status until 1894, when it became part of Coyutla. Tecolutla was not a *pueblo* in 1746, but had become one by 1827. Chumatlán has had an eventful political life. It was a municipality until 1890, when it was annexed to Coxquihui; it remained under the authority of Coxquihui until 1922 and was then transferred to the jurisdiction of Coyutla, to which it belonged until 1935, when it regained municipal status. Gutiérrez Zamora was created in 1877 on lands taken from Papantla and Tecolutla. Cazones comprises lands on both sides of the river after which it is named. It was created in 1936 on lands withdrawn from Papantla (right bank) and Tuxpan (left bank). The urban enclave of Poza Rica—a product of the oil business—attained municipal status in 1951.

15. Wolf, *Peasants*, 18–21. In this typology, *neotechnic* agriculture is characterized by "increasing reliance on the energy supplied by combustible fuels and the
skills supplied by science" (19).

16. García, "Los climas del estado de Veracruz"; Contreras Arias, *Mapa de las
provincias climatológicas de la República Mexicana.*

17. García, "Los climas del estado de Veracruz," 6–8. See also Wallén, "Some
Characteristics of Precipitation in Mexico," 53–56; Page, "Climate of Mexico"; and
Vivó, "Weather and Climate of Mexico and Central America."

18. García, "Los climas del estado de Veracruz," fig. 11. For average annual
precipitation figures throughout Mexico, see Contreras Arias, *Mapa de las provincias climatológicas de la República Mexicana*, 1–53. On aridity in Mexico, see, e.g.,
Whetten, *Rural Mexico*, 6–8; and Orive Alba, *La política de irrigación en México*,
1–9. On the spatial distribution of annual precipitation in general, see Granger,
"Precipitation Distribution," 691–93.

19. These calculations are based on data collected by Enriqueta García (see
"Los climas del estado de Veracruz," appendix 1).

20. Kelly and Palerm, *The Tajin Totonac*, 47; Wallén, "Some Characteristics of
Precipitation in Mexico," 51, 64–77, 83–85. Regarding the reliability of *temporal*
agriculture, Wallén thought that "on the central plateau the precipitation conditions
definitely are the best in all Mexico," since summer-fall precipitation is generally
sufficient and variability is very low. In Papantla, where summer rain variability is
high, winter maize crops tend to be more reliable than summer ones, despite the fact
that on average it rains much more during the summer (see de la Peña, *Veracruz
económico*, 1:93, 2:31, 41–43; also Kelly and Palerm, *The Tajin Totonac*, 117–21).

21. Estado de Veracruz, *Estadística del estado libre y soberano de Veracruz*,
1:109.

22. For a discussion of classification systems and tropical rain forests, see Wag-
ner, "Natural Vegetation of Middle America," 216–32; Rzedowski, *Vegetación de
México*, 151–58, 159–78; Gómez Pompa, *Ecología de la vegetación del estado de
Veracruz*, 51–57; and Ramamoorthy et al., *Biological Diversity of Mexico*.
Richards, *The Tropical Rain Forest*, is not specifically about Mesoamerica but is
nevertheless useful.

23. Kelly and Palerm, *The Tajin Totonac*, 49. One of the climbing orchids that
populated this habitat was the wild vanilla.

24. See, e.g., AGN, Ramo de Tierras, vol. 1225, exp. 16. In the *Relación de Papantla* of 1581, Juan de Carrión noted that, aside from the forest vegetation, "ay
abundancia de pastos" (pastures are abundant) (Carrión, *Descripción del pueblo de
Gueytlalpan*, 61). There is some debate as to whether these savannas are truly a climax vegetation rather than one induced by fires and human intervention. For a discussion, see Beard, "The Savanna Vegetation of Northern Tropical America," especially 202–3; Gómez Pompa, *Ecología de la vegetación del estado de Veracruz*,
59–61, 70–71; and Gómez Pompa, "La vegetación de México," 97–98.

25. This is not to say that these coastal flatlands are intrinsically unsuitable for
agriculture, nor to suggest that cultivation techniques other than slash-and-burn
were unknown; indeed, there is ample evidence that water-management systems on
the floodplains near the mouths of the Tecolutla, Nautla, and other Veracruz rivers

may have sustained year-long agriculture on permanent fields as early as the beginning of the first millennium A.D., and plantation-style agriculture has prospered there more recently. Still, slash-and-burn appears to have always been the predominant method of crop production in the basin, and the historical record suggests that cultivators of that type have tended to stay away from these grassy plains, preferring instead to settle and plant in forest sites whenever possible (settlement patterns are discussed below). On ancient coastal hydroagriculture, see, e.g., Siemens, "Wetland Agriculture in the Lowlands of Pre-Hispanic Mesoamerica"; Wilkerson, "So Green and Like a Garden"; and Siemens, "Modelling Pre-Hispanic Hydroagriculture," 27–90. On the parallel case of the lowland Maya, see Harrison and Turner, *Pre-Hispanic Maya Agriculture*; and Farriss, *Maya Society under Colonial Rule*, 125, 448–49 n. 30.

26. Kelly and Palerm, for instance, compiled a list of the numerous species of trees and vines (lianas) found in what little *monte alto* remained in Tajín at the time of their visit, providing local Spanish and Totonac names (see *The Tajín Totonac*, 346, appendix C). Gómez Pompa offers a brief analysis of the composition of a stand in the environs of Poza Rica, as well as a list of species found in *Brosimum alicastrum* forests (*Ecología de la vegetación del estado de Veracruz*, 51, 55).

27. Already in the early 1960s, when the modern scientific study of tropical lowland ecology was still a very young profession in Mexico, geographer Robert C. West considered the vegetation of northern Veracruz "so greatly modified by man" that, in his view, it was by then "practically impossible to estimate the nature of its original cover" ("The Natural Regions of Middle America," 378). Faustino Miranda's seminal field work on the tropical rain forests of Chiapas, for example, started only in the 1940s. For a brief bibliographic discussion of the history of ecological research in Mexico, see Rzedowski, *Vegetación de México*, 13–20.

28. Wilken, *Good Farmers*, 226ff. See also Geiger, *The Climate near the Ground*.

29. Kelly and Palerm, *The Tajín Totonac*, 362.

30. Data are from ibid., 109. It should be noted that these figures represent time spent clearing secondary vegetation. There, the underbrush is typically thicker than in *monte alto*, but the trees are also younger and shorter, and thus it may be assumed that felling the *monte alto* must have involved less *roza* and more *tumba* work, irrespective of the tools employed. For a modern example, see López Patiño and García Pérez, "El maíz en la Congregación Vicente Herrera," 115–16. These questions are sometimes addressed in studies of ancient Maya agriculture. See, e.g., Hester, "Agriculture, Economy and Population Density of the Maya," 266–71, 288–92; Sanders, "The Cultural Ecology of the Lowland Maya"; and Rojas Rabiela, *Las siembras de ayer*.

31. Clearing usually takes place in the spring, to allow sufficient time for the cut vegetation to dry and be burned before the arrival of the summer rains. For a more detailed account of the clearing process, see Palerm, "Agricultural Systems and Food Patterns," 29–31; and Kelly and Palerm, *The Tajín Totonac*, 107–9. For a general discussion and bibliography, see Conklin, "El estudio del cultivo de roza."

32. Kelly and Palerm, *The Tajín Totonac*, 108.

33. Wilken, *Good Farmers*, 55–57. Wilken notes that "the fertilizing ash from slash-and-burn farming is more a by-product of clearing than deliberately created

soil amendment" (56). See also Nye and Greenland, *The Soil under Shifting Culti-vation*, 66–70, on which Wilken relies.

34. For a description of the espeque and its use, see Cruz León, *Los instrumen-tos agrícolas en la zona central de Veracruz*, 198–200, 202; also Kelly and Palerm, *The Tajín Totonac*, 108, 111.

35. Cleared forest fields can turn (or be turned) into grasslands, but not under normal *roza* practices (see Palerm, "Agricultural Systems and Food Patterns," 32; Kelly and Palerm, *The Tajín Totonac*, 114). The development of grasslands is asso-ciated with the expansion of cattle ranching, which in the Tecolutla basin began in earnest only in the late nineteenth century.

36. On cultivation, see Kelly and Palerm, *The Tajín Totonac*, 113; de la Peña, *Veracruz económico*, 2:33–38, 41–42; and Montesinos et al., "El maíz en el mu-nicipio de Papantla," 192. On the *coa*, used elsewhere—e.g., in Tepoztlán—for planting maize, see Kelly and Palerm, *The Tajín Totonac*, 108–9; and Cruz León, *Los instrumentos agrícolas en la zona central de Veracruz*, 200–2. These calcula-tions of work time are based on estimates obtained by Kelly and Palerm in Tajín and they are broadly in agreement with figures supplied by de la Peña, once the lat-ter are adjusted to include the extra work involved in clearing *monte alto*. Neither takes into account the additional time spent on daily cultivation chores, without which the *escarda* sessions would absorb even more labor time.

37. On the regeneration of tropical forest vegetation see, e.g., Sarukhán, "Estu-dio sucesional."

38. On tropical soil fertility, see Nye and Greenland, *The Soil under Shifting Cultivation*; also Sánchez, *Properties and Management of Soils in the Tropics*; and Van Wambeke, *Soils of the Tropics*. Stevens, "The Soils of Middle America," though dated, is still worth reading.

39. De la Peña, *Veracruz económico*, 2:39ff. For a comparative discussion of yield declines, see Sánchez, *Properties and Management of Soils in the Tropics*, 374–75.

40. Nye and Greenland have described the logic of shifting fields as follows: "A farmer will tend to abandon a plot when the return from the considerable labour of clearing and cultivating a new one exceeds the return from his labour in weeding the existing one" (*The Soil under Shifting Cultivation*, 76; see also Kelly and Palerm, *The Tajín Totonac*, 100–1). For a case study of the connections between la-bor expenditures in weeding and clearing, crop yields, and field shifting in the low-land tropics of Mexico, see Emerson, "A Preliminary Survey," 51–62.

41. Kelly and Palerm, *The Tajín Totonac*, 123; also Fontecilla, *Breve tratado so-bre el cultivo y beneficio de la vainilla*, 118–19.

42. Conklin, *El estudio del cultivo de roza*. Conklin's piece is primarily a bibli-ography. See also Watters, *Shifting Cultivation in Latin America*; Haney, "The Na-ture of Shifting Cultivation in Latin America"; and Wolf, *Peasants*, 20–25.

43. According to recent research, the population of El Tajín peaked at 10,000–15,000 inhabitants; not all of them should be considered urban dwellers, however (see Bruggemann, "Análisis urbano del sitio arqueológico del Tajín").

Papantla was elevated to the rank of "city" in 1910, but its population then was a mere 5,500.

44. The Spanish word *pueblo* can create confusion in this context, since it can

mean both "people" and "village" or "town." For a good historical discussion of its usage, see García Martínez, *Los pueblos de la sierra*, especially 78–79 and 157ff.; also, Kourí, "Interpreting the Expropriation of Indian Pueblo Lands in Porfirian Mexico," 77–82.

45. Estado de Veracruz, *Estadística del estado libre y soberano de Veracruz*, 1:106.

46. See, e.g., Gibson, *The Aztecs under Spanish Rule*; Taylor, *Landlord and Peasant in Colonial Oaxaca*; and Taylor, *Drinking, Homicide, and Rebellion in Colonial Mexican Villages*, especially ch. 1.

47. In these cases, the village was referred to as the *cabecera* (head village). For a discussion of the use of these terms, see Gibson, *The Aztecs under Spanish Rule*, 33ff., and below.

48. *Memoria leída por el C. Gobernador del Estado . . . 13 de Octubre de 1871*, 2:1108–12. The original spelling has been respected.

49. Charles Gibson has noted that "this kind of status depended partly on size . . . and partly on local campaigns for privilege" (*The Aztecs under Spanish Rule*, 32). Papantla was elevated to the rank of *villa* sometime between 1868 and 1874. For most of the nineteenth century, *ayuntamientos* in Veracruz were restricted to district seats (*cantón* or *partido*), to a few relatively populous jurisdictions (usually with no less than two or three thousand inhabitants), and to places that had obtained the privilege before 1808. These jurisdictions were generally called *pueblos* before the 1850s and *municipalidades* or *municipios* thereafter. All other *pueblos* or *municipios* were managed at various times by *alcaldes* or *jueces de paz*, and after 1861 by a small body of *regidores* and a *síndico*, which went by the name of *municipalidad* but had essentially the same powers and obligations as an *ayuntamiento*. For a list of the *ayuntamientos* and *municipalidades* of Veracruz in 1870, see *Memoria . . . Noviembre 30 de 1870*, 2:857. Beginning in 1874, all municipal corporations—regardless of size—would be labeled *ayuntamientos*.

For the legislative history of systems of local administration in the nineteenth century, see Estado de Veracruz-Llave, *Colección de leyes, decretos y circulares*, in particular, the following: Decree No. 43 of 17 March 1825, art. 1–6; *Ley para la organización, policía y gobierno interior del estado* of 26 May 1825, ch. 5, art. 32–37; Law of 20 March 1837, art. 122, 177–83; *Reglamento de ordenanzas municipales para los ayuntamientos* of 30 December 1840; Decree No. 57 of 17 December 1848, art. 1, 5; Decree of 7 September 1855, art. 2–3; *Estatuto orgánico* of 10 October 1855, art. 7; Decree of 24 November 1855; *Constitución política del Estado de Veracruz* (1857), art. 59; Decree of 24 October 1859, art. 1–4; *Ley orgánica para la administración interior del Estado libre y soberano de Veracruz* (no. 43) of 29 June 1861, ch. 4, art. 25–28; Decree of 2 December 1868 (no. 120); *Constitución política del Estado libre y soberano de Veracruz Llave* (1873), art. 3; *Ley orgánica de administración interior del Estado* (no. 35) of 30 December 1873, ch. 5, art. 25–29; and *Ley orgánica para la administración municipal del Estado* (no. 120) of 24 December 1874. For a general context, see Blázquez Domínguez and Gidi Villarreal, *El poder legislativo en Veracruz*, one of the very few monographs on this subject.

50. This description is based on L. Garcés's drawing, "Vista general de Papantla," published in Rivera Cambas, *Historia antigua y moderna de Jalapa*, vol. 2,

opposite p. 126; on data from the Governor's annual reports to the state legislature
for 1870, 1871, and 1886; and on Luis Salas García's books *Cachiquín* and *Juu Papantlán*. There are descriptions of the village of Papantla in 1830 (Estado de Veracruz, *Estadística del estado libre y soberano de Veracruz*, pt. 1, 14–15) and 1845
(Bausa, "Bosquejo geográfico y estadístico del Partido de Papantla," 382–83, 395,
399), which are also very useful.

51. Sanders, "Settlement Patterns," 53–54ff.

52. Bausa, "Bosquejo geográfico y estadístico del Partido de Papantla," 380.

53. On *congregaciones* or *reducciones*, see, e.g., Cline, "Civil Congregations of
the Indians in New Spain"; and Gerhard, *A Guide to the Historical Geography of
New Spain*, 26–27, 219–20. Bernardo García Martínez provides an excellent analysis of the historical process of *congregación* in the Sierra de Puebla, including the
upper piedmont of the Tecolutla basin (see *Los pueblos de la sierra*, 151–79). To the
extent that *congregaciones* (in the old sense) were attempted around Papantla, their
fate probably resembles that of their counterparts among the lowland Maya; that is,
they succumbed to the forces of dispersal (see Kelly and Palerm, *The Tajin Totonac*,
38–39; and Farriss, *Maya Society under Colonial Rule*, 207–14).

54. See the *Ley orgánica de administración interior del Estado* of 30 December
1873, art. 1–2, art. 36, sec. 43, and art. 37–39. In essence, these state that the *municipalidades* are to be divided by the *ayuntamiento* into territories (*demarcaciones*)
called *congregaciones*. See also this law's predecessor, the *Ley orgánica para la administración interior del Estado libre y soberano de Veracruz* of 29 June 1861, art.
7, as well as the *acuerdo* of 5 July 1861. The legacy of this wholesale creation of
congregaciones was still evident in the mid-1940s, when Moisés de la Peña complained that "in many . . . [municipalities] . . . the *congregaciones* are really
rancherías—with houses dispersed over large areas—which by convention and for
administrative purposes are so denominated" (*Veracruz económico*, 1:199). In those
years, less than one-fifth of the population of the *congregación* of Tajín, to the west
of Papantla, resided in a hamlet; "the rest," wrote Kelly and Palerm, "live widely
scattered on outlying parcels of land, the more remote as much as three hours on
foot from the *fundo* (hamlet)" (*The Tajin Totonac*, 59).

55. Because of the rudimentary way in which these early population tallies were
organized, it is impossible to know how many actually lived in these villages in
1871. It is worthwhile noting that civil congregations were carried out in Mecatlán,
Coahuitlán, Chumatlán, and other piedmont communities in the 1590s, and that
these were probably more successful than those attempted in the coastal plains. Perhaps this also helps explain the scarcity of *rancherías* recognized as such. For a description of the process of *congregación* in Chumatlán, see "Visita a la Congregación de Chumatlán" (the original is found in AGN, Ramo Tierras, vol. 24, exp.
4). See also García Martínez, *Los pueblos de la sierra*, 160ff.

56. This is a high estimate because it assumes, rather improbably, that most of
those assigned by the census to a *cabecera* were in fact village residents. In addition,
this estimate does not take into account the likely undercounting of those who lived
scattered in remote locations. In this regard, it is worth noting that a report prepared for the merchant guild of Veracruz in 1804 suggests that only 11 percent of
the basin's inhabitants lived in villages (see "Noticias estadísticas de la Intendencia

de Veracruz"103–5). On *cachikin* or *calchikin*, see Aschmann, *Diccionario to-tonaco de Papantla*; and García Martínez, *Los pueblos de la sierra*, 73 n. 11, 305.

57. Carrión, *Descripción del pueblo de Gueytlalpan*, 62. This text is also known as the *Relación de Papantla*. For earlier descriptions and sources, see García Payón's notes in this edition, especially n. 36 and n. 42. In the early 1530s Papantla consisted of fifteen *estancias* with a total of 210 houses (55 n. 36).

58. Torquemada, *Monarquía Indiana*, 1:249.

59. AGN, Ramo Criminal, vol. 304, exp. 2, 91–120, 211, 303–19; also AGN, Ramo Civil, vol. 1465, exp. 15.

60. For a 1773 map of some of Papantla's *rancherías*, see AGN, Ramo Tributos, vol. 10, exp. 5, 52.

61. These calculations are adapted from Kelly and Palerm, *The Tajin Totonac*, 101. See also Palerm, "Aspectos agrícolas del desarrollo," 12–19; and Farriss, *Maya Society under Colonial Rule*, 125ff.

62. For a related discussion, see Farriss, *Maya Society under Colonial Rule*; also Farriss, "Nucleation versus Dispersal."

63. Sources: for 1743, Villaseñor y Sánchez, *Theatro americano* 2:317–20; for 1804, "Noticias estadísticas de la Intendencia de Veracruz," 103–5; for 1826, "Noticia estadística que el Gobernador del Estado libre y soberano de Veracruz presenta al Congreso de la Unión . . . (1827)," in Blázquez Domínguez, *Estado de Veracruz: Informes de sus Gobernadores*, 1:3; for 1830, "Tabla estadística que manifiesta el censo de los pueblos y rancherías del Cantón de Papantla . . . ," in Estado de Veracruz, *Estadística del estado libre y soberano de Veracruz*, 1:110ff; for 1837, Bausa, "Bosquejo geográfico y estadístico del Partido de Papantla," 379–80; for 1868, *Memoria . . . 13 de marzo de 1869*, 2:703; for 1871, *Memoria leída por el C. Gobernador del Estado . . . 13 de octubre de 1871*, 2:1108–12; and for 1873, *Memoria . . . 17 de setiembre de 1873*, 3:1726.

64. This is assuming that 10 percent of a hypothetical population of forty thousand were village residents. For a discussion of population density in Veracruz during pre-Hispanic and early colonial times, see Sanders, "The Anthropogeography of Central Veracruz," 44ff.; also Kelly and Palerm, *The Tajin Totonac*, 7–12. On modern densities across rural Mesoamerica, see Sanders, "Settlement Patterns."

65. *Memoria leída por el C. Gobernador del Estado . . . 13 de Octubre de 1871*, 38ff.

66. On Indian flight in sixteenth-century Totonacapan, see Kelly and Palerm, *The Tajin Totonac*, 10. For a general discussion of flight as a strategy, see Farriss, *Maya Society under Colonial Rule*, 72–73.

67. Mota y Escobar, "Memoriales del obispo de Tlaxcala"; "Visita a la Congregación de Chumatlán (1599)," *BAGN* 14, no. 2 (1943): 13–48; Villaseñor y Sánchez, *Theatro americano*, 2:317–20. On the *pardo* militia, see AGN, Ramo Criminal, vol. 303, exp. 222–27; also Vinson, "Las compañías milicianas."

68. Kelly and Palerm, *The Tajin Totonac*, 30–32; Villaseñor y Sánchez, *Theatro americano*, 2:317–20; Mota y Escobar, "Memoriales del obispo de Tlaxcala"; and García Martínez, *Los pueblos de la sierra*, 123–35. See also Estado de Veracruz, *Estadística del estado libre y soberano de Veracruz*, 1:106; and Bausa, "Bosquejo geográfico y estadístico del Partido de Papantla," 399–400.

69. The orientation of these travel routes reflects ancient conquests as well as migratory and trade patterns. For a discussion of the early history of the area, see Kelly and Palerm, *The Tajín Totonac,* 14–24; and Krickeberg, *Los Totonaca,* ch. 3.

70. Carrión, *Descripción del pueblo de Gueytlalpan,* 63, 61. For an interesting, if florid, description of the trail and river crossings between Huauchinango and Xicotepec, Puebla, in 1871, see García Cubas, "Impresiones de un viaje a la sierra de Huauchinango,"73ff.

71. For the complicated early history of these roads, see Rees, *Transportes y comercio entre México y Veracruz,* ch. 1.

72. Kelly and Palerm, *The Tajín Totonac,* 39, 16–26; García Martínez, *Los pueblos de la sierra,* 138, 147.

73. Note that the fallow requirements of the *roza* system are also part of the explanation. For a good example of the argument for indolence, see Bausa, "Bosquejo geográfico y estadístico del Partido de Papantla," 401–4.

74. Carrión, *Descripción del pueblo de Gueytlalpan,* 61; see also 69.

75. For a discussion of the patterns of economic exchange among the lowland Maya, see Farriss, *Maya Society under Colonial Rule,* 119–24.

76. See, e.g., Palerm, "Etnografía antigua Totonaca en el oriente de México," 167; also José García Payón's comments in Carrión, *Descripción del pueblo de Gueytlalpan,* 69 n. 55.

77. Carrión, *Descripción del pueblo de Gueytlalpan,* 70; Mota y Escobar, "Memoriales del obispo de Tlaxcala"; and García Martínez, *Los pueblos de la sierra,* 146.

78. AGN, Ramo Criminal, vol. 304, exp. 3, 390–91.

79. On the trade of these forest products around the middle of the eighteenth century, see Villaseñor y Sánchez, *Theatro americano,* 2:318. There was also a small trade in animal skins for tanning. On the wax trade from Papantla to Puebla and Mexico City, see Quirós, "Memoria sobre el fomento agrícola de la Intendencia de Veracruz," 138.

80. See, e.g., AGN, Ramo Criminal, vol. 714, exp. 4, 80–102, 111–30.

81. AGN, Ramo Criminal, vol. 304, exp. 3, 387–89; vol. 304, exp. 2, 139; vol. 303, exp. 4, 339–40; vol. 304, exp. 2, 340; see also AGN, Ramo Civil, vol. 1465, exp. 9, 15.

82. AGN, Ramo Civil, vol. 1465, exp. 15, 9. These documents are reproduced in Florescano, *Fuentes para la historia de la crisis agrícola,* 1:155–75.

83. AGN, Ramo Alcabalas, vol. 354, exp. 3, 188–97; exp. 4, 198–207; exp. 7, 247–55; exp. 9, 272–85; Ramo Alcabalas, vol. 228, exp. 73–83. See also Garavaglia and Grosso, *Las alcabalas novohispanas.*

84. Carrión, *Descripción del pueblo de Gueytlalpan,* 65–66; Carrión also wrote that "pastures are abundant" (61).

85. Mota y Escobar, "Memoriales del obispo de Tlaxcala," 191–306.

86. See, e.g., Estado de Veracruz, *Estadística del estado libre y soberano de Veracruz,* pt. 1, 107–8.

87. See Villaseñor, *Theatro americano,* 2:318; also Estado de Veracruz, *Estadística del estado libre y soberano de Veracruz,* 1:107–8. It is telling that the term "hacienda" is rarely used.

88. Given the importance of communal land tenure in the history of Mesoamerican agriculture, it is remarkable how little is known about the process of allocating cropland for individual use during the colonial period and after, especially under a system of cultivation involving field rotation and fallowing. The distribution of land was probably a source of friction, but as long as there was plenty available to satisfy everyone's minimal needs, quality and location were likely to be the main issues.

89. On ploughing, see Haudricourt and Delamarre, *L'homme et la charrue à travers le monde*; for Mexico, see Stresser-Péan, "El arado criollo en México y en América Central"; also Cruz León, *Los instrumentos agrícolas en la zona central de Veracruz*; and Rojas Rabiela, *Las siembras del ayer*.

90. AGN, Ramo Tierras, vol. 1225, exp. 16, 1–27.

91. AGN, Ramo Criminal, vol. 303, exp. 2–5; vol. 304, exp. 2–3; vol. 315, exp. 2. For a detailed analysis, see Ducey, "Viven sin ley ni rey"; also Ducey, "From Village Riot to Regional Rebellion," ch. 2. On the 1787 rebellion, see also Archer, *The Army in Bourbon Mexico*, 94–97; and Hamnett, *Roots of Insurgency*, 79–80.

92. Ducey, "Viven sin ley ni rey," 42. Ducey's essay examines Papantla's electoral and fiscal conflicts between 1760 and 1790.

93. For a detailed analysis of Papantla's insurgency, see Ducey, "From Village Riot to Regional Rebellion," ch. 3; also Ducey, "Village, Nation, and Constitution"; and, more generally, Guedea, *La insurgencia en el Departamento del Norte*; and Trens, *Historia de Veracruz*, vol. 3.

94. "Orden de 18 de Diciembre [1830]," in *Legislación del Estado de Veracruz*, 3:241.

95. Bausa, "Bosquejo geográfico y estadístico del Partido de Papantla," 379; Estado de Veracruz, *Estadística del estado libre y soberano de Veracruz*, table following pt. 1, 110.

96. Ducey, "Village, Nation, and Constitution," 466–67, 492–93.

97. On Mariano Olarte's rebellion of 1836–38, see Ducey, "From Village Riot to Regional Rebellion," ch. 4; also Escobar Ohmstede, "El movimiento olartista," 51–74; Flores, *La revolución de Olarte en Papantla*; and Trens, *Historia de Veracruz*, vol. 5, chs. 2, 3. Ducey's study describes at length the local conflicts over elections, taxes, trade, the tobacco monopoly, and administrative autonomy which fueled Olarte's Federalist rebellion, as well as the deep anti-Spanish sentiment that seems to have animated it.

98. It should be emphasized that these conflicts and alliances often crossed ethnic boundaries, as Olarte's rebellions amply demonstrate. Concrete disputes over the conduct of local government and the politics of trade—and not ethnicity *per se*—defined the actual battle lines.

99. On the rebel settlements, see Ducey, "From Village Riot to Regional Rebellion," ch. 3, especially the tables based on amnesty lists; Ducey, "Village, Nation, and Constitution," 473–74; and Bausa, "Bosquejo geográfico y estadístico del Partido de Papantla," 377, 379. According to Bausa, greater Papantla's population declined precipitously during the early postcolonial decades. Bausa alludes to a generalized social and economic ruin brought about by the "continuous civil dissensions" of the times, and he mentions a cholera epidemic in Papantla that wiped out "a third of its population" in 1833 ("Bosquejo geográfico y estadístico del Partido de

Papantla,"377, 382, 390). Undercounting due to dispersal may also be part of the explanation.

100. Estado de Veracruz, *Estadística del Estado libre y soberano de Veracruz,* pt. 1, 110; Bausa, "Bosquejo geográfico y estadístico del Partido de Papantla," 380.

101. Bausa, "Bosquejo geográfico y estadístico del Partido de Papantla," 404, 421.

102. Ibid., 420–22.

103. Estado de Veracruz, *Estadística del estado libre y soberano de Veracruz,* pt. 1, 110.

104. Bausa, "Bosquejo geográfico y estadístico del Partido de Papantla," 391ff.

105. On internal roads and the trail to Misantla, see Estado de Veracruz, *Estadística del Estado libre y soberano de Veracruz,* pt. 1, 107–8, and 100, respectively; also Bausa, "Bosquejo geográfico y estadístico del Partido de Papantla," 425–26; on Tuxpan and the Huasteca, see Soto, *Noticias estadísticas de la Huasteca,* 131–35. On cabotage, see Estado de Veracruz, *Estadística del estado libre y soberano de Veracruz,* pt. 1, 109; and Bausa, "Bosquejo geográfico y estadístico del Partido de Papantla," 383–84, 396–97. The sandbanks at the mouth of the Tecolutla river allowed in only fairly small vessels, and navigation up the river was limited to primitive craft with very shallow drafts.

106. For graphic descriptions of traffic along this sierra, see Villaseñor y Sánchez, *Theatro americano,* 2:296; and Trens, *Historia de Veracruz,* 4:114.

107. Bausa, "Bosquejo geográfico y estadístico del Partido de Papantla," 397–98. For a description of the approach to Teziutlán in the 1870s, see García Cubas, "Una excursión a tierracaliente," 174–76.

108. Bausa, "Bosquejo geográfico y estadístico del Partido de Papantla," 393, 406–8. On Papantla's modern marketplaces, see Salas García, *Juu Papantlán,* 410–13; also Velázquez, "Mercados y tianguis en el Totonacapan veracruzano." For an anthropological perspective on marketplace organization in general, see, e.g., Nash, "Indian Economies"; and Smith, "How Marketing Systems Affect Economic Opportunity in Agrarian Societies." The lack of specialization and the self-sufficient orientation of the Totonac agriculturalists of the basin—then the vast majority of the population—explain in part the historic absence of native markets. A number of the piedmont *pueblos* would in time establish such markets, but it is not clear exactly when these were started.

109. Estado de Veracruz, *Estadística del estado libre y soberano de Veracruz,* pt. 1, 107.

110. Estado de Veracruz, *Estadística del estado libre y soberano de Veracruz,* pt. 1, 108, 110; Bausa, "Bosquejo geográfico y estadístico del Partido de Papantla," 409.

111. The exact areas and boundaries of these estates are not known, so this map shows only their approximate location. The sources are Estado de Veracruz, *Estadística del estado libre y soberano de Veracruz;* and Bausa, "Bosquejo geográfico y estadístico del Partido de Papantla."

112. Estado de Veracruz, *Estadística del estado libre y soberano de Veracruz,* pt. 1, 107–8; Bausa, "Bosquejo geográfico y estadístico del Partido de Papantla," 409. The spelling of some of these names has varied over time. The *propios* were com-

munal lands traditionally rented out to private individuals in order to obtain funds with which to cover certain communal expenses. After Independence, the *propios* came to be administered by the new municipal authorities. Aside from the *propios*, community lands typically included the *fundo legal*, the *ejido*, and the *tierras de común repartimiento*. The latter were those devoted to the family *milpas*. For a discussion, see, e.g., Powell, *El liberalismo y el campesinado*, 43–44.

113. According to the local census of 1871, 12 percent of Papantla's municipal population lived on these private lands.

114. On rents, see, e.g., ACAM, no. 14 (Papantla), pp. 14–15; ACAM, no. 150 (Mesa Chica y anexos); ACAM, no. 164 (Pueblillo); ACAM, no. 309 (Pabanco); ACAM, no. 166 (Joloapan y anexos); and ACAM, no. 344 (Paso del Correo y anexos).

115. It is interesting to consider that between the 1820s and the mid-1840s most of the lands below the Tecolutla River (and beyond) belonged to a single owner, General Guadalupe Victoria, who received them as a reward for his military leadership in Veracruz during the wars of Independence. They were gradually sold off after his death, and a number of the estates (including Larios and Malpica) ended up in the hands of Church corporations. Those were sold again in the late 1850s, when the Lerdo Law was applied to expropriate religious institutions. Over time, a certain fragmentation of some of the estates closer to Papantla is evident. In general, merchants from Papantla and Teziutlán were the principal buyers of these southern lands. Turnover, however, was high. On Guadalupe Victoria, see Bausa, "Bosquejo geográfico y estadístico del Partido de Papantla," 384, 409; also, incidentally, Hoffmann, "Entre mar y sierra," 139ff.; for transactions tied to the Lerdo Law, see, e.g., ANP 5/6/1857, 7/19/1859, and 2/21/1860, the last two about the Larios and Malpica estates.

116. ACAM, no. 42 (Jamaya). This singular case (no others have been documented) is discussed in Ducey, "Tierras comunales y rebeliones," 212.

117. Tutino, *From Insurrection to Revolution in Mexico*, ch. 6, especially 228–41; also, e.g., Ducey, "Tierras comunales y rebeliones," 210–16; and Ducey, "From Village Riot to Regional Rebellion," ch. 4.

CHAPTER THREE

1. AJP, Juzgado de Primera Instancia del Cantón de Papantla, "Ynventario y avalúo del intestado Don Francisco Naveda Somarriba, practicados judicialmente," 29–31 March and 11–13 May 1880.

2. A few words on weights and measures might be useful at this point. Until late in the nineteenth century, it was customary for traders in Mexico to buy and sell vanilla in nominal units of one thousand beans (*millares*, sing. *millar*), instead of by weight. Given that the size and weight of individual vanilla beans can vary considerably, the weight of the millares was far from uniform. That makes it impossible to determine very accurately the magnitude of these early export shipments. Changing classification and packing systems add to the problem. Up until around 1850, vanilla was classified according to size, appearance, aroma, etc. (e.g., *fina*, *fina chica*, *zacate*), and each class was often bundled separately. This made the millares even more disparate in terms of weight. To compensate, though, low quality millares

sometimes contained more than a thousand pieces, according to established formulas. By the 1860s, however, all except for the worst classes of vanilla were mixed together in each bundle. To complicate matters further, it is probable that the average weight of the millar diminished somewhat over time, due to a notable increase in premature harvesting in the course of the nineteenth century. All these factors make comparisons over time less than perfect, but do not invalidate them altogether, especially when their aim is to identify broad trends.

Fontecilla considered that the average weight of a millar of cured vanilla was around 4 kilograms, and various other sources suggest similar figures. After careful consideration, it has seemed wise to adopt his estimate. It will be used throughout for comparative purposes. For details, see Fontecilla, *Breve tratado sobre el cultivo y beneficio de la vainilla*, 106ff., especially 111–12; Fontecilla, *Informes de Agapito Fontecilla al C. Ministro de Fomento*, 8–9; Humboldt, *Ensayo político sobre el Reino de la Nueva España*, 294–95; and de la Peña, *Veracruz económico*, 2:136–37. The writings of Karl Kaerger (1900) and R. López y Parra (1900) provide the same estimate, which they both borrow from Fontecilla.

3. Production—as opposed to export—figures for vanilla have seldom been available, largely because of the disaggregated nature of cultivation and the secretive business practices of merchants. Early on, wild vanilla was an important part of the trade, so not all that was harvested was actually "produced." In addition, premature picking—usually the work of thieves—always ruined a part of the harvest. This was already a problem in the late eighteenth century. All in all, though, virtually all of Mexico's cured vanilla has been destined for export, and thus—spoilage aside—export series provide a good overall indication of the scale of production. They are not, however, reliable indicators of the size of individual harvests.

4. See Table A.1; also Lerdo de Tejada, *Comercio exterior de México*, docs. 2–7; and Humboldt, *Ensayo político sobre el Reino de la Nueva España*, 5:12:497–98.

5. For a contemporary description of the vanilla trade and its origins, see Quirós, "Memoria sobre el cultivo y beneficio de la vainilla."

6. Humboldt, *Ensayo político sobre el Reino de la Nueva España*, 292.

7. Exactly how much so, however, it is difficult to ascertain. Based on information gathered during his stay in Xalapa and Veracruz (early 1804), Humboldt conjectured that New Spain's average yearly output was 910 millares, which would be approximately 3,650 kilograms. José María Quirós's January 1806 report to the governing board of the Veracruz Consulado presents a similar estimate. Yet both writers seem to have based their calculations on the performance of exports in recent years (i.e., 1802–1804), which were, in retrospect, extraordinary ones (see Table A.2). In light of the fact that the export statistics for the following two and a half decades show consistently lower figures, a few explanations come to mind. One is simply that both Humboldt's and Quirós's estimates were overly optimistic, which is hardly implausible. Another is that the political and commercial turmoil of the 1810s and early 1820s disrupted not just trade but also production (cultivation and gathering), arresting or even reversing temporarily a gradual process of growth evident by the turn of the century. Finally, it is also possible that both of the aforementioned interpretations hold true (see Humboldt, *Ensayo político sobre el Reino de la Nueva España*, 295–96; Quirós, "Memoria sobre el cultivo y beneficio de la vainilla," 127).

8. See the report titled "Cantón de Misantla, su gefe el ciudadano Angel de Ochoa y Ortega," in Estado de Veracruz, *Estadística del estado libre y soberano de Veracruz*, 1:80–104. A description of Misantla's new coat of arms (which is still in use) appears on p. 84.

9. Humboldt, *Ensayo político sobre el Reino de la Nueva España*, 295. Interestingly, the German botanist Dr. Christian Julius Wilhelm Schiede, who unlike Humboldt did visit Misantla and Papantla (in early 1820), considered that Papantla produced the best vanilla (see "Botanische Berichte aus Mexico," 575).

10. These calculations are based on export figures obtained from the following sources: for 1787–90, Humboldt, *Ensayo político sobre el Reino de la Nueva España*, 5:12:498; for the rest, Lerdo de Tejada, *Comercio exterior de México*, docs. 15–35. For the cochineal column, the data on *grana fina* (the best) was used. Wherever possible, figures on *vainilla de primera* are provided; in all other cases, either class is not specified or all classes are listed in aggregate. On the cochineal trade, see a similar but longer data series (1800–75) compiled in Herrera Canales, *El comercio exterior de México*, 65–66; also, more generally, Barbro Dahlgren's compilation, *La grana cochinilla*.

11. AGN, Ramo General de Parte, vol. 34 (1743); AGN, Ramo Criminal, vol. 304, exp. 2; vol. 340 (1768); Quirós, "Memoria sobre el cultivo y beneficio de la vainilla," 127–28; and Bruman, "The Culture History of Mexican Vanilla," 373–75.

12. See, e.g., "Orden de 30 de Setiembre de 1824, relativa a impedir el corte de vainilla antes de su sazón, y penas a los contraventores," in *Legislación del Estado de Veracruz*, 1:114–15; an 1835 edict reproduced in Salas García, *Cachiquín*, 17–18; and Fontecilla, *Breve tratado sobre el cultivo y beneficio de la vainilla*, 108–10. A new edict was issued in 1856, with identical results.

13. The few export figures available for the years in question refer only to value, not weight, and it is hard to know how much vanilla they represent. See, e.g., for 1851, Lerdo de Tejada, *Comercio exterior de México*, doc. 39; and for 1857–60, Díaz, *Versión francesa de México*, vol. 1, tables 6, 10, 14, and 18. Herrera Canales's analysis—cited above—is also based on value data.

14. Fontecilla, *Breve tratado sobre el cultivo y beneficio de la vainilla*, 106.

15. Ibid., 111.

16. Ibid., 111ff., 123.

17. On Jicaltepec (and later San Rafael), see Skerritt, *Colonos franceses y modernización en el Golfo de México*; Demard, *Aventure extraordinaire*; Demard, *Jicaltepec, terre d'Argile*; Bernot, "Datos sobre la colonización de Jicaltepec"; Génin, *Les français au Mexique*, 386ff.; and Estrada García, *Monografía del municipio de Martínez de la Torre*. Two useful contemporary descriptions of agriculture (vanilla, tobacco, coffee, and sugarcane) in San Rafael and nearby districts are Barba et al., "Prácticas de los alumnos," 37:3–74 (dated July 1888); and Ortiz Izquierdo, "Instrucciones sobre algunos importantes cultivos," 45:73–117 (dated March 1889).

18. "Cantón de Misantla, su gefe el ciudadano Angel de Ochoa y Ortega," in Estado de Veracruz, *Estadística del estado libre y soberano de Veracruz*, 1:83–84; Trens, *Historia de Veracruz*, 4:114–15; also, more generally, Ramírez Lavoignet, *Misantla*; and González de la Lama, "Rebels and Bandits," ch. 1.

19. Fontecilla, *Breve tratado sobre el cultivo y beneficio de la vainilla*, 126–43.

Many in Papantla consider Juan Pérez the inventor of the *poxcoyon*, but this practice clearly had older, indigenous roots.

20. Ibid., 113.

21. This calculation is based on the following: 1 estajo (100 square varas, or 0.77 hectares) planted with vanilla may yield an average of 400 fruits on the third year (its first crop), 1,000–1,500 on the fourth, and 2,000–3,000 at its peak on the fifth and sixth years, after which its productivity declines gradually. Actual yields, of course, can vary considerably. Fontecilla, who provides these figures, estimated an average yield for years three through ten of 1,000 fruits per annum per estajo. Assuming that Papantla produced between 1,250,000 and 1,500,000 vanillas around this time (5,000–6,000 kilograms), it follows that the area under cultivation would have been roughly 1,000 hectares. For estajo yields, see Fontecilla, *Breve tratado sobre el cultivo y beneficio de la vainilla*, 122–23.

22. "Tabla estadística que manifiesta el censo de los pueblos y rancherías del Cantón de Papantla," in Estado de Veracruz, *Estadística del estado libre y soberano de Veracruz*, 1:110ff.

23. Bausa, "Bosquejo geográfico y estadístico del Partido de Papantla,"379, 381. According to Bausa, there were two other Spaniards who had opted to become Mexican citizens. "They are the only ones," he wrote, "who have wanted to."

24. Fontecilla, *Breve tratado sobre el cultivo y beneficio de la vainilla*, 101; Salas García, *Cachiquín*, 39.

25. See, e.g., ANP, protocols dated 9/30/1847, 1/18/1848, 1/29/1848, 8/13/1856, 11/3/1856, 12/2/1857, 12/19/1859, and 12/21/1860; also Secretaría de Hacienda y Crédito Público, *Memoria presentada al Exmo. Sr. Presidente sustituto de la República por el C. Miguel Lerdo de Tejada*, 521.

26. For biographical details, see AJP, Juzgado de Primera Instancia del Cantón de Papantla, "Ynventario y avalúo del intestado Don Francisco Naveda Somarriba, practicados judicialmente," 29–31 March and 11–13 May 1880; also AJP, Juzgado de Primera Instancia del Cantón de Papantla, "Juicio escrito de intestado del comerciante Don Francisco Naveda Somarriba," Libro 25, no. 2 (Civil), 1880; and RPP 1878, nos. 17 and 22. On Manuel Zorrilla, see Hoffmann, "Entre mar y sierra," 144ff.

27. On Spanish immigration in the nineteenth century, see Lida, *Una inmigración privilegiada*; also Miño Grijalva et al., *Tres aspectos de la presencia española en México*. On immigration and colonization in general, see Berninger, *La inmigración en México*; González Navarro, *La colonización en México*; de la Peña, "Problemas demográficos y agrarios"; and González Navarro, *Los extranjeros en México y los mexicanos en el extranjero*.

28. The relevant decree and plans—including a rosy report describing conditions at the site—can be found in Secretaría de Fomento, *Memoria*, docs. 18 and 19, pp. 18–24. For a detailed study of the Texquitipan colonization project, see Zilli Manica, *La Villa Luisa de los Italianos*.

29. RPP 1881, no. 42; 1883, no. 34; Zilli Manica, *La Villa Luisa de los Italianos*, 33–35.

30. Secretaría de Fomento, *Memoria*, docs. 19–20; doc. 20 is the text of the contract. See also Zilli Manica, *La Villa Luisa de los Italianos*, 24–40.

31. Zilli Manica, *La Villa Luisa de los Italianos*, 96–97.

32. RPP 1881, no. 42. Much of what has been written about the *colonia modelo* is confused, confusing, or contradictory. In fact, very little is known about the whole episode, though Zilli's recent book *La Villa Luisa de los Italianos*, based on some archival research, does shed new light on many basic questions. Moisés de la Peña visited Gutiérrez Zamora in the 1940s and spoke to some of the descendants of the Texquitipan colonists and of another group of Italians who arrived around 1880. They told him the family stories they had been told, and de la Peña used these embellished fragments of memory to craft his own tale. Despite some evident inaccuracies and questionable assertions and assumptions (documents contradict various aspects of the tale), it remains an important source of information on the Italians who were sent to the ill-fated *colonia modelo* (see de la Peña, *Veracruz económico*, 1:236ff.; also de la Peña, "Problemas demográficos y agrarios," 217–24). Accounts of the Italian experience (prior to Zilli Manica's *La Villa Luisa de los Italianos*) rely almost entirely on de la Peña, whether or not they realize or acknowledge it. See, e.g., Revel-Mouroz, *Aménagement et Colonisation du Tropique Humide Mexicain*, ch. 5, sec. 1; García Rodríguez et al., *El municipio de Gutiérrez Zamora*, 5–6; Ramírez Lavoignet, *Tecolutla*, 37–39; Zilli Manica, *Italianos en México*, 26–27; and Skerritt, "Colonización y modernización," 47.

33. See Furber's autobiography, *I Took Chances*, 93.

34. De la Peña, "Problemas demográficos y agrarios," 217.

35. Ibid., 218–23; de la Peña, *Veracruz económico*, 1:236; Ramírez Lavoignet, *Tecolutla*, 41–42. Some of de la Peña's dates and facts are incorrect, so his assertions should not be accepted uncritically.

36. Fontecilla, *Breve tratado sobre el cultivo y beneficio de la vainilla*, 106.

37. Unfortunately, there are no data with which to construct a price series for this period. However, there are some numbers which suggest wide fluctuations. Fontecilla notes that during the 1840s and 1850s the price of vanilla in Veracruz ranged between 22 and 140 pesos per millar, i.e., roughly 7:1. For the same period, prices in France ranged from 32 francs to 260 francs per kilogram (see *Breve tratado sobre el cultivo y beneficio de la vainilla*, 111–12).

38. Bausa, "Bosquejo geográfico y estadístico del Partido de Papantla," 407–8.

39. Ibid., 415, 403, 406.

40. Ibid., 415; Fontecilla, *Breve tratado sobre el cultivo y beneficio de la vainilla*, 149.

41. Fontecilla, *Breve tratado sobre el cultivo y beneficio de la vainilla*, 111, 155–58.

42. Ortiz Izquierdo, "Instrucciones sobre algunos importantes cultivos," 45:109 (dated March 1889); Secretaría de Fomento, *Disposiciones*; López y Parra, *La vainilla*, 40–41.

43. Fontecilla, *Breve tratado sobre el cultivo y beneficio de la vainilla*, 111–12.

44. Ibid., 107.

45. Bausa, "Bosquejo geográfico y estadístico del Partido de Papantla," 408.

46. Ibid., 419. Interestingly, a hundred years later Moisés de la Peña would describe Papantla's Totonacs in almost exactly the same terms: "Thanks to vanilla . . . they live well . . . ; no Indians are better dressed or cleaner than these . . . ; their

dwellings are not the miserable hovels that one sees elsewhere" (*Veracruz económico*, 1:98, 228–29).

47. Fontecilla, *Breve tratado sobre el cultivo y beneficio de la vainilla*, 110.

48. Estado de Veracruz, *Estadística del estado libre y soberano de Veracruz*. 1:110.

49. See Bausa, "Bosquejo geográfico y estadístico del Partido de Papantla," 420.

50. Ibid., 408, 420. On Misantla, see *El Sol*, no. 1125, 13 July 1826, which is quoted in Trens, *Historia de Veracruz*, 4:115: "The huge profits those people make with vanilla are all wasted, because they bury all their money without showing even their children where they have put it, so that when the head of the family dies his offspring remain as poor as ever, and the rest of the country has lost too, because this wealth will remain out of circulation."

51. See, e.g., Bausa's long tirade against the Indians' "lethargy," "conformity," "lack of a work ethic," and "scant ambitions" ("Bosquejo geográfico y estadístico del Partido de Papantla," 404).

52. Flores, *La revolución de Olarte en Papantla*, 76.

53. See, e.g., Hale, *Mexican Liberalism in the Age of Mora*, ch. 7.

54. Bausa, "Bosquejo geográfico y estadístico del Partido de Papantla," 408.

CHAPTER FOUR

1. ACAM, no. 14 (Papantla), p. 111ff. (also marked as p. 117).

2. Fontecilla, *Breve tratado sobre el cultivo y beneficio de la vainilla*, 103, 106–7.

3. See, e.g., Fontecilla, *Informes de Agapito Fontecilla al C. Ministro de Fomento*, 9–10.

4. See Appendix Tables A.8 and A.9; also *Memoria . . . 17 de Setiembre de 1873* (sección de producciones agrícolas e industriales, table 1), 4:1788–99, 1812.

5. Demard, *Jicaltepec, terre d'Argile*, 176–80; Bernot, "Datos sobre la colonización de Jicaltepec," 32–33. Demard writes that Messrs. Levet, Mahé, and Lavoignet are said to have made the trip sometime around 1877. They happened to see the vanilla plants in Paris, whereby they became interested in artificial pollination. Upon their return, he adds, they charged their compatriots "ten dollars each" to teach them the technique. Bernot tells a somewhat different and more intriguing story. According to him, the colonists had learned that in France vanilla was fertilized by hand, and thought that this practice could make their stands more—and more consistently—productive. They had read about artificial pollination in one of Louis Figuier's popular classics, *Le savant du foyer*, and had tried to replicate it without success. Then, sometime between 1874 and 1877, Mr. Mahé traveled to Paris and was taught the proper method, which he passed on to his fellow colonists upon returning to their settlement by the Nautla. By the time a group of students from the Escuela Nacional de Agricultura visited the French colonies in 1887, hand pollination was already commonly practiced (Barba et al., "Prácticas de los alumnos," 37:10–11, 15–16 [dated July 1888]).

6. Demard states that one of the sons of François Denis went to Papantla to sell this method of fertilization, and that in a few days he managed to earn the *belle fortune* of "eight hundred dollars," but he does not specify when this is supposed to

have happened (see, e.g., Demard, *Jicaltepec, terre d'Argile,* 179; Bernot, "Datos sobre la colonización de Jicaltepec," 33; Bruman, "The Culture History of Mexican Vanilla," 371–72, who tells a different story and mistakenly argues that it happened in the 1840s; and de la Peña, "Problemas demográficos y agrarios," 208–9ff., from where Demard seems to have taken a good part of his story).

7. Fontecilla, *Informes de Agapito Fontecilla al C. Ministro de Fomento,* 1–2ff. López y Parra's treatise *La vainilla,* first published in 1900, shows that the spread of artificial fecundation beyond San Rafael was a very recent phenomenon (see pp. 49, 62ff.). See also *PO,* 12 August 1899, 1–2; and Kaerger, *Agricultura y colonización en México en 1900,* 137.

8. Fontecilla, *Informes de Agapito Fontecilla al C. Ministro de Fomento,* 8–9. The two-thirds estimate refers to the years leading up to 1883; Papantla's share probably grew even larger during the late 1880s.

9. For Jicaltepec and San Rafael's production figures in the early 1880s, see *Memoria . . . 17 de Septiembre de 1882* (sección de "colonias extranjeras"), 4:2082–83.

10. Fontecilla, *Informes de Agapito Fontecilla al C. Ministro de Fomento,* 6.

11. U.S. Congress, House, *Annual Report on the Commercial Relations between the United States and Foreign Nations . . . September 30, 1874,* 878.

12. See "Líneas de vapores que tocan en puertos mexicanos," in Secretaría de Hacienda y Crédito Público, *Memoria,* 434–36; also U.S. Congress, House, *Annual Report upon the Commercial Relations of the United States with Foreign Countries . . . 1878,* 418–19 ("Steam Navigation"). It is worth noting that at that time U.S. lines were the only ones subsidized by the Mexican government. Three British lines—the Royal Mail Steam Packet and two other monthly merchant services out of Liverpool—as well as the St. Nazaire French line, all called at Veracruz. St. Nazaire and the Royal Mail were subsidized by their own governments.

13. On Tuxpan's roads, see, e.g., Soto, *Noticias estadísticas de la Huasteca,* 131–35. On Tuxpan's commerce and navigation, see, e.g., the U.S. consular report for 1876–77, in U.S. Congress, House, *Report upon the Commercial Relations of the United States with Foreign Countries . . . 1877,* 748–50, as well as U.S. Congress, House, *Annual Report on the Commercial Relations between the United States and Foreign Nations . . . September 30, 1874,* 875–80; also Kourí, "El comercio de exportación en Tuxpan." A tonnage comparison illustrates the effect of steamship traffic on trade. In 1876–77, the twenty-eight steamers in question exported a total of 33,416 tons of commodities, an average of nearly 1,200 tons per ship. Four French sailing vessels, meanwhile, took only 996 tons of merchandise (roughly 250 tons per ship), while U.S.-flag sailboats—of which there were twenty-six—carried a total of 1,818 tons, less than 70 tons per vessel on average. For the vanilla trade, however, the sheer increase of regular traffic was probably more important than the overall expansion in carrying capacity.

14. U.S. Congress, House, *Annual Report on the Commercial Relations between the United States and Foreign Nations . . . September 30, 1874,* 879–80.

15. *Memoria . . . 17 de Setiembre de 1873,* 3:1248–50.

16. See, e.g., ANP 1877, nos. 101, 108, 109, 114; ANP 1878, no. 42; and *PO,* 6 April 1878, 4, all on Pedro Tremari's bankruptcy.

17. On the importance of German trading houses in nineteenth-century Veracruz, see Von Mentz et al., *Los pioneros del imperialismo alemán en México*, especially Pt. 2, "El capital comercial y financiero alemán en México," of which pp. 149–59 are devoted to Veracruz. In the 1870s, over 40 percent of the principal trading firms in Veracruz were German—e.g., Watermeyer y Cía., Duhring y Cía., and G. Krönke y Cía. Among the Spanish firms operating in the port city was Zorrilla y Cía. of Teziutlán.

18. On Fontecilla, see ANP 1877, no. 14 (appendix); on Naveda, see AJP, Juzgado de Primera Instancia del Cantón de Papantla, "Ynventario y avalúo del intestado Don Francisco Naveda Somarriba, practicados judicialmente," 29–31 March and 11–13 May 1880. In 1881 Román Silvera—Naveda's brother-in-law—told the court that Naveda's vanilla stock for 1880 had not been duly shipped to and sold "in New York" and a considerable financial loss was therefore expected. Silvera, who had recently become the family's trustee, promised that he would take care of Naveda's outstanding business as soon as he finished the "urgent task" of curing and selling abroad his own 1881 stock (see AJP, Juzgado Permanente de Primera Instancia del Cantón de Papantla, "Juicio escrito de intestado del comerciante Don Francisco Naveda Somarriba," Libro 25, no. 2 [Civil], 1880+; and also RPP 1878, no. 17; for another example, see ANP 1885, no. 8).

19. *OPDR* 19 (1 June 1881): 755; also, e.g., "Cultivation of Vanilla in Mexico," *OPDR* 23 (2 May 1883): 1111; "Vanilla Beans," *OPDR* 30 (13 October 1886): 40; and "The Vanilla Bean and How it Flourished in Old Mexico," *OPDR* 33(25 January 1888): 51.

20. "The Advance in Vanilla Beans," *OPDR* 30 (28 July 1886): 5.

21. *OPDR* 30 (22 September 1886): 38.

22. "Vanilla Beans," *OPDR* 31 (1 June 1887): 48.

23. *OPDR* 34 (25 July 1888): 46. The Dodge & Olcott advertisement is also from this issue.

24. See, e.g., Cosío Villegas, ed., *Historia moderna de México*, vol. 2 of *El Porfiriato, Vida económica*, 665–66.

25. Fontecilla, *Breve tratado sobre el cultivo y beneficio de la vainilla*, 114–15.

26. See, e.g. López y Parra, *La vainilla*, 35–37.

27. In 1895 the *Reporter* reminded its readers that "twenty two years ago [1873] . . . thirty-two dollars per pound was paid" ("The Outlook for Vanilla Beans," *OPDR* 48 [11 November 1895]: 5).

28. *OPDR*, vols. 17–38 (1880–1890); also Fontecilla, *Informes de Agapito Fontecilla al C. Ministro de Fomento*, 5. Low quotes for whole beans ("ordinary grades") range from US$9.00 per pound in early 1880 to US$7.00 in early 1887 and US$4.50 in early 1890. Cuts are offered at between US$3.00 and US$8.50 in 1886 and between US$3.00 and US$5.00 in 1890.

29. "Vanilla Bean Prospects," *OPDR* 39 (1 April 1891): 6.

30. For that reason, the price index assembled in Colegio de México, *Estadísticas económicas del Porfiriato* (358–59) is not very useful. This index takes the aggregate export value declared at Customs and divides it by the total weight of the shipments to produce unit prices (pesos per kilogram). It is not clear how these values were calculated or what exactly they represented, since vanilla was often sent on

consignment and final prices (and profits) depended on actual sales made in New York. The index does reflect the broad price trends of the period, but the individual unit prices it provides are generally misleading; this is in part because no distinction can be made between the various classes of vanilla, since the composition of shipments (percentages of cuts, *ordinaria*, and top grades) is not known. From a commercial point of view, these distinctions made all the difference, especially during these years, when the gap in prices according to class was still very wide. In understanding the organization and evolution of the business, New York prices (by category) are a more accurate and suggestive guide.

31. INEGI, *Estadísticas históricas de México*, 2:854–55.

32. Fontecilla, *Informes de Agapito Fontecilla al C. Ministro de Fomento*, 5–6.

33. See. e.g., RPP 1874, no. 8; 1877, no. 18; 1880, no. 1; and ANP 1878, no. 21; 1883, no. 24; 1884, nos. 12, 19.

34. For 1873, *Memoria . . . 17 de Setiembre de 1873*, 4:1815; for 1889, *Memoria . . . 18 de septiembre de 1890* (annex no. 7, Sección de Estadística), 7:3695–3702; for 1894, *Memoria . . . 16 de septiembre de 1894* (annex no. 13, Sección de Fomento y Estadística), 8:4553–55.

35. See Castro, "Dictamen de la Comisión Especial de Agricultura," 74–76.

36. The fresh chiles were dried to make them lighter, more durable, and easier to transport. In this case, growers seem to have performed much of the drying. Back in the mid-1840s, Bausa wrote that the *chilpotle* was produced exclusively around Espinal and that its trade was fairly small. In 1889 greater Papantla's production was estimated at 12,500 kilograms, but the actual figure is likely to have been much higher. Espinal was still the principal area of chile cultivation (the *chiltepín*, which was also harvested, grows wild) (Bausa, "Bosquejo geográfico y estadístico del Partido de Papantla,"403, 407; and Blázquez Domínguez, *Estado de Veracruz: Informes de sus Gobernadores*, 7:3699). Unlike with tobacco, the *chilpotle* trade had other important routes besides Teziutlán, in particular from Coyutla up the Sierra Norte in Puebla. The mule traffic along these western trails grew notably during the Porfiriato and the early decades of the twentieth century (see Bravo Marentes, *Arrieros somos*; also Velázquez, *Cuando los arrieros perdieron sus caminos*).

37. RPP 1878, no. 41; 1871, no. 18; and ANP 1883, no. 22 (appendix). Lalanne owned part of Larios y Malpica, while Hinojosa owned Tulapilla.

38. RPP 1880, nos. 30, 32; see also, e.g., RPP 1879, no. 50. A native of Orizaba, Antonio Maldonado was almost certainly Papantla's first resident business lawyer. Until al least 1878, he was also the only one. According to a government report, he received his degree in late 1848, which, as of 1878, made his the eleventh longest practice in the state of Veracruz. It is not known, however, exactly when he resettled in Papantla. His clients were the top merchants of Papantla, as well as their counterparts in Teziutlán and Veracruz, whom he represented whenever they had legal matters to attend to in the basin (see, e.g., RPP 1878, no. 41). By 1880, Vicente Lombardo was also doing legal work in the basin, mostly with the Italians of Gutiérrez Zamora. On Maldonado, see Blázquez Domínguez, *Estado de Veracruz: Informes de sus Gobernadores*, vol. 2, tables following p. 1144, and 4:1974, which show that in 1871 and 1878 the Cantón of Papantla only had one lawyer.

39. RPP 1879, no. 60; also ANP 1879, nos. 11, 43; 1880, no. 86. On feeder

grasses, see ANP 1883, no number, document of 4 January 1884 describing Avelino Pérez's pasturelands in Espinal. For data on 1869, *Memoria . . . 13 de Marzo de 1869*, 2:694; for 1873, *Memoria presentada . . . 17 de Setiembre de 1873*, 4:1815; for 1888, *Memoria . . . del 1 de julio de 1886 a 30 de junio de 1888*, 7:3744; for 1890, *Memoria . . . 18 de septiembre de 1890*, 7:3708; see also *Memoria . . . de 1 de Enero de 1889, a 30 de Junio de 1890*, 8:4172. On the subsequent development of the *engorda* business, see, e.g. de la Peña, *Veracruz económico*, 1:563ff.

40. For a description of how *aguardiente* used to be made, see, e.g. Bausa, "Bosquejo geográfico y estadístico del Partido de Papantla," 405–6; also Estado de Veracruz, *Estadística del estado libre y soberano de Veracruz*, 1:110.

41. The data come from various state governor reports in Blázquez Domínguez, *Estado de Veracruz: Informes de sus Gobernadores*, vol. 4 (see *Memoria* of 1878, Sección de Fomento, doc. 20, "Noticia general de los establecimientos industriales que existen en el Estado"), and for 1890, vol. 7, pp. 3699, 3707.

42. RPP 1873, no. 11. On Silvera's sawmill, see Luis Mier y Terán's gubernatorial report in Blázquez Domínguez, *Estado de Veracruz: Informes de sus Gobernadores*, vol. 4 (see *Memoria* of 1878, Sección de Fomento, doc. 20, "Noticia general de los establecimientos industriales que existen en el Estado"). On Silvera's family, see RPP 1880, no. 41. On logging by the Cazones river, see RPP 1878, no. 11. For data on Tuxpan's timber exports during the Porfiriato, see Kourí, "El comercio de exportación en Tuxpan."

43. *Memoria . . . noviembre 30 de 1870*, 2:763, 851.

44. U.S. Congress, House, *Annual Report on the Commercial Relations between the United States and Foreign Nations . . . September 30, 1874*, 880.

45. For a general discussion of the early development of oil extraction and marketing in the United States and Mexico see, e.g., Brown, *Oil and Revolution in Mexico*, especially ch. 1. On El Cuguas, in particular, see Furber, *I Took Chances*, chs. 17, 19–20.

46. *PO*, 28 February 1878.

47. On Autrey's medical practice, see Blázquez Domínguez, *Estado de Veracruz: Informes de sus Gobernadores*, 4:1977; and Naveda and González Sierra, *Papantla*, 32–33; on his business, see Blázquez Domínguez, *Estado de Veracruz: Informes de sus Gobernadores*, vol. 4 (see *Memoria* of 1878, Sección de Fomento, doc. 20, "Noticia general de los establecimientos industriales que existen en el Estado," and p. 2191); also Salas García, *Cachiquín*, 60–61.

48. Contreras, "Memoria que rinde el Jefe Político del Cantón de Papantla . . . 1 de Noviembre de 1881," 223; also Blázquez Domínguez, *Estado de Veracruz: Informes de sus Gobernadores*, 5:2552 (1885–86).

49. See AJP, Juzgado de Primera Instancia, "Ynventario y avalúo del intestado Don Francisco Naveda Somarriba, practicados judicialmente," 29–31 March and 11–13 May 1880.

50. On political offices, see, e.g., Blázquez Domínguez, *Estado de Veracruz: Informes de sus Gobernadores*, 4:2112, and 5:2280, 2460, 2501; for Decree No. 114 (15 December 1874) and No. 44 (30 October 1877) on the vanilla tax, see Labastida, *Colección de leyes, decretos, reglamentos*. On the merchants' reactions,

see *PO*, 24 January 1878, 1–2; 1 August 1878, 3; and ANP 1877, nos. 30–33, 37, 41–45, 47, 49–50.

51. Blázquez Domínguez, *Estado de Veracruz: Informes de sus Gobernadores*, 5:2552; and Salas García, *Cachiquín*, 41. According to Salas, Agapito Fontecilla personally directed the construction of the church tower, which was completed in 1879.

52. Decree No. 39 of 22 December 1826, *Sobre repartimiento de terrenos de comunidad de indígenas y baldíos*; Law of 4 April 1856; Decree No. 58 of 2 July 1861; and Circular of 19 August 1867, all in Blázquez Domínguez and Corzo Ramírez, *Colección de leyes*. For a general overview—and the typical interpretation—of the legal history of communal disentailment in Veracruz, see Florescano, "El proceso de destrucción de la propiedad comunal."

53. Article 14 of the accompanying regulations asked *jefes políticos* "to persuade the Indians that they must divide their lands and settle their legal disputes now that they've been granted a new grace period, since by letting the previous deadlines pass they had already lost the right to their lands" (Decree No. 152, 17 March 1869, in Blázquez Domínguez and Corzo Ramírez, *Colección de leyes*).

54. *Memoria . . . Noviembre 30 de 1870*, 2:767–68, 890–92.

55. *Memoria . . . 18 de Setiembre de 1882*, 4:2205.

56. For a description of the "mixed" tax regime of the early 1870s—and of the governor's budget woes—see Blázquez Domínguez, *Estado de Veracruz: Informes de sus Gobernadores*, 3:1223ff.

57. See the Hacienda sections and statistical tables in the *Memorias* for 1867–1890, in Blázquez Domínguez, *Estado de Veracruz: Informes de sus Gobernadores*, vols. 2–8; also Ochoa Contreras, "Cambios estructurales," which discusses the tax reforms of these years (Ochoa's analysis is useful, but it contains a number of errors). For a discussion of tax reform at the federal level, see Carmagnani, *Estado y mercado*.

58. For remarks on this issue, see, e.g., *Memoria . . . Noviembre 30 de 1870*, 2:768; and *Memoria . . . 18 de Setiembre de 1882*, 4:2089–90

59. See, e.g., AGEV—Gobernación y Justicia, caja 4 (Reparto Comunales Papantla, 1894): Lázaro Muñoz's letter, 4 July 1878.

60. The figures for 1871–85 come from the governors' reports in Blázquez Domínguez, *Estado de Veracruz: Informes de sus Gobernadores*: for 1871, see 2:1108–12; for 1873, 3:1726; for 1878, 4: table 19; for 1882, 4:2164; and for 1885, 5:2657–60. Figures for 1895–1900 come from federal censuses: for 1895, see Ministerio de Fomento, *Censo general . . . (1895)*; and for 1900, Secretaría de Fomento, Colonización e Industria, *Censo y división territorial . . . en 1900*.

61. ACAM, no. 14 (Papantla), pp. 125–26 (also marked as p. 114).

62. See, e.g., Velasco Toro, "Indigenismo y rebelión totonaca de Papantla"; also, Chenaut, "Comunidad y ley en Papantla a fines del siglo XIX."

63. RPP 1880, no. 1.

64. See, e.g., Katz, "The Liberal Republic and the Porfiriato," 96–97.

65. ACAM, no. 14 (Papantla), surveys of the boundaries of the *congregaciones*; also, RPP 1878, nos. 4, 18, 37.

66. AGEV—Gobernación y Justicia, caja 4 (Reparto Comunales Papantla, 1894): government memorandum, 4 December 1877, p. 2.

67. Blázquez Domínguez, *Estado de Veracruz: Informes de sus Gobernadores,* 2:1149.

68. Decree No. 33 of 27 December 1873, No. 109 of 5 December 1874, and No. 132 of 7 December 1875, in Blázquez Domínguez and Corzo Ramírez, *Colección de leyes.*

69. Article 3, Decree No. 68 of 2 July 1874, in Blázquez Domínguez and Corzo Ramírez, *Colección de leyes.*

70. On the *condueñazgo,* see, e.g., de la Peña, *Veracruz económico,* 1:135–39; also, Escobar Ohmstede and Schryer, "Las sociedades agrarias en el norte de Hidalgo." On the *condueñazgo* of Cacahuatal, see, e.g., RPP 1878, nos. 15, 20, 21, 28.

71. On this subject, see Blázquez Domínguez, *Estado de Veracruz: Informes de sus Gobernadores,* 4:2089–90.

72. For a partial listing, see Blázquez Domínguez, *Estado de Veracruz: Informes de sus Gobernadores,* 8:4279–94.

73. ACAM, no. 14 (Papantla); also, AGEV—Gobernación y Justicia, caja 4 (Reparto Comunales Papantla, 1894); and caja 11 (Ingenieros Militares, 1905), 23 October 1880.

74. These dates may not be exact. It is not clear whether Mecatlán formed *grandes lotes* as well; by 1894, its communal lands were already divided into individual plots. Santo Domingo had boundary disputes with communities in neighboring Puebla, and Espinal had a long-standing land dispute with Jamaya, so neither of them carried out a *reparto* at this time. Coyutla and Gutiérrez Zamora, meanwhile, did not have communal lands of their own to divide (Blázquez Domínguez, *Estado de Veracruz: Informes de sus Gobernadores,* 8:4288–90).

75. On the *roza,* see, e.g., de la Peña, *Veracruz económico,* 1:136; Velasco Toro, "Indigenismo y rebelión totonaca de Papantla," 87–88; and Chenaut, "Comunidad y ley en Papantla a fines del siglo XIX," 78.

76. AGEV—Gobernación y Justicia, caja 4 (Reparto Comunales Papantla, 1894): government memorandum, 4 December 1877, p. 2.

77. See ACAM, no. 14 (Papantla), *condueñazgo* privatization deeds (*actas de posesión*).

78. ACAM, no. 14 (Papantla). The notion of forming *juntas de indígenas* to carry out the division of communal lands went back to the law of April 4, 1856 (Articles 14–16), but Decree No. 152 had eliminated this requirement, allowing Ayuntamientos to undertake land subdivisions on their own (Article 2). For text of laws and decrees, see Blázquez Domínguez and Corzo Ramírez, *Colección de leyes.* Evidently, this was not feasible in the case of Papantla, and the old idea of creating *juntas* was revived, albeit with some modifications.

79. AHSDN, Archivo de Cancelados: Expediente personal del extinto Mayor de Infantería Simón Tiburcio; also, Simón Tiburcio, "Recuerdo de mi vida en la época del llamado Imperio y apuntes para la historia militar del Cantón de Papantla," reproduced in Salas García, *Juu Papantlán,* 147–63. A photograph of Tiburcio in military uniform appears on p. 145. See also RPP 1871 and 1874; and Olivo Lara, *Bi-*

ografías de veracruzanos distinguidos, 388. On warfare in Papantla and neighboring areas during the 1860s, see Alatorre, *Reseña de los acontecimientos*; also, Thomson and LaFrance, *Patriotism, Politics, and Popular Liberalism in Nineteenth-Century Mexico*, chs. 5–7.

80. AHSDN, Archivo de Cancelados: Expediente personal del extinto Capitán Primero Pablo Hernández Olmedo; Expediente personal del extinto Capitán Primero Antonio Jiménez.

81. ACAM, no. 14 (Papantla), pp. 119–20 (also marked as p. 140).

82. RPP 1877, nos. 7, 19; 1881, no. 42; also, Bausa, "Bosquejo geográfico y estadístico del Partido de Papantla," 409; and AHSDN, Archivo de Cancelados: Expediente personal del extinto Mayor de Infantería Simón Tiburcio.

83. Decree No. 39 of 22 December 1826 (Veracruz), Article 4; also, federal law of 25 June 1856, Article 8, in Blázquez Domínguez and Corzo Ramírez, *Colección de leyes*.

84. ACAM, no. 14 (Papantla), pp. 139ff. (also marked as pp. 190–91ff.). Quite probably, some of these lands were already occupied by townspeople and the establishment of an *ejido* was a way of perpetuating this practice.

85. ACAM, no. 14 (Papantla), pp. 139 (also marked as p. 119).

86. ACAM, no. 14 (Papantla), *actas de deslinde*.

87. ACAM, no. 14 (Papantla). In the original documents the size of each *lote* was calculated in *sitios de ganado mayor* (sgm) or in *varas cuadradas*. Here, the *sitios de ganado mayor* have been converted into hectares (1 sgm = ± 1,756 hectares).

88. For the Commission's estimates, see ACAM, no. 14 (Papantla); actual figures are taken from the individual land subdivisions of the 1890s, for which more accurate surveys (involving actual measurements) were conducted (see DRTP, *condueñazgo* files; also, Chenaut, "Comunidad y ley en Papantla a fines del siglo XIX," 80, table 7).

89. ACAM, no. 14 (Papantla), p. 139 (also marked as p. 119) back. See also AGEV—Gobernación y Justicia, caja 4 (Reparto Comunales Papantla, 1894): letter from the Junta to the Jefe Político, 22 February 1876.

90. AGEV—Gobernación y Justicia, caja 4 (Reparto Comunales Papantla, 1894): government memorandum, 4 December 1877, p. 4.

91. ACAM, no. 14 (Papantla), p. 145 (also marked as p. 122), back.

92. See Table 2.1. Cuespalapan, Puxtla, Rincón, Aguadulce, Mascapan, Isla de Juan Rosas, Paso del Correo, and Estero were also in this category.

93. Fontecilla y Vidal's background highlights the sad irony of this outcome. Son of a Spanish merchant, he was born in Papantla but was sent to Spain as a small child, where he grew up and was educated. After receiving a degree in accounting, he traveled widely in Europe, the United States, and Canada, and only then did he settle in Papantla, already a grown man. Following in his father's footsteps, he quickly became one of the basin's leading vanilla merchants and political figures. In the 1880s, he would occupy the posts of mayor and *jefe político* in Papantla. He was one of the 241 original *condueños* of lot 5, Zapotal y Cazonera (see Olivo Lara, *Biografías de veracruzanos distinguidos*, 321–22; also ACAM, no. 14 [Papantla], p. 125 [also marked as p. 156]).

94. Extraordinary session of Papantla's Municipal Council, 19 April 1877, in

ACAM, no. 14 (Papantla), p. 122ff. (also marked as p. 145ff.); and AGEV—Gobernación y Justicia, caja 4 (Reparto Comunales Papantla, 1894).

95. AGEV—Gobernación y Justicia, caja 4 (Reparto Comunales Papantla, 1894): memorandum, 4 December 1877; letters of 12 December 1877 and 21 December 1877; memorandum, 18 May 1878; also Trens, *Historia de Veracruz*, Vol. VII, Ch. 4.

96. AGEV—Gobernación y Justicia, caja 4 (Reparto Comunales Papantla, 1894): letter from the Junta, 29 April 1878; letter from Lázaro Muñoz, 4 July 1878; also, ACAM, no. 14 (Papantla), pp. 123–24 (also marked as pp. 148–52).

97. ACAM, no. 14 (Papantla), pp. 123–24 (also marked as pp. 148–52, 34–38).

98. The Italian colonists and their backers did not stand still, however. Seeking to obtain direct political control over these territories, they persuaded the state legislature to set up a separate municipality comprising the *lotes* in which they had their farms. In July 1877, the *municipio* of Tecolutla—which included El Cristo, Anclón y Arenal, and Arroyo Grande—was renamed Gutiérrez Zamora, and Cabezas was elevated to the rank of *pueblo*. The *congregaciones* of Boca de Lima and Cazonera, until then a part of Papantla, were also placed under the jurisdiction of Gutiérrez Zamora (Decree No. 22, 21 July 1877, in Blázquez Domínguez and Corzo Ramírez, *Colección de leyes*). Tecolutla became a separate municipality again in 1879, but Gutiérrez Zamora retained some of the *congregaciones*. Significantly, this redistricting took place just as the fate of municipal shares was being debated. Although by law the Ayuntamiento of Papantla remained in charge of dividing these lands, this maneuver nevertheless gave the Italians a political base from which they could subsequently defend their interests.

99. ACAM, no. 14 (Papantla), p. 122 (also marked as p. 147).

100. Blázquez Domínguez, *Estado de Veracruz: Informes de sus Gobernadores*, 4: table 19.

101. ACAM, no. 14 (Papantla), *condueñazgo* name lists. These numbers may not be exact because in a few cases it is hard to tell whether a name refers to a man or to a woman.

102. ACAM, no. 14 (Papantla), *actas de posesión*.

CHAPTER FIVE

1. AGEV—Gobernación y Justicia, caja 11 (Ingenieros Militares, 1905), 23 October 1880.

2. AGEV—Gobernación y Justicia, caja 4 (Reparto Comunales Papantla, 1894): government memorandum, 4 December 1877, pp. 4–5.

3. DRTP, lot 24, Sombrerete, Caristay y Aguacate: Acta de otorgamiento de poder, August 1879. On Salas, see ACAM, no. 14 (Papantla), p. 119 (also marked as p. 137).

4. ACAM, no. 14 (Papantla), p. 116 (also marked as p. 130).

5. ANP 1880, no. 90 (*bases de administración*, sociedad agrícola de Benito Juárez, Chote y Mesillas).

6. See, e.g., ANP 1882, nos. 17, 18, 22 (Coxquihui); RPP 1886, nos. 9, 69 (Coatzintla); and *PO*, 14 July 1891.

7. ANP 1880, no. 88 (*bases de administración*, sociedad agrícola de San Miguel y San Lorenzo).

8. Kelly and Palerm, *The Tajín Totonac*, 54 n. 88. González's recollections are broadly in harmony with the historical record, but Kelly and Palerm's analysis of this period is riddled with factual errors as well as with misinterpretations of their informant's tale.

9. Chenaut, "Costumbre y resistencia étnica," 162–64; Chenaut, "Fin de siglo en la costa totonaca"; Chenaut, "Comunidad y ley en Papantla a fines del siglo XIX"; Chenaut, "Orden jurídico y comunidad indígena en el Porfiriato"; and Chenaut, *Aquellos que vuelan*. See also Velasco Toro, "Indigenismo y rebelión totonaca en Papantla"; Velasco Toro, "La política desamortizadora y sus efectos en la región de Papantla"; Florescano, "El proceso de destrucción de la propiedad communal"; and Naveda and González Sierra, *Papantla*. All of these works share the same set of assumptions.

10. ANP 1880, no. 79; RPP 1881, no. 53.

11. ANP 1880, no. 84.

12. AJP, Juzgado de Primera Instancia del Cantón de Papantla, "Conciliación promovida por el tesorero municipal contra los condueños del lote #23 por pesos," March–June 1885.

13. AGEV—Gobernación y Justicia, caja 4 (Terrenos, 1894): memo citing Rafael Mendizábal's report, 12 October 1889; also, CPD, 16:7733–34 (1891).

14. ANP 1886, nos. 39, 81, 86; RPP 1886, nos. 27, 66, 67, 68; 1888, no. 4; 1889, no. 56. Tiburcio and his partners operated in Nextlalpan and Palma Sola.

15. See, e.g., de la Peña, *Veracruz económico*, 1:135–36. De la Peña explains how property shares were sometimes divided into fractions for inheritance purposes. Incidentally, in the twentieth century the post-Revolutionary *ejidos* would face the same issue.

16. See Blázquez Domínguez, *Estado de Veracruz*, 4: table 19 (for 1878), and 5:2609–10 (for 1885).

17. AGEV—Gobernación y Justicia, caja 11 (Ingenieros militares, 1905): Informe de Ignacio Muñoz, 17 December 1894; also, *Memoria . . . 16 de septiembre de 1896*, 9:4661.

18. For details and sources, see Chapter 4 n. 57; also, CPD, 11:11198–99 (1886).

19. On rural property taxes, see Decree No. 81 of 21 December 1886, in Blázquez Domínguez and Corzo Ramírez, *Colección de leyes*; also, for 1873, Blázquez Domínguez, *Estado de Veracruz: Informes de sus Gobernadores*, 3:1227, 1231; for 1886, ibid., 5:2434–39, which includes a discussion on value assessments and the difficulties involved in forming a land register; and for 1888, ibid., 6:2923. By 1887, the state tax rate was 0.3 percent 1,000, but the Ayuntamientos could charge (and keep) an additional percentage.

20. CPD, 16:12225–28 (1891) (Juan Enríquez to Porfirio Díaz); 7733–34 (1891); 19:17021–29 (1894) (Teodoro Dehesa to Porfirio Díaz); 21:5056 (1896) (Papantla residents to Porfirio Díaz); also, AGEV—Gobernación y Justicia, caja 4 (Consulta a la Legislatura, 1894), 31 March 1896.

21. Decree No. 142 of 28 June 1875, in Blázquez Domínguez and Corzo Ramírez, *Colección de leyes*; for 1878, Blázquez Domínguez, *Estado de Veracruz: Informes de sus Gobernadores*, 4:1935–36; and for 1882, ibid., 4:2212ff.

22. For 1885, Law No. 12 of 30 May 1885, in Blázquez Domínguez and Corzo Ramírez, *Colección de leyes*; for 1886, Blázquez Domínguez, *Estado de Veracruz: Informes de sus Gobernadores*, 5:2364–65; and for 1888, ibid., 6:2929.

23. For all of 1884, the old 1.5 percent tax yielded a total of $33,305.29 pesos, whereas during 1885–86 (the first twelve months after it was enacted) the new personal tax raised $114,364.60 pesos (see Blázquez Domínguez, *Estado de Veracruz: Informes de sus Gobernadores* 5:2511–14). For tax figures by category, see Ochoa Contreras, "Cambios estructurales," tables 6 and 7, 62–63 and 66–67, respectively, which present data from the governors' reports (also available in Blázquez Domínguez's collection).

24. See Blázquez Domínguez, *Estado de Veracruz: Informes de sus Gobernadores*, as follows: for 1881 and 1882, vol. 4, tables 9 and 10 (opposite p. 2146); for 1885 and the first semester of 1886, vol. 5, tables 35 A, B, and C (opposite p. 2517); and for the second semester of 1886, as well as for 1887 and 1888, 6:3205, 3216, and 3230. For 1889 and 1890, see M. Sánchez, "Memoria que rinde el Jefe Político del Cantón de Papantla . . . 1 de abril de 1891," 341–44.

25. See Decrees of 15 February 1871 and 19 June 1871, and Decree No. 38, 1884, in Blázquez Domínguez and Corzo Ramírez, *Colección de leyes*; also, for 1871, Blázquez Domínguez, *Estado de Veracruz: Informes de sus Gobernadores*, 2:917; for 1884, ibid., 4:2251–52; and for 1886, ibid., 5:2511–14.

26. For 1886 and 1887, see Decree No. 66 of 19 November 1886, and Decree No. 52 of 5 November 1887, in Blázquez Domínguez and Corzo Ramírez, *Colección de leyes*; for 1888, see Blázquez Domínguez, *Estado de Veracruz: Informes de sus Gobernadores*, 6:2918–19, 2923, 3058–59; and for 1891, M. Sánchez, "Memoria que rinde el Jefe Político del Cantón de Papantla . . . 1 de abril de 1891," 341.

27. On mortgages and sales of vanilla plantings (without the land) connected with credit or cash advances, see, e.g., ANP 1883: nos. 7, 25, 48; 1883 (appendix): nos. 5, 6, 24; 1884: nos. 12, 19; 1885: no. 8; also, ANGZ 1879: no. 15; 1889: nos. 1, 2, 3, 4, 5; and 1890: no. 24.

28. For sales of *condueñazgo* shares, see, e.g., DRTP, lots 13 and 15; also, ANGZ 1883: nos. 4, 8, 9, 12, 15; 1885: nos. 1, 6, 12; 1886: no. 3; 1887: nos. 3, 14; and 1888: nos. 11, 12. Chapter 6 examines this topic in more detail.

29. PO, 16 January 1886 ("Proclama de Manfort"); and 15 May 1886 ("Lo que proclama el C. Antonio Díaz Manfort"); also, González de la Lama, "Los papeles de Díaz Manfort," 490, 513–14. An appendix to González's article reproduces a series of documents taken from Díaz Manfort after he was killed.

30. PO, 14 January 1886, 16 January 1886, 21 January 1886, and 15 May 1886; González de la Lama, "Los papeles de Díaz Manfort," 484–88, 505–21.

31. AHSDN, Archivo de Cancelados: Expediente personal del extinto Capitán Primero Pablo Hernández Olmedo; PO, 27 April 1886, 29 April 1886, and 4 May 1886.

32. For 1887, see Blázquez Domínguez, *Estado de Veracruz: Informes de sus*

Gobernadores, 5:2228–89; *PO*, 6 May 1886, 13 May 1886, and 15 May 1886; González de la Lama, "Los papeles de Díaz Manfort," 478–79, 505–21. Also, González de la Lama, "Rebels and Bandits," ch. 4.

33. CPD, 10:7911–23 (1885), 8189–90 (1885), 8478–82 (1885), 9246 (1885); also, Blázquez Domínguez, *Estado de Veracruz: Informes de sus Gobernadores*, 5:2282–92.

34. On *rastro* fees, see Decree No. 36 (1883), Decree No. 11 (1884), and Decree No. 6 (22 May 1885), in Blázquez Domínguez and Corzo Ramírez, *Colección de leyes*; also, for 1888, Blázquez Domínguez, *Estado de Veracruz: Informes de sus Gobernadores*, 6:2927–28. On Colipa's rebel butcher, see González de la Lama, "Los papeles de Díaz Manfort," 485–86.

35. The *pueblos* of Misantla were also privatizing their communal lands in these years, but not in the form of *condueñazgos*. Instead, individual plots were distributed directly (see Blázquez Domínguez, *Estado de Veracruz: Informes de sus Gobernadores*, 8:4286–87).

36. The official account of these events appears in Blázquez Domínguez, *Estado de Veracruz: Informes de sus Gobernadores*, 5:2716, 2759–63. For another analysis, see Chenaut, "Fin de siglo en la costa totonaca," 114–17; also, Naveda and González Sierra, *Papantla*, 35.

37. AGN, Ramo Buscas, vol. 16, exp. 14 (23 March 1887).

38. CPD, 13:424–25 (1888) and 1840–41 (1888).

39. In 1891, when a new commission was organized to bring Papantla's land disputes to the attention of authorities in Mexico City, some of its members acknowledged that they had been duped: "It is true that we have been the victims of a scam and have been defrauded by some *tinterillos*, among them X; he promised to obtain copies of our titles from the National Archive, and even though we gave him large sums of money, nothing good ever came of it" (*MR*, 11 July 1891). "X" was almost certainly Miguel W. Herrera.

40. AGN, Ramo Buscas, vol. 16, exp. 43 (31 August 1887). Mariscal's Ministry was then in charge of the archive.

41. For 1886, Blázquez Domínguez, *Estado de Veracruz: Informes de sus Gobernadores*, 5:2280; and *PO*, 23 March 1886; also, Naveda and González Sierra, *Papantla*, 36. Although he was born in Papantla, Fontecilla y Vidal was—like his father—a Spanish national.

42. CPD, 12:9609, 9604 (1887).

43. Blázquez Domínguez, *Estado de Veracruz: Informes de sus Gobernadores*, 5:2759.

44. Historians have speculated about the significance of these dates. For a discussion, see González de la Lama, "Los papeles de Díaz Manfort," 499ff.

45. AHSDN, Archivo de Cancelados: Expediente personal del extinto Capitán Primero Pablo Hernández Olmedo; Blázquez Domínguez, *Estado de Veracruz: Informes de sus Gobernadores*, 5:2760.

46. Blázquez Domínguez, *Estado de Veracruz: Informes de sus Gobernadores*, 5:2759–63; *PO*, 12 January 1888; CPD, 13:424–26 (10–11 January 1888).

47. *PO*, 21 January 1888; CPD, 13:1569 (1840–42), 2652 (1888).

48. *MR*, 11 July 1891.

49. AGA, Grupo Documental Histórico de Terrenos Nacionales, Ejidos 1.24 (26) no. 19 (1888).

50. AGN, Ramo Buscas, vol. 17, exp. 68 (13 November 1888). The following documents were located: Ramo Tierras, vol. 971, exp. 4, ff. 1–34 (1773–74); Ramo Tierras, vol. 1048, exp. 9, ff. 1–8 (1779); Ramo Tierras, vol. 1225, exp. 16, ff. 1–27 (1787–92); Ramo Tierras, exp. 3, f. 376v. (sic); and Ramo Mercedes, exp. 82, ff. 149–50 (1778).

51. AGN, Ramo Buscas, vol. 17 exp. 68 (24 November 1888; 7 March 1889); also, vol. 18, exp. 39 (27 March 1889).

52. For 1871, Blázquez Domínguez, *Estado de Veracruz: Informes de sus Gobernadores*, 2:1108–12, and exp. 47 (tables opposite p. 1144); for 1885, 5:2609, 2622–29. Numerous "cooks" and "domestic servants" were not included in the "males with listed jobs" category for 1885, since most were in all likelihood women.

53. For 1885, Blázquez Domínguez, *Estado de Veracruz: Informes de sus Gobernadores*, 5:2622–29.

54. M. Sánchez, "Memoria que rinde el Jefe Político del Cantón de Papantla . . . 24 de junio de 1890," 319 (in García Morales, *Memorias e informes*).

CHAPTER SIX

1. Fontecilla, *Informes de Agapito Fontecilla al C. Ministro de Fomento*, 11.

2. *OPDR* 42 (28 November 1892): 7; *OPDR* 47 (1 April 1895): 6; *OPDR* 48 (11 November 1895): 5; *OPDR* 53 (14 February 1895): 14; also, Noble and Lebrija, "La sequía en México y su previsión," 145.

3. "Vanilla Bean Predictions Realized," *OPDR* 42 (28 November 1892): 7.

4. "The Position of Vanilla Beans," *OPDR* 47 (1 April 1895): 6.

5. For 1889–90 through 1892–93, Secretaría de Estado y del Despacho de Hacienda y Crédito Público, *Exportaciones . . . (1889–90/1892–93)*; for 1893–94 through 1895–96, Secretaría de Estado y del Despacho de Hacienda y Crédito Público, *Estadística fiscal . . . (1893–94/1895–96)*; for 1896–97 through 1897–98, Secretaría de Estado y del Despacho de Hacienda y Crédito Público, *Comercio exterior . . . (1896–97/1897–98)*; for 1898–99 through 1899–1900, Secretaría de Estado y del Despacho de Hacienda y Crédito Público, *Comercio exterior y navegación . . . (1898–99/1899–1900)*; and for 1900–01 through 1909–10, Secretaría de Estado y del Despacho de Hacienda y Crédito Público, *Boletín de estadística fiscal*.

6. "The Outlook for Vanilla Beans," *OPDR* 48 (11 November 1895): 5.

7. "A Circular from Mexican Shippers of Vanilla Beans," *OPDR* 53 (14 February 1898): 14.

8. *Consular Reports: Commerce, Manufactures, Etc.*, vol. 60, no. 226 (July 1899): 583. The consul was correcting U.S. newspaper reports suggesting that all of the plants had been destroyed.

9. Kaerger, *Agricultura y colonización en México en 1900*, 136–37. See also "El cultivo de la vainilla," *PO*, 12 August 1899; and López y Parra, *La vainilla*, 62ff. López y Parra's text reflects the debates—and the anxieties—generated by the

spread of artificial pollination after 1900. "Let us hope," he wrote, "that the artificial fecundation of vanilla never becomes dominant among us [in Mexico]" (p. 65).

10. See, e.g., "The Position of Vanilla Beans," *OPDR* 53 (14 February 1898): 5.

11. "The Unusual Status of Vanilla Beans," *OPDR* 78 (26 December 1910): 8.

12. "Vanilla Bean Prospects," *OPDR* 39 (1 April 1891): 6.

13. New York prices were obtained from a survey of numerous *OPDR* issues published between 1890 and 1910; for 1899–1910 some of the data are collected in *OPDR* 78 (26 December 1910): 9. Whole bean price figures for 1893 and the high price for 1900 could not be obtained. *Picadura* prices for 1891 and 1893 could not be located.

14. "The Position of Vanilla Beans," *OPDR* 47 (1 April 1895): 6.

15. "The Outlook for Vanilla Beans," *OPDR* 48 (11 November 1895): 5.

16. "The Position of Vanilla Beans," and "A Circular from Mexican Shippers of Vanilla Beans," *OPDR* 53 (14 February 1898): 5 and 14, respectively.

17. See, e.g., *OPDR* 70 (10 September 1906); *OPDR* 70 (15 September 1906); and *OPDR* 71 (3 June 1907).

18. INEGI, *Estadísticas históricas de México*, 2:854–55.

19. Blázquez Domínguez, *Estado de Veracruz: Informes de sus Gobernadores*, 5:2767–70.

20. Preamble to the governor's bill, in Blázquez Domínguez, *Estado de Veracruz: Informes de sus Gobernadores*, 7:3876–81; also, CPD, 17:486–88 (27 January 1892).

21. For a partial accounting, see Blázquez Domínguez, *Estado de Veracruz: Informes de sus Gobernadores*, 8:4278–94 (for 1894), and 9:4653–67 (for 1896).

22. Scholars have attributed great importance to the federal circulars of 28 October 1889 and 12 May 1890, arguing that these led directly to a rash of subdivisions. But in Veracruz most of the provisions of Fomento's circulars had already been included in the law of July 1889. For a discussion of the confused relationship between federal and state disentailment regulations issued during these years (including the crucial question of who had the right to issue new property titles), see CPD, 14:9249, 9416, 12386–89 (September–November 1889). For the text of the federal circulars, see de la Maza, *Código de colonización y terrenos baldíos de la República Mexicana*. See also Phipps, "Some Aspects of the Agrarian Question in Mexico," 113ff; Simpson, *The Ejido*, 29–30; Whetten, *Rural Mexico*, 86; and Valadés, *El porfirismo*, 1:276–77.

23. For instance, Victoria Chenaut states that the subdivision of the *condueñazgos* was "the direct result of legislation enacted by the state government" (Chenaut, "Fin de siglo en la costa totonaca," 111–12 n. 10). Likewise, José Velasco Toro argues that during Enríquez's tenure, "it was ordered that the *condueñazgos* be divided into individual lots"; the law of 1889, he asserts, made this obligatory ("Indigenismo y rebelión totonaca de Papantla," 95; also, Velasco Toro, "La política desamortizadora y sus efectos en la región de Papantla," 148). See also Florescano, "El proceso de destrucción de la propiedad comunal," 13–14, and Chenaut, "Comunidad y ley en Papantla a fines del siglo XIX," 78–79.

24. For 1882, Blázquez Domínguez, *Estado de Veracruz: Informes de sus Gobernadores*, 8:4287; see also ibid., 4:2089.

25. ACAM, no. 14 (Papantla); also, DRTP, Ejido.

26. See, e.g., Decree No. 5 of 9 June 1894, in Blázquez Domínguez and Corzo Ramírez, *Colección de leyes.*

27. AGEV—Gobernación y Justicia, caja 11 (Ingenieros militares, 1905): Informe de Ignacio Muñoz, 17 December 1894; this report is also excerpted in Blázquez Domínguez, *Estado de Veracruz: Informes de sus Gobernadores,* 9:4661ff.

28. See, e.g., CPD, 16:7733–34 (4 July 1891).

29. For 1890, see "Memoria[del] Jefe Político del Cantón de Papantla," *PO,* 9 June 1891, and 11 June 1891. For 1891, see *PO,* 17 March 1892; Blázquez Domínguez, *Estado de Veracruz: Informes de sus Gobernadores,* 8:3965, 3967; *PO,* 12 December 1891; and Salas García, *Cachiquín,* 41–54. The church clock was finally purchased and installed in 1895.

Salas García reproduces various documents from the Registro Público de la Propiedad, showing how the railroad company obtained land grants from various *condueñazgos* along the projected route. In November 1893, Papantla's Ayuntamiento and Chamber of Commerce petitioned the government to have the route redrawn so that the railroad would go through the Villa (see Blázquez Domínguez, *Estado de Veracruz: Informes de sus Gobernadores,* 8:4339). It was all for nothing, since the Tecolutla–Espinal road was never completed (it did not get very far), and the Teziutlán–Nautla (after 1898, the Teziutlán–Tecolutla) line was never started. In the end, Teziutlán was as far as the railroad would reach; that line—finally finished around 1901—helped to solidify Teziutlán's domination of the lowland trade. On Romero Rubio's involvement with the *Interoceánico,* see, e.g., Tischendorf, *Great Britain and Mexico in the Era of Porfirio Díaz,* 45 ff; also, more generally, Calderón, "Los Ferrocarriles,"; and Schmidt, *The Social and Economic Effect of the Railroad in Puebla and Veracruz, Mexico, 1876–1911,* ch. 2.

30. AGEV—Gobernación y Justicia, caja 4 (Terrenos, 1894): report from Marcelino Sánchez, no. 5107, 6 May 1889 and 9 May 1889; memo citing Rafael Mendizábal's report, no. 9927, 15 May 1889 and 12 October 1889; and memo from Pedro Coyula to Juan Enríquez, 16 October 1889.

31. See, e.g., ANGZ 1883: nos. 4, 8, 9, 10, 11, 12, 13, 15, 16; 1884: no. 5; 1885: nos. 1, 3, 6, 12, 14; 1886: nos. 3, 5; 1887: nos. 3, 6, 7, 12, 14; 1888: nos. 9, 11, 12; and 1889: no. 4. Similar transactions can also be found in the Registro Público de la Propiedad. On the Colonia San Antonio, see also AGA, Grupo Documental Histórico de Terrenos Nacionales, Diversos 1.29 (26), no. 283 (1883). When Moisés de la Peña visited Gutiérrez Zamora in the 1940s, he was informed that the Italian colonists had obtained their land shares thanks to the intervention of Porfirio Díaz, but the available evidence tells a different story (de la Peña, "Problemas demográficos y agrarios," 218–19).

32. CPD, 14:9249, 9416, 12386–89 (September–November 1889); see also Decree No. 50, 20 November 1890, in Blázquez Domínguez and Corzo Ramírez, *Colección de leyes.*

33. *PO,* 7 June 1890.

34. RPP 1890, nos. 29, 44–46, 60, 66, 73, 78, 79, 92, 94; ANGZ 1890: nos. 3, 6–8, 19, 20, 21, 24, 43.

35. *PO,* 11 September 1890.

36. "Memoria[del] Jefe Político del Cantón de Papantla," *PO*, 11 June 1891.

37. AGEV, Gobernación—Tierras, caja 9, no. 12–13–24/1890, letter from Marcelino Sánchez to Sección de Fomento, December 1890.

38. AGEV—Gobernación y Justicia, caja 5 (Terrenos, 1896): Angel Lucido Cambas to Secretario de Gobierno, 6 September 1892; telegram from Víctor Assenato to Juan Enríquez, 17 February 1892; also, Blázquez Domínguez, *Estado de Veracruz: Informes de sus Gobernadores*, 8:4289–90. Zozocolco's *lotes* were also privatized in the early 1890s; Alejandro Coiffier was the surveyor in charge.

39. AGEV—Gobernación y Justicia, caja 5 (Terrenos, 1896): "Padrón formado por la Administración de Rentas de Papantla con motivo del fraccionamiento individual en los lotes denominados 'El Cristo' y 'Palo Hueco' de la jurisdicción de Gutiérrez Zamora," 19 July 1892. For title registrations, see RPP 1890–1892.

40. "Memoria[del] Jefe Político del Cantón de Papantla," *PO*, 18 June 1891. The "coffee & tobacco (total—production)" row is a composite: for 1887 it shows total revenues under Decree No. 66, all of which went to the State Treasury; for 1888–90 it calculates total revenues under Decree No. 52, of which 8 percent was kept by the municipal treasurers, and 20 percent of the rest (listed therein) belonged to the state. A full explanation of these laws is provided in Chapter 5.

41. *MR*, 21 February 1890, 2.

42. See, e.g., *PO*, 16 June 1891.

43. *OPDR* 39 (1 April 1891): 6.

44. *PO*, 21 July 1891.

45. DRTP, Ejido. The contract was signed on 5 August 1890.

46. Veracruz State Circular No. 26, 11 August 1890, in Blázquez Domínguez and Corzo Ramírez, *Colección de leyes*.

47. "Memoria[del] Jefe Político del Cantón de Papantla," *PO*, 9 June 1891; the *Memoria* was dated 1 April 1891.

48. DRTP, Tlahuanapa; and DRTP, Chote y Mesillas: annotated *condueñazgo* certificate belonging to Francisco Pérez Zepeta, 17 June 1887; and notarized sale thereof, 5 April 1890.

49. CPD, 10:11762, 11796–97 (December 1885); 11:4583 (11 May 1886); 15:10807 (26 July 1890) and 10922 (30 August 1890); 21:20917 (21 December 1896); also, AGN, Ramo Buscas, vol. 19, exp. 74 (1 July 1890). On the Sonora Commission, see Hu-DeHart, *Yaqui Resistance and Survival*, 120ff.

50. Aboites Aguilar and Morales Cosme, "Amecameca, 1922," 69–71; also, CPD, 21:20917 (21 December 1896).

51. See de la Maza, *Código de colonización y terrenos baldíos de la República Mexicana*; also, Secretaría de Agricultura y Fomento, *Colección de leyes . . . del año de 1863 a 1943*. A precise definition of public-land categories can be found in the text of the public land law of 26 March 1894, Articles 1–5, in Villamar, *Las leyes federales vigentes*. For a general discussion of the implementation of the public-land laws and a detailed study of the activities of private survey companies in other parts of Mexico, see Holden, *Mexico and the Survey of Public Lands*.

52. Holden, *Mexico and the Survey of Public Lands*, 28–29; also, *MR*, 25 June 1891 and 11 July 1891.

53. CPD, 16:16017 (15 December 1891) and 16018 (18 December 1891);

21:20917 (21 December 1896); also, Aboites Aguilar and Morales Cosme, "Ame-cameca, 1922," 70. On Julio López's rebellion, see, e.g., Reina, *Las rebeliones campesinas en México,* 64–82.

54. CPD, 16:5737 (30 June 1891), 7728–30 (4 July 1891), 7733–34 (4 July 1891), and 7735–37 (18 July 1891); "Los disturbios de Papantla," *MR,* 25 June 1891; and "Los sucesos de Papantla," *MR,* 4 July 1891.

55. "Noticias de Papantla," *MR,* 23 July 1891; CPD, 16:5737 (30 June 1891).

56. "Rumores de un levantamiento en Papantla," *MR,* 20 June 1891; "Pueblos sublevados," *MR,* 21 June 1891, which cites a report from Puebla's newspaper, *El Presente;* also, *MR,* 25 June 1891 and 23 July 1891; CPD, 16:6069–71 (June 1891), 6279 (17 June 1891), and 6784 (27 June 1891).

57. Kelly and Palerm, *The Tajín Totonac,* 54 n. 88.

58. *MR,* 4 July 1891, citing the *PO;* also, *MR,* 23 July 1891; AHSDN, Archivo de Cancelados: Expediente personal del extinto Mayor de Infantería Simón Tibur-cio, and Expediente personal del extinto Capitán Primero Pablo Hernández Olmedo.

59. CPD, 16:8057 (6 July 1891), 5737 (30 June 1891), and 7733–34 (4 July 1891).

60. "Los disturbios de Papantla," *MR,* 25 June 1891. The text of the letter raises a number of interesting questions. Although it is dated "Coyuxquihui, June 6," it describes events that did not take place until the third week of June, such as the arrival of the warships carrying federal troops. This suggests that it was not written—or at least not completed—in Papantla. Its language and style of argu-mentation point to Galicia as the likely author. For Díaz's reaction to this letter, see CPD, 16:6277 (27 June 1891).

61. "Los sucesos de Papantla," *MR,* 4 July 1891, citing the *PO.*

62. "Remitido aclaratorio," *MR,* 11 July 1891. A month or so after the letter's publication, a scared Mateo Xochihua was brought before a judge in Papantla to testify about the veracity of the allegations made therein. He was a *labrador* from the *congregación* of Palmar, one of the hotbeds of unrest. Not surprisingly, he de-nied having anything to do with the letter and readily contradicted every one of its assertions. Significantly, however, he did not speak a word of Spanish and did not know how to write (see *PO,* 18 August 1891). Moreover, the prose style of this let-ter bears a striking resemblance to that of the previous one. It is also telling that when Xalapa's letter was published in Mexico City (*MR,* 4 July 1891), a note from Galicia was appended to it, which concluded by saying: "We will see what the Indi-ans of Papantla have to say about all of this."

63. The *Periódico Oficial* would later seek to discredit Xochihua and Malpica's letter with the claim that Galicia was "without a doubt . . . the author of the letter." This was probably true, but the point, while not insignificant, did not in and of it-self disprove any of the letter's concrete allegations. The government also claimed to have a letter from Galicia to the leaders of the uprising asking for $400 pesos in or-der to measure their lands. In all, said the *Periódico,* Galicia had probably received about $1,000 pesos (see *PO,* 14 July 1891).

64. Here, Galicia seems to be using the term *"egidos"* to refer to the *tierras de repartimiento* that became *grandes lotes,* and not to Papantla's rather modest post-

1870s *ejido*. This usage of the word was not common locally and shows the author's unfamiliarity with the organization of land tenure in Papantla.

65. "Remitido aclaratorio," *MR*, 11 July 1891.

66. On vanilla prices, see *PO*, 21 July 1891. Xochihua and Malpica's letter stated that the merchant Emilio Arenal had been fined $300 pesos by the authorities because he had bought some vanilla at $5 pesos per hundred. As it turns out, the fine was imposed by his fellow cartel members, and Arenal ended up not paying it. For Xalapa's response to Galicia's accusations, see *PO*, 14 July 1891; and CPD, 16:7728–30 (4 July 1891). The *Periódico* insisted on the fairness of the state's tax system, arguing that taxes were lower in Veracruz than in most other states in the Republic. As to the land surveys, it reiterated that the *grandes lotes* were private property, and that the *ejidos* (i.e., the one carved out during the first *repartos*) were by law the property of the municipality; there were thus "no *demasías* to claim, and no arrangements to be made with the Ministry of *Fomento*" (*PO*, 14 July 1891).

67. "Los sucesos de Papantla," *PO*, 14 July 1891; "Noticias de Papantla," *MR*, 23 July 1891. See also "Las contribuciones y la instrucción pública en Papantla," *MR*, 17 July 1891, another letter probably written by Galicia.

68. CPD, 16:8270 (13 July 1891), 8271 (22 July 1891), 7735–36 (18 July 1891), 7737 (21 July 1891), 7741 (25 July 1891), and 7742 (19 July 1891).

69. CPD, 16:9675 (8 August 1891) and 12225–28 (15 October 1891); also, AGEV—Gobernación y Justicia, caja 4 (Terrenos, 1894), 21 August 1891 (Galicia's map receipt).

70. CPD, 16:12225–28 (15 October 1891), 16133 (1 December 1891), and 16145 (4 December 1891); also, *PO*, 17 March 1892.

71. "Noticias de Papantla," *MR*, 10 September 1891; Kelly and Palerm, *The Tajín Totonac*, 54 n. 88.

72. "Los sucesos de Papantla," *MR*, 9 October 1891, citing a letter from Papantla published in *El Universal*. The author of the letter is not identified.

73. CPD, 16:16017 (15 December 1891) and 12225–28 (15 October 1891); *MR*, 9 October 1891; AHSDN, Archivo de Cancelados: Expediente personal del extinto Capitán Primero Pablo Hernández Olmedo; and Kelly and Palerm, *The Tajín Totonac*, 54 n. 88.

74. *PO*, 29 September 1891; *MR*, 9 October 1891.

75. CPD, 16:12225–29 (15 October 1891) and 12230–31 (10 October 1891).

76. *PO*, 20 October 1891; CPD, 16:12225–28 (15 October 1891).

77. "Los disturbios en Papantla," *MR*, 6 November 1891.

78. *MR*, 30 October 1891, 10 September 1891, and 28 October 1891; also *PO*, 17 March 1892.

79. "Noticias de Papantla," *MR*, 25 November 1891, citing a piece published in *El Nacional*; "Los presos de Papantla," *MR*, 24 December 1891, quoting an article from Puebla's newspaper *El Presente*; CPD, 16:14396 (26 November 1891).

80. CPD, 16:16017 (15 December 1891) and 16018 (18 December 1891).

81. CPD, 16:14390 (14 November 1891), 14401 (18 November 1891), 16144 (3 December 1891), 14183 (20 November 1891), and 16019 (31 December 1891).

82. *PO*, 14 January 1892.

83. See, e.g., CPD, 19:16961–66 (7 November 1894); also, AGEV—Gober-

nación y Justicia, caja 5 (Terrenos, 1896): Lucido Cambas memo to Gobernación, no. 265, 22 October 1892.

84. *PO*, 11 February 1892, 17 March 1892, 24 March 1892, and 7 April 1892; Blázquez Domínguez, *Estado de Veracruz: Informes de sus Gobernadores*, 8:4290; CPD, 17:477 (4 January 1892); and AGEV—Gobernación y Justicia, caja 5 (Terrenos, 1896): Maraboto to Enríquez, no. 2044, March 1892.

85. AGEV—Gobernación y Justicia, caja 5 (Terrenos, 1896): Lucido Cambas memo to Gobernación, no. 265, 22 October 1892; caja 4 (Visitador Vélez, 1893): Vélez reports, no. 1749, 23 April 1893, and no. 2133, 1 April 1893; also, DRTP, Chote y Mesillas; DRTP, Tlahuanapa; and DRTP, Cerro del Carbón.

86. AGEV—Gobernación y Justicia, caja 5 (Terrenos, 1896): Maraboto to Gobernación, no. 27, 27 January 1892; Manuel Sosa to Enríquez, no. 2044, 11 February 1891 and reply, 20 February 1892; Antonio García to Enríquez, no. 2877, 1 March 1892, and reply, 22 March 1892; Juan Jiménez et al. to Enríquez, no. 2403, 24 February 1892, and reply, 3 March 1892; Maraboto to Enríquez, no. 2044, March 1892; and telegrams from Maraboto to Enríquez, 17 February 1892 and 19 February 1892.

87. AGEV—Gobernación y Justicia, caja 5 (Terrenos, 1896): Maraboto to Enríquez, no. 2044, March 1892.

88. RPP 1888, no. 4; 1889, nos. 56, 72; 1890, no. 82; 1892, nos. 59, 60, 61, 155, 156; 1893, nos. 9, 25; 1902, no. 113; CPD, 19:16965–66 (1894).

89. CPD, 17:3744 (2 March 1892), 5490 (7 April 1892), 5493 (10 April 1892), and 11654–56 (28 January 1893); also, *PO*, 14 June 1892.

90. Olivo Lara, *Biografías de veracruzanos distinguidos*, 350; Pasquel, *Xalapeños distinguidos*, 399–401. Lucido Cambas was acting *jefe político* for two months, after which his appointment was made permanent.

91. AGEV—Gobernación y Justicia, caja 5 (Terrenos, 1896): Lucido Cambas to Gobernación, no. 355, 19 August 1892.

92. CPD, 17:10453 (26 July 1892), 12320 (29 July 1892), 12324 (10 August 1892), 12338 (18 August 1892), 12340 (22 August 1892), 12341 (20 August 1892), 13762–63 (29 August 1892), 14047 (22 August 1892), and 11657 (20 July 1892).

93. CPD, 17:13765–66 (13 August 1892) and 13763–64 (29 August 1892).

94. AGEV—Gobernación y Justicia, caja 5 (Terrenos, 1896): Lucido Cambas to Gobernación, no. 355, 19 August 1892; Lucido Cambas to Gobernación, no. 810, 6 September 1892; Lucido Cambas to Gobernación, no. 1254, 29 October 1892; Lucido Cambas to Gobernación, no. 1674, 1 December 1892; Huerta to Dehesa, no. 55, 24 December 1892; and Lucido Cambas to Gobernación, no. 63, 26 December 1892.

95. AGEV—Gobernación y Justicia, caja 5 (Terrenos, 1896): Lucido Cambas to Gobernación, no. 265, 22 October 1892; caja 4 (Visitador Vélez, 1893): Gobernación to Dehesa, no. 1003, 6 March 1893. Also, CPD, 17:11664 (12 November 1892), 11672 (30 September 1892), 15434 (27 October 1892), 16478–79 (27 October 1892), 17265–68 (29 November 1892), 17026 (29 November 1892), 17901 (15 November 1892), 19076 (6 December 1892), 19082 (15 December 1892), 19083 (21 December 1893), 19084–85 (17 December 1892), and 19146 (19 December 1892).

96. CPD, 17:13998 (5 September 1892), 17201–02 (7 November 1892), 19088 (20 December 1892), 18641 (13 December 1892), and 11673 (13 December 1892).

97. CPD, 17:11665 (1 January 1893), 11666 (12 January 1893), 11667 (17 January 1893), 11654–56 (28 January 1893), 19096 (28 December 1892), and 19097 (31 December 1892); "Disturbios en Papantla," *MR*, 2 February 1893, citing a story that appeared in Puebla's newspaper *El Presente* (31 January 1893); "El orden público en Papantla," *MR*, 8 February 1893, printing a response from the *PO*; "Revuelta en Papantla," *MR*, 9 February 1893, citing the *Eco Popular*; "Revuelta en Papantla," *MR*, 12 February 1893, quoting *El Demócrata*; "Más sobre Papantla," *MR*, 17 February 1893; "El secretario del Ayuntamiento en Papantla," *PO*, 16 February 1893; "Sobre Papantla," *PO*, 18 February 1893, citing *El Diario del Hogar* and *El Monitor Republicano*; and CPD, 18:4175 (11 March 1893).

98. CPD, 18:4187 (23 March 1893), 4188 (25 March 1893), 7447 (10 May 1893), and 7492–93 (29 May 1893); RPP 1893, nos. 25, 69, 114; and AHSDN, Archivo de Cancelados: Expediente personal del extinto Mayor de Infantería Simón Tiburcio.

99. AGEV—Gobernación y Justicia, caja 5 (Terrenos, 1896): State Treasurer to Dehesa, no. 886, 23 February 1893; Lucido Cambas to Gobernación, no. 90, 21 March 1893; caja 4 (Consulta, 1894): Arturo Nuñez to Dehesa, no. 1760, 5 July 1894; caja 4 (Visitador Vélez, 1893): Lucido Cambas to Gobernación, no. 1346, 23 February 1893; Gobernación to Vélez, no. 1519, 11 April 1893 and 14 April 1893; Lucido Cambas to Gobernación, no. 115, 19 April 1893; Vélez to Gobernación, no. 1682, 19 April 1893; Vélez to Gobernación, no. 1749, 23 April 1893; Vélez to Gobernación, no. 2133, 1 May 1893; Vélez to Gobernación, no. 2134, 6 May 1893; Vélez to Gobernación, no. 2135, 14 May 1893; Gobernación to Lucido Cambas, no. 2135, 26 May 1893; Vélez to Gobernación, no. 156, 2 June 1893; Vélez to Gobernación, 20 May 1893; Vélez to Gobernación, no. 2284, 27 May 1893; Vélez to Gobernación, no. 197, 5 July 1893; caja 5 (Terrenos, 1896): Lucido Cambas to Gobernación, 5 August 1895. Also, DRTP, Cazones y Migueles, and Sombrerete, Caristay y Aguacate: Actas generales del reparto individual, July 1893 and July 1895.

100. CPD, 18:6661–62 (6 May 1893), 6931 (9 June 1893), 7638–40 (7 June 1893), and 17019 (30 October 1893); 21:5389 (25 April 1896) and 9956 (30 May 1896); AGEV—Gobernación y Justicia, caja 4 (Visitador Vélez, 1893): Tribunal Superior to Dehesa, 30 May 1893; Vélez to Gobernación, 3 June 1893; Vélez to Gobernación, no. 2395, 3 June 1893; Vélez to Gobernación, 10 June 1893; Vélez to Gobernación, no. 2642, 17 June 1893; Vélez to Gobernación, no. 2651, 24 June 1893; Vélez to Gobernación, no. 2766, 1 July 1893; Vélez to Gobernación, 8 July 1893; Vélez to Gobernación, no. 1473, 15 July 1893. Also, DRTP, Tlahuanapa: Registro de *condueños*, 15 August 1893, and Acta general de división, March 1894.

101. CPD, 18:13851 (23 September 1893), 14552–53 (14 October 1893), and 14554 (18 October 1893).

102. AGEV–Gobernación y Justicia, caja 11 (Ingenieros militares, 1905): Lucido Cambas to Gobernación, no. 541, 26 October 1895; also, Blázquez Domínguez, *Estado de Veracruz: Informes de sus Gobernadores*, 9:4663–64.

103. CPD, 18:6690–91 (22 May 1893) and 448 (9 January 1893); 17:11654–56 (28 January 1893), 17201 (7 November 1892), and 19422 (1 December 1892).

104. CPD, 18:14552–53 (14 October 1893), 16807 (13 November 1893), and 16808 (4 November 1893).

105. AGEV—Gobernación y Justicia, caja 4 (Consulta, 1894): Dehesa to Legislature, no. 2138, 9 December 1893; Arturo Nuñez to Dehesa, no. 1760, 5 July 1894; Gobernación to Lucido Cambas, no. 1760, 19 July 1894. Also, DRTP, Chote y Mesillas: Acta de división individual, 29 January 1894; DRTP, Tlahuanapa: Acta general de división, 20 March 1894.

Decree No. 48 of 27 December 1894 brought back the "incentives" offered by Decree No. 50, including municipal titles. Under the new law (which did not impose any deadlines), ex-*condueñazgo* properties valued at under $200 pesos were exempted from the Registro Público fee. Now, however, every property title—regardless of the value it represented—would have to be registered.

106. Ley sobre ocupación y enajenación de terrenos baldíos (26 March 1894), in Villamar, *Las leyes federales vigentes*; PO, 13 September 1894; AGA, Grupo Documental Histórico de Terrenos Nacionales, Baldíos 1.29 (26), no. 153 (1894); and Diversos 1.29 (26), no. 300 (1894); CPD, 19:14481 (22 September 1894), 14497 (27 September 1894), and 16119–21 (28 September 1894).

107. CPD, 19:15362–63 (3 October 1894), 15492 (28 October 1894), and 16195–97 (27 October 1894).

108. CPD, 19:16961–66 (7 November 1894), 17008–11 (25 November 1894), 17012–14 (15 November 1894), 17015–37 (November 1894), 17529 (10 November 1894), 18162 (12 November 1894), 19722–23 (3 December 1894), 19019–20 (17 December 1894), 20024–25 (18 December 1894), and 20038–41 (22 December 1894); 20: 264 (22 January 1895), 282 (7 January 1895), and 5273–74 (16 March 1895); also, AGA, Grupo Documental Histórico de Terrenos Nacionales, Diversos 1.29 (26), no. 300 (1894); and AGEV–Gobernación y Justicia, caja 11 (Ingenieros militares, 1905): Informe de Ignacio Muñoz, 17 December 1894.

109. *MR*, 11 August 1895; CPD, 20:264 (22 January 1895), 1437 (18 January 1895), 5273 (16 March 1895), 5274 (7 February 1895), 9756 (3 June 1895), and 10060 (22 May 1895); DRTP, Tlahuanapa: Acta de conformidad, 21 January 1895; Furber, *I Took Chances*, 93–94; AGEV–Gobernación y Justicia, caja 11 (Ingenieros militares, 1905): Pedro Tremari to Subregidor de Aguacate, no. 410, 19 June 1895; also, DRTP, Chote y Mesillas: Acta de conformidad, 5 July 1895; DRTP, Cazones and Sombrerete: Acta general de reparto, 10 July 1895; and Blázquez Domínguez, *Estado de Veracruz: Informes de sus Gobernadores*, 9:4663–64.

110. AGEV–Gobernación y Justicia, caja 5 (Terrenos, 1896): Lucido Cambas to Gobernación, 5 August 1895.

111. AGEV–Gobernación y Justicia, caja 11 (Ingenieros militares, 1905): Mateo Morales et al. to Dehesa, no. 2267, 13 July 1895; Lucido Cambas to Gobernación, no. 2478, 2 August 1895; and Gobernación to Mateo Morales et al., 8 August 1895.

112. AGEV–Gobernación y Justicia, caja 11 (Ingenieros militares, 1905): Gobernación to Dehesa, no. 2120, 3 July 1895; Dehesa to Minister of War, 4 July 1895; Gobernación to Ignacio Muñoz, 19 August 1895; Gobernación to Lucido Cambas, *reparto* instructions, no. 3144, 7 October 1895. Also, CPD, 20:11295 (9

July 1895) and 11296 (12 July 1895); Blázquez Domínguez, *Estado de Veracruz: Informes de sus Gobernadores*, 9:4663; and *MR*, 11 August 1895.

113. AGEV–Gobernación y Justicia, caja 11 (Ingenieros militares, 1905): Lucido Cambas to Gobernación, no. 537, 24 October 1895; Lucido Cambas to Gobernación, 26 October 1895; Benigno Rivera to Ignacio Muñoz, 18 November 1895; Gobernación to Lucido Cambas, no. 3574, 21 November 1895; Lucido Cambas to Gobernación, no. 603, 30 November 1895. Also, DRTP, Ojital y Potrero: Acta de conformidad, 26 December 1895; Acta del Ayuntamiento, 16 January 1896; DRTP, Escolín: Acta general de reparto, 18 January 1896; Acta de conformidad, 30 January 1896.

114. DRTP, Escolín: Registro de los accionistas, 24 January 1896; DRTP, Ojital y Potrero: Registro de los accionistas, January 1896.

115. DRTP, Talaxca y Arroyo Colorado: subdivision contract, 23 January 1896; DRTP, Pital y Mozutla: subdivision contract, 27 January 1896. Pital's perimeter map was completed in April 1896. See also Blázquez Domínguez, *Estado de Veracruz: Informes de sus Gobernadores*, 9:4664; DRTP, Cerro del Carbón; and AGEV–Gobernación y Justicia, caja 4 (Consulta, 1894): Lucido Cambas to Gobernación, no. 349, 23 January 1896; Gobernación to Lucido Cambas, 31 January 1896; caja 11 (Ingenieros militares, 1905): Muñoz to Dehesa, no. 1063, 30 March 1896; and Blázquez Domínguez, *Estado de Veracruz: Informes de sus Gobernadores*, 9:4662, 4665.

Around the same time, Muñoz asked Dehesa to modify the package of fiscal incentives offered to shareholders who subdivided their *lotes*, exempting all ex-*condueñazgo* parcel titles from the Registro Público fee regardless of the value of the new properties being registered. Muñoz argued that the current threshold ($200 pesos) was problematic, so it was eliminated (Decree No. 10 of 6 June 1896, in Blázquez Domínguez and Corzo Ramírez, *Colección de leyes*). Large landowners benefited the most (see AGEV–Gobernación y Justicia, caja 11 [Ingenieros militares, 1905]: Muñoz to Dehesa, 5 March 1896; Gobernación to Dehesa, no. 823, 6 March 1896; and Registro Público to Gobernación, no. 937, 14 March 1896).

116. AGEV–Gobernación y Justicia, caja 11 (Ingenieros militares, 1905): Gobernación to Lucido Cambas, no. 3056, 28 September 1895; Mateo Morales et al. to Dehesa, no. 3421, 30 October 1895; Mateo Morales and Fernando Vicente to Dehesa, no. 3695, 27 November 1895.

117. AGEV–Gobernación y Justicia, caja 4 (Consulta, 1894): Mateo Morales et al. to Porfirio Díaz, no. 1247, 31 March 1896; also, CPD, 21:5056–57 (31 March 1896).

118. CPD, 21:5086 (11 April 1896), 5065 (17 April 1896), 5055 (22 April 1896), 5058 (25 April 1896), and 6936–37 (16 May 1896); also, AGEV—Gobernación y Justicia, caja 11 (Ingenieros militares, 1905): Manuel Seguera et al. to Dehesa, 3 June 1896; Manuel Seguera to Dehesa, no. 1738, 4 June 1896; Lucido Cambas to Gobernación, no. 1963, 19 June 1896.

119. CPD, Telegramas: 3236–37 (15 June 1896), 3261 (16 June 1896), and 3320 (20 June 1896); DRTP, Talaxca y Arroyo Colorado; DRTP, Pital y Mozutla; DRTP, Santa Agueda; DRTP, Cerro del Carbón; DRTP, Arroyo Grande de Boca de Lima:

Nombramiento de la Junta Directiva, 8 June 1896; Subdivision contract, 11 June 1896; DRTP, Concha, Aguacate y Totomoxtle: Nombramiento de la Junta Directiva, 25 May 1896; also, *MR*, 10 July 1896; and *OPDR* 53 (14 February 1898): 14.

120. CPD, Telegramas: 3376–78 (24 June 1896), 3450 (26 June 1896), 3500 (28 June 1896), and 3605–08 (1 July 1896); also, "La sublevación de Papantla," *MR*, 10 July 1896; "La revuelta de Papantla," *MR*, 14 July 1896; and Blázquez Domínguez, *Estado de Veracruz: Informes de sus Gobernadores*, 9:4672

121. CPD, Telegramas: 3396–98 (25 June 1896) and 3457 (26 June 1896); AGEV–Gobernación y Justicia, caja 11 (Ingenieros militares, 1905): Muñoz to Dehesa, no. 2301, 4 August 1898; also, Blázquez Domínguez, *Estado de Veracruz: Informes de sus Gobernadores*, 9:4672; "Sobre los disturbios de Papantla," *MR*, 3 July 1896, citing *El Universal*; "La sublevación de Papantla," *MR*, 10 July 1896, quoting from Papantla's *El Oriente* (7/1/1896); and *MR*, 14 July 1896 and 23 July 1896.

122. CPD, Telegramas: 3572 (30 June 1896); *MR*, 10 July 1896 and 14 July 1896.

123. CPD, Telegramas: 3376–78 (24 June 1896) and 3500 (28 June 1896); AHSDN, Archivo de Cancelados: Expediente personal del extinto Capitán Primero Pablo Hernández Olmedo; and Expediente personal del extinto Capitán Primero Antonio Jiménez; also, Blázquez Domínguez, *Estado de Veracruz: Informes de sus Gobernadores*, 9:4672–73; "Disturbios en Veracruz," *MR*, 1 July 1896; "Sobre los disturbios en Veracruz," *MR*, 2 July 1896; and *MR*, 3 July 1896 and 10 July 1896.

124. CPD, Telegramas: 3605–08 (1 July 1896), 3609 (1 July 1896), and 3679–80 (2 July 1896); AHSDN, Archivo de Cancelados: Expediente personal del extinto Capitán Primero Pablo Hernández Olmedo; Salas García, *Juu Papantlan*, 203–4, who cites María de la Luz Lafarja's "Gran Señora Mi Ciudad," which reproduces a series of notes on the rebellion of 1896 written by her sister Manuelita; and CPD, 21:11275–77 (14 July 1896). See also Modesto González's recollections in Kelly and Palerm, *The Tajin Totonac*, 54 n. 88. In his biennial report to the state legislature, Governor Dehesa went out of his way to praise these local forces for their role in suppressing the insurrection of other individuals "of the Indian race," citing Jiménez and Hernández Olmedo for their distinguished service.

125. CPD, Telegramas: 3834–35 (13 July 1896), 3872 (15 July 1896), 3941 (17 July 1896), and 3972 (18 July 1896); AHSDN, Archivo de Cancelados: Expediente personal del extinto Capitán Primero Pablo Hernández Olmedo; CPD, 21:11247–48 (21 July 1896); and Salas García, *Juu Papantlan*, 203.

126. CPD, 21:11275–77 (14 July 1896), 11276 (21 July 1896), 12013–15 (16 July 1896), and 11985 (25 July 1896); CPD, Telegramas: 3940 (17 July 1896) and 4209–10 (30 July 1896).

127. CPD, 21:11985 (25 July 1896), 15845 (31 July 1896), 15846 (5 August 1896), and 16713 (19 October 1896); AHSDN, Archivo de Cancelados: Expediente personal del extinto Capitán Primero Pablo Hernández Olmedo; and Expediente personal del extinto Capitán Primero Antonio Jiménez; also, Blázquez Domínguez, *Estado de Veracruz: Informes de sus Gobernadores*, 9:4672–73; "Los asuntos de Papantla," *MR*, 21 July 1896, citing *El Nacional*; "Consignación del Ingeniero Galicia a Veracruz," *MR*, 25 July 1896; "De Veracruz," *MR*, 2 August 1896; "Los

sublevados de Papantla," *MR*, 14 August 1896, citing *El Universal*; and "Llegada del 4to batallón," *MR*, 15 August 1896.

128. CPD, Telegramas: 4209–10 (30 July 1896), 4280 (3 August 1896), and 4341 (8 August 1896); AHSDN, Archivo de Cancelados: Expediente personal del extinto Capitán Primero Pablo Hernández Olmedo; DRTP, Poza Larga y Cazuelas: Nombramiento de la Junta Directiva y Contrato, 19 August 1896; DRTP, Pital y Mozutla: Registro general de los condueños and Acta de conformidad, 28 August 1896; DRTP, Talaxca y Arroyo Colorado: Acta de conformidad, 25 August 1896; Registro de los condueños, 28 August 1896; Acta de posesión, 29 August 1896.

129. AHSDN, Archivo de Cancelados: Expediente personal del extinto Mayor de Infantería Simón Tiburcio; Expediente personal del extinto Capitán Primero Pablo Hernández Olmedo; and Expediente personal del extinto Capitán Primero Antonio Jiménez; also, Camp, *Mexican Political Biographies, 1884–1934*, 124; AGEV–Gobernación y Justicia, caja 11 (Ingenieros militares, 1905): Guillermo Vélez to Gobernación, no. 3315, 3 September 1901; also, CPD, 21:17635–66 (5 October 1896), 13771 (6 August 1896), 13641 (25 August 1896), 17136 (13 October 1896), and 20917 (21 December 1896); CPD, Telegramas: 4417 (12 August 1896); and *MR*, 19 August 1896 and 20 December 1896.

130. DRTP, Arroyo Grande Boca de Lima: Acta de conformidad, 7 March 1897; Acta de posesión, 13 March 1897; Padrón de los condueños, 20 March 1897.

131. DRTP, Santa Agueda: Acta de conformidad and Registro de condueños, 9 March 1897; Acta de posesión, 15 March 1897; DRTP, El Palmar: Acta de conformidad and Padrón de condueños, 14 March 1897; Acta de posesión, 20 March 1897; DRTP, El Cedro: Acta de conformidad, 23 March 1897; Acta de posesión, 3 April 1897; Padrón nominal, 15 April 1897; DRTP, Concha, Aguacate y Totomoxtle: Acta general y Registro, 13 April 1897; Acta de posesión, 29 April 1897; DRTP, Poza Larga y Cazuelas: Acta de conformidad and Registro general, 4 May 1897; Acta de posesión, 12 May 1897; also, AHSDN, Archivo de Cancelados: Expediente personal del extinto Capitán Primero Pablo Hernández Olmedo.

132. DRTP, Polutla, Taracuán y Poza Verde: Acta de conformidad, 19 July 1897; Registro de accionistas, 30 September 1897; DRTP, Carrizal y Volador: Acta de conformidad and Padrón de los condueños, 19 October 1897; Acta de posesión, 23 December 1897.

133. DRTP, Cerro del Carbón: Nombramiento de la junta y contrato, 27 April 1897; Acta de conformidad, 1 March 1898; Padrón, 4 March 1897; Acta de posesión, 7 March 1898.

134. DRTP, *lote* files; ACAM, no. 14 (Papantla). "Actual area" figures are close approximations, since the documents do not always include lands set aside for *fundos legales* and other special uses. For the same reason, the number of parcels listed may not be exact in every case. The figures under "hectares per share" have been rounded off; except in Chote y Mesillas, all parcels in each *lote* were of the same size.

135. AGEV–Gobernación y Justicia, caja 11 (Ingenieros militares, 1905): Muñoz to Dehesa, no. 3102, 11 October 1897; "Noticia de las órdenes que se han dado por el Gobierno a la Tesorería General para ministrar a las Juntas Directivas...cantidades destinadas a gastos de fraccionamiento de terrenos," 18 November 1899;

Guillermo Vélez to Gobernación, no. 2752, 10 July 1901; Rafael Rosas to Gobernación, no. 3043, 20 August 1901; Guillermo Vélez to Gobernación, no. 3315, 13 September 1901; Guillermo Vélez to Gobernación, no. 2335, 26 April 1902; Gobernación to Dehesa, no. 5647, 21 December 1903.

136. AGEV–Gobernación y Justicia, caja 11 (Ingenieros militares, 1905): Muñoz to Dehesa, 10 November 1897; Fernández Leal to Dehesa, no. 3572, 2 December 1897; Muñoz to Dehesa, no. 2301, 4 August 1898; Muñoz to Dehesa, no. 2328, 6 August 1898; caja 6 (El Cedro, 1898): Fernández Leal to Dehesa, no. 2684, 29 August 1898.

EPILOGUE

1. RPP 1912, no. 149; Furber, *I Took Chances*, 93–94, 145; and RPP 1897–1910, passim. Furber's company also bought many ex-communal land parcels from various neighboring *congregaciones* in Papantla and Coatzintla, including Poza Rica.

Bibliography

ARCHIVAL SOURCES

Archivo de la Comisión Agraria Mixta, Xalapa [ACAM]
Archivo de Notarías de Gutiérrez Zamora [ANGZ]
Archivo de Notarías de Papantla, Papantla [ANP]
Archivo General Agrario, Mexico City [AGA]
Archivo General de la Nación, Mexico City [AGN]
Archivo General del Estado de Veracruz, Xalapa [AGEV]
Archivo Histórico, Secretaría de la Defensa Nacional, Mexico City [AHSDN]
Archivo del Juzgado de Papantla, Papantla [AJP]
Colección Porfirio Díaz, Universidad Iberoamericana, Mexico City [CPD]
Documentos sobre el reparto de tierras del pueblo de Papantla, Papantla [DRTP]

This is an extensive collection of original documents detailing the parcelization of Papantla's communal lands. It was kept by Papantla's public notaries since the late nineteenth century, and it was last located in the house of Sr. Rufino Zárate, Papantla's Notario no. 1.

Mapoteca Ing. Antonio García Cubas, Sociedad Mexicana de Geografía y Estadística, Mexico City [SMGE]
Registro Público de la Propiedad, Papantla [RPP]

NEWSPAPERS AND PERIODICALS

Boletín del Archivo General de la Nación [BAGN]
Oil, Paint, and Drug Reporter (New York) [OPDR]
El Monitor Republicano (Mexico City) [MR]
Periódico Oficial del Gobierno del Estado de Veracruz [PO]

OTHER SOURCES

"A Half-Century of Ice Cream Technology." Ice Cream Trade Journal 51 (June 1955): 52–54.
Aboites Aguilar, Luis, and Alba Morales Cosme. "Amecameca, 1922: Ensayo sobre centralización política y estado nacional en México." Historia Mexicana 49, no. 1 (1999): 55–93.
Acosta, José de. Historia natural y moral de las Indias. Mexico, D.F.: FCE, 1985.
Alatorre, Ignacio. Reseña de los acontecimientos ocurridos en las líneas del norte y del centro del estado de Veracruz en los años de 1863 a 1867. Veracruz, 1868.
Alcocer, Ignacio. "Las comidas de los antiguos mexicanos." In Historia general de las cosas de Nueva España, Bernardino de Sahagún, 5 vols. Mexico, D.F.: Pedro Robredo, 1938.

————. "Consideraciones sobre la medicina azteca." In *Historia general de las cosas de Nueva España*, Bernardino de Sahagún, 5 vols. Mexico, D.F.: Pedro Robredo, 1938.

Alonso, Ana María. *Thread of Blood: Colonialism, Revolution, and Gender on Mexico's Northern Frontier*. Tucson: University of Arizona Press, 1995.

Archer, Christon I. *The Army in Bourbon Mexico, 1760–1810*. Albuquerque: University of New Mexico Press, 1977.

Armillas, Pedro. "Notas sobre sistemas de cultivo en Mesoamerica: Cultivos de riego y humedad en la cuenca del río de las Balsas." *Anales del Instituto Nacional de Antropología e Historia* 3 (1949): 85–113.

Aschmann, Herman P. *Diccionario totonaco de Papantla, Veracruz: Castellano–Totonaco, Totonaco–Castellano*. Mexico, D.F.: Instituto Lingüistico de Verano, 1973.

Barba, R., et al. "Prácticas de los alumnos de la Escuela N. de Agricultura sobre algunos cultivos tropicales en el Estado de Veracruz." In Vol. 37 of Secretaría de Fomento, Colonización e Industria, *Informes y documentos relativos a comercio interior y exterior: Agricultura, minería e industrias*. Mexico, D.F.: Secretaría de Fomento, Colonización e Industria, 1888.

Bausa, José María. "Bosquejo geográfico y estadístico del Partido de Papantla (1845)." *Boletín de la Sociedad Mexicana de Geografía y Estadística* 5, 1st ser. (1857): 374–427.

Beard, John S. "The Savanna Vegetation of Northern Tropical America." *Ecological Monographs* 23, no. 2 (1953).

Belmonte Guzmán, María de la Luz. *La organización territorial de Veracruz en el siglo XIX*. Xalapa: Universidad Veracruzana, 1987.

Bernal, Ignacio, and Eusebio Dávalos Hurtado, eds. *Huastecos, totonacos y sus vecinos*. Mexico, D.F.: Sociedad Mexicana de Antropología, 1953.

Berninger, Dieter. *La inmigración en México, 1821–1857*. Mexico, D.F.: SEP, 1974.

Bernot, Carlos Ernesto. "Datos sobre la colonización de Jicaltepec—San Rafael." Unpublished manuscript, 1970.

Blázquez Domínguez, Carmen, ed. *Estado de Veracruz: Informes de sus Gobernadores, 1826–1986*. 22 vols. Xalapa: Gobierno del Estado de Veracruz, 1986.

Blázquez Domínguez, Carmen, and Ricardo Corzo Ramírez, eds. *Colección de leyes y decretos de Veracruz, 1824–1919*. 15 vols. Xalapa: Universidad Veracruzana, 1997.

Blázquez Domínguez, Carmen, and Emilio Gidi Villarreal. *El poder legislativo en Veracruz, 1824–1917*. Xalapa: Gobierno del Estado de Veracruz, 1992.

Bourgaux, Albert. *Quatre siécles d'histoire du cacao et du chocolat*. Brussels, 1935.

Bouriquet, Gilbert. *Le vanillier et la vanille dans le monde*. Vol. 46, *Encyclopédie Biologique*. Paris: Editions P. Lechevaner, 1954.

Brady, Nyle C. *The Nature and Properties of Soils*. 8th ed. New York: Macmillan, 1974.

Bravo Marentes, Carlos, ed. *Arierros somos . . . : El sistema de arriería de la Sierra Norte de Puebla*. Mexico, D.F.: Dirección General de Culturas Populares, 1988.

Brillat-Savarin, Jean Anthelme. *The Physiology of Taste, or Meditations on Tran-*

scendental Gastronomy. Translated by M. F. K. Fisher. San Francisco: North Point Press, 1986.

Brinsmade, Robert B. *El latifundismo mexicano: Su origen y su remedio.* Mexico, D.F.: Secretaría de Fomento, 1916.

Brown, Jonathan C. *Oil and Revolution in Mexico.* Berkeley: University of California Press, 1993.

Bruggemann, Jürgen K. "Análisis urbano del sitio arqueológico del Tajín." In *Proyecto Tajín,* edited by J. K. Bruggemann. Mexico, D.F.: Instituto Nacional de Antropología e Historia, 1991.

Bruman, Henry. "The Culture History of Mexican Vanilla." *Hispanic American Historical Review* 28, no. 3 (1948): 360–76.

Bungener, L. *History of the Council of Trent.* New York: Harper, 1855.

Buzell, Frank. "Origin and Development of the Ice Cream Industry." *The Ice Cream Trade Journal* 5 (1909).

Calderón, Francisco. "Los Ferrocarriles." In *"El Porfiriato: Vida Económica, vol. 1,"* in *Historia moderna de México,* edited by Daniel Cosío Villegas. Mexico, D.F.: Editorial Hermes, 1965.

Camp, Roderic A. *Mexican Political Biographies, 1884–1934.* Austin: University of Texas Press, 1991.

Cárdenas, Juan de. *Problemas y secretos maravillosos de las Indias.* 1591; reprint, Mexico, D.F., 1913.

Carmagnani, Marcello. *Estado y mercado: La economía pública del liberalismo mexicano, 1850–1911.* Mexico, D.F.: El Colegio de México/FCE, 1994.

Carrión, Juan de. *Descripción del pueblo de Gueytlalpan (Zacatlán, Juxupango, Matlaltán y Chila, Papantla), 30 de Mayo de 1581 (Relación de Papantla).* Edited by José García Payón. Xalapa: Universidad Veracruzana, 1965.

Castorena, Guadalupe, and Enrique Florescano, eds. *Análisis histórico de las sequías en México.* Mexico, D.F.: SARH, 1980.

Castro, Rafael de. "Dictamen de la Comisión Especial de Agricultura." *Boletín de la Sociedad Mexicana de Geografía y Estadística* 12, 1st ser. (1866).

Chalot, Charles. *Culture et préparation de la vanille.* Paris: É. Larose, 1920.

Chang, Jen-Hu. "Agroclimatology." In *The Encyclopedia of Climatology,* edited by John E. Oliver and Rhodes W. Fairbridge. New York: Van Nostrand Reinhold, 1987.

———. *Climate and Agriculture: An Ecological Survey.* Chicago: Aldine, 1968.

Chenaut, Victoria. *Aquellos que vuelan: Los Totonacos en el siglo XIX.* Mexico, D.F.: CIESAS, 1995.

———. "Comunidad y ley en Papantla a fines del siglo XIX." In *La costa totonaca: Cuestiones regionales II,* edited by Luis M. Gatti and Victoria Chenaut. Mexico, D.F.: CIESAS/SEP, 1987.

———. "Costumbres y resistencia étnica: Modalidades entre los totonaca." In *Entre la ley y la costumbre: El derecho consuetudinario indígena en América Latina,* edited by Rodolfo Stavenhagen and Diego Iturralde. Mexico, D.F.: Instituto Indigenista Interamericano, 1990.

———. "Fin de siglo en la costa totonaca: Rebeliones indias y violencia regional,

1891–1896." In *Procesos rurales e historia regional: Sierra y costa totonacas de Veracruz*, edited by Victoria Chenaut. Mexico, D.F.: CIESAS, 1996.

———. "Orden jurídico y comunidad indígena en el Porfiriato." In *Pueblos indígenas ante el derecho*, edited by Victoria Chenaut and María Teresa Sierra. Mexico, D.F.: CEMCA/CIESAS, 1995.

Chowning, Margaret. *Wealth and Power in Provincial Mexico: Michoacán from the Late Colony to the Revolution*. Stanford, Calif.: Stanford University Press, 1999.

Clavijero, Francisco Javier. *Historia Antigua de México*. Edited by Mariano Cuevas. Mexico, D.F.: Porrúa, 1964.

Cline, Howard F. "Civil Congregations of the Indians in New Spain, 1598–1606." *Hispanic American Historical Review* 29, no. 3 (1949): 349–69.

———. *The United States and Mexico*. 1953; reprint, New York: Atheneum, 1963.

Colmenero de Ledesma, Antonio. *Tratado de la naturaleza y calidades del chocolate*. Madrid, 1631.

Conklin, Harold C. *El estudio del cultivo de roza*. Vol. 11, *Estudios y monografías*. Washington, D.C.: Unión Panamericana, 1963.

El conquistador anónimo: Relación de algunas cosas de la Nueva España y de la gran ciudad de Temestitan México. Escrita por un compañero de Hernán Cortés. . . . Mexico, D.F.: Editorial América, 1941.

Consular Reports: Commerce, Manufactures, Etc. 122 vols. Washington, D.C.: Government Printing Office, 1893–1903.

Contreras, Joaquín. "Memoria que rinde el Jefe Político del Cantón de Papantla al C. Gobernador del Estado de Veracruz, 1 de abril de 1891." In *Memorias e informes de jefes políticos y autoridades del régimen porfirista, 1877–1911*, vol. 1, edited by Soledad García Morales and José Velasco Toro. Xalapa: Universidad Veracruzana, 1991.

Contreras Arias, Alfonso. "La función económica del Servicio Meteorológico en la agricultura." In *Los problemas agrícolas de México: Anales de la economía mexicana*, patrocinado por la Secretaría de Acción Agraria del Partido Nacional Revolucionario. Mexico, D.F.: Partido Nacional Revolucionario, 1934.

———. *Mapa de las provincias climatológicas de la República Mexicana*. Mexico, D.F.: Secretaría de Agricultura, 1942.

Correll, Donovan S. "Vanilla—Its Botany, History, Cultivation, and Economic Import." *Economic Botany* 7, no. 4 (1953): 291–358.

———. "Vanilla: Its History, Cultivation and Importance." *Lloydia* 7, no. 3 (1944): 236–64.

Cosío Villegas, Daniel. "El porfiriato: Su historiografía o arte histórico." In *Extremos de América*. Mexico, D.F.: Tezontle, 1949.

———, ed. *Historia moderna de México*. 9 vols. Mexico, D.F.: Editorial Hermes, 1955–72.

Cossío, José L. *¿Cómo y por quienes se ha monopolizado la propiedad rústica en México?* Mexico, D.F., 1911.

Council of Trent. *The Canons and Decrees of the Council of Trent*. Literally translated into English by Theodore Alois Buckley. London, 1851.

———. *El sacrosanto y ecuménico Concilio de Trento*. Madrid, 1787.

Crespo, Horacio, "Los pueblos de Morelos: La comunidad agraria, la desamortización liberal en Morelos y una fuente para el estudio de la diferenciación social campesina." In *Estudios sobre el zapatismo*, edited by Laura Espejel. Mexico, D.F.: INAH, 2000.

Crespo, Horacio, Luis Aráoz, and Brígida von Mentz, eds. *Morelos: Cinco siglos de historia regional*. Cuernavaca: CEHAM/Universidad Autónoma del Estado de Morelos, 1984.

Crosby, Alfred W., Jr. *The Columbian Exchange: Biological and Cultural Consequences of 1492*. Westport, Ct.: Greenwood, 1972.

Cruz León, Artemio. *Los instrumentos agrícolas en la zona central de Veracruz*. Mexico, D.F.: Universidad Autónoma de Chapingo, 1989.

Dahlgren, Barbro. *La grana cochinilla*. Mexico, D.F.: Porrúa, 1963.

Dampier, William. *Dampier's Voyages*. 22 vols. London, 1906.

Darwin, Charles. *The Effects of Cross and Self Fertilization in the Vegetable Kingdom*. 2nd ed. London: J. Murray, 1878.

———. *The Various Contrivances by which Orchids are Fertilized by Insects*. 2nd ed. rev. London: J. Murray, 1877.

"Datos sobre la producción de vainilla." In Vols. 27 and 28 of Secretaría de Fomento, Colonización e Industria, *Informes y documentos relativos a comercio interior y exterior: Agricultura, minería e industrias*. Mexico, D.F.: Secretaría de Fomento, Colonización e Industria, 1887.

Dávila Padilla, Agustín. *Historia de la fundación y discurso de la provincia de Santiago de Mexico, de la Orden de Predicadores, por las vidas de sus varones insignes, y casos notables de Nueva España*. 1596; reprint, Mexico, D.F.: Editorial Academia Literaria, 1955.

de la Maza, Francisco. *Código de colonización y terrenos baldíos de la República Mexicana: Años de 1451 a 1892*. Mexico, D.F.: Secretaría de Fomento, 1893.

de la Peña, Guillermo. *Herederos de promesas: Agricultura, política y ritual en Los Altos de Morelos*. Mexico, D.F.: CIS/INAH, 1980.

de la Peña, Moisés T. "Problemas demográficos y agrarios." *Problemas agrícolas e industriales de México* 2, no. 3–4 (1950): 9–324.

———. *Veracruz económico*. 2 vols. Mexico, D.F., 1946.

Deans-Smith, Susan. *Bureaucrats, Planters, and Workers: The Making of the Tobacco Monopoly in Bourbon Mexico*. Austin: University of Texas Press, 1992.

Delteil, Arthur. *La vanille: Sa culture et sa préparation*. 5th ed. Paris: A. Challamel, 1902.

Demard, Jean-Christophe. *Aventure extraordinaire d'un village Franc-Comtois au Mexique: Champlitte, Jicaltepec, San Rafael, 1832–1888*. Langres, France: D. Guéniot, 1984.

———. *Jicaltepec, terre d'Argile: Chronique d'un village français au Mexique*. Paris: Editions du Porte-Glaive, 1987.

Desvaux, M. "Quelques notions nouvelles sur les vanilles et la culture de l'espèce commerçable." *Annales des Sciences Naturelles*, 3ème série (Botanique), vol. 6 (1846): 117–23.

Díaz, Lilia, ed. *Versión francesa de México: Informes económicos, 1851–1867*. 2 vols. Mexico, D.F.: Secretaría de Relaciones Exteriores, 1974.

Díaz del Castillo, Bernal. *Historia verdadera de la conquista de la Nueva España.* Madrid: Espasa-Calpe, 1955.

Dictionnaire universel théorique et pratique du commerce et de la navigation. 3rd ed. Paris: Librairie Guillaumin, 1873.

Ducey, Michael T. "From Village Riot to Regional Rebellion: Rural Social Protest in the Huasteca, Mexico, 1760–1870." Ph.D. diss., University of Chicago, 1992.

———. "Liberal Theory and Peasant Practice: Land and Power in Northern Veracruz, Mexico, 1826–1900." In *Liberals, the Church, and Indian Peasants: Corporate Lands and the Challenge of Reform in Nineteenth-Century Spanish America,* edited by Robert H. Jackson. Albuquerque: University of New Mexico Press, 1997.

———. "Tierras comunales y rebeliones en el norte de Veracruz antes del Porfiriato, 1821–1880: El proyecto liberal frustrado." *Anuario (Centro de Investigaciones Históricas, Universidad Veracruzana)* 6 (1989).

———. "Village, Nation, and Constitution: Insurgent Politics in Papantla, 1810–1821." *Hispanic American Historical Review* 79, no. 3 (1999): 463–93.

———. "Viven sin ley ni rey: Rebeliones coloniales en Papantla, 1760–1790." In *Procesos rurales e historia regional: Sierra y costa totonacas de Veracruz,* edited by Victoria Chenaut. Mexico, D.F., 1996.

Edelstein, Ludwig. "Hippocrates of Cos." In *The Encyclopedia of Philosophy,* edited by Paul Edwards. New York: Macmillan, 1967.

Elliot, J. H. *Europe Divided, 1559–1598.* London: Fontana/Collins, 1968.

———. *Imperial Spain, 1469–1716.* New York: St. Martin's, 1963.

Emerson, R. "A Preliminary Survey of the Milpa System of Maize Culture as practiced by the Maya Indians of the Northern Part of the Yucatan Peninsula." *Annals of the Missouri Botanical Garden* 40 (1953): 51–62.

Emmart, Emily W., ed. *The Badianus Manuscript.* Baltimore: Johns Hopkins University Press, 1940.

Escobar Ohmstede, Antonio. "El movimiento olartista: Origen y desarrollo, 1836–1838." In *Procesos rurales e historia regional: Sierra y costa totonacas de Veracruz,* edited by Victoria Chenaut. Mexico, D.F.: CIESAS, 1996.

———, ed. *Indio, nación y comunidad en el México del siglo XIX.* Mexico, D.F.: CEMCA/CIESAS, 1993.

Escobar Ohmstede, Antonio, and Frans Schryer. "Las sociedades agrarias en el norte de Hidalgo, 1856–1900." *Mexican Studies/Estudios Mexicanos* 8, no. 1 (1992): 1–21.

Espejel, Laura, ed. *Estudios sobre el zapatismo.* Mexico, D.F.: INAH, 2000.

Estadísticas económicas del Porfiriato: Comercio exterior de México, 1877–1911. Mexico, D.F.: El Colegio de México, 1960.

Estrada García, Manuel. *Monografía del municipio de Martínez de la Torre, Veracruz.* N.p., 1982.

Falcón, Romana, and Raymond Buve, eds. *Don Porfirio presidente, nunca omnipotente: Hallazgos, reflexiones y debates, 1876–1911.* Mexico, D.F.: Universidad Iberoamericana, 1998.

Farriss, Nancy M. *Maya Society under Colonial Rule: The Collectice Enterprise of Survival.* Princeton, N.J.: Princeton University Press, 1984.

———. "Nucleation versus Dispersal: The Dynamics of Population Movement in Colonial Yucatan." *Hispanic American Historical Review* 58 (1978): 187–216.

Feldkamp, Cora L. "Vanilla: Culture, Processing, and Economics—A List of References." Library List no. 13, U.S. Department of Agriculture Library. Washington, 1945.

"Fifty Years of Ice Cream Freezing." *Ice Cream Trade Journal* 51 (June 1955): 82–84.

Figuier, Louis. *Le savant du foyer, ou notions scientifiques sur les objets usuels de la vie.* Paris: Hachette, 1862.

Flores, Jorge. *La revolución de Olarte en Papantla, 1836–1838.* Mexico, D.F.: Imprenta Mundial, 1938.

Florescano, Enrique. *Precios del maíz y crisis agrícolas en México, 1708–1810.* Mexico, D.F.: El Colegio de México, 1969.

———, ed. *Fuentes para la historia de la crisis agrícola de 1785–1786.* 2 vols. Mexico, D.F.: Archivo General de la Nación, 1981.

Florescano, Enrique, and Isabel Gil Sánchez, eds. *Descripciones económicas regionales de Nueva España: Provincias del Centro, Sudeste y Sur, 1766–1827.* Mexico, D.F.: INAH, 1976.

Florescano, Sergio. "Las divisiones políticas del estado de Veracruz, 1824–1917." *Dualismo* 6, no. 1 (1977): 39–110.

———. "El proceso de destrucción de la propiedad comunal de la tierra y las rebeliones indígenas de Veracruz, 1826–1910." *La Palabra y el Hombre* 52 (October–December 1984): 5–18.

Fontecilla, Agapito. *Breve tratado sobre el cultivo y beneficio de la vainilla.* Mexico, D.F., 1861.

———. *Informes de Agapito Fontecilla al C. Ministro de Fomento.* Mexico, D.F., 1887(?).

Foster, Nelson, and Linda Cordell, eds. *Chilies to Chocolate: Food the Americas Gave the World.* Tucson: University of Arizona Press, 1992.

France. Direction Générale des Douanes. *Tableau des marchandises étrangères importées en France, et des marchandises françaises exportées à l'étranger.* 7 vols. Paris, 1818–24.

———. *Tableau général du commerce de la France avec ses colonies et les pouissances étrangeres.* 71 vols. Paris, 1825–95.

———. *Tableau général du commerce et de la navigation.* 15 vols. Paris, 1896–1910.

Fraser, Donald. "La política de desamortización en las comunidades indígenas, 1856–72." *Historia Mexicana* 21, no. 4 (1972): 615–52.

Friedrich, Paul. *Agrarian Revolt in a Mexican Village.* Englewood Cliffs, N.J.: Prentice-Hall, 1970.

Fuentes y Guzmán, Francisco Antonio de. *Recordación florida: Discurso historial y demostración natural, material, militar y política del Reyno de Guatemala.* 2 vols. Guatemala: Sociedad de Geografía e Historia, 1932–33.

Furber, Percy. *I Took Chances: From Windjammers to Jets.* Leicester: Edgar Backus, 1954.

Galván Rivera, Mariano. *Ordenanzas de tierras y aguas.* Paris: Librería de Rosa y Bouret; Mexico, D.F.: Librería del Portal de Mercaderes, 1855.

Garavaglia, Juan Carlos, and Juan Carlos Grosso. *Las alcabalas novohispanas (1776–1821).* Mexico: AGN/Banca Cremi, 1987.

García, Enriqueta. "Los climas del estado de Veracruz." *Anales del Instituto de Biología—UNAM (Serie Botánica)* 41, no. 1 (1970): 3–42.

García Cubas, Antonio. "Impresiones de un viaje a la sierra de Huauchinango." In *Escritos Diversos de 1870 a 1874.* Mexico, D.F.: Imprenta de I. Escalante, 1874.

———. "Una excursión a tierracaliente: De Teziutlán a Nautla." In *Escritos Diversos de 1870 a 1874.* Mexico, D.F.: Imprenta de I. Escalante, 1874.

García Martínez, Bernardo. "Consideraciones corográficas." In *Historia general de México,* edited by Daniel Cosío Villegas. Mexico, D.F.: El Colegio de México, 1988.

———. *Los pueblos de la sierra: El poder y el espacio entre los indios del norte de Puebla hasta 1700.* Mexico, D.F.: El Colegio de México, 1987.

García Morales, Soledad, "Análisis de la estadística de 1907: Haciendas y hacendados." In *Veracruz: Un tiempo para contar,* edited by Mirna Benítez, Carmen Blázquez, Abel Juárez, and Gema Lozano. Mexico, D.F.: Universidad Veracruzana/INAH, 1989.

García Morales, Soledad, and José Velasco Toro, eds. *Memorias e informes de jefes políticos y autoridades del régimen porfirista, 1877–1911.* 6 vols. Xalapa: Universidad Veracruzana, 1991.

García Rodríguez, Leandro, et al., eds. *El municipio de Gutiérrez Zamora.* Monografías del Estado de Veracruz. Xalapa: CEPES, 1973.

Geiger, Rudolf. *The Climate near the Ground.* Cambridge, Mass.: Harvard University Press, 1965.

Génin, Auguste. *Les français au Mexique: Du XVIe siècle a nos jours.* Paris: Nouvelles Éditions Argo, 1933.

Gerhard, Peter. *Geografía histórica de la Nueva España, 1519–1821.* Translated by Stella Mastrangelo. Mexico, 1986.

———. *A Guide to the Historical Geography of New Spain.* Cambridge: Cambridge University Press, 1972.

Gibson, Charles. *The Aztecs under Spanish Rule.* Stanford, Calif.: Stanford University Press, 1964.

Gómez Pompa, Arturo. *Ecología de la vegetación del estado de Veracruz.* Mexico, D.F.: Cía. Editorial Continental, 1978.

———. "La vegetación de México." *Boletín de la Sociedad Botánica de México* 29 (1965): 76–120.

González de Cossío, Francisco. *Historia de la tenencia y explotación del campo desde la época precortesiana hasta las leyes del 6 de enero de 1915.* Mexico, D.F.: INEHRM, 1957.

González de la Lama, Renée. "Los papeles de Díaz Manfort: Una revuelta popular en Misantla (Veracruz), 1885–1886." *Historia Mexicana* 39, no. 2 (1989): 475–521.

González de la Lama, Renée. "Rebels and Bandits: Popular Discontent and Liberal Modernization in Nineteenth-Century Veracruz, Mexico." Ph.D. diss., University of Chicago, 1990.

González Navarro, Moisés. *La colonización en México, 1877–1910.* Mexico, D.F., 1960.

———. *Los extranjeros en México y los mexicanos en el extranjero, 1821–1970.* 2 vols. Mexico, D.F.: El Colegio de México, 1993–94.

———. "Tenencia de la tierra y población agrícola (1877–1960)." *Historia Mexicana* 19, no. 1 (1969): 62–86.

González Roa, Fernando. *El aspecto agrario de la Revolución Mexicana.* Mexico, D.F.: Dirección de Talleres Gráficos, 1919.

González Roa, Fernando, and José Covarrubias. *El problema rural de México.* Mexico, D.F.: Secretaría de Hacienda, 1917.

Gourou, Pierre. *Les pays tropicaux.* Paris: Presses Universitaires de France, 1947.

Granger, O. E. "Precipitation Distribution." In *The Encyclopedia of Climatology*, edited by John M. Oliver and Rhodes W. Fairbridge. New York, 1987.

Guardino, Peter F. *Peasants, Politics, and the Formation of Mexico's National State: Guerrero, 1800–1857.* Stanford, Calif.: Stanford University Press, 1996.

Guedea, Virginia. *La insurgencia en el Departamento del Norte: Los Llanos de Apán y la Sierra de Puebla, 1810–1816.* Mexico, D.F.: UNAM/Instituto Mora, 1996.

Guerra, François-Xavier. *Le Mexique de l'Ancien Régime à la Révolution.* 2 vols. Paris: L'Harmattan, 1985.

Hale, Charles A. *Mexican Liberalism in the Age of Mora, 1821–1853.* New Haven, Ct.: Yale University Press, 1968.

Halperin, Rhoda, and James Dow, eds. *Peasant Livelihood: Studies in Economic Anthropology and Cultural Ecology.* New York: St. Martin's, 1977.

Hamnett, Brian. *Roots of Insurgency: Mexican Regions, 1750–1824.* Cambridge: Cambridge University Press, 1986.

Haney, Emil B. "The Nature of Shifting Cultivation in Latin America." Land Tenure Center Papers, no. 45. University of Wisconsin, Madison, 1968.

Harrison, Peter D., and B. L. Turner, eds. *Pre-Hispanic Maya Agriculture.* Albuquerque: University of New Mexico Press, 1978.

Haskins, Charles H. *The Renaissance of the Twelfth Century.* Cambridge, Mass.: Harvard University Press, 1927.

Haudricourt, André, and Mariel Jean-Brunhes Delamarre. *L'homme et la charrue à travers le monde.* Paris: Gallimard, 1955.

Hernández, Alicia. *Anenecuilco: Memoria y vida de un pueblo.* Mexico, D.F.: El Colegio de México, 1991.

Hernández, Francisco. *Historia natural de Nueva España.* Vol. 3, *Obras Completas.* 1651; reprint, Mexico, D.F., 1959.

———. *Rerum medicarum Novae Hispaniae thesaurus.* Rome, 1651.

Herrera Canales, Inés. *El comercio exterior de México, 1821–1875.* Mexico, D.F.: UNAM, 1977.

Hester, Joseph A. "Agriculture, Economy, and Population Density of the Maya." *Carnegie Institution Yearbook* 51 and 52 (1951–52).

Hippocrates. *Hippocrates*, with an English translation. Translation by William Henry Samuel Jones and Edward Theodore Withington. 4 vols. Cambridge, Mass.: Harvard University Press, 1948–1953.

Hoffmann, Odile. "Entre mar y sierra: Nacimiento de la región de Martínez de la Torre, Veracruz." In *Las llanuras costeras de Veracruz: La lenta construcción de regiones*, edited by Odile Hoffmann and Emilia Velázquez. Xalapa: ORSTOM/ Universidad Veracruzana, 1994.

Hoffmann, Odile, and Emilia Velázquez, eds. *Las llanuras costeras de Veracruz: La lenta construcción de regiones*. Xalapa: ORSTOM/Universidad Veracruzana, 1994.

Holden, Robert H. *Mexico and the Survey of Public Lands: The Management of Modernization, 1876–1911*. DeKalb: Northern Illinois University Press, 1994.

Hu-DeHart, Evelyn. *Yaqui Resistance and Survival*. Madison: University of Wisconsin Press, 1984.

Humboldt, Alexander von. *Ensayo político sobre el Reino de la Nueva España*. 4th ed. Mexico, D.F.: Porrúa, 1984.

INEGI (Instituto Nacional de Estadística, Geografía e Informática). *Anuario estadístico del estado de Veracruz*. Mexico, D.F.: INEGI, 1991.

———. *Estadísticas históricas de México*. 2 vols. Mexico, D.F.: INEGI, 1990.

———. *Síntesis geográfica, nomenclátor y anexo cartográfico del estado de Veracruz*. Mexico, D.F.: INEGI, 1988.

Jackson, Robert H., ed. *Liberals, the Church, and Indian Peasants: Corporate Lands and the Challenge of Reform in Nineteenth-Century Spanish America*. Albuquerque: University of New Mexico Press, 1997.

Jellicoe, Geoffrey, Susan Jellicoe, Patrick Goode, and Michael Lancaster. *The Oxford Companion to Gardens*. Oxford: Oxford University Press, 1986.

Joseph Burnett Company. *Vanilla and Other Flavoring Extracts*. Boston, n.d.

Kaerger, Karl. *Agricultura y colonización en México en 1900*. Mexico, D.F.: Universidad Autónoma Chapingo/CIESAS, 1986.

Kapp, Bernard. "Les relations économiques extérieures du Mexique (1821–1911) d'après les sources françaises." In *Ville et commerce: Deux essais d'histoire hispano-américaine*, edited by Bernard Kapp and Daniel Herrero. Paris: Klincksieck, 1974.

Katz, Friedrich. "The Liberal Republic and the Porfiriato." In *The Cambridge History of Latin America*, vol. 5, edited by Lelie Bethell. Cambridge: Cambridge University Press, 1986.

———. *The Life and Times of Pancho Villa*. Stanford, Calif.: Stanford University Press, 1998.

———. "Rural Rebellions after 1810." In *Riot, Rebellion, and Revolution: Rural Social Conflict in Mexico*, edited by Friedrich Katz. Princeton, N.J.: Princeton University Press, 1988.

———, ed. *Porfirio Diaz frente al descontento popular regional, 1891–1893: Antología documental*. Mexico, D.F.: Universidad Iberoamericana, 1986.

Kelly, J. N. D. *The Oxford Dictionary of Popes*. Oxford: Oxford University Press, 1986.

Kelly, Isabel, and Angel Palerm. *The Tajin Totonac: Part 1. History, Subsistence, Shelter, and Technology*. Institute of Social Anthropology, Publication no. 13. Washington, D.C.: Smithsonian Institution, 1952.

Kiel, Leopoldo. *El estado de Veracruz.* Mexico, D.F.: Cía. Nacional Editora "Aguilas," 1924.

Knapp, Arthur William. *Cocoa and Chocolate: Their History from Plantation to Consumer.* London: Chapman and Hall, 1920.

Knight, Alan. *The Mexican Revolution.* 2 vols. Cambridge: Cambridge University Press, 1986.

Knowlton, Robert. "La division de las tierras de los pueblos durante el siglo XIX: El caso de Michoacán." *Historia Mexicana* 40, no. 1 (1990): 3–25.

———. "La individualización de la propiedad corporativa civil en el siglo XIX: Notas sobre Jalisco." *Historia Mexicana* 28, no. 1 (1978): 24–61.

Kourí, Emilio H. "El comercio de exportación en Tuxpan, 1870–1900." In *El siglo XIX en las Huastecas,* edited by Antonio Escobar Ohmstede and Luz Carregha. Mexico, D.F.: CIESAS/Colegio de San Luis, 2002.

———. "Interpreting the Expropriation of Indian Pueblo Lands in Porfirian Mexico: The Unexamined Legacies of Andrés Molina Enríquez." *Hispanic American Historical Review* 82, no. 1 (2002): 69–117.

Krickeberg, Walter. *Los Totonaca.* Mexico, D.F.: Museo Nacional de Arqueología, Historia y Etnografía, 1933.

Labastida, Luis. *Colección de leyes, decretos, reglamentos, circulares, órdenes y acuerdos relativos a la desamortización de los bienes de corporaciones civiles y religiosas y a la nacionalización de los que administraron las últimas.* Mexico, D.F.: Tip. de la Oficina Impresora de Estampillas, 1893.

Le Roy Ladurie, Emmanuel. *Times of Feast, Times of Famine: A History of Climate since the Year 1000.* New York: Doubleday, 1971.

Lecomte, Henri. *Le vanillier: Sa culture, préparation et commerce de la vanille.* Paris: C. Naud, 1901.

Legislación del Estado de Veracruz, desde el año de 1824 hasta la presente época. Multiple vols. Xalapa, 1881–82.

León, Nicolás. *Manual para el cultivo y beneficio de la vainilla en el estado de Michoacán.* Mexico, D.F.: Vargas Rea, 1943.

Lerdo de Tejada, Miguel. *Comercio exterior de México, desde la Conquista hasta hoy.* Mexico, D.F.: R. Rafael, 1853.

Lida, Clara, ed. *Una inmigración privilegiada: Comerciantes, empresarios y profesionales españoles en México en los siglos XIX y XX.* Madrid: Alianza Editorial, 1994.

Lira, Andrés. *Comunidades indígenas frente a la ciudad de México: Tenochtitlán y Tlatelolco, sus pueblos y barrios, 1812–1919.* Mexico, D.F.: El Colegio de México/Colegio de Michoacán, 1983.

Lloyd, G. E. R. *Magic, Reason, and Experience: Studies in the Origins and Development of Greek Science.* Cambridge: Cambridge University Press, 1979.

López de Gómara, Francisco. *Historia de la conquista de México.* Mexico, D.F.: Pedro Robredo, 1943.

López Patiño, Bartolo, and Pedro García Pérez. "El maíz en la Congregación Vicente Herrera, Papantla, Veracruz." In *Nuestro maíz: Treinta monografías populares,* vol. 2. Mexico, D.F.: Museo Nacional de Culturas Populares, 1988.

López y Parra, Rodrigo. *La vainilla: Su cultivo y beneficio en la República Mexicana*. Mexico, D.F.: Imprenta "El Monograma," 1900.

Lynch, John. *Spain under the Habsburgs*. 2 vols. New York: New York University Press, 1984.

Mallon, Florencia. *Peasant and Nation: The Making of Postcolonial Mexico and Peru*. Berkeley: University of California Press, 1995.

Mallory, L. D., and Karolyne Walter. "Mexico's Vanilla Production—Ancient Indian Industry Thrives in All its Picturesqueness." *Foreign Commerce Weekly*, 20 June 1942.

Markusen, Ann. *Regions: The Economics and Politics of Territory*. Totowa, N.J.: Rowman and Littlefield, 1987.

Márquez Hernández, Carlos, et al. "Mito, historia y realidad en el cultivo del maíz: Francisco Sarabia, Papantla, Veracruz." In *Nuestro maíz: Treinta monografías populares*, edited by Guillermo Bonfil Batalla. Mexico, D.F.: Museo Nacional de Culturas Populares, 1988.

Mártir de Anglería, Pedro. *Décadas del nuevo mundo*. 2 vols. Mexico, D.F.: Porrúa, 1964–65.

McBride, George McCutchen. *The Land Systems of Mexico*, Research Series, no. 12. New York: American Geographical Society, 1923.

Memoria de la Tesorería General del Estado, presentada a la H. Legislatura el 18 de Setiembre de 1882. In *Estado de Veracruz: Informes de sus Gobernadores, 1826–1986*, edited by Carmen Blázquez Domínguez. Xalapa, 1986.

Memoria general de la administración pública del Estado libre y soberano de Veracruz Llave . . . de 17 de Setiembre de 1882. . . . . In *Estado de Veracruz: Informes de sus Gobernadores, 1826–1986*, edited by Carmen Blázquez Domínguez. Xalapa, 1986.

Memoria general de la administración pública del Estado libre y soberano de Veracruz Llave . . . de 17 de Setiembre de 1884. . . . . In *Estado de Veracruz: Informes de sus Gobernadores, 1826–1986*, edited by Carmen Blázquez Domínguez. Xalapa, 1986.

Memoria leída por el C. Gobernador del Estado ante la H. Legislatura del mismo el día 13 de Octubre de 1871. . . . . In *Estado de Veracruz: Informes de sus Gobernadores, 1826–1986*, edited by Carmen Blázquez Domínguez. Xalapa, 1986.

Memoria presentada a la H. Legislatura del Estado libre y soberano de Veracruz-Llave el 18 de septiembre de 1890 por el Gobernador Constitucional General Juan Enríquez. In *Estado de Veracruz: Informes de sus Gobernadores, 1826–1986*, edited by Carmen Blázquez Domínguez. Xalapa, 1986.

Memoria presentada a la H. Legislatura del Estado libre y soberano de Veracruz Llave el 16 de Setiembre de 1894 por el Gobernador Constitucional C. Teodoro A. Dehesa. . . . . In *Estado de Veracruz: Informes de sus Gobernadores, 1826–1986*, edited by Carmen Blázquez Domínguez. Xalapa, 1986.

Memoria presentada a la H. Legislatura del Estado libre y soberano de Veracruz Llave el 16 de Septiembre de 1896 por el Gobernador Constitucional C. Teodoro A. Dehesa. . . . In *Estado de Veracruz: Informes de sus Gobernadores, 1826–1986*, edited by Carmen Blázquez Domínguez. Xalapa, 1986.

Memoria presentada a la H. Legislatura del Estado libre y soberano de Veracruz

Llave, por el Gobernador Constitucional C. Francisco de Landero y Cos, el día 17 de Setiembre de 1873. . . . In *Estado de Veracruz: Informes de sus Gobernadores, 1826–1986,* edited by Carmen Blázquez Domínguez. Xalapa, 1986.

Memoria presentada a la H. Legislatura del Estado libre y soberano de Veracruz Llave por el C. Tesorero General Manuel Leví . . . *de 1° de Enero de 1889, a 30 de Junio de 1890.* . . . In *Estado de Veracruz: Informes de sus Gobernadores, 1826–1986,* edited by Carmen Blázquez Domínguez. Xalapa, 1986.

Memoria presentada a la Honorable Legislatura del Estado de Veracruz-Llave por el C. Gobernador Constitucional General Juan Enríquez en la sesión del 17 de Setiembre de 1886. . . . In *Estado de Veracruz: Informes de sus Gobernadores, 1826–1986,* edited by Carmen Blázquez Domínguez. Xalapa, 1986.

Memoria presentada al H. Congreso del Estado de Veracruz Llave, por su Gobernador Constitucional el C. Francisco Hernández y Hernández, el día 13 de Marzo de 1869. . . . In *Estado de Veracruz: Informes de sus Gobernadores, 1826–1986,* edited by Carmen Blázquez Domínguez. Xalapa, 1986.

Memoria presentada por el C. Gobernador del Estado libre y soberano de Veracruz-Llave a la H. Legislatura del mismo en Noviembre 30 de 1870. . . . In *Estado de Veracruz: Informes de sus Gobernadores, 1826–1986,* edited by Carmen Blázquez Domínguez. Xalapa, 1986.

Memoria que comprende el periodo administrativo, del 1_de Julio de 1886 a 30 de Junio de 1888, presentada a la H. Legislatura del Estado de Veracruz Llave, por el Gobernador Constitucional . . . *C. Juan Enríquez.* . . . In *Estado de Veracruz: Informes de sus Gobernadores, 1826–1986,* edited by Carmen Blázquez Domínguez. Xalapa, 1986.

Mendieta y Nuñez, Lucio. *El problema agrario de México.* Mexico, D.F., 1926.

Menegus Bornemann, Margarita. "Ocoyoacac: Una comunidad agraria en el siglo XIX." *Historia Mexicana* 30, no. 1 (1980): 33–78.

Menéndez y Pelayo, Marcelino. *Historia de los heterodoxos españoles.* 8 vols. Santander, 1946–48.

Mexico. Estado de Veracruz. *Estadística del estado libre y soberano de Veracruz.* Xalapa, 1831.

Mexico. Estado de Veracruz. El Gobernador. *Noticia estadística que el Gobernador del Estado libre y soberano de Veracruz presenta al Congreso de la Unión de la 8a. obligación del artículo 161 de la Constitución federal.* . . . Xalapa, 1827.

Mexico. Estado de Veracruz-Llave. *Colección de leyes, decretos y circulares del Estado de Veracruz.* Xalapa and Veracruz, 1824–.

Mexico. Estado de Veracruz-Llave. Secretaría de Gobierno. Departamento de Estadística. *Sinopsis de la división territorial del Estado, comprendiendo los Cantones, Municípios, Congregaciones, Haciendas, y en general, todos los poblados existentes en el mismo, el 1° de Enero de 1900.* . . . Xalapa: Estado de Veracruz-Llave, Secretaría de Gobierno, Departamento de Estadística, 1902.

Mexico. Ministerio de Fomento. *Censo general de la República Mexicana (1895).* Mexico, D.F., 1897.

Mexico. Secretaría de Agricultura y Fomento. *Colección de leyes sobre tierras y demás disposiciones relacionadas con las mismas; comprende del año de 1863 a 1943.* Mexico, D.F., 1944.

————. *Regiones económico agrícolas de la República Mexicana (memoria descriptiva)*. 2 vols. Mexico, D.F., 1936.

Mexico. Secretaría de Estado y del Despacho de Hacienda y Crédito Público. *Boletín de estadística fiscal, año fiscal de . . . (1900–01/1909–10, annual)*. Mexico, D.F., 1901–10.

————. *Comercio exterior, año fiscal de . . . (1896–97/1897–98, annual)*. Mexico, D.F., 1901.

————. *Comercio exterior y navegación, año fiscal de . . . (1898–99/1899–1900, annual)*. Mexico, D.F., 1901–2.

————. *Estadística fiscal: Exportación, año fiscal de . . . (1893–94/1895–96, annual)*. Mexico, D.F., 1895–99.

————. *Exportaciones en el año fiscal de . . . (1889–90/1892–93, annual)*. Mexico, D.F., 1891–94.

————. *Noticia de la exportación de mercancías en el año fiscal . . . (1877–1878/1888–1889, annual)*. Mexico, D.F., 1881–90.

————. *Noticia de la importación y exportación de mercancías, en los años fiscales de 1872 a 1873, 1873 a 1874 y 1874 a 1875*. Mexico, D.F., 1880.

Mexico. Secretaría de Fomento. *Disposiciones sobre designación y fraccionamiento de ejidos de los pueblos, mandadas compilar y publicar por el Sr. Ministro de Fomento Gral. Carlos Pacheco*. Mexico, D.F., 1889.

————. *Memoria de la Secretaría de Estado y del Despacho de Fomento, Colonización, Industria y Comercio de la República Mexicana*. Mexico, D.F., 1857.

Mexico. Secretaría de Fomento, Colonización e Industria. *Censo y división territorial del Estado de Veracruz, verificado en 1900*. Mexico, D.F., 1904.

————. *Informes y documentos relativos a comercio interior y exterior: Agricultura, minería e industrias*. Multiple vols. Mexico, D.F., 1885–91.

Mexico. Secretaría de Hacienda y Crédito Público. *Memoria de Hacienda y Crédito Público, 1878–1879*. Mexico, D.F., 1880.

————. *Memoria presentada al Exmo. Sr. Presidente sustituto de la República por el C. Miguel Lerdo de Tejada. Dando cuenta de la marcha que han seguido los negocios de la Hacienda Pública, en el tiempo que tuvo a su cargo la secretaria de este ramo*. Mexico, D.F., 1857.

Meyer, Jean. "Haciendas y ranchos, peones y campesinos en el Porfiriato: Algunas falacias estadísticas." *Historia Mexicana* 35, no. 3 (1986): 477–509.

————. *Problemas campesinos y revueltas agrarias, 1821–1910*. Mexico: SEP, 1973.

Miller, Philip. *The Gardener's Dictionary; Containing the Methods of Cultivating and Improving the Kitchen, Fruit and Flower Garden, as also the Physic Garden, Wilderness, Conservatory, and Vineyard. . . .* 2nd ed. London, 1739.

Minifie, Bernard W. *Chocolate, Cocoa, and Confectionery: Science and Technology.* 2nd ed. Westport, Ct.: AVI Publishing, 1980.

Miño Grijalva, Manuel, et al., eds. *Tres aspectos de la presencia española en México durante el Porfiriato: Relaciones económicas, comerciantes y población.* Mexico, D.F.: El Colegio de México, 1981.

Molina Enríquez, Andrés. *Los grandes problemas nacionales.* Mexico, D.F.: Imprenta de A. Carranza e Hijos, 1909.

Montañez, Carlos, and Arturo Warman. *Los productores de maíz en México: Restricciones y alternativas.* Mexico, D.F.: Centro de Ecodesarrolo, 1985.

Montesinos, Elda, et al. "El maíz en el municipio de Papantla." In vol. 2 of *Nuestro maíz: Treinta monografías populares,* edited by Guillermo Bonfil Batalla. Mexico, D.F.: Museo Nacional de Culturas Populares, 1988.

Montoya Hernández, Felipe. "Vanilla: Shanat." Agronomy thesis, Escuela Nacional de Agricultura (Chapingo), 1945.

Morren, Charles. Research Report. *Comptes Rendus Hebdomadaires des Séances de l'Académie des Sciences* (Paris) 8 (January-June 1839): 841–42.

———. "On the Production of Vanilla in Europe." *Annals of Natural History,* ser. 1, 3 (1839): 1–9.

———. "Sur la fructification de la vanille obtenue a moyen de la fécondation artificielle." *Comptes Rendus Hebdomadaires des Séances de l'Académie des Sciences* (Paris) 6 (1838): 489–92.

Morton, Marcia, and Frederic Morton. *Chocolate: An Illustrated History.* New York: Crown Publishers, 1986.

Mota y Escobar, Alonso de la. "Memoriales del obispo de Tlaxcala, fray Alonso de la Mota y Escobar." *Anales del Instituto Nacional de Antropología e Historia* 1 (1939–40): 191–306.

Motolinía, Fray Toribio de. *Historia de los indios de la Nueva España.* Mexico, D.F.: Porrúa, 1969.

Nash, Manning. "Indian Economies." In vol. 6 of *Handbook of Middle American Indians,* edited by Manning Nash. Austin: University of Texas Press, 1967.

Naveda, Adriana, and José González Sierra. *Papantla.* Xalapa: Archivo General del Estado de Veracruz, 1990.

Noble, Gontran, and Manuel Lebrija. "La sequía en México y su previsión." Pts. 1 and 2. *Boletín de la Sociedad Mexicana de Geografía y Estadística* 83 (January–June 1957): 1–3; 84 (July–December 1957): 1–3.

"Noticias estadísticas de la Intendencia de Veracruz." In *Descripciones económicas regionales de Nueva España: Provincias del Centro, Sudeste y Sur, 1766–1827,* edited by Enrique Florescano and Isabel Gil Sánchez. Mexico, D.F., 1976.

Nugent, Daniel. *Spent Cartridges of Revolution: An Anthropological History of Namiquipa, Chihuahua.* Chicago: University of Chicago Press, 1993.

Nye, P. H., and D. Greenland. *The Soil under Shifting Cultivation,* Technical Communication no. 51. Buckinhamshire: Commonwealth Agricultural Bureaux, 1960.

Ochoa Contreras, Octavio. "Cambios estructurales en la actividad del sector agrícola del estado de Veracruz, 1870–1900." *Dualismo* 5, no. 1 (1974): 23–87.

Olivo Lara, Margarita. *Biografías de veracruzanos distinguidos.* Mexico, D.F.: Museo Nacional de Arqueología, Historia y Etnografía, 1931.

O'Neill, James D. "Escobar y Mendoza." In *The Catholic Encyclopedia.* New York: Robert Appleton, 1909.

———. "Fast." In *The Catholic Encyclopedia.* New York: Robert Appleton, 1909.

Orive Alba, Adolfo. *La política de irrigación en México.* Mexico, D.F.: FCE, 1960.

Orozco, Wistano Luis. *Legislación y jurisprudencia sobre terrenos baldíos.* 2 vols. Mexico, D.F.: Imprenta de El Tiempo, 1895.

―――. *Los ejidos de los pueblos*. Mexico, D.F.: Ediciones el Caballito, 1975.

Ortiz de la Tabla Ducasse, Javier, ed. *Memorias políticas y económicas del Consulado de Veracruz, 1796–1822*. Seville: Escuela de Estudios Hispano-Americanos de Sevilla, 1985.

Ortiz Espejel, Benjamin. *La cultura asediada: Espacio e historia en el trópico veracruzano (el caso de Totonacapan)*. Mexico, D.F.: CIESAS/IEAC, 1995.

Ortiz Izquierdo, José. "Instrucciones sobre algunos importantes cultivos en el Estado de Veracruz." In Vol. 45 of Secretaría de Fomento, Colonización e Industria, *Informes y documentos relativos a comercio interior y exterior: Agricultura, minería e industrias*. Mexico, D.F.: Secretaría de Fomento, Colonización e Industria, 1889.

Ott, Michael. "Gregory XIII." In *The Catholic Encyclopedia*. New York: Robert Appleton, 1909.

Pagden, Anthony. *European Encounters with the New World*. New Haven, Ct.: Yale University Press, 1993.

Page, J. "Climate of Mexico." *Monthly Weather Review*, Supplement no. 33. Washington, 1929.

Palacios, Enrique Juan. *Puebla: Su territorio y sus habitantes*. Mexico, D.F., 1917.

Palerm, Angel. "Agricultural Systems and Food Patterns." In vol. 6 of *Handbook of Middle American Indians*, edited by Manning Nash. Austin: University of Texas Press, 1967.

―――. "Aspectos agrícolas del desarrollo de la civilización prehispánica en Mesoamerica." In *Agricultura y civilización en Mesoamerica*, edited by Angel Palerm and Eric Wolf. Mexico, D.F.: SEP, 1972.

―――. "Etnografía antigua Totonaca en el oriente de México." In *Huastecos, totonacos y sus vecinos*, edited by Ignacio Bernal and Eusebio Dávalos Hurtado. Mexico, D.F.: Sociedad Mexicana de Antropología, 1953.

Palerm, Angel, and Eric Wolf. *Agricultura y civilización en Mesoamerica*. Mexico, D.F.: SEP, 1972.

Pasquel, Leonardo. *Xalapeños distinguidos*. Mexico, D.F.: Editorial Citlaltepetl, 1975.

Pérez Milicua, Luis. *Compendio de geografía física, política y económica del estado de Veracruz*. 3rd ed. Mexico, D.F.: Librería de la Vda. de Ch. Bouret, 1921.

Phipps, Helen. "Some Aspects of the Agrarian Question in Mexico: A Historical Study." *University of Texas Bulletin*, no. 2515 (1925): 7–157.

Pomet, Pierre. *Le marchand sincère, ou traite general des drogues simples et composées*. Paris, 1695.

Powell, T. G. "Los liberales, el campesinado indígena y los problemas agrarios durante la reforma." *Historia Mexicana* 21, no. 4 (1972): 653–75.

―――. *El liberalismo y el campesinado en el centro de México, 1850 a 1876*. Mexico, D.F., 1974.

―――. "Mexican Intellectuals and the Indian Question, 1876–1911." *Hispanic American Historical Review* 48, no. 1 (1968): 19–36.

Precope, John. *Hippocrates on Diet and Hygiene*. London: Zeno, 1952.

Purnell, Jennie. "With All Due Respect: Popular Resistance to the Privatization of Communal Lands in Nineteenth-Century Michoacán." *Latin American Research Review* 34, no. 1 (1999): 85–121.

Quirós, José María. "Memoria sobre el cultivo y beneficio de la vainilla." In *Memorias políticas y económicas del Consulado de Veracruz, 1796–1822*, edited by Javier Ortiz de la Tabla Ducasse. Seville: Escuela de Estudios Hispano-Americanas de Sevilla, 1985.

———. "Memoria sobre el fomento agrícola de la Intendencia de Veracruz." In *Memorias políticas y económicas del Consulado de Veracruz, 1796–1822*, edited by Javier Ortiz de la Tabla Ducasse. Seville: Escuela de Estudios Hispano-Americanas de Sevilla, 1985.

Ramamoorthy, T. P., et al., eds. *Biological Diversity of Mexico: Origins and Distribution*. Oxford: Oxford University Press, 1993.

Ramírez Lavoignet, David. *Misantla*. Mexico, D.F.: Editorial Citalalépetl, 1959.

———. *Tecolutla: Monografía histórica*. Xalapa, 1981.

Ramírez Melgarejo, Ramón. *La política del estado mexicano en los procesos agrícolas y agrarios de los totonacos*. Xalapa: Universidad Veracruzana, 2002.

Raynal, Guillaume-Thomas François. *A Philosophical and Political History of the Settlements and Trade of the Europeans in the East and West Indies*. Translated by John O. Justamond. London: T. Cadell, 1777.

Rees, Peter. *Transportes y comercio entre México y Veracruz, 1519–1910*. Mexico, D.F.: SEP, 1976.

Reina, Leticia. *Las rebeliones campesinas en México, 1819–1906*. Mexico, D.F.: Siglo XXI, 1980.

Revel-Mouroz, Jean. *Aménagement et Colonisation du Tropique Humide Mexicain*. Paris: Institute des Hautes Etudes de L'Amerique Latine, 1972.

Reyes Heroles, Jesús. *El liberalismo mexicano*. 3 vols. Mexico, D.F.: UNAM, 1957–61.

Ricard, Robert. *La "conquête spirituelle" du Mexique*. Paris: Institute d'Ethnologie, 1933.

Richards, P. W. *The Tropical Rain Forest: An Ecological Study*. Cambridge: Cambridge University Press, 1952.

Ridley, Henry N. *Spices*. London: Macmillan, 1912.

Rivera Cambas, Manuel. *Historia antigua y moderna de Jalapa y de las revoluciones del Estado de Veracruz*. 5 vols. Mexico, D.F.: I. Cumplido, 1869.

Rojas Rabiela, Teresa. *Las siembras de ayer: La agricultura indígena del siglo XVI*. Mexico, D.F.: SEP, 1988.

———. "La tecnología agrícola mesoamericana en el siglo XVI." In *Historia de la agricultura: Época prehispánica–siglo XVI*, edited by Teresa Rojas Rabiela and William T. Sanders. Mexico, D.F.: INAH, 1985.

Rolfe, R. Allen. "A Revision of the Genus *Vanilla*." *The Journal of the Linnean Society of London: Botany* 32 (1896): 439–78.

Rossignon, Julio. *Manual del cultivo del café, cacao, vainilla y tabaco en la América española*. Paris: Librería de Rosa y Bouret, 1859.

Rzedowski, Jerzy. *Vegetación de México*. Mexico, D.F.: Editorial Limusa, 1978.

Sahagún, Bernardino de. *Historia general de las cosas de Nueva España*. Mexico, D.F.: Porrúa, 1985.

Salaman, Redcliffe N. *The History and Social Influence of the Potato*. Cambridge: Cambridge University Press, 1949.

Salamini, Heather Fowler. *Agrarian Radicalism in Veracruz, 1920–1938.* Lincoln: University of Nebraska Press, 1971.

Salas García, Luis. *Cachiquín.* Xalapa, 1986.

———. *Juu Papantlán (Apuntes para la historia de Papantla).* Mexico, D.F.: Gráfica Editorial Mexicana, 1979.

Sánchez, Pedro A. *Properties and Management of Soils in the Tropics.* New York: Wiley, 1976.

Sanders, William T. "The Anthropogeography of Central Veracruz." In *Huastecos, totonacos y sus vecinos,* edited by Ignacio Bernal and Eusebio Dávalos Hurtado. Mexico, D.F.: Sociedad Mexicana de Antropología, 1953.

———. "The Cultural Ecology of the Lowland Maya: A Reevaluation." In *The Classic Maya Collapse,* edited by P. T. Culbert. Albuquerque: University of New Mexico Press, 1973.

———. "Settlement Patterns." In vol. 6 of *Handbook of Middle American Indians,* edited by Manning Nash. Austin: University of Texas Press, 1967.

Sarukhán, José. "Estudio sucesional de un área talada en Tuxtepec, Oaxaca." In *Publicación Especial No. 3.* Mexico, D.F.: Instituto Nacional de Investigaciones Forestales, 1964.

Sauer, Carl O. *Agricultural Origins and Dispersals.* New York: American Geographical Society, 1952.

Schenk, Frank. "La desamortización de las tierras comunales en el estado de México (1856–1911): El caso del distrito de Sultepec." *Historia Mexicana* 45, no. 1 (1995): 3–37.

Schiede, Christian Julius Wilhelm. "Botanische Berichte aus Mexico, mitgetheilt vom Dr. Schiede." *Linnaea* 4 (1829): 554–83.

Schivelbusch, Wolfgang. *Tastes of Paradise: A Social History of Spices, Stimulants, and Intoxicants.* New York: Pantheon, 1992.

Schmidt, Athur. *The Social and Economic Effect of the Railroad in Puebla and Veracruz, Mexico, 1876–1911.* New York: Garland, 1987.

Schryer, Frans J. *Ethnicity and Class Conflict in Rural Mexico.* Princeton, N.J.: Princeton University Press, 1990.

———. "Peasants and the Law: A History of Land Tenure and Conflict in the Huasteca." *Journal of Latin American Studies* 18, no. 2 (1986): 283–311.

———. *The Rancheros of Pisaflores: The History of a Peasant Bourgeoisie in Twentieth-Century Mexico.* Toronto, 1980.

Semo, Enrique, ed. *Historia de la cuestión agraria mexicana: La tierra y el poder, 1800–1910.* 9 vols. Mexico, D.F.: Siglo XXI Editores/CEHAM, 1988.

Siemens, Alfred H. *Between the Summit and the Sea: Central Veracruz in the Nineteenth Century.* Vancouver: University of British Columbia Press, 1990.

———. "Modelling Pre-Hispanic Hydroagriculture on Levee Backslopes in Northern Veracruz, Mexico." In *Drained Field Agriculture in Central and South America,* edited by J. P. Darch. Oxford: B.A.R., 1983.

———. "Wetland Agriculture in the Lowlands of Pre-Hispanic Mesoamerica." *Geographical Review* 73, no. 2 (1983): 166–81.

Silva Herzog, Jesús. *El agrarismo mexicano y la reforma agraria.* Mexico, D.F.: FCE, 1959.

————, ed. *La cuestión de la tierra.* 4 vols. Mexico, D.F.: Instituto Mexicano de Investigaciones Económicas, 1960–62.

Simpson, Eyler. *The Ejido: Mexico's Way Out.* Chapel Hill: University of North Carolina Press, 1937.

Sims, Harold D. *La expulsión de los españoles de México, 1821–1828.* Mexico, D.F.: FCE, 1974.

Skerritt, David. "Colonización y modernización del campo en el centro de Veracruz (siglo XIX)." *Siglo XIX—Cuadernos de Historia* 2, no. 5 (1993): 39–57.

————. *Colonos franceses y modernización en el Golfo de México.* Xalapa: Universidad Veracruzana, 1995.

————. "Tres culturas: Un nuevo espacio regional (el caso de la colonia francesa de Jicaltepec—San Rafael)." In *Las llanuras costeras de Veracruz: La lenta construcción de regiones,* edited by Odile Hoffmann and Emilia Velázquez. Xalapa: ORSTOM/Universidad Veracruzana, 1994.

Smith, Carol. "How Marketing Systems Affect Economic Opportunity in Agrarian Societies." In *Peasant Livelihood: Studies in Economic Anthropology and Cultural Ecology,* edited by Rhoda Halperin and James Dow. New York: St. Martin's, 1977.

Sotelo Inclán, Jesús. *Raíz y razón de Zapata.* Mexico, D.F.: Editorial Etnos, 1943.

Soto, Manuel. *Noticias estadísticas de la Huasteca y de una parte de la sierra alta formadas en el año de 1853.* Mexico, D.F.: J. M. Sandoval, 1869.

Southworth, J. R. *El Estado de Veracruz-Llave.* Mexico, D.F., 1900.

Stevens, Rayfred L. "The Soils of Middle America and their Relation to Indian Peoples and Cultures." In vol. 1 of *Handbook of Middle American Indians,* edited by Robert C. West. Austin: University of Texas Press, 1964.

Stresser-Péan, Guy. "El arado criollo en México y en América Central." In *Homenaje a Isabel Kelly,* edited by Yólotl González. Mexico, D.F.: INAH, 1989.

Swahn, Jan Öjvind. *The Lore of Spices: Their History and Uses around the World.* New York: Crescent Books, 1991.

Tamayo, Jorge L. *Datos para la hidrología de la República Mexicana.* Publicación no. 84. Mexico, D.F.: Instituto Panamericano de Geografía e Historia, 1946.

————. *Geografía general de México.* 2 vols. Mexico, D.F.: Talleres Gráficos de la Nación, 1949.

Tannenbaum, Frank. *The Mexican Agrarian Revolution.* New York: Macmillan, 1929.

Taylor, William B. *Drinking, Homicide, and Rebellion in Colonial Mexican Villages.* Stanford, Calif.: Stanford University Press, 1979.

————. *Landlord and Peasant in Colonial Oaxaca.* Stanford, Calif.: Stanford University Press, 1972.

Thompson, Guy P. C., and David LaFrance. *Patriotism, Politics, and Popular Liberalism in Nineteenth-Century Mexico: Juan Francisco Lucas and the Puebla Sierra.* Wilmington, Del.: Scholarly Resources, 1999.

Thompson, J. Eric S., ed. *Thomas Gage's Travels in the New World.* Norman: University of Oklahoma Press, 1958.

Thorndike, Lynn. *Science and Thought in the Fifteenth Century.* New York: Columbia University Press, 1929.

Tischendorf, Alfred. *Great Britain and Mexico in the Era of Porfirio Díaz.* Durham, N.C.: Duke University Press, 1961.

Torquemada, Juan de. *Monarquía Indiana.* 3 vols. Mexico, D.F.: S. Chávez Hayhoe, 1943.

Torres, Blanca. *México en la Segunda Guerra Mundial.* Mexico, D.F.: El Colegio de México, 1979.

Toussaint-Samat, Maguelone. *A History of Food.* Oxford: Blackwell Reference, 1992.

Trens, Manuel B. *Historia de Veracruz.* 7 vols. Xalapa: Secretaría de Educación y Cultura, 1992.

Turnbow, Grover Dean, Paul Hubert Tracy, and Lloyd Andrew Rappetto. *The Ice Cream Industry.* 2nd ed. New York: J. Wiley and Sons, 1947.

Tutino, John. *From Insurrection to Revolution in Mexico: Social Bases of Agrarian Violence, 1750–1940.* Princeton, N.J.: Princeton University Press, 1986.

U.S. Bureau of the Census. *Foreign Commerce and Navigation of the United States.* 38 vols. Washington, 1865/66–1902/03 [reports for these dates were issued by Bureau of Statistics of the Department of the Treasury].

U.S. Congress. House. *Annual Report on the Commercial Relations between the United States and Foreign Nations, made by the Secretary of State, for the year ending September 30, 1874.* 43rd Cong., 2nd sess., 1875. H. Doc. 157.

————. *Annual Report upon the Commercial Relations of the United States with Foreign Countries for the year 1878.* 46th Cong., 2nd sess., 1879. H. Doc. 90.

————. *Letter of the Secretary of State. . . . for the Year ending September 30, 1858.* 35th Cong., 2nd sess., 1859. H. Doc. 85.

————. *Letter of the Secretary of State . . . for the Year ending September 30, 1859.* 36th Cong., 1st sess., 1860. H. Doc. 4.

————. *Letter of the Secretary of State . . . for the Year ending September 30, 1861.* 37th Cong., 2nd sess., 1862. H. Doc. 45.

————. *Letter of the Secretary of State . . . for the Year ended September 30, 1862.* 37th Cong., 3rd sess., 1863. H. Doc. 63.

————. *Report of the Secretary of State, transmitting a statement from the Superintendent of Statistics of the Commercial Relations of the United States with Foreign Nations, for the Year ending September 30, 1856.* 34th Cong., 3rd sess., 1857. H. Doc. 60.

————. *Report upon the Commercial Relations of the United States with Foreign Countries for the year 1877.* 45th Cong., 2nd sess., 1878. H. Doc. 102.

————. *Report upon the Commercial Relations of the United States with Foreign Countries for the year 1878.* 46th Cong., 2nd sess., 1879. H. Doc. 90.

U.S. Department of the Treasury. *Report of the Secretary of the Treasury, transmitting a Report from the Register of the Treasury, of the Commerce and Navigation of the United States for the year ending . . . .* Washington, 1863–1866 [published annually].

Valadés, José C. *El porfirismo: Historia de un régimen.* 3 vols. Mexico, D.F.: Antigua Librería de Robredo de J. Porrúa e Hijos, 1941–48.

Vanderwood, Paul J. *Disorder and Progress: Bandits, Police, and Mexican Development.* Lincoln: University of Nebraska Press, 1981.

———. *The Power of God against the Guns of Government: Religious Upheaval in Mexico at the Turn of the Nineteenth Century.* Stanford, Calif.: Stanford University Press, 1998.

Van Wambeke, Armand. *Soils of the Tropics: Properties and Appraisal.* New York: McGraw-Hill, 1992.

Vavilov, Nikolai I. *The Origin, Variation, Immunity, and Breeding of Cultivated Plants.* Waltham, Mass.: Chronica Botannica, 1951.

Velasco Toro, José. "Indigenismo y rebelión totonaca de Papantla, 1885–1896." *América Indígena* 39, no. 1 (1979): 81–105.

———. "La política desamortizadora y sus efectos en la región de Papantla, Ver." *La Palabra y el Hombre* 72 (Nueva Época) (October–December 1989): 137–62.

Velázquez, Emilia. *Cuando los arrieros perdieron sus caminos: La conformación regional del Totonacapan.* Zamora: Colegio de Michoacán, 1995.

———. "Intercambio comercial y organización regional en el Totonacapan." Master's thesis, El Colegio de Michoacán, 1992.

———. "Mercados y tianguis en el Totonacapan veracruzano." In *Procesos rurales e historia regional: Sierra y costa totonacas de Veracruz,* edited by Victoria Chenaut. Mexico, D.F.: CIESAS, 1996.

Vicens Vives, Jaime., ed. *Historia social y económica de España y América.* 2nd ed. 5 vols. Madrid: Editorial Vicens Vives, 1972.

Villamar, Aniceto. *Las leyes federales vigentes sobre tierras, bosques, aguas, ejidos, colonización y el gran registro de la propiedad: Colección ordenada y anotada.* 2nd ed. Mexico, D.F.: Herrero Hnos., 1910.

Villaseñor y Sánchez, José Antonio de. *Theatro americano: Descripción general de los reynos y provincias de la Nueva España y sus jurisdicciones.* 2 vols. Mexico, D.F.: Imprenta de la Viuda de D. J. Bernardo de Hogal, 1746–48.

Vinson, Ben. "Las compañías milicianas de pardos y morenos en la Nueva España." In *Población y estructura urbana en México, siglos XVIII y XIX,* edited by Carmen Blázquez, Carlos Contreras Cruz, and Sonia Pérez Toledo. Xalapa: Universidad Veracruzana, 1996.

"Visita a la Congregación de Chumatlán." *Boletín del Archivo General de la Nación* 14 (Primera Serie), no. 2 (1943): 13–48.

Vivó, Jorge A. "Weather and Climate of Mexico and Central America." In *Handbook of Middle American Indians,* edited by R. C. West. Austin: University of Texas Press, 1964.

Von Mentz, Brígida, et al., eds. *Los pioneros del imperialismo alemán en México.* Mexico, D.F.: CIESAS, 1982.

Wagner, Philip L. "Natural Vegetation of Middle America." In *Handbook of Middle American Indians,* edited by R. C. West. Austin: University of Texas Press, 1964.

Walker, David. "Business as Usual: The Empresa del Tabaco in Mexico, 1837–1844." *Hispanic American Historical Review* 64, no. 4 (1984): 675–705.

Wallén, Carl Christian. "Some Characteristics of Precipitation in Mexico." *Geografiska Annaler* 38, no. 1–2 (1955): 51–85.

Warman, Arturo. *Y venimos a contradecir: Los campesinos de Morelos y el estado nacional.* Mexico, D.F.: CIS/INAH, 1976.

————. *La historia de un bastardo: Maíz y capitalismo*. Mexico, D.F.: UNAM/FCE, 1988.

Waterbury, Ronald. "Non-revolutionary Peasants: Oaxaca Compared to Morelos in the Mexican Revolution." *Comparative Studies in Society and History* 17, no. 4 (1975): 410–42.

Watters, R. F. *Shifting Cultivation in Latin America*, FAO Forestry Development Paper no. 17. Rome, 1971.

Weber, N. A. "Brancaccio." In *The Catholic Encyclopedia*. New York: Robert Appleton, 1909.

Wells, Allen, and Gilbert M. Joseph. *Summer of Discontent, Seasons of Upheaval: Elite Politics and Rural Insurgency in Yucatan, 1876–1915*. Stanford, Calif.: Stanford University Press, 1996.

West, Robert C. "The Natural Regions of Middle America." In *Handbook of Middle American Indians*, edited by R. C. West. Austin: University of Texas Press, 1964.

Whetten, Nathan L. *Rural Mexico*. Chicago: University of Chicago Press, 1948.

Whitmore, Helen B. "Vanilla-Bean Production and Trade." *Foreign Agriculture* 10, no. 1 (1946): 11–16.

Whymper, Robert. *Cocoa and Chocolate: Their Chemistry and Manufacture*. London: J. and A. Churchill, 1912.

Wickizer, Vernon Dale. *Coffee, Tea, and Cocoa: An Economic and Political Analysis*. Stanford, Calif.: Stanford University Press, 1951.

Wilken, Gene C. *Good Farmers: Traditional Agricultural Resource Management in Mexico and Central America*. Berkeley: University of California Press, 1987.

Wilkerson, Jeffrey K. "So Green and Like a Garden: Intensive Agriculture in Ancient Veracruz." In *Drained Field Agriculture in Central and South America*, edited by J. P. Darch. Oxford: B.A.R., 1983.

Wolf, Eric R. *Peasants*. Englewood Cliffs, N.J.: Prentice-Hall, 1966.

Womack, John, Jr. *Zapata and the Mexican Revolution*. New York: Knopf, 1969.

Zarco, Francisco. *Historia del Congreso Extraordinario Constituyente, 1856–1857*. 2 vols. Mexico, D.F.: Imprenta de Ignacio Cumplido, 1857.

Zilli Manica, José B. *La Villa Luisa de los Italianos: Un proyecto liberal*. Xalapa: Universidad Veracruzana, 1997.

————, ed. *Italianos en México: Documentos para la historia de los colonos italianos en México*. Xalapa: Ediciones San José, 1981.

Index

Page numbers in *italics* refer to illustrations and tables.

lion resulting from attempts to control,
68; U.S.–Mexico sea trade, 114–15.
See also vanilla
transit fees, 173
Tremari, Pedro, 94; and *acciones concejiles*, 151; *latifundio* assembled by,
282; letter on Mexican vanilla, 196; as
mayor of Papantla, 262; Palma Sola
and Nextlalpan bought by, 247, 262;
in parcelization of Ojital y Potrero,
265; parcelization supported by, 262,
263; San Miguel and San Lorenzo
bought by, 239, 262; strategy to keep
vanilla prices high, 195; and uprising
of June 1896, 271; value of property
of, 211; as vanilla merchant, 94, 96; in
vanilla producers' cartel, 214
Tulancingo, 60
Tulapilla estate, 76, 77, 180
Tutino, John, 78
Tuxpan: cattle ranching in, 125; in
Papantla vanilla trade, 92, 99, 115,
117, 118; personal tax causes uprising
in, 177; J. J. Puigdengolas & Co., 125;
in road system, 60, 74; shipments of
Mexican vanilla by port, 1872–1900,
300; steamboat service to, 115, 206,
327*n*13; telegraph service in, 116;
timber exported through, 126; topography of Veracruz state, *59*; in vanilla
trade, 115
Tuxtepec, Revolution of, 142, 149, 180
Tyler & Finch, 119

United States: New Orleans, 114, 115;
Pure Food and Drug Act of 1906, 198;
sea trade with Mexico, 114–15; as
vanilla consumer, 87–88, 111–12, 113,
114, 116, 191–98; vanilla exports to
France, 290–91, 294–95; vanilla
imports, *193*, *293*, *296–97*. *See also*
New York City
United States Pharmacopoeia, 20

Valles, Juan, 263
vanilla, 5–33; *acahuales* for planting, 46,
186; advertisements for, 118–19, *120*;
artificial, 29; as artisanal product,
29–30, 31–32; beans, 6, 302*n*8; beginning of commercial exportation of, 27;
boom of 1870–90, 109–14, 158;
chocolate associated with, 9–10,
20–24, 27, 28; in colonial trade,

63–64; commercial standards adopted
for, 13, 30; in communal landholding's
demise, 1, 104–6, 108, 132, 140, 150,
155, 158, 280; on *condueñazgos*,
162–63; economic and social transformation resulting from, 2, 3, 86–87, 90,
103–6, 160; economics of processing,
32–33; European botanists interested
in, 16–17; evolution of business in
1870s and 1880s, 114–29; exportation
to Spain, 10, 13–14; export merchants,
12, 99, 117, 122, 372; exports of New
Spanish, *287*; fluctuations in trade in,
82; French colonies producing, 18, 19,
28, 29, 109–14, 192; French imports
of, *289*, *292*, *294–95*; geography of
collection of, 9–10; grower's manuals,
6; as herbal medicine, 19–20; in ice
cream, 28, 29; industrial uses for,
119–20; as labor-intensive crop, 15;
legal opening of harvest, 97; literature
on Mexican industry, 5–6; making of
the spice, 30–33; Mexican exports of,
190, *288*, *298–99*; Mexican trade,
81–90; Mexican war of independence
interrupting trade in, 28, 82; mortgaging and sales of plantings, 123, 137,
174; Papantla cartel to fix price of,
213–14; Papantla trading in, 80–106;
premature picking of, 85, 86, 100;
price decline for green, 226, 227;
price decline for Mexican, 1870–90,
120–21, 328*n*28; prices for in
Veracruz, 98–99, 325*n*37; prices for
Mexican, 1890–1910, 192–98, *194*,
195, *196*, 213; production after
parcelization, 281; production and
exports growing under *condueñazgo*,
158–59; production and reproduction
of, 6–19; profit margins for, 97–99,
122; regulating trade in, 85–86; as relatively unimportant before Conquest,
23–24; rotation with corn cultivation,
15, 101; shipments of Mexican by
port, 1872–1900, *300*; shipments to
France, 1831–70, *290–91*; social structure mirrored in economy of, 84–85;
Spaniards come into contact with, 7;
speculators in, 100, 102, 105, 116,
202–3, 230; tax on, 128–29; theft of,
85, 86, 105, 123, 158; as traditional
and potentially revolutionary, 84, 103;
ups and downs of, 1890–1910,